written in 1995

ECONOMIC GROWTH IN THE THIRD WORLD,
1850–1980

A Publication of the Economic Growth Center, Yale University

ECONOMIC GROWTH IN THE
THIRD WORLD,
1850–1980

LLOYD G. REYNOLDS

Yale University Press   New Haven and London

Designed by James J. Johnson
and set in Times Roman type by the Composing Room of Michigan.
Printed in the United States of America by
Braun-Brunfield, Inc., Ann Arbor, Michigan.

Library of Congress Cataloging in Publication Data

Reynolds, Lloyd George, 1910–
    Economic Growth in the Third World, 1850–1980

    (A Publication of the Economic Growth Center, Yale
University)
    Bibliography: pp. 441–56.
    Includes index.
    1. Developing countries—Economic conditions.
2. Economic history—1750–1918. 3. Economic history—
1918–   . I. Title. II. Series.
HC59.7.R475 1985   338.9′009172′4   84–19542
ISBN 0–300–03255–2 (alk. paper)

*The paper in this book meets the guidelines for
permanence and durability of the Committee on
Production Guidelines for Book Longevity of the
Council on Library Resources.*

10   9   8   7   6   5   4   3   2

Contents

List of Tables   vii

Foreword   ix

Preface   xi

PART I   OVERVIEW

    1. The Study of Long-Term Growth   3
    2. The Era of Extensive Growth   15
    3. The Timing of Turning Points   31
    4. The Pattern of Intensive Growth   49

PART II   EARLY DEVELOPERS, 1850–1950

    5. Argentina, Brazil, Mexico   81
    6. Chile, Colombia, Cuba, Peru   108
    7. Sri Lanka, Burma, Malaysia, Thailand   135
    8. Taiwan, South Korea, Philippines: With Notes on Algeria,
       Morocco, Venezuela   166
    9. Nigeria, Ghana, Ivory Coast   202
   10. Kenya, Uganda, Tanzania, Zimbabwe, Zambia   227

PART III   RECENT DEVELOPERS, 1950–1980

   11. China   268
   12. India   293
   13. Egypt, Turkey, Iraq, Iran   318
   14. Pakistan, Indonesia, and Seven Nonstarters   350

PART IV   RETROSPECT

   15. Comparative Growth Performance, 1950–80   387
   16. The Functions of Government   419

Bibliography   441

Index   457

Tables

1	A Chronology of Turning Points	32
2	Selected Measures of Output Growth	390
3	Changes in Welfare: Some Physical Indicators	393
4	Output by Sector of Origin	396
5	Output by End Uses	400
6	Demographic Behavior	404
7	Growth Rates of Agricultural Production and Food Production	407
8	Export Performance, 1950–80	410

Foreword

This volume is one in a series of studies supported by the Economic Growth Center, a research organization within the Yale Department of Economics. The Center was created in 1961 to analyze, both theoretically and empirically, the process of economic growth and the economic relations between the developing and economically advanced countries. The research program emphasizes the search for regularities in the process of growth and changes in economic structure by means of cross-sectional and intertemporal studies and the analysis of policies that affect that process. An increasing share of the research involves statistical study of the behavior of households and firms as revealed in sample surveys by means of the application of microeconomic theory. Current projects include research on technology choice and transfer, household consumption, investment and demographic behavior, agricultural research and productivity growth, commodity market stabilization, labor markets and the returns to education and migration, income distribution, and international economic relations, including monetary and trade policies. The Center's research faculty hold appointments in the Department of Economics and accordingly have teaching as well as research responsibilities.

The Center administers, jointly with the Department of Economics, the Yale master's degree training program in International and Development Economics, in which most students have experiences as economists in foreign central banks, finance ministries, and public and private development agencies. It presents a regular series of workshops on development and trade and on microeconomics of labor and population and includes among its publications book-length studies, reprints by staff members, and discussion papers.

T. PAUL SCHULTZ, DIRECTOR

Preface

Most writing on economic development since 1950, being concerned with recent events and future prospects, has a short time horizon. Yet many countries of Asia and even of Latin America are old countries with growth records going back to the late nineteenth century or beyond. And there is a growing supply of country monographs in which this record is documented as fully as the fragmentary statistics permit.

Several years ago it occurred to me that it would be useful to draw together this historical material and inquire what can be learned from it, a task that to my knowledge no one else has performed. So I proceeded to read and summarize several hundred monographs, some of general scope but most of them relating to particular economies. This book consists primarily of brief outlines of the growth experience of various countries, omitting detail and trying to go for the jugular.

I am well aware that such an enterprise is open to the charge of superficiality. Country specialists will doubtless feel, correctly, that I have not done justice to the fine shadings of growth experience in their particular country. But I believe that what I have said about each country is tolerably accurate, if necessarily incomplete because of the severe constraint of space. The advantage to students of being able to get a quick overview of the larger third-world countries seemed to me to outweigh the costs imposed by brevity of treatment. Anyone who wants really to understand the experience of a particular country will obviously need to consult the sources listed in the bibliography.

Such an immersion in detail naturally tempts one to generalize. So in four chapters at the beginning of the book and two chapters at the end, I inquire what lessons one can draw from the countries' experiences. Some of the ideas in the early chapters have already been published in "The Spread of Economic Growth to the Third World, 1850–1980," *Journal of Economic Literature* 21 (September 1983), pp. 941–81. I am grateful to the American Economic Association for permission to reprint portions of pages 959–64 in that article.

I am grateful also to the Mellon Foundation for financing what must have seemed at the outset a high-risk enterprise. A number of colleagues have provided helpful criticisms at various stages of the work. Janet Armitage and Adrienne Cheasty bore the brunt of the bibliographical and statistical work, and Roberta Milano-Ottenbreit handled the manuscript with her usual care and efficiency. I owe a special debt to Dr. Mary T. Reynolds for a fine analytical index.

PART I
OVERVIEW

1

The Study of Long-Term Growth

Until recently economic history meant the economic history of Western Europe and the United States. This was what we were taught in graduate school and what we dutifully retaught our students. Other parts of the world were outside the mainstream—they were the province of orientalists, Africanists, and other regional specialists, whose work was little regarded by economists.

After 1945 this situation began to change, essentially for political reasons. During the next twenty years the number of independent countries multiplied remarkably, as one colony after another became self-governing. Quite soon the new countries decisively outnumbered the old. The United Nations and its specialized agencies provided a forum in which new countries could voice their complaints and their needs. With the growing political-military rivalry between the North Atlantic Treaty Organization and the Soviet blocs, nonaligned nations tended to be regarded as potential allies or enemies, and competition for their allegiance became a major diplomatic sport. The "foreign-aid boom" may have owed a little to humanitarian sentiment, and even a little to economic analysis, but it owed much more to international politics.

Social scientists, like judges, follow the election returns; and these strong political tides soon rippled over into the world of scholarship. There was a rapid multiplication, especially in the United States, of research centers, foundation and government grants, specialists and courses in economic development, and advisory missions to foreign countries. The research literature on non-Western economies grew from a trickle in the late 1940s to a flood by the 1960s.

This literature focused heavily on recent events and current problems. Much of it, indeed, was devoted to researching the future in that it explored policies and programs for future growth. A conventional wisdom of economic development grew up rather rapidly. Third-world countries were viewed as lined up, more or less equally, at the threshold of economic growth. They had a future, but no past. Third-world countries were structurally different from the "more-developed countries" and would have to develop along different lines. Old rules of the game no longer applied. In particular, foreign trade could no longer be relied on as an

3

engine of growth because of the bleak outlook for primary exports. Development policies must emphasize reduction of imports and greater self-sufficiency.

In fact, little was known about the economic structure or past growth record of most third-world countries. As Ian Little comments, "A priori postulation and premature stereotyping ran far ahead of empirical research. Hypotheses were accepted as facts, and it has taken years of patient work to undermine the myths thus created. . . . Subsequent research and events have shown that most of the presumptions . . . were wrong."*

Beginning around 1960, the intellectual climate began to change. "Neo-classical economics," previously ignored or explicitly rejected, was rehabilitated and applied to empirical problems. An increasing flow of research revealed, not surprisingly, that economic behavior in third-world economies had much in common with economic behavior elsewhere. Alongside those who were researching the future, some economists turned to researching the past. A growing number of solid monographs on particular countries, often going back to 1900 or beyond, appeared.

This country-specific literature has now accumulated to impressive proportions. The bibliography at the end of this volume, which includes only material available in English, runs to more than four hundred books. There is plenty of reading material to support courses on the economic history of particular regions or of the third world as a whole; and such courses are appearing in increasing numbers, as options or supplements to the standard European and American courses. But no one to my knowledge has undertaken to review and digest the country material and to fit it into a systematic framework. This is the main object of the present study. The discussion may also serve as a corrective to some earlier misconceptions. As against the view that "life began in 1950," I hope to show that the third world has a rich record of prior growth, beginning for most countries in the 1850–1914 era. I hope also to show that growth patterns in third-world countries bear some resemblance to those observed earlier in Europe and North America.

An immersion in the country literature inevitably tempts one to generalize. What does it all add up to? How and why does a country's per capita income, previously stationary, embark on a sustained uptrend? Can economic growth, once initiated, be counted on to continue indefinitely? As per capita income continues to rise, is there a standard pattern of change in the composition and distribution of output? Have growth patterns since World War II differed significantly from those observed before World War II?

These are large questions, which no one study can hope to resolve. But the temptation to suggest answers is there, and I have not resisted it entirely. In later chapters I shall occasionally suggest generalizations, which for brevity must be stated in a way that may appear dogmatic. The reader should understand that these

*Ian M. D. Little, *Economic Development* (New York: Basic Books, 1982), pp. 118–19.

generalizations are less firm in my own mind than they may appear on paper. Further, there are hardly any general statements to which one cannot find exceptions in one country or another. I shall look at such exceptions and try to do justice to the rich variety of country experience.

SCOPE OF THE STUDY

The countries with which I am concerned go by a variety of names. *Underdeveloped* was abandoned rather early as carrying a stigma. *Less developed* is still commonly used. But less developed than what? By what tests, or in what dimensions? The United Nations and other political bodies tend to use the more complimentary term *developing,* but it unfortunately does not describe all countries in the group. *Third world* is a political term, meant to designate countries that are neither part of the OECD (Organization for Economic Cooperation and Development) or of the Soviet–East European bloc. Although I shall use it here for brevity, it has little economic meaning. The countries included under this rubrik, which comprise most of the world's surface and population, differ widely in size, resource base, income level, growth rate, and economic structure.

It is best to admit frankly that the definition of our universe is geographic. It embraces the continents of Asia, Africa, and Central and South America, excluding only Vietnam and North Korea because of poor documentation and South Africa because of its relatively high income level and special socioeconomic characteristics. The late-developing countries of southern and eastern Europe are analogous in some ways to those considered here, but to include them would have stretched an already large undertaking to unmanageable proportions.

Even the three continents I am considering are unmanageable in the sense of including 120 independent countries. To simplify the task, I have generally excluded countries with a population in 1980 of less than ten million. (I have cheated slightly in order to secure a reasonable representation of African countries. Ivory Coast, Zambia, and Zimbabwe, which are included, are somewhat below the ten million mark.) This tactic gets rid of some 80 countries at one stroke, reducing the sample to 41. The exclusion is unfortunate in that small economies have special characteristics, notably heavier dependence on foreign trade. But it does not appear to bias the sample with respect to economic success. Comparative analysis of country growth rates over the period 1950–80 shows no significant relation between growth rate and country size. The spectacular performance of Singapore and Hong Kong is offset by miserable performance in some other small economies.

The countries included, then, are as follows:

Latin America	Argentina, Brazil, Chile, Colombia, Cuba, Mexico, Peru, Venezuela
North Africa and Middle East	Algeria, Egypt, Iran, Iraq, Morocco, Sudan, Turkey

| *Africa (sub-Saharan)* | Ethiopia, Ghana, Ivory Coast, Kenya, Mozambique, Nigeria, Tanzania, Uganda, Zaire, Zambia, Zimbabwe |
| *Asia* | Afghanistan, Bangladesh, Burma, China, India, Indonesia, Japan, Malaysia, Nepal, Pakistan, Philippines, South Korea, Sri Lanka, Taiwan, Thailand |

Present-day country names have been employed here; in some cases they differ from names used during the colonial period. Problems of boundary change on the Indian subcontinent have been taken into account. Taiwan is a province of China rather than a country but has followed a separate development path for almost a century, which seems worth reporting. Some might question the inclusion of Japan, whose high and sustained growth rate has led it to be classified since 1950 among the advanced industrial countries. But Japan's economic success should not rule it out of consideration with the 1880–1940 era, any more than the remarkable success of Taiwan and South Korea should rule them out for the 1950–80 period.

In addition to limiting country coverage, some restriction of scope was necessary to hold the study within manageable bounds. The main focus is on economic growth, in the simplest Kuznetsian sense of an increase in capacity to produce. But this restriction is not as serious as it might appear. Almost everything that happens in an economy will affect its growth rate. So the question of how economic growth begins and how it proceeds over the course of time will lead into areas as diverse as agricultural productivity, the typical sequence of industrialization, patterns of foreign trade, sources and uses of public revenue, and the ways in which growth can be stimulated or retarded by government action.

The emphasis on growth is not meant to downgrade such other important dimensions of national economic performance as institutional improvement, the level of employment, and the distribution of income. Indeed, a good deal will be said about these things. Reliable data on income distribution, however, are limited to recent decades and to a few countries and are still too fragile to support sweeping generalizations.

A further restriction, evident from the bibliography, is that I have relied mainly on writings by economists and economic historians, with only sporadic forays into related social science disciplines. This no doubt imparts a certain bias to the discussion. I have tended to follow the economists' habit of assuming that economies everywhere behave more or less similarly and that, if they are sufficiently insulated from political shock and other exogenous disasters, they will go about the business of development and growth. In this view third-world countries are much like those of the first world and will, with a modicum of external aid and internal stability, follow in the path of their predecessors.

Although there is an element of truth in this view, it is also in some ways limited. One perceptive reviewer of this manuscript commented that most third-world societies do not have the value systems required to generate economic development from within; and also that I had not taken adequate account of political variables. He remarked that

> some of these countries (Argentina is an example) have seen their promise blighted by internecine conflict. They have been, as it were, derailed; and with luck, may yet get back on the rails. But this raises the question whether political stability is not also related to internal characteristics. . . . [The author] could do much more to stress the degree to which appropriate and effective forms of government are a function not only of experience, but also—and once again—of values. I am thinking here of such things as the shift from office as property (an opportunity for personal enrichment) to office as function (a bundle of tasks and obligations). Or of the shift from personal power to the rule of law.

I have much sympathy with these comments. But one person can do only so much; and the ideal volume would never have been finished. In the two concluding chapters I have tried, in a very amateur way, to assess the impact of political variables on a country's growth performance. But the study is no doubt still too "economic" in tone. Perhaps in time someone with broader social science skills will be able to put more flesh on this bare-bones narrative.

THE CONCEPTION OF GROWTH

Studies of national economic growth tend to begin with the point at which one observes a sustained rise in per capita income and to focus on experience after that point. But what is going on "before the curtain rises"? Rarely, if ever, does the rise in per capita income begin from a situation of stationary population size and national output. Anything resembling the "classical stationary state" would be hard to find in modern times. Rather, one observes in most countries during the eighteenth and early nineteenth centuries that population is growing slowly and national ouput is rising at about the same rate. A situation in which population and output are growing at roughly the same rate, with no secular rise of per capita output, I define as *extensive growth*.

Kuznets's view is that this is genuine growth, deserving of study. A similar view is taken in an interesting study by Ashok Guha (1981), who regards growth as biological adaptation to environment. A species that is able to reproduce itself and increase in numbers is a successful species.

I share this view for several reasons. Empirically, the era in which population and output are growing without a rise in per capita output is usually quite long (in China, it is said to have lasted for some six centuries before 1949). To omit this period, then, is to omit a substantial part of the growth story. Analytically, the conventional procedure in which the rate of population growth is simply deducted from the rate of gross domestic product (GDP) growth to arrive at what is *defined* as "economic growth" reduces population growth to secondary importance. A broader definition, under which economic growth begins when population growth begins, has the merit of restoring population analysis to a more prominent place. Finally, some developments that arise during an era of extensive growth, if not strictly prerequisite to a later rise in per capita output, are at least helpful in facilitating it. There is considerable continuity in the evolution of an economy.

Of the 41 countries in our sample, seven seem still to be in the extensive-growth era. But in the remaining countries, at various points in time between 1850 and 1965, the beginnings of a sustained rise in per capita output can be observed— sustained in the sense that, although year-to-year growth rates are uneven, per capita output does not fall back to its initial level. I call the point at which this happens the *turning point.* In chapter 3 I shall date the turning point for each country, but it should be understood that there is nothing magical about this date. Rather, I mean to draw attention to a period of a decade or so before and after the date. The turning point can be identified only in retrospect; it will usually be a decade or more before a trend is certain rather than a temporary upswing to be followed by relapse.

I call the sustained rise in per capita output after the turning point *intensive growth.* This does not mean that the future beyond the turning point is entirely predictable. There is predictability in the sense that, so long as per capita output continues to rise, there will be systematic changes in the composition and uses of national output, the broad contours of which have been charted by Kuznets, Chenery, and others. But the growth rate of per capita output will fluctuate in response to swings in the world economy, harvest variations, resource discoveries, and other circumstances. In addition to such fluctuations, there are countries—Japan, Taiwan, Korea—in which the trend rate of growth has accelerated over the long run. There is one notable case, Argentina, in which growth has decelerated gradually over the past century. There are also cases, such as Ghana, Uganda, and Zambia, in which growth has changed to stagnation or decline. The turning point is not an insurance policy for all future time.

My schema thus includes three chronological stages: an era of extensive growth, followed (in cases of success) by a turning point, followed by an era of intensive growth extending in most cases to the present day. I find this schema useful in organizing historical experience and will follow it in later chapters. But it also invites misunderstanding, because the same terms have been used with different meanings by other economists. So some further distinctions are in order.

Readers of the literature on agriculture will recall the distinction between the *extensive margin of cultivation,* on which previously unused land is being brought into production, and the *intensive margin of cultivation,* on which more labor and other variable inputs are being applied to previously cultivated acres. Here *extensive* and *intensive* are clearly being used in a quite different sense. The extensive and intensive margins do not form a chronological sequence. They coexist at each point in time and are extended in a balanced way that equates marginal productivity of the variable factors on the two margins.

There is still some danger of confusion, because expansion of acreage on the extensive margin of cultivation is usually a prominent feature of my era of extensive growth. Eventually, as population continues to grow, all cultivable land is occupied and the extensive margin vanishes. Continued increases in agricultural output are then dependent on application of more variable inputs at the intensive margin, accompanied by innovation in crops and production methods. It is quite possible, even usual, for efforts in these directions to succeed in raising food output in line with population growth. We may thus see a continuation of *extensive growth* (in my sense) accomplished by continuing effort on the *intensive margin* of cultivation.

Thus there is no necessary correspondence in time between the end of the frontier and the end of my extensive-growth era. There are cases—Egypt, for example—in which land was fully occupied long *before* the turning point. But there are many more cases in which the end of the frontier came well *after* the turning point. Indeed, a surprising number of third-world countries still have reserves of unused land.

A word now about turning points. My turning point marks the transition from a stationary to a rising trend of per capita output, a transition that is arguably important. But after my turning point, that is, within the intensive-growth era, there are additional dates that have sometimes been regarded as turning points and that are also important. One of these is the point at which declining birthrates overtake declining deathrates, so that the rate of natural increase begins to fall. This point, which in northwestern Europe and North America was passed before 1900, has been passed by some third-world countries only since 1960, and in most of those countries it still lies in the future. Another significant date is that at which the agricultural labor force, which goes on increasing for a long time after our turning point, finally begins to shrink in absolute size. This marks a late stage of intensive growth, a stage at which the suction of labor demand into urban activities is strong enough to absorb more than the natural increase of population in rural areas.

Perhaps most significant is the Lewis (1954) turning point, which appears also in the Fei-Ranis (1964) model as the "commercialization point," at which an assumed initial pool of surplus labor has been drained dry and the real wage level begins to rise. I shall have more to say about this concept in chapter 4. The relevant point here is that this is also a late stage of the growth story. In Japan, for example, I date the turning point at 1880, but the Lewis turning point was reached only in the 1920s. I date the turning point for Taiwan in 1895, and for Korea in 1910, the dates of Japanese colonization; but Taiwan and South Korea reached the Lewis turning point only in the late 1960s. For China, my turning point is 1949, but the Lewis turning point has not yet been reached.

Walt Rostow's "takeoff" concept (1956) has not fared well in the literature, but a word should be added about it. Rostow tends to identify growth with industrialization and to date a country's takeoff as the point at which one sees a substantial development of factory industry. In my schema, the turning point is typically characterized by an acceleration of agricultural (or occasionally mineral) output and a rising foreign-trade ratio. Rising income from exports does broaden the domestic market for manufactures, but the initial supply response comes mainly from handicraft workshops and small-scale industries. There is usually a lag of several decades before factory industry becomes prominent, though this lag has been shorter since 1950 than it was in earlier times.

Thus Rostow's takeoff datings (1978) are typically too late, sometimes much too late, from my point of view. A few examples may be useful:

Country	Reynolds Turning Point	Rostow Takeoff
Argentina	1860	1933–50
Brazil	1880	1933–50
Mexico	1873	1940–60
South Korea	1910	1961–68
Taiwan	1895	1953–60
Thailand	1850	1960–70

Further, Rostow posited a "takeoff into self-sustained growth." This implies that, once the plane is off the ground, it moves up smoothly to a stable cruising altitude. My turning point carries no such guarantee. Some countries in my sample have managed to do less well in recent decades than they were doing at an earlier time, and in some cases per capita output fell during the 1970s.

My turning-point dates are early, most of them falling between 1850 and 1914. This will raise at least two questions in readers' minds. First, until recently most of these areas were colonies rather than independent countries. In 17 cases my turning point falls within the colonial era. Can a country really develop in a significant sense under colonial rule? Second, in almost every case the turning point is associated with a sharp rise in exports of agricultural or mineral products. Much of the recent development literature is critical of growth led by primary exports. Such a growth pattern is sometimes regarded as "colonial" or "neo-colonial," benefiting the industrial countries rather than the primary-product suppliers, and even as unviable over the long run. These questions deserve more attention than is feasible in an introductory chapter and will be considered at some length in chapter 3.

THE METHOD OF ANALYSIS

Having defined economic growth, I now must consider how to set about analyzing it. In my view, countries are the basic unit of study, and national time series are the main raw material.

Economic growth occurs within units of varying size: farms and business enterprises, cities, regions, countries. But among these, the nation is most significant. *Nation* is used here to include colonies, a view I shall try to justify in chapter 3. Some degree of political unification, of continuity in government, of external peace and internal order seems necessary before growth can begin. Further, economic interaction is more intense within national boundaries than across them. And a nation can in principle control economic events within its borders but not beyond them. Thus efforts to understand long-term growth must start from the experience of individual countries. National case studies are the building blocks for growth analysis.

This view, however, is open to challenge from two directions. Some would urge regional units as at least equally important. In large countries such as India, China, or Brazil there are well-known differences in regional income levels and growth rates, and the significance of national averages may well be questioned. Indeed, regional income differences probably tend to widen during the early decades of intensive growth. But over the longer run they tend to narrow again; and they narrow precisely because the regions are part of a nation, making possible relatively free movement of factors and the application of national economic policies to reduce inequality. The disequalizing effects of growth, emphasized by Myrdal and others, do not seem to dominate over the long run.

An opposite and perhaps more trenchant criticism is that analysis should focus on the world economy and that it is the position of a country within this larger structure that determines its economic fate. Several strands of thought recur in this literature: the argument that most third-world countries were long exploited by the colonial powers and that many are still exploited under a system of "neo-colonialism"; the "dependencia" or "unequal exchange" view that third-world nations are inherently disadvantaged in the world trading system; the view, advanced most recently by Immanuel Wallerstein (1979), that the core-periphery distinction is fundamental and that the exploited peripheral countries are essential to the functioning of the core countries. It follows that all countries cannot develop simultaneously.

A critical review of this literature would require a separate essay. On the whole, I find it unconvincing. Much of it appears doctrinaire and nonempirical, more concerned with reasoning from general principles than with careful observation of reality. It flies in the face of the evidence of massive economic progress in many countries since 1945.

Even if one finds the core-periphery schema useful, one must admit that nations do not remain locked in position within this schema. Japan would certainly have been classified as peripheral in 1880. Today, it is part of the core. Quite a few other middle-income countries have achieved at least "semi-core" status. The world economy offers opportunities as well as constraints, but nations differ in their ability to take advantage of these opportunities. The world economic boom of 1850–1914, and the more recent boom of 1945–73, offered increased opportunities to move from extensive to intensive growth. Yet in each of these periods, some countries were able to climb onto the growth escalator while others were not. What makes the difference? Generalized complaints about exploitation of third world countries do not provide a satisfactory answer.

In reviewing historical experience, I have been impressed with the degree of *mobility* among national economies. Countries are continuously reranking themselves in the national-income league, through widely differing rates of progress. This is at least as true of third-world countries as of the "developed" countries, where there has also been considerable reranking since 1945. The interesting question is why the growth rate of per capita income should differ so widely among countries. It would seem that efforts at explanation should focus not on the world economic environment, which to some extent is common to all, but on the internal dynamics of each national economy.

Having chosen countries as the unit, and having compiled a list of 41, I turn next to the question, What would we like to know about them? The ideal data bank would consist of long time series for each country, measuring a rather obvious list of economic magnitudes, beginning at some point in the period of extensive growth and continuing through the turning point to the present day. What we actually have falls far short of this ideal. For the long period before 1940, the data are quite fragmentary. They relate mainly to things which governments tend to measure for administrative purposes, including the following.

1. *Population*. For most parts of the world other than tropical Africa there are estimates of population size going back for several centuries. Dana Durand (1974) has reviewed these estimates and has assigned quality grades, A through D, to countries and major regions. The ratings for 1750 are quite poor, with many areas receiving C and D grades and only Japan getting an A. By 1900, however, the ratings are much better, with no D grades and only three Cs. This improvement over time would no doubt hold true also for trade statistics and other economic data, though I have not found any Durand-type ratings. This qualitative change in time-series data obviously increases the difficulty of drawing conclusions from them. What appears to be an increase in quantity may partly reflect more complete enumeration.

2. *Foreign Trade*. Foreign trade is measured in the course of applying export and import duties, a major source of government revenue in earlier times. In addition to value totals, which raise serious problems of deflation, there are often physical series for principal export and import products. The data are somewhat impaired by smuggling activities, but the fact that trade flows are recorded by both participating countries permits cross-checking for accuracy. The primary data on trade have been worked over quite thoroughly by Kuznets (1967), Lewis (1969), Maizels (1968), and others, and economic historians have usually exploited the data available for their countries.

3. *Government Finance*. Again, accuracy of reporting varies with the political structure and with honesty and competence in public administration. The best

accounts are usually for colonial areas where the metropolitan government, concerned that the colony should be self-supporting, required a detailed accounting of revenues and expenditures.

4. *Agricultural Acreage and Output.* This area is not very well documented. Instead of the continuous time series we would like to have, there are fragments of information for scattered years and on a variety of subjects. They include: total cultivated acreage; percent of acreage that is irrigated; acreage devoted to each major crop—interesting because there is often considerable change in the composition of output even during the period of extensive growth; occasionally, estimates of yields per acre for particular crops. Information on yields is sparse, however, and historians tend to assume constant yields in the absence of a better alternative and in the absence of significant evidence of technical progress.

Information on national output, then, reduces to output of export products, government output, and limited information on domestic food production. Manufacturing production, which at this stage is carried on mainly in households and handicraft workshops, is essentially unmeasured; so too is trade and production of private services. Thus the conclusions one finds in economic histories of individual countries are almost invariably qualitative, taking the form ''there is no indication of an increase in per capita output *before* such-and-such date'' or ''per capita income seems to have been rising appreciably *after* such-and-such date.'' Here the historian is trying to judge what the time series of total and per capita output would look like if they were actually available. And I, standing on the shoulders of the country specialists, can only report these judgments without trying to improve them.

For the years since 1945 the situation is better. The United Nations and its specialized agencies, as well as the International Bank for Reconstruction and Development (IBRD), International Monetary Fund (IMF), OECD, and other organizations, regularly collect national accounts and a great variety of other economic measurements from almost every country. The quality of the national accounts, to be sure, still varies widely from country to country. But imperfect numbers, interpreted with due caution, are better than no numbers at all. I shall mine this data bank at some length in a later chapter.

Frustration at the scarcity of really long time series has led to widespread resort to cross-section studies as a partial substitute. In the 1950s, indeed, this was the only possible course. Countries were arranged in order of per capita income in U.S. dollars as of a particular year, and per capita income was then used as an independent variable to explore differences in economic structure.

Such studies are interesting and important in their own right. They have confirmed many systematic differences in the structure of production and employment for countries at differing income levels. In general, recent work by Chenery and others supports the earlier findings of Clark, Hoffman, and Kuznets.

It is wrong, however, to regard cross-section analyses as a satisfactory substitute for longitudinal studies. The reasons are partly technical and statistical—

distortions in the conversion of national currencies to U.S. dollar equivalents, differences in regression coefficients derived from cross-section as against time-series data, and so on. But the matter goes deeper than this. Cross-section analysis at a single point in time cannot reproduce the richness of events over time. It cannot answer such key questions as why a particular country reaches a turning point at one time rather than another or why, during a particular time period, some countries grow considerably faster than others. Nor can it illuminate the qualitative changes in economic and political institutions that typically accompany growth and that may either accelerate or impede it. Each country is a historically unique individual whose growth experience will not be replicated precisely by any other country. This sense of identity is lost when Ghana becomes simply X_{33} in a supposedly homogeneous universe.

There is no satisfactory substitute for comparative analysis of national time series. This is the method pioneered by Kuznets in his classic studies of long-term growth in the "developed" countries. We can try to work in the spirit of Kuznets, even though the data do not allow us to replicate the precision of his results.

2

The Era of Extensive Growth

The era in which population and output are growing at about the same rate is a long one. It typically lasts for a century or more, and in some countries extensive growth has been documented over several centuries. I propose to ask several questions about such a period:

1. How is the economy organized? What do we mean by such terms as *premodern, traditional,* or *subsistence economy?*
2. How and why does population begin to grow? How is food output increased to keep pace with population?
3. What changes do we observe in the organization of industry, trade, and other nonagricultural sectors? For example, does power-driven factory production ever appear before the turning point?
4. Finally, several analytical problems;
   a. When per capita income fails to rise, does this indicate the absence of significant change? Under these circumstances are we dealing with a ''stationary state''?
   b. In classical economic models, population growth usually was associated with a change in per capita income—positive or negative, depending on the model. How can the economy increase in size without an appreciable change in per capita income?
   c. In what sense, if at all, can developments during the extensive-growth era be regarded as a preparation, or a precondition, for the later turning point to intensive growth?

ECONOMIC ORGANIZATION

What does the economy look like during a period of extensive growth? Some of the terms commonly used for this stage of development are not really very descriptive. We often speak of these economies as ''traditional'' or ''conventional,'' the implication being that actions are guided by customary rules rather than economic

15

calculation. In particular, the small peasant farmers who make up most of the population are portrayed as following traditional farming routines. This scenario surely overstates the role of custom and understates the importance of economic rationality. There is now abundant evidence that small peasant producers, in view of what they know and the constraints they face, behave just as economically as American farmers. In a situation where crop failure can mean disaster and even starvation, peasant farmers are sensibly averse to risk. But they are quite responsive to *demonstrated* opportunities for income improvement. As we shall see, introduction of new crops and methods for the intensification of cultivation is usually going on even during the extensive-growth period. And the later transition to intensive growth is heavily dependent on a "normal" farmer response to income incentives.

Another familiar term is *subsistence economy*. This has a dual connotation: people consume what they produce, and they live in some sense at a minimum or conventional level of "subsistence." Both statements contain an element of truth, but both are also treacherous. The ratio of home production to home consumption rarely approaches 100 percent, and it is certainly not invariant among countries or over time. The conventional level of "subsistence" is also flexible. In adverse periods, it can be depressed farther than one might have thought possible in advance. And it is quite flexible upward when conditions are improving.

It is better to say that the economy is dominated at the stage of extensive growth by *household production*. Each family produces not only most of its own food, but most of its housing and clothing, plus a wide range of services—education, healing, recreational activity, religious observance. We commonly observe that at this stage 80–90 percent of the population live in rural areas, on isolated farms or in small villages close to farmland. This was true in Europe in 1700, and the 80 percent ratio still holds in China today. This percentage is sometimes wrongly regarded as indicating the size of the agricultural sector. All it really means is that most economic activity is family activity. A careful record of time use by rural family members will reveal that agricultural activities take perhaps 50–60 percent of the total, the remainder going to "industrial" and service activities.

It follows that the apparent shrinkage of the agricultural sector and the swelling up of other sectors as economic growth proceeds is partly fictitious. In part, the shift represents a transfer of activities from households to specialized commercial producers, whose activities are more readily detected and measured. But people always have clothes and they always have housing, no matter how these goods are produced.

The prominence of household production is not inconsistent with a substantial amount of marketed output, a widespread development of markets, and trade and transport over long distances. Nor is it inconsistent with substantial changes in commodities, techniques, market organization, and trade routes over the course of time. What some might view as a "primitive" economy is in fact quite complex, sophisticated, and responsive to change.

In the case of Western European countries, this view would be readily accepted. It is well known that these economies became increasingly diversified, commercialized, and linked by trade relations during the sixteenth and seventeenth
centuries. Well before the industrial era European economies experienced substantial development of towns and town markets, extensive development of manufacturing by handicraft methods, substantial interchange of goods between town
and country, creeping technical progress in agriculture, internal trade along rivers
and canals, and overseas trade around the shores of the Mediterranean and the
Baltic and North seas.

There is a tendency, however, to assume that similar statements cannot be
made about third-world countries, that their pre-turning point economies were less
commercialized, more static, more agriculture-oriented than were their European
counterparts. As evidence to the contrary, let us look briefly at three cases: China
during the Ming and Ching dynasties; West Africa before 1900; and the contemporary Sherpa economy of northern Nepal.

China

The case of China has been documented by Albert Feuerwerker (1968, 1969),
Dwight Perkins (1969, 1975), Alexander Eckstein (1977), and others. The six
centuries before 1949 can be regarded as an era of extensive growth, which had
been going on more or less continuously since establishment of the Ming dynasty
in 1368. Over this period the population of the country increased about eight
times. What did the economy look like during these centuries?

Agriculture was central, but far from all-important. Feuerwerker estimates
that agricultural output was about two-thirds of national output in the 1880s. This
is close to Eckstein's estimate of 65 percent for 1933, suggesting the absence of
significant structural change. The percentage of rural *population,* of course, was
substantially higher—perhaps 80 percent of the total, as indeed it is today. But the
rural population was doing many things besides growing foodstuffs.

Industry, which at this stage meant handicrafts, accounted for perhaps 7–8
percent of national output. This work was done mainly in individual farm households. But there was also cooperative activity by a number of households in rice
milling, wheat milling, and salt and pottery production; and there were some
larger workshops in urban areas. The trading activities, to be described later,
constituted another 7–8 percent, and transport perhaps 5 percent, of national
output. Government in the late nineteenth century was raising in taxes about 7.5
percent of national output, a figure not out of line with tax ratios in European
countries during the nineteenth century.

The most notable feature of the centuries before 1900 was the gradual peopling of the country. The population in 1400 is estimated at 65–80 million, heavily
concentrated in the lower Yangtze valley and along the east coast. From these
areas people spread out to the south and southwest, west into the "rice bowl" of
Szechwan, and north into the North China Plain. The process was still continuing

in 1900 with expansion into Manchuria and Sinkiang, though land here was of lower quality than that settled earlier. The average growth rate of population before 1900 was about 0.4 percent by year, held to this level by occasional wars and famine as well as endemic diseases. The 1913 population is estimated at 430 ± 25 million.

If we assume, as China scholars generally do, that per capita food consumption changed little over this long period, then agricultural output must have risen roughly in line with population. How was this increase accomplished? The most obvious source is an increase in cultivated acreage, which grew about fourfold between 1400 and 1950. More interesting, however, is that yields per acre roughly doubled over this period, indicating that the "traditional economy" was not immune to technical change. Perkins (1969) notes several kinds of change:

1. Some improvement of seeds, partly developed and diffused within China, partly imported from abroad.
2. Introduction of new crops from America after 1600. Corn and potatoes were especially important, partly because they could be grown in areas not hospitable to other crops. As the frontier gradually closed and the man / land ratio rose after 1850, farmers adjusted to the decreasing availability of new land partly by shifting to crops (including cash crops such as cotton and raw silk) that yielded more food or income per acre and at the same time required more labor for their cultivation.
3. A gradual extension of double-cropping, accompanied by irrigation projects to provide the necessary control of water supply. By 1900 irrigation had been extended to almost all feasible acreage. Population growth in a sense *produced* more double-cropping by providing more labor both for seasonal peaks of cultivation and for water-control projects.
4. An increase of inputs, notably fertilizer inputs. More people produced more night soil! So did more pigs, whose numbers apparently kept up with population growth. Perkins suggests that, without this side benefit, pork production would have been unprofitable.

Trade was carried on in a stable hierarchy of markets, ranging from local to international in scope. Perhaps three-quarters of total trade went on in some 70,000 local markets, in which peasants and handicraftsmen exchanged their surplus produce. Local trade absorbed perhaps 20 percent of farm output, and this proportion seems not to have changed much over the centuries. Trade was thoroughly monetized and commercialized but restricted in geographic scope.

Longer-distance trade was restricted by transport costs and involved only objects of sufficient value to warrant the cost. Trade moved mainly along waterways, notably the vast Yangtze network, by vessels ranging from tiny sampans to large freighters. In northern China, less well supplied with waterways, most goods had to be moved by carts, which was slow and expensive. It is estimated that only 5–7 percent of national output went into interprovincial trade and perhaps 1–2 percent into foreign trade. Even by 1900 the trade network had changed only a little at the seacoast fringes and not at all within the country.

The government apparatus presiding over this economic activity was a meritocracy populated by the small educated elite. Perhaps because of the sheer size of the country, provincial and local governments were relatively more important than in smaller countries. Regular (or irregular) tribute was paid to the Emperor, but the Emperor was far away. Scholars estimate that even in the 1890s only 40 percent of tax revenues went to the central government. Government did little to promote economic growth, but it was adequate for maintenance of the economy at a relatively constant level of per capita output.

West Africa

A more surprising illustration comes from West Africa. One might visualize the economic organization of this region in precolonial times as unusually primitive and custom-bound, with tribal villages existing in economic isolation and following an unchanging production routine. But evidence assembled by A. G. Hopkins (1973) suggests that the reality was rather different.

As of 1800–50, West Africa was sparsely populated. Hours worked were low, varying with the season, but averaging perhaps half a day over the course of the year. This did not reflect a strong preference for leisure but resulted partly from physical debility due to tropical diseases and partly from resource constraints, which limited the opportunity for productive activity. There were substantial concentrations of population. Of the Hausa population in what is now northern Nigeria, about half lived in towns, of which Kano with 30,000 people was the largest. Yorubaland had a dozen towns of 20,000 or more. Ibadan, the principal city, had 70,000 people and city walls with a circumference of 24 miles. There was also much mobility among the population, associated mainly with shifting pasturage of livestock and with trading activities.

Production occurred mainly within the household, support of whose members was an overhead cost that was spread over a variety of activities. There was also a market for nonfamily labor, though this was mainly a slave rather than a hired-labor market. Slavery was a long-established institution, especially in areas where development of an exchange economy had created more employment opportunities than could be met by local free labor. Slaves were preferred because the cost of acquiring and maintaining them was less than the cost of hiring labor for wages.

Agriculture was the basic economic activity, with cereals predominating in the northern savanna and root crops, which yield more calories per acre, predominating in the forest. Cattle raising, an ancient activity, was restricted to areas free of tsetse fly and usually involved migration in search of adequate pasture. The early food crops had come mainly from Asia by way of the Middle East. Through contact with European traders many new crops were introduced, especially from

South America. Successful innovations included corn, cassava, groundnuts, tobacco, and cocoa. The crops that survived and spread did so for the good reason
that the value of output exceeded the cost of production. This responsiveness to
change refutes the idea of a static "traditional" economy.

At least seven different methods of cultivation were practiced in different
parts of West Africa, ranging from shifting use of virgin land to permanent,
intensive cultivation. The average length of the fallow period, a good measuring
rod for comparing different systems, seems to have been mainly a function of
population density, availability of fertilizer from animal or other sources, and the
range of crops produced. Permanent cultivation was associated with a rather dense
population, good fertilizer supply, and a variety of crops. Here again we see an
economic adaptation to the environment.

Africans seem to have been quite good farm managers. The charge of primitive technology is based mainly on their limited use of the plow. But the evidence
suggests that this was a rational decision, reflecting the fact that deep plowing was
not suited to fragile tropical soils, or that the plow was too costly relative to
available alternatives, or both. Nor is it accurate to say that productivity was
hampered by "communal tenure" of land. Although land ownership was usually
vested in the village, cultivation rights to particular strips were clearly allocated
among families and could even be inherited.

Regarding industry Hopkins notes in *An Economic History of West Africa*
that "pre-colonial Africa had a range of manufacturing industries which closely
resembled that of pre-industrial societies in other parts of the world . . . based on
clothing, metal working, ceramics, construction, and food processing." Kano
was a major textile center, a kind of Manchester of West Africa. Leather goods
were prominent in cattle-raising areas. Pottery production was widely diffused
throughout the region. While most of these handicraft activities were carried on
within family units, they were often regulated by guild rules that any European
would have recognized as familiar.

The extensive development of trade and markets should be emphasized as an
offset to stereotypes of purely subsistence production. Local trade was carried on
in regular town markets, to which people walked from a radius of ten miles or so,
bringing in foodstuffs and carrying back craft products. Nearby towns arranged to
rotate their market days to avoid overlapping.

Perhaps more surprising, there was an organized network of long trade
routes, covering distances as great as from the Lake Chad area to Dakar or from
Kano to the Mediterranean coast. This long-distance trade usually moved in
caravans, which individual traders could join for part or all of their journey. The
caravans provided protection from bandits and other economies of joint effort.
There were recognized trade centers along these routes for the assembly, breakup,
or reexport of shipments; an elaborate system of local agents and commission men;
banking and credit facilities; even a code of commercial morality. Transport was
by boat along water routes, by head porterage in the forest, by donkeys and camels
in the savanna and desert.

The people who participated in this trade can be classified as:

1. "Target marketers," who made a few trips in the dry season carrying cloth, salt, kola nuts, or whatever, to acquire a certain sum of money for a specific purpose.
2. Regular traders, whose commercial operations were integrated vertically with some specialized production activities. Thus a producer might gradually accumulate a stock of iron implements, weapons, or whatever, and then sell them when market conditions were favorable.
3. Specialized and substantial professional traders, with no connection with production. These could be regarded as business firms, with an established operating routine, a head-office staff, and a network of buying and selling agents scattered along their trade route.
4. Official traders buying or selling on behalf of some royal house. At this stage a high proportion of state revenue came either directly from trade or from taxes levied on traders.

The Sherpas of Northern Nepal

A word finally on a small but interesting economy still in the extensive-growth stage, one that is perhaps as untouched by modernization as that in any part of the world. Walking through the Sherpa country gives one the impression of having stepped back several centuries to some area of medieval Europe. My expertise on this economy comes from four long treks into the Himalaya, each lasting about five weeks and covering several hundred miles over mountain trails, that I made accompanied only by my wife and a caravan of Sherpa guides and porters. Our guide on these expeditions, Sherpa Ang Lakpa of Khumjung village, is an experienced mountaineer who speaks Tibetan, Sherpa, and Nepali as well as English, French, and German. He was invaluable in putting economic questions for me to villagers and traders and translating their replies, as well as in explaining his own domestic economy.

The Sherpas are descended from Tibetans who from about 1850 onward moved south over the Himalayan passes; they occupy the higher valleys, at altitudes of 8,000 to 15,000 feet. Most of their family labor time (including heavy labor by women as well as men) is spent in food production. Millet and other coarse grains can be grown in the lower altitudes; potatoes, almost as important to the Sherpas as to the Irish, can be grown at 12,000 feet. The yak, which good Buddhists must not kill or eat, is in all other ways a most useful animal. It provides milk, blood (drawn from the veins, as the Masai do in Africa, and mixed with porridge to provide animal protein), and hair (the main raw material for cloth spinning and weaving).

Almost everything that is consumed is home-produced. Clothing, Tibetan-style boots, and carpets are woven in the household on simple hand looms. The sturdy, Swiss-style houses needed to withstand winter weather are built by the householder with the help of neighbors and a few specialized artisans in the village. Recreation and other "services" are also home-produced. They include village feasts, which each family is obligated to provide in turn, depleting its liquidity for some years to come; and religious festivals at local monasteries, which the villages support mainly by contributions of food.

Trade with lower regions to the south is severely constrained by lack of transport. The terrain is so steep and broken that it is not feasible to build roads suited to wheeled vehicles. Whatever moves must move over footpaths on the backs of people, donkeys, or crossbred cattle used as pack animals. So in the short (in miles) journey from southern to northern Nepal, a kilo of rice or wheat doubles in price; and a glass window (one of the few signs of Sherpa affluence) or a large piece of lumber carried on a porter's back from Kathmandu triples in price.

Some rice and wheat does come in. And villagers from lower altitudes also bring chickens, eggs, goats, and other supplies to the great weekly market at Namche Bazaar, where local people sit on the hillside and estimate the day's prices by the number of sellers approaching up the valley. The only other significant imports to Sherpa land are metal tools and cooking utensils, bits of hardware for door hinges, and salt.

Money is widely used, mainly in the form of Nepalese rupees, though the black-market value of foreign currencies is also well known. Economic motivation is pervasive. People know to a penny the difference between the price of a commodity in one area and another, and if the spread is sufficient to cover transport costs, goods will move. Income differences are sufficient to be noted and envied. Everyone is eager to have a bit more land, glass windows and copper cooking utensils in the home, an additional yak, or a crossbred pack animal that can be used to supplement family income.

As one lives with these honest, kindly, cheerful people, one is bound to ask, "In what way are they poor?" Any comparative tabulation of worldwide per capita income would put them near the bottom of the list. What does this mean? They are eating reasonably well, their clothing is adequate for the climate, their houses are substantial and durable. Education is still almost absent. Few adult Sherpas have ever been in a school, and such language and arithmetical skills as they have are self-taught. Health conditions are also poor, with tuberculosis and goiter especially common. There is only one small, foreign-financed hospital with two doctors for all the villages in the Everest region. Life expectancy is short. In these respects the Sherpas are indeed poor, though not as badly off as the gross national product (GNP) figures would suggest.

Examples could be multiplied—from India, from Java, from Egypt, and elsewhere. But the cases cited here are perhaps sufficient to dispel misconceptions about the pre–turning point economy. Production does *not* consist only of grubbing food from the soil. People produce and consume a wide range of goods and services. The economy is *not* uncommercial and unmonetized. A considerable percentage of output is exchanged among households. Local trade is always important, and long-distance trade is often quite important. Individual and family calculations are *not* "uneconomic." There is abundant evidence that poor and illiterate people can make precise calculations of economic advantage. The economy is *not* unresponsive to innovation, as shown particularly by the spread of new crops imported from other parts of the world and the gradual intensification of cultivation systems.

POPULATION AND FOOD SUPPLY

Population Growth

During the era of extensive growth, population is increasing by definition; and this increase begins very early. Durand (in *Population Problems,* 1967) estimates that population was growing at a low rate almost everywhere in the world from at least 1750 onward. (A possible exception is tropical Africa, for which estimates before 1900 are quite dubious.) Growth rates were low by modern standards. In Europe, the average growth rate was about 0.7 percent per year from 1800 to 1850 and 0.8 percent from 1850 to 1900. Kuznets's estimate (in Easterlin, 1980) for the less-developed countries places their average population growth at 0.35 percent from 1800 to 1850 and 0.56 percent from 1850 to 1900.

The great killers are famine, war, and plague. Where these are somewhat under control, population tends to grow through a modest excess of births over deaths. During the extensive-growth stage of development, the fertility rate is mainly the result of uncontrolled reproduction. People are not sure that they will have as many surviving children as they would prefer to have. In Easterlin's terminology, the desired number of children, C_d, is greater than the natural fertility rate, C_n; so the former is dominant, and there is no incentive for population control.

To speak of a "natural fertility rate" does not imply that it is a universal constant determined by biology alone. Even the uncontrolled birth rate is influenced by such things as: (1) the percentage of women who marry; (2) average age at marriage, which varies presently from around 30 in Ireland to 25 in the United States to 20 in tropical Africa; (3) the rate at which fecundity declines with age; (4) the average interval between births, which is influenced by social factors such as breast-feeding customs and taboos on intercourse during breast-feeding, and so may vary from less than two years to more than three years; (5) the probability of husband or wife dying before the end of the child-bearing period. Because of these factors, uncontrolled birth rates range from about 35 to 55 per thousand.

The mortality rate is somewhat influenced by economic factors. Famine, traditionally an important cause of death, has been gradually eliminated by reductions in the cost of transporting food within and among countries. More recently, improvements in nutrition, sanitation, and literacy have reduced child mortality from diarrhea and other diseases. To a large extent, however, the determinants of mortality are exogenous, related to the progress of medical science; and this progress is somewhat discontinuous. Thus after a gradual sag of mortality rates up to 1914 we see a marked drop after 1920 and another marked drop after 1945.

Although in general we shall argue for similarity between "early developers" and "late developers," the population growth rate is one respect in which the timing of a country's turning point makes a decided difference. Countries that reached the turning point before 1914 did so when the population growth rate was still low, typically below 1 percent. For output to accelerate sufficiently to outrace population and initiate intensive growth was thus no great feat.

But since 1920, and especially since 1945, population growth in third-world countries has accelerated sharply. Medical progress has impinged on every country, regardless of its income level or growth rate. For countries already well launched on intensive growth, including most of Latin America and parts of East and Southeast Asia, high population growth rates did not pose an insuperable problem. But for latecomers, those still in the extensive-growth phase in 1945, the problem of getting started has been formidable. This is one reason that some of the post-1945 turning points remain precarious and that some countries have not yet reached the turning point.

Growth of Food Supply

We have defined extensive growth as a situation in which population growth is matched by growth of national output and in particular of food supply. When we see population growing, how do we know that this second condition is met? The data for some of the larger third-world countries, such as Brazil, India, China, and Indonesia, have been worked over with considerable care. Typically, studies suggest that food output per capita was either stationary or rising very slowly in the premodern period. Usually, however, we have to resort to negative reasoning. *If* population growth had been accompanied by marked deterioration of living standards, one would expect this deterioration to have been reported by informed observers. While reports of short-term hardships arising from drought and other natural disasters are common in the literature, reports of a secular decline in living standards are rare. In general, growing populations manage to feed themselves at near-stationary levels.

How is this feat accomplished? Least interesting, though very important historically, is the simple extension of the cultivated area. As of 1900, most of the countries in our sample still had reserves of unused land, and some countries of Africa and South America still do. The spreading out of population over a larger area, with at least a proportionate increase in agricultural output, is familiar from American history and presents no analytical problems.

More interesting is intensification of cultivation, which tends to accompany acreage expansion and becomes dominant when the frontier finally closes. Using length of the fallow period as an indicator of intensity, one can lay out a spectrum of cultivation systems ranging from slash-and-burn through bush fallow to short fallow, annual cropping with no fallow period, and multicropping. Ester Boserup (1964, 1981) has argued persuasively that movement along this spectrum is an endogenous result of population growth. The population increase that requires larger food supplies also tends to produce them by bringing about a shift toward more intensive land use. She uses cross-section analysis across countries to test the relation between population density and the cultivation system, with good results.

More intensive cultivation systems, of course, require larger factor inputs per unit of land. Labor inputs present no problem. More mouths to feed are accompanied by more hands to cultivate, a state that has reached a high point in Chinese or Javanese rice growing, which resembles gardening more than farming. When the soil is no longer allowed to recuperate through fallow periods, larger fertilizer inputs become necessary—at this stage, mainly organic rather than chemical fertilizer. Multicropping, and even annual cropping in areas of deficient rainfall, typically requires large investments of labor in drainage and irrigation facilities. The historical literature reports heavy investment in irrigation in the nineteenth century in Egypt, Iraq, Sri Lanka, India, China, and Java.

By such methods it is possible to raise crop yields *per acre* in the most intensive cultivation systems several times over yields in less intensive systems. Yield *per farm worker* will tend to fall, but perhaps not very much. Ishikawa (1981) has made cross-country studies of rice cultivation in which yield per hectare on the vertical axis is charted against available hectares per farm worker on the horizontal axis. The results conform quite closely to a rectangular hyperbola, sometimes called an "Ishikawa curve." Data for the same country, such as Japan or Taiwan, in successive time periods show a similar pattern. Yield per hectare moves upward to the left along the Ishikawa curve as land availability decreases.

A further possibility for increasing yield in changes in the agricultural product mix. Potatoes and other root crops yield substantially more calories per acre than do most grain crops, and thus a reallocation of land among crops can raise caloric availability. Another way in which densely populated countries adjust is through de-emphasis of livestock production. Boserup finds a strong inverse relation between population density and pasture area/cultivated area and livestock/person ratios. Large animals are a very inefficient way of converting acreage into calories, though pigs and chickens are somewhat more efficient. Densely populated areas tend to get a high proportion of their animal protein from fish.

Several of these possibilities are indicated by the experience of China, which was summarized in the previous section. Over the six centuries before 1949, output per cultivated acre roughly doubled. This was accomplished through a combination of seed improvement, introduction of new crops, extension of double-cropping made possible by irrigation, and an increase of labor and fertilizer inputs per acre. There was technical change, but of a gradual and traditional sort. "Modern" technical change, in which yields are raised rapidly by a combination of seed improvement, application of chemical fertilizers and pesticides, and improved cultivation methods, was not important in any of our countries during the extensive-growth era.

Industrial output grows along with population and agricultural output, and there is a gradual shift in the locus of manufacturing activity from the household to specialized workshops and cottage industry. Since clothing is a major consumer good, textiles tend to take the lead in this process. The putting-out system, in which a merchant supplies materials to home spinners and weavers and then collects and markets their product, is familiar to readers of European economic history; but it was by no means confined to that continent. Quite similar systems existed in China, India, and many other third-world countries. One typically finds in addition to textiles an array of other handicraft industries supplying household necessities.

Handicraft production in turn gives way gradually to factory production, with textiles and raw-material processing in the lead. Handicraft products are often forced to compete first with imported factory goods and later on with the output of domestic factories. Whether factory production appears during the period of extensive growth depends on the era we are discussing. In the substantial number of countries that reached the turning point before 1900, factories were almost absent at the turning point and did not become important for several decades thereafter. This is why it is wrong to take the onset of industrialization as marking the beginning of intensive growth for these countries. But when we come to the years 1900–50, by which time modern industrial techniques were increasingly well known throughout the world, we find considerable development of factory production in countries such as Egypt, Turkey, India, and China when they were still in the extensive-growth phase. And since 1950 efforts to initiate intensive growth have been strongly identified with forced-draft industrial development.

The volume of internal trade and transport grows with the volume of production, and may indeed grow somewhat faster, as urban centers develop and households begin to shed some of their nonagricultural functions. Trade networks are elaborated and perfected. Further, as European traders voyaged around the world from 1500 onward, most of the countries discussed here developed some external trade, typically involving exchange of primary products for manufactured consumer goods. The volume of such trade may have grown somewhat faster than domestic output, but it was still marginal rather than central to the economy. Only after about 1850 do we observe, in one country after another, a marked rise in the export/GDP ratio, which I shall argue in chapter 3 was often important in initiating growth.

The public sector remained small. Nineteenth-century governments, whether indigenous or colonial, collected only a small percentage of national income, mainly from head taxes, land taxes, and trade taxes. Expenditures were mainly for the military, the civil service, and consumption of the ruling group, with little remaining for economic or social purposes. But there was some building of roads, railroads, ports, and warehouses for trade and military uses. Interestingly enough, some colonial governments were more active on this front than were most independent countries.

Since national accounts are typically lacking for the period of extensive growth, we cannot say what is happening to the sectoral composition of output or the sectoral distribution of the labor force. But it is a reasonable surmise that the economy shows little structural change. One implication of extensive growth is that part of the growth in the labor force is being absorbed in nonagricultural activities. Extension of settlement over a larger land area means some increase in transport requirements. Growth of total output and income means more people are engaged in trade and trade-related activities. The service sector is large and expansible, though at this stage it involves mainly personal services. We have already noted the gradual transfer of some types of manufacturing and repair work from the household to independent artisans and also some increased absorption of family labor time in manufacturing for the market, as under the putting-out system.

In all these ways the demand for labor is growing, and it may well grow as rapidly as the available labor supply. The "surplus-labor" economy, so prominent in recent development literature, had not yet appeared on a substantial scale. Only in Egypt, Java, and some regions of India and China were there complaints of overpopulation. In other third-world countries, and especially in Africa and Latin America, population density was low relative to land resources. As intensive growth got under way, the common complaint was of labor scarcity.

THREE ANALYTICAL PROBLEMS

Absence of Economic Change?

The economic literature contains several models of an essentially changeless economy—the classical stationary state, Schumpeter's "circular flow of economic life," the Walrasian general equilibrium system. In these systems population, capital stock, and technology are constant, and the economy grinds out the same menu of goods period after period. It is worth emphasizing that economies in the extensive-growth era do not correspond to any of these models. Output per capita is unchanged in the sense of fluctuating about a level trend line. But other types of economic change, usually gradual and undramatic, pervade the economy.

Numerous examples of such change were given in the previous section. Population is spreading out gradually over a larger land area—from Java to the outer islands of Indonesia, from central China to the north and southwest, from Upper Burma to Lower Burma, from Buenos Aires to the pampas of Argentina, and so on. In agriculture, cultivation methods and crop mix are usually changing. There may also be institutional changes, such as clarification of individual titles to land, which was an important nineteenth-century development in some countries. There is an elaboration of handicraft production of manufactures, sometimes under the auspices of merchant entrepreneurs. There is gradual improvement of roads, ports, and other infrastructure. There is growing contact with other economies along seacoast fringes.

These changes stand out particularly in the "late developers"—India, China, Indonesia, Egypt, Turkey Iraq, Iran. Although per capita income in these countries was not appreciably higher in 1950 than in 1900, in other respects their economies had changed significantly: important governmental changes, accelerated population growth, better infrastructure, an enlarged and changed pattern of exports, more-intensive land use usually accompanied by irrigation development, even the beginnings of factory industry.

"Change without Change"

How can the economy grow in absolute size, and even undergo the significant changes just noted, without any appreciable uptrend in per capita income? By previous economic reasoning, population growth *was* expected to change per capita income, usually in a negative direction. In early classical models, any temporary improvement in living standards led to more rapid population growth, which forced a return to the subsistence level of the stationary state. Malthus, the classical economist most concerned with population, argued that man's reproductive capacity would lead naturally to a doubling of population in each generation. But food output can be increased only at a slower rate. So, unless the population growth rate is held down by voluntary restraint, it will be cut back forcibly by famine and disease.

Why has historical reality not conformed very closely to the Malthusian predictions? One reason, less important today than in the past, is widespread availability of uncultivated land of good quality. Malthus, writing in the English context, naturally thought in terms of a fully settled country. A second reason, ruled out by the implicit classical assumption of static technology, is the possibility of technical progress in agriculture. The Boserup hypothesis that population growth itself tends to generate such changes is relevant here. Further, the agglomeration of population may generate modest economies of scale in transport, trade, and small-scale industrial activities. If Adam Smith was right about the relation between market size and division of labor, one might expect a gradual rise of productivity in the nonagricultural sectors, perhaps sufficient to offset any tendency toward diminishing returns in agriculture as intensity of cultivation increases. These considerations may help to explain the deviation of actual economic growth from Malthusian predictions.

The Question of Preconditions

To what extent can developments during the period of extensive growth be regarded as a preparation for, or a prerequisite for, the turning point to intensive growth?

The answer depends on how the question is put. One could ask: does extensive growth tend to develop naturally, almost automatically, into intensive growth, so that from existence of the former one can predict eventual appearance of the latter? I suspect that the answer to this question is no. There seems no reason to believe that per capita income *must* begin to rise or that extensive growth could not continue indefinitely.

But suppose one asks instead: are developments during this era of extensive growth *helpful* at later stages of growth? Is the economy in some sense better prepared for takeoff at the end of the period than it was at the beginning? The answer to this more modest question may well be yes. Some events of this period are decidedly helpful to later growth. In regard to Europe, Eric Jones (1981) has emphasized that a great deal of gradual change was going on before the so-called modern period. This stage-setting was spread over several centuries. It included: the solidification of nation-states and some increase in the optimum size of states; the growing autonomy of the market economy from the political systems, achieved partly through the spread of rural industry outside the control of the urban guilds; the growth of what Jones terms ''ghost acreage'' in the newly discovered continents overseas, which greatly increased the land per man available to Europeans; and creeping changes in technology, partly by trial and error, but increasingly as the result of more abstract speculation. ''Small but productive technical changes were constantly being made in the more advanced regions, though many are scarcely discernible in the documented sources and are individually too minor to figure among the stylized facts of technical change during the Industrial Revolution, which rears up as a cliff face in the textbooks where it should emerge instead from swelling foothills'' (p. 65).

The same view is warranted, I think, for most third-world countries. Important conditioning factors during the period of extensive growth include: (1) nation-building, which in many countries is a recent and precarious process, still going on with varying degrees of success; (2) small technical changes that add up to what we might call ''the importance of the inconspicuous''; (3) changes in crops, water-control systems, and cultivation methods, which enable food output to at least keep up with population; (4) gradual reduction of transport costs and extension of long-distance trade; (5) growth of manufacturing production outside the household, or even within the household through the putting-out system.

These factors are perhaps especially important for countries that have *recently* embarked on intensive growth after a long prior exposure to the world economy. For example, India in 1947 had a tradition of national unity and democratic government, a well-staffed civil service, a substantial educational system, much physical infrastructure, a long tradition of handicraft manufacturing, and the beginnings of factory industry, notably in textiles. Some of these things could be said also of China, Pakistan, Egypt, Turkey, and other recent developers. They were taking off, not from a situation of stagnation, but from an economy already visibly in motion.

3

The Timing of Turning Points

Modern economic growth began in the United Kingdom in the mideighteenth century, and in France in the late eighteenth century. By 1850 it had spread to most of northern and western Europe, North America, and Australia. Southern and Eastern Europe were to come along later. Western economists and historians often assumed that nothing much was happening in the third world, Japan being regarded as an exception to the general rule. The other countries of Asia, Africa, and Latin America were seen as marginal—mere suppliers of raw materials to the developing industrial countries. Thus when Western economists turned their attention to third-world countries after 1945, they assumed that the era of economic development was just beginning for the rest of the world. The countries of the third world were all lined up at the starting gate, preparing to "take off" into an era of sustained growth.

This chronology, in which Europe and North America develop very early and other countries follow only after a century-long delay, is seriously distorted. First, turning points within Europe itself were spread out over a period of about two centuries. Very roughly, intensive growth spread from northwest to southeast. France, Belgium, and Switzerland were early followers of the United Kingdom, their intensive growth dating from about 1800. By the 1830s Austria, the states of western Germany, and the United States had joined the growth procession. The Scandinavian countries and Australia came along in midcentury, Canada around 1870. Intensive growth in Hungary, Russia, and Italy seems to have been under way by the 1880s; that in Poland and Czechoslovakia, which did not exist as independent countries before World War I, can be dated from the 1920s (though the Bohemian region of Czechoslovakia was already growing in the nineteenth century). Not until after 1945 were Rumania, Bulgaria, and Yugoslavia drawn strongly into the growth current. The spread of intensive growth from the initial "core" to peripheral areas to the south and east was gradual and long drawn out.

Meanwhile, a similarly long drawn out process was under way on other continents. Intensive growth began in Chile about 1840, in Argentina about 1860. By 1900 most other Latin American countries, as well as Japan and most of

Southeast Asia, had joined the procession. In Africa, intensive growth began in the 1890s under colonial auspices, the present African countries being in fact colonial creations. Intensive growth in Korea dates from 1910, in Zambia, Morocco, and Venezuela from the 1920s. Another important group, including the Asian giants, India and China, as well as Egypt, Turkey, Iraq, Iran, Pakistan, and Indonesia, embarked on intensive growth only after 1945. And seven of the countries in our sample still have not done so, remaining in the extensive-growth era. In the third world the sequence of turning points has been spread out over a century and a half and is by no means complete. Thus we see that the procession of turning points in Europe *overlaps* heavily with the corresponding procession in the third world.

My early dating of turning points for most third-world countries is admittedly controversial and will raise several questions in readers' minds. The most substantial of these relate, first, to the fact that more than half of these countries were still colonies at my turning-point date. Can a country really embark on intensive growth under colonial auspices? Second, my datings depend rather heavily on an increase in the growth rate of primary exports from the country in question. It has sometimes been argued that primary exports are of doubtful benefit to a developing country and do not provide a reliable basis for sustained growth.

The evidence suggests that export expansion usually is a major factor in initiating intensive growth; but there are exceptions, and the reasons for these need to be explored. The best procedure is perhaps to set forth the chronology of turning points as I visualize it and then to consider possible objections and qualifications.

TABLE 1   A Chronology of Turning Points

1840	Chile	1900	Uganda
1850	Malaysia	1900	Zimbabwe
1850	Thailand	1910	Korea
1860	Argentina	1920	Morocco
1870	Burma	1925	Venezuela
1876	Mexico	1925	Zambia
1880	Algeria	1947	India
1880	Brazil	1947	Pakistan
1880	Japan	1949	China
1880	Peru	1950	Iran
1880	Sri Lanka	1950	Iraq
1885	Colombia	1950	Turkey
1890	Nigeria	1952	Egypt
1895	Ghana	1965	Indonesia
1895	Ivory Coast	—	Afghanistan
1895	Kenya	—	Bangladesh
1895	Taiwan	—	Ethiopia
1900	Cuba	—	Mozambique
1900	Philippines	—	Nepal
1900	Tanzania	—	Sudan
		—	Zaire

THE CHRONOLOGY OF TURNING POINTS

The dates listed in table 1 are subject to the qualifications noted in chapter 1 about the use of a single year. The turning point is actually a period of a decade or so around the cited year, during which one observes a significant and continuing rise in per capita income.

The striking fact emerging from the table is that about two-thirds of the countries that have thus far reached a turning point had done so by 1914. Between 1914 and 1945, on the other hand, only three countries appear on the list. After 1945 the procession speeds up again, with eight countries reaching the turning point soon thereafter.

I shall argue that this chronology stems from three major epochs in the world economy, whose main features will be reviewed briefly.

World Economic Boom, 1850–1914

It is clear in retrospect that the 1850–1914 era was unusually favorable to worldwide diffusion of economic growth. Output in the early-developing countries of Europe and North America was rising rapidly, and with it their demand for imports of primary products. Kuznets (1966) estimates the median growth rate of output in these countries from 1860 to 1914 at about 3 percent per year, which meant a median growth of about 2 percent a year in per capita terms.

Rapid economic growth in Europe and North America opened up the possibility of enlarged trade with other continents. But this possibility could scarcely have been realized without an improvement and cheapening of transport. This involved replacement of sailing ships by steam-driven steel ships, which reduced ocean-freight rates by 1913 to about 30 percent of their 1870 level; a worldwide railroad boom, which peaked in the years 1870–1914 and which produced even more spectacular reductions in overland transport costs; and building of a worldwide telegraph network linking would-be sellers and buyers. Completion of the Suez Canal in 1869 was a particularly important development for Asian countries trading with Europe.

Available estimates of growth in the volume of international trade have been analyzed by Kuznets (1967). They show the sum of exports and imports growing at an average rate of 50.3 percent per decade from 1850 to 1880 and 39.5 percent per decade from 1881 to 1913. The ratio of world trade to world output was thus rising quite rapidly. Kuznets estimates that this ratio had reached 33 percent by 1913.

Trade was of course dominated by the countries of Europe and North America, which accounted for about three-quarters of combined exports and imports. Latin America, Africa, and Asia accounted for about 20 percent of trade in 1876–80 and 22 percent in 1913, not far from their proportion in recent decades. The implication of these figures is that third-world countries were keeping up with the general pace of world trade. This conclusion is confirmed by the investigations of Lewis (1969), who finds that the volume of tropical exports grew at 3.6 percent per year from 1883 to 1913. Agricultural exports grew a bit more slowly than this, but mineral exports grew more quickly. Indeed, during this period total exports from the tropical countries grew at almost exactly the same rate as industrial production in the advanced countries. Although terms of trade between primary products and manufactures show short-term fluctuations, Lewis (1970) concludes that there was no appreciable change in terms over this period as a whole.

The third-world countries that embarked on intensive growth before World War I fall into three groups.

1. *Latin America*. All the Latin American countries in our sample, with the exception of Venezuela. The turning-point dates in most cases mark the beginning of political stability after the prolonged civil wars that followed independence. Growth was invariably export-led, the nature of the exports varying from case to case. Argentina and Chile were able to grow and export wool, wheat, meat, and other temperate-zone products. Brazil relied on tropical products, initially sugar, with coffee becoming dominant from the 1840s onward. Coffee also dominated the early export trade of Colombia. Minerals were important in Chile—at first nitrates, later copper. Minerals dominated Mexico's nineteenth-century exports, though agricultural products, cattle, and timber gradually grew in importance. Peru also had a combination of agricultural and mineral exports. Cuba was a sugar island. But everywhere exports, directed mainly toward European and North American markets, were the key to economic expansion.

2. *Asia*. Four of the Asian countries that were drawn into the world export boom lie in an arc—from Ceylon through Burma and Malaya to Thailand.* Their turning points can be dated generally from the 1850s, though Ceylon had large and growing coffee exports from the 1830s onward. In Burma and Thailand a rising flow of rice exports came mainly from peasant producers expanding into uncultivated land, a pattern to be repeated later in West Africa. In Malaya the early export product was tin, produced mainly by relatively small entrepreneurs of Chinese origin, but by 1900 rubber had emerged as a second major product. Ceylon's exports came initially from large foreign-owned plantations—coffee plantations from 1830–70, tea plantations after the coffee trees had been ruined by plant disease. Toward the end of the century, however, smallholder production of coconuts, rubber, and other crops became increasingly important, and by 1913 the export list was quite diversified.

Next, there is the case of Japan, so well documented in the literature that details would be superfluous. But it is worth noting that Japan, like the other countries listed, showed a consistently strong export performance. Exports plus

---

*In some cases the name of a country after independence differs from the name during the colonial era. In such cases I have used the old name (Ceylon, Malaya, Tanganyika, and so on) in discussing the earlier period and the new name (Sri Lanka, Malaysia, Tanzania) in discussing events since independence.

imports were about 10 percent of GNP in the 1870s, but had risen to 30 percent by 1910–13. Over the years 1881–1914, Japanese exports grew about twice as rapidly as world exports. Up to 1900 Japan's export growth is mainly the story of raw silk, after 1900 mainly the story of cotton textiles.

Taiwan and the Philippines round out the Asian experience. Taiwan was ceded to Japan after China's defeat in the Sino-Japanese war of 1894–95. Japan energetically set out to turn the island into a rice bowl for the home country. The Philippines passed under American control after Spain's defeat in the Spanish-American War of 1898. There followed a period of rapid export-led growth, dominated by sugar and aided by a preferential trade agreement with the United States.

3. *Africa.* Toward the end of the century several areas of Africa were drawn into the intensive-growth process. Algeria in North Africa; Nigeria, Ghana, and Ivory Coast in West Africa; Kenya, Uganda, and Tanganyika (Tanzania) in East Africa; and Southern Rhodesia (Zimbabwe) in Central Africa. To speak of these as "countries" is to speak of colonial creations. Europeans drew the boundaries, established unified administration over numerous tribal areas, and created an impression of nationhood that, although it took on some substance over the years, was never as strong as that inherited from the ancient kingdoms of Asia.

Most of the Asian and Latin American countries mentioned participated in the pre-1914 boom for periods of forty to sixty years. The new African colonies were latecomers who participated for a generation or less. They nevertheless got in on the tail end of the boom. Their exports rose sharply up to 1914, giving them an initial momentum that they never entirely lost. Wheat, fruits, and wine from Algeria; palm products, cocoa, coffee, and timber from West Africa; cereals from Kenya, cotton from Uganda, sisal and coffee from Tanganyika; cereals, gold, and other minerals from Southern Rhodesia—all flowed into international trade in growing volume. Exports from Ghana, Nigeria, Ivory Coast, and Uganda came almost entirely from African smallholders, who brought additional land under cultivation in the pattern observed earlier in Southeast Asia. In Algeria, Kenya, and Southern Rhodesia, on the other hand, substantial white settlement created dualistic economies in which most of the exports came from European-owned farms.

The Longest Depression, 1914–45

This phrase, borrowed from Lewis (1978a), is adequately descriptive. Nineteen fourteen to 1945 was a bleak period for the world economy, marked by two world wars, the Great Depression, and a marked slowdown in the growth of world production and trade. The growth rate of industrial production in the "developed" countries fell from 3.6 percent in 1883–1913 to 2.7 percent in 1913–29 and 1.3 percent in 1929–38. This drop is significant in view of Lewis's finding that the growth rate of primary exports from tropical countries is closely related to growth of industrial production in the advanced economies. And in fact the growth rate of tropical exports fell from 3.7 percent per year in 1883–1913 to 3.2 percent in 1913–29 and 1.9 percent in 1929–37. This decline in export volume was accompanied by a mild sagging of the terms of trade of primary products against manufactures even before 1929 and by a sharp drop after 1929. The import capacity of third-world countries was sharply reduced.

Under these depressed conditions, countries that had been growing quite rapidly before 1914 now grew more slowly. It is significant, too, that only a few additional countries reached the turning point during this period, and these cases can be attributed to special circumstances. Korea was formally taken over by Japan in 1910 and, as in the earlier case of Taiwan, Japan set about to develop the country as an auxiliary to the Japanese economy. A French protectorate was established in Morocco in 1912 as part of a deal among the European powers, and effective control over most of the territory had been gained by 1920. Here, as earlier in Algeria, French settlers in effect implanted a new, "modern" economy on top of the indigenous economy, initiating a growth process whose benefits went disproportionately to the Europeans.

In Venezuela, which had remaind a stagnant backwater dominated by military dictators and an agricultural oligarchy, the discovery of oil in the early 1920s set off a rapid transformation of both the economy and the political structure. Venezuela was the first great oil exporter and remains a key member of OPEC, which it took the initiative in founding in the 1960s. In Zambia (then Northern Rhodesia), rich copper deposits began to be exploited by foreign-owned companies in the late 1920s. While these properties have now passed from foreign to national ownership, copper remains a dominant factor in the economy.

The Greatest Boom, 1945–73

The evolution of the world economy after World War II is still fresh in mind and can be reviewed very briefly. The years 1945–73 saw an unprecedented boom in world production and trade, a "second golden age" with growth rates well above those of the "first golden age" of 1850–1914. The average annual growth rate of GNP in the OECD countries from 1950 to 1973 was 4.9 percent, compared with an 1870–1913 average of 2.5 percent and a 1913–50 figure of 1.9 percent. These high output rates—plus lowering of trade barriers, plus continued reduction of transport costs (supertankers, container ships, jet aircraft, great expansion of road mileage and truck transport)—produced an even faster growth in the volume of international trade. Angus Maddison (1982) shows the export volume of the OECD countries rising at 8.6 percent per year from 1950 to 1973. Thus export/GNP ratios rose substantially.

Exports from third-world countries, while still growing rapidly by historical standards, grew somewhat less rapidly than developed-country exports, with the result that their percentage of world exports fell from 25.3 percent to 17.7 percent.

There was some diversification of the export mix. Manufactured goods formed only 7.6 percent of third-world exports in 1955, but by 1970 their share had risen to 16.7 percent (and the percentage was to double again by 1980). Meanwhile exports of foodstuffs had fallen from 36.7 percent to 26.5 percent of the total, reflecting not only demand constraints but also increasing domestic food consumption associated with population growth and rising per capita incomes. The great grain-surplus areas are now the United States, Canada, Australia, and Europe. Thus the old distinction between "developed" exporters of manufactures and "less-developed" exporters of primary products has become increasingly blurred. The terms of trade between primary products and manufactures show no marked trend over the period 1945–73.

The boom crested in 1973, and the median growth rate in the OECD countries from 1973 to 1980 fell to about half its previous level—in fact, to almost precisely the rate that had prevailed from 1870 to 1913. There was a corresponding turnaround in world trade. Maddison (1982) shows the average annual growth of OECD exports falling from 8.6 percent in 1950–73 to 4.8 percent in 1973–79. World exports grew even more slowly, at 4.0 percent per year.

Different groups of third-world countries fared quite differently in the 1973–80 period: (1) oil exporters did very well in income terms, though not always well in terms of economic policy; (2) countries that had established a substantial industrial base by 1973, often grouped together as "newly industrializing countries" or NICs, have also done well—their median growth rate since 1973 is well above that of the OECD countries; (3) other oil-importing countries in the third world have found their growth rates retarded and have been kept afloat partly by short-term borrowing, which can scarcely continue to increase at recent rates; (4) countries that had not yet reached the turning point by 1973 have fared worst, and their chances of reaching it now appear even bleaker than before.

The main effect of the 1945–73 golden age was to speed up growth in countries that had already embarked on intensive growth at various points between 1850 and 1950. Virtually all countries—the OECD countries, Eastern Europe and the Soviet Union, as well as third-world countries that had already reached the turning point—experienced a sharp increase in GNP growth rates. In the euphoria of this period it was perhaps natural to suppose that third-world growth before 1950 had been negligible. But what had actually happened, for the nineteenth-century and early-twentieth-century developers, was that a previously moderate growth rate of per capita income accelerated after 1950 to a markedly higher level.

However, the view that "development began in 1950," while largely illusory, is not entirely so. Eight countries reached the turning point in the 1950–80 period, including China and India, plus Pakistan and Indonesia. In both China and undivided India one could make a case for a slight rise in per capita income from 1900 to 1940. But the increase, if present at all, is so slight that in my judgment the turning point for India and Pakistan should be dated from independence in 1947 and for China from the revolution of 1949.

There is some ambiguity about the correct dating of turning points for four of the eight countries—Egypt, Turkey, Iraq, and Iran. These countries experienced some political and economic modernization from the 1920s onward. But the 1929 depression and the 1939 war followed so soon afterwards that they had scarcely made a significant beginning before 1945. It seems most reasonable, then, to locate their turning points in the postwar period.

The case of Indonesia is also complex and somewhat ambiguous. Exports from Indonesia rose from 1880 to 1930 at a quite respectable rate. But to an unusual degree these exports came from foreign-owned mines and plantations, and a large share of the proceeds remained in foreign hands. Particularly in densely populated Java, the benefits to the local population seem to have been meager. As a matter of judgment, then, I prefer to locate Indonesia's turning point after the achievement of independence. Even then, GNP per capita did not begin to rise perceptibly until the overthrow of President Sukarno and installation of the present regime in the mid-1960s.

Some Laggards

I note finally that seven countries in our sample remain in the phase of extensive growth and show no sign of a sustained rise in per capita income. These countries are Afghanistan, Nepal, Bangladesh, Ethiopia, Sudan, Mozambique, and Zaire. There does not seem to be any single reason for their failure to achieve intensive growth. Rather, failure results from varying combinations of geographic remoteness (Afghanistan, Nepal, most of Ethiopia, Zaire, and Sudan), absence of transport facilities and other infrastructure (all seven countries except Bangladesh), internal political turmoil (absent only in Nepal and post-1970 Sudan), the flight of colonial authorities with no real preparation for independence (Mozambique, Zaire), primitive government (Afghanistan, Ethiopia, Nepal), and massive misgovernment (Zaire).

In the bleaker post-1973 environment these countries, and some smaller countries in similar plight, will have serious difficulty in reaching the turning point. The end of the growth-diffusion story is not yet in sight.

THE QUESTION OF TIMING

The most intriguing question in growth economics is why a turning point occurs in a particular country at a particular time. Why, under the favorable world conditions of 1850–1914, did some countries embark on intensive growth while others did not? Why was this true once more during the boom of 1945–73? Why have turning points been spread out over more than a century, and why in some countries have they not yet occurred?

A review of the country histories assembled as part of this exercise suggests two clues. First, the turning point is almost always associated with some significant political event. In only four of our 41 countries does this seem not to have been true. Second, the turning point is usually associated with a marked rise in exports. Although rising world demand impinges on all countries, each country differs in its ability to make an appropriate production response. This point will be explored further in a later section.

Among "significant political events" the most interesting cases, though not the largest in number, involve a transfer of power within the country from a less-progressive to a more-progressive regime. Cases that fall under this heading include: installation of the modernizing ruler Rama IV as king of Thailand (1851); the Meiji Restoration in Japan (1868); collapse of the Ottoman Empire and emergence of Kemal Atatürk as ruler of Turkey (early 1920s); emergence of Iraq from the Ottoman Empire as an independent state under British tutelage (early 1920s); installation of the Pahlevi dynasty in Iran (1925); the communist-led revolution in China (1949); overthrow of the monarchy and installation of President Nasser in Egypt (1956); overthrow of President Sukarno and installation of President Suharto in Indonesia (1967).

In Latin America, independence in most countries was followed by a prolonged period of recurring civil war, lasting as late as 1876 in Mexico and 1885 in Colombia. The turning point usually dates from the emergence at long last of a stable government able to exercise effective control of the country for an extended period.

Most numerous are the cases in which intensive growth can be dated from the time of colonization by a foreign power: namely, the ten European-created African countries listed earlier plus Burma, Malaysia, Taiwan, Korea, Cuba, and the Philippines (the last two involving transfer from one colonial power to another rather than fresh colonization). Granting all necessary qualifications about distribution of the increased income from growth, the fact of increased capacity to produce can scarcely be questioned.

In two cases—India and Pakistan—initiation of intensive growth was roughly synchronous with decolonization. Finally, there are four cases (Ceylon, Brazil, Venezuela, and Peru) in which major political events did not occur around the turning-point date.

QUALIFICATIONS AND OBJECTIONS

We turn now to possible objections, and several necessary qualifications, to the argument advanced above. The first relates to the continuation of extreme poverty in many third-world countries. If Sri Lanka has really been developing for more than a century, how can it still rank so low in per capita income? Second, we must look briefly at the controversy over the impact of colonialism. Third, we must look into the requirements for export-led growth and why these requirements are met in some cases but not in others.

Why Still So Poor?

The IBRD World Development Report for 1981 contains the usual listing of countries ranked by per capita income in 1979 U.S. dollars. Of these, 36 are classified as "low-income countries," with per capita incomes in the range of $100–400 per year. Twenty-one of these countries fall outside the sample taken here, usually because they do not meet the size criterion. Seven more are the countries listed earlier as not having reached the turning point. But this still leaves eight countries in our sample that, although they have passed the turning point according to my chronology, are still very poor: Burma, China, India, Indonesia, Pakistan, Sri Lanka, Tanzania, and Uganda. Half of these, to be sure, are post-1945 developers that have not had time to move far beyond their starting point. Burma and Uganda have had a disastrous recent experience after a long period of earlier growth. But a case like Sri Lanka, with an average annual per capita income of $230, is admittedly puzzling.

Certainly people in Western Europe and the United States are much better off than people in Sri Lanka, though not as much better off as the World Bank tables suggest. Simon Kuznets and more recently Irving Kravis and his colleagues on the International Comparisons Project suggest that conversion from local currencies to U.S. dollars at official exchange rates exaggerates the actual difference in consumption levels. Moreover, the degree of distortion increases with the disparity in per capita income. Adjustment to a purchasing-power basis suggests that the "official" per capita figures for the lowest-income countries should be two to three times their current levels to make them at all comparable with figures for the richest countries.

Certainly, too, per capita income in the advanced industrial countries has risen faster than it has in Sri Lanka over the past century. The income gap has been widening. But such comparisons do not bear directly on the question of what has been happening in Sri Lanka itself. Here the economic histories of the country suggest that per capita income did begin to rise significantly around 1880 and that it has risen intermittently ever since. Between 1950 and 1980, for which data are reasonably reliable, average per capita income grew at more than 2 percent per year.

The other significant development is the growing inequality of incomes that seems to characterize most, though not all, developing countries in the early stages of intensive growth. As of 1880, there was something approaching a flat plateau of poverty across the population. The increases in income since that time have been unequally distributed, and hills and valleys in the distribution have become more prominent. There may well be some Sri Lankans, especially small farmers with little marketed output, who are living today much as their forefathers lived a century ago. Those who argue that growth is illusory tend to focus on these lowest strata. But many others—sizable commercial farmers, factory workers, business and professional people, civil servants, other white-collar groups—have moved up in the income scale, while at the same time growing in relative numbers. The lower-middle and upper-middle income brackets are more thickly populated than they used to be.

In addition to higher per capita consumption of private goods and services by these groups, we should not overlook important increases in consumption of public services. Public education and public health services have been substantially strengthened in Sri Lanka, as in most other third-world countries. This must have brought some benefit to even the poorest groups in the population.

The Question of Colonialism

We cannot enter here into a full-dress discussion of colonialism, which has its own large and controversial literature, but several comments are in order. First, we cannot safely generalize about all colonies at all times. We cannot toss all the colonial powers into one basket. Japan has always been growth-oriented, in colonial areas as well as at home; and it is clear that Japanese rule helped to initiate intensive growth in both Korea and Taiwan. In Cuba and the Philippines, intensive growth dates from transfer of the colonies from Spanish to American rule. The British were also typically growth-minded. But they tended to delegate much authority to local administrators, and so policy varied from one area to the next and even in the same colony at different times. (The case of India, which did not achieve intensive growth during the colonial era, has tended to dominate the anticolonial literature; but India is rather a special case, and most other British colonies did better.) Going downward in the scale of interest—and success—in colonial development, we may list the Germans, French, Belgians, Dutch, and Portuguese. Angola, Mozambique, and Zaire have not yet achieved intensive growth, and in Indonesia growth remains precarious. General statements professing to apply to all colonial powers and to all periods clearly cannot be true.

Second, one should distinguish several different questions that can be asked about colonial rule:

1. Did areas under colonial rule achieve a turning point and embark on intensive growth? Some did, and some did not, as is true also among countries that remained independent.
2. Could these areas have grown more rapidly had the colonial powers made indigenous economic growth a prime objective? Here the answer usually is, "Yes, more could have been done than actually was done." But here again, one must distinguish among countries and time periods. In Britain's African colonies there was a clear progression from a relative lack of interest in economic advancement of "the natives" before 1914 to a more substantial interest and even some infusion of development funds from 1920 to 1940, to strong interest in economic development and preparation for eventual independence from 1945 to 1960. For whatever reason, the two world wars were distinct punctuation marks in colonial policy.

3. Would these areas have developed more rapidly before 1950 if they had been independent countries rather than colonies? Any answer to this counterfactual question is conjectural, especially for "countries" that did not exist before colonization. But the record of countries that never fell under colonial rule—Ethiopia, Afghanistan, Nepal, pre-1949 China—is not impressive. There is no magic in independence.

Colonial rule usually made several positive contributions. It often established clear political boundaries for the first time, and experience of unified administration within these boundaries contributed to a growing sense of nationhood. Even the nationalist groups that arose in opposition to colonial rule often furnished the nucleus of later independent governments. Colonial authorities often introduced new export crops—coffee, tea, cocoa, sugar, rubber, and so on—or devised land-settlement schemes that stimulated production of traditional crops, such as rice, for export. Colonial governments usually engaged in considerable construction of physical infrastructure, notably roads, railroads, river navigation, and port facilities. Suppression of internecine warfare and maintenance of internal order were favorable to economic activity and were important in speeding population growth. Also favorable to population growth was reduction of famine through improved food transport and the spread of Western medical facilities, which became increasingly important after 1900.

There are also negative items on the scorecard. There was typically an income drain from the colony through repatriation of profits on foreign investment and in other ways. Some of the new export industries had a distinct enclave character. Even that portion of export proceeds that remained within the colony was unequally distributed within the population. The colonial authorities did little to shelter domestic handicrafts from competition from imported factory goods. They were also typically hostile to domestic industrialization, preferring continued import of manufactures from the metropolis. Education, particularly secondary and higher education, was usually undersupported. Even more serious, the colonial authorities often encouraged immigration to fill intermediate positions between the top jobs, held by Europeans, and unskilled labor, which alone was considered suitable for the "natives." This policy produced a three-tier racial division of labor, as in British East Africa or Burma, where the rulers were British, most traders, clerks, and skilled workers were Indian, while the indigenous population were farmers and laborers. Throughout Southeast Asia the Chinese filled this intermediate role, and natives of the colonies were largely walled off from occupational advancement.

The net score from adding these pluses and minuses varies from country to country, and each case must be considered on its own merits. It will be useful in this connection to look at the 41 countries in our sample. For 16 of these the colonialism issue is not relevant. Except for Cuba, the Latin American countries were not colonies after about 1820. Nine additional countries were under colonial control only briefly, or indirectly, or not at all: China, Japan, Thailand, Afghanistan, Nepal, Iran, Iraq, Turkey, and Ethiopia.

Of the countries that were colonies, 17 reached the turning point during the colonial era whereas eight did not. Those which did not include the three successor states of the Indian subcontinent—India, Pakistan, and Bangladesh—plus Indonesia, Egypt, Sudan, Mozambique, and Zaire. The fact that several very large countries appear in this group has no doubt contributed to an impression that colonial rule usually prevented economic growth, a conclusion that does not seem to be true.

All these colonies are now ex-colonies; and it is interesting to ask whether they have grown more quickly since independence than they did under colonial rule. In making such a comparison, one must recall that decolonization set in during the late 1940s and that from 1945 to 1973 world output and trade grew at an unusually fast rate. One might expect, therefore, that growth in ex-colonies would have been faster after independence than before; but this could have resulted mainly from participation in the world economic boom rather than from independence per se. Setting this point aside, and overlooking the fact that post-1950 growth estimates are somewhat firmer than those for earlier periods, a gross comparison is possible for 20 countries (four ex-colonies did not reach the turning point in either era, and Zimbabwe's independence is so recent that nothing can be said). The expectation of more rapid recent growth is confirmed for 11 of these countries. For three additional countries (Kenya, Sri Lanka, and Malaysia), the post-1950 growth rate of per capita income is not very different from that in the colonial period. This leaves six countries (Burma, Cuba, Ghana, Tanzania, Uganda, and Zambia) whose performance has deteriorated since independence, for reasons that differ in detail but can be characterized broadly as political.

The legacy of colonialism is perhaps most dubious in Africa. True, Africans in large numbers were drawn into the monetary economy, as wage earners and as producers of marketed crops. A purely arithmetical calculation shows a rise in per capita income, evidenced in larger consumption of simple consumer goods plus some improvement of public services. At the same time the racist occupational stratification that developed in most colonies was stultifying and demeaning to Africans. Public education and training of local leadership was badly neglected, which helps to explain the fragility of political systems in the postindependence period. It is no accident that the economies whose performance has deteriorated since 1960, or that have failed even to reach the turning point, are heavily concentrated in Africa.

Stimulus to Growth from Primary Exports

In countries that reached the turning point before 1940, intensive growth was usually associated with a sharp rise in primary exports, in absolute terms and as a percentage of GDP. Exports came to be regarded as the "engine of growth." In the development literature of vintage 1950–65, however, it was fashionable to regard growth led by primary exports as unfeasible over the long run, or at any rate as inferior to other possible growth paths. The criticisms of primary exports included the following arguments: primary products are often produced by foreign-owned enterprises, with the result that much of the income flows abroad rather than stimulating the domestic economy; market prospects for primary products are poor because of low income elasticities of demand as well as material-saving technical change in the industrialized countries; because of slow growth of demand plus the difficulty of controlling supplies, terms of trade for primary products relative to manufactures are bound to deteriorate over the long run; sharp fluctuations in the value of exports, arising from wide swings in world prices as well as harvest variations, are disruptive to the economy; continued reliance on primary exports perpetuates a quasi-colonial pattern of dependence on the industrialized countries, from which an independent nation should try to break free.

The most substantial of these criticisms involves the wide swings in world prices for primary products and the consequent fluctuations in export receipts. These swings generate cycles in primary-producing countries similar to the business cycles generated by investment fluctuations in industrialized countries. But in neither case do fluctuations necessarily prevent growth, and a variety of counter-cyclical measures are available. The "dependency" argument is heavily political and, I think, somewhat superficial. Any country, including Japan and the United States, is "dependent" in the sense that its export volume is responsive to fluctuations in the world economy. But exploitation of comparative advantage and other gains from integration into the world economy more than outweighs the consequences of exposure to these fluctuations. A country can deliberately unlink itself from the world economy by trade barriers, thus achieving what is best described as isolation rather than independence; but isolation tends to lower the growth rate rather than raise it, as later chapters will make clear.

Nor have events since 1945 borne out the forecast of poor market prospects for primary products. The demand equations that Lewis fitted for the years 1886–1965 have continued to predict quite accurately. Primary exports have continued to grow at almost exactly the same rate as industrial production in the industrialized countries. Agricultural exports have grown a bit less rapidly, but mineral exports have grown more rapidly.

At any time, to be sure, a *particular* primary product may face sluggish world demand, as may be true for a particular kind of manufacture. A country practicing monoculture also faces the prospect of growing competition from other countries producing sugar, coffee, rubber, or whatever. But a country is not locked into producing any one product in perpetuity. Country economic histories reveal two interesting phenomena. The first is rotation of leadership among primary exports. At any one time a single product may bulk large in a country's export bill, but the product does not necessarily remain the same over time. Thus Argentina moved from wool to wheat to chilled meat; Mexico shifted from metals to agricultural products to petroleum; in Peru, leadership has rotated among several farm crops, several metals, and most recently a large fish meal industry.

The second important phenomenon is *diversification* of primary exports over time, meaning that instead of a single dominant export the country has a half-dozen or more important exports. Diversification does not happen in every case. Several of the oil economies have stuck with oil, copper remains dominant in Zambia and Chile, cocoa in Ghana, and sugar in Cuba. But diversification is prominent in well over half our countries and is strongly associated with export success. Especially impressive cases of primary export diversification include Brazil, Mexico, Peru, Sri Lanka, Malaysia, Thailand, Ivory Coast, Pakistan, and Indonesia.

The terms-of-trade argument has been going on for generations. Around 1900 J. M. Keynes predicted that the primary products/manufactures terms of trade must move increasingly in favor of primary products because natural resources are limited whereas manufacturing output can be multiplied indefinitely. Around 1950 Prebisch and others were predicting precisely the opposite. Most recently the ''limits of growth'' school has been predicting exhaustion of mineral resources; although these models usually employ only quantities and no prices, a rise in the relative price of minerals (and, because of the ''population bomb,'' foodstuffs as well) would logically follow.

Empirical studies by Kindleberger (1978) and others, however, fail to reveal any long-run tendency in the terms of trade. Over the past century there have been sharp fluctuations in response to boom, depression, and war. But the view that prices of primary products have undergone a secular deterioration is not sustained. Generalized complaints about the undependability of primary exports, then, are not substantiated by the evidence. The fact remains that, from 1850 to 1914 and again from 1945 to 1973, some countries achieved substantial gains in per capita output fueled by primary exports while others did not. Exports clearly can serve as an ''engine of growth'' or at least, in Kravis's phrase, as a ''handmaiden of growth.'' But they will not always do so.

What makes the difference? Relevant factors seem to include (1) supply elasticities within the country. A sharp increase in foreign demand for a product may evoke a large supply response, or it may not. (2) The size of the export sector relative to the size of the economy will make a difference. (3) The disposition of the export proceeds—how much remains in the domestic economy to raise incomes and stimulate local demand—is clearly very important. Let us consider these points in turn.

1. As Lewis (1978b) has emphasized, the challenge of rising export opportunities must be met by an adequate production response within the country, which may or may not occur. Examination of our country cases suggests several things which influence a country's supply responsiveness:

a. Natural-resource supplies. This is most clearly a factor for mineral exporters, but it is important also for exporters of agricultural products. For example, the tropical crops for which world demand was rising rapidly from 1850 to 1914 usually required either irrigated land or land with adequate natural water supply. Where there was a plentiful supply of unused, well-watered land, as in West Africa, Ceylon, Burma, and Thailand, export volume could be increased rapidly by bringing more land under cultivation. But where virtually all the good land was already occupied, as in Egypt or Java, possibilities of export expansion were limited. In other cases the export response was sluggish because land-ownership patterns prevented peasant producers from getting access to land, as in the Philippines or Venezuela.

b. Diversity of resources and products. It is true that Brazil rode the coffee wave and West Africa rode the cocoa wave for long periods of time. But reliance on a monoculture is precarious, partly because of the certainty of growing competition from other countries. Successful exporters succeed partly by gradual diversification of exports, which reduces the importance and the associated risk attaching to any one product.

c. Government capacity and government policy. Nothing is easier than to prevent or stifle economic growth. A government that is unable to maintain internal order, that lacks minimal administrative capacity, that is so little interested in growth that it fails to provide the necessary physical and human infrastructure, or that follows trade and tax policies strongly biased against exports can readily prevent a country from reaching a turning point. There are numerous examples of success and failure in these respects among both colonial administrations and independent governments.

2. The relative size of the export sector is self-evidently important. A small engine will have difficulty moving a large train. If exports are only a few percent of GDP, even a high rate of export growth will mean only a small increase in per capita income. The size of the export sector is related partly to geographic size of the country and the ratio of coastline to hinterland. China, for example, has a huge hinterland that until recently was linked to the coast mainly by river transport. It is estimated that around 1900 only about 2 percent of China's national product entered into international trade. The trade ratio of India seems to have been somewhat higher but, partly because of supply and transport difficulties, the export growth rate from 1870 to 1914 was below that of most other third-world countries. So the stimulus to this large and sluggish economy was quite limited. Even since 1950, growth in per capita income in neither country can be attributed to any extent to export growth. In India, the export/GDP ratio *fell* considerably between 1950 and 1980, to a current level of only about 5 percent. China's trade ratio is also very low, though it has risen somewhat since 1975.

Read This

Quite different is the situation of smaller economies such as Taiwan, Thailand, Malaysia, Sri Lanka, Ivory Coast, Ghana, Peru, or Chile—not to mention Hong Kong, Singapore, and dozens of others that fall below our size limit. Here the export/GDP ratio quickly reached 20–30 percent, sometimes even 50 percent, and a substantial percentage of the population was drawn into export production. Models of export-led growth offer a good description of the experience of these countries.

3. Finally, much depends on the disposition of the export proceeds. *Returned value* to the domestic economy can be defined as net exports (value of goods sold abroad *minus* value of imported materials used as inputs) less transfers accruing to foreigners (such as repatriation of profits by foreign owners). Returned value, calculated as a percentage of net exports, is a key statistic that many authors have attempted to estimate. Its size is influenced by foreign or domestic ownership of productive assets. It is influenced also by the labor intensity of the production process and by the extent of linkages to other sectors via input purchases. Historically, foreign-owned petroleum enterprises come closest to the model of a pure economic enclave with minimum spread effects to the domestic economy. Plantation agriculture is somewhat more favorable to domestic growth. Still more favorable is small-scale peasant production of export crops.

Returned value depends also on how far government chooses to tax export income in one way or another. It is thus partly a policy variable, not just a fact of nature.

Critics of primary exports have tended to focus on the enclave cases, but these are by no means predominant. By far the most common situation, exemplified especially by West Africa and Southeast Asia (but found also in countries as diverse as Colombia, Pakistan, and Taiwan), is one in which agricultural exports come from owner-occupied farms of moderate size. The responsiveness of small farmers to income incentives has been demonstrated repeatedly. In these cases returned value is high, accruing primarily to the farmers but secondarily to government through export taxation.

Of 30 countries in our sample characterized by export-led growth, 21 depended almost entirely on agricultural exports. In 10 countries export crops were grown almost exclusively by peasant producers on small farm units. In 11 additional countries small farm units coexisted with larger commercial farms or plantations (Sri Lanka, Tanzania) or sugar estates (Philippines, Cuba).

In four countries (Indonesia, Malaysia, Peru, Mexico) agricultural exports, coming partly from small farmers, were combined with substantial mineral exports. Only five countries (Chile, Venezuela, Zambia, Iraq, Iran) were almost exclusively mineral exporters.

The most interesting feature of the mineral economies is the way in which governments gradually appropriated more of the export proceeds. To induce initial exploration and investment, the government usually offered very favorable royalty terms to private companies. Once a company had invested, however, its properties were hostage to subsequent tax increases. The company retained some leverage through its ability not to increase its investments or to curtail production and thereby reduce the country's export receipts. A threatened tax increase was often countered by an "investment strike." The dispute was eventually settled on terms involving some increase in taxation, investment was resumed, and the stage was set for the next round in the bargaining game. Thus governments that had initially received only a few percent of the rents from mineral exploitation eventually came to receive 50 percent or more. The eventual outcome was usually nationalization of company properties.

This process has been described in detail for Venezuela by Franklin Tugwell (1975), for Chile by Markos Mamalakis and Clark Reynolds (1965), for Iraq by Edith and E. F. Penrose (1978), and for Iran by Julian Bharier (1971). It scarcely corresponds to the picture sometimes presented of helpless governments subservient to foreign interests.

To sum up: although the turning point is *usually* associated with a marked rise in the export/GDP ratio, this is not an invariable rule. It has not been true in India, where the trade ratio has declined during the intensive-growth era. China has also followed a relatively autarkic, inward-looking development path. Other exceptions among recent developers include Egypt and Turkey, whose export/GDP ratios in 1978–80 were only about half as high as in 1950–52. Closed-economy models of internally generated growth would be relevant to these cases. In a large majority of cases, however, export performance is the best single clue to the initiation and continuation of intensive growth.

4

The Pattern of Intensive Growth

What happens after the turning point? We are looking at 34 countries scattered over three continents and most of the earth's surface. Intensive growth in these countries began at different times, ranging from 1840 to 1965. How far can we generalize over such a broad sweep of space and time?

A number of statistical regularities have been revealed by the work of Kuznets, Chenery, and others. As per capita income rises there is a gradual shift in the composition of national output, with the agricultural sector shrinking and the industrial and service sectors growing in relative importance. A similar shift occurs in the uses of output, with a relative decline in the share of private consumption and an increase in the shares of public consumption and investment.

But when we look below these macroeconomic totals we find a great deal of variation: in the pattern of institutional change, in the pace of sectoral shifts, in the sources of increased agricultural and industrial output, in the product composition of output, in foreign trade and financial flows, in the orientation of economic policy and the frequency of policy shifts. This rich variety of country experience stands out clearly in the country case studies and can be fully appreciated only by reading them. In an effort at summation, I shall venture some generalizations that seem to hold true for most countries in the sample. But there is hardly any statement to which one cannot find exceptions, and these will be duly noted.

One interesting question relates to the difference between pre-1945 and post-1945 experience. The post-1945 era brought general decolonization, a faster tempo of world economic growth, new institutions for transfer of capital and technology, a new climate of opinion emphasizing the responsibility of government to promote economic growth. Thus late developers were arriving at the turning point under different conditions from those facing early developers; and the post-1945 growth path of the early developers was affected in important ways. At the end of this chapter I shall offer some summary comments on development then and now.

POPULATION AND LABOR SUPPLY

Even in the last century, the beginnings of intensive growth typically brought some acceleration in the rate of natural increase in population. A gradual sag in mortality rates was mainly responsible. The reasons included improved transport facilities to move food to areas that might otherwise have experienced famine; gradual spread of vaccination against infectious diseases from the late nineteenth century onward; reduction of infant mortality through improved water supply, sewer systems, and maternity clinics; growing availability of curative services by doctors and hospitals; and improvements in nutrition, education, and personal health care, all raising natural resistance to disease. Improvements in health and nutrition may also bring some increase in (unregulated) fertility rates. There are examples of rising fertility in our country cases; but on the whole fertility changes appear minor compared with the effect of declining mortality.

But while endogenous changes would have produced some acceleration of population growth in developing countries, they cannot explain anything like the rates of increase actually observed. These rates have been due mainly to discontinuous jumps in the progress of medical science, associated particularly with the two world wars and impinging on third-world countries as an exogenous factor provided virtually free of charge by international agencies. Medical progress produced a marked reduction of deathrates in the 1920s and an even more dramatic reduction after 1945; reductions occurred even in countries that have not yet reached the turning point. The average rate of population increase in third-world countries is estimated by Kuznets (in Easterlin, 1980) at only about 0.6 percent per year from 1850 to 1900. By the 1920s it had risen to 1.3 percent. By 1950–55, it had risen to 2.0 percent and by 1970–75 to 2.6 percent, as crude deathrates fell from an average of 31 per thousand in 1937 to 16 per thousand from 1970 to 1975.

This sharp acceleration of population growth has placed late-developing countries in a different position from that of their predecessors. Late developers have had to run faster to outpace population growth and achieve increases in per capita income. In general, third-world countries have responded successfully to this challenge. The rates of GDP growth achieved since 1945 would have appeared sensational in the nineteenth century. After deducting high rates of population growth, however, the growth rates of GDP per capita are only moderate. The detailed country data to be presented in chapter 15 show also that there is no significant relation between the rate of population growth and the rate of increase in per capita income, that is, countries with higher population growth have managed on average to offset this increase by faster growth of total output. This observation supports a similar conclusion reached earlier by Kuznets for the "developed" countries.

Higher rates of population growth have also altered the labor-supply situation. While "surplus labor" can be defined in a variety of ways, I take it as meaning unutilized labor time that does *not* reflect a preference for leisure but rather lack of opportunity for productive employment. In the pre-1940 era surplus labor was limited to a few densely settled areas: Egypt, Java, parts of China and India. Latin America, Africa, and even much of Asia had reserves of unused land that could readily absorb population growth. Indeed, managers of mines and plantations commonly complained of the scarcity of labor. What this often meant, however, was unwillingness to pay wages high enough to attract people from a relatively comfortable living in agriculture. It was for this reason that Brazil imported slaves and later European immigrants, that Ceylon imported Tamil laborers from southern India, that Malaya imported Chinese, and so on.

Since 1945, however, accelerated population growth has produced surplus-labor conditions in more and more countries. The effects of surplus labor are seen in underutilization of agricultural labor, excessive migration to the cities, over-crowding of "traditional" trade and service activities, and open unemployment. The pressure for employment tends also to produce compulsory overstaffing of industrial enterprises, particularly public-sector enterprises, as well as govern-ment agencies. As always, there are exceptions. A few countries with unusually high growth rates, notably Taiwan and South Korea, have exhausted the surplus-labor pool and entered the era of labor scarcity. But such situations are unusual.

It is usually thought, following the well-known Lewis model, that surplus labor is accompanied by a constant real wage rate. In some countries one does observe this, but in others one does not. Where agricultural productivity is rising, a rise in agricultural wages may put pressure on the urban wage level. Large em-ployers may voluntarily pay a premium wage in order to recruit, stabilize, and motivate an industrial labor force. It is possible also for the urban real wage level to be forced upward prematurely through political mechanisms. Unions of workers in government and large-scale industry, often concentrated in and near the capital city and often linked to political parties, are in a good position to win minimum-wage legislation and high pay scales in government, which often serves as wage leader for the economy. This premature forcing up of urban wage scales tends to restrict urban employment opportunities while at the same time increasing the incentive to rural-urban migration. It thus aggravates the problem of urban unem-ployment and underemployment.

To end this section on a more cheerful note: in the older industrial countries, after an initial spurt of population growth associated mainly with declining mor-tality, the birthrate began to follow the deathrate downward, eventually reducing population growth to a modest 1 percent or so per year. This process seems now to be setting in among third-world countries. In 15 countries in our sample, including almost all the rapidly growing countries, the rate of natural increase was *lower* in 1980 than in 1960. In some cases the decline was quite sharp: in Chile from 2.5 to 1.5 percent, in Colombia from 3.2 to 2.2 percent, in Brazil from 3.0 to 2.1 percent, in South Korea from 3.0 to 1.7 percent, in Thailand from 2.9 to 2.2 percent. All the other Latin American countries in our sample show declines, as do Malaysia, Indonesia, Taiwan, Turkey, Philippines, and Sri Lanka. Although data for China are not precise, there is no doubt that birthrates and the population growth rate have been reduced substantially by the government's active population-control program.

The reasons for declining birthrates no doubt vary from country to country and could be revealed only by careful case studies. The limited evidence suggests that, while family-planning programs have had some effect, the main factors are associated with rising per capita income and resemble those operating earlier in the "developed" countries: lower infant mortality, which reduces the number of births needed to achieve a desired family size; urbanization, which leads to a decline in birthrates because children are more expensive and less useful in cities than in the country; better education, which tends to raise people's aspirations both for themselves and their children; and especially improved education and higher socioeconomic status for women, which seems strongly associated with lower birthrates.

In regard to population, then, the normal pattern is for the growth rate to rise for a considerable time after the beginning of intensive growth. Eventually, however, developments associated with rising per capita income have a retarding influence on the birthrate. The decline in the birthrate eventually exceeds the parallel decline in the deathrate (which is still continuing even in developed countries), and the rate of natural increase begins to fall. Experience in the older industrial countries suggests an eventual leveling off of the population growth rate at something like 1 percent per year.

AGRICULTURE AND FOOD SUPPLY

Over the course of intensive growth, while the agricultural sector is shrinking in relative terms, output is normally rising in absolute terms. Rising agricultural output serves several familiar functions. First, except for a limited number of oil-mineral economies, agriculture is initially the main source of rising exports. Some of these export crops may have been newly introduced to the economy—cocoa in West Africa, tea in Sri Lanka, rubber in Malaysia, sugar in Cuba and Philippines—but others may be traditional food crops, such as rice, which are produced in increasing volume to meet rising foreign demand. In a land-surplus situation, which has existed in most countries until quite recently, production for export is added on to domestic food production rather than displacing it.

Second, agriculture is the main, often the exclusive, source of food supply for the growing population. In a poor country with low nutritional levels, income elasticity of demand for food is quite high, perhaps in the range of 0.6–0.7. For example, if population is growing at 2 percent and per capita income is also growing at 2 percent, food demand will be rising at more than 3 percent per year. If food output rises less rapidly than demand, the internal terms of trade will turn in favor of agriculture, with upward pressure on food prices and money wage rates; this will tend to choke off industrial growth, as Ricardo predicted. The food constraint can be relaxed, of course, through food imports, but this course also has costs and risks.

Finally, a growing population needs more jobs as well as more food, and for a long time agriculture remains the main source of increased employment. True, migration to the cities sets in early. If a country's population is growing at 2 percent the rural population may be growing at only 1.5 percent. But since 80 percent of the population is rural in the first instance, the rural sector still accounts for a lot of people in absolute terms. Additional employment for them has to come from some combination of increase in cultivated acreage, application of more labor inputs per acre, and diversion of rural labor time into small-scale industry and other nonagricultural activities. In some cases—Japan after 1880, Taiwan after 1950, China after 1950—this absorption of farm-family labor time in non-farm activities has been quite important. Although densely populated China has not yet achieved full employment, a study by Rawski (1979) indicates that it was much closer to it in 1979 than in 1950.

Whereas the development literature of the 1950s emphasized industrialization as the key to progress, the recent tendency has been to place increasing emphasis on agriculture. It is now standard doctrine that agriculture plays a central role as provider of exports, foodstuffs, and employment.

When we look at production experience, however, we find some surprises. Even in the 1970s, when the "green revolution" had worked its benign effect in many areas, five of the 19 countries with highest GDP growth rates were raising food production at less than 3 percent per year. Of the 18 countries at the bottom of the growth league, 16 were raising food output at less than 3 percent. Thus more than half the countries in our sample were not meeting what could be considered a modest standard of agricultural performance.

In some cases, to be sure, there is a plausible explanation. Countries with a strong position in oil or mineral exports can trade these products for food imports, thus relaxing the pressure on food production. This would apply to such cases as Iraq, Nigeria, Egypt, Algeria, Chile, and Peru, in all of which food imports have been rising rapidly. Even so, food imports use foreign exchange that could be put to other uses. Further, any interruption of the export flow can place the country in a precarious position.

In another eight countries, per capita income growth from 1960 to 1980 was near zero or even negative. This group includes Zambia, Zaire, Nepal, Mozambique, Sudan, Uganda, Ghana, and Afghanistan. In these cases low growth in agriculture is part of a pattern of low GDP growth and, indeed, is a large component of poor overall performance. These cases provide negative confirmation of the key importance of agriculture.

The most interesting countries are those which have achieved modest growth of GDP per capita in spite of substandard agricultural performance, thus apparently contradicting the conventional wisdom. In this group are Kenya, Morocco, Tanzania, India, and Burma. These cases might be regarded as showing that strong growth of agricultural output is not *essential* for overall growth. But agricultural growth is still very *helpful*. The GDP growth rate of these countries could have been considerably higher if agricultural performance had been better.

This having been said, agricultural output normally rises during intensive growth, and in the more successful economies it rises at a good rate. For the dozen most rapidly growing countries in our sample (excluding the oil economies), the median annual growth rate of food output in the 1970s was 4.5 per cent. And even some of the oil countries did quite well, as for example Indonesia (3.6 percent), Iran (4.0 percent), and Venezuela (4.0 percent).

This leads to the next question: where do output increases come from, and why are some countries able to raise output more rapidly than others? Agricultural organization is important, with owner-operated farms clearly superior, though tenancy systems that assure security of tenure and moderate rentals can also perform well. Land reserves are always helpful, though their exploitation requires investment in infrastructure. Technical progress is always necessary and must be relied on increasingly as the frontier closes. Government can contribute in important ways: by changing agricultural organization so that more income accrues to the cultivator; by investment in irrigation and drainage, roads, warehouses, and marketing facilities; by agricultural research and extension services; and by helping to ensure adequate supplies of credit, seeds, fertilizers, and other inputs. The converse of this is that government can readily choke off agricultural growth by doing the wrong things or by sheer neglect.

The pattern of agricultural organization existing at the turning point may already be favorable to intensive growth. In quite a few Asian and African countries (Burma, Thailand, Nigeria, Ghana, Ivory Coast, Uganda) small, owner-operated farms have always predominated. Another group had a combination of small and medium-sized farms (Chile, Argentina, Brazil, Peru, Colombia, India, Pakistan). In still other cases foreign-owned plantations were established to grow export crops, while food was produced mainly by small indigenous farmers (Sri Lanka, Malaysia, Philippines, Indonesia). The least favorable situations were those in which large landowners dominated a mass of peasant cultivators (Mexico, Venezuela, Egypt, Iran) or in which European settlers had appropriated much of the best land and developed a modern agricultural economy on top of the traditional indigenous economy (Algeria, Morocco, Kenya, Zimbabwe). These last situations were unstable in the sense that they could not survive the transition to independent rule.

Where the initial situation is unfavorable, usually because of excessive landlordism, there has often been a major "land reform" early in the intensive-growth era. Land reform typically takes the form of a ceiling on landholdings, with holdings above the ceiling purchased or confiscated by government and subdivided into small farms whose new owners pay for the land over a period of years. A nominal purchase sometimes turns into a confiscation, as in cases where the large landowners are paid off in government bonds whose value later shrinks through continuing inflation. Reforms of this type, intended to provide strong incentive to small cultivators, occurred in Japan (1873), Mexico (nominally after the 1910 revolution, but implemented mainly in the 1930s and 1940s), Taiwan (1949–53), South Korea (early 1950s), Egypt (1952), Iraq (1958 and 1970), Iran (1960 and 1965), and Kenya (1960 onward). These reforms are generally judged to have made a substantial contribution to the subsequent rise in agricultural output.

A different type of reform has involved transformation of formerly private (and, in some cases, foreign-owned) holdings into cooperative or communal farms. This happened in China after 1949, Cuba after 1958, Algeria after 1962, Mozambique after 1975, and Tanzania ("villagization program" of the 1970s). The only one of these cases that can be considered moderately successful is China, where agricultural output has rather more than kept pace with population since 1950. In the other cases the results have been poor.

A word now about the input sources of output growth. In examining the literature I was surprised to find that almost every country had surplus land as of 1900 and that quite a few still had surplus land in 1950. The closing of the frontier has been very gradual. But the process is inexorable, and in one country after another the possibilities of further expansion of acreage are being exhausted. As this happens, the burden of raising agricultural output is shifted increasingly to technical progress. Generalizing for the third world as a whole, we can say that over the past century the contribution to output of increases in acreage has become steadily less important, while the contribution of higher yields per acre through technical progress has become steadily more important.

In addition to the growing importance of new technology, the nature of technical progress has changed substantially. Until recently yield increases came mainly from traditional technical progress, of the type illustrated by our discussion of China in chapter 2: modest improvement of seeds through selection and transference; irrigation and drainage to regulate water supply; larger per acre inputs of labor and organic fertilizer; shifts in the cropping pattern toward crops yielding more calories per acre; more continuous use of land, with shorter fallow periods. Since World War II, however, there has been a rapid development of modern or science-based technical progress, involving systematic and sustained research and experimentation. The Mexican center for wheat and corn research (CYMMIT) and the Philippine center for rice research (IRRI) developed new seed varieties that provided large increases in crop yields. The success of these ventures has stimulated establishment of other international centers for research on sugar, potatoes, and a variety of tropical crops.

Use of these new seeds, often called "high-yielding varieties" (HYV), typically requires a "package" of complementary inputs—water supply, chemical fertilizers, pesticides, more-intensive tillage. These must be applied in carefully regulated proportions to achieve optimal results. Further, it appears that a country cannot simply "borrow" seed varieties developed elsewhere. Considerable research and experimentation within the country is necessary to domesticate the new strains to local soil and climate conditions. Countries that have moved energetically to incorporate HYV seed into their agricultural systems have been able to achieve remarkable yield increases within a few years. The most dramatic examples come from Southeast Asia (Thailand, Burma, Taiwan, Philippines, Indonesia), but India, Pakistan, Turkey, and Egypt have also made substantial gains.

I noted above that accelerated population growth since 1945 has made the food-supply problem more urgent than before. At the same time, intensified technical progress in agriculture has provided at least a potential answer to this need. But one cannot be uniformly optimistic. There are a number of countries, particularly in sub-Saharan Africa, where yields per acre are static or even declining and where domestic food supplies are falling increasingly behind the growing population's needs.

In addition to reforming tenure systems, building rural infrastructure, and supplying modern inputs and new technology, government can influence the cash returns from farming through purchase of output by government marketing boards, farm price controls (or lack of such controls), pricing of government-supplied fertilizer and other inputs, exchange-rate policies (which determine the return from agricultural exports), and industrial-protection policies (which affect the prices farmers must pay). Harsh policies that tax farmers heavily can discourage cash-crop production and even cause a reversion to subsistence farming. A shift toward more generous policies, which a good many countries made in the 1960s and 1970s, can lead to a sharp rise in output. This point will be elaborated and illustrated in chapter 16.

THE INDUSTRIAL SECTOR

"Industry" must be viewed broadly as including household and handicraft production as well as factory output. Indeed, the early developers often had few or no factories at the turning point. For countries reaching the turning point after 1945, such as China, India, Egypt, Turkey, and Indonesia, there was already a modest development of factory industry. But even in these cases handicrafts still provided most of industrial output.

The rapid expansion of foreign trade typically associated with the turning point has two main consequences. To the extent that revenue from exports is returned to the economy, domestic demand for all goods and services, including manufactures, is increased. But tradable goods need no longer be obtained from domestic sources. Handicraft producers have to compete with imports, whose volume tends to rise in tandem with export volume. Although the *market share* of handicraft producers declines, there is not necessarily an absolute decline in output. Since total demand is rising, the volume of handicraft production may be maintained or even continue to grow slowly. Further, the impact of import competition is uneven by product and region. It is usually most severe in textile spinning, where the cost advantage of factory goods is very large, and hand spinning is often wiped out quickly. The decline of hand weaving proceeds more slowly, partly because availability of cheap machine-produced yarn helps the weavers to survive in competition. Producers of bulky products or producers located far from the seacoast get some protection from transport costs and may be little affected by imports. Handicraft producers of export specialties, such as Iranian carpets, will also continue to flourish.

As demand continues to grow and as the market is confirmed and mapped out by imports of manufactures, domestic factory production eventually makes its appearance. But this happens only with a considerable lag. Peru and Argentina had very small industrial sectors before 1930. Malaya, Thailand, and all the African countries except Southern Rhodesia and Kenya had scarcely any factory industry as late as 1940. Still, factories eventually appear and expand. Domestic industry grows mainly in response to rising demand; but it grows also by taking over an increasing share of the market from handicrafts and from imports. The progress of import substitution can be traced by looking at the percentage of, say, cotton-cloth consumption supplied by imports. This figure, typically falling over time and eventually approaching zero, appears in many countries' economic histories. It should be emphasized that import substitution is a normal process that will spread from products with small optimum scale of plant to those requiring larger scale, even in the absence of special stimulus. Substitution usually is stimulated in varying degree by protective tariffs, which, while they may be imposed mainly for revenue purposes, do raise domestic prices of manufactures above the world price, making it easier for domestic industries to survive. Industrialization has also been stimulated by special crises that reduced availability of foreign supplies. The two world wars, which sharply reduced the flow of manufactures from the industrialized countries, left a market gap that was filled in some third-world countries by rising domestic production. The collapse of primary-product prices during the Great Depression, which sharply reduced most countries' capacity to import, also led to a spurt in domestic industrialization, especially in Latin America.

Rising industrial output as a percentage of GDP is sometimes seen as a growth of "big business." But for a long time after industrialization begins, the number of really large establishments is limited. Industrial censuses usually show that the great majority of manufacturing enterprises are very small. The structure of manufacturing can properly be characterized as "dualistic." On one hand are enterprises with several hundred workers, with a relatively high capital/labor ratio, relatively high output per worker, and relatively high wage rates. On the other hand are a multitude of small shops with markedly lower capital/labor ratios, labor productivity, and wage rates. The small establishments typically provide more than half of factory employment, though because of their lower productivity they may provide only a quarter or less of factory output.

Notable too is the very gradual shrinkage of the handicraft and cottage-industry sector, which even today provides a surprising amount of employment in many third-world countries. A few examples may be worth citing. In Chile in 1970, after more than a century of intensive growth, about half of all industrial workers were in some 70,000 very small workshops, about 40 percent of which were producing clothing and shoes. In Colombia in the late 1960s, when factory employment was around 300,000, there were still an estimated 150,000–200,000 handicraft workers. These workers, however, produced only about 15 percent of manufacturing output, implying relatively low output per worker. In Nigeria in 1965, some 900,000 rural households were engaged in cottage industries. This compares with 100,000 in urban enterprises with 10 workers or less, and only 76,000 in firms employing more than 10 people. In the Philippines in 1970, handicraft and cottage industries with 1–4 workers provided an estimated 70 percent of industrial employment. In Morocco at the time of independence in 1956, the number of handicraft workers was reported as "substantially larger" than the number of factory workers. In Iran, too, handicraft workers were said to outnumber factory workers as recently as 1970.

Who were the early industrial entrepreneurs? In some countries foreign enterprise was quite important. American investment was prominent in the Philippines and Cuba after 1900. The early factories in Taiwan and Korea were Japanese-owned. The British were prominent manufacturing investors in Kenya, Nigeria, and the Rhodesias, as were the French in Algeria, Morocco, and Ivory Coast. In a larger number of cases, however, the entrepreneurs were homegrown. This was generally true in Latin America, provided we count recent immigrants as part of the local population. Immigrants from Portugal, Spain, and Italy, who often brought capital as well as business experience, played a considerable part in the industrialization of Brazil, Argentina, and Chile. Local enterprise predominated also in Southeast Asia, provided again we count people of Chinese origin as "local." Families that had migrated permanently from China were the main entrepreneurs in Malaya and Thailand as well as Singapore and Hong Kong; and they made important contributions in Taiwan, Philippines, and Indonesia. Although there was some British investment in manufacturing in India, Indian entrepreneurs predominated increasingly with the passage of time. In China, too, British and Japanese investors established some of the first textile mills, but Chinese gradually took over most of the manufacturing sector. In Pakistan, which had little industry at independence, the new manufacturing entrepreneurs were entirely local.

In the post-1945 period, most newly independent countries have been suspicious of or even hostile to foreign investment. Many foreign-owned enterprises have been partially or wholly nationalized, and indigenous businessmen have taken over increasingly. There has also been a substantial increase in government entrepreneurship, which is local by definition.

There is nothing unusual to be said about the sources of labor and capital inputs, nothing that would distinguish industrialization in third-world countries from the similar process in Europe or America. Leaving aside foreign-capital inflows, the initial domestic capital for new industries came usually from trade or agriculture. As had been true earlier in England and Western Europe, many of the early industrialists were merchants, often engaged previously in import trade. From serving the domestic market through imports, they turned rather naturally to serving it through local factories, using their accumulated capital to finance the initial construction. Wealthy landowners—the "coffee barons" of Brazil, the "sugar barons" of Peru, and so on—also turned their capital toward manufacturing when it became profitable to do so. Once established, the new industries grew in classical fashion through reinvestment of their large profits.

Labor supply, in the sense of sheer numbers, was rarely a problem. From the outset factories were able to offer wage rates well above those in agriculture and other alternative occupations and thus to attract a surplus of applicants. The difficulties were rather those of training, motivation, and supervision, which early industrialists often underestimated. Finding labor apparently cheap, they tended to use it inefficiently. Only gradually, and often under the pressure of rising wages, did they pay enough attention to personnel management to develop reasonable levels of proficiency. The much-discussed "labor problems" of industry in developing countries usually turn out on examination to be largely "management problems."

The normal sequence of products in an industrializing economy is quite predictable. Textiles are usually the leading sector, because clothing is a basic need and the domestic market is large. Further, the capacity to produce cotton and other fibers is widely distributed throughout the world, which means that domestic raw materials are usually available. In addition to an assured domestic demand for cloth—often demonstrated initially by large cloth imports—the emergence of textiles is facilitated by relatively small minimum efficient scale of plant, a well-known technology, ready availability of used as well as new textile machinery, and limited requirements of skilled labor.

Other early industries are concerned mainly with agricultural processing for home use or for export—rice milling, flour milling, sawmilling, palm-oil extraction, and so on. These are followed by the production of light consumer goods, such as shoes, clothing, beverages, leather goods, ceramics, furniture, and household utensils, as well as building materials and simple agricultural implements. As the market continues to grow, additional industries appear in a sequence charted by Walther Hoffman (1958) and Hollis Chenery (1960, 1979). "Middle industries," such as chemicals and petroleum products, appear next, followed eventually by "late" or heavy-goods industries, dominated by metals, machinery, and transport equipment.

In comparing the course of manufacturing growth since 1950 with that in earlier periods, one observes both similarities and differences. The basic sequence—textiles, other consumer goods, intermediate goods, capital and durable consumer goods—does not seem to have changed. Countries normally move through this sequence, with domestic production replacing imports at successively higher stages. But since 1950 there has been a more systematic effort to guide the process of industrial expansion, not only in late-developing countries but in third-world countries in general. In earlier periods, although there were general trade and exchange-rate policies that might help or hamper manufacturing growth, there was little effort to discriminate among branches of manufacturing. After 1950, with more activist governments and more attention to overall development planning, arose a widespread belief that some paths to expansion are preferable to others and that governments should guide the sequence as well as the overall tempo of industrialization.

Partly because of this proindustry policy bias, partly because of the increased resources made available by rapidly rising exports and foreign borrowing after 1950, the pace of movement through the sequence from handicrafts to light industry to heavy industry was considerably accelerated as compared with earlier eras. And in some countries the sequence itself was altered to the extent that heavy industry was expanded faster than would have happened without government intervention—and often faster than market size warranted. The socialist economies of Eastern Europe have sometimes been described as "prematurely heavy-industry oriented." The same could be said of a number of third-world countries.

Another characteristic of post-1950 manufacturing expansion was a marked increase in the public-sector share of assets and output. Before 1940 third-world manufacturing industries were almost entirely in private hands. Since 1950 in most countries government has not only been the main source of industrial finance, through government investment banks, commercial banks, and direct budget allocations, but has gone beyond fulfilling this role to ownership and management of manufacturing establishments. The public-sector share of manufacturing is often 20 or 25 percent and sometimes reaches 75 or 80 percent. The reasons vary from country to country: a long-standing statist tradition, as in Turkey and other remnants of the Ottoman Empire; socialist ideology of the British Labour Party type, as in India; a desire to transfer industry from foreign to national ownership, which tended to be interpreted as public ownership, as in Egypt or Burma; and a perhaps natural tendency for government investment banks to acquire majority equity ownership and thus responsibility for management, as in Mexico or Brazil.

These publicly owned manufacturing industries on the whole have not operated very efficiently, with the result that there have been recent reversals of policy in a number of countries. This range of problems will be examined further in chapter 16.

THE FOREIGN SECTOR

Since early intensive growth is normally export-led, a rising trade ratio follows almost by definition. During the 1870–1914 era, third-world countries that had entered on intensive growth typically had population growth rates of around 1 percent, GDP growth rates of 2–3 percent, but export growth rates of 3–4 percent. The export/GDP ratio was thus typically rising.

After 1945, export pessimists such as Prebisch argued that growth led by primary exports was no longer feasible. The rules of the game had changed. But the export record since 1945, presented in some detail in chapter 15, fails to confirm this gloomy prognosis. In most countries the export/GDP ratio was higher in 1980 than in 1950. Significantly, this was true especially of countries *with high growth rates*. Of the 19 countries with the highest growth of per capita income, 15 had a higher export/GDP ratio in 1980 than in 1950. Thus exports were still operating as a leading sector. Countries in which the export/GDP ratio declined are clustered toward the bottom of the growth-rate table. In India, for example, with a below-average growth of per capita output, the export/GDP ratio fell from 6.7 percent in 1950–52 to 4.9 percent in 1978–80. This decline is related to inward-looking economic policies unfavorable to exports, described more fully in later chapters. Most of the other cases are African countries, where the falling export ratio is symptomatic of political disorganization and low economic growth. Examples are Tanzania, Zambia, Uganda, Zaire, and Ghana. But in the more successful African countries, Kenya and Ivory Coast, the trade ratio has risen.

Arguments about the limited stimulating effect of primary exports often seem to assume that a country keeps on exporting the same products in perpetuity and that, if returned value to the domestic economy is initially low, it will remain low. But neither of these premises is realistic. One of the more striking features of the oil-mineral economies is the demonstrated ability of governments to extract a growing share of the export proceeds by taxation and by raising the price of labor and other domestic inputs. A few examples: in *Chile,* returned value from the copper industry rose from 38 percent in 1925 to about 80 percent by the late 1950s. In *Peru* returned value, which comes from agricultural and fishery products as well as minerals, had risen to 53 percent by 1960 and 81 percent by 1973. In *Venezuela* the government share of net income in the oil industry rose from a low initial level to 51 percent in 1950 and 80 percent in 1973. In *Iraq,* the privately owned Iraq Petroleum Company paid only a low fixed royalty; but in 1951 the government succeeded in enforcing a fifty-fifty sharing of profits, and when the oil company proved resistant to further concessions it was nationalized in 1972. In *Iran,* too, the British-owned Anglo-Iranian Oil Company paid only a meager royalty up to 1950; but when the company refused to concede a larger share, it was nationalized and the government share of oil revenue jumped sharply. In none of the countries studied has the trend been in the opposite direction.

A second striking development is that many countries, and especially the more successful exporters, have managed to diversify their export bill over time. Thus even where the export of goods that were dominant in the early days has grown slowly or even declined, the growth rate of total exports has been maintained by adding on new products. Again a few examples, drawn from our country case studies, will be helpful. In *Brazil,* where coffee, sugar, cotton, and cocoa still formed 89 percent of exports in 1960, the share of these traditional goods had fallen to 36 percent by 1976. New exports include soybeans and derivatives (17 percent), iron ore (10 percent), and manufactures (30 percent). *Mexico* in the 1870–1910 era was mainly a mineral exporter. But by the 1950s, due mainly to an active government policy of agricultural development, Mexico was exporting a diversified list of agricultural and livestock products and minerals were of minor importance. Still more recently have come oil and growing exports of manufactures, in addition to a large tourist industry. In *Ivory Coast* the "big three"—cocoa, coffee, and logs—were traditionally close to 100 percent of exports. But today these goods are exported increasingly in processed rather than raw form, and the country has added cotton, palm products, and fruit as well as growing exports of manufactures. The *Philippines* traditionally exported sugar, copra, and coconut oil, to which have now been added logs, plywood, copper concentrates, and manufactures (about 20 percent of exports.)

In *Pakistan,* raw cotton fell from 40 percent of exports in 1950 to 14 percent in 1980. Rice exports are now larger than cotton exports, and still more important are finished manufactures (42 percent) and semifinished goods (16 percent). In *Sri Lanka,* traditional tea, rubber, and coconut exports have fallen from 95 percent to 60 percent of the total. New agricultural exports, as well as manufactured exports, have been rising rapidly. In *Malaysia* tin and rubber, which were 90 percent of exports in 1950, have now fallen below 50 percent. New exports include timber, palm oil, petroleum, and manufactures. *Thailand*'s traditional export of rice, which for many decades accounted for about 70 percent of all exports, has now fallen below 20 percent. New exports include maize, kenaf, cassava, rubber, timber, and manufactures (about 22 percent of the total).

These examples make clear that many third-world countries have succeeded not only in diversifying their exports of primary products but also in penetrating the huge world market for manufactures. The most spectacular examples are South Korea and Taiwan, where manufactures now form close to 90 percent of all exports. The "gang of four," which includes these countries plus Singapore and Hong Kong, now supplies about half of all third-world exports of manufactures (a percentage that is probably at its peak and will fall as manufacturing capacity expands elsewhere). But quite a few other countries have succeeded in raising manufactures from a few percent of exports in 1950 to 20–30 percent by 1980. The list includes Mexico, Brazil, Colombia, Egypt, Turkey, Pakistan, Sri Lanka, Thailand, and Philippines.

In terms of dynamic comparative advantage, one might expect labor-intensive manufactures to migrate increasingly to third-world countries having abundant labor and relatively low wage rates. The main retarding factors are import quotas and other restrictions imposed by the developed countries, plus the time and effort needed to bring third-world industries up to a competitive level of productivity and costs. In addition to competing in developed-country markets, it should be possible for third-world countries increasingly to exchange manufac-

Read this

tures with each other. Already a good share of manufactured exports from Brazil are to other Latin American countries, from Ivory Coast to other African countries, from Egypt and Pakistan to the Arab oil states, and so on.

Rising exports mean rising capacity to import. The import/GDP ratio tends to parallel the export/GDP ratio, rising when exports are buoyant, falling when exports are doing poorly. More interesting is the commodity composition of imports, which changes in a predictable way. In the early decades of intensive growth, consumer goods and especially textiles usually dominate the import list. But as the country develops its own light industries, consumer-goods imports decline steadily as a percentage of total imports and as a percentage of domestic supply of consumer goods. The composition of imports shifts toward capital goods, fuels, and intermediate goods needed as inputs to manufacturing. These items now dominate the import list in most third-world countries, with consumer goods only a quarter or less of all imports. The main exception is a number of countries that, as noted earlier in the chapter, have allowed food production to lag behind population growth, with the result that food imports may constitute 20 or 30 percent of the import bill.

Imports tend to run ahead of exports, the balance being closed by foreign borrowing. It is natural for a developing country to be a borrower for quite a long period. The United States, Canada, and Australia were large net borrowers during the nineteenth century, and so were several countries in Eastern Europe. This has also been the general rule in the third world, the main exception being Japan, which was unusually successful in mobilizing domestic capital and in earning foreign exchange through a rapid increase in exports. More recently, China has developed mainly from internal resources, except for substantial Soviet credits in the 1950s and a modest infusion of Western capital in the post-Mao period.

Much has been written on capital transfers from developed to developing countries. Anything that could be said within the limits of space here would have to be quite superficial, and so it is perhaps best to say nothing. The literature suggests that foreign capital, while quite helpful to some countries at some times, has rarely been critical. The key requirements for growth lie in the domestic economy and polity; and where these requirements are absent, foreign capital is unlikely to be used effectively.

I have tended in this section to view export-led growth as the standard case and to view a rising export/GDP ratio as helpful, if not essential. So it is important to note exceptions. China's trade ratio since 1950 has been low. India's trade ratio has been low and declining. A similar decline is evident in Egypt and Turkey over the 1950–80 period. It is no doubt easier for a large country, with diverse resources and a large internal market, to follow an autarkic, inward-looking development path. India and China can do things that would not be feasible for Jamaica or Gambia. Even in the Indian case, however, most economists conclude that more outward-looking policies and more concern for exports would have made possible a higher growth rate than that actually achieved.

My interpretation implies also a standard *pattern* of growth, broadly similar for most developing countries. Other writers, however, have tried to distinguish several distinct *patterns* of growth and to classify countries on the basis of which pattern they fit. Such efforts usually rely mainly on the differing behavior of the foreign sector. Thus Paauw and Fei (1973) distinguish between (1) continued reliance on growth of primary exports, (2) import-substitution policies aimed at accelerating the growth of the industrial sector, and (3) export substitution, in which manufactured goods increasingly replace primary products in the export bill.

I prefer to regard these not as *alternative* growth patterns but as successive *stages* in a historical sequence. A country begins by exporting primary products, since they are all it has. As income from exports broadens the domestic market, the industrial sector grows through the normal import-substitution sequence outlined in the previous section. This sequence can no doubt be accelerated by protectionist trade policies, but it is not clear that a specific degree of import restriction warrants placing a country in a separate category, especially in view of the variability of policy over time. Many countries that followed restrictionist policies for a decade or two after 1945 concluded eventually that continued growth of the industrial sector required development of export capacity in manufactures, aided by a more outward-looking policy stance.

A successfully developing country, then, tends to move through the three Paauw-Fei stages in sequence, ending up with a large component of manufactured exports. Taiwan and South Korea are classic examples, but a dozen other "newly industrializing countries" are now following the same trajectory. Countries differ, however, in the tempo of movement through the sequence. These differences stem partly from the richness and variety of the natural-resource base. A country with a strong resource base can afford to be more leisurely about manufacturing development, which will occur in any event unless thwarted by obtuse policies. Size of country is also a major consideration. Larger size, by providing a large domestic market, tends to hasten the rate of industrialization and broaden its pattern, so that even "late" industries arrive fairly soon.

The large country–small country dimension and the rich resources–poor resources dimension yield a four-box classification of countries that could prove useful. The growth experiences, and especially the industrialization experiences, of countries in different boxes probably do differ in a systematic way. To this extent one may be justified in speaking of *patterns* of growth.

THE PUBLIC SECTOR

Government functions as a producer of public and quasi-public goods and as an important investor in physical capital. Looking first at the former function: it is familiar knowledge that the public consumption/GDP ratio in developed countries is substantially higher today than it was fifty years ago. High income elasticity of demand for education and health services, a tendency to stretch the public-good concept to cover more and more things, and the fact that most of the cost of public goods is labor cost and so reflects wage scales that typically rise faster than prices, all contribute to this result.

In the third world, too, there is a marked difference between earlier times and the post-1945 situation. Estimates of national income before 1940 are rare; but where they have been made, it appears that public consumption was rarely more than 5 percent of GDP. Colonial governments tended to service mainly the European population, which was concentrated in urban areas. The peasant in the countryside received much less attention. Education in particular was notably underdeveloped. But one can scarcely say that independent countries were more enterprising. The Latin American countries, for example, had very small public sectors before 1940, and their public consumption/GDP ratios are still relatively low.

Since 1950 we do have national-income estimates for almost all countries and tables showing the distribution of income among private consumption, public consumption, and capital formation. A tabulation of the data for the countries in our sample appears in chapter 15. The relative importance of public output has risen substantially over time. By 1950, the median public consumption/GDP ratio for countries in our sample was already about 10 percent. By 1980 the median had risen to 13 percent. Of the 30 countries for which a comparison can be made, 26 show an increase in the ratio over this period. Although these are nominal figures, there was no doubt also a rise in the real level of public services. In most countries real per capita income was rising; and demand for education, health services, and other public goods is quite income-elastic. Further, where national governments had replaced colonial governments, these new governments were likely to be more responsive to public demands. The demonstration effect of the richer countries and the activities of international bodies such as the World Health Organization (WHO) and the United Nations Educational, Scientific, and Cultural Organization (UNESCO) must also have stimulated expansion of public output.

There is marked intercountry variation in the public output/GDP ratios. The 1980 ratios ranged all the way from 28 percent in Zambia and 22 percent in Morocco to 8 percent in Colombia, Ghana, Sri Lanka, and the Philippines. Except for Argentina, the Latin American countries have relatively low public-goods output. Other countries with low ratios include Thailand, Pakistan, Sudan, India, Sri Lanka, Ghana, and the Philippines. There is no obvious economic basis for these intercountry differences, which do not correlate closely either with 1980 per capita income levels or with 1950–80 growth rates.

The allocation of expenditures differs rather widely among countries, but a few generalizations can be made. The largest allocations are typically for defense, general administration, and education. Defense is the most variable item, taking less than 10 percent of the budget in Mexico, Colombia, Kenya, and Ivory Coast, but about 30 percent in Turkey, Thailand, and South Korea, and close to 50 percent in Taiwan, Pakistan, and Iran. General administration typically takes 10–20 percent of the budget, and the median figure for education is also around 20 percent. Large educational expenditure is explained by high population growth rates, which result in a large school-age component in the population, and by the fact that universal primary education is in most countries a high-priority objective. There is wide intercountry variation, however, with most Latin American countries unusually light on education and Philippines, Malaysia, Taiwan, and Ivory Coast unusually heavy. Health, housing, and other social services typically take 5–10 percent of the budget, and economic services something like 20 percent. This amount is usually distributed fairly equally among agriculture, roads and infrastructure, and other economic purposes, though again there is considerable intercountry variation.

Turning to government's role as investor, we again note a marked change in recent decades. We have inadequate data for the pre-1940 era, but it is estimated that gross capital formation as a percentage of GDP probably did not exceed 10 percent in most third-world countries. In Argentina, Brazil, Mexico, Taiwan, and Korea the rate may have been somewhat higher. Most investment, moreover, was private. Governments built roads and public buildings, made irrigation improvements in some countries, and sometimes contributed capital to railway construction. In many cases, however, government simply encouraged private railway companies through land grants, profit guarantees, or guarantee-of-bond issues.

Table 5 shows a large increase in the postwar period in gross capital formation rates. By 1950 the median rate for the countries in our sample was already 14 percent. By 1980, the median rate for the top half of our sample—19 countries with highest growth of per capita income—was 28 percent, though this falls to 21 percent for the next nine countries in the growth-rate ranking and to 12 percent for the nine least successful economies. These nominal gross capital formation/GDP ratios are somewhat higher than the real ratios because of the relatively high prices of capital goods in third-world countries. Even so, countries in the top half of our sample were investing, in real terms, about the same proportion of GDP as the richer industrial countries.

Government has participated heavily in, and in some countries has been largely responsible for, this upsurge of investment. Regular government departments build roads and bridges, urban streets and sewage systems, schools and hospitals, public buildings and military installations. In addition, many economic activities are organized as semiautonomous public corporations. The public sector now normally includes rail transport, electric power, and other public utilities; frequently includes mining and some branches of manufacturing; and sometimes extends to banking and trading activites. These corporations also have substantial investment programs, which are included in measuring the percentage of total gross domestic capital formation (GDCF) accounted for by public-sector capital formation (PSCF).

For the mixed economies in our sample (that is, excluding Cuba and China), the PSCF/GDCF ratio is usually in the range of 30–50 percent. Countries toward the lower end of the range are of two sorts: (1) Latin American countries that are already quite industrialized and have a vigorous private sector—thus the PSCF/GDCF ratio is about 30 percent in Colombia and Mexico and about 35 percent in Brazil: and (2) other countries with a strong private-enterprise orientation, such as South Korea and Thailand, where the ratio is also about 30 percent. Countries at the high end of the range include Turkey (50 percent), which has a strong statist tradition and many public manufacturing corporations; Ivory Coast (50 percent), which is still in the stage of infrastructure building; pre-1979 Iran (60 percent), where the large oil revenues flow in the first instance into government channels; and India (more than 60 percent), which has a large public manufacturing sector.

This prominence of government as investor is not new. The conventional picture of early European and American growth as a private, capitalist development overlooks the importance of government in organizing, helping to finance, and (in most countries) eventually owning railway systems and other forms of infrastructure. True, the PSCF/GDCF ratio for early developers was low by modern standards, usually in the range of 10–20 percent. But in two countries, Japan and Australia, it was substantially higher, rising at times to almost half of total investment. Moreover, in most of the presently developed countries, the PSCF/GDCF ratio has risen over the course of time. For 15 of these countries, which I analyzed in a previous study,* the ratio is now typically in the range of 30–40 percent.

The fact remains that, in third-world countries today, the PSCF/GDCF ratio is substantially above what it was in the richer countries *at a comparable stage of development.* One reason is the extension of the concept of the public sector to include not only public utilities but parts of mining, manufacturing, and other economic activities.

The large increase in government spending on current services and on investment implies a corresponding increase in government revenues. Space does not permit an extended discussion of revenue performance. Briefly, the current revenue/GDP ratio has risen substantially in most countries since 1945. By 1980 the median ratio for countries in our sample was almost 20 percent, though there is the same intercountry variation observed on the expenditure side. Revenues have been increased partly by considerable diversification of tax structures, with the share of revenue coming from a fall in import and export taxes and a rise in the share of taxes on income and wealth.

In only a few cases—South Korea, Taiwan, Brazil—is government revenue sufficient to cover both current and capital expenditures. A sizable public-sector deficit is the general rule. Part of the deficit can usually be covered by domestic

*Lloyd G. Reynolds, "Public Sector Saving and Capital Formation," *Government and Economic Development,* ed. Gustav Ranis (New Haven: Yale University Press, 1971), pp. 516–51.

nonbank borrowing, the feasibility of which depends on private saving propensities, on the existence of financial institutions for transfer of savings, and on offering savers an adequate real rate of return. Foreign borrowing contributes in greater or lesser degree. The last resort is central-bank borrowing, which beyond a certain point generates inflationary pressure. Country experience in this respect varies widely. The more successful economies typically use bank financing only moderately and show marked price stability. Heavy reliance on banks and high inflation rates are most common among countries that are relatively poor, that are growing slowly or not at all, and that show poor economic management by government.

THE BEHAVIOR OF TOTAL OUTPUT

Can we say anything, after this sector-by-sector review, about the typical behavior of GDP in the course of intensive growth? Not very much. We have estimates only for the post-1950 period, which for most countries is a small part of the intensive-growth era. So we are forced to surmise about what the figures for earlier periods would look like if they were available. I surmise that this hypothetical record would broadly resemble that which Kuznets has compiled for the developed countries from about 1860 onward. Specifically:

1. There is an initial period, which can be as long as two or three decades, during which the growth rate of per capita output rises from near zero to some "normal" level, that is, normal for the particular country and for the era in question. For countries whose intensive growth began before 1914, "normal" might have meant 2 percent per year (roughly the average rate for the Kuznets countries). For countries whose intensive growth began after 1945, 3–4 percent per year is normal.

   This initial increase is typically associated with export behavior. The export sector usually grows at a considerably faster rate than does GDP, which means that the export/GDP ratio is rising. The high growth rate of the export sector, plus its growing weight in the economy, gradually pulls up the overall GDP growth rate. But because of supply constraints, and occasionally because of demand constraints as well, the export/GDP ratio does not continue to rise indefinitely. As it levels off, the GDP growth rate also tends to level off at a normal or characteristic rate for the country, but a rate that varies among countries.

   This mechanism of export-propelled, or at least export-lubricated, growth seems to have operated since 1945 in much the same way as before 1945. India and China, however, stand out as notable exceptions in the recent period.

2. When I speak of a "normal" growth rate for a country, I do not mean one that is stable or invariant. Just as in the developed countries, third-world growth rates have been responsive to long swings in the world economy. Countries that embarked on intensive growth before 1914 and that had attained growth rates normal for that era grew less rapidly in the years 1914–45 as developed-

country growth slowed down. After 1945 growth rates rose again, and in most countries they were higher than ever before. There are also marked short-term fluctuations in growth rates, associated mainly with fluctuations in primary-product prices and export proceeds, that resulted partly from economic fluctuations in the developed countries affecting their demand for primary products. The most dramatic of these was the 1929–33 downswing, but the recent 1979–82 downswing was also substantial.

3. In any era one chooses, growth rates differ substantially among third-world countries. This is readily documented for recent decades. Growth rates of real GNP per capita from 1960 to 1980 range from 7.0 in South Korea to 0.2 in Zambia and − 1.0 in Ghana. To explain these intercountry differences is perhaps the most challenging problem in growth analysis. We shall explore this problem further in chapter 15.

   Such characteristic differerces in national growth rates appear also in the countries studied by Kuznets. For many decades Japan and Sweden have had relatively high growth rates, while Britain has stood near the bottom of the league.

4. Although the picture of a growth rate rising initially and then "settling down" at a characteristic level fits most countries, it does not fit every country. There are cases in which a country's growth rate has *accelerated* over the course of time, to a degree greater than can be explained by world economic fluctuations. The most famous example is Japan, for which case Ohkawa and Rosovsky coined the term *growth acceleration*. The two Japanese offshoots, Taiwan and South Korea, have followed a similar path. Their recent growth rates, like that of Japan, have been much above those of other apparently comparable countries. Mexico and Brazil might also be added to this list.

   There is at least one notable case of growth *deceleration*. Argentina's growth rate was highest before 1914, dropped off sharply from 1914 to 45, and has continued at a subnormal level in recent decades. Rated as comparable with Canada and Australia in 1914, Argentina has now fallen far behind these countries and may soon drop below Brazil. There are also a few cases of *reverse development,* in which per capita income was rising for a long period but has recently gone into decline. In Uganda during the Amin regime of 1971–79, the processes regarded as characteristic of development went into reverse: people moved back from the monetary economy to the subsistence economy, monetized output dropped sharply, investment and exports almost disappeared. A similar process of undevelopment, on a less dramatic scale, seems to be under way in Ghana.

THE DISTRIBUTION OF INCOME

Thus far I have detoured around issues of income distribution, partly because of the complexity of these issues, partly because of limited information for most countries. But there is some relevant literature, which justifies a brief comment.

In thinking about income distribution in a third-world country, it is useful to decompose it into: (1) distribution among rural households, which still predominate greatly in most countries; (2) distribution among urban households; and (3) the urban-rural gap, which is typically large. For countries with a system of sample surveys, (1) and (2) can be measured by Gini coefficients for the rural and urban sectors and (3) is measured by the difference in median household income in the two sectors. Each of the three measures has a different set of determinants, and the three will not necessarily move in the same direction—that is, toward an increase or reduction of inequality—over the course of time.

Kuznets advanced a well-known hypothesis that inequality of personal incomes tends to increase in the early stages of economic growth. A possible explanation might run in terms of the Lewis model, in which business profits swell the number of high-income recipients while surplus labor retards the advance of real wages. But eventually, Kuznets thought and Lewis would probably agree, as full utilization of labor is approached, real wages are bid up and profit margins shrink, the process goes into reverse, and inequality begins to decrease. The Gini coefficient of household incomes thus traces an inverse U-shape, first rising (greater inequality) but reaching a peak and then falling continuously. Kuznets was able to document the second phase of falling inequality quite satisfactorily for the developed countries. The phase of growing inequality is plausible but harder to document because the data diminish in quantity and quality as we go back in time.

The Kuznets hypothesis seems also to hold for most third-world countries, though I shall note some interesting exceptions. In considering typical developments during the early decades of intensive growth, it will be useful to decompose the story into the three components distinguished above.

In the rural sector, the most important determinant of income is the distribution of property ownership. Labor being relatively abundant and land and capital relatively scarce, the property share of agricultural income is higher than in the developed countries. In a study of Colombia, Berry and Urrutia (1976) found that 62 percent of farm income was attributable to land and capital (including the human capital of farm operators) and that the "pure labor share" was only 38 percent. Moreover, land and capital ownership is highly skewed and accounts for most of the income of the top income recipients. Even the labor share is somewhat skewed by unequal division of land because, as farm size decreases, family members are able to work fewer hours per year on the farm. Thus, even if the hourly return to labor were equal across farm sizes, the small farmer would earn less.

Where land distribution is quite unequal, income inequality may grow over time because the larger farmers absorb technical progress faster than the smaller farmers. Larger incomes make it easier to finance purchases of fertilizer, improved seed, and other modern inputs. Larger farmers also tend to dominate the boards responsible for allocating farm credit and input supplies and are able to place themselves at the head of the queue. In the Philippines, for example, an employment mission from the International Labour Organization (Ranis, 1973) found clear indications of growing inequality in the rural sector. Between 1956 and 1971 the Gini coefficient for rural households rose from 0.38 to 0.46. The authors of the ILO report surmised that large farmers were adopting new agricultural technology and raising crop yields faster than were smaller farmers. Regionally, too, the poorest agricultural regions have had the lowest rate of increase in median income. There is similar evidence from India, Pakistan, Mexico, and a number of other countries.

In Taiwan, South Korea, and Thailand, on the other hand, the distribution of rural income is considerably more equal. Thailand has always been a land of small farmers, without great disparity in farm sizes. Taiwan and South Korea undertook land reforms in the 1950s that established small, owner-occupied farms as the dominant mode of production. A land-reform program usually brings a one-time shift toward greater equality of rural incomes.

In the urban sector the distribution of income, and changes in this distribution over time, depend mainly on: (1) the labor and property shares of income in the private business sector, which usually shifts in favor of profits in the early decades of growth; (2) the gap between wage levels for jobs in "modern" industry and government and the earnings of self-employed workers in traditional trade, handicraft, and service activities (Again, this gap is likely to grow in the first instance, as wages in the modern sector rise in response to rising productivity and political pressures, while earnings in self-employment are held back by the competition of migrants from the countryside.); and (3) the growth rate of modern employment, absolutely and as a percentage of the urban labor force. In a few countries, notably Taiwan and South Korea, this growth has been fast enough to exhaust surplus labor in the economy, producing a more rapid rise of real wages in both industry and agriculture and a consequent shift toward income equality.

The size of the rural-urban gap depends on developments in each sector and is influenced to some extent by government policy. In the 1950s and 1960s many third-world governments severely restrained prices paid to farmers in order to ensure cheap food for urban consumers and substantial profits for government marketing boards. This widening of the urban-rural gap both discouraged farm production and stimulated cityward migration. On the other hand, policies that pay farmers close to world prices and that, by stimulating technical progress, raise crop yields and farm incomes will tend to stabilize the urban-rural gap or even reduce it. The level of modern-sector wages in urban areas is also partly a policy variable. Where the urban wage level is pushed upward prematurely, even with large amounts of surplus labor, the urban-rural gap will widen.

Although one can find reasons for supposing that the gap will usually widen in the early period, evidence is scanty and somewhat mixed. Moreover, this evidence relates almost entirely to years since 1950, which for countries where intensive growth began before 1914 is a rather late stage. In Malaysia, Snodgrass (1980) found that the ratio of median urban to median rural household income rose from 1.84 in 1957–58 to 2.24 in 1976. The Philippines study, on the other hand, reported a modest narrowing of the gap from 2.45 in 1956 to 2.08 in 1971.

I have perhaps said enough to suggest that the overall distribution of income in a country results from a complex interplay of forces. Although forces making for growing inequality may still dominate in most countries, this is not invariably the case. It may be useful to add a word on Taiwan, where income distribution is about as equal as in the United States, and on China, where greater equality has been a high-priority policy objective.

The extent of income equalization in Taiwan, and the reasons for it, is documented in an interesting study by Fei, Ranis, and Kuo (1979). Income from agriculture was equalized considerably by the land-reform program. Important also was the policy of decentralized industrialization, which enabled a growing number of farm family members to find wage employment in nearby industries. The percentage of rural income derived from nonagricultural employment rose steeply, until by 1972 it slightly exceeded income derived from agriculture. Moreover, this rural nonagricultural activity is highly labor intensive. Since such wage income is more equally distributed than income from property or agriculture, its growing importance has reduced the rural Gini coefficient.

In urban areas the wage share of income has risen moderately and, in addition, both wage income and property income have become somewhat more equally distributed. These trends are related to the rapid growth of labor-intensive industrial exports, plus the subsequent shift from a labor-surplus to a labor-scarce economy and the resulting rapid rise in real wages. Another unusual feature of the Taiwan case is the smallness of the urban-rural income gap, which is only about 15 percent. The overall Gini coefficient for household incomes in 1972 was 0.29, placing Taiwan clearly in the "developed-country" range.

In China, there was a one-time shift toward greater equality in the 1950s. In the countryside, rich landowners disappeared and income differences based on land ownership were eliminated. In the cities, property income and private business income disappeared, and the new salary scales for managers and officials provided lower salary premiums than had existed previously. China succeeded also in establishing a poverty floor through rationing of certain necessities—grain, cooking oil, cotton cloth—and through free or heavily subsidized provision of health facilities, education, urban housing, and urban transport. This minimum standard of living is low, but the extreme poverty that one sees in many other Asian countries has been eliminated. China, it has been said, has succeeded in cutting off the two tails of the usual income distribution.

It is not clear, however, that there has been much further movement toward equality since the 1950s. Rural income differences are still wide, depending mainly on agricultural productivity in various regions. Dwight Perkins (in Dernberger, 1980) has estimated that the six richest agricultural counties in the country have a per capita income six times as high as that in the six poorest counties. Urban income differences are smaller and the urban wage-salary structure has remained relatively stable, though there is a slight tendency for the lowest wage rates to increase faster than higher rates. The urban-rural gap seems to have diminished somewhat, mainly due to government price policies favorable to agriculture. An IBRD study estimated that the ratio of urban to rural household incomes in the late 1970s was 1.7. This is not much different from ratios reported for a number of other Asian countries: Bangladesh, 1.5; India, 1.8; Sri Lanka, 1.7; Indonesia, 2.1; Philippines, 2.1; Malaysia, 2.2.

DEVELOPMENT THEN AND NOW

I return now to a question raised at the outset: how far has the pattern of intensive growth in third-world economies since 1945 differed from that observed before 1945?

There are obviously similarities and differences. On the side of similarity: most (not all) countries conform to something like a standard pattern of intensive growth, and this seems to have been true in recent decades as in earlier decades. This pattern can be summarized as follows: the rate of population growth accelerating for a long time, but eventually peaking and then tending to decline; food output keeping reasonably apace with population growth before 1940, but falling behind in perhaps half our sample countries during the recent decades of high population growth; increases in agricultural output depending increasingly on technical progress as land availability decreases; manufacturing output rising faster than agricultural output, with a gradual shift toward larger-sized establishments and heavier types of industry, but with handicrafts and small-scale industry remaining important for a long time; the export/GDP ratio rising steeply (again, with exceptions) and then stabilizing at a rather high level appropriate to the still small (economic) size of most third-world economies; the export menu increasingly diversified, and moving eventually into significant exports of manufactures; imports running ahead of exports, implying some dependence on foreign borrowing; government playing an increasingly important role as producer of public goods, property owner, and investor, especially in the post-1945 era; the growth rate of GDP and GDP per capita rising for some time and then stabilizing at a "characteristic" level, which differs considerably among countries, and which is subject to both long swings and short-term fluctuations; increasing inequality in household income distribution, though again with important exceptions. A few countries, which have grown rapidly enough to exhaust the surplus-labor pool and enter the era of labor scarcity, have experienced an accelerated increase in the average level of real wages and sometimes also a reduction of wage differentials among occupational groups, both of which tend to equalize the household distribution.

So what is new since 1945? The impression that things are different now arises partly, I think, from the faster tempo of world economic growth in the 1945–73 period, in which most third-world countries participated. Many of the sequences of change—for example, the sequence from handicraft production to light industry to heavy industry—that were observed in the early developers from 1850 to 1914 are still observed in the 1945–80 era. But the movie projector has been speeded up, as it were, and structural change has proceeded at a faster rate than before.

But this is not the whole story. There have been additional changes, partly political and intellectual in character, but with economic consequences. Three in particular deserve comment.

1. The achievement of national independence by over half the countries in our sample had several consequences. Even where self-government came peacefully, and still more where it was achieved by military struggle, there was a natural desire to break with the colonial past, to achieve economic as well as political independence. This tended to import to economic policy a bias against trade and primary exports and in favor of industrialization in the immediate postindependence period. Further, since much of the economy had previously been under foreign control while government was now under national control, there was a tendency to identify assertion of sovereignty with transfer of economic activity to government hands. The alternative of transferring economic enterprises from foreign to domestic private owners was often not seriously considered. The relative expansion of the public sector in many ex-colonies since 1950 has more to do with nationalism than with socialist ideology, though the latter sometimes came in as reinforcement. Finally, the new national governments, even where dictatorial in character, were more responsive to popular pressure than the previous colonial administrations had been. This shows up in rapid expansion of health services, education, and other public services; in price controls and subsidization for the benefit of urban consumers; and often in forcing up of wage levels in government and industry.

2. A new climate of opinion took hold, a conventional wisdom of economic development whose main features were outlined in chapter 1. The influence of this structure of thought probably peaked around 1960, after which it was undermined increasingly by continuing research and by the record of economic success or failure in particular countries. But meanwhile it had given a special twist to economic policy in many countries: high growth targets and large five-year plans for economic development, designed partly to prove the essentiality of large-scale foreign aid; a distrust of markets and private initiative and a preference for detailed government regulation; a mystique of industrialization and a tendency to premature development of heavy industry; a tendency to regard agriculture as a resource reservoir that could be relied on to supply food and labor to urban activities, but without active measures to stimulate production; protectionist trade policies and overvalued exchange rates, which worked against exports and encouraged indiscriminate import substitution.

3. A new combination of forces impinged on third-world countries from the

developed world: advances in medical science, which for the time being led to much higher rates of population growth; advances in agricultural technology and new international organizations for disseminating this technology throughout the world; continued reduction of transport and communications costs; new channels for government-to-government transfers of long-term capital; and perhaps most important, a higher tempo of economic growth in the developed countries, which raised demand for primary products much faster than had seemed possible around 1950. On the whole, the world situation was more favorable to intensive growth in third-world countries than it had been before 1940; and even countries that made policy errors were able to do moderately well. The data in chapter 15 will show, however, that some countries took much better advantage of this favorable environment than did others, while some failed to progress at all.

PART II
EARLY DEVELOPERS, 1850–1950

We embark now on a medium-depth exploration of country experience. Among other things, this section will illustrate the great variation of economic structure and economic performance. Even a brief glimpse of economies as diverse as Brazil, Nigeria, and Indonesia should destroy the illusion of a homogeneous group of "less-developed countries." For the reader who wishes to look more deeply into a particular country, the sketches included here may serve as an appetizer and a guide to the literature.

A further purpose is to document the generalizations advanced in chapters 1–4. In undertaking this work, I chose to complete the country analyses in chapters 5–14 first. Chapters 1–4 (as well as chapters 15 and 16) could not have been written until this groundwork had been laid.

The treatment is chronological, beginning usually in the middle or late nineteenth century and continuing to the present. The structure I have imposed on each country "story" is semi-uniform, rather than completely standardized, and rests on the phases of growth outlined in chapter 1.

1. Discussion of *extensive growth* is limited to countries that reached the turning point quite recently and that have a long and reasonably well documented record of prior growth. This group includes such interesting cases as Egypt, India, China, and Indonesia. But for the majority of countries, which reached the turning point before 1914, I have usually ignored the era of extensive growth and started the story with the turning point.
2. In examining the circumstances surrounding the *turning point* I focus on the sources of increased foreign demand for the country's products and on the internal conditions that permitted an adequate supply response.
3. The era of *intensive growth* is quite long in most countries, ranging from 30 to 130 years; so it has usually proved convenient to divide it into two or more subperiods. Because most colonies achieved political independence only after World War II, and because the international politicoeconomic milieu after the war was decidedly different from that of prewar years, I have usually used 1950

as a breaking point. But in the long-independent Latin American countries, the shift away from open, export-dominated economies began with the Great Depression, and for these countries the significant breaking point is 1930. Within each subperiod, I try to highlight important developments in population, agricultural output, industrial output, government activities, and foreign trade.

The country stories are thickly studded with dates and numbers. Sources of some of the most important statements are cited in the text, but to provide references in every case would have made the manuscript almost unreadable. The reader can take it that data have been extracted judiciously from the sources listed in the bibliography. The only exception is that data for very recent years have sometimes been taken from World Bank country mission reports, which are unpublished internal documents but which are available for consultation by research scholars. I have striven for accuracy in detail and caution in general statements; but anyone who questions my interpretation of a country's experience is free to retrace my tedious journey through the literature.

5

Argentina, Brazil, Mexico

The countries of Latin America differ in size, resources, topography, and other important respects. But they also have marked similarities, and it will be useful to comment briefly on these common features. This section draws particularly on Furtado (1976) and Stein and Stein (1970).

EARLY GROWTH IN LATIN AMERICA

That Latin American countries developed early is not surprising. A European population expanding into a resource-rich continent and able to mobilize labor from the indigenous Indian population and imported African slaves was able to generate an export surplus and a comfortable living for the ruling elite. The colonies were export-oriented and Europe-oriented from the outset. After attainment of political independence in the period 1810–25, the export surplus grew in volume and more of it could be retained for local use.

Central and South America are often grouped with North America and Australia as "areas of new settlement," whose growth could almost be taken for granted. But several differences among these continents should be noted, differences that still shape the political economy of Latin America. First, along the western fringe from Mexico through Peru to Bolivia there was a large indigenous population. The Spanish conquerors used this population as a source of forced labor for mining, agriculture, porterage, and other activities. European settlement disrupted the traditional Indian economy and, together with the introduction of European diseases, led to a large drop in population. But by 1700, with a decline of mining, development of subsistence agriculture, and increased natural resistance to new diseases, the Indian population stabilized and began to increase. In thinly settled Brazil, population grew mainly through importation of African slaves for work on plantations producing sugar and other tropical crops.

The outcome was a social stratification that, in looser form, continues to the present day. At the top was a tiny white elite, initially immigrants from Portugal or Spain, reinforced gradually by descendants born in the colonies (Creoles). The mass of the population was Indian or Negro. In between there developed an intermediate group of mestizos and mulattos. From this group came skilled workers, supervisors, artisans, mule drivers, petty merchants, and traders—to fill jobs below the dignity of the whites but which "the masses" were judged incapable of performing. As of 1700, about 6 percent of the population was white, about 6 percent of mixed blood, and 88 percent African or Indian. Over the next two centuries the European population grew through immigration, while the mixed-blood group also increased in relative size; but the three-tier stratification is still important.

Second, in contrast to the small-scale agriculture that developed in North America, Latin America early developed a pattern in which most land was owned by a small number of large landowners. The Crown granted large tracts of land, together with their Indian inhabitants, to colonial administrators and court favorites, who coerced the labor they needed (or, in Brazil, imported slave labor) from people who were allocated small plots on which to grow their own subsistence. The latifundia-minifundia pattern thus became the main form of agricultural organization. Nor did it disappear when the colonies achieved independence. In addition to the old landholders, influential city families were able to buy large amounts of land from impoverished smallholders or from expropriated Church properties. The dualistic pattern of large and small landholdings has continued to a degree not found in most parts of Asia or Africa.

Third, most of the colonies after independence developed a distinctive type of government involving oligarchic rule by a small elite. Although the constitutions of the new states may have resembled that of the United States, the reality was considerably different. A change of regime usually occured through a coup rather than an election, and it usually meant displacement of one faction within the elite by a rival faction. Personal leadership, often associated with military status, was always important.

Turning to indicators of growth, population appears to have been growing from about 1700 onwards. Durand (in *Population Problems*, 1967) estimates the annual rate of increase for Central and South America at 0.8 percent from 1750 to 1800, rising to 0.9 percent from 1800 to 1850—about twice the average rate for the world as a whole during these periods, though below the rates achieved in North America. The impression of sustained population growth is supported by estimates for individual countries.* The "big countries" as of 1850 were Mexico and Brazil, each with more than seven million people, while Argentina with one million was still very thinly settled.

A continuing flow of exports—gold, other metals, sugar, cotton, cocoa, hides, indigo—were channeled through Seville and Lisbon to other parts of Eu-

---

*For estimates for individual countries, see in particular N. Sanchez-Albornoz, *The Population of Latin America: A History* (Berkeley: University of California Press, 1974); and Colin McEvedy and Richard Jones, *Atlas of World Population History* (New York: Facts on File, 1978).

rope. There was a return flow of luxury consumer goods for the colonial elite; but imports were typically only about one-quarter of exports, indicating that the grantee class was able to save a large proportion of its income, which was transferred to Spain and Portugal. The object was to build up wealth at home rather than to invest in the colonies.

Over the course of time the initial Spanish and Portuguese monopoly of colonial trade was weakened by British penetration. The Methuen treaty of 1703 between England and Portugal gave the British access to markets in Brazil as well as Portugal. The 1713 Treaty of Utrecht between England and Spain gave the British the right to send specified quantities of merchandise and slaves to specified colonial ports. Spain later attempted to withdraw this right and to maintain its position as entrepôt, but with indifferent success. From Jamaica and other beachheads in the Caribbean, the British continued to press in, and smuggling and privateering flourished alongside official trade. After 1763 intercolony trade was permitted, and colonials (Creoles) were allowed to ship to Spain. Thus a new class of merchants emerged in the colonies.

Trade was a key issue in the breakaway movements that developed in the colonies after 1800. The decisive political event was French occupation of Spain and Portugal during the Napoleonic Wars. The Spanish Bourbons were deposed in 1808, and the juntas that succeeded them had only limited authority abroad. The Portuguese court fled to Brazil, effectively breaking ties with the home country. This encouraged Creole leaders in the colonies, who were now numerous and influential compared with the official colonial administrators, to think about seizing power and achieving the control of trade they had long desired. In one colony after another, breakaway movements developed from 1810 onward. These were sometimes suppressed temporarily by force of arms, but in the end repression did not succeed. By 1825 almost all the former colonial "provinces" were self-governing countries. In this struggle the Creoles were generally able to coopt the mestizos, who also hoped for greater upward mobility. The masses took little part in the movement, simply obeying whoever seemed to be in control.

The leaders of independence movements, however, often fell out among themselves along regional, factional, or family lines. Civil wars continued in most parts of the continent until around 1850 and in some countries until late in the century. This infighting partly accounts for the differing dates at which countries embarked on intensive growth. The turning point in a particular country often corresponds to the end of the last civil war and the establishment of political stability.

Economic historians tend to regard the years around 1850 as a watershed in Latin American development. There are several reasons for this dating. For a time after 1820 the British seemed almost to have taken over Latin America. They dominated the seas and supplied two-thirds of Latin American imports of manufactures. British merchants proliferated in the coastal cities, though internal trade remained in Spanish or Portuguese hands. The rapidly expanding British economy might seem to have provided a promising market for Latin American exports, but expansion of exports was hampered by the fact that Britain could draw on its own colonial empire for raw materials. Cotton textiles, the leading British industry, could get cheap slave-grown cotton from the United States, which was also closer in terms of transport. Thus in some measure the Latin American takeoff had to await the spread of industry to other parts of Europe and North America, which gradually weakened British dominance and diversified the pattern of world trade. By midcentury France, Germany, the United States, and other countries were emerging as alternative markets for exports and sources of imports.

A second factor was the gradual consolidation of new power structures, which provided more stable governments for the Latin American states. Consolidation took several decades after independence but was beginning to be accomplished in some countries by 1850. The predominant pattern was the rise of a mercantile bourgeoisie, liberal in outlook and oriented toward Europe and toward foreign trade. Interested in exports, the bourgeoisie turned naturally to alliances with large landowners, gradually building up effective power systems. Stein characterizes the new governments as "oligarchic republics," usually federal in form but centralized in reality. A strong executive normally dominated the legislature. The national executive was empowered to appoint provincial governors and other lower officials. The franchise was very restricted, with perhaps 2–4 percent of the population participating in elections by the late-nineteenth century. The controlling elite was Creole, though it was now more permeable by suitably "whitened" mestizos. Politics was sometimes violent, but involved mainly factionalism *within* the elite, the factions representing local power bases and shifting family alliances.

The final conditioning factor was the accelerated growth of world output and world trade from midcentury onward, which was described in chapter 3. Growth rates rose both in the industrializing countries and in the suppliers of raw materials as a result of a marked acceleration of population growth, a rapid expansion of the fund of transmittable technical knowledge, and an intensification of international specialization. Progress in rail and ocean transport, which greatly reduced unit transport costs, played a central role. As one after another Latin American country achieved internal stability, it was drawn into this powerful current of expanding trade.

Following Furtado, we can distinguish three patterns in different parts of the continent:

1. Countries exporting temperate-zone agricultural products—Argentina and Uruguay. These followed a pattern of development typical of the United States and Canada—extensive cultivation, technology similar to that found in the United States, high productivity from the outset, and high growth rates throughout the period of export expansion.
2. Countries exporting tropical agricultural products—Brazil, Colombia, Vene-

zuela, Cuba, and the other Caribbean islands. These products were less promising in the sense that their prices continued to reflect the low wages prevailing in the traditional economies of these countries.
3. Mineral exporters—Mexico, Peru, Bolivia, and Chile. Mining, which requires relatively large units as well as technical expertise, tended to be dominated by foreign companies. Thus export growth in these countries had a strong enclave character and the spread effects were limited, except to the extent that government intervened to compel local purchase of inputs or to share in profits through taxation.

These background comments permit us to focus on events since 1850 in the following country analyses.

ARGENTINA

Turning Point: circa 1860

The richest region of Argentina in colonial times was the provinces of the extreme northwest, bordering on Peru and Chile. These provinces sent mules for use in the mines to Potosí, Bolivia, and other mining centers; and they exported mainly hides and skins, the only products that could bear the transport costs from this remote area. But from about 1800 onward there was a gradual reorientation of the economy toward Buenos Aires and the adjacent coastal provinces. Between 1780 and 1823, the population of Buenos Aires province grew at 6.5 percent per year, while Buenos Aires city more than doubled in size to 163,000.

Development was impeded, however, by some fifty years of civil war following the 1810 revolution against Spain. Only in the 1860s did the country enter on a period of reasonably stable government. It seems appropriate to date the turning point at around 1860 both for this reason and because of the appearance of wool as an important new export. Sheep-raising gathered momentum during the 1830s, partly through the efforts of Scottish and Irish settlers. But the major expansion of wool exports came between 1850 and 1870. By 1870 Argentina had as many sheep as the United States (about 40 million), and by 1900 it was second only to Australia. The growth of the wool industry was the first of several waves of export expansion that carried the economy forward during the "golden age" of 1860–1914, a period in which Argentina's per capita output rose faster than it has at any time since 1914.

Intensive Growth, 1860–1930

Wool exports, in thousand metric tons per year, rose from 45 in 1860–69 to 90 in 1875–79, 129 in 1885–89, and 211 in 1895–99. The next wave of expansion, which got underway in the 1880s, involved grain, primarily wheat and corn. The increasing scarcity of grain in the industrializing countries of northwestern Europe was met initially by drawing on Eastern Europe and later on North America. But eventually the suction of demand reached Argentina, which with a great expanse of largely vacant land was a natural source of supply.

The expansion of grain cultivation and export was a complex process, with several interrelated aspects. It involved:

1. A large inflow of settlers from Europe. Argentina, with a population of only 2.5 million in 1880, received 3.2 million immigrants between 1880 and 1910, mainly from Spain and Italy.
2. Settlement and cultivation of new land. Most of this land had already been allotted to large landowners, so settlers tended to enter the system as tenants rather than (as in the United States and Canada) as homesteaders. There were areas, however, in which owner-occupied farms became the dominant pattern. In any event the tenancy market was active and competitive and tenancy did not seriously hamper incentives to produce.
3. Extensive railroad building in the interior, to bring grain to Buenos Aires for shipment. Much of the construction was financed by direct British investment, and Britain also provided engineering expertise and railroad equipment. The government of Argentina also sold bonds to investors in Britain and elsewhere and used part of the proceeds for rail construction.
4. Development of enlarged shipping capacity and a new pattern in which ships carried grain in one direction and immigrants in the other.

Grains and flour increasingly dominated the export bill, amounting by 1900 to about half of total exports. The next wave of export expansion was set off by the arrival of the refrigerator ship. Chilled beef began to be exported, primarily to Britain, shortly before World War I, and by the 1920s was about 10 percent of all exports. As new export products were added, older ones did not disappear. Thus while almost all of Argentina's exports were of rural origin, the list was increasingly diversified—hides and skins, wool, wheat, corn, flour, chilled meat. By the late 1920s still other lines—cotton, butter, fruits—were showing promise. This diversification reduced Argentina's exposure to price fluctuations for any one product.

The pattern of farming was extensive, not unlike that in Canada or the United States, and operating units were large. In the pampean zone, farms of a thousand hectares or more occupied 61 percent of the farm acreage, and even an average farm was 100–500 hectares. Outside the pampean zone, where cattle and sheep ranching were dominant, average sizes were even larger. Here holdings of a thousand hectares or more comprised 90 percent of total acreage.

Technical progress seems to have come mainly from word-of-mouth communication, purchase of improved animals and seeds from abroad, and efforts of salesmen for farm machinery and other inputs. Government research and extension services appeared late and had relatively little impact. Practically no fertilizers were used in the pampean sector. Despite inattention to technology, however, yields of the major crops in the 1920s were roughly the same in Argentina and the United States. Argentina was a bit ahead in corn and oats, a bit below in wheat and barley.

During the late nineteenth century Argentina's product and factor markets became thoroughly integrated into the world economy. By 1900 about one-quarter of rural output was being exported in raw form and another quarter with varying degrees of processing. About half remained for domestic consumption. About 30 percent of exports were destined for Britain; but Germany, France, the United States, Belgium, Netherlands, and Italy were also substantial markets. While the United States took only 8.8 percent of Argentina's exports in 1927–29, it supplied 24.6 percent of its imports. This unfavorable trade balance with the United States and the strongly favorable balance with the United Kingdom were readily cleared through the international payments mechanism.

Argentina's imports amounted consistently to about one-quarter of its GNP. The composition of the import bill reflects an open economy in the early stages of manufacturing development. It is striking that as late as 1929 textiles and textile products still formed about one-quarter of all imports. Food, tobacco, and beverages accounted for 13.4 percent. The 16.2 percent for machinery and vehicles reflects partly the rapidly growing import of automobiles. The remainder is spread across the whole commodity range, reflecting an across-the-board *lack* of manufacturing capacity within the country.

The Argentine labor market was closely linked with those of the European countries, notably Italy and Spain. Argentina faced a perfectly elastic supply of labor at the going real wage in Italian and Spanish cities, plus a small differential. We have already noted the huge flow of permanent settlers in the years 1880–1914, of whom about 30 percent came from Spain and 45 percent from Italy. In 1914 foreign-born people formed 30 percent of Argentina's total population and 50 percent of the population of Buenos Aires. Further, the integration with the Spanish and Italian labor markets was sufficiently close that large numbers of workers came to Argentina just for the harvest season, after which most of them returned home. It is estimated that during 1900–10 an annual average of 100,000 seasonal workers entered and left Argentina within a year. A further result is that from 1860 to 1930 Argentina was essentially a full-employment economy in which there was a simple remedy for temporary unemployment: go back home. This is quite different from the labor market pattern in most developing countries.

The capital inflow to Argentina was also large. Diaz (1970) estimates that gross fixed-capital formation as a percentage of GDP, in constant prices, was in the range of 17–19 percent during 1900–14. Domestic saving, however, was only about 10 percent of GDP. Thus it appears that close to half of fixed-capital formation in Argentina was foreign-financed. Indeed, in 1913 the total of long-term foreign investment in Argentina was about half the value of the country's fixed-capital stock. About 60 percent of this capital came from the United Kingdom and almost all of the rest from other European countries, investment from the United States being still very small in 1914. The railroad system was largely British-owned; and foreign investors also bought large amounts of Argentine government bonds, the proceeds of which went partly into infrastructure investment.

Manufacturing output during this period grew only a little faster than GDP and was linked rather closely with export expansion. Meat-packing plants, flour mills, and wool-washing establishments shipped a large part of their output abroad. Railroad construction and repair, other export-oriented infrastructure facilities, and housing and urban facilities for immigrants also provided a stimulus to manufacturing. But as of 1900 manufacturing output was still only about 15 percent of GDP and rose only to 19 percent by 1929. The light and export-oriented nature of manufacturing appears clearly from the composition of manufacturing output in 1914. Foodstuffs, beverages, and tobacco were 56.5 percent. Other resource-based products—leather, wood products, stone, glass, and ceramics—were 18.8 percent. Clothing was 7.9 percent, but textiles only 1.7 percent, contrary to the usual leading role of this industry in manufacturing development. About 55 percent of domestic consumption of textiles was still being imported at this time. Output in the metals-machinery group was insignificant.

Manufacturing growth came mainly from export expansion plus growth of the domestic market, with import substitution playing a minor role. Significantly, the import/GDP ratio changed very little, falling from 26 percent in 1900–04 only to 25 percent in 1925–29.

To those who identify economic development with industrialization, then, it might seem that Argentina's development was quite limited. Yet total and per capita output grew at substantial rates. From the 1860s onward we have reasonably reliable estimates of population, merchandise exports, merchandise imports, and crop acreage. Drawing on these sources, Diaz (1970, p. 3) concludes that: "It may be guessed that real GDP grew at an annual average rate of at least 5 percent during the fifty years preceding the outbreak of World War I." With population growing at an annual rate of 3.4 percent, the GDP growth rate left a considerable margin for improvement of per capita incomes.

For the early-twentieth century, where data are somewhat better, Diaz estimates that real GDP grew between 1900–04 and 1910–14 at 6.3 percent per year as a result of differing sectoral growth rates: agriculture, 3.4 percent; manufacturing, 7.7 percent; mining, 11.5 percent; construction, 11.6 percent; and services, 6.8 percent. Population was also growing unusually rapidly during this period, at 4.3 percent per year. But this figure still leaves a 2 percent annual gain in per capita income, as high as the median for Kuznets's group of "developed" countries.

The end of Argentina's "golden age" is often dated at 1914; but 1929 is perhaps a better dating. World War I did bring a marked drop in growth from 1914 to 1921, as happened in other countries as well. But during 1921–29, total and per capita output grew at about the pre-1914 rate.

Intensive Growth, 1930–80

The shift from export-led growth to a more inward-looking development strategy emphasizing import-substituting industrialization is conventionally dated from World War II. In Latin America, however, the shift occurred earlier and was associated with the impact of the Great Depression. Export prices collapsed more sharply than did import prices. Between 1929 and 1933 the terms of trade of the Latin American countries fell by amounts ranging from 21 to 45 percent. Export volume also fell in the early 1930s and, although volume recovered in the late 1930s, the terms of trade remained depressed. In this period Argentina's close ties with Britain involved some disadvantage. Britain turned protectionist in 1931 and began to rely more heavily on Commonwealth countries for sources of supply. At the same time its position as the dominant importer of some Argentine products, such as chilled beef, enabled it to drive a hard bargain on prices. Britain was also able to insist that Argentina continue its interest payments on British debt, at a time when debt repudiation or at least postponement was common in other countries.

The reduction in Latin America's capacity to import during the 1930s, followed by physical shortages of supplies from 1939 to 1945, produced a sharp turn toward self-sufficiency. Although the policies adopted by various countries differ in detail, they show a strong family resemblance: imposition of foreign-exchange controls and deliberate management of the exchange rate; import restriction through higher tariffs, import quotas, and exchange allocation; activist fiscal and monetary policies to counter depression; and encouragement of manufacturing through tax and credit incentives as well as trade controls. In response to these measures manufacturing output in most countries grew considerably faster than GDP during the 1930s and 1940s; and import substitution made a much larger contribution to manufacturing growth than in previous decades.

I shall not review Argentina's post-1930 growth record in detail, partly because of space considerations, partly because the record is well documented in studies by Diaz and others. It is well known that Argentina's performance over the past fifty years has been substandard compared with most other Latin American countries. Thus a few comments on this point may be in order.

As of the 1920s Argentina, Canada, and Australia were often grouped as promising ''areas of new settlement'' having similar income levels and growth prospects. But their subsequent paths diverged sharply. In 1928, per capita income in Australia was only one-third above that in Argentina. But in 1980, Australia's per capita income was almost double the Argentine level.

An even more dramatic comparison is with Argentina's neighbor, Brazil. In 1928, per capita income in Brazil was only 30 percent of the Argentine level. By

1980, Brazil had pulled almost even as a result of its much stronger growth performance. Diaz (in Ranis, 1983) estimates the growth rates of per capita income in the two countries as follows:

	Argentina	*Brazil*
1928–55	0.5	2.5
1955–73	2.2	4.4
1973–80	0.9	4.1

In looking for clues, one is struck first by Argentina's weak export performance. In 1928–29 Brazil's per capita exports were only 17 percent of Argentina's; by 1975–79 they were almost equal. Argentina's per capita exports in 1975–79 were only half as large as they had been at the beginning of the century. This drop can scarcely be blamed on the state of world markets, which were booming after 1945 and which should have been as good for wheat, beef, and wool as for coffee. Argentina's lag might be ascribed partly to differing factor endowments. Brazil in 1928 was still a Lewis-type economy with abundant surplus labor and could make large productivity gains by transferring labor from lower- to higher-productivity sectors. Argentina, on the other hand, was approaching neo-classical conditions and was reallocating labor from a highly productive agricultural sector to activities whose superior productivity is doubtful. Estimates for 1910–14 and 1925–29 indicate that output per worker in agriculture was in both periods about equal to the economy-wide average and distinctly *above* output per worker in manufacturing.

Much of the blame, however, must be placed on Argentine policy. On the political side, Argentina's policy was nonaligned and anti-American. Argentina declined to join the Food and Agriculture Organization (FAO), IBRD, or IMF, limiting both markets in the United States and capital availability from the United States and international organizations. The Perón regime deliberately depressed farm prices for agricultural products, in the interest of providing cheap food for the urban workers who formed its main political clientele. This naturally reduced production incentives. Per capita production of cereals in 1950–54 was only 46 percent of the 1935–39 level. Livestock did better, but total agricultural output per capita fell 11 percent over this period, with a consequent reduction of exports. In industry, indiscriminate import substitution in consumer durables, capital goods, and intermediates with little attention to resource costs involved wasteful use of capital and transfer of labor from more- to less-productive activities.

At the most basic level, poor economic performance reflects serious political disorganization. Consider the record: a military coup in 1930; hybrid military-civilian conservative regimes from 1930 to 1943; the nationalist and populist Perón regime from 1943 to 1955; efforts to restore non-Perónist civilian rule under military tutelage from 1955 to 1966; direct military rule in 1966–73; a restoration of Perónist rule from 1973 to 1976; a new coup and a return to military rule from

1976 to 1983. As Diaz (1983) comments, "The secular trend has been toward greater instability, faster turnover of economic policy makers, and a more fragmented polity." No government has had sufficiently broad and deep popular support to engage in the subtle maneuvers necessary to achieve sustained per capita growth.

BRAZIL

Extensive Growth

Brazil is one of the world's largest countries, rich in resources, thinly populated, and still not pressing seriously on its resource base. Population was growing even in the seventeenth century, largely through the Portuguese slave trade with Africa. In the eighteenth century population is estimated to have doubled, from 1.25 million in 1700 to 2.5 million in 1800. After that the growth rate accelerated markedly, reaching 7.25 million in 1850 and 18 million in 1900.

During these early centuries the country passed through a series of export cycles. Sugarcane, introduced in 1520, was grown in the northeastern provinces with slave labor on large plantations, averaging 80–100 slaves each. The export proceeds went mainly to plantation owners, merchants, and shippers and financed the continued import of slaves plus luxury consumer goods for the small European population. The spread effects were thus limited. Sugar continued to flourish through most of the seventeenth century, but meanwhile it had been introduced into the Caribbean islands owned by the Spanish, British, French, and Dutch. The Caribbean had shorter shipping routes plus preferential treatment in the home markets of the colonial powers. So after about 1675 Brazilian sugar went into decline, a decline from which the northeast has never really recovered.

Gold was discovered in Minas Gerais province in the 1690s, and gold exports rose rapidly to a peak around 1760. This gold cycle shifted the center of economic activity from the northeast to the center-south of the country, symbolized by movement of the administrative center from Salvador to Rio de Janeiro in 1763. Mining was organized differently from sugar, in units that could be as small as a single prospector, depending on the owner's capital. It was carried on mainly by Europeans and the European population, which in 1700 was only 100,000, had by 1800 grown to about a million. The income from gold was more widely distributed than that from sugar, thereby contributing to larger spread effects. A growing demand for food in the towns and mining centers and for mules to transport gold to distant ports stimulated farming and livestock growing in the center of the country.

Gold declined in its turn and was followed by a "coffee cycle," which got under way in the 1830s and with which Brazil's modern economic growth really begins. Meanwhile, unlike the Spanish colonies, Brazil had made the transition to independence without bloodshed. When Napoleon occupied Lisbon in 1807, the capital of the Portuguese Empire was moved to Rio de Janeiro. After the European peace settlement, the king returned to Portugal in 1821, leaving his son behind in Rio as regent. But when continued Portuguese control of the colony proved distasteful to the Brazilian population, the son in 1822 declared himself emperor of an independent Brazil as Dom Pedro I. He and his son Dom Pedro II remained as nominal rulers until 1889, when the monarchy was finally abolished as part of a modernization that included abolition of slavery in 1888.

Turning Point: circa 1880

The date of Brazil's turning point is debated among scholars. The earliest estimates, by Celso Furtado (1963), place it as early as 1850. Furtado estimates that between the 1840s and the 1890s the physical volume of exports rose by 214 percent, while there was a 58 percent improvement in the terms of trade, yielding an increase of 396 percent in real income generated in the export sector. His national-income estimates show total output growing at 3.5 percent per year, population at 1.5 percent, and output per capita at 2.0 percent over this period.

The Furtado estimates, however, have been disputed by later writers. Leff (1982) considers them too high, resulting from overemphasis of the export sector as against the more slowly growing domestic sector. He places the growth rate of per capita income at less than 1 percent per year, with substantial variation among subperiods—high growth from 1863 to 1878, followed by negative growth from 1879 to 1899, then high growth once more from 1900 to 1913. Published estimates by Contador and Haddad and unpublished estimates by Raymond Goldsmith show short-term fluctuations in output per capita but no sustained uptrend during the years 1850–1900.*

I am nevertheless inclined to place the turning point in the 1880s, which saw the beginning of the coffee boom in São Paulo state, as well as the abolition of slavery and the end of the empire. One must recognize, however, that the growth of this period had a strong regional character. It was most rapid in São Paulo, less rapid in other central and southern states, while in the northeast per capita output seems to have been falling.

Intensive Growth to 1930

Coffee was introduced into Brazil soon after 1700, and for a century after that it was grown mainly for local consumption. But with the decline of gold and with the European peace settlement of 1815, coffee broke into the export market. From the 1830s onward coffee exports mounted rapidly in a prolonged boom that lasted until the 1920s. Exports (in thousand bags of 60 kilos) rose from a total of 10,430

---

*In *Revista Brasileria de Estatistica* 36 (1975). The Goldsmith estimates, which the author kindly made available to me, will be published in due course.

for the decade 1831–40 to 27,339 for 1851–60 to 51,631 for 1881–90. By 1914 about half of all cultivated land in Brazil was in coffee, and two-thirds of agricultural output was exported.

Until about 1880 coffee was grown mainly to the north and west of Rio, on plantations using slave labor. But as the supply of suitable land was exhausted, the industry moved south to São Paulo and westward within that state. In the 1860s British engineers with British capital built a railroad over the escarpment separating the central plateau of São Paulo from the port of Santos; and in the next several decades a rail network penetrated deep into the São Paulo coffee zone. By 1890, Santos had pulled ahead of Rio as a coffee port, and the gap widened in later years.

Most of the coffee initially was grown on large estates, though smallholder cultivation was also present. People with substantial capital and political influence were best able to establish and defend land titles and to finance the period between planting of coffee trees and full-scale production. Land supply was no problem, but labor supply was a considerable problem. There was some use of slaves in the years before abolition and some local supply of free laborers, including migrants from the less-prosperous northeast. But the ultimate resort was European immigration, actively promoted by the landowners with government assistance. Immigration to São Paulo alone rose from 13,000 in the 1870s to 609,000 in the 1890s, with Italy the most important source. This supply was sufficient to hold the coffee wage rate rather stable and to maintain the profitability of the industry.

The economy received further stimulus from the great rubber boom of 1890–1910, which drew many people from the northeast and other states into the Amazon region. With the motor age, demand for rubber was rising rapidly, and Brazil's wild rubber trees were initially the main source of supply. Rubber prices soared, reaching an all-time high of £512 per ton in 1909–11. Meanwhile, however, rubber seeds had been smuggled from Brazil to England and, after a period of research and experimentation, were introduced into Ceylon, Malaya, and other colonial areas around 1895. When Asian rubber began to reach the market in substantial volume around 1910, the price collapsed, falling by 1921 to one-sixth the 1910 level. Brazilian rubber, unable to compete with the cheaper Asian product, rapidly lost its market.

With coffee, Brazil finally had a product whose export proceeds were widely distributed. There was a growing stream of wage payments to coffee-farm workers and also to workers on the railroads, ports, and other servicing facilities. Wage income created a mass market for basic consumer goods, which stimulated cash-cropping in agriculture and the growth of factory industry. As usual, textiles were in the forefront of industrialization. From 48 mills with 3,172 workers in 1885, the industry grew to 240 mills with 82,257 workers in 1915. By this time domestic mills were supplying about 85 percent of Brazil's textile consumption. Other important early industries were clothing, shoes, and food processing, which together with textiles produced about two-thirds of industrial output in 1914. Many of the early Brazilian industrialists started out as importers who at a certain stage found it more profitable to produce domestically than to import. Rich coffee growers often used their accumulated capital for manufacturing investment; and immigrant entrepreneurs were of some importance.

Sporadic bursts of tariff protection from the 1840s onward were no doubt helpful but seem to have been less important than sheer growth of the domestic market. Helpful also were occasional devaluations of the Brazilian currency vis-à-vis the pound, which stimulated industrialization by making imports more expensive. Devaluation also raised coffee prices in local currency and helped to sustain the profitability of coffee growing.

The coffee cycle continued in all essentials through the 1920s; and not until the 1930s was there a decisive break with the export-dominated pattern. At the all-time peak in 1928, coffee exports amounted to three-quarters of all exports; and exports had risen to 12.5 percent of GDP. Manufacturing continued to grow at a moderate rate—about 4.6 percent per year from 1911 to 1920, 3.0 percent per year from 1920 to 1929. Manufacturing growth was linked with coffee not only via increased domestic demand due to wage income but also because exports provided the foreign exchange needed to import capital goods. Thus peak periods for coffee exports tended also to be peak periods for capital-goods imports and expansion of industrial capacity.

Brazil's strategy, immediately profitable but ultimately self-defeating, was to use its dominant market position to hold the world coffee price above a long-run equilibrium level. Already in the early 1900s this tactic had led to efforts to restrict coffee marketings. When the flood of coffee exports threatened to break the coffee price, the state of São Paulo established the first "valorization scheme" to buy up coffee and hold it off the market. This was to be a model for later plans at the federal level. Maintaining a high world price, however, stimulated planting of coffee in a dozen other countries, and Brazil's market share began a long decline from three-quarters of world supply in the 1900s to only one-third in the 1960s.

Intensive Growth, 1930–80

Continued prosperity of the coffee industry led to heavy planting of coffee trees in the middle and late 1920s. The eventual increase in production, plus growing supplies from other coffee-producing countries, plus the onset of the Great Depression, brought a collapse of prices and piling up of unsold coffee stocks in Brazil. Government reaction to this crisis initiated a new pattern of growth, mainly generated from within and for the first time aimed consciously at industrial development.

The federal government intervened for the first time in the coffee market, guaranteeing a minimum price to growers, buying up surplus coffee, and actually destroying part of the unsold stock. Devaluation of the currency also helped to sustain the cruzeiro income of coffee growers. While about half of the coffee-support program was financed by an export tax on coffee, the remainder was financed by credit expansion. Furtado seems to be correct in arguing that the support program played the role of Keynesian pyramid building in sustaining domestic income. The drop in Brazil's GNP was considerably milder and briefer than that in the United States and other industrial countries.

The drop in import capacity led also to foreign-exchange licensing and to severe restrictions on manufactured imports. This restriction of supply, plus the cruzeiro devaluation, raised the price of imported goods relative to domestic goods and thus made manufacturing more profitable. The main immediate effect was fuller use of existing plant capacity. But by the late 1930s, when import capacity had recovered somewhat, there were substantial imports of capital goods for use in plant expansion. Between 1929 and 1939, Brazil's output of textiles rose by 147 percent, of metal products by 300 percent, and of paper products by 700 percent. Industry remained basically light industry, though the metals and machinery group had risen from 10 percent to 18 percent of manufacturing output. The effects of World War II were similar to those of World War I—fuller use of existing plant capacity, but not much capacity expansion because of reduced availability of capital goods. The growth rate of manufacturing output from 1939 to 1945 was 5.2 percent per year.

After a burst of unrestricted imports from 1945 to 1947, which exhausted the exchange reserves accumulated during the war, Brazil embarked on a conscious policy of import-substituting industrialization—mainly, substitution in intermediates, capital goods, and automobiles, since import substitution in nondurable consumer goods was already virtually complete. The techniques, whose relative importance varied somewhat over time, included: (1) import licensing, under which competing imports were severely restricted while materials and productive equipment were admitted at relatively low prices; (2) an overvalued exchange rate, which also benefitted importers of equipment while serving as a tax on agricultural exporters; (3) very high tariff protection on finished consumer goods, with lower rates on intermediates and still lower rates on capital goods; (4) heavy government investment in infrastructure, plus establishment of public corporations in iron-ore mining (1942), steel (1946), and petroleum (1954)—financed in part by a government development bank (BNDE), established in 1952; and (5) inflation, which seems to have contributed to a shift toward profits. Between 1949 and 1959, physical output per manufacturing worker rose 90 percent, the average real wage rose by 26 percent, and wages as a percent of value added fell by 18 percent. This redistribution toward profits was veiled by the fact that *nominal* wage rates were rising rapidly.

The heavy emphasis on import substitution, accompanied by relative neglect of agriculture and of exports, continued from about 1947 to 1962. During this period manufacturing output rose at almost 10 percent a year, contributing to a 6 percent annual rise in GDP. There was a marked shift toward heavy industry. By 1963 the metals and machinery group produced 37 percent of manufacturing output and chemicals 15 percent, while textiles plus food processing had dropped to 25 percent. The extent of import substitution is shown by the fact that imports of intermediate goods as a proportion of total supply dropped from 26 percent in 1949 to 9 percent in 1962. For capital goods the drop was even more spectacular, from 59 percent to 13 percent.

These results were no doubt accomplished at some resource cost. One study (Winpenny, 1972) found that unit production costs in Brazil typically exceeded those of the same industry in the United States, the excess cost being correlated with the rate of effective protection. In general, capital goods were not as overpriced as consumer goods. Another study (Bergsman, 1970) estimated the costs of protection at 8–10 percent of GNP in 1967. But only a small part of the cost of protection resulted from static misallocation, while most of it consisted in monopoly profits plus avoidable higher production costs.

There was a lull in growth from 1962 to 1967, associated with the resignation of President Quadros in 1962, the overthrow of President Goulart by a military coup in 1964, and the time required for the policies of the new regime to become effective. These policies included: (1) inflation control—reduction of the federal budget deficit, reduction of the deficits in public-utility enterprises by raising selling prices, improvement of tax collection, tightening of credit, and a squeeze on the wage sector; (2) modernization and strengthening of capital markets, including widespread indexation of interest rates and securities yields; and (3) a shift toward emphasis on exports, notably through a more realistic exchange-rate policy involving adoption of a "crawling peg" system. Most export taxes were abolished, and exporters were now favored with subsidized credit and tax incentives.

Under these policies there was a renewed spurt of economic growth. Real GDP rose at 11 percent per year from 1968 to 1973 and at 7.7 percent from 1973 to 1977. While industry grew at a considerably faster rate than agriculture, agriculture also did well, averaging 5.4 percent growth from 1968 to 1977. By 1977 industry produced 37.0 percent of GDP, agriculture 12.2 percent. The capital-formation rate hovered around 25 percent for most of the 1970s. The domestic savings rate rose to 21 percent of GDP, about half of which was government saving through social-security funds and other channels. The boom was strongest in São Paulo province, where most of manufacturing has always been concentrated—initially because of its good infrastructure and the availability of coffee money for investment, later because of availability of input supplies, financial and marketing services, and other economies of agglomeration. By the mid-1970s there were complaints of acute labor shortage; and this may partly explain why real wages rose much more rapidly after 1965 then before that time.

Especially impressive was the turnaround in the foreign sector. From 1947 to 1962 policymakers, accepting the pessimism of export-led growth of Prebisch and others, tended to neglect and even penalize exports. Exports were treated as a residual, whatever was left after domestic needs were satisfied. So export volume stagnated, and the export/GDP ratio declined. With the more outward-looking policies followed after 1964, this trend was reversed. Between 1965 and 1976, the trade ratio (exports plus imports/GDP) rose from 16 percent to 25 percent. There was a particularly sharp rise in manufactured exports, which by 1976 were almost 30 percent of the total. Other "new exports" included soybeans and derivatives (17 percent) and iron ore (10 percent). Coffee and other traditional primary products (cotton, cocoa, sugar), which as recently as 1960 were 89 percent of all exports, had now fallen to 36 percent. This diversification of export products was accompanied by a substantial diversification of markets. The share going to the United States has been falling and by 1976 was considerably below that of Western Europe. Japan and the Middle East are now also substantial markets.

Discussions of recent Brazilian experience tend to focus on industrialization. But the accomplishments on this front might well have been impossible without improved agricultural performance. As elsewhere in Latin America, Brazilian agriculture is quite dualistic. Latifundia of 1,000 hectares or more occupy about 40 percent of the farm land, though most of this land is in pasture with only a small cultivated area. Some 10 percent of the rural labor force are permanent wage-earners, and another 15–20 percent are seasonal workers. About two-thirds, however, are owner-operators, most of whom have holdings of 10 hectares or less. These proportions vary considerably by region, with latifundia especially prevalent in the northeast, smallholdings prevalent in São Paulo and the south.

Until recently government policy toward agriculture was neglectful or actually exploitative. There was some contribution through rural road building, occasional subsidization of fertilizer prices, and price supports for coffee and some other crops. But these contributions were outweighed by the adverse effects of export taxes, the overvalued exchange rate, and price ceilings on food products in the cities. Here again the post-1964 regime shifted policy in a favorable direction. Agriculture benefitted from abolition of export taxes, adoption of the crawling-peg system, and lifting of food-price controls. There was also a marked expansion of rural credit facilities, which previously existed mainly on paper. The real value of new loans increased sixfold between 1960 and 1975. Moreover, much of this lending was at negative real rates of interest, amounting to an income transfer to the agricultural sector.

The growth rate of agricultural output since 1960 has averaged about 5 percent per year. The highest growth rates have been for food products—soybeans, rice, corn, milk, beef, and pork. The export crops—coffee, cocoa, and sugar—have had markedly lower growth rates. The fact that food prices have risen about in line with the general price index suggests that food output is keeping up with domestic demand. It is less encouraging that almost all the increased output has come from acreage expansion. Brazil has always been, and still is, a frontier economy. As of 1965 it was estimated that only 49 percent of the arable land area was actually in use. Between 1950 and 1970 the number of farms more than doubled and the amount of land under cultivation rose by 124 percent. There have been appreciable yield increases only for coffee, sugarcane, and (recently) corn, and yields of some crops have declined. This mediocre productivity performance is due partly to a lag in the use of modern inputs. Fertilizer use did increase fourfold between 1960 and 1975 but is still low on an international scale. There are, however, substantial regional differences. Fertilizer use, farm mechanization, and crop yields are all considerably higher in São Paulo than elsewhere, partly because the state government has taken an active interest in research and in input supplies. A notable feature of the Brazilian economy is the pervasive influence of government. It would be hard to find an economy that is more truly "mixed." The importance of government is quite inadequately reflected in the current budget. Indeed, output of government services has actually *fallen* from 11.7 percent of GDP in 1949 to 9.7 percent in 1973. Transfer payments have risen substantially, from 3.1 percent to 8.9 percent of GDP, reflecting the emergence of a modern social-insurance system. More significant, however, is government's role as *banker* and as owner of public enterprises. Government banks provide about 70 percent of investment funds and 65 percent of loans for working capital. A recent study of the 5,113 largest firms in Brazil showed that government's share of asset ownership was 37 percent. The largest public-sector shares are in public utilities (88 percent), mining (62 percent), chemicals and petroleum (55 percent), and metal products (34 percent).

Public ownership, as Baer (1979) argues convincingly, does not for the most part reflect ideological preference but represents rather a pragmatic response to particular circumstances. In railroading, and later in electric power, the following sequence of events occurred: government assumed power to regulate rates; political pressures caused rates to be set at unprofitable levels; the private companies lost money, and so eventually were bought out by government. World War II led to state expansion into ownership of shipping lines, soda-ash production, and iron-ore mining for nationalistic and national-security reasons. During the industrialization drive, BNDE helped to meet the unusually large capital requirements of two integrated steel mills, and the bank gradually became the main stockholder. And so on. If the present-day structure does not seem particularly logical, this may be because it was never derived from logical principles. But it works.

We have come a long way from the sugar-and-coffee economy of 1850. But I hope to have shown that Brazil's dramatic growth since 1945 is only the latest stage in a long historical process.

MEXICO

The unusually interesting case of Mexico deserves more space than is available here. It is also relatively well documented, illustrating my earlier statement that success breeds bibliography.

Turning Point: circa 1876

After the earlier decimation of the Indian population, Mexico's population seems to have been growing from at least 1700 onward. During the nineteenth century it more than doubled, from an estimated 5.5 million in 1800 to 13.5 million in 1900. Extensive growth clearly was under way, but the transition to intensive growth was long retarded by political instability. The revolt against Spanish rule was followed by fierce fighting from 1810 to 1821, which devastated the country. During the next fifty years Mexico had more than fifty governments, with thirty different individuals serving as president. The period included foreign occupation of parts of the country at various times and border wars with the United States, which ended in the loss of large territories that had been part of colonial Mexico.

This turbulent era was ended by the accession in 1876 of Porfirio Díaz, who with one brief interregnum served as president until 1911. This period, the "Porfiriato," saw the beginnings of intensive growth, led mainly by mineral exports but with agricultural exports becoming increasingly important. The dictatorial character of the regime, and in particular its neglect of the peasant masses, led to the revolution of 1911. The revolution could be regarded as a second turning point in that it established a new institutional structure that in large measure survives to the present day.

Revolution, however, did not lead immediately to growth. Bloody fighting from 1911 to 1921 reduced both population and agricultural output. Production had begun to recover by the late 1920s but fell again in the early years of the Depression, which sharply reduced export possibilities. From 1911 to 1940, then, the average annual growth rate of total and per capita output was *below* that during the Porfiriato. But during these years an institutional structure was established that proved unusually conducive to rapid growth from 1940 onward. The period since 1940, sometimes termed "the Mexican miracle," is a third distinct epoch in the country's economic growth. Let us look at the main features of these three periods.

The Porfiriato, 1876–1911

What did the Díaz regime do to integrate and develop the economy? The stability of the new regime and its guarantees to private investors stimulated a large inflow of foreign investment, particularly in mining and railroad construction. The isolated local economies that existed in 1875 were brought closer together by an active transportation program, which increased railroad mileage from 400 in 1876 to 15,000 in 1910. Economic integration was furthered also by the abolition of internal customs barriers, which had been decreed in the constitution of 1857, but only now began to be actively enforced. Monetary policy, under which the peso was allowed to fall to about half its initial value, was favorable to exports. Land policy, which favored private rather than communal ownership, created both a land market and a detached labor force. But the resulting high concentration of land ownership and the large flow of displaced peasants to the cities contributed to political instability and eventually to overthrow of the regime.

Mexico's rugged topography, which divides the country into semi-isolated regions, makes transportation facilities especially important. The Díaz regime undertook initially to promote railways either directly or through subsidies to state governments; but results were slow to appear. So after 1880 policy shifted to subsidies to private companies, partly in the form of land grants, which attracted substantial amounts of British and American capital. Railroads were developed primarily in an east-west direction, passing through already settled areas and linking coastal ports with the interior. Fear of the United States delayed any northward expansion; but eventually lines pushed north to the U.S. border and linked up with American railways. Private construction by numerous companies produced a rather disorganized network with considerable duplication of routes. So government gradually attempted to consolidate companies and buy out part of their capital. The eventual result was a national railway system (Ferrocarriles Nacional de México, formed in 1909), with majority government ownership but continuing private participation from the United States and Great Britain.

The drastic reduction of transport costs had predictable results: relocation of industries away from the coast, rise of new industries and new mining centers. Mining development was furthered by a law of 1892 by which the government relinquished its previous control of subsoil rights. This act stimulated a large inflow of foreign capital, predominantly from the United States but also from the United Kingdom. Export volume grew during the Porfiriato at 6.6 percent per year and also became more diversified. In 1878 silver alone formed 60 percent of all exports; by 1910 its share had fallen to 33 percent, though silver production had increased two-and-a-half times. Hemp, coffee, cattle, rubber, copper, and lead had emerged as significant exports, together forming 56 percent of the 1910 total. Agricultural exports came mainly from the large haciendas to be described in a moment. Although much of the export earnings went abroad, a significant part was distributed within the country—to mine workers, to hacienda owners and laborers, to suppliers of inputs to the export industries (including transport), and to government in tax payments.

All this broadened the internal market for manufactures. Manufacturing was encouraged also by high external tariffs, abolition of internal customs duties and the great reduction of transport costs. Real manufacturing output grew during the Porfiriato at an estimated 3.6 percent per year, considerably above the 2.6 percent rate for GDP. There was substantial import substitution, particularly in textiles, clothing, processed foods and beverages, tobacco, cement, and other building materials. The textile industry flourished, and imports of cotton cloth fell from 32 percent of domestic consumption in 1889 to 3 percent in 1911. All consumer goods, which had formed 75 percent of Mexican imports in 1877–78, had fallen to 43 percent by 1910–11. Industrial profits were high. Initial investment in manufacturing came mainly from Mexican sources, and reinvestment of earnings fueled the growth process.

The inflow of foreign capital was much larger, relative to the size of the economy, than had been true in the United States during its takeoff period. Hansen (1971) estimates that foreign investment formed about two-thirds of total investment during the Porfiriato. As of 1911, about 38 percent of the accumulated foreign investment was from the United States, 29 percent from the United Kingdom, and 27 percent from France. About 33 percent of foreign capital went into railroads, 24 percent into mining and metallurgy, and 15 percent was portfolio investment in Mexican public debt. Only 4 percent went into manufacturing, which remained largely a Mexican preserve.

In agriculture, concentration of land ownership was furthered by two actions:

1. The "reform laws" of 1855–57, which disfranchised both the Catholic Church and the communal landholdings of the Indian villages. All land was now to be turned over to private ownership. Proponents of the law seem to have visualized a new class of small yeoman farmers. But what actually happened was that many poor and illiterate Indian "owners" sold out quickly, and most of the land passed into the hands of large holders.
2. A Díaz program initiated in 1883 for surveying, subdivision, and sale of public lands. Within a decade about 20 percent of the entire area of Mexico had passed into the hands of land-survey companies.

What emerged was a system in which about half of the rural population lived on a few thousand haciendas, some of them millions of acres in size. The hacienda was a large, relatively self-sufficient production unit with a resident labor force tied to the land by debt bondage, characterized by absentee ownership, backward production methods, and cautious management aimed at steady and predictable returns rather than maximum returns. These large units tended to concentrate on commercial crops. Between 1877 and 1907, production for export grew at 6.5 percent per year, and production of raw materials for domestic industry grew at 2.5 percent. But food output per capita certainly did not increase, and Reynolds (1970) and Hansen surmise that it actually declined.

During the Porfiriato, GDP seems to have grown at some 2.6 percent per year. With population growing at 1.4 percent, this would mean growth of 1.2 percent per year in per capita output. During 1900–10, for which estimates are somewhat firmer, Reynolds shows GDP growing at 3.3 percent, population at 1.1 percent, GDP per capita at 2.2 percent—about as fast as in North America and Western Europe during the same period. The pattern of growth, however, was quite unbalanced: mining and commercial agriculture grew rapidly, manufacturing somewhat less rapidly, food output very slowly. On this ground, and on the ground that development had largely bypassed the mass of the rural population, one could argue that the Porfiriato did not after all represent a turning point to intensive growth. I would be inclined to argue the contrary view, but not very strongly.

Revolution, Recovery, and Reform, 1911–40

While the economy may have progressed under Díaz, the political situation was increasingly unstable. The Díaz land policies displaced large numbers of small cultivators, forcing them into wage employment. The terms of trade turned against agricultural exports around 1895, putting pressure on rural wages. Food output per capita appears to have been declining. Large numbers of handicraft workers were displaced by the growth of factory industry as well as by imports. All this contributed to land hunger, rural unrest, and eventually to revolution.

The years from 1911 until the late 1920s were marked by armed conflict, destruction of property, loss of perhaps a million lives, and fear and insecurity for large and small landowners alike. Curiously enough, the output of the mining and petroleum enclaves, which protected themselves with private armies, grew at 5.6 percent a year between 1910 and 1925. But manufacturing grew at only 1.7 percent and agricultural output at only 0.1 percent per year. The situation was saved only by the fact that, because of civil-war casualties, population growth was also close to zero.

The years 1925–40 were also disappointing in terms of production. By the time the economy had begun to recover in the late 1920s it was hit by the world-wide Depression of 1929. Exports dropped sharply, and national output did not recover to earlier levels until 1940. In addition, the institutional reforms of the period—acceleration of land reform, nationalization of railroads in the early 1930s, and of foreign petroleum companies in 1938—had an "announcement effect" that was adverse to production, though their long-range effects were beneficial. Between 1925 and 1940 manufacturing output grew at 4.3 percent, agricultural output at 2.7 percent, mining and petroleum at −1.9 percent. Overall, GDP grew at 1.6 percent a year, and population also grew at 1.6 percent, so that 1940 output per capita was at about the 1925 level. Looking beneath the aggregates, however, it is encouraging that food availability had grown at about 1 percent a year, while the country's reduced capacity to import after 1929 gave a distinct stimulus to manufacturing, similar to that observed earlier in the case of Brazil.

The main feature of this period, however, was not so much progress in production as development of an institutional framework that was to prove conducive to rapid growth after 1940. Perhaps most significant was the institutionalizing of political stability through a dominant political party, the PRI. The PRI rests on three legs: a labor organization, a farmers' organization, and a "popular" organization in which government employees are quite important. This tripartite structure operates at federal, state, and local levels, and in principle controls the nomination of candidates for public office. But in reality, control seems to operate from the top down. The president serves for a six-year term and may not succeed himself. Each president picks his successor by a somewhat mysterious "insider" process; and this procession of six-year presidents has continued unbroken since the installation of Cárdenas in 1934. The president also has a dominant voice in selecting members of the federal legislature and governors of the states; and the governors have similar powers in their jurisdictions. Other parties exist, and regular elections are held, but the official candidates almost invariably win. The executive branch dominates the legislature at all levels of government. "Uncooperative" legislators, labor leaders, or whoever find themselves quietly edged out of the power structure.

While business groups are not included in the official power structure, government is strongly responsive to their views and interests. One gets an impression of almost Japanese-like symbiosis of the public and private sectors. It is taken for granted that those selected for high office will come out rich, mainly through using personal contacts to participate in quite legal business transactions.

Next most important in the 1925–40 period was the transformation of the agrarian structure. Mexican land reform has consisted in reducing the size of the haciendas and redistributing the expropriated land to smallholders under the *ejido* form of tenure. Formally, land is owned by the village community; but it is assigned in plots of 5–7 hectares to individual cultivators, who have effective security of tenure. (There are also some truly collective ejidos for plantation-type crops that can benefit from large-scale organization and management.) Legislation to this effect had been on the books since 1915, but little had been done about it. As of 1930, ejido land was still only 13 percent of the cultivated area. Under the Cárdenas regime (1934–40) the process was systematized and accelerated. By 1940, ejido land formed 47 percent of the total. Some further redistribution has occurred since, notably under the López Mateos administration (1958–64), but not on the scale of the Cárdenas period.

Other important developments of this period included:

1. The nationalization of foreign-owned railroads, mines, and petroleum enterprises. Nationalization produced an outcry from the companies and a temporary stoppage of foreign-capital inflow. But in time compensation agreements for the seized assets were negotiated, and since 1945 foreign capital has returned to large volume.
2. The foundations were laid for a system of government investment banking that has played a key role in post-1940 development. The Bank of Mexico was founded in 1925, with sole right of note issue and the normal central banking functions. The Nacional Financiera, a major institutional innovation, was founded in 1934. Many other specialized investment banks for particular sectors, including agricultural credit banks, were to follow in later years.
3. The power of the hacienda owners was finally broken. Among other things, this created a free labor market. By 1940, less than a million peasants still lived on haciendas. Most had now received their own land, while the landless were at least free to seek wage employment.
4. An interesting development underlined by Hansen was the appearance of a sizable middle class, which grew from an estimated 8 percent of the population in 1895 to 16 percent in 1940. Meanwhile, those who could be classified as "upper class" had shrunk from 1.44 to 1.05 percent of the population.

Intensive Growth since 1940

The growth rate since 1940 has been much higher than in the initial period 1876–1911, and the pattern of growth has been distinctly different. Recent growth has been mainly generated from within, and the export/GDP ratio has tended to fall. Growth has been unusually balanced, with agricultural performance above that in most developing countries. Import-substitution policies have been moderate, with tariffs averaging only about 25 percent, realistic exchange rates at most times, and a relatively low rate of inflation. The economy continues to be a Lewis-type economy, with surplus labor, a lag of wage rates behind productivity, high industrial profits, and a high rate of reinvestment. The distribution of income remains among the most unequal in Latin America. The benefits of income growth have accrued mainly to the middle and upper-middle classes.

The rate of natural population increase has risen from about 2.5 percent in 1940 to about 3.5 percent today, reflecting mainly mortality behavior. As in most other countries, the crude deathrate has fallen sharply from around 23 per thousand in 1940 to about 8 per thousand today. Meanwhile, fertility remains almost unchanged in the 43–44 per thousand range. Life expectancy at birth has risen from around 40 years in 1940 to more than 60 years today. Mexico has not been a land-scarce economy, and population growth has been accommodated in good measure by increasing the cultivated acreage. Between 1929 and 1959, for example, cultivated acreage increased by 92 percent. Proximity to the United States also provides outlets for labor through temporary seasonal work or permanent emigration. Even so there remains a pool of surplus labor, estimated by Clark Reynolds at five million rural families in the late 1960s. The availability of these people for transfer to commercial agriculture or industry reduces pressure on wage levels. It is estimated that such intersectoral transfers accounted for about one-third of the increase in average national productivity since 1940.

Agriculture's output growth has been unusually high—close to 6 percent in the 1940s, near 5 percent since that time. While some of this increase has gone into exports, there has also been an increase in per capita food availability and an improvement of diets for most of the population. The agriculture/industry terms of trade have fluctuated within a moderate range, with no trend in either direction. The agricultural structure is markedly dualistic, with large commercially oriented farms predominant in the north and small-scale ejido cultivation dominant in the center and south.

Government agricultural policy has itself been dualistic. On the one hand, land reform has served to build mass support for the system and to ensure peasants a minimum subsistence. On the other hand, there has been heavy investment in rural infrastructure, which has benefited mainly the larger commercial farmers, many of whom occupy newly irrigated land. This strand of policy is production-oriented, while the former is people-oriented. Federal investment in roads and irrigation as a percentage of total federal investment rose from 22 percent in 1925–

29 to 45 percent in 1935–39, then fell back gradually to 20 percent in the 1960s, although it continued to rise in absolute terms. This public investment called forth an even larger amount of complementary private investment, and much of the post-1940 output increase can be interpreted as a lagged response to this investment.

Contrary to practice in many countries, there has been a substantial net transfer of funds *to* the agricultural sector through government budgets. This has probably been more than offset, however, by a flow of private-sector savings in the other direction. Hansen estimates that the overall rural-urban transfer of funds in the years 1942–61 was $250 million, or 2–3 percent of domestic fixed investment. Thus Mexican agriculture seems to have performed all the "functions" that appear in development models: a plentiful supply of labor, which has restrained wages and maintained high profits and high reinvestment; higher levels of food consumption and better diets for the population; agricultural exports, which have grown at more than 6 percent a year and risen from 25 percent to more than half of total exports; a flow of inputs for domestic manufacturing, notably cotton and sugarcane; a substantial savings transfer; and rising rural purchasing power, which has broadened the market for domestic manufactures.

Increased agricultural output is largely accounted for by larger inputs, including increased labor inputs per hectare by ejido cultivators. Technical progress, "the residual," seems to account for about 30 percent of output growth. Interestingly enough, although absolute productivity levels are substantially higher in the commercial-farm sector, the small-scale ejido cultivators show just as high a rate of technical progress.

A substantial industrial sector already existed in 1940, producing about 17 percent of GDP. Except for automobiles and a few other consumer durables, import substitution in consumer goods was virtually complete. Since 1940, industrial growth has speeded up to 6–7 percent per year, somewhat higher than agricultural growth though not dramatically higher. There has been the usual shift toward heavier industries, with the metal-machinery and chemical shares rising and textiles and food processing falling. Output growth is almost entirely explained by input growth, "the residual" accounting for only about 10 percent of the growth rate. The capital stock has risen more rapidly than output, the labor force a good deal more slowly. As in other countries, manufacturing has not proven very labor-absorbing, and most of the labor transferred from agriculture has gone into service activities.

Government has aided industrial growth in several ways. There have been the usual tax exemptions and import concessions, though Timothy King judges that these were not of major importance. There is moderate tariff protection, and more importantly an import licensing system. This system seems to have been used rather sensibly, including occasional use as a threat against local producers who are notably inefficient or who take undue advantage of monopoly positions. The Mexican price of manufactured products is typically 20–30 percent above the import price. This varies widely among products—50 percent for automobiles, less than 10 percent for fertilizers. In general, Mexico's import-substitution policies have been more pragmatic and moderate than in many other countries. Government has also made a substantial contribution through the investment banks to be described in a moment.

To some extent, however, government was pushing on an open door, in the sense that economic conditions favored industrial growth. These conditions include: rapid growth of the domestic market, including a rural market that provides an estimated 30 percent of consumer demand; the lag of real wages behind productivity, which permitted high profits and high reinvestment; the presence of a large and active group of Mexican entrepreneurs (foreign investment is less than 10 percent of manufacturing investment, and foreign ventures require at least 51 percent Mexican participation); and the gradual development of export capacity, with the result that manufactures now provide a rising percentage of the export total.

A word now about the foreign sector. Until the oil boom of the late 1970s, the export/GDP ratio had been falling and one could no longer regard growth as export-led. The pattern of exports had also changed remarkably from earlier years. After 1950 tourism emerged as the largest single earner of foreign exchange, amounting by 1965 to 38 percent of total exports. Among merchandise exports, a diversified list of agricultural and livestock products now amounted to two-thirds of nonoil exports. The share of mineral exports had fallen dramatically, with gold and silver almost out of the picture. Manufactured exports, while still only 10 percent of the total, had the highest percentage rate of growth and were clearly destined to become a major factor. The development of "border-zone" factories adjacent to the United States, which permitted Mexico in effect to export labor, was an important source of export growth.

The structure of commodity imports has also changed in predictable ways. By 1965 capital goods were 39 percent of the total, raw materials and intermediates 38 percent, and consumer goods only 14 percent. Imports have tended to run substantially above exports, the gap being closed by long- and short-term capital inflows, mainly from the United States. The influx of capital has included long-term private investment, purchase of Mexican government securities, and loans to Nacional Financiera and other government-owned financial intermediaries. Mexico has been sufficiently credit-worthy to have ready access to the New York financial market (though heavy borrowing led eventually to the massive peso devaluation and repayment crisis of 1982).

The importance of the public sector varies with the indicator one uses. Government's fiscal ability is limited. The export and import duties that earlier provided the bulk of revenue have been eroded over time, and the income and profit taxes that now provide about half of revenue are not easy to collect. Government current expenditures are less than 10 percent of GDP, one of the lowest figures in Latin America and only about half the median for countries of this size and income level. But if one looks instead at capital formation, government looms considerably larger. In the 1940s, public investment was typically 50–55 percent of the national total. With the upsurge of private investment since 1945, the government's share has fallen but remains in the range of 30–40 percent. About two-thirds of this is investment by public corporations rather than by the central government. Infrastructure industries and petroleum are publicly owned, and government also has a substantial ownership share in steel, automobiles, and several other heavy industries.

An especially interesting feature of Mexico's public sector is the network of financial institutions that provides not only capital but guidance and occasionally equity participation in private industries. The oldest and largest of these is Nacional Financiera, established in 1934; but this was followed by creation of additional financieras for particular sectors. Nacional Financiera itself is infrastructure-oriented, about half of its funds going to power, transport, and communications, though it also invests in heavy industry and irrigation. It draws funds from both domestic and foreign sources and makes substantial profits overall. Other financieras, in addition to long-term and short-term lending, sometimes take an equity participation in private enterprises. Financiera officers often sit on the boards of enterprises to which it supplies capital, and private business executives sit on the board of the financiera. Similar relations exist within the private sector, where manufacturing firms are typically linked with banks and finance companies in a way reminiscent of the Japanese Zaibatsu. There are a half-dozen dominant groups of this sort in Mexico, with funds moving readily from industry to industry within the group.

All in all, a remarkable success story, with many special features that underline the uniqueness of each country's experience.

6

Chile, Colombia, Cuba, Peru

We proceed to review other Latin American countries with turning points before 1900. Venezuela, a laggard that reached the turning point only in the mid-1920s, will be considered in chapter 8.

CHILE

Chile is a temperate-zone country, somewhat remote from the main routes of world trade. It is a middle-income country that has been growing for a long time and that could scarcely have been considered ''underdeveloped'' even in 1914. It is a slowly growing economy and, although growth has been slightly faster since 1945 than before that date, the marked speedup that we see in many other countries is not evident. It is a consumption-oriented economy, with an extensive social-security system and low personal savings and without an aggressive policy of public investment.

Turning Point: *circa* 1840

The period of post-independence warfare in Chile was relatively short, and political stability had been restored by 1840. That year also saw the reestablishment of normal commercial relations with Peru, the traditional export market. The California gold rush of 1849, which produced a demand for wheat and other food products, gave a further stimulus to the economy. Thus economic historians tend to date the sustained rise of per capita output from the 1840s.

Intensive Growth since 1840

The Chilean story has been well documented by Mamalakis (1976) and others, so the treatment here will be brief. Further, since the World War II watershed is less marked in Chile than in other Latin American countries, I shall treat the 140 years of intensive growth as a single period.

Population grew steadily from 1830 to 1920, but at a low rate, typically 1.2–1.3 percent per year. As in other countries, this rate accelerated slightly after World War I and more markedly after World War II, as mortality fell without an immediate response of birthrates. Population growth peaked at 3 percent a year from 1959 to 1964. Birthrates then began to fall, and Chile is now well into the demographic transition, with a current rate of natural increase below 2 percent. The population was 83 percent urban in 1970, both population and industry being heavily concentrated in Santiago, Valparaíso, and Concepción.

The growth of total and per capita output for earlier periods is conjectural. Ballisteros and Davis estimate that during the nineteenth century per capita output was rising at 1 percent per year. Mamalakis considers this figure too low and thinks that it was probably closer to 2 percent. He has attempted a more precise estimate for years since 1915, basing his efforts on extensive research into Chilean statistics. His tables show GDP rising in the range of 3–4 percent per year up to 1945 and continuing in the same range since 1945 except for an increase to 5.0 percent in the decade 1960–70. Because the population growth rate has been higher in recent decades, there has actually been a slight *downtrend* in the growth rate of GDP per capita.

Chile has always depended heavily on exports, which have developed in three stages: a wheat era, a nitrate era, and a copper era. In colonial times, wheat and other food products moved north from Chile to the mining areas of Peru. This tie was broken for a time after independence; but in 1840 Peru agreed to lower its tariff on Chilean wheat and this traditional market was partly regained. The California gold rush of 1849 produced a demand for agricultural exports to the West Coast, and Chile was the closest source of supply. Australia was also a substantial and growing market in this period. Wheat thus remained a major export product from about 1860 to 1900. After the turn of the century exports declined because of powerful competition from Argentina and Canada, low-cost producers with shorter trade routes to Europe; because the opening of the Panama Canal reduced Chile's advantage in Pacific markets; and because the growing Chilean population ate into the output of a laggard agricultural sector. Today Chile is a substantial food importer.

Nitrate deposits were discovered in Antofagasta in the 1870s. After victory over Peru and Bolivia in the War of the Pacific (1879–84), which led to incorporation of the nitrate areas into Chilean territory, exports rose rapidly from 510,000 tons in 1884 to 2,702,600 tons in 1913. They remained at about that level until 1929 and then fell sharply under the combined impact of the Depression and the development of cheaper synthetic fertilizers. The collapse of this large industry was a considerable economic disaster.

Government initially tried to own and operate the nitrate fields, but results were unsatisfactory and the government holdings were sold off in the 1890s, mainly to British companies. The companies were quite heavily taxed. An estimate for the period 1890–1920 shows that about 30 percent of the value of output was taken in taxes, which formed about half of all government revenue. Adding payments for labor (12 percent of output value) and other production inputs, it appears that more than half of value added in the industry remained in the country.

Copper was mined in Chile by locally owned concerns as early as the 1830s. In the 1860s Chilean copper was 40 percent of world supply and 65 percent of British imports. But by 1880 the easily workable, small-scale copper deposits were substantially exhausted. The modern story of copper, under foreign rather than local auspices, dates from the entry of the Braden Company in 1904, quickly followed by Anaconda and Kennecott. From that time the big three dominated the industry and exports rose rapidly, especially from 1920 to 1929. Chile was once more the largest copper producer.

The returned value from copper to the Chilean economy was initially quite low. Although wage rates are higher than in other industries and have risen substantially over time, labor productivity has risen so rapidly that the wage share of output has fallen. Blue-collar employment in the mines has also declined over the years, as capital-labor substitution has been encouraged by high wages and heavy social-security charges. Returned value as a percentage of output was nevertheless raised substantially through heavier taxation. The industry was not taxed at all before 1925, perhaps because of the continuing large yield of nitrate taxes, but from the late 1930s taxes were increased sharply. By the late 1950s taxes were taking about 30 percent of the value of output, and other components of returned value another 30 percent. The tax burden was severe enough to reduce new investment in the mines and to produce a running controversy between government and the companies, leading eventually to nationalization of the industry.

These successive waves of expansion raised Chile's exports at rates usually in the range of 6–9 percent per year from 1850 to 1929. After the collapse and recovery of the 1930s, export growth was resumed. Total exports (in millions of U.S. dollars at 1961 prices) rose from 335.4 in 1940 to 1,090.0 in 1970, an average growth rate of 3.8 percent per year. While part of the export proceeds leaked abroad, enough remained in Chile to give a substantial stimulus to domestic demand.

The growth of the industrial sector has been prolonged, gradual, undramatic—as is true of most other aspects of the economy. Flour mills and other agricultural processing establishements appeared as early as 1840, followed by the usual sequence of textiles, clothing, shoes, beverages, and other light consumer-goods industries. By 1907 industry and construction already employed 17.6 percent of the labor force, as against the 37.7 percent employed in agriculture. A striking feature of the industrial structure was the continued persistence of large numbers of small-scale artisans. In 1927 about two-thirds of the industrial labor force—155,000 out of 230,000—was employed in establishments with four or fewer workers.

The years since 1945 have seen the appearance of chemicals, metalworking, and other heavy industries. The Chilean Development Corporation (CORFO), founded in 1939, established the first steelworks in 1950 and encouraged the development of Concepción as a metalworking center. Postwar governments followed import-substitution policies, favoring industry with subsidized credit and low-cost imports of materials and machinery while restricting imports through a complex system of quotas, foreign-exchange controls, licenses, and tariffs. Under this regime, manufacturing output grew at 8.14 percent per year in the 1950s and 5.42 percent in the 1960s and increased its share of GDP to 25.3 percent, compared with agruculture's share of 9.3 percent, in 1970. The resulting industrial structure appears overprotected, overdiversified for the size of the country, not very efficient, and unable to develop export capacity.

The artisans are not gone. In 1970 about half of all industrial employees were in some 70,000 very small establishments (of which about 40 percent were producing clothing and shoes). The larger industrial establishments, as usual, have not been very labor-absorbing. The employment elasticity of manufacturing with respect to output from 1960 to 1970 was a rather typical 0.56 percent. Overpricing of labor through the minimum wage and social-security systems may have contributed to this result. Chile is a well-developed welfare state without the productive capacity that underwrites such a state in the richer industrial countries.

Between 1930 and 1970 manufacturing absorbed only 25 percent of the growth in the labor force. Net labor absorption in agriculture was zero. This has contributed to an inflation of service employment, including a tendency to use government as the "employer of last resort." (The short-lived Allende regime coped with the problem by simply ordering industrial establishements to hire more workers; but this produced a roughly proportionate drop in labor productivity.) Open unemployment was running at 5–8 percent in the 1960s and had risen to 10–14 percent in the mid-1970s.

One of the more puzzling features of the economy is the poor performance of Chilean agriculture, which drags down the overall growth rate and dissipates foreign exchange in food imports. Moreover, performance seems to have worsened over time. Between 1910 and 1930 agricultural output grew at a bit under 3 percent per year. From 1940 to 1973 the average rate was only 2.2 percent. Meanwhile demand was growing at about 4 percent (2.5 percent due to population and 1.5 percent due to income growth). The growing gap has been filled by food imports, which by 1972 were absorbing 30 percent of export earnings. As Mamalakis (1976, p. 131) comments, "Whatever gains in economic independence Chile seemed to achieve through industrial growth and import substitution it lost through agricultural import desubstitution." Agriculture has been unable to perform the functions it is expected to perform in models of successful development.

The reasons for this poor performance are complex, imperfectly known, and in any event cannot be explored here. A typical latifundista system with much absentee ownership is not conducive to high productivity. Belated and inadequate efforts at land reform were made only in the late 1960s. The policy of focusing on import substitution contains well-known biases against agriculture. Government seems also to have been unusually negligent in developing agricultural research and extension, credit facilities, and import supplies.

Recent Chilean experience has been dominated by political controversy. Allende's socialist regime, whatever the merit of its reform program, had a very disorganizing effect on production. The coup that overthrew Allende installed a repressive military regime quite at variance with Chile's long democratic tradition. The new regime made a sharp turn toward reduction of government subsidies and controls and increased reliance on prices and markets, administered by technocrats who were popularly labeled "the Chicago boys," because many of them had been trained in economics at the University of Chicago. These policies contributed to an unusually high (for Chile) GDP growth rate in the middle and late 1970s and was widely hailed as a successful experiment in free-market economics. In the early 1980s, however, the world recession plus some apparent errors in foreign-exchange policy produced an unusually severe recession. Chile is not yet out of the woods. But perhaps it never has been.

COLOMBIA

The economic history of Colombia falls into three distinct phases: (1) extensive growth over most of the nineteenth century, with per capita income stationary or even declining mildly; (2) a turning point around 1885, with export-led growth dominated by coffee lasting until 1929; and (3) the post-1930 period, marked by expansion of manufacturing, a good overall growth rate, and a diversification of exports in terms of both products and destinations.

Extensive Growth

Population was growing throughout the nineteenth century at rates in the range of 1.0–1.5 percent per year. (To jump ahead, the growth rate accelerated to somewhat above 2 percent in the 1920s and 1930s. There was a further acceleration after 1945 associated with mortality reduction, and the growth rate peaked at 2.8 percent from 1951 to 1964. But by 1980 Colombia was well into the demographic transition, with a crude birthrate of about 30 per thousand, compared with earlier rates of 40–45, and a population growth rate from 1975 to 1980 of 2.2 percent.)

McGreevey (1971) judges that from 1830 to 1885 there was some decline in economic welfare. Political conditions were quite unstable, with a president rarely serving out his term. The average tenure of presidents was 14 months in the period 1830–63 and 16 months in 1863–84. (The later increase in political stability is indicated by the fact that since 1900 the average presidential tenure has been 38 months, not very different from the expected 48-month term.)

Successive administrations represented shifting alliances among the elite groups of merchants, large landowners, clerics, and politicians. Neither the small urban middle class nor the rural peasantry had a significant influence on policy. The policies favored by the elite were not such as to generate intensive growth. Land that previously had been reserved for the Indian population for communal use was now turned into transferable private property, with the result that much of it was sold off to large landholders and many Indians became landless laborers. Anticlerical feeling combined with land greed led to expropriation of church lands in 1864, and these plus crown lands also tended to be sold cheaply in large parcels. The latifundia-minifundia division in agriculture crystallized during this period and has continued to the present day.

The elite were free-trade liberals, and effective tariff rates averaged only about 15 percent. Low tariffs led to a flood of imports from 1850 onward. About two-thirds of these were textile imports, and the proportion of domestic consumption provided by imports rather than local artisan production rose from 25 percent in 1855 to 70 percent in 1890. Finally, the elite favored a weak central government, with power concentrated in regional governments, which they could readily control. The federal government was systematically stripped of its taxing powers, which were either abolished or transferred to lower levels of government. The central government was unable to carry out public works and its army, which fluctuated in the range of 6,000–10,000 men, was quite inadequate to police regional and local disputes, which were decided by battles among private armies.

Population was concentrated in the highland areas because of the prevalence of malaria in the lowlands. Transport costs were high because of the rugged topography. The country was still thinly settled, the farm area being only one-seventh as large in 1870 as in 1960. Large landholders tended to occupy the better valley lands, which were devoted mainly to cattle raising, forcing the small farmers up onto the hillsides. There were several export boomlets—in gold up to 1840, in tobacco from 1840 to 1875 (which failed because poor quality control caused the Colombian crop to lose out in competition with Java), in cotton during the American Civil War, in quinine, indigo, sugar, and cocoa. But these had little spillover effect on the subsistence economy, and Colombia did not succeed in developing a reliable export staple.

The Turning Point: *circa* 1885

Political conditions were somewhat stabilized by the advent of the Nuñez regime in 1884 (though there was renewed civil war from 1899 to 1903, before the presidency of Rafael Reyes in 1904 ushered in thirty years of unbroken Conservative Party rule). The turning point to intensive growth is usually identified with the rise of coffee production in Antioquia province during the 1880s. Coffee is a good peasant crop. There are no appreciable economies of scale, and coffee can be grown alongside food crops—indeed, interplanting of food crops with coffee trees was to become a standard feature of Colombian agriculture. Coffee needs a light volcanic soil, 40 inches or so of rainfall, and moderate temperatures, which at this latitude are found between 1,000 and 1,800 meters. Much of the land in Antioquia fits this description. Antioquia was also a relatively prosperous area as a result of previous gold-mining activities that had produced experimentation with joint-stock enterprises and a strong entrepreneurial tradition. Its population growth in the midnineteenth century was already more than twice as high as the national average. Smallholders also had relatively good access to land. While there was thus a strong regional aspect to export development, coffee growing was rather wisely diffused throughout highland areas adjacent to Antioquia.

Intensive Growth, 1885-1930

As coffee growing took hold, government contributed by encouraging railroad building. Railroad mileage rose from 202 kilometers in 1885 to 1,212 in 1915, reducing the cost of getting coffee to the coast from $70 a ton to $19 a ton, with a consequent higher return to growers. Coffee exports rose from 107,000 bags in 1880 to 1,100,000 bags in 1915, by which time they formed 55 percent of export earnings. This percentage rose as high as 80 percent in later years as the coffee export boom continued, paralleling the 1900–29 boom in Brazil and contributing to the eventual oversupply and collapse of prices.

Colombian coffee production was largely a small-scale peasant activity. The first coffee census, taken in 1932, counted some 150,000 coffee farms, most of which were less than ten hectares in size. So many farms meant that the export proceeds were widely distributed throughout the population, and gave a strong stimulus to domestic demand. McGreevey (1971) estimates that "in the half-century from the 1870's to the early 1930's a fifth to a quarter of Colombia's rural population was brought out of subsistence cultivation and into the market for coffee."

It is not surprising, then, that the first textile mills were established in Medellín by Antioquian entrepreneurs soon after 1900. Coffee money provided both demand and a source of investible funds. Important manufacturing establishments were soon founded in Bogotá, Cali, and Barranquilla. But while factory production grew along normal light-industry lines, artisan production continued to supply a large share of manufacturing output. The census of 1870 counted 305,000 artisans, of whom about two-thirds were women, engaged mainly in textiles as a sideline to agricultural production. Under the pressure of import competition, the number of artisans fell by about one-third. But it then stabilized at around 200,000—190,302 in 1912, 197,000 in 1925, and 224,000 in 1938—much larger than the number of factory employees at these dates. The only indication of what these people were doing comes from a census of some 18,000 artisan enterprises in the city of Santander in 1892, which shows the following distribution: soft-fiber textiles, 41.6 percent; hard-fiber textiles, 27.9 percent; clothing and tailoring, 9.6 percent; food, beverages, and tobacco, 5.7 percent; soap and candles, 7.1 percent;

pottery and tile- making, 3.3 percent; woodworking and carpentry, 2.3 percent; iron and other metalworking, 1.5 percent.

Part of the development of this period included the improvement of transport facilities:

1. The introduction of steam-powered boats for coastal and river transport, particularly on the Magdalena River, which reduced river-freight rates by about one-quarter.
2. Railroad construction, which began in the 1880s but proceeded rather slowly, partly because construction was left to private entrepreneurs with government providing only land subsidies. Only one-quarter of the eventual mileage had been built by 1910. The main period of railroad building was the 1920s, at which time the government of Antioquia played a prominent role. There was always a close connection between coffee expansion and railroad construction. The railroads made the expansion possible by cutting transport costs by 75 percent, while coffee provided most of the freight traffic for the railroads.
3. The opening of the Panama Canal in 1914 was a very significant event.* Colombia's western ports became much more viable, and their percentage of ocean traffic grew rapidly as compared with the northern ports.
4. Road construction is more recent, the roads remaining in miserable condition for most of this period. Not until 1945 did highway ton-miles rise above railway ton-miles.

It would be convenient to summarize the growth of the economy from 1885 to 1930 in terms of GDP and GDP per capita, but no one has ventured to make such estimates. It is almost certain that per capita income was rising, though with fluctuations associated with the varying fortunes of exports (in which gold, petroleum, bananas, and other products were important along with coffee.) It is certain also that growth was uneven regionally, with Antioquia enjoying a rate well above the national average. Further, a considerable part of the population—small subsistence farmers in the interior of the country—was largely left out of the growth process.

Intensive Growth, 1930–80

Accounts of the economy tend to pass lightly over the 1929–45 period. We can surmise that, as elsewhere in Latin America, the collapse of exports in the early 1930s must have stimulated domestic industrialization and a turn toward more

---

*What is now Panama was originally part of Colombia. Its secession and creation of a separate republic was stage-managed by the United States in order to secure the canal concession on more favorable terms. This led to a prolonged dispute, which ended with payment by the United States of a $25 million indemnity to Colombia in 1922.

inward-looking policies and that intensive growth, while interrupted in the aggregate and reoriented in detail, was not brought to a halt. I shall pick up the story around 1950, since most recent studies focus heavily on the 1950–80 period.

After a period of guerrilla warfare ("la violencia"), in which many thousands were killed, the political situation was stabilized by an agreement under which the presidency rotates automatically between the Liberal and Conservative parties. Both parties are dominated by a civilian elite that has managed to keep the military under control. The lower strata of society have relatively little leverage, and the main outlines of policy reflect elite preferences: light taxation, a small public sector, a small military budget, inattention to agriculture and especially to small-scale agriculture, and opposition to land reform.

Colombia has four rather distinct agricultures: coffee growing for export, by small and large farmers; livestock raising, rather large scale and mainly for domestic consumption; "commercial" farming of other crops, involving considerable mechanization and use of modern inputs; and traditional small-scale production of food crops. These differ substantially in scale, productivity, income level, and rate of increase in income. Coffee farmers did best in the 1950s and 1960s, livestock producers next best, and small traditional farmers least well. Even this last group has probably gained somewhat, but the evidence is weak. Some of the most important policy problems involve a possible shift in the "mix" of farm types—for example, taking land out of livestock production, where it is used extensively with low yield per hectare, and turning it over to smallholders who would crop it more intensively.

The pattern of inputs and productivity is typically dualistic. As farm size decreases, labor inputs per hectare increase steadily. For cropped land, the labor/hectare ratio is five to ten times as high on the smallest units as on the largest. Given a declining marginal productivity of labor, this allocation of labor time is inefficient. Output *per hectare* is substantially higher—as much as double—on the smallest units; and this is true of coffee growing as well as of food crops. But output *per unit of labor* is substantially lower, contributing to marked inequality of incomes.

Despite migration to the cities, population has continued to pile up on the land. The rural population has been growing at about 1 percent a year, compared with 4 percent growth of the city population. The main alternatives for easing pressure on the land are purchase of large holdings and their subdivision into smallholdings and colonization of new land. Colombia still has a good deal of unoccupied land, but bringing it into use requires substantial public investment in roads and other infrastructure. Activities are under way on both fronts, though scarcely on a scale adequate to the need.

Agricultural output has grown at a moderate rate—about 3 percent a year from 1950 to 1967, almost 4 percent a year after the shift in 1967 to more outward-looking policies. Part of this increase has come from movement of farm workers from lower-productivity to higher-productivity areas. (The variation in male daily wage rates among departments, which gives some indication of productivity, is almost 3:1; and research studies indicate that labor migration is strongly related to wage differences.) There has also been substantial technical progress since 1950, including mechanization on the larger farms, aided by enlarged credit facilities, and introduction of improved barley, wheat, and corn varieties.

With this modest growth of output it is a little surprising that Colombia has remained self-sufficient in food and indeed has shifted from a net import to a net export position. The explanation may be partly that, at Colombia's present income level, the income elasticity of demand for food is rather low. Berry estimates it at about 0.5.

As in other Latin American countries, export pessimism prevailed in the immediate postwar period, and until 1967 the main emphasis was on import-substituting industrialization. The devices used are familiar: high tariffs, foreign-exchange licensing, an overvalued exchange rate, tax and credit incentives to industry. The drive for industrialization produced a certain number of "horror stories," industries introduced prematurely on an inadequate scale, with high costs relative to world price levels. These included automobiles, petrochemicals and some other chemicals, electric appliances, such as refrigerators and washing machines, synthetic fibers, and some alcoholic beverages. But these sectors comprise only about one-third of value added in manufacturing, and Diaz Alejandro (1976) comments that "what is really remarkable is how much of Colombian manufacturing operates near world prices." This is confirmed by an IBRD study which compared domestic prices with import prices for a long list of manufactured goods. For most goods, the domestic price was equal to or up to one-and-a-half times the foreign price. Automobiles, however, were four times as expensive and trucks two-and-a-half times as expensive.

Manufacturing output grew quite rapidly during this period, though the growth rate declined from 7.25 percent per year in 1950–56 to 5.68 percent in 1956–67. As usual, industrial employment grew much less rapidly than output—only 1 percent a year from 1956 to 1967. A rapid increase in labor costs may have contributed to this result. The real hourly wage rate in manufacturing almost doubled between 1958 and 1971. Fringe benefits are also substantial, amounting to about 40 percent of base rates. The gap between earnings in manufacturing and traditional activities, which was estimated in 1970 at about 3:1, has been widening. Limited labor absorption in industry, together with heavy migration to the cities, has produced the usual problems: open unemployment in the cities running at around 10 percent (though research indicates that part of this is "luxury unemployment" of educated young people who can afford to wait for "good" white-collar jobs); a decline in labor force participation rates, which are low compared with most other Latin American countries; and the forcing of labor into self-employment in the "spongy" sectors of the economy. A 1970 ILO employment study of Colombia, prepared by an interagency team, reported that self-employed workers as a proportion of total employment amounted to 31 percent in commerce, 24 percent in construction, 21 percent in transport, and 17 percent even in manufacturing.

The structure of manufacturing is markedly dualistic. In most branches of industry small and large firms coexist, sometimes making different products (small pots and pans *versus* washing machines and refrigerators), but sometimes competing directly, as in shoes or furniture. Output per worker in the largest plants is two to four times as high as that in the smallest. Large firms also pay substantially higher wages, but the wage gap is not as large as the productivity gap. In addition, the large firms seem to get somewhat better workers, they have better access to capital, and they use considerably more capital per worker. So they are very profitable—earnings of 30–40 percent on capital are not uncommon. High profits, associated in some cases with monopoly positions, plus quite well organized trade unions and a public policy under which hiring of strikebreakers is forbidden, help to account for the rapid increase in real wages noted earlier.

There is even a three-level industrial structure, in the sense that handicraft production continues to be important. In the late 1960s, when factory employment was around 300,000, there were still an estimated 150,000–200,000 handicraft workers. Their share of manufacturing output, however, had fallen from 25 percent in 1950 to 15 percent in 1968, implying a productivity level only one-third that of factory workers.

On the trade front, there was a shift in 1967 toward an outward-looking stance favorable to exports. The change was signaled by adoption of a flexible exchange-rate system, under which the value of the Colombian currency fell within a few years by more than 40 percent. Export incentives were introduced and other policies readjusted. The effect of this policy shift was quite dramatic. Merchandise exports, whose dollar value had risen hardly at all from 1956 to 1967, now began to rise at more than 7 percent per year. Contrary to the view of export pessimists, the indications are that demand for Colombia's actual and potential nontraditional exports is quite price-elastic. It was these exports that shot up most rapidly after 1967. The share of coffee, which in 1960 was still 72 percent, had fallen by 1976 to 46 percent. The share of manufactured exports had risen to 21 percent; and other resource-based "minor exports"—bananas, sugar, tobacco, cotton—had also risen rapidly. There was also a marked diversification of export markets, with the share going to the United States falling rapidly and the Common Market share rising.

Even manufacturing grew faster with the opening of export outlets. Its growth rate rose from 5.68 percent in 1956–67 to 7.62 percent in 1967–72. The growth rate of primary production rose from about 3 to about 4 percent, and the growth of real GDP rose from 4.57 percent to 6.08 percent. Diaz Alejandro (1976, p. 224) gives a plausible interpretation of this improved performance.

Higher growth rates in foreign exchange receipts, primarily derived from merchandise exports, allowed the government systematically to follow more expansionary fiscal and monetary policies than had been possible from 1956–67. Such stimuli, and the positive reactions they triggered in private expenditure, led to a higher level of resource utilization almost across the board within the Colombian economy. Widespread pockets of under-utilized labor, capital, and land were gradually brought into production without any major sector being required to contract so as to release resources for better use elsewhere. The foreign exchange scarcity of 1956–67 forced fiscal and monetary policies sporadically to apply severe limits on aggregate demand; these restrictions were clumsy in the sense that nearly all sectors suffered, whether or not they were heavy users of foreign exchange.

These macroeconomic gains from liberalization, Diaz argues, were more important than the static resource-allocation effects on which trade theory has traditionally focused.

The public sector is relatively small, decentralized, and conservatively managed. In terms of either current or capital expenditure, the departments and municipalities are about equal to the federal government, and the autonomous public corporations are somewhat larger than either. Public consumption as a percentage of GDP is among the lowest in Latin America. The current surplus is normally sufficient to finance most public investment, the remainder being covered by moderate foreign borrowing. Public investment is about one-quarter of total investment, and public savings about one-quarter of total savings, these proportions having risen somewhat since 1950.

Colombia's growth record is superior and has improved since the turn toward export-oriented policies in 1967. The average annual growth rate of GDP was 4.5 percent in 1960–65, 5.5 percent in 1965–70, 6.4 percent in 1970–75, and 6.0 percent in 1975–80—indicating an increase in per capita output during the 1970s of almost 4 percent, well above the average for the ''developed'' countries.

CUBA

Cuba is an extreme example of specialized monoculture. Its dependence on sugar is almost as great as Saudi Arabia's dependence on oil. Sugar has traditionally formed between one-quarter and one-half of GDP and 70–90 percent of Cuban exports. To an unusual degree the economy has revolved around fluctuations in world demand for sugar and the sugar price level. While this dependence had some unfavorable consequences, sugar had by 1950 produced a level of per capita income in Cuba higher than that of any other tropical country.

The country's political history falls into three stages. From its first settlement until 1898 it was a Spanish colony. After 1898 the United States exercised predominant political and economic influence. Nominally independent, Cuba was in fact a quasi colony. The revolution of 1958 led to expropriation of the large U.S. investments in Cuba, a complete break with the United States, and a shift to economic dependence on the Soviet Union.

Extensive Growth

Sugar did not have an early success in Cuba, mainly because of shortage of labor. The Spanish administration initially did not follow the Portuguese policy of importing slave labor, which led to early sugar development in Brazil. During the seventeenth and eithteenth centuries Cuba's abundant land was devoted mainly to cattle raising. The population of the island in 1700 was only 100,000, which by 1800 had grown to about 400,000. Tobacco began to be cultivated in the eighteenth century, mainly by smallholders, and it was expanded considerably from 1800 to 1850. The rise of sugar dates from about 1820, when importation of slaves for the first time provided a flexible labor supply for the industry. Output rose from 90,000 tons in 1827 to 300,000 tons in 1850 and the number of sugar mills rose from 870 to 1,500.

After about 1850, however, the industry began to run into trouble. The rapid rise of European beet sugar in midcentury brought a sharp break in prices. Cuban slave labor was relatively inefficient and, after the freeing of the slaves in 1880, had to be bought on market terms. The supply of suitable land also began to run out.

The response was a reorganization of the industry, with greater concentration of production. This brought a renewed expansion of output from about 1880 onward. Small sugar mills were eliminated and replaced by larger *centrales,* which bought cane on contract from the *colons.* Some colons owned their own land, but increasingly land belonged to the centrales, which rented it on sharecropping terms. By 1890 the number of mills had fallen from 1,500 to 400 (and was to continue falling to 157 by 1925). Labor supply was augmented by massive importation of free or semifree ("contract") labor from Yucatán, Jamaica, and even China. There was also extensive development of railroad lines, often owned by the centrales, which reinforced the dependence of the colons.

Turning Point: *circa* 1900

The reorganization and expansion of the sugar industry in the 1880s may have raised per capita output in the island, but statistical documentation is weak. This was also a period of internal political disturbance. It is safer, therefore, to date the turning point from the United States takeover after the Spanish-American War of 1898. The substantial integration of Cuba into the American economy, although it had some disadvantages, did bring an assured outlet for sugar and a substantial inflow of investment; it initiated a period of export-led growth that continued until the 1958 revolution.

Intensive Growth, 1900–58

Cuba was occupied by American troops from 1898 to 1902. As a condition for ending the military occupation, Cuba was obliged to write into its constitution a provision that the United States might intervene at any time to ensure a government able to protect life, liberty, and property. This provision encouraged American investment in sugar and infrastructure industries, since investors felt assured of U.S. government protection. But it was also a severe restriction of Cuban sovereignty. After an armed rebellion against the Cuban government, the country was reoccupied from 1906 to 1909. In response to the Negro Rebellion of 1912, U.S. troops and battleships were sent in to protect American sugar and mining interests. The troops entered Cuba once more during World War I, remaining from 1917 to 1922.

On the economic side, under a Reciprocal Trade Agreements Act of 1902, Cuba and the United States gave a 20 percent tariff preference to each others' products. Significantly, this preference applied to Cuban raw sugar but not to refined sugar, the intent being to confine refining operations to the United States. By 1909, all of Cuba's sugar was going to the United States, which also provided the bulk of Cuba's imports. Although preferred access to the American market was an advantage, it also increased Cuba's dependence, since its continuation depended entirely on U.S. trade policy. This became clear in the 1930s, when Cuba's market share was restricted and it was obliged to unload sugar on the world market at depressed prices.

Before resuming the sugar story, let us outline other developments of the "American period." Population more than tripled between 1900 and 1950. The crude deathrate fell from 23.7 per thousand in 1900–04 to 13.3 in 1930–34, reflecting improved nutrition and medical facilities. There was a further decline to 11.3 in 1950–54. The sharp post–World War II decline observed in most other third-world countries is not present here, since by 1930 Cuba was already approaching "developed-country" levels. Birthrate behavior is also appropriate to a relatively high income country, the rate falling from 44.6 per thousand in 1900–04 to 31.3 in 1930–34. The rate of natural increase thus trended upward only slightly, peaked at 2.1 percent from 1950–60, and then fell as birthrates continued their downward course.

The United States invested heavily in Cuba after 1900; Canada, Britain, and other sources invested smaller amounts. U.S. investment rose from $50 million in 1898 to $205 million in 1911 to $1,140 million in 1927. Of this, about $600 million was invested in sugar, $120 million in railroads and shipping, $115 million in public utilities, $50 million in mines, and $50 million in real estate and mortgages. By 1925 about half of all the capital invested in sugar came from the United States, and about half of the mills were under U.S. (or, in a few cases, joint U.S.-Cuban) control. Most of the American owners were either sugar-refining companies, which were integrating backward both in the United States and abroad, or banks that had taken over land because of default on loans, especially after the sharp price drops of 1920–21 and 1929–30.

The vulnerability of the economy is suggested by its unusually high trade ratio with exports plus imports/GDP running in the range of 70 to 90 percent. The dominant export was raw sugar, which amounted to 90 percent of the total in some years. Imports were more diversified, and by 1950 about one-quarter of imports were foodstuffs, reflecting the heavy specialization of Cuban agriculture in sugar. There was little development of factory industry. Writings on Cuba scarcely mention industry, which is significant in itself. It is interesting, too, that Wallich (1950), writing in the late 1940s and suggesting possible future directions for Cuban development, urged more development of light manufacturing industries. Heavy industry he considered unfeasible because of the limited size of the market. In estimating the composition of GDP as of 1938, he places sugar growing and processing at 22.4 percent, other agricultural production at 13.4 percent, and industry (other than sugar) at 12.6 percent, most of which must have been handicraft production of clothing and other household needs.

The government sector was small, Wallich estimating it at 10.7 percent of GDP in 1938. Export and import taxes provided 70–80 percent of government revenue until the 1930s, when falling sugar prices cut the share to about 50 percent. Although no details of government expenditure are available, Birnberg and Resnick (1975) state that ''government expenditures emphasized construction of the railroads, roads, harbors, sewers, telephones, and aqueducts used to promote the development of sugar exports.'' In their view Cuba conforms to a model of colonial development in which exports provide government revenue and revenue is plowed back into infrastructure to support further increase of exports in an expanding circular process.

The overall picture is one of export-dominated growth and, while some of the export proceeds leaked abroad in profits and dividends, enough remained in the economy to generate growth of infrastructure, commerce, finance, urban services, and a large tourist trade. Since import capacity rose along with exports, Cuba was able to import manufactured consumer goods as well as a considerable part of its food supply; imports reduced pressure to promote local industry or to raise productivity in food-crop production.

Sugar production and exports rose rapidly up to 1929. Output rose from 1 million tons in 1903 to 2.4 million in 1913, 4.0 million in 1919, and 5.0 million in 1925, an average annual growth rate of 7.1 percent. The share of sugar exports going to the United States, however, fell from an initial 100 percent to 78 percent in 1929. As Cuban production continued to grow, part of the output had to be diverted to Europe at lower prices. Cuba's share of the U.S. market peaked at 56 percent in 1922–26 and then began a long, sustained decline.

The growth of world demand for cane sugar slowed after about 1920 due to slow increase of population and income in the industrial countries plus continued expansion of beet-sugar production in the United States and Europe. The onset of the Great Depression brought a sharp price drop in 1929–30. Of particular importance to Cuba, however, was loss of its preferred position in the U.S. market. The Hawley-Smoot Tariff Act of 1930 substantially raised the tariff on Cuban sugar. In 1934 the United States adopted a system of import quotas for sugar based on average imports from each supplier in 1931–33. Since imports from Cuba during this base period had already been reduced by the Hawley-Smoot tariff, Cuba received a relatively small quota. Hawaii, Puerto Rico, and the Philippines, which as possessions of the United States had not been affected by the tariff, received more favorable treatment. Between 1929 and 1934 their share of the U.S. market rose from 23 to 42 percent, U.S. production rose from 19 to 28 percent of total supply, and Cuba's market share fell to 29 percent. In absolute terms, Cuba's exports to the United States were about half as large in the 1930s as they had been in the 1920s. The squeeze was sufficiently severe that Cuba took steps to restrict sugar acreage and output.

Although there are no GDP data for this period, Dominguez (1978) concludes that "there was a decade and a half of trendless economic change" lasting until 1948. After that time, however, per capita income growth was resumed and continued up to the 1958 revolution. Dominguez's estimates show the index of per capita income rising from 100 in 1946 to 134 in 1957. The index of real non-agricultural wages rose from 100 in 1946 to 162 in 1958, and real wages in agriculture were also rising from 1949 onward. The wage-salary share of national income rose from 55.3 percent in 1945 to 62.3 percent in 1958, leading Dominguez to conclude that "even those at the bottom of the social structure had benefitted from this period of relative prosperity."

On the eve of the revolution, then, Cuba had one of the highest per capita incomes in Latin America. In terms of educational facilities, health facilities, and social-security protection it was one of the top three Latin American countries. But one could also point to weaknesses in the economy. The heavy dependence on sugar, which Mesa-Largo (1981) estimates at 28–29 percent of GNP and 84 percent of exports in 1950–58 left the economy vulnerable to U.S. quota policies and swings in world sugar prices. Sugar had small backward linkages. Even bags for sugar were imported, along with all the machinery and transport equipment. Forward linkages were also small since raw sugar was refined mainly in the United States. There was substantial surplus labor. Mesa-Largo estimates that in 1958 open unemployment amounted to 16 percent and underemployment to an additional 14 percent of the labor force. The population was polarized between a small upper class of unenterprising owners and a large mass of low-skilled laborers. The governing oligarchy was responsive mainly to the sugar interests, internal and external, and to other U.S. investors.

Economic Growth since 1958

The sources of the 1958 revolution and the reasons for its easy victory will no doubt be debated by historians for some time. At any event, 1958 marks a distinctly new period of economic history, whose outlines are now becoming clearer through the work of Mesa-Largo and others.

Economic policy has passed through several phases. The initial emphasis was on collectivization of production. Even agriculture was 70 percent collectivized by

1963. All other types of production, including petty trade and repair services, were fully collectivized. There was no central planning at this stage, though there was a limited amount of sector and unit planning. A strong emphasis was placed on reducing income disparities and on setting a minimum consumption level through comprehensive rationing. The investment/GDP ratio fell considerably.

After several years of agitation led by Che Guevara, Premier Castro in 1966 adopted a Maoist policy line. Money incentives were deemphasized, wage differences were reduced, moral incentives were stressed, and farmers' private plots were abolished. During this period, which lasted until 1970, production was seriously disorganized and GDP fell substantially. Poor economic performance no doubt contributed to a shift in 1971 to a generally Soviet pattern of economic organization. The tendencies of the previous period were reversed. Farmers were allowed to sell above-quota output on private markets. Interest, profit, and economic accounting were restored to their normal role in enterprise management. Bonus funds were established. Management was decentralized by splitting the previous 300 state enterprises into some 3,000 units. Small-scale private repair and construction services, without employees, were permitted. A start was made on serious annual planning. Under the new system production recovered from 1971 to 1975 then leveled off from 1975 to 1979.

Turning from policies to accomplishments, we note first that there has been little progress in diversifying the production pattern or in reducing external economic dependence. Official tables on the sector distribution of output since 1960 show only small sectoral shifts. The industrial sector is still small. Textile and shoe production seems not to have risen over the twenty years. Beer and liquor are up, but cigars and rubber tires are down. Cement, steel products, electricity, fertilizers, and some consumer durables show sizable percentage increases but from a very small base.

In agriculture, sugar is still king; it continues to provide 75–85 percent of all exports. Production has fluctuated widely from year to year, in the range of four to eight million tons, with no visible trend. An initial antipathy to sugar was followed by an effort to push sugar in order to earn foreign exchange. The crash program of 1970 did yield an all-time high of 8.5 million tons but drained the rest of the economy of resources; so this policy was abandoned, and production has since returned to a more normal level. Food production was adversely affected by the Maoist period. The pig and poultry population fell drastically between 1965 and 1970 and, although poultry have now recovered to the 1965 level, pigs have not yet done so. Food imports continue to be about one-quarter of total imports. The only area of food production that has done well is fisheries, which have been aided by use of newer and larger boats.

As for external dependence, the export/GDP ratio was 30.6 percent from 1954 to 1958, fell to 14.1 percent by 1962, then recovered to 33.8 percent in 1978. The import ratio went through a similar cycle and stood at 35.1 percent in 1978. There is a consistent negative trade balance, compensated by foreign credits.

Comparing 1959 with 1974, machinery and transport equipment rose only from 19 percent to 21 percent of total imports, while fuels and minerals rose from 9 to 10 percent. These figures confirm the small size of the industrial sector and the lack of the drive for industrialization one commonly finds in a socialist economy.

While external dependence has not been reduced, the direction of dependence has shifted. About 50 percent of total trade is with the Soviet Union, 20 percent with other socialist economies, and 30 percent with market economies (though the market economies provide about 40 percent of Cuba's imports). The Soviet Union subsidizes Cuba by buying sugar at more than the world price and by selling oil at less than the world price. There is typically a trade deficit with both sets of trading partners. As of 1977, Cuba owed about $5 billion to the Soviet Union and $4.2 billion to market economies, principally Spain and Argentina.

Open unemployment was reduced during the 1960s by forbidding dismissal of workers and by absorbing the unemployed into the state sector. This of course affects output per worker, which fell drastically between 1962 and 1970. Since 1970 productivity has recovered somewhat in industry, but not in agriculture. Post-1971 economic policies have also brought some reappearance of open unemployment, primarily of young people in the cities.

Turning to macroeconomic data, we note first a marked slowdown of population growth. The Castro regime initially showed the orthodox Marxist opposition to birth control, but by the early 1970s it had shifted to the view that population is a problem. Abortions, contraceptive pills, and IUD's are now freely available. This may partly account for a drop in the crude birthrate from 26.1 per thousand in 1958 to 15.3 in 1978. Thus the rate of natural increase has fallen from about 2 percent to about 1 percent per year. There has also been a "brain drain" from Cuba of more than 500,000 emigrants, including about half the doctors and large numbers of teachers, other professionals, managers, and technicians.

Following socialist practice, the national accounting totals run in terms of gross *material* product (GMP). The only figures available, however, are in current prices; and the official contention that, since there has been little inflation, these can be taken as equivalent to real values is scarcely credible. To form an opinion of changes in per capita income, then, one has to fall back on physical indicators. The FAO index of agricultural output, with 1959 as 100, stood in 1976 at 105.7; but because of population growth the index of per capita output had fallen from 100 to 73.8. This drop in real income is supported by estimates of calorie availability per capita, which show a decline between 1958 and 1978; and it is supported also by production data for individual crops, most of which show a level or declining trend. The only products that show an increase in total (but not necessarily in per capita) output are fish, eggs, citrus fruits, potatoes, and tomatoes.

I noted earlier that textile and shoe production show no upward trend, which means a substantial decline in per capita terms. Imports of consumer goods (other than food) have fallen from 31 percent to 13 percent of total imports. Further indications can be obtained from the rationing system. Rationing in Cuba is pervasive, covering not only basic food items but almost everything else in daily use: cigarettes, cigars, gasoline, detergent, soap, toilet paper, toothpaste, clothing, and shoes. Rations were cut during the disorganized 1960s, touched bottom in 1969, then recovered; but for almost every item the 1978 ration was still only equal to or below the 1962 level. The rationing system is accompanied by a three-level price system: (1) the ration of each good is sold at a relatively low official price; (2) supplies permitting, the state stores will sell amounts above the ration at a substantially higher price ("parallel price"); (3) still higher prices prevail on the black market and in private farmers' markets. Thus it is obviously difficult to infer the size of real incomes from data on money incomes.

The physical data suggest that, over the period 1958–78, real income per capita probably fell moderately. The main qualification is that supply of some public services, notably educational services, has increased. Government has done somewhat less well on health services and quite poorly on housing, where there is a large and growing deficit. The rural-urban gap has been reduced by the agricultural minimum wage and by extension of education and other social services to the countryside. The gap between the lowest and highest urban wages is also smaller than before. Thus it is possible that the very poorest groups in the population may have gained, even though average per capita income has probably fallen.

PERU

Peru is really three countries:

1. The coastal region, which contains virtually all of factory industry and large-scale estate agriculture (sugar and cotton), as well as a large part of food production. Population is concentrated in the Lima-Callao area, which produces well over half the output of the "corporate sector." When we speak of economic growth, we are speaking mainly of this region.
2. The Andean highlands (the "sierra"). Apart from the mining centers, this region is dominated by herding and food production by simple, traditional methods. Its income level is markedly below that of the coastal region, its growth has been slower, and the income gap has widened.
3. The tropical lowlands east of the Andes, which are very thinly populated and which thus far have failed to yield the oft-predicted riches of the Amazon.

Although nineteenth-century export growth in Peru places it clearly within the time period of this chapter, in other aspects the country appears to be a late developer—late in industrialization, late in moving away from laissez-faire toward interventionism, late in eroding the power of the traditional elite, late in paying serious attention to agrarian reform. This slowness of modernization is no doubt related to an unusually high rate of export expansion, which has prolonged the era of export-led growth. From 1830 to 1870 the quantum index of Peruvian exports grew at almost 7 percent a year. Again, from 1890 to 1929 both the quantum and value indexes grew at about 7 percent a year. After a period of relative stagnation from 1930 to 1950, export growth was resumed at an even higher rate, the quantum index rising from 103 in 1950 to 395 in 1970. Small wonder that successive governments, largely dominated by exports interests, tended to focus on export promotion rather than import substitution.

The export growth rate, in turn, is linked to an unusual diversity of export products. The list of products that have been important at one time or another includes guano, sugar, cotton, wool, gold, silver, copper, lead and zinc, iron ore, rubber, petroleum, and fish meal. Each product has had its ups and downs, but some were usually expanding while others were declining, thus maintaining the momentum of overall growth.

Extensive Growth

The export story begins with the "age of guano"; guano—deposits of bird droppings that may extend hundreds of feet in depth—is a rich source of nitrogen fertilizer and for a while Peru had a virtual monopoly on its supply. After independence in 1821, Peru was racked for some time by civil wars and disputes with Chile. By 1840, however, a settlement had been reached with Chile providing for normal commercial relations. The guano boom began in 1840 and ended around 1880, when the deposits were substantially exhausted. Peru then turned toward nitrates, but lost its rich nitrate area to Chile in the War of the Pacific (1879–84). Peru sank back into being an agricultural country whose main exports, apart from the traditional silver, were sugar, cotton, and wool.

The spread effects of the guano-export revenue were quite limited. Guano was sold through foreign consignees, initially British, later the Dreyfus firm in Paris. These firms set the selling price and, being interested mainly in volume, set it quite low. Their expenses, sales commissions, and interest charges on advances to the Peruvian government absorbed a good deal of the sales proceeds. The Peruvian government did receive a share, which in fact provided about 80 percent of government revenue, but this money seems to have been used mainly for transfer payments: repayment of foreign loans dating from the early independence era; indemnities to Peruvians who had lost property during the civil wars; and indemnities to former slave-owners after the abolition of slavery in 1855. The only important developmental expenditure was construction of two railway lines—a line from Lima to the interior mining centers and a line from Arequipa to Cuzco.

Turning Point: *circa* 1880

It is not plausible, then, to regard the guano boom as a turning point toward intensive growth, which is more properly dated from around the end of the Pacific War. The agricultural exports that grew in importance during the 1880s and 1890s provided a much larger returned value to the Peruvian economy and gave a strong stimulus to domestic demand, initiating a period of rapid and diversified growth—in exports, in manufacturing, in infrastructure, in commerce and finance—under predominantly local ownership and control.

Because of Peru's continuing dependence on exports and its failure to make the shift toward industrialization made by most other Latin American countries in the 1930s, we shall depart from our usual subdivision of the intensive-growth era. Instead of a chronological break, which in the Peruvian case did not occur, we shall deal first with export performance over the past century and then with domestic sectors of the economy.

Intensive Growth since 1880: The Export Story

Peru's agricultural and mineral exports have differing ownership and production characteristics, which influence their returned value to the domestic economy. Mining enterprises, though often initiated by Peruvians, had by 1910 come mainly under foreign control. Agriculture, on the other hand, is locally owned. Sugar is a large-scale plantation industry, but the profits of the "sugar barons" tend to be invested widely in manufacturing and other industries. Cotton production is generally smaller in scale than sugar and has high returned value and also strong forward linkages to textile production. Wool, including alpaca and sheep wool, is grown in the high Andes by both small-scale Indian producers and larger-scale hacienda owners.

The takeover of silver, copper, and petroleum production after 1900 came about through large firms (predominately from the United States) buying out smaller-scale Peruvian producers, who usually sold out quite cheerfully. Thorp and Bertram (1978) surmise that the foreign firms valued the future income stream from the mines more highly than did the local producers, enabling both sides to make what seemed to each a good bargain. Government tolerated the takeover activity and made additional mining concessions to the foreign firms on what seem in retrospect to have been very generous terms.

From 1890 to 1930 export volume grew at about 7 percent a year; but the total masks quite different performance of individual products. The Amazon region of Peru participated with Brazil in the great rubber boom of 1890–1910. In 1910 rubber was 18 percent of Peru's exports, but within a few years its share had fallen almost to zero. Oil, on the other hand, spurted from zero in 1900 to 30 percent of exports in 1930. Agricultural exports grew somewhat in importance relative to mineral exports, but this masks a relative decline in sugar and a marked expansion of cotton. Sugar production leveled off after 1920 because of growing competition from beet sugar and other cane producers. Cotton continued to do well because of rising domestic consumption as well as strong demand for Peruvian long-staple cotton on the world market. Cotton acreage rose from 23,000 hectares in 1901 to 127,000 hectares in 1930; and cotton exports, only one-quarter of sugar exports in

1900, were 50 percent larger by 1930. On the minerals front, silver production peaked in 1900–04 and then began a long decline. Falling silver production was counterbalanced by sustained expansion of copper, which was insignificant in 1890 but two-and-a-half times as large as silver by 1930.

The Great Depression brought the usual sequence of declining export value in the early 1930s followed by recovery later in the decade. But Peru's exports recovered less rapidly than those of most other Latin American countries. An index of dollar value of exports, with 1933 as 100, stood in 1948 at only 258 for Peru, compared with 411 for Argentina, 506 for Brazil, 478 for Chile, and 384 for Mexico. The years 1930–50, then, were a period of relative stagnation both in export volume and in general economic growth.

The share of cotton and sugar in exports rose from 28.5 percent in 1930 to 50.5 percent in 1950, but again the two products fared quite differently. Sugar production stagnated because Peru received only a small U.S. quota. A good deal of land was diverted from sugar to cotton, which benefited from U.S. price-support schemes in the 1930s and became the mainstay of Peru's west-coast region. On the mineral side, the copper-silver share of exports fell from 20.1 percent in 1930 to 9.4 percent in 1950, but the lead-zinc share rose from 6.8 to 11.7 percent. Oil fell from 29.7 percent to 13.1 percent of total exports. Oil output grew substantially during the 1930s because the government, in need of revenue, pressured the International Petroleum Company to produce more under threat of punitive taxation or expropriation. But after 1942, when an initial 20-year tax concession expired, taxes were raised substantially. The company reacted by reducing new exploration, and output declined as old fields were worked out. Because of the relative decline of oil and minerals, the proportion of Peru's exports produced by foreign firms dropped from 60 percent in 1930 to 30 percent in 1950.

After a mild flirtation with economic interventionism in the 1940s, the Peruvian government had by 1950 returned to a traditional laissez-faire stance favoring foreign investment and exports. Aided by the world economic boom, exports rose with unprecedented speed. Sugar and cotton exports continued to grow, though their percentage share of exports dropped sharply from 53 percent in 1945 to 17 percent in 1974. Sugar production doubled, though exports increased only 50 percent, as more sugar was absorbed by domestic demand. Cotton expanded up to 1960, after which the world market deteriorated and the price became unattractive relative to other crops. By 1971 cotton acreage had been cut in half. Yields per hectare for both sugar and cotton continued to rise, as they had been doing in the 1930s and 1940s.

The striking developments of this period, however, were a sensational recovery of mining output and the great fish-meal boom of 1955–70. Between 1945–49 and 1965–69 copper production increased eight times, silver and lead three times, and zinc five times. By 1970 metals were more than half of total exports. The fish-meal boom got under way about 1955, with the annual anchovy catch rising from a half-million tons per year in 1955–59 to more than 11 million tons at the peak in

1970–71, while the number of processing plants rose from 17 to 154. In 1970 fish meal was 32 percent of total Peruvian exports. The factors responsible for this boom included (1) a rapid increase in demand for fish meal, primarily as food for pigs and poultry; (2) technological breakthroughs, which included larger fishing boats with sonar equipment and development of strong nylon nets; (3) availability of secondhand equipment from the dwindling sardine industry in California (whole factories were shipped down the coast and reassembed in Peru); and (4) ample commercial bank credit, which made it easy for small operators to enter the industry. About half the entrepreneurs were of middle-class origin, though the Peruvian elite also participated along with some foreign firms.

The industry declined after 1970, as fickle ocean currents carried the anchovies away from the Peruvian coast. But it still provided 10 percent of Peruvian exports in 1978–80. Another 10 percent came from coffee, a relatively new export product. With new oil discoveries plus the large price increases, petroleum's share rose to 22 percent, a bit above the 20 percent share of copper. So the twists and turns of Peru's export growth continue.

More significant than export growth itself is the disposition of the export proceeds. How much came back to the Peruvian economy in wage-salary payments, purchase of supplies and services, and tax payments to the Peruvian government? We know a good deal about this from the detailed research of Thorp and Bertram (1978). Their data permit several conclusions. First, returned value was substantial, particularly in the later decades of the period. Overall, they estimate it at 53 percent in 1960 and 81 percent in 1973. Second, the returned value percentage varies widely among products. At one pole are cotton and fish meal, where it is about 90 percent. Cotton acreage is locally owned and requires few imported inputs, since local guano is the main fertilizer. Fish meal also depends heavily on local supplies, including a sizable boat-building industry. At the other pole, petroleum comes closest to the stereotype of an economic enclave with minimal spread effects. From 1916 to 1934, returned value from the International Petroleum Company averaged only 16 percent (though today, with national ownership, this is no longer true.) Mining operations occupy a middle range between these extremes.

Third, the returned-value percentage has increased markedly over time, mainly as a result of increasing government participation. Initially, the foreign companies were taxed very lightly. As late as 1939 the tax burden was only 4 percent of export earnings. Under the system of oligarchic government by the elite, Peruvian presidents seem to have been more interested in serving out their five-year terms than in long-run growth of the economy. Peaceful relations with foreign investors contributed to this goal. In the 1940s, however, parties with a broader base of middle-class support began to dominate Peruvian politics, and there was more interest in extracting a surplus from the export sector and using it for domestic development. By 1945 the tax burden on foreign companies had risen to 14 percent of exports. Export sectors were also taxed indirectly by ceiling prices on their local sales and by maintenence of a fixed (overvalued) exchange rate.

After 1960 government moved to increase further taxation on the mining companies. The companies responded by an "investment strike" while they bargained for better treatment, and mineral output leveled off on a plateau. The annual growth rate of mineral production dropped from 13.4 percent in 1950–55 and 15.6 percent in 1955–60 to 2.8 percent in 1960–65 and 3.5 percent in 1965–70. This stalemate was broken when, after the military coup of 1968, the new government nationalized several of the major mining companies and declared all unexploited mineral resources to be state property. The government share of export revenue is presumably a good deal larger today than in 1968, though recent figures are not available.

Intensive Growth since 1880: Domestic Sectors

Here we note first a typical acceleration of population growth. Peru's population is estimated to have grown from 1.5 million in 1800 to 3.75 million in 1900, an average annual growth of 0.9 percent per year. This rate rose gradually as health improvements reduced the mortality rate, and between 1930–40 and 1940–50 population grew at 1.6 percent per year. After World War II mortality continued to decline toward "developed-country" levels, the crude deathrate averaging 11.1 per thousand from 1965 to 1970. With birthrates almost unchanged, the population growth rate rose to 2.4 percent from 1950 to 1960, 2.9 percent from 1960 to 1970, and 2.8 percent from 1970 to 1980. Peru is thus late in entering the demographic transition, as in so many other respects.

What was happening meanwhile to food supply? Information is poor. Agricultural statistics focus on the export crops. Area devoted to "other crops" usually appears as a residual, and there is little information on yields or output. There is no evidence that the growth of sugar and cotton acreage diverted land from food production. Land was sufficiently plentiful that food-crop acreage and export-crop acreage could expand side by side. From 1890 to 1930 food output seems to have grown slowly, but population was also growing slowly in this period. During the relatively stagnant years 1929–44, sugar and cotton acreage were almost stationary. Acreage under food crops in the coastal areas rose by 67 percent, or about 3.5 percent per year, and output may have grown at about the same rate, since there is little evidence of technological change. In the sierra, there is little indication of change in either acreage or technology. So, if food output for the country as a whole grew faster than population (which is not certain), it did not grow very much faster.

From 1944 to 1971, land devoted to "other crops" increased by about 50 percent, or 1.4 percent per year. FAO data show food output growing at 2.3 percent per year in the 1950s, 3.2 percent in the 1960s, but only 0.7 percent in the 1970s. With population growing at 2.8 percent, this is clearly an unsatisfactory performance. FAO data show food availability per capita as 4 percent *lower* in 1978–80 than in 1964–66.

In view of the sluggishness of food production, it is surprising that at no time did the internal terms of trade turn markedly in favor of agriculture. The general price level has floated upward, but food prices have risen no faster than nonfood prices. Part of the explanation may be that some segments of the population, notably the population of the sierra, have not experienced much increase in per capita income, which has held down the growth of food demand. Another factor has been availability of food imports as a safety valve. It is significant that food imports as a percentage of total imports rose from 13 percent in 1900 to the range of 20–25 percent in the 1920s. Food imports were still 20 percent of total imports in 1970, which means a very large increase in absolute terms.

Peru, in short, has behaved somewhat like contemporary oil-exporting countries, and for that matter like Chile. A strong export position has permitted inattention to agricultural performance, any demand-supply gap in foodstuffs being filled by imports. While the Peruvian government has taken an interest in irrigation projects and subsidized fertilizer supplies for export crops, it has taken remarkably little interest in food-crop agriculture.

The same inertness of policy is evident in the industrial sector, where Peru does not conform to the "standard" Latin American pattern. During the early 1930s Peru actually reduced government spending faster than export earnings fell. Argentina, Brazil, Chile, and Mexico, on the other hand, resorted in varying degrees to deficit finance and also manipulated exchange rates and trade controls to stimulate domestic industrialization. During the 1940s the more progressive, middle-class regimes that came to power in Peru took some interest in industrial promotion, but the measures were mild compared with the "crash programs" of some other Latin American countries. Peru remained devoted to specific tariff rates, which were rapidly eroded by inflation. Peruvian industries thus had little protection, and the more industrialized Latin American countries took advantage of this weakness to invade the Peruvian market. Not until the 1960s was there a coherent industrialization policy supported by substantial tariffs, tax incentives, and a development bank—steps that had been taken much earlier in other countries.

Even without strong promotional efforts, however, the growth of the domestic market led to a sustained, gradual, long drawn out process of industrialization from the 1890s onward. As usual, textiles were the leading sector, the more so because of availability of local cotton and wool. The progress of the industry, and also its moderate pace, can be seen by noting the domestically supplied share of textile consumption at various dates, which rose from near zero in 1890 to 47 percent in 1908, then more gradually to 56 percent in 1930, then sharply again to 93 percent in 1945. Import substitution in this field thus took about sixty years.

There was a parallel expansion of other light consumer-goods industries—rapid from 1890 to 1910, more gradual from 1910 to 1930, rapid again from 1930 to 1945. Expansion of light industry is suggested by the proportion of consumer goods in total imports, which fell from 57.6 percent in 1891 to 39.0 percent in 1907 to 29.0 percent in 1930 to 23.0 percent in 1945. Light-industry output grew quite rapidly after 1929 for the usual reasons—reduced capacity to import and a falling exchange rate, leading to higher prices for imported goods—though the rate of increase was lower in Peru than in Latin American countries that industrialized more aggressively. The World War II years, when import availability was again reduced, saw the appearance of a number of new industries—tires, toiletries and pharmaceuticals, some basic chemicals. The average growth rate of industrial output from 1938 to 1950 was 6 percent per year.

In 1950, industrialization was less far along in Peru than in comparable Latin American countries; and post-1950 governments continued to be oriented mainly toward export promotion rather than import-substituting industrialization. Still, manufacturing continued to grow and there was a mild shift toward heavier types of industry. Between 1950 and 1968, capital goods and consumer durables rose from 6.7 percent to 12.9 percent of output, while chemicals, petroleum products, and other intermediate goods rose from 19.0 percent to 25.1 percent. Some foreign firms diversified considerably—for example, the Grace Company went into chemicals, paper, paper products, machinery, textiles, and paint. The local elite also took a more favorable view of nonexport production, signaled by the passage of an Industrial Promotion Law in 1959. This law had the usual tax and tariff incentives, applied rather indiscriminately, since it extended to old as well as new industries, even including export processing. Sharp tariff increases were made in 1964 and 1965. Also important was expansion of financial institutions and a sharp increase in the flow of personal savings into these institutions, which rose from 2 percent of personal income in 1961 to 4 percent in 1965. The number of foreign firms entering Peru rose sharply from 23 in 1955–59 to 73 in 1960–64, to 89 in 1965–69. By 1968 foreign and "mixed" firms were producing about half of manufacturing output.

Although the trend of per capita income has been upward since at least 1890, no one has ventured a quantitative estimate of the growth rate. Only from 1950 onward do we have systematic national accounts. These show GDP rising at 4.9 percent per year both in the 1950s and 1960s, which means an increase of about 2 percent per year in per capita income. But GDP rose at only 3.0 percent during the 1970s—that is per capita income was virtually stationary following the 1968 military takeover.

Income increases were quite unequally distributed among the population. A study of the period 1950–66, reported in Thorp and Bertram, shows the following annual rates of increase in per capita real income: modern-sector employees, 4.1 percent; workers in the urban traditional sector, 2.0 percent; small farmers, 0.8 percent; farmers in the sierra with less than five hectares of land, zero. No group seems to have suffered an absolute decline in real income; but income inequalities obviously widened.

The year 1968 marked a sharp turning point in economic organization and policy. President Belaúnde was sent into exile and a military government took over. Apart from being independent and nationalist, the new regime does not seem to have any clear ideology—whether left, right, or center. By the mid-1970s it had taken over the position previously held by foreign capital in mining, oil, electricity, and railways; had taken over most of the banking system, virtually all export marketing, and the entire fishing industry; and had decreed that foreign capital in manufacturing industries must retreat to minority ownership. The regime seems to have hoped for a revival of *domestic* private enterprise, but it is not surprising that this failed to develop. The end result was a large stride toward state capitalism, with the state share of enterprise ownership in the modern sector (40 percent) well above that of domestic private capital (35 percent) and with foreign capital reduced to a minor role. Under an Agrarian Reform Law of 1969, the large sugar estates were turned into worker cooperatives, and most other large landholdings were also expropriated. The operative effect of this law, however, is still unclear.

It is not surprising that these changes were somewhat disorganizing to production. The quantum index of exports declined during the 1970s, and the average annual growth rate of GDP fell to 4.6 percent in 1970–75 and to 1.2 percent in 1975–79. Given the country's resources, it seems likely that growth will be resumed at a higher rate. But it is unclear how soon this will happen or what institutional structure (especially in agriculture) will eventually emerge.

7

Sri Lanka, Burma, Malaysia, Thailand

The countries that embarked on intensive growth during the second half of the nineteenth century lie in two parts of the world. One group, located in Central and South America, was discussed in chapters 5 and 6. The second group, considered here, lies in an arc across South and Southeast Asia, from Sri Lanka in the west to Thailand in the east. Sri Lanka, Burma, Malaysia, and Thailand are relatively small, resource-rich countries that achieved high export ratios on the basis of agricultural exports (and in the case of Malaysia, mineral exports as well). Moreover, to an unusual degree these exports came from small peasant producers, so that returned value to the economy was high. The opening of the Suez Canal in 1869 and the great reduction of shipping costs as sail was replaced by steam were major facilitating factors in export growth.

Why do we not extend our picture of colonial development still further eastward to include French Indochina? There is evidence of intensive growth from about 1880 in the Mekong Delta region (Cochin China). Lightly settled at the time of colonization, this land was opened up by the French through extensive canal dredging, which provided both drainage and water transport to market. Between 1880 and 1937 the population of this region increased by 267 percent, cultivated acreage by 421 percent, rice exports by 545 percent. In the more densely settled northern kingdoms of Annam and Tonkin, on the other hand, the evidence is that food output at most kept pace with population. One gets the impression of a sluggish, rather self-contained economy resembling China (under whose control the area had been for centuries) rather than Southeast Asia. Laos and Cambodia were isolated and backward, as indeed they remain today. Our judgment, then, is that regional development in Cochin China is not sufficient to make a case for intensive growth in Indochina as a whole.

A second consideration is that after 1940 the region was racked by almost continuous warfare—against the Japanese, against the French, against the Americans, in addition to civil warfare in Laos and Cambodia. In view of the devastation resulting from these conflicts, it would not be surprising to find that per capita income has risen little if any since 1940. In any event, the statistical documentation is inadequate to test this surmise.

SRI LANKA (CEYLON)

Nineteenth-century Ceylon was a labor-scarce, land-abundant country in which plantation agriculture and smallholder agriculture could expand alongside each other with no constraint on resources.

Turning Point: *circa* 1880

The British seized Ceylon from the Dutch in 1796 and began developmental activity as early as 1820. But the first export boom in coffee began only in the 1840s. Most of the coffee came from British-owned estates (which could be bought at low prices from the colonial government), though about one-quarter of exports came from smallholder production. Coffee-rust disease, however, destroyed the industry in the 1870s and led to a search for a new export crop. Tea emerged as the preferred alternative. It can be grown at altitudes of 2,500–6,000 feet, it thrives on rain (which cocoa does not), it has economies of scale in processing, and picking continues throughout the year, which permits employment of a stable labor force. The rising demand for tea by industrial workers in Britain seemed to promise an assured market. Cheapened transport through the Suez Canal for tea exports and the return flow of imports was also a stimulating factor.

Tea thus became a well-established industry, and was soon joined by a variety of other export crops. The unusually high rate of export growth from 1880 to 1913 warrants dating the turning point at around 1880.

Intensive Growth, 1880–1950

Falling tea prices from 1882 to 1905, which reduced export receipts and estate profits, led to a search for still other export crops. One such was rubber, which was introduced from Brazil via London in the 1890s and benefited from the rubber price boom. Rubber acreage grew from 1,000 hectares in 1900 to 94,000 hectares in 1913. Rubber requires little capital, and it is a lowland crop, so it did not compete with tea for highland acreage. Rubber was grown by some of the tea companies, by a new indigenous capitalist class, and also by smallholders, who had about 20 percent of the 1913 acreage. The second expanding export was coconut products, indigenous to the island. Acreage in coconut trees grew from 200,000 hectares in 1900 to 384,000 hectares in 1913. The coconut is also a lowland crop and essentially a peasant crop, though there were some large holdings.

By 1913, then, Ceylon's exports were reasonably diversified. Tea provided about 35 percent, rubber 26 percent, coconut products 20 percent, and other products 19 percent. The growth rate of exports from 1880 to 1913 was an unusually high 5.4 percent, much above the rate of population growth, which was only about 0.5 percent a year from 1870 to 1900 and about 1.0 percent from 1900 to 1920. To anticipate a bit, I shall note that export growth—dominated still by these three product groups—continued from 1913 to 1939, though at a slightly lower rate. Snodgrass (1966) estimates that over the years 1888–1939 exports grew at 5.1 percent per year. This "modern sector," moreover, was producing about half of estimated GDP. Even if we assume that per capita output in the traditional sector did not increase at all, we come out with a GDP growth rate of 3.2 percent per year, or about 2 percent per year in per capita terms.

We must penetrate behind these aggregates, however, because Ceylon is sometimes portrayed as a case of enclave growth in which most of the indigenous population did not participate. It is true that the coffee and tea estates were staffed initially by Tamil laborers imported from southern India. (Indigenous farmers were doing well enough from traditional agriculture so that the prospect of becoming wage laborers was not attractive.) Further, since the Tamils did not like the type of rice grown in Ceylon, most of their food was imported from India. The estates also imported many of their other supplies, exported almost all their output, and remitted most of their profits to Britain.

Granting all this, I believe that the local spread effects were important and that they can be documented along several lines:

1. Smallholders produced a substantial proportion of exports. They produced about 10 percent of the tea, 20 percent of the rubber, and 60 percent of coconut products—perhaps one-fifth of exports overall. By 1913 some 200,000 peasants were growing export crops, compared with 450,000 who continued as subsistence rice producers. Export producers also had a much higher average income than the food producers.
2. The local Sinhalese began gradually to participate as estate laborers. Their initial reluctance to do so is quite understandable. With no scarcity of good rice land, subsistence farming offered returns above the wage level offered on the estates. So planters in Ceylon imported Indians, as Brazilian planters for the same reason had imported first slaves and later European immigrants. But in the twentieth century this situation was changed by growing population pressure. The man/land ratio in subsistence agriculture, which had remained almost constant up to 1921, began to rise rather steeply after that. This stimulated movement of labor both to the cities and into estate work. By the 1930s, about 100,000 Sinhalese were working as estate laborers, forming about one-fifth of the estate labor force.
3. I noted earlier the rise of a Ceylonese planter class alongside the expatriate planter class. These people went mainly into the newer crops, rubber and coconuts, rather than into tea. Craig (in Lewis, 1970) comments that "Ceylon seems to have gone further than any other South Asian country . . . in producing a middle class of indigenous agriculturalists," whose profits were available for reinvestment in other lines of production.

4. The rising tide of exports served to finance a rising, though not equal, flow of imports. About half of these imports were traditional consumption items, notably rice and textiles. (Ceylon, like some other export-rich countries, has traditionally used rice imports to supplement local production.) Part of these imports, of course, went to the estate laborers. But a good deal must have spilled over to the local population, urban and rural.

5. The impression of rising local incomes and a broadening domestic market is confirmed by the early growth of manufacturing industries. By 1911 there were already 170,000 workers employed in manufacturing, of whom 48,000 were in the textile and clothing industries. Between 1881 and 1911, manufacturing employment rose at 2.8 percent per year, more than double the growth rate of the labor force.

   The growth of off-farm employment opportunities has been documented also by Snodgrass (1966). Comparing 1901 with 1946, the proportion of the labor force engaged in smallholder agriculture fell from 37.7 to 21.3 percent. The proportion employed as estate workers rose slightly from 26.7 to 30.0 percent. But the proportion employed in "other sectors" rose from 35.6 to 48.7 percent, suggesting a considerable increase in urbanization and in trade and service as well as manufacturing employment, a normal accompaniment of rising per capita incomes.

6. Finally, government was active in infrastructure development. The colonial administration in Ceylon was normally in a comfortable financial situation. Revenue, derived mainly from export and import taxes, rose rapidly with rising trade volume. Unlike neighboring India, debt interest and defense expenditure were small items, leaving revenue available for road and railway building, irrigation activity, and port development in the new city of Colombo. The main object of this activity was to facilitate exports, but the benefits spilled over into other sectors. Government was also unusually active in education. School enrollment increased two-and-one-half times between 1890 and 1910, and in 1911 the male literacy rate was already 47 percent. Ceylon still has one of the highest educational levels in Asia.

It appears, then, that the colonial period brought an improvement in living standards, not only for the expatriates, but for most of the indigenous population. On the eve of World War II, however, Ceylon remained a classic export economy, with a small industrial sector, a small public sector, a heavy concentration of resources in export agriculture, and an export ratio in the range of 40–50 percent of GDP.

Intensive Growth, 1950–80

Limited self-government for internal affairs by an elected legislature had been granted to Ceylon by Britain in 1931. Full independence was achieved in 1948 and the country's name changed to Sri Lanka. From this point on the nation was ruled by a government that was not constrained by the budget-balancing rules of the colonial era, that could operate an independent monetary policy (using a central bank established in 1950), that could stimulate industry through protectionist policies, that could levy heavier taxes on foreign-owned plantations and use the proceeds for development purposes. In these and other ways government became a central rather than an incidental feature of the economy.

Constitutional government has been maintained, with two major parties and several minor parties competing for office. Of the major parties one has a conservative, private-enterprise orientation while the other has a democratic-socialist orientation resembling that of the British Labour Party. The conservatives held office until 1956, then were out of office for most of the 1960s and 1970s, returned to power in 1977, and were reelected for a further term in 1982.

There have been short-run fluctuations in the rate of economic growth, partly associated with changes in the political regime. Over the long run, however, growth has been sustained at a moderate rate—an average annual increase of about 4 percent in GDP and 2 percent in GDP per capita. There has been considerable restructuring of the economy along predictable lines. Only a few of the recent developments can be outlined within our space limits.

The immediate postwar period brought a population explosion, due mainly to virtual eradication of malaria through DDT spraying of mosquitoes. The number of malaria cases dropped from 2.5 million in 1945 to less than 20,000 in 1955. The overall deathrate fell from about 20 to about 10 per thousand and has continued to fall slightly. The crude birthrate remained in the range of 36–38 per thousand, where it had been ever since 1900. As a result of health improvements after World War I, the rate of natural increase had already risen from 0.9 percent from 1900 to 1920 to 1.3 percent from 1920 to 1940. But it jumped to an alarming 2.7 percent in the 1950s.

During the 1960s, however, Sri Lanka entered the demographic transition, perhaps aided by its relatively high level of education and health services. By 1980 the crude birthrate had fallen to 26 per thousand and the rate of natural increase to 1.8 percent per year, with further declines in prospect. Another development affecting population was restriction of further immigration from India, intended to increase employment opportunities for the Sinhalese. (The government did not succeed, however, in repatriating the 700,000 Tamils already in Sri Lanka, since India refused to recognize them as Indian citizens.)

The population spurt aggravated the problem of food supply. Ceylon had long depended on imports for a substantial percentage of its rice supply, but now rice imports began seriously to strain the balance of payments, cutting into the margin for needed imports of intermediate and capital goods. Government was thus forced to turn its attention to raising domestic paddy production. The pattern of agricultural organization is favorable, in that the percentage of owner-operators is high. But the average holding is very small. Some 85 percent of paddy holdings are 2 acres or less in size.

Government's contribution in these circumstances consisted in expansion of the acreage under cultivation through colonization schemes; extensive development of irrigation, which by 1980 covered about 60 percent of total rice acreage; assuring farmers of a guaranteed purchase price; provision of subsidized fertilizer supplies, the use of which quadrupled between 1957 and 1970; and introduction of high-yielding rice varieties. As a result of all this, food production has been one of the more flourishing sectors of the economy. Paddy acreage has almost doubled since 1946, output has considerably more than doubled, and domestic output has risen from about 50 percent of domestic consumption in 1946 to more than 90 percent in 1980. There have been even larger increases in production of "minor crops" and of livestock products, suggesting some progress toward diversification of diets.

Rice production did particularly well after election of the conservative government in 1977. The new government emphasized private trading rather than state trading in rice, and by 1980 less than 10 percent of the rice crop moved through government procurement channels. The long-standing system of retail price control and rice rationing was abolished in 1979 and replaced by a food-stamp program similar to that of the United States to benefit those below a certain income level. Retail prices rose significantly, holding farm gate prices well above the guaranteed support level, which was also raised by stages. Between 1978 and 1981, rice production grew at 7.3 percent per year, above the 6.5 percent growth rate of GDP. About three-quarters of this increase came from higher yields, about one-quarter from increase in rice acreage.

Meanwhile acreage and output of export crops has been rather stagnant. Both tea and rubber production have been hampered by the need for replanting of older trees. Sri Lanka has been less aggressive in replanting rubber trees than has Malaysia and has suffered in consequence. The rubber-tea-coconut percentage of total exports, formerly about 95 percent, had fallen by 1979 to 62 percent, while "nontraditional exports" (including manufactures) have risen rapidly. Thus the previous imbalance between export-crop production and domestic-food production and the heavy concentration of exports in a few products have been somewhat redressed.

The manufacturing sector is rather "Indian" in that some areas are reserved to government, and public corporations produce a substantial share of industrial output. A number of government-owned plants established during World War II—for the production of cement, leather products, oils and fats, ceramics, plywood—were reorganized in 1955 as public corporations. In 1957, the newly elected socialist government announced three lists of industries: (1) those reserved for government operation—iron and steel, cement, chemicals, fertilizers, salt, mineral sands, sugar, power, alcohol, and rayon; (2) those open to public corporations, mixed corporations, and private corporations—textiles, tires and tubes, bicycles, ceramics, glassware, paper, and another dozen or so light industries; and (3) some 82 industries, mostly producing light consumer goods, that were reserved for private enterprise (though negotiation with government over tax and tariff concessions was necessary for profitable operation in these areas).

I have not seen data on how far public and private enterprises have occupied the areas assigned to them in principle, nor on what percentage of industrial output comes from the public sector. (All public utilities, of course, are government-operated, and the former private tea estates are now operated by two public corporations.) Nor is it clear how far cottage and handicraft industries, formerly very important, have survived alongside factory production. The percentage of GDP produced by manufacturing, which in 1940 was well below 10 percent, had risen by 1980 to 18 percent. There has been a substantial shift from production of consumer goods toward production of intermediates and even some capital goods. In 1979, textiles plus the food-beverage-tobacco group were only 40 percent of manufacturing output. Chemicals, petroleum products, rubber, and plastics were 45 percent of the total, and the metals-machinery group was about 15 percent. Except in a few fields, average plant size is quite small, typically below 100 workers.

Open unemployment is substantial, though the percentage has fallen somewhat since 1977, and an accelerated rise of real wages also suggests tightening of the labor market. Typically, the highest unemployment rate is among secondary school graduates or dropouts. Some 70 percent of the unemployed are in this category. University graduates form less than 1 percent of the unemployed because there are relatively few of them; but the unemployment rate in 1980 among university graduates aged 20–29 was about 30 percent. The well-developed educational establishment seems to be producing graduates whose expectations and skills are not well adapted to the structure of labor demand.

There was a substantial upturn in the economy after 1977, when a newly elected conservative government introduced a more outward-looking, regulation-free policy package. Elements in the package included: (1) unification of exchange rates at a more realistic level; (2) import liberalization; (3) establishment of a duty-free processing zone north of Colombo; (4) higher interest rates to encourage saving and better allocation of capital; (5) abolition of price controls on most products and revision of other government-determined prices (such as water rates and electricity rates) to reflect scarcity values; and (6) a considerable reduction of consumer subsidies. Petroleum subsidies were abolished, and rice and sugar subsidies were abolished for people in the upper half of the income distribution. Fertilizer subsidies have been raised, to stimulate agricultural production. Even so, total subsidies dropped from 35.7 percent of government revenue in 1977/78 to 18.9 percent in 1980/81. The budget has benefited also from giving greater autonomy and responsibility to public corporations, which must now finance capital formation from their own resources or from borrowing. Transfers of capital funds from the government budget have ceased.

The response to these changes was quite substantial. GDP, which had risen at only 2.9 percent per year from 1970 to 1977, rose at 6.5 percent from 1978 to 1981. The gross capital formation/GDP ratio rose from an average 14.5 percent from 1970 to 1977 to 28.7 percent in 1981. "Nontraditional exports," including manufactures from the new duty-free zone, rose from $40 million in 1970 to $372 million in 1979. Imports shifted toward capital goods and intermediates, though food imports are still 20 percent, and other consumer goods 15 percent, of the total.

The future is not free of problems. Traditional exports are rather stagnant. Rice imports are still necessary. Unemployment of the educated is substantial. The post-1977 program, heavily underwritten by foreign lenders, involves a rising debt-service ratio that cannot continue to rise indefinitely. Still, Sri Lanka's growth record, now well over a century old, seems likely to continue.

BURMA

For almost a century Burma was a British colony, governed as part of the Indian Empire. The British took over two coastal provinces adjacent to India in 1825–26, the remainder of Lower Burma in 1852, and Upper Burma in 1885. Northern or Upper Burma, the traditional center of Burmese population and government, had an essentially feudal organization in the pre-British period. Lower Burma was largely unsettled in 1850 but was to fill up rapidly and become the country's rice bowl later in the century. Proximity to India, and a government policy that not merely permitted but subsidized immigration, led to an overflow of Indian surplus labor into the Burmese economy. The resulting racial division of economic functions resembles that in British East Africa: British at the top, Burmese at the bottom, and Indians performing most of the intermediate functions. Thus, when we say that "the population" benefited from economic growth, we must bear in mind that these strata benefited unequally, with the smallest benefit flowing to the indigenous population.

Turning Point: *circa* 1870

When the British arrived in 1852, Lower Burma had a small population on a large area of potentially fertile land. Government policy was to encourage smallholder settlement on this land by surveying and plotting it and by confirming transferable titles of ownership, which had not existed previously. Progress initially was slow, since there was no ready market for output beyond subsistence needs. The decisive event was the growth of steam navigation and particularly the opening of the Suez Canal in 1869, which opened a large European market for Burmese rice. The price of rice, which in the 1860s had been 50–55 rupees per hundred baskets, rose by 1880 to 85 rupees. After this no government stimulus was needed. Population flowed in rapidly, mainly through migration from Upper Burma. The growth of rice acreage in Lower Burma is illustrated in the following table.

Year	Cultivated Area (thousand acres)	Average Annual Increase in Previous Decade (thousand acres)
1852–53	600	–
1872–73	1,500	45
1882–83	2,860	136
1892–93	4,467	160
1902–03	6,649	218
1912–13	7,913	126
1922–23	8,936	102

Intensive Growth, 1870–1950

Although the rate of expansion peaked in the 1890s, rice output and exports continued to grow vigorously in the early twentieth century. Rice exports rose from 400,000 tons a year in 1865–66 to 817,000 tons in 1891, 2,500,000 tons in 1921, and reached 3,500,000 tons in some years of the 1930s. Rice sales brought the Burmese peasant almost more money than he could readily spend. Concentration on rice production was so intense that many household items formerly produced at home were now imported. By 1900 foreign trade was five to six times as large as it was in the 1860s. Andrus (1956, p. 16) comments: "It appears that there was an increase in the standard of living and at the same time new, hitherto unknown commodities were introduced."

The kind of agriculture that developed in Lower Burma has been labeled by Furnivall (1957) "industrial agriculture"—"a vast area of thick jungle with secure rainfall rapidly brought under cultivation by peasant cultivators with seasonal labor and a ready supply of capital producing a single crop for the export market." Initially, the landowners and tenants were Burmese, though this changed somewhat in later years. The Indians entered as moneylenders ("chettyars") and traders and also as seasonal laborers. There was an unlimited supply of Indian workers, who were willing to work for less than what the Burmese considered a reasonable standard of living; and government stimulated the movement by subsidies to the shipping companies that brought in the migrant labor. By the late nineteenth century, Indian immigration was already approaching 100,000 a year, and in the 1920s it exceeded 300,000 a year, of whom at least half seem to have remained in Burma. The colonial government, in addition to maintaining law and order, had an active Public Works Department that protected large areas of the Irrawaddy Delta from flooding. British companies also provided riverine transport from rice-growing areas to the ports and operated large rice-milling establishments.

The course of events in Upper Burma was less dramatic. Lands there had long been settled, under complex tenure arrangements carried over from feudal times. The proportion of landowners who were also cultivators was much higher than in the delta. Large estates were rare; those that did exist belonged to old feudal families rather than (as in the delta) to rich businessmen. There was some tenancy, but of a rather humane sort. Most tenants had *de facto* tenure even when they were nominally on an annual lease, and landowners usually did not extract the full economic rent of the land.

The traditional crops of Upper Burma were cotton, rice, millet, and sesame. Variations in topography and water supply permit a wider range of crops there than in the delta. Many new crops were introduced during the British period, including sugarcane, groundnuts, some types of beans, and pigeon peas. Groundnuts, a profitable crop introduced only in 1906, had expanded to 781,000 acres by 1940–41. As Furnivall comments, "This ready assimilation of new crops and new methods of cultivation shows that cultivators in Upper Burma are comparatively free from the reproach of undue conservatism which is so often levelled at farmers."

Although rice acreage in Upper Burma increased from 1,357,000 acres in 1890 to 2,459,000 in 1930, the region was not self-sufficient and continued to draw rice as well as imported consumer goods from Lower Burma. In return, it supplied Lower Burma with vegatable oils and other nonrice crops. Upper Burma also exported cotton, groundnuts, and a variety of other products. Thus by the 1930s agriculture in Upper Burma was substantially commercialized, though the percentage of output marketed was well below that in Lower Burma. But production was carried on within a traditional organization of agriculture and even traditional farm boundaries carried over from earlier times.

From several good economic histories we can form an impression of what the economy looked like on the eve of World War II. Population had been growing at a moderate rate since the first British censuses. The average growth rate from 1850 to 1900 is estimated at 1.1 percent per year. This rose only a little after 1900, reaching 1.4 percent per year from 1931 to 1941. At no time did land scarcity or food scarcity impose any check on population growth; and uncontrolled fertility at rates estimated as high as 50 per thousand left a comfortable margin over mortality. It is interesting that the population, in addition to being well fed, was relatively well educated. In 1931 the literacy rate was already 71 percent for males, though only 21 percent for females. In addition to the Buddhist monastic schools, there were thousands of one-teacher and two-teacher schools in the villages. The towns had schools teaching in English above fourth grade, and the University of Rangoon in 1931 had 3,000 students, but with a curriculum oriented heavily toward law and the humanities rather than science, engineering, or medicine.

As for patterns of landholding, the aim of establishing peasant proprietorship in Lower Burma was by no means fully achieved. Transferability of titles facilitated buying up of land as an investment by city businessmen, and a good deal of land also came into the hands of chettyar moneylenders through farmers defaulting on loans, especially during the depressed 1930s. Furnivall estimates that in the 1930s about 40 percent of the land in the delta was held by large landowners, who either operated it or let it out to tenants on rather onerous terms. Annual tenancy was the general rule and, unlike practice in Upper Burma, landlords seem to have exacted the full economic rent. The tenants now included a good many Indians as well as Burmese. The Indians had a competitive advantage by being willing to work for less, and they tended to be preferred by Indian and even by some Burmese landowners. Most land, to be sure, was still operated by smallholders; but much of this land was so heavily mortgaged that the owner's equity was quite small.

"Manufacturing" at this time was done mainly by more than a half-million handicraft workers. While imports did cut into the market for handicraft products, they were far from eliminating it. Much of the handicraft work, particularly in textiles, was part-time and seasonal activity carried on in conjunction with agriculture. Cotton spinning and weaving, for example, employed some 230,000 people, of whom all but 4,000 were women. For only 40,000 of these women, however, was textiles their principal occupation, and only 1 percent lived in urban areas. Other important handicraft workers, with 1931 employment levels, were lacquer workers (66,000); tailors, milliners, and dressmakers (51,000); carpenters, turners, and joiners (43,000); distillers (36,000); tobacco workers (20,000); jewelry workers (22,000); plus blacksmiths, potters, and makers of metal cooking utensils and tableware.

The 1931 census also counted about 1,000 "factories" with 90,000 workers. But 85 percent of these were rice mills, cotton gins, and sawmills engaged mainly in export processing. Factory production of consumer goods proper was still in its infancy.

Export trade had by 1940 become considerably more diversified through appearance of new export products; so while rice continued to expand in absolute terms, its share declined considerably. In the period 1937–41, rice was 47 percent of total exports and other crops, 5 percent. But about 45 percent of exports now came from Western-owned enterprises in petroleum products (26 percent), minerals and ores (11 percent), timber and rubber (8 percent). The import pattern was typical, with textiles and clothing about half of all imports and other consumer goods forming most of the remainder. Between 50 and 60 percent of total trade was with India, about 15 percent with the United Kingdom, and the balance widely scattered.

The public sector also followed a conventional colonial pattern. About half of all revenue came from customs duties and land taxes, though excise and income taxes also made sizable contributions. Most of the expenditures were for the army, police, education, and general administration. Very little was spent on agriculture or on other development projects.

A word, finally, on the racial division of labor, which affected both income distribution in colonial times and the economic heritage of Burma at independence. The British and a limited number of other Westerners dominated not only the upper ranks of public administration but also petroleum, mining, lumbering, modern banking, shipping, and much of foreign trade. The Burmese were mostly at the bottom of the ladder, as farmers, farm laborers, and general laborers. They also carried on a good deal of the retail trade in the villages, especially trade in Burmese-produced rather than imported goods. The Indians operated at several levels. They were the main moneylenders in the informal sector. They engaged in export and import trade, wholesale trade, and even a good deal of the retail trade in Lower Burma. They provided most of the clerical work force, walling off the Burmese from what would otherwise have been a normal channel of occupational advancement. They competed with the Burmese for factory jobs, which caused considerable ill feeling, especially during the depressed 1930s. They also formed, as noted above, part of the tenant population and most of the seasonal agricultural labor.

All this contributed to what Myint (1964) has labeled the most basic form of underdevelopment—underdevelopment of *people*. The occupational distribution of the *Burmese* labor force was skewed away from the more remunerative and skill-intensive types of work. The effects of stratification were more important than the drain of funds from the country through profits of foreign enterprises and immigrant remittances, which Richter (in Shand, 1969) estimates at about 6 percent of GDP during the 1930s.

Intensive Growth, 1950–80

World War II brought Japanese occupation of much of the country and widespread devastation. Independence for India and Pakistan in 1947 was followed quickly by independence for Burma in 1948, which brought a complete turnover of government personnel and drastic policy changes. Economic performance since independence has been poor—well below the level of other Southeast Asian countries— though there appears to have been a moderate improvement since 1975.

At the deepest level, the reasons for poor performance are administrative and political. Unlike India, Burma never developed an indigenous bureaucracy under British rule. The departure of British and Indian administrators after 1948 left a vacuum, which was filled by amateurs whose "learning by doing" involved substantial economic cost. The country has never been entirely pacified since World War II. There has been continuing warfare with the hill tribes in outlying provinces, widespread banditry in the countryside, as well as much smuggling and black marketing to avoid cumbersome government controls. An incipient two-party parliamentary system broke down in the late 1950s because of fission within the parties, personal rivalries among established leaders, and lack of a mechanism by which able younger people could succeed to leadership. A coup in 1962 ushered in a period of "temporary" military rule that in fact continued for more than a decade. All ministries and government enterprises were now managed by army officers who, however loyal or honest, were lacking in technical expertise. This system was not basically changed by adoption of a new constitution in 1974, which inaugurated what Silverstein (1977) terms "constitutional dictatorship: the second phase of military rule.'' Burma was declared a one-party state, to be governed by the Burma Socialist Program Party, which selects all candidates for legislative office and wields all executive power. Military men appear to dominate the party structure, and their control of economic administration has been little changed.

The stance of Burmese governments since 1948, and especially since 1962, has been strongly nationalist and inward-looking. There has been an expressed desire to break away from the ''colonial'' pattern of heavy dependence on foreign trade and to move toward a more autonomous economy with a blend of agriculture and industry. In practice, this policy has meant neglect of rice exports and of agriculture in general, accompanied by rather ineffectual efforts at import substitution. Particularly after 1962 there was increasing distrust of foreigners, virtual elimination of tourism, and an effort to isolate Burma from the world economy.

Major institutional changes were made after 1948 in both agriculture and industry. In agriculture, former tenants were confirmed in what amounts to ownership, though in principle all land belongs to government. The burden of interest and rent payments was much reduced. There was also substantial land redistribution. Foreign landholdings, belonging mainly to Indians who had fled the country, were expropriated, and ceilings were set on the size of Burmese holdings. Between 1948 and 1965 the number of farms more than doubled and they also became more equal in size, most falling in the range of two to four hectares.

Apart from giving the peasants security of tenure, however, government did little else for them. There was little attention to irrigation, input supplies, or technical progress. Government marketing boards took over the purchasing and distribution of rice and offered prices much below world-market levels, partly to hold down food costs for the urban population. Low official prices, plus rather chaotic purchasing and grading policies, plus long distance to the government procurement centers led farmers to divert land to other crops, to black-market their rice, or simply to retreat into subsistence farming. As Richter (in Shand, 1969, p. 175) comments, ''dacoity [banditry], agrarian reform, lack of market incentives and employment opportunities outside farming, have created a situation in which a cultivated area, not greatly enlarged since the colonial period, is shared amongst a much larger farm population . . . secured on their holdings, who are disinclined or unable to invest in raising the productivity of their land.''

Paddy production recovered slowly after the war and did not reach the 1938 level until 1962–63. After that, rice acreage and output remained essentially stagnant. Meanwhile, the population growth rate had risen to 1.9 percent per year in the 1950s and to 2.2 percent in the 1960s and 1970s. So more and more of the rice crop was eaten at home. Rice exports as a percentage of production fell from 66 percent from 1936 to 1940 to 22 percent in 1965 to 1966. By 1975 rice exports were down to 300,000 tons, or about one-tenth the level of the 1930s. The decline of exports restricted Burma's ability to import the consumer goods to which the population had become accustomed, with the usual result of shortages, black markets, inflated prices, urban discontent, and occasional riots. Burma was indeed delinking itself from the world economy, a policy sometimes advocated as desirable for third-world countries, but which in this case was clearly counterproductive.

The Burmese today are not ill fed. Indeed, figures of calorie availability per capita show some improvement since 1950. Nor is Burma a land-scarce country. Richter estimated that in the mid-1960s there were still some seven million hectares of unused cultivable land, compared with ten million then under cultivation. But government policies were doing little to activate potential production.

In industry there was widespread socialization after 1948. Although this may have been inspired partly by ideology, it is perhaps best understood as a nationalist reaction against the traditional pattern of foreign ownership of business. Since the Burmese now owned the government, a policy of transferring industry to Burmese control could reasonably be interpreted as transferring it to government control. During the period of civilian control, government embarked on import-substituting industrialization, though without any coherent plan or any assurance of adequate supplies of raw materials. It built a textile mill, a cold-rolled steel mill, and a pharmaceutical plant; and it also sought to revive the war-damaged oil refineries, expand timber mills, and create a wood-products industry. The 1962 coup brought increased government intervention. The government took over all banks, took charge of rice milling as well as marketing, took over all export-import trade, nationalized all gasoline filling stations, the marine fishing industry, and a number of manufacturing plants. The result is a very mixed economy. In 1980, state enterprises produced the following percentages of sector output: power and communications, 100.0; finance, 99.0; mining, 86.0; construction, 75.3; manufacturing, 56.2; trade, 42.6; transportation, 40.8 (with buses and taxis in private hands); forestry, 36.4.

The industrial sector is still relatively small. Manufacturing, which provided 5 percent of GDP in 1950, had increased its share to only 10 percent in 1980. Manufacturing is almost entirely light industry. Privately owned plants, while they have been starved in terms of credit and foreign exchange, continue to produce close to half of manufacturing output. Artisan production must also be quite important, though there are no recent figures that could be compared with earlier data.

The lackluster performance of the industrial sector arises from several sources. Since much of industry is still engaged in agricultural processing, the slow growth of agricultural output has led to low rates of capacity utilization in processing plants. Scarcity of imported inputs, arising from poor export performance and limited foreign-exchange availability, has had a similar result. Government has also paid inadequate attention to transport development. The war damage to the railway system was repaired quite early. But there has been only limited highway construction, there are few vehicles apart from government and military vehicles, and there has been little investment in new boats and port facilities for river transport. Added to all this is inexperienced management by military administrators and the inattention to costs and tendency toward deficits that seems usually to plague state economic enterprises.

To end on a happier note: there was a marked policy shift around 1975, leading to improved economic performance in recent years. Whether because of the 1974 change in regime or because of a realization that past policies had been ineffective, the government of Burma opened discussions with a consortium of Western lenders organized by the World Bank. The outcome was that the government initiated a series of economic reforms, including important tax and pricing reforms, while the consortium underwrote a substantial loan program.

The most striking result of the new policies was a marked rise in agricultural output and productivity. A "package program" for rice (the "Whole Township Program") was initiated and by 1980–81 had been extended to 46 percent of the paddy acreage. The program included dissemination of high-yielding rice varieties, increased supply of fertilizer at a subsidized price, and high-priority provision of consumer goods to project areas to complement rising farm incomes. Purchase prices for rice were raised and by 1975 were roughly double the 1970 level. Controls over private sales to the free market were relaxed. As a result, the rice yield per hectare rose within a few years by one-third, and total paddy output rose about 40 percent.

As a result of this success in rice, the program was extended to production of groundnuts, maize, wheat, sesame, cotton, beans, and pulses, most of which have also shown substantial increases in yield and output. From 1978 to 1981, agricultural output rose at about 8 percent a year, well above the growth rate in most other sectors and in GDP. The increase in agricultural output also benefited agro-based processing industries, whose operating rates rose substantially.

A further result of the new program was a rise in the gross capital formation rate by 1981 to about 24 percent of GDP. About three-quarters of this increase was public-sector capital formation, of which almost half was financed by foreign funds. The allocation of public-sector capital formation appears reasonably balanced—about 35 percent to manufacturing, 20 percent to agriculture, 17 percent to infrastructure, 10 percent to mining. Exports, which had deteriorated seriously, recovered by 1981 to 9 percent of GDP, of which 43 percent came from rice, 23 percent from teak, and the balance from other sources. Imports were running at 14 percent of GDP, with capital goods forming 60 percent and consumer goods only 5 percent of the total.

The average annual GDP growth rate, which was only 2.6 percent from 1960 to 1970 and 2.1 percent from 1971 to 1976 (meaning that *per capita* output was essentially stagnant), rose to 6.3 percent from 1976 to 1981. Many problems remain in the economy: financial weakness of many of the State Economic Enterprises; persistent shortages of imported intermediate inputs and spare parts (especially for the private sector); some prices still held at artificially low levels; a rapid increase in bank credit to the public sector; a rising debt-service ratio. But Burmese experience suggests that a government whose ineptitude has hampered the economy for a long time can reverse course and achieve at least a temporary, perhaps a continuing, recovery of production.

MALAYSIA

Malaysia is a rather conservative democracy, export-dominated, rich in resources, including reserves of uncultivated land, benefiting from good infrastructure and a strong civil service inherited from colonial days, and with a superior growth record both before and after political independence.

Turning Point: circa 1850

Foreigners were first attracted to the Malay Peninsula by the strategic value of the Strait of Malacca as a gateway to the Far East and the spice islands of Indonesia. For a long time occupation was limited to coastal forts and trading posts, notably at Malacca, Penang, and Singapore. After prolonged conflict, an agreement was reached under which the Dutch retained Sumatra while the British retained posts on the eastern side of the strait. These Straits Settlements were taken over by the Colonial Office from the British East India Company in 1867.

Meanwhile, a flourishing tin-mining industry had grown up along the western coast of Malaya, controlled mainly by Chinese immigrants who entered in substantial numbers in the 1840s and 1850s. The trade led to conflicts among the princely rulers of the numerous Malay states, conflicts between the Malays and Chinese, and even among the Chinese themselves. Appeals to the British for protection led to gradual extension of British control into the interior. From 1875 onward, one sultan after another was persuaded to accept a British "resident" who became the effective governor. In 1895 four states were united in the Federated Malay States, and the addition of four more states ceded by Thailand in 1909 rounded out the area of modern Malaya.

The initiation of intensive growth around 1850 is suggested by population data. It took two-and-a-half centuries for population to double from an estimated 500,000 in 1600 to 1,000,000 in 1850. By 1900, however, population had increased by 150 percent to 2.5 million. Much of the increase was the result of Chinese immigration, partly directly from China, partly from Singapore and other Straits Settlements whose populations had long been mainly Chinese.

Intensive Growth, 1850–1950

From 1850 until around 1900 the great industry was tin. The Chinese entered the industry as both entrepreneurs and laborers. They had the advantages of long experience with a monetized economy, a superior technology of chain pumps for mine drainage and brick kilns for smelting, and a high degree of ethnic solidarity. The previous Malay producers were largely driven from the industry, and even would-be British producers found it hard to survive in competition. In 1913 the Chinese still controlled three-quarters of tin output, and 95 percent of tin miners were Chinese. In later decades, however, the European percentage of output increased substantially with the introduction of dredging and other capital-intensive techniques.

Average annual exports of tin rose from 7,000 tons in the 1870s to 42,000 tons in the 1890s, by which time Malaya exported more tin than all other countries combined. Growth was more moderate after 1914, but has continued to the present day, and Malaysia is still the headquarters of and the dominant voice in the tin cartel.

Tin was joined eventually by rubber as a second great revenue producer. Brazilian seeds had found their way to Kew Gardens in London, and from there to Ceylon and Malaya in the 1870s. H. N. Ridley, director of the Singapore Botanical Gardens from 1888 onward, became known as "rubber Ridley" because of his eager propagation of the new crop. The great expansion of acreage, however, dates from around 1900, propelled by the rise of the motor industry and a skyrocketing of rubber prices. Total rubber plantings in Southeast Asia, mainly in Malaya and Ceylon, rose from 5,000 acres in 1900 to a million acres in 1910, to which another half-million acres was added in 1911. Expansion continued later on at a more moderate rate. By 1940 rubber acreage in Malaya alone was 3.5 million acres, almost five times the 786,000 acres planted to rice.

Most of the rubber output came from substantial "estates," or plantations, ranging from 500 to 5,000 acres in size. As of 1914, these were about 70 percent European-owned and 20 percent Chinese-owned. The estate workers were mostly Tamil laborers from southern India, adding a third element to Malaya's multiracial mixture. There were some Chinese estate workers, but in general the Chinese had superior opportunities in other areas. The native Malays, too, generally preferred their established pattern of village life and subsistence cultivation to wage labor in rubber production or tin mining.

There are few economies of scale in planting, cultivating, and tapping rubber trees. So there was some smallholder output from the beginning, about equally divided between Chinese and Malays; and the percentage of output from smallholdings tended to grow over time. Smallholder production was stimulated especially by the Stephenson rubber restriction scheme of the late 1920s, an early attempt to cartelize the industry by agreement among Malaya, Indonesia, and other major producers and to raise rubber prices by reducing output. The estate producers were readily controlled, but the smallholders declined to cooperate. The rapid increase in the output of the latter, plus the impact of the Great Depression, broke the cartel within a few years. By 1953 some 200,000 smallholders were engaged in rubber production, raising the percentage of export revenue returned to the domestic economy.

With fluctuations arising from war and depression, Malaya continued to ride the export tide right through the colonial period, as indeed it has largely continued to do. But the export economy would not have been possible without services provided by the colonial administration. The basic service was maintenance of internal order, which permitted peaceable economic activity. Beyond this, government was active in railroad construction. Beginning in 1885 several lines were built into the interior to serve the tin mines. These were amalgamated in 1901 into the Federated Malay States Railways. A rapid expansion of trunk lines followed, and by 1930 Malaya had an excellent railway system. Government also built roads, cleared rivers, encouraged coastal and river transport, built post offices, schools, and hospitals, these activities being financed mainly by export taxation. On the institutional side, there was early development of a British-dominated banking system. The currency was tied to the pound, and Malaya functioned as part of the London capital market. There was free repatriation of profits, which encouraged foreign investment. Another important institution was the "managing-agency" system developed earlier in India. Under this system each management company provided expert management to a considerable number of plantations, mines, and other enterprises. Distant British investors could invest with more confidence because of the availability of this service. Finally, the colonial civil service, inherited by independent Malaya, has been judged by some to be the best in the colonial world.

The colonial economy was almost completely open as regards trade, capital movements, and immigration, and it was highly export-oriented. The export/GDP ratio was typically around 50 percent. The strong export position permitted the great bulk of consumer goods to be imported. This was true even of food, where rice imports typically equalled about half of domestic consumption. Essentially, the rural Malay population ate home-produced rice while the Chinese and Indian half of the population ate imported rice. Although the colonial government was active in rubber research and development, it did little to stimulate domestic food production. Agriculture was not a high-priority claimant on public funds. It was not considered expedient to encourage commercial rice growing by the Chinese, agriculture being regarded as a Malay preserve. When falling tin and rubber prices produced a foreign-exchange squeeze in the early 1930s, there was some discussion of restricting rice imports and trying to substitute domestic production. But this would have raised food prices and put upward pressure on money wage rates. The powerful tin and rubber industries, interested above all in cheap labor, naturally opposed such a move and in the end nothing was done.

The export orientation also militated against any substantial development of domestic manufacturing. As of 1947, only 6.7 percent of the labor force was employed in industry. A considerable proportion of these were handicraft workers, and most of the others were employed in very small establishments. If industrialization were used as criterion, then, Malaya had not yet "taken off." Yet there had been a substantial increase in per capita income, though immigrants gained more than the indigenous population.

A less-fortunate legacy of the colonial period was a community divided along racial lines. By 1910 Malays were only 60 percent of the population and, as Chinese and Indian immigrants continued to pour in, they seemed doomed to permanent minority status. But with the advent of the Great Depression, many Indian laborers were sent home from 1930 to 1932 and free immigration to Malaya was ended in 1933. The country was left with a population about 50 percent Malay, 40 percent Chinese, and 10 percent Indian. The Chinese, however, were overwhelmingly dominant in trading and other business activities, as well as in tin mining. The Malays were predominantly farmers and also provided most of the soldiers and police. The Indians, predominantly rubber-estate laborers, had the lowest economic status.

Intensive Growth, 1950–80

During World War II Malaya was occupied by the Japanse and suffered much war damage. After the war, movement toward independence was delayed by a communist-led insurgency that took ten years to bring under control. The new nation finally emerged in 1957. Its boundaries have changed somewhat over the years. Singapore was initially part of the Federation of Malaya but withdrew after a few years, when it appeared that its financial contribution was exceeding any benefits received. As the British gradually withdrew from their colonies in Borneo, these were incorporated in 1963 into the Malay state, now called the Federation of Malaysia. These eastern areas substantially increased the country's geographic size; however, they are still relatively undeveloped, and the great bulk of economic activity is concentrated in traditional Malaya, now Western Malaysia.

The key issue of Malay-Chinese relations was settled in 1957, at least for the time being, by a political compromise. The Chinese got citizenship rights, a continuation of meritocracy in the public service (which benefited the more educated and upwardly mobile Chinese), and a laissez-faire business system. The Malays got recognition of their special indigenous status and establishment of Islam as the state religion and of Malay as the official language, with English to be phased out gradually. But Malay grievances continued to accumulate. The governing coalition lost the election of 1969, which was followed by race riots and declaration of a state of emergency. When political order was restored, the government embarked on an ''affirmative-action'' program intended to increase the proportion of Malays in higher-level jobs in the public service and elsewhere, to raise the Malay share of industrial ownership, and to speed replacement of English by the Malay language. Many of the policy actions since 1970 can be understood only in terms of their relative benefits to the Chinese and Malay populations.

The main contours of the economy have changed relatively little since independence, so little that the country is sometimes referred to as ''neocolonial.'' It is still a relatively open, private-enterprise economy with substantial foreign investment. It is strongly export-oriented, and the manufacturing sector is relatively smaller than in most other third-world countries. The balance-of-payments position is strong, government finances are strong, and prices are relatively stable. The GDP growth rate since 1960 has averaged 7.1 percent per year, well above the median for our sample.

Despite the ending of mass immigration, population spurted sharply after 1945 as deathrates were reduced rapidly to developed-country levels. The population growth rate peaked at 2.8 percent in the 1960s but fell back to 2.4 percent in the 1970s, and a further decline is in prospect. Family planning has spread particularly rapidly among the Chinese, with the result that the Chinese percentage of Malaysia's population is falling gradually relative to the more-prolific Malays.

The export/GDP ratio, while falling slightly since 1950, has remained close to the 50 percent level. Rubber has continued to do well, thanks to a vigorous government program of replacing older rubber trees with new plantings. At the peak of this program, replanting absorbed 16 percent of all development expenditure. While rubber acreage has expanded only moderately, productivity per acre has grown since 1960 at about 5 percent per year. Equally significant, however, is the marked diversification of exports over time. Tin and rubber, which in 1950 were 90 percent of all exports, have now fallen to less than 50 percent. With recent oil discoveries, petroleum has appeared as a major export. Timber and palm-oil exports have risen rapidly. Even more interesting, there are substantial and growing exports of manufactures. Malaysia's manufacturing sector, which has received relatively little protection, has been forced to be efficient from the outset and so has acquired export capacity.

Agriculture has received much more attention than it did during the colonial period. In the first four five-year development plans, it consistently received 20 to 25 percent of total expenditure, with about 50 percent going to infrastructure and 15 percent to health, education, and housing. Until recently industry received very little, industrial development being left to private enterprise. Industry's allocation rose in the 1970s, however, as part of the campaign to promote Malay-owned businesses.

The political reason for giving attention to agriculture is that it is largely in Malay hands. Improving the incomes of Malay farmers is thus an important step toward redressing racial imbalance. Large areas of virgin land suitable for rubber and palm-oil production have been cleared and provided with roads, electricity, and public buildings. This land is then subdivided and sold to Malay smallholders, many of them previously landless, who are thus enabled to participate in export production. Rice production has also been increased by the encouragement of colonization of new land as well as irrigation of previously settled areas and double-cropping. As a result, food production grew at 5.3 percent per year in the 1960s and at 6.1 percent in the 1970s, the highest rate in our sample. While there are still substantial rice imports, dependence on imported rice is gradually being reduced.

The industrial base at independence was small. Manufacturing employed some 6 percent of the labor force and produced about the same percentage of GDP.

One-third of the industrial workers were self-employed, and most others worked in very small shops. Only 79 establishments in the country had more than 100 employees. Apart from export processing, the products were mainly light consumer goods plus building materials protected by transport costs.

In this situation many third-world governments would have chosen forced-draft industrialization. Malaysia did not do so. The explanation is partly economic—there was no balance-of-payments constraint limiting imports of manufactures. But it is also partly political. The industrialists and most of their employees were Chinese. Raising their incomes by the usual protectionist devices would benefit the Chinese but injure the Malays through higher consumer-goods prices. It would also raise the money wage level, which would injure the powerful tin and rubber interests. Protectionism was generally opposed by the import merchants, who were doing well under free trade; and it was opposed also by treasury officials interested in maximizing the revenue from import duties, which would be reduced if rates were raised too high.

These forces help to explain the moderate nature of industrial-promotion policies. Government did not embark at all on direct ownership of industry. It did create a category of "pioneer industries" that received both tax incentives and a diversified package of supporting services. Tariffs were also raised after the mid-1960s, and by 1974 the average effective rate was about 40 percent, compared with virtually zero in 1965. A careful study by Hoffman and Fe (1980) concludes, however, that the tax and tariff incentives "were largely redundant in the sense that most of the investment would have taken place without them." Perhaps the most important thing government did was to provide political stability and efficient administration, plus an open economy that provided both free access to raw materials and capital goods and free repatriation of profits.

Modern manufacturing has been largely created by foreign investment, and most industrial capital is still foreign-owned. Hoffman and Fe concluded that expansion of foreign corporations has sometimes led to displacement of local companies. The profit outflow is also a substantial negative item on the balance of payments, but this is more than offset by the flow of manufactured exports generated by the new enterprises.

Under this regime, Malaysian manufacturing has expanded along normal lines. Its contribution to GDP in 1980 was 16 percent, which is about the norm suggested by Chenery for a country of this size and income level. There was the usual shift toward larger establishments and toward heavier types of industry. The chemicals, petroleum, metals, machinery, and transport equipment industries now provide more than one-third of manufacturing output. The main driving force behind industrial expansion has been rapid growth of the domestic market, which has become increasingly important relative to import substitution and export expansion. Overall, Malaysia conforms to the pattern indicated by comparative advantage, exporting labor-intensive products and importing capital-intensive ones.

As in other countries, manufacturing in Malaysia has absorbed only a small proportion of the growing labor force. Underemployment, indicated partly by rising open-unemployment rates in urban areas, is still growing.

Turning to the public sector, government has succeeded in mobilizing more than 20 percent of GDP as current revenue. In addition, tax sources are more diversified than they were a generation ago, with direct taxes on income and wealth now contributing more than taxes on foreign trade. Current expenditure amounts to about 15 percent of GDP and, in areas where quantitative indicators are available, these funds appear to be used effectively. Primary-school enrollment is now virtually universal, and secondary enrollment has risen from 5 percent of the relevant age group in 1950 to 50 percent today. Mortality rates, and particularly infant mortality, have been much reduced. By 1980 life expectancy at birth had risen to 68 years, which is close to developed-country levels and well above the level in most third-world countries.

Government is also an important investor but, in accordance with the country's private-enterprise stance, it provides one-quarter to one-third of total capital formation rather than the half or more found in many other countries. Public investment is financed partly from the current budget surplus and partly from noninflationary domestic borrowing, with little reliance on foreign finance.

Although in general I avoid the issue of income distribution in this book, an unusually thorough investigation of Malaysian data by Donald Snodgrass (1980) warrants brief comment. Family survey data indicate that inequality has increased since independence in almost every dimension. Tables on the occupational distribution of male workers show the Chinese constituting a high proportion of employment in administrative and managerial work (61 percent), clerical work (37 percent), sales and related activities (51 percent), and manufacturing (62 percent). The ratio of Chinese to Malay household incomes rose from 2.16 in 1957–58 to 2.49 in 1976. The urban-rural gap, which in large measure is a Chinese-Malay gap, has risen from 1.84 in 1957–58 to 2.24 in 1976. Gini coefficients have risen in both the urban and rural sectors. It appears that the top 10 percent of households were able to increase their incomes by 51 percent between 1957 and 1970 and to capture 49 percent of the total income growth over this period. These trends, which support Kuznet's hypothesis of growing inequality in the early decades of development, are unusually well documented in the Malaysian case.

THAILAND

For most of its existence Thailand has been a land-abundant, labor-scarce economy, almost entirely agricultural, and with 95 percent of its cultivated area devoted to rice. Its government has been archaic, rather inert, but permissive of economic activity on condition of specified payments to the crown. Its history provides a test of the possibility of economic expansion without significant political modernization.

James Ingram's classic study (1971) provides a good picture of the Thai economy in 1850. King Rama IV (also known as Mongkut and celebrated in "Anna and the King of Siam") ascended the throne in 1851 under a system of absolute monarchy that continued until 1932. Under him was a feudal structure of nobles and officials who subsisted on a flow of goods to Bangkok that amounted to taxes in kind. Rice was the staple food crop, grown mainly with river floodwater on the central plain. Any freeman was entitled to occupy 25 rai, equal to about ten acres. Land belonged in principle to the king, but the cultivator had tenure rights extending even to the right to mortgage. In return, the peasant provided labor and other services to the local noble as the king's representative. Manufacturing was entirely handicraft and carried on largely in agricultural households. Specialized, full-time artisans were found mainly in noble households and the royal court. Internal trade was largely in the hands of Chinese merchants under a grant from the king, who in principle had a monopoly of all economic activity. Intervillage trade was small relative to intravillage trade and moved mainly along waterways. Foreign trade, also relatively small, was in the hands of the king or his concessionaires. Exports were quite diversified and, except for rubber, most of today's exports appear on the 1850 list.

Thailand (then Siam) was a buffer state between the British in Burma and the French in Indochina. King Mongkut managed to ensure at least nominal independence by signing a treaty with the British in 1855 giving them extraterritorial status under their own consul, allowing them to buy and sell produce anywhere in the kingdom, and restricting export and import duties to 3 percent, which limited a major source of government revenue. A British "financial adviser" became in effect the budget director. Similar treaties, of less practical consequence, were signed later on with the United States, Japan, France, and other European powers. Mongkut's accommodating stance, however, did not prevent the Western powers from nibbling away pieces of his territory. France established protectorates in Laos and Cambodia, previously tributory to Bangkok, and in 1907 took over four eastern Thai provinces, which were added to Cambodia. In 1909 four provinces in the Malay Peninsula were ceded to Britain and became part of Malaya.

Turning Point: *circa* 1850

The choice of 1850 as Thailand's turning point is suggested by the ascension of a modernizing ruler, King Mongkut, in 1851; by the key treaty with Britain in 1855, which opened the country to foreign trade; and by the acceleration of rice exports from the 1850s onward, which ran well ahead of the rate of population growth. Moreover, these were peasant-produced exports, so that returned value to the economy was high.

Intensive Growth, 1850–1950

Over the century between 1850 and 1950 Thailand was characterized by a marked continuity of economic trends and a lack of major structural change. Population grew slowly in the nineteenth century through natural increase supplemented by a continuing flow of Chinese immigrants. Population is estimated to have increased from six million in 1850 to eight million in 1900, a growth rate of 0.56 percent per year. In the twentieth century population growth accelerated, from eight million in 1900 to 18.5 million in 1950, a growth rate of 1.64 percent per year.

Population growth was readily accommodated by growing more rice on more land. The striking feature of this period, however, was that rice acreage and output grew much faster than was necessary for domestic consumption. Rice exports rose from less than 5 percent of the crop in 1850 to about 50 percent by 1900. The demand for rice came mainly from other Asian countries, notably China and Malaya. The development of Malaya, with its large surplus of tin and rubber and its large food deficit and the marked cheapening of ocean transport were the most important factors stimulating the growth of Thai exports.

The growth of rice exports, in thousands of piculs (1 picul = 60 kilos) per year, was as follows:

Period	Exports (thousand piculs)
1857–59	990
1865–69	1,630
1875–79	3,530
1885–89	5,320
1895–99	8,000
1905–09	14,760
1915–19	15,790
1925–29	23,390
1935–39	25,370

These high growth rates, well above the rate of population growth, provide a *prima facie* case for rising per capita incomes, even though peasant producers received only about half of the export price. The growth of exports did not encroach on domestic rice consumption per capita, which seems if anything to have risen over the period. The Thai people have always been well nourished— and they continue to be, as anyone traveling in the country today can testify.

For several decades after 1850 the growing foreign demand for rice was met mainly from paddy produced in the heart of the central plain, around the ancient capital of Ayutthaya, north of Bangkok. Much unused land was available at this time, and population simply grew and spread out over the plain. By the 1880s, however, the central plain was substantially occupied. Settlement then spread to a large area of unclaimed land east of Bangkok, which amounted eventually to about 25 percent of the rice land in central Thailand. Opening of this land required transport, which meant mainly digging east-west canals to link rivers running from north to south. Lacking funds for such a large enterprise, government turned it over to private entrepreneurs, among whom princes and nobles were prominent, along with Chinese traders and others. These developers were given the right to sell the land assigned to them, with government taking a percentage of the profit. This colonization boom peaked in 1890–1910. After 1900, rice cultivation was also extended farther to the north and northeast as railroads were built into these areas, financed mainly by bonds floated in London. The total area planted to rice rose from 5.8 million rai in 1850 to 11.5 million in 1910–14 to 25.5 million in 1935–39 to 34.6 million rai in 1950.

How could rice acreage and output grow so much faster than population? Where did the labor come from? Peasants seem to have responded to market incentives by putting in more labor time per capita, by trading leisure for income. In addition, more household labor time became available as imported consumer goods decreased the need for household production. Seasonal peaks of labor demand were met partly by migratory labor from areas of the northeast not suited to rice production.

Most of the peasant producers owned their land, though there were also a good many tenants, especially in the "colonized" areas, where land was sometimes sold in large blocks to owners who subdivided and rented it. These producers proved quite responsive to market demand, for example, by shifting from the traditional sticky rice to the nonglutinous rice demanded by the export market. Capital requirements for entering production were low, amounting mainly to purchase of a plow and a bullock, which could be covered by one year's cash return from the crop. The simple production techniques changed little over the course of time. Rice yields per rai remained roughly stable in the central plain, though they declined significantly in the north and northeast as cultivation was extended to less and less suitable land.

Rice growing was sufficiently profitable that Thai peasants showed marked reluctance to leave the village for urban employment. This kept urban labor scarce and wage rates relatively high. Urban wage labor was performed almost entirely by Chinese immigrants, who entered in increasing numbers, attracted by wages higher than could be earned at home. There were trading as well as wage-earning opportunities. In the rice trade, Chinese performed the middleman functions of going upriver, buying paddy from the farmers, transporting it to rice mills in Bangkok or nearby, and eventually exporting the finished rice. Ingram estimates that the farmer got about half the export value of the crop, the rest going to the trader, the miller, and the exporter. The Chinese trader also sold imported consumer goods to the farmer, advanced credit, bought land, and functioned as a multipurpose businessman. To an extent unusual in Southeast Asia the Chinese, who still dominate business life, have managed to blend into the local population by intermarriage and by adopting Thai names and customs. An outsider to the culture cannot readily determine who is of Chinese origin and who is not.

While rice was typically about 70 percent of total exports, tin provided about 10 percent and teak around 5 percent; because we know that rice exports were growing rapidly in volume, the stability of these percentages implies a rapid increase in absolute terms. The tin industry is located in the Thai portion of the Malay Peninsula, and its evolution is similar to that in Malaya—domination first by Chinese entrepreneurs, then by Western companies as dredging techniques raised capital costs. Teak, located in the north near the Laotian border, is in the hands of Chinese, Burmese, and some Western companies. Rubber emerged in the 1920s and grew rapidly to about 30 percent of total exports by 1950. It is located along the Malaysian border and is mainly in the hands of Thai smallholders, though Chinese smallholders have about one-quarter of the acreage. This modest diversification of exports before 1950 foreshadows a more substantial diversification in later years.

The rapid rise of exports made possible a large increase in imports. At the outset more than 90 percent of imports were manufactured consumer goods. This situation changed only gradually and moderately over the years. In 1938 consumer goods were still 72 percent of imports, with capital goods 13 percent, and raw materials, fuels, and other intermediates 15 percent. There was typically a surplus of exports over imports, offset by substantial home remittances by the Chinese immigrants. Fluctuations in the value of rice exports seem not to have caused serious difficulties. A drop in export receipts, by reducing incomes in Thailand, also reduced demand for imported consumer goods. In this sense the balance of payments was self-equilibrating. Further, with the notable exception of cotton cloth, the imported consumer goods did not form part of the basic consumption package. When imports were curtailed there was mainly a temporary reduction in what could be regarded as luxury consumption. The possibility of acquiring these luxury items, however, served as an important incentive in stimulating rice production.

The most important import item was textiles, especially cotton cloth. Imported cloth was finer though less durable than the coarse home-woven cloth, it was cheaper, and it offered bright colors, which were more attractive than the somber colors produced by Thai dyes. Thus imports took over a growing share of the market, particularly in the central plain with its easy water transport and large money income from rice. Penetration to the north and northeast was slowed by high transport costs and the risk of banditry, but these problems were eased by the spread of railroads after 1900.

Domestic demand for textiles, of course, increased greatly over the period 1850–1950 because of the tripling of population and the rise in income levels. Thus the *absolute* level of handicraft production seems never to have fallen, and on the contrary increased considerably. But its market *share* fell from 1850 until about 1920, while the share of imports rose. After 1920, however, domestic production and especially domestic weaving made something of a comeback, as indicated by a marked expansion of cotton growing in the north and a substantial growth of imported yarn. Domestic cloth was competitive partly because the opportunity cost of the household labor used in producing it was close to zero. By 1950 about 60 percent of Thai cloth consumption was home-produced, and entirely by handicraft methods, since no textile mills had yet been established.

Apart from cloth and clothing, most of the goods in daily use continued to be produced at home or in the village. These included such things as kitchen utensils, mats, baskets, pottery, thatched roofing, wooden sandals, woven hats, boats, and bullock-drawn carts.

Throughout this long period, 85 percent of the population continued to be engaged in agriculture, forestry, and fishing. Factory industry was virtually absent. As of 1937, only 1.6 percent of the labor force was employed in manufacturing, and almost all of these were in mills processing rice, sugar, lumber, and rubber. Apart from these activities there were only a dozen or so industrial enterprises in the country.

The "public sector" remained small and primitive. The king governed as an absolute monarch until a coup in 1932, and after that as a constitutional, but quite influential, ruler. About 40 percent of royal revenue came from gambling and the opium monopoly, with excises, customs duties, and land taxes each contributing about 15 percent. When the British treaty limiting import duties to 3 percent expired in 1926 tariffs were raised considerably, reaching an average level of 28 percent by the late 1930s and contributing 25 percent of government revenue. The main expenditures were for the court and the military. Education was a tiny item. Over the years 1890–1940 only about 11 percent of the budget went for capital formation, primarily for irrigation. Railroad building, as noted earlier, was financed by foreign bond issues.

This limited productive role, however, does not mean that government was unimportant in the economy. Mongkut and his successor, Chulalongkorn, were strongly prorice and proexport. They maintained the traditional right of citizens to occupy unused land up to 25 rai (ten acres) per household. Slavery and the corvée system were gradually abolished over the last half of the nineteenth century, which increased the number of potential farmers. Land taxes were kept low, averaging only about 5 percent of annual crop value, compared with 30 percent or more in some other Asian countries. Further, new land brought under cultivation was exempt from taxation for the first year and taxed at a reduced rate for an additional three years. The court encouraged canal building between rivers, which provided transportation and helped to regulate water supply. It also encouraged expansion of the rail network, which by 1940 amounted to 3,130 kilometers and served most of the area not served by waterways.

Thailand's experience up to 1950 supports the view that intensive growth should not be identified with industrialization. Factory industry was almost absent, but income growth was substantial. True, a disproportionate share of the increased income went to a limited circle of nobles, officials, Chinese businessmen, and large landowners. But there is evidence also of modest, undramatic improvement in living standards for the mass of the farm population. Nutrition levels were at least maintained, and possibly improved. There was opportunity to consume a wider array as well as large amounts of consumer goods, including some exotic or luxury items. There was opportunity also to substitute imports for home production in some areas, and the fact that these substitutes were preferred suggests some gain in welfare.

Intensive Growth, 1950–80

Although there was modest progress before World War II, this progress was much accelerated after 1945. Population growth speeded up, but output speeded up even more. Particularly from 1960 onward, Thailand's growth rate of per capita income was one of the highest in the developing world.

The population story is not unusual. From 1850 to 1900 population grew at an average rate of only 0.6 percent per year. During the interwar period, the growth rate rose to about 2.0 percent per year, mainly through reduction of mortality. After 1945 there was a further sharp increase, resulting from a decline in mortality almost to "developed-country" levels, with the birthrate showing its characteristic lag in response. The population growth rate peaked in the 1960s at 3.0 percent. A decline to 2.5 percent in the 1970s, however, suggests that Thailand has now entered the demographic transition.

Agricultural output grew at 4.5 percent per year in the 1950s and at 5.1 percent in the 1960s and 1970s, well ahead of population growth. Not only does Thailand have no food problem, but it has been able to supply an increasingly diversified flow of agricultural exports. This is due partly to a good supply of land. The cultivated area has grown at about the same rate as the farm population, with the result that the average size of holding has remained roughly constant. There is moderate inequality in the size distribution of holdings, but not the extreme inequality found in some other countries. About 85 percent of the farmers are owner-operators, who have shown themselves quite adept in allocating acreage among crops on the basis of relative profitability. For the first time in Thai history there has been a substantial increase in crop yields. The rate of output growth since 1950 has been roughly double the growth rate of acreage and of the farm labor force.

Rice acreage has continued to expand, though more slowly than it did before 1950. Yields per acre began to rise around 1960, and they rose during the 1960s at almost 4 percent per year, accounting for two-thirds of the output increase from seven million tons to 13 million tons per year. The productivity increase can be attributed to several factors: growing imports of fertilizer (though fertilizer use is still low compared with Taiwan or Japan); a continuing effort to adapt new IRRI rice strains to Thai conditions; a much more active government irrigation policy, which raised the irrigated area from 3.8 million rai in 1947 to 14.0 million rai in 1969; an expansion of the rural road network to some 10,000 miles, reducing transport costs; and rapid extension of primary education and adult literacy.

A subject of continuing controversy has been the "rice premium," an export tax amounting to 25–35 percent of the value of exports, which serves to depress the domestic rice price below the world price by this amount. Assuming that middlemen's margins are competitively determined, which appears to be true, the burden of the tax falls on farmers. Government likes the system because, in addition to yielding revenue, it makes for cheaper food and a lower urban wage level, which is encouraging to industry. Its opponents contend that it is inequitable and reduces production incentives.

For whatever reasons, rice growing does appear to be less profitable than most other crops. A study covering the crop years 1965–67 shows the following average income (in bahts) yielded by one rai of land: rice, 291; maize, 325; cassava, 611; sugarcane, 606; cotton, 501; kenaf, 569; rubber, 377; vegetables, 852. Farmers have sensibly responded by allocating more land to nonrice crops. These include export crops, such as maize, kenaf (a jutelike fiber), cassava, and rubber; and crops for home use, such as cotton, coconuts, sugarcane, fruits, and vegetables. The acreage devoted to such crops increased four times between 1950 and 1970, while rice acreage rose only 20 percent and nonrice crops accounted for 88 percent of the total acreage increase. The value of livestock output plus fruit and vegetable output was by 1970 equal to the value of rice output. In export terms, this shift has meant a sharp drop in the rice percentage of total exports and a sharp increase in the share of other agricultural products. In terms of domestic consumption it has meant a diversification of diets, of which rice is still the central component, by increased consumption of meat, fruits, vegetables, sugar, fats, and oils.

From 1950 to 1970 the export/GDP ratio fluctuated in the range of 16–19 percent, without trend. In the 1970s, however, it rose above 20 percent, reaching 23 percent by 1979. Export volume rose sharply in the same period and was only partially offset by a moderate decline in the terms of trade. The most interesting development was a marked diversification out of rice into other export products. By 1970 a half-dozen other primary products had become important, their total export value exceeding that of rice, whose export share fell below 20 percent. Further, with the gradual industrialization of the economy, exports of manufactured goods rose from near zero in 1960 to 22 percent of all exports in 1979.

The import pattern shows the usual shift away from consumer goods as import-substituting industries were established in one field after another. By the 1970s machinery and transport equipment accounted for one-third of imports and all capital goods for about half. The fuel share of imports also rose to about 25 percent with the oil-price jumps of 1974 and 1979. In contrast to the pre-1940 era, with its typical trade surplus, Thailand since 1950 has typically had a current-account deficit. Thailand has provided a congenial climate for foreign private investment, and there has been a substantial inflow of private long-term capital. The remainder of the deficit has been closed by moderate foreign borrowing.

Thailand entered the postwar era with very little factory industry. Apart from raw-materials processing there were only a few establishments producing such things as sugar, beer, liquor, matches, cigarettes, and soap. But government now embarked on a policy of deliberate industrialization. This policy was interpreted initially as meaning establishment of government-owned industries, which would be in the hands of Thai officials rather than Chinese businessmen. But these early industries were quite inefficient and became a substantial drain on the treasury, so by the late 1950s government had shifted to policies favoring private initiative.

Elements in the new policy package included: (1) a Promotion of Industrial Investment Act of 1959, which offered tax advantages plus duty-free entry of capital goods and raw materials to industries selected for "promotion"; (2) a companion measure guaranteeing that government would not compete with private industry in "promoted" activities, nor would it nationalize them—government's role would be limited to investing in infrastructure to support the private sector; and (3) moderate tariff protection, with the rate schedule escalating in the usual way. By 1969 the average rate of effective protection was estimated at 42 percent for capital goods, 86 percent for nondurable consumer goods, and 109 percent for consumer durables. Domestic industry was favored also by a variety of licensing and bank-credit arrangements.

Under this regime, manufacturing output has grown since 1960 at about 11 percent per year and has raised its share of GDP from about 10 percent in 1950 to 20 percent in 1980. About two-thirds of industrial investment has come from local sources and about one-third from abroad, primarily from Japan and secondarily from the United States and Taiwan. The marginal propensity to save since 1960 has been estimated as high as 0.30, and by 1979 gross domestic saving was 21 percent of GDP. Thailand is also well supplied with entrepreneurs, mainly of Chinese origin but now blended into the local population, as described earlier. An ingenious system has developed in which a Chinese business owner often has a Thai "silent partner" in government, who shares in the profits in exchange for political protection. What some Westerners might criticize as corruption appears to most Thais as a sensible and workable arrangement. Most domestic businesses are still owned by individuals or partnerships rather than by public corporations. Profit rates are high compared with those in more industrialized countries.

Manufacturing enterprises were initially very small. A 1964 study found only 239 establishments with 100 or more employees, and these employed only 15 percent of all manufacturing workers. Since that time large establishments have become somewhat more prominent, and there has been a gradual shift toward heavier types of industry. Even in 1980, however, the metals-machinery-transport equipment group still formed only a small percentage of manufacturing output. Perhaps because of the smallness of the domestic market, perhaps because decisions have been guided by profit calculations, perhaps because of the moderate and outward-looking tone of public policy, there has been less of a headlong rush into heavy industry than in some other third-world countries.

The public sector is also moderate in size. The government revenue/GDP ratio rose from 11.0 percent in 1952 to 13.9 percent in 1980. Four-fifths of revenue comes from indirect taxes, but the contribution of import and export duties has fallen somewhat while that of internal excises has risen. Income and profit taxation is light. Current expenditure has been held to a level that normally yields a considerable surplus to help in financing capital expenditure. Government capital expenditure in the 1970s has been running at around 7 percent of GDP, rather less than one-third of total capital formation in the country. Overall, there is a public-sector deficit of the order of 3–4 percent of GDP, about three-quarters of which is typically financed by domestic borrowing and one-quarter by foreign borrowing. The World Bank, the United States, and West Germany have been the largest lenders.

As I noted earlier, Thailand ranks near the top of the league in overall growth rate. The average annual increase in GDP was 8.4 percent from 1960 to 1970 and 7.2 percent from 1970 to 1980. Thus between 1960 and 1980, income per capita rose at an average of 4.7 percent per year.

Government is oligarchic, and abrupt changes of government are not unknown. But popular attachment to the monarchy provides an element of stability. The occasional coups are of the good-natured Latin American variety, with little bloodshed and the ousted premier flying off to a prosperous exile. There is a good supply of economic technocrats, partly foreign-trained but now trained increasingly at Thammasat and Chulalongkorn universities. I have already noted the presence of a vigorous business community, which government has tended to encourage rather than to stifle. The owner-based agricultural sector, providing exports, raw materials for local industry, food supplies, and an expanding market for domestic manufactures, has also played a key role in overall growth.

8

Taiwan, South Korea, Philippines

With Notes on Algeria, Morocco, Venezuela

This chapter will focus on the experience of Taiwan, Korea (up to 1940, South Korea since 1950), and the Philippines. I shall comment more briefly on three additional cases—Algeria, Morocco, and Venezuela—partly because of space constraints, partly because of scantier source materials.

Why no discussion of the important and well-documented case of Japan? To take account of the large literature on Japan would have required at least a chapter, which would have further enlarged an already long book. In an earlier study (Reynolds, 1977) I did devote a chapter to the Japanese experience, which can be read as a companion to this volume.

In generalizing about intensive growth in chapter 4, I drew on early Japanese experience, particularly from the years 1880–1920. By 1950, however, Japan had clearly passed out of the "less-developed" category and was classified among the advanced industrial countries. In the comparative analysis of third-world growth from 1950 to 1980 in chapter 15, therefore, Japan is excluded.

TAIWAN

Taiwan's spectacular post-1950 performance has distracted attention from the fact that it also, for the period, had an unusually high growth rate from 1900 to 1940. Relying mainly on an excellent monograph by Samuel Ho (1978), I shall try to correct this undue emphasis on recent events.

Turning Point: *circa* 1895

Taiwan's population was growing in the eighteenth and nineteenth centuries, mainly through migration from other provinces of southern China. By 1811 there were already two million people in this small island. Taiwan was closed to foreigners until its ports were opened by treaties of 1858 and 1860. British and American merchants then took over most of the long-distance trade, but the "junk trade" to Hong Kong and Amoy remained in Chinese hands. The main export items were tea (50 percent) and sugar (25 percent), while opium was half of all imports. Internal transport was virtually absent, and the island remained a collection of isolated communities rather than an integrated economy.

Taiwan was unable to respond in a sustained way to the stimulus of external trade because of production conditions in the basic crops. Rice was grown by traditional Chinese methods, with little productivity increase, and after feeding themselves the peasants were unable to generate much of an export surplus. Sugar was also a stagnant industry, with no uptrend in output from 1870 to 1895 because of primitive methods in both growing and cane crushing. Unlike traditional rice and sugar, tea developed as a peasant crop in direct consequence of the opening of trade with the West. Output and exports expanded as more land was allocated to tea. But the Chinese merchants and peasant producers took little interest in the quality-control problems involved in picking, selection, and packing. So the product deteriorated, and Taiwan lost out in the world market to Ceylon, India, and Japan.

Until 1895, then, the picture is one of extensive growth, with population growing but with little change in per capita output. After Japan's victory over China in 1895 Taiwan (then Formosa) passed into Japanese hands. The new rulers set out to turn the island into an economic asset and to integrate it with the Japanese economy. As Ho (1978, p. 26) comments, "most important, the colonial government, with vastly different objectives and preferences than the Imperial Chinese government, was involved actively in developing the island. It was the agent, the entrepreneur that mobilized resources and made development possible."

As I proceed I shall note interesting parallels between economic trends in Taiwan and those which had occurred earlier in Japan itself. These similarities are no accident, but represent rather a transfer to Taiwan of the ingenuity that the Japanese had already shown in their own development.

Intensive Growth, 1895–1940

The magnitude of the development effort after 1895 is suggested by the fact that expenditures of the colonial government varied between 12 and 18 percent of estimated GDP, an unusually high level for this era. The tax system was regressive. Some 70–80 percent of current revenue came from land taxes and from profits of government monopolies, that is, from the Taiwanese farmer and consumer. Profits were taxed very lightly, as they always have been in Japan. Expenditures for development typically formed more than 40 percent of total expenditure, which again is a remarkably high figure for the period. Top priority went to transport and communications, which received 40–60 percent of development funds. Starting from zero in 1895, Taiwan by 1940 had 12,076 kilometers of roads and 907 kilometers of railway. The main purpose of the transport system was to move farm produce to the ports and to speed the commercialization of agriculture. Agriculture itself received one-third of development expenditure, partly for irrigation. Irrigated land as a proportion of all cultivated land rose from 32 percent in 1906 to 64 percent in 1942. There was considerable attention, too, to human-resource development. Between 1905 and 1940 the crude deathrate fell from 31 per thousand to 17, while the literacy rate rose from 1 percent to 27 percent.

The strategy of development was to transform Taiwan into an agricultural appendage of the Japanese economy, thus helping to close Japan's growing food deficit. The situation was favorable in that, unlike in many colonial areas, in Taiwan the basic export crops were peasant crops. But much had to be done to inform, motivate, and assist peasant producers and integrate them into a commercialized economy. An early step was to transform the previous three-tier system of land ownership into a two-tier system. The rentiers in the top tier were paid off in bonds, which subsequently lost most of their value through inflation. This scheme resembles the land reforms instituted in Japan itself in the 1880s, which laid the foundations of modern Japanese agriculture. There continued, however, to be a rather skewed distribution of land ownership, which changed little during the colonial period. Some 2 percent of farm families with holdings of more than 10 hectares owned 36 percent of the land, while the 60 percent of families with less than 1 hectare owned only 14 percent. As of 1937–40, about 56 percent of cultivated land was rented, while 44 percent was owner-operated.

The road-building and irrigation programs helped to raise cultivated acreage from 519,000 hectares in 1910 to 837,000 hectares in 1942. By that time almost two-thirds of the land was irrigated, and the multiple-cropping index had risen to 125. After about 1920, however, little new land was available and output increases had to come mainly from technical progress. On this front the authorities did several things:

1. They established a strong network of agricultural experiment stations and extension agents, patterned on Japanese experience. By the end of the colonial period there was one extension agent for every 32 farm families.
2. They introduced improved strains of rice from Japan and improved sugarcane varieties from Java. Chemical fertilizers were imported from Japan, and later on fertilizer factories were built in Taiwan.
3. They established a system of farmers' cooperative associations, which played an important role in spreading technical knowledge, managing input supplies, and providing farm credit. The associations served as effective intermediaries between government officials and technicians and the peasant producer.

The results of this promotional activity were impressive. Agriculture continued to dominate the economy and to provide about 70 percent of GDP. Between 1900 and 1920 agricultural output rose at 2–2.5 percent per year. Between 1920 and 1940 the growth rate rose to 3.8 percent per year, mainly through higher crop yields per hectare. Output growth significantly exceeded population growth, and generated a growing export surplus. Production was also increasingly commercialized. By 1940 some 75 percent of rice output and almost 100 percent of sugar output was marketed. The farmers, to be sure, did not get all of the rapidly growing farm income. Ho (1978, p. 68) comments that "the net agricultural surplus nearly always absorbed one-fifth of the rapidly expanding agricultural production. Numerous mechanisms helped transfer the net surplus from agriculture: agricultural taxes, the savings of both individual and corporate landlords, and the strong monopsonistic power of buyers of agricultural goods." The main export crop was sugar, and Japanese-owned sugar companies were given exclusive buying rights over specified areas. But colonial policy was judicious in that it left farmers a sufficient share of increases in output to induce continued growth.

Trade grew rapidly, in absolute terms and as a percentage of GDP. Between 1900 and 1939 export value increased eighteenfold, with 90–95 percent of the exports going to Japan. The main export crop was sugar, whose output grew at 4.5 percent per year from 1905 to 1940, compared with a 2.7 percent growth of rice production. Sugar formed about 50 percent of total exports, rice 25 percent, other food products 10 percent. It may seem strange that food also formed about one-third of *imports* until one recalls that there was a substantial Japanese population of business and professional men, administrators, and technicians who demanded goods to which they were accustomed at home. Among manufactured imports, while textiles were important, the proportion of fertilizers, machinery, and transport equipment was well above that in other colonial areas. There was typically an export surplus, amounting to about one-quarter of exports, representing in part profit transfers by Japanese-owned enterprises.

Big business was mainly Japanese, little business Taiwanese. Six large Japanese companies accounted for 80 percent of paid-up capital in manufacturing, and Japanese ownership was dominant also in mining, electric power, banking, and commerce. Japanese dominated the administrative, professional, and technical occupations, with the Taiwanese confined to farming, manual labor, and petty trade.

The manufacturing sector was strongly agriculture-oriented. About half of output in the 1930s came from sugar processing, another quarter from processing rice and other food products. But there was considerable development of ceramics, chemicals, and fertilizer production; and after 1935, with war imminent, Japan began moving machine-building and other strategic industries to Taiwan as well as Korea. There was a large handicraft sector. As late as 1930 the number of handicraft workers still equaled the number of factory workers, even though all establishments with five or more workers were classified as "factories." By 1940, however, factory employment had pulled well ahead.

There was a substantial inflow of Japanese capital in the early stages of colonization. Ho estimates the figure at 80 million yen per year from 1896 to 1910. By the 1920s and 1930s, however, industrial investment was being financed mainly from savings generated in Taiwan. Domestic investment was made possible by rapid increases in labor productivity, a lag of wages behind productivity, consequent high profit rates, and high reinvestment from profits—all paralleling

Japan's industrial experience. From 1920 to 1939, labor productivity in manufacturing rose at 3.3 percent per year, while real wages rose at 1.5 percent. Profits were typically in the range of 20–45 percent of paid-up capital; and on average about 55 percent of profit was reinvested. Even so, dividend payments were large enough so that by the late 1930s there was an average net outflow of investment income from Taiwan of some 50 million yen per year.

The colonial economic record can be summarized in a few numbers: from 1903 to 1940, total product in constant prices increased by about 45 percent per decade; population grew at 26 percent per decade, mainly because of Japanese-sponsored health improvements that cut the mortality rate in half. Thus output per capita grew at 19 percent per decade—an unusually strong performance for that period and equaling the average for the "developed" countries. Growth was unusually rapid from about 1915 to the early 1930s, as Taiwan shared in the impetus that World War I gave to Japanese economic growth.

The benefits of income growth, of course, went disproportionately to the Japanese; but the Taiwanese also gained significantly. Farmers kept a considerable share of their rising cash income and also learned more productive techniques. The average Taiwanese farmer by 1940 was a very different person from his counterpart in 1900. The real wage rate rose in agriculture as well as in industry. The average increase in agriculture was 1.3 percent per year from 1910 to 1939. While per capita food consumption did not change much from its level of 2,000 calories per day, diets were diversified as rice was supplemented increasingly with sweet potatoes and other new foods. Per capita availability of cotton cloth more than doubled, there was a great increase in the number of bicycles, and marked improvement in health and education. Thus Ho (1978, p. 91) seems warranted in concluding that "in the colonial period the average Taiwanese improved his general economic conditions moderately and in a few areas, such as education and health, significantly."

Intensive Growth, 1950–80

The outlines of Taiwan's rapid post-1950 development are well known and can be recapitulated briefly. During the 1950s considerable attention was paid to land reform and to strengthening the agricultural base. Conventional import-substitution policies were followed, but these were more moderate than in most other countries and did not turn the internal terms of trade against agriculture. During the late 1950s and early 1960s a variety of reform measures were introduced to liberalize trade and establish a more realistic set of relative factor prices. Taiwan adopted a unified and realistic exchange rate, relaxed exchange controls, reduced effective protection, and raised interest rates substantially. Manufacturing production and exports responded strongly to this policy package. While agricultural exports continued to rise, they were overshadowed increasingly by exports of labor-intensive manufactures, a process that has been labeled "export substitution." By 1968 Taiwan had exhausted its surplus-labor pool and entered a period of labor scarcity and sharply rising real wages. Exports and GDP continued to grow rapidly in the 1970s, with little retardation from the 1974 and 1979 oil-price shocks.

The growth rate of GDP accelerated during the 1950s and since 1960 has usually been in the range of 8–10 percent per year. Investment, which was about 12.5 percent of GDP in 1952, had risen to 25 percent by the 1970s. The domestic savings rate rose in tandem with the investment rate. Although there has been considerable foreign investment from Japan, the United States, and elsewhere, the bulk of investment has been financed from domestic saving. The public sector is moderately large but not growing relatively, public consumption remaining in the range of 16–17 percent of GDP. Exports, only about 10 percent of GDP in the 1950s, had risen above 30 percent by the 1970s. From 1960 to 1975 commodity exports grew at an average rate of 18.7 percent per year. Meanwhile there was a dramatic shift in the composition of exports. Primary products, which were 90 percent of exports in 1952, had fallen to 20 percent by 1977, the other 80 percent being manufactured goods. Manufacturing expansion in the 1950s and 1960s was oriented toward labor-intensive products and processes. Unlike the situation in many other third-world countries, the rate of increase in manufacturing employment was nearly as high as that in manufacturing output.

The reasons for Taiwan's unusual success have been widely debated. One view is that it can be explained in terms of conventional trade theory. A country that has abundant labor and that adopts an outward-looking policy stance can expect to benefit from its comparative advantage in labor-intensive manufacturing. There is undoubtedly an element of truth in this view and some other policy morals for other labor-surplus countries. But, as Hla Myint has argued persuasively to me, this approach assumes too readily that, once biases and distortions are removed, comparative advantage will *automatically* assert itself. To take advantage of an abundant labor supply it is necessary to combine an adequate supply of food with institutional adaptations to reduce the capital and human costs of putting this labor to work. Labor-intensive methods cannot be taken as given. Correct factor pricing is important. Further, in both agriculture and industry, it is necessary to seek out and disseminate appropriate labor-intensive technology.

Formal trade theory assumes that the domestic economic organization of the trading country is already fully developed: the economy is operating on the frontier of production possibilities, pure competition prevails throughout, and so on. But this is not the case. Labor-intensive producers in industry and agriculture tend to be relatively small. To cater to the needs of many dispersed small-scale producers creates additional demands on the domestic economic system to provide an adequate network of transport, marketing, credit, and informational facilities. Without this institutional infrastructure, which can be regarded as a nontradable input, Taiwan's export sector could not have expanded as it did.

We must look, then, at what Taiwan's government did in the areas of agriculture, fiscal-monetary policy, and trade policy. The land reforms of 1949–53 included establishment of rent ceilings, subdivision and sale of former Japanese-owned lands, and the placing of size limits on other large holdings, with the surplus distributed to smallholders. The reforms affected 48 percent of farm households and 25 percent of the cultivated area. The amount of tenant-cultivated land was reduced from 44 percent to 14 percent; and small- to medium-size owner-operated farms were established as the dominant pattern of organization.

Land redistribution, however, might have had little effect without a variety of other productivity-raising measures. The farmers' cooperatives, which under the Japanese had been run largely from the top down, were reorganized as genuinely farmer-controlled, multipurpose organizations that supplied inputs, purchased outputs, and provided short-term credit. Their establishment and operation was supervised by a key government agency, the Joint Commission on Rural Reconstruction, staffed by American and Taiwanese agricultural technicians. Government also improved rural infrastructure, supported basic and applied agricultural research, diversified production into new and profitable crops such as asparagus and mushrooms, and provided a growing amount of off-farm employment for family members by encouraging a decentralized pattern of industrialization.

The results of these measures were quite striking. A study by Fei, Ranis, and Kuo (1979) notes that, in the immediate postreform years 1952–64, crop and livestock output increased by 68 percent, with an increase of only 17 percent in the man-days of labor utilized and virtually unchanged land acreage. Agriculture was able to provide improved diets for the local population (calorie availability per person per day rose from 1,980 in 1950 to 2,350 in 1970) and a growing export surplus, while at the same time liberating part of the growing rural labor force for industrial employment.

In the monetary area, a high-interest-rate policy was used to check inflation and encourage savings. Inflation was brought under control by 1952, and its average rate fell from 12 percent in the 1950s to 4 percent in the 1960s. The savings/GDP ratio, only around 5 percent in the 1950s, accelerated sharply during the 1960s and reached 30 percent in the mid-1970s, a good part of this consisting of reinvestment by the highly profitable industrial sector. High interest rates also encouraged economy in the use of capital—reflected, for example, in the purchase of secondhand textile machinery, which was cheaper and more labor-using than the newest equipment.

The shift to an outward-looking trade stance in the late 1950s has already been noted. In 1955 the currency was devalued, and a new law provided for rebate of the commodity tax, import duties, and defense tax on export products and raw materials used in such products. In 1958 there was a further devaluation, combined with establishment of a unified exchange rate and liberalization of imports. Exports were helped also by a policy of wage restraint, under which trade unions and strikes were not allowed to interfere with availability of the abundant labor supply. Real wage rates in manufacturing rose only moderately up to 1968, well below the rate of productivity increase. The competitive advantage of cheap labor was brought to bear fully by maintaining a low real rate of exchange and by keeping domestic inflation under control.

Two other features of the postwar record are worth noting. First, Taiwan has moved into the demographic transition with unusual speed. As of 1950, the rate of natural population increase was around 3 percent per year because mortality rates had been much reduced by public-health measures during the Japanese period while birthrates showed little change. But after 1960 birthrates began to fall sharply, due partly to a vigorous government program of family planning, but due also to the growing affluence, urbanization, and education of the population. The rate of natural increase is now below 2 percent and is continuing to decline toward "developed-country" levels.

Second, instead of the increased inequality in income characteristic of accelerated development in most countries, Taiwan shows a shift toward greater income equality. This does not result to any extent from fiscal redistribution through government, of which there has been little, but rather from characteristics of the growth path itself. The extent of income equalization and the reasons for it are documented by Fei, Ranis, and Kuo, who draw on an annual survey of household incomes that reports the sources of income as well as its amount, making it possible to compute "factor Ginis." The Gini coefficient for all household incomes, which was 0.56 in 1953 and 0.44 in 1959, had fallen to 0.29 by 1972, again putting Taiwan in the "developed-country" range. This decline, moreover, occurred in both the rural and urban sectors. As farm families increasingly provided labor to nearby industrial activities, the percentage of rural income derived from wages rose steeply, until by 1972 it slightly exceeded income derived from agriculture. Since wage income is more equally distributed than income from property or from agriculture, its growing importance tended to reduce the rural Gini. In addition, the Gini for income derived from agriculture was reduced by the land-redistribution program of 1949–53 and has continued to fall since that time, indicating a broadly based process of agricultural improvement that benefited farms of all sizes.

In urban areas the wage share of income has risen moderately and, in addition, both wage income and property income have become somewhat more equally distributed. These trends are related, of course, to the rapid growth of labor-intensive industrial exports, the shift from a labor-surplus to a labor-scarce economy, and the rapid rise in real wages. Another unusual feature of the Taiwan case is the smallness of the urban-rural income gap, which amounts to only about 15 percent.

SOUTH KOREA

Korea, like Taiwan, has experienced two takeoffs—the first after its annexation by Japan, the second in the post-1945 period.

Turning Point: *circa* 1910

Korea, long a feudal "hermit kingdom" virtually closed to foreigners, was opened to trade by an 1876 treaty with Japan. There followed a period in which China, Japan, and Russia competed for dominance, with Korea appearing as "a shrimp among whales." This issue was decided by Japanese victories in the Sino-Japanese and Russo-Japanese wars. The 1905 treaty ending the latter war recognized Japan's paramount interest in Korea, and a Japanese resident-general became the effective ruler of the country. In 1910 the emperor of Korea was deposed, and the country was formally annexed to Japan.

Intensive Growth, 1910-40

Colonial development passed through several phases. Until about 1920 the main emphasis was on agricultural development, to supply Japan with rice and industrial raw materials. During the 1920s there was considerable development of light consumer-goods industries, notably textiles and food processing. After 1931 there was rapid development of heavy industry, partly for military purposes. Korea had good mineral supplies, cheap electric power, and cheap labor, and it was strategically located between Japan and Manchuria, which had been occupied by Japan in 1931. After the outbreak of war with China in 1937, and with the United States in 1941, it became even more important to develop war industries away from the vulnerable Japanese mainland.

In examining the main strands of development, we begin as usual with agriculture. Between 1912 and 1918 the colonial government carried through a land survey and established legal guarantees of private ownership. In the course of this the authorities, profiting by the vagueness of previous land laws, were able to lay hands on some 354,000 hectares of land, much of which was sold to Japanese. By 1935 some 62 percent of the large landholdings of 250 acres or more were Japanese-owned. But the government also enlisted the cooperation of the Korean nobles by providing legal guarantees for their tenancy system. Tenancy increased from 39 percent of farm households in 1913-17 to 56 percent in 1938.

The tenancy system was rather harsh, with the rental share of output generally above 50 percent. There were also heavy land taxes, which provided about half of government revenue. The results, as reported by Paul Kuznets (1977), included: a decline in the average consumption of food grains by Koreans; disincentives to production that were considerably stronger than those in Taiwan, where expropriation of the surplus was less harsh and direct; a plentiful labor supply to industry from impoverished tenants; and substantial emigration from Korea. By the 1930s there were a million Koreans in Manchuria and half a million in Japan.

Wheat growing was dominant in the north, rice growing in the south. A long-term plan to raise rice production, including land improvement and agricultural extension programs, was initiated in 1920. There were also programs to increase output of cotton and silk, to supply Japan's textile industries. Despite the disincentives just noted, total agricultural production doubled between 1910 and 1940, while rice production more than doubled. But the increase benefited mainly Japanese rather than Korean consumers. The proportion of rice exported to Japan rose from 16 percent in 1910–15 to 44 percent in 1930–36. In the period 1925–40, more than half of Japan's rice imports came from Korea. Kuznets estimates that about three-quarters of the growth in output can be attributed to increased factor inputs (mainly labor and capital inputs, since land supply was relatively fixed) and one-quarter to technical progress. As compared with Taiwan, rates of productivity growth and output growth were lower, and the squeeze on domestic consumers was more severe.

In regard to industry, the colonial authorities initially imposed a licensing system for all new establishments, to discourage manufacturing and to keep Korea as a source of food and raw materials and a market for Japanese manufactures. In 1920, however, this system was abolished, restrictions on capital exports to Korea were lifted, and Korea was brought within the Japanese tariff zone. These measures led to considerable Japanese investment in Korea during the 1920s, much of it devoted to processing local raw materials. After the world slump of 1929, production and marketing controls were imposed on Japanese industry with a view to curbing competition and reducing bankruptcies. But since these controls did not extend to Korea, many Japanese companies moved to establish subsidiaries there. There was a substantial expansion not only of textiles and food processing but also of cement, fertilizer, and chemicals. After 1937, and still more after 1941, the government emphasized expansion of the metal and machinery industries to supply military goods.

As of 1938 there were 3,135 Japanese-owned business firms in Korea, compared with 2,278 Korean-owned firms. In terms of paid-up capital, however, the average Japanese firm was six times as large as the average Korean firm. Japanese owners thus controlled about 90 percent of industrial capital, though the presence of Korean entrepreneurs was to prove helpful in the postwar period.

Manufacturing output grew faster than that of any other sector. Over the period 1910–40, the average growth rate was 10.4 percent per year. Only mining, at 10.1 percent, came anywhere near this figure. In consequence, manufacturing's share of GDP rose from about 7 percent in 1910–12 to 29 percent in 1939–41. Thus the sensational expansion of Korean industry since 1960 has a parallel in earlier times.

Growth was accompanied by the usual structural changes. In 1920, handicraft and cottage industries still provided half of manufacturing output. By 1940, though their output had risen substantially in absolute terms, their share of output had fallen to one-quarter. As for type of product, the light-industry share, initially close to 100 percent, had fallen below 50 percent by 1940. Manufacturing expansion in the 1930s was dominated initially by fertilizers and other chemicals, later on by metals, machinery, and war goods. There was some specialization between the south and the north, which had most of the electric-power supply. The south was dominant in textiles, printing, machine tools, and processed foods, but the north produced 80 percent of the chemicals and almost 90 percent of basic metals. The postwar division of the country, of course, disrupted this well-established division of labor.

Volume of trade rose more than tenfold between 1910 and 1940. The great bulk of this trade was with Japan, which took 90 percent of Korea's exports and supplied 70–80 percent of its imports. The ratio of exports to commodity output rose from 4.2 percent in 1910–12 to 21.0 percent in 1938–40, while the import ratio rose from 11.3 percent to 29.1 percent. There was a consistent trade deficit, financed in part by the inflow of private Japanese capital.

Initially, food formed 50–60 percent of exports and other raw materials 15–20 percent, Korea thus fulfilling its role of complement to the Japanese economy. But this situation changed quite rapidly in the 1930s. Between 1930 and 1940 manufactures rose from 21 percent of exports to 55 percent, of which about half was semifinished and the other half finished products. Manufactures always formed 70–80 percent of imports, but there was a marked shift toward a higher proportion of capital goods in the 1930s, when the Japanese began to push development of heavy industry.

The expansion of production and trade was supported by investment in infrastructure and implanting of modern economic institutions. Ports were improved, roads and railroads were constructed. The country's currency was linked to the yen, and a central bank was established as early as 1909. Human capital, on the other hand, was relatively neglected. Separate schools were maintained for Japanese and Koreans, and instruction in both was in Japanese. Even by 1937 only about one-third of the relevant age group were enrolled in primary schools. At the university level, Koreans were outnumbered by Japanese, who dominated the higher rungs of the occupational ladder.

Population growth accelerated as Japanese-sponsored health facilities reduced the crude death rate to the range of 18–22 per thousand. Kuznets estimates that population grew at 2.0–2.5 percent per year during the colonial period, though the data are clouded by substantial emigration. He estimates GDP growth at about 4 percent per year, which would mean something less than 2 percent growth of income per capita. A later study by Kim and Roemer (1979) estimates per capita income growth at 1.6 percent from 1910 to 1940.

Increments in income were of course unequally distributed between Japanese and Korean residents and among different groups in the Korean population. Those who transferred to urban wage employment no doubt experienced a substantial rise in income. But the position of the average peasant may have improved little.

Intensive Growth, 1950–80

The division of the country at the end of World War II was in some ways disadvantageous to South Korea. It was left with two-thirds of Korea's population but only half of its usable land. It was also left with little heavy industry or electric power, whose development had been concentrated in the north. The 1950–51 war brought further devastation, destroying about half of the manufacturing plants in South Korea. By 1953 output per capita had at most regained the 1939 level. The rest of the 1950s was mainly a period of reconstruction, during which the economy was sustained by large inflows of aid from the United States.

The rapid growth that we now consider characteristic of South Korea dates from the early 1960s. The Park regime assumed power in 1963. Since that time government has been dictatorial but stable, and the main lines of policy have been substantially unchanged. Much has been made, correctly, of the shift around 1963 from a policy of moderate import substitution to an outward-looking, export-oriented policy. The changes included devaluation of the won and establishment of a floating exchange rate, trade liberalization with preferences for imports of machinery and intermediate goods, and a battery of tax, credit, and tariff incentives for manufactured exports. The policy package included also a sharp increase in real interest rates to encourage domestic saving and tax increases to provide a substantial surplus in the current budget to be used for capital formation.

The last two decades have seen a GDP growth rate in the Japan-Taiwan range, manufacturing growing about twice as fast as GDP, and a sharp rise in the trade ratio, with manufactures now forming more than 90 percent of total exports. By 1980 South Korea was much above Chenery's norms, for a country of its size and income level, with regard to the manufacturing/GDP and export/GDP ratios. This story has been told so many times that it can be summarized here very briefly.

In agriculture, land reform in the early 1950s led to the sale of a large area of formerly Japanese-owned land to smallholders. Owner-occupied farms became the dominant form, and tenancy was reduced to about 12 percent of the cultivated area. Holdings are very small, however, averaging only 2.2 acres, and one-third of farms are below 1 acre in size.

Only about one-fifth of South Korea's land area is arable, and it is fully occupied. After about 1967, too, the farm labor force began to decrease as the rapid expansion of industry drained people into urban employment. Output increases, then, have had to come from greater use of "modern" inputs, such as improved seeds, fertilizers, and pesticides, plus some expansion of irrigation and double-cropping and some diversification into noncereal products. The productivity record is quite good. Rice yields are about the same as in Taiwan, about double those in Thailand and Indonesia, and only 20 percent below the level of Japan. Wheat yields are also at the Taiwanese level. A government price-support system has kept the rural-urban terms of trade roughly constant.

Food output has risen at about 4 percent per year, but it has been insufficient to keep up with a domestic demand spurred by rapidly rising incomes, much less to produce the kind of export surplus that fueled Taiwanese growth in the 1950s. Food imports have been rising and, while self-sufficiency is still proclaimed as a policy goal, it seems farther and farther away. The goal itself may be unreasonable. Nineteenth-century Britain and twentieth-century Japan did very well by trading manufactures for food, and this may be a reasonable course also for South Korea.

Manufacturing, as already suggested, took off around 1964 and since then has shown a growth rate roughly equal to that in Taiwan and a strong export orientation. By the mid-1970s about one-third of value added was being exported, and manufactures formed more than 90 percent of all exports. Partly because of availability of the world market, light industries still provide the bulk of manufacturing output. But there has been a moderate shift toward metals, oil products, fertilizers and other chemicals, shipbuilding, and other transport equipment. Machinery output has not grown very fast, because a low-tariff policy has favored machinery imports. Thus far locally produced machinery has been too high in price and too low in quality to stand up well against import competition.

Government enterprises are important, particularly in heavy industry. As of the early 1970s two government fertilizer companies produced virtually all fertilizer, a government oil refinery monopolized that industry, a government shipbuilding company had 64 percent of industry capacity, and a mineral-refining company controlled 70 percent of its industry. Data assembled by Kuznets suggest that, contrary to experience in some other countries, these government enterprises are generally profitable. Profit/sales ratios run in the range of 1–20 percent and are usually in line with those of comparable private companies. Most private enterprises are closely held family organizations, Korean-owned. Government has been skeptical of foreign investment, especially Japanese investment, and foreign capital does not play a large role in the manufacturing sector.

Plant sizes are quite large. For all manufacturing, a distribution of output among "small," "medium," and "large" establishments looks much like a corresponding distribution in the United States. Output levels naturally vary by type of industry. Clothing, footwear, and furniture plants are relatively small. But textile plants are large, and so are those in fertilizers, chemicals, and heavy industry.

South Korean industry benefited initially from surplus labor and constant real wages. But rapid growth of output meant a rapid, though less than proportionate, growth of manufacturing employment. Between 1963 and 1972, output of mining and manufacturing grew at 17.4 percent a year, employment at 8.4 percent. By 1967 the surplus labor pool was substantially exhausted, and real wages began to rise in both agriculture and industry. But the wage level was not spurred on by minimum-wage legislation or trade-union pressure. Wages lagged behind productivity, making possible high profit rates that contributed to reinvestment. Corporate saving is the largest component in the unusually high rate of domestic saving, though personal saving and government saving are also important. In addition to retained earnings, both private and government enterprises have access to long-term funds from the Korean Development Bank, a government-owned financial intermediary.

The growth rate of manufacturing output is reasonably well explained by (1) a high capital-formation rate; (2) a substantial rise in the utilization rate of capital equipment (the obverse of which is an unusually low incremental capital-output ratio (ICOR) for the manufacturing sector); and (3) rapid employment growth combined with improvement in the educational level of the labor force. After taking account of these variables, the unexplained residual is small.

The public sector shows a rapid growth of current revenue from the early 1960s onward. This was not due mainly to increases in tax rates or diversification of tax sources. Indirect taxes and customs duties have continued to play a major role. Indeed, in a comparative international study by Lotz and Morss (*IMF Staff Papers*, November 1967, and *EDCC*, April 1970), South Korea was ranked low in "tax effort." Rather, revenue came flooding in because of high output growth and rapid expansion of the tax base, as has traditionally been true in Japan. At the same time, current expenditure has been well contained. Government consumption as a percentage of GDP fell from 13.6 percent in 1953–55 to 9.2 percent in 1968–70. There were substantial budget deficits from 1953 to 1963, closed by large inflows of aid from the United States. From 1963 onward, however, current revenue pulled increasingly ahead of current expenditure. Government saving was soon large enough to more than cover government capital formation, and government became increasingly a net lender to the private sector.

The GDCF/GDP ratio rose from a low level in the mid-1950s to about 25 percent in the mid-1970s. Gross domestic saving rose less rapidly, despite a good savings performance by government, corporations, and households. About one-third of investment was still foreign-financed, and the debt-service ratio had risen substantially.

The allocation of government expenditure, current and capital, shows one-third going to infrastructure and other economic services, which is about in line with comparable countries. The 20 percent allocated to education, however, is unusually high, and the high educational enrollments from primary school through university must have contributed to the country's economic success. Defense, with 17 percent, is also on the high side, though pressure here is eased by United States sharing of defense costs.

Regarding trade, the sensational rise of manufactured exports from the early 1960s onward has already been noted. In the first instance these exports were light-industry products. Clothing, wigs, cotton and other textiles, and plywood sheets formed 80 percent of manufactured exports in 1970. After that time, however, there were growing exports of steel plate and sheets, electronic products, machinery and transport equipment, and ships. The import content of exports, however, is quite high. Net foreign-exchange earnings from exports are only about half their gross value. Exports grew at 40 percent per year in the 1960s and at 37 percent in the 1970s. The export/GDP ratio, about 1 percent in 1950, had risen to 28.1 percent by 1980.

Manufactures form 55–65 percent of total imports. Within this total, the proportion of consumer goods has remained stable at around 20 percent, the proportion of investment goods has jumped sharply, and there has been a drop in intermediates, such as fertilizer, petroleum products, and paper, where import substitution is virtually complete. Imports have risen even faster than exports, and there is a consistent deficit in merchandise trade. From 1953 to 1962 the deficits were very large, with exports sometimes only 10 percent of imports, a situation made possible only by massive infusions of United States aid totaling almost $5 billion. After the mid-1960s, however, American grants and soft loans were tapered off and the trade deficit was closed increasingly by normal foreign borrowing. The main long-term lenders have been the United States, Japan, West Germany, and international agencies.

South Korea experienced the usual post-1945 acceleration of population growth, which reached 3.1 percent in 1955–60. Since 1960, however, the crude birthrate and the population growth rate have been falling, and South Korea appears well along in the demographic transition. Thus the high GDP growth rate is largely reflected in a rapid rise of per capita income. The increments to income have not been uniformly distributed within the population. Entrepreneurial incomes seem to have risen relative to labor incomes. The earnings of manufacturing workers and other urban incomes have risen relative to those of farmers and farm laborers. In the early 1970s rural incomes per capita were estimated at only 77 percent of urban incomes. One reason for the disparity may be that South Korean industry is heavily concentrated in Seoul, Inchon, Pusan, and other cities. Farm families thus do not have as much access to manufacturing employment as those in contemporary Taiwan or in late-nineteenth-century Japan.

Comparative studies, however, show that South Korea's income distribution is one of the more equal in the developing world. The typical pattern in third-world countries is that the bottom 40 percent of the population receive 10–12 percent of personal income. However, the Chenery-Ahluwalia study (1974) found that in South Korea the bottom 40 percent received 18.0 percent of income, compared with 20.4 percent in Taiwan (and around 20 percent in most of the developed capitalist countries.) Reasons for this relatively good showing may include: the land-reform program, which created a large number of small family farms; a great expansion of education, which raised the literacy rate from 30 percent in 1953 to 80 percent in 1963, by which time South Korea's human-resource development had exceeded the norm for a country with three times its per capita GNP; and a successful shift into labor-intensive exports, which rapidly exhausted the surplus-labor reservoir and initiated a sustained rise in real wages.

PHILIPPINES

The Spaniards entered the Philippines from America in 1568, conveniently overlooking the fact that the famous papal division of the world placed the islands in the Portuguese zone. Their activities were mainly confined to central Luzon, and much of the archipelago was never occupied. The Spanish functioned as rulers, soldiers, and missionaries. The Chinese, who came in quite early, together with their mixed-blood descendants, took over virtually all trade and artisan activities as well as many service functions. Filipinos generally followed traditional agricultural activities.

For almost three centuries the islands were mainly an entrepôt. Chinese traders, and later British traders, brought exotic goods from China and India. The galleons carried these goods to Mexico, bringing back silver in return. The few local exports were mainly gathered rather than produced—birds' nests, tortoiseshell, seashells, sea slugs, small amounts of gold.

Turning Point: *circa* 1900

After the islands were formally opened to trade in 1834, British and American merchant houses appeared and an export trade in local produce developed. The value of exports (in million pesos) rose from 1.0 in 1825 to 5.9 in 1855 to 36.6 in 1895. As of 1895, sugar and abaca were about 75 percent of exports, tobacco and coffee about 13 percent. Sugar, which soon emerged as the dominant export crop, was grown in Negros on European-owned plantations using recruited wage labor. In Luzon, however, share tenancy predominated because of the difficulty of persuading subsistence farmers to work for wages. Abaca is a labor-intensive product involving clearing the forest, planting the suckers, weeding, harvesting, and stripping the stalks. A husband, a wife, and a knife are all that is needed, and so this is mainly a smallholder crop. Over the nineteenth century a good deal of land and labor was shifted from rice to export crops, and after 1855 the Philippines was a net importer of rice, mainly from Saigon.

Because nineteenth-century export production was localized in a few areas of the archipelago, and because it remained small relative to national output, I do not regard its growth as marking a turning point for the Philippine economy.

The transfer of the islands to American control after the Spanish-American War of 1898 did bring a turning point to intensive growth, led by exports and dominated by sugar. Philippine products were granted a 25 percent preference in the American market until 1909, free entrance within quota limits from 1909 to 1913, and full free trade thereafter. Under this regime foreign trade grew rapidly and was reoriented from Britain and Spain toward the United States. Exports rose from an annual average of 51 million pesos in the early 1900s to 312 million pesos per year from 1936 to 1941. Sugar expansion was eventually checked by the Agricultural Adjustment Act of 1934, which set quota limits for each country exporting to the United States. As of 1935–37, however, sugar still formed 38 percent of Philippine exports, while abaca, coconut oil, and copra formed another 37 percent.

Intensive Growth, 1900–40

The agriculture-based character of early economic growth is suggested by R. W. Hooley's (1968) national-income estimates. He shows agricultural output growing at 5.1 percent per year from 1902 to 1918, compared with 4.1 percent growth for manufacturing and 4.4 percent for GDP. Output increases up to 1940 seem to have been accomplished entirely by acreage expansion, with little evidence of technical progress. Land was still abundant, and the cultivated acreage tripled from 1.3 million hectares in 1902 to 3.9 million hectares in 1938. Cultivated acreage, indeed, rose faster than labor inputs, so that the land/labor ratio and the output/labor ratio were both rising. Nor does export expansion seem to have encroached on food production. The percentage of land devoted to export crops did rise from 35 percent in 1902 to 41 percent in 1938. But the share of rice was virtually constant, while that of corn rose from 8.0 to 20.5 percent of total acreage.

As of 1939 about 60 percent of all land was cultivated by owners and 40 percent by share tenants, but the ratio varied by type of crop. Landlordism was strongest in sugar, where 61 percent of the land was worked by tenants. But the tenancy share was only about 50 percent in corn, 40 percent in tobacco and rice, 20 percent in abaca and coconuts. Holdings were small but not tiny, averaging about three hectares for tenants and 4.5 hectares for owners. American colonial policy discouraged large plantation holdings and imposed a size ceiling on grants of public land to corporations. Although some concentration did develop through evasion of ceilings and distress sales of land by smallholders, it never rose to Latin American proportions. The rising income from exports was thus rather broadly distributed among the farm population.

In sugar, Philippines remained a low-productivity supplier. In 1929–34 the average yield in quintals per hectare was 361, about on a level with Cuba (381), but little more than half of Taiwan (683) and less than one-third of yields in Java (1,327) and Hawaii (1,357). There was a modest improvement in rice yields, from 0.76 tons per hectare in 1902 to 1.10 tons in 1936–41. The Philippines remained a rice importer throughout the period, though imports were somewhat smaller from 1920 to 1940 than from 1900 to 1920.

From 1902 to 1918 the growth of secondary industry was confined almost entirely to rice mills and sugar mills. But the next twenty years saw the beginnings of import substitution in light consumer goods. By 1939 the islands were producing dairy products, soy sauce, canned fruits, vegetables, fish, matches, liquor and beverages, leather products, paints and varnishes, fertilizers, agricultural implements, clothing, footwear, glass products, and furniture. But food, beverages, and tobacco still formed two-thirds of manufacturing output and (untypically) textiles were virtually absent. In addition to factory production there was a large handicraft industry, which at this time provided far more employment than did factories. The largest handicraft was embroidery, followed by "native textiles," mat making, tailoring, hat making, and umbrella making. Factories were heavily concentrated in Manila, which, if we omit sugar mills and rice mills, produced 70 percent of manufacturing output.

United States investment went mainly into export industries—mining, plantations, sugar centrales—or into public utilities. Very little went into manufacturing. In addition to the $537 million of American investment in 1939, there was about $200 million of Chinese investment (largely in wholesale and retail trade), and about $100 million of Japanese investment. A sizable profit drain is suggested by the fact that there was usually a substantial surplus in merchandise trade.

Growth was less vigorous from 1918 to 1938 than it had been from 1902 to 1918, being interrupted by the mild slump of 1920–21 and later by the Great Depression. Hooley's estimates show GDP not quite keeping up with population growth, which had accelerated from its nineteenth-century level of about 1.5 percent growth per year to 2.1 percent from 1918 to 1938. World War II and Japanese occupation brought widespread devastation, followed by several years of gradual recovery, with the result that the postwar economic story begins about 1950.

Intensive Growth, 1950–80

Meanwhile the Philippines had been granted independence in 1946. Although independence brought greater autonomy in economic policymaking, it also meant a reduction of preferences in the American market. Free trade was to continue for eight years, followed by a gradual diminution of tariff preferences over the next twenty years. (Indeed, sugar interests in the United States had been among the strongest advocates of Philippine independence, for they wished to place Philippine producers clearly outside the American trade system.) The new political system bore clear marks of American influence: a strong, popularly elected executive; a separately elected legislature; a relatively small public sector; and heavy emphasis on private enterprise. During the 1970s, however, the system was transformed into a presidential dictatorship. Opposition leaders were suppressed, and elections had only a ceremonial significance.

The 1950–80 growth record, while less impressive than that of Taiwan or Korea, is well above that of any prior period. Population growth accelerated once more to 2.7 percent in the 1950s and 3.0 percent in the 1960s, with only a slight decline in the 1970s. GDP grew at a bit more than 6 percent per year in the 1950s, dropped to 5 percent in the 1960s, then rose above 6 percent again in the 1970s. Over the whole period, then, GDP per capita has grown at about 3 percent per year. It will be useful to examine this record sector by sector.

Agriculture varies considerably over the 2,000-mile expanse of the Philippine Islands. Average farm income per household in the richest region is about double that in the poorest region. The lowest-income region (the eastern Visayas) has relatively small average farm size, a relatively low level of irrigation and fertilizer use, and a high rate of out-migration, losing about one-eighth of its population between 1960 and 1970. Farm families, unlike those in Taiwan or nineteenth-century Japan, get relatively little income from nonagricultural activities. A survey in the early 1970s showed that the average farm household in the

Philippines got only 11 percent of its income from (nonagricultural) wages, 3 percent from trade, and 2 percent from handicrafts.

Tenure systems have not changed much from colonial times. Landholding is quite concentrated. The 5 percent of landowners with 12 hectares or more have about half of the land, while the 67 percent with less than 3 hectares have only 20 percent. About 39 percent of the land is under tenancy, but 56 percent of rice land is farmed by tenants. Unlike results in some other countries, studies in the Philippines have shown that tenure form makes little difference to output per hectare, inputs of farm-family labor, and other variables. So while land reform might be desirable on distributional grounds, it appears that it would not raise output materially.

The traditional pattern of raising output by extending the cultivated area continued until around 1960. Between 1948–50 and 1957–59, the annual growth rate of key variables was as follows: output, 4.5 percent; cultivated area, 3.8 percent; farm labor force, 3.0 percent; total inputs, 4.1 percent; total factor productivity, 0.4 percent. By 1960, however, the possibilities of acreage expansion were largely exhausted. Between 1957–59 and 1970–72 the annual increase of cultivated area dropped sharply to 1.4 percent, and the farm labor force grew by only about 1 percent as migration to the cities intensified. The main burden of raising output was thus shifted to productivity. With some lag, productivity did largely take up the slack, particularly after about 1965 as new, high-yielding rice varieties were introduced. Between 1957–59 and 1970–72, land productivity rose at 2.6 percent per year and labor productivity at 2.2 percent. This resulted from several interrelated developments: a 50 percent increase in the irrigated area; an increase in the proportion of rice land irrigated, from 24 percent to 44 percent, permitting a marked increase in multiple-cropping; planting of about 60 percent of rice land to high-yielding varieties; and a tripling of fertilizer consumption.

Productivity levels are still low on an international scale. In the early 1970s, rice yields per hectare were still the lowest in Southeast Asia and less than half the Taiwanese level, while corn yields were less than one-third those of Taiwan. Overall, the average Taiwanese farmer was producing twice as much as the average Philippine farmer. This could, of course, be regarded as encouraging in the sense of leaving much room for future increases in output.

Agriculture serves the dual function of providing food for the cities and earning foreign exchange to pay for the imports needed for economic development. It has performed better on the second front than on the first. Primary exports grew at an annual rate of 5.5 percent from 1950 to 1972, especially important because the Philippines has failed to develop substantial export capacity in manufactures. But the supply of food to the urban sector grew more slowly. Indeed, between 1950 and 1970 food output per capita did not increase at all. Low productivity in agriculture resulted in a marked shift in the internal terms of trade in favor of that sector, imperiling industrial development. The food/manufactures price ratio, with 1955 as 100, had risen to 135 by 1971. Things improved in the

1970s as the new agricultural technology raised food output more rapidly. Food production, which had grown at only 3.1 percent per year in the 1950s and 3.2 percent in the 1960s, grew at 4.5 percent in the 1970s. Food output per capita rose 14 percent between 1970 and 1980.

Industrialization has been promoted in a variety of ways: a tariff structure with high rates on consumer goods and relatively low rates on capital goods and intermediates; long periods in which the peso was overvalued, which favored importation of inputs for industry while penalizing exports; exchange controls imposed to meet balance-of-payments crises by which "nonessential" goods were severely restricted, which increased the profitability of producing them domestically; and special tax and other incentives for favored industries.

During the "easy phase" of import substitution in light consumer goods, which lasted until about 1960, manufacturing grew rapidly and raised its share of GDP by several points. But the growth rate slowed gradually, and after 1960 manufacturing grew less rapidly than GDP and was in no sense a leading sector. Growth was constrained by limitations of the domestic market, by inability to develop export capacity, and by a chronic shortage of foreign exchange, which limited imports of necessary inputs, leading to low utilization of plant capacity. The tendency of food prices to rise, forcing up money wages faster than product prices could be raised, also reduced the profitability of manufacturing.

Government trade and exchange policies, and the industrial structure that has emerged under them, have been criticized by students of the economy. Power and Sicat (1971), for example, point out that:

1. Manufacturing industries are inward-looking, convinced of their inability to export. In part, this lack of confidence reflects the overvalued exchange rate. At an equilibrium exchange rate, exporting would be easier.
2. The structure of protection tends to produce "finishing touches" industries that depend excessively on imported inputs and hence yield little foreign-exchange saving. Artificially cheap imported inputs are addictive, and those who benefit from them naturally resist pushing import substitution back to earlier stages of production.
3. Industry is overconcentrated in Manila.
4. Manufacturing employment is growing slowly due partly to the cheapness (in pesos) of imported capital goods. Manufacturing employment since 1960 has grown only about as fast as the labor force, leading to substantial open unemployment plus underemployment of people forced into self-employment in the "informal sector."
5. Technical and economic inefficiency has arisen from protected markets, suboptimum scale, and oligopolistic market structure.

Today's manufacturing structure is dualistic to an unusual degree. As of 1969–71, large enterprises with 200 or more workers, which are favored in various ways by government, accounted for only 17.5 percent of employment but produced 70.1 percent of value added. Handicraft and cottage industries with one to four workers provided 70 percent of employment but only 5.6 percent of output. The number of people in these household enterprises is still rising in absolute terms, though falling as a proportion of manufacturing employment. Their apparent low productivity must partly reflect underutilization of labor time, which could be improved if demand warranted and if bottlenecks in materials supply were removed. The excellent ILO employment report on the Philippines organized by Gustav Ranis (1973) contains an interesting discussion of the policies needed to foster small-scale enterprise.

Manufacturing industry is largely locally owned, with American and other foreign investment a minor and decreasing factor. Of the new Filipino entrepreneurs, about two-thirds appear to be "nouveau riche" while one-third are from monied families connected especially with sugar planting. The fact that many such families are engaged both in sugar and in protected manufacturing tends to blunt the natural antagonism between export and import interests. Entrepreneurs seem to have been the most substantial beneficiaries from manufacturing growth. Real wage rates in manufacturing show no consistent upward movement. But since urban wages are roughly double the rural level, workers who transfer between sectors make a large one-time gain.

Exports continue to play a leading role in the sense that they have been rising faster than GDP. The growth rate of merchandise exports rose from 4.5 percent per year in the 1950s to 7.5 percent in the 1960s to 17.7 percent in the 1970s, with the result that the export/GDP ratio rose from 9.6 percent in 1950–52 to 14.0 percent in 1978–80. The Philippines has lagged behind most other Southeast Asian countries in developing capacity to export manufactures, though again performance improved during the 1970s. Manufactured goods as a percentage of all exports rose from 6.4 percent in 1970 to 20.8 percent in 1979.

Export growth has been restrained by the alternation of restrictive and liberalized foreign-trade regimes, under which the peso has been overvalued for extended periods of time. Research studies suggest that exports are quite sensitive to the exchange rate. Baldwin (1975) estimates that, with an equilibrium exchange rate throughout the period, exports would have been from $120 million to $180 million a year above their actual level. Despite periods of trade liberalization, the Philippines has never made the decisive turn toward outward-looking policies that have occurred in some other countries.

Although the balance-of-payments problem has been contained, it has never disappeared. There is typically a moderate deficit in merchandise trade. This deficit is partially closed by United States military expenditures and by remittances from Filipinos employed abroad. Occasional payments crises are met by short-term borrowing plus exchange restrictions. There has been little inflow of long-term capital from either private or official sources. Although some private capital came in during the import-substitution push of the 1950s, after 1960 the net capital movement was outward.

There has been some diversification of primary exports, with logs, plywood, and copper concentrates growing in importance; but sugar, copra, and coconut oil are still quite important. There has been little change in terms of trade, with the result that value of exports has roughly paralleled the physical quantum. The composition of imports has changed in the usual way. Consumer goods, which were 37 percent of the total in 1949, had fallen to 12 percent by 1967–69, representing almost complete import substitution in most lines. Over the same period machinery imports rose from 10 to 20 percent of the total and raw materials from 1 to 13 percent. Imports of intermediate goods are unusually high, running consistently at around 50 percent of the total. The high share of intermediate goods represents the previously noted "finishing touches" character of Philippine manufacturing, which shows no tendency to diminish.

The Philippines is a "small-public-sector" country, and a "low-infrastructure-investment" country. Government revenue as a percent of GDP has risen only moderately, from 9.0 percent in 1952 to 13.8 percent in 1980. Direct taxes are only about one-quarter of total tax collections, with no tendency for their share to rise over time. Budget allocations, averaged over several years, show 25–30 percent going to defense, police, and administration and 30–35 percent going to education. The Philippines, perhaps reflecting United States influence, has an unusually well developed educational system, with virtually complete enrollment in primary schools, about 60 percent enrollment in secondary schools, numerous colleges and universities, and an adult literacy rate of 88 percent. The University of the Philippines has one of the best economics faculties in the third world and turns out a good supply of economic technocrats for government service as well as private entrepreneurs.

The allocation to agriculture, on the other hand, averaged only 6 percent of expenditure, and only 7–8 percent went to transport and communications. Total investment in infrastructure was only about 1 percent of GNP, with about half of this going for highways and most of the remainder for irrigation projects. While there is a competent economic-planning staff in the central government, grassroots capacity to plan and execute development projects appears to be low. The economy remains very much a private-enterprise economy. "Private enterprise," however, must be construed in a Latin American sense. There is a strong symbiosis of the business and governmental elites, with much two-way movement of money and personnel.

VENEZUELA

Turning Point: *circa* 1925

Unlike the Latin American countries discussed previously, Venezuela in 1920 was still a very underdeveloped country with no sign of a turning point toward intensive growth. This must be attributed partly to an unusually comprehensive and rigid latifundia system in agriculture. The rural population, some 90 percent of the total population, consisted mainly of peons who were allowed to cultivate small plots of land in return for supplying labor time and a share of their crop to the landowner. This semifeudal system meant low incomes and a very limited market for nonagricultural products. Such manufacturing as existed was almost entirely of a handicraft nature. Mortality rates were high and population growth rates correspondingly low, typically less than 1 percent per year. Political authority was exercised by a series of military dictators, whose interest in economic development was minimal. Dictatorial rule, indeed, lasted until 1958, when the overthrow of Pérez Jiménez initiated a new era of democratic government.

The era of intensive growth was initiated by the discovery of oil in the early 1920s. Since that time Venezuela has emerged as a classic "oil economy," more similar to the Arab oil states than to other countries of Latin America. The predominance of oil shows up in all the statistical tables: oil providing one-quarter of GDP, while agriculture provides less than 10 percent; oil constituting more than 90 percent of exports and some 60 percent of government revenue; an investment rate in the 25–30 percent range, heavily oriented toward oil and petrochemical production. Oil will consequently form a large part of our story here.

Intensive Growth, 1925–80

The story of oil production divides into two phases: a sensationally rapid rise up to the end of the Jiménez dictatorship in 1958 and a leveling off of output during the era of democratic rule. Annual crude-oil output, in millions of barrels, rose from 19 in 1925 to 183 in 1940, to 547 in 1950, to 1,011 in 1959. Since that time it has fluctuated in the range of 1,000–1,300 million barrels, with only a slight uptrend. This changed behavior reflects a complex blend of company and government strategies. The way in which successive democratic governments moved in on the foreign companies to extract a growing share of profits is a fascinating story, well told by Franklin Tugwell (1975). The international oil companies tended to respond to this pressure by reducing their exploration expenditures in Venezuela and by substituting Arab for Venezuelan oil in their output mix. Middle East oil was cheaper in production-cost terms as well as in tax terms. Venezuelan oil, on the other hand, had lower transport costs to the United States market.

While the companies at times restricted output for bargaining reasons, government also had an interest in restraining it for conservation reasons. It has long been recognized that the reserves are finite. It is now estimated that, without further discoveries, reserves will run out in less than twenty years. So government strategy has been to "sow the oil" through development expenditures, with a view to having a diversified and viable economy when oil production ceases. In pursuit of this strategy, the Venezuelan oil minister took the lead in convening a meeting at Caracas in 1960, at which the Organization of Petroleum Exporting Countries (OPEC) was founded. He wanted a full-blown cartel, with fixed prices supported by production quotas for each country. The Arab producers were not ready for production control, however, and so nothing came of the idea during the 1960s. (Even today, despite OPEC's success on the price front, it has been difficult to negotiate and enforce agreements on national output quotas.)

Returned value to the Venezuelan economy was initially quite low. In recent decades, however, it has ranged from 60 to 70 percent of the value of output and has tended to increase over time. Hansen (in Martz and Myers, 1977) shows it rising from 2.2 million bolivars in 1950 to 14.2 million in 1973. In constant prices, the increase was more than fourfold. Most of this returned value consisted of taxes to government. Successive administrations tried with considerable success to penetrate the mysteries of corporate bookkeeping, to devise new and more effective forms of taxation, and to increase the government share of net income. In 1950 the government share was 51 percent, while corporate profit after taxes was 41 percent. But the government share rose to 67 percent by 1960 and to 80 percent by 1973—considerably above the government share of profits in the Arab oil-producing countries, which was 56 percent in 1958 and 72 percent in 1970. The companies thus had an incentive to use Middle East rather than Venezuelan oil insofar as markets and transport costs permitted.

Labor costs were a substantial item, but one that declined in relative importance over time. Between 1956 and 1973, employment in petroleum was cut roughly in half, despite a moderate increase in output. Other local costs, including exploration costs, were also substantial but not rising. Exploration costs, indeed, peaked at the end of the dictatorship and fluctuated at a lower level after that time.

Petroleum income was consistently more than half of total government income, with the proportion tending to rise over time. By 1973 it had reached about 70 percent. Expansion of the petroleum sector thus brought a rapid increase in government's fiscal capacity. Under the dictatorship, about half of revenue was allocated to current expenditure and the remainder to investment. With the appearance of democratic governments more responsive to popular pressures, the current budget began to outstrip the capital budget. By 1970 about two-thirds of revenue was going for current expenditure. Even so, public consumption in 1980 was only 13 percent of GDP. Of the capital budget, about one-quarter goes into roads and ports, another quarter into other physical projects (irrigation, building construction, sanitation systems), and about half into indirect or financial investment through a variety of development corporations. The overall investment rate of the economy is high, typically near 25 percent of GDP.

When one examines Hansen's tabulation of federal government expenditure by functions, the most interesting feature is the high proportion (more than one-third) going to education, health, housing, and other social purposes. This investment is reflected in relatively high school enrollment and adult literacy rates and superior health facilities. Infrastructure gets about 14 percent of total expenditure and agriculture 10 percent, with little going into manufacturing, where private enterprise predominates. Administration takes about 20 percent, and debt servicing plus revenue sharing with the states takes another 20 percent. The government's economic-planning agency, although it makes the usual macroeconomic projections, is primarily concerned with multiyear capital budgeting and with coordinating current and capital expenditures.

Agriculture was relatively neglected under the dictatorship and, while output was growing, about one-quarter of the country's food supply was imported. This situation changed somewhat after 1960, when democratic governments initiated a modest agrarian reform, increased allocations for irrigation and agricultural credit, initiated an import-substitution campaign in foodstuffs, and subsidized commercial farming in a variety of ways. But food supply has not been regarded as an urgent problem, perhaps because of the ease with which imports can be financed from oil revenues. In addition, the strength of the bolivar on foreign exchanges, again deriving from oil revenues, militates against the exportation of coffee, cocoa, and other crops. Agricultural output has grown a bit less rapidly than total output, and by 1980 had fallen to only 6 percent of GDP. Because of the drain of labor to the cities, which has produced a moderate decline in the farm labor force since 1960, output per worker in agriculture has been rising about as rapidly as in other sectors. But the productivity gap remains wide, productivity in agriculture being only about one-sixth of that in nonagricultural activities.

An import-substitution program was launched in the 1950s, and there has been considerable expansion of manufacturing since that time. Government has pushed development of petrochemicals and steel, taking advantage of good iron-ore deposits. There has been substantial import substitution in light consumer goods such as tires, textiles, clothing, and footwear, as well as expansion of nontraded goods such as beer, other beverages, cement, bricks, and other building materials. But manufacturing has not grown much faster than output in general and still forms only about 15 percent of GDP. To a remarkable degree Venezuela has become a service-producing economy. Trade, private services, and government services amount to more than half of GDP and about two-thirds of GDP if oil's share is excluded.

Population growth showed the typical post-1945 acceleration, reaching the remarkable level of 4.0 percent per year during the 1950s, then falling to 3.4 percent in the 1960s and 3.3 percent in the 1970s. The GDP growth rate was about 8 percent in the 1950s, 6 percent in the 1960s, and 5 percent in the 1970s. Between 1960 and 1980 per capita income grew at 2.6 percent per year. While there has been some diversification of output, growth remains distinctly lopsided, with oil still playing the star role. Oil's percentage contribution to GDP fell moderately up to 1973 but soared again with the oil-price explosion. Future prospects are tied to the course of oil revenues and to the disposition of these revenues by government, which since the oil nationalization of 1975 is entirely a matter of national policy.

Turning Point: *circa* 1880

Unlike Tunisia or Morocco, the area that now constitutes Algeria was not a unified state before the entrance of the French in 1830. Modern Algeria is a French creation. Its economic history can be divided into: (1) a period of warfare with local tribes and gradual extension of the area under French control, from about 1830 to 1880; (2) extensive French settlement, development of a "modern" French-dominated economy on top of the indigenous economy, and a modest rise of per capita output from 1880 to 1940; (3) accelerated, French-dominated economic growth after 1945, ended by the bitter French-Algerian war and achievement of national independence in 1962; and (4) Algerian-controlled economic growth since 1962, dominated increasingly by oil production and oil revenues and showing some interesting parallels with Venezuela.

Intensive Growth, 1880–1962

By 1880 the French had succeeded in pushing the indigenes back to the edge of the Sahara. The colonial government had decided to encourage French settlement in the area rather than to preserve it as an Arab state under French "protection." The loss of Alsace and Lorraine to Germany in 1870 brought substantial emigration from those areas, and France had begun to experience population pressure. Part of this pressure spilled over into Algeria. From 1875 onward the French proportion of Algeria's growing population hovered around 10 percent, and the French formed about one-third of the urban population. By 1914 the pattern of French settlement was well established. The French owned more than one-quarter of the agricultural land, which was divided into relatively large farms oriented toward production of export crops. They dominated trade, banking, and government service and even formed about half of the skilled labor force. The native Moslem population was heavily agricultural, on small, low-productivity farms, and in the cities was relegated to the lower tiers of the occupational structure.

Algeria was regarded as an integral part of France. It was divided into *départements* with the same status as other French *départements,* including representation in the French parliament. The Algerian franc was tied to the French franc, and there was free movement of commodities, capital, and labor. While this retarded the growth of factory industry in Algeria, as well as damaging handicraft production there, it also provided an outlet for surplus labor. The number of Algerians employed in France grew steadily and by the 1950s was approaching a half-million.

Economic growth before 1940 was heavily agricultural and oriented toward noncereal crops in which French farmers tended to specialize. The area under vines grew from 40,000 hectares in 1880 to 400,000 hectares in 1940, and wine production increased six times. Citrus fruits, introduced around 1925, had a high rate of output growth, as did potatoes and tobacco. Cereal production grew more slowly, probably at best keeping up with population growth. There was substantial development of infrastructure—roads, railroads, ports, electric power, communications facilities. While some traditional handicrafts stagnated or declined in the face of import competition, "modern" crafts and small-scale industry grew rapidly. Samir Amin (1970) estimates that the output of this sector, in constant prices, increased fivefold between 1880 and 1955. Large-scale manufacturing, however, was still largely absent in 1940.

Estimates of overall output growth are necessarily crude. Amin (1970) estimates that *material* production outside of agriculture (crafts and industries, mining, power, construction) grew at 3.1 percent per year from 1880 to 1955. When this figure is averaged out with lower growth in agriculture and services, his estimate of total output growth is only 1.9 percent. Since population was growing at an estimated 1.6 percent, any increase in per capita income was clearly modest. Moreover, increments to income were distributed heavily toward French rather than Moslem residents. On these grounds one could argue that my dating of the turning point is too early and that Algeria should instead be placed in the post-1945 category.

There was a marked acceleration after 1945 in the growth rates of population, total output, and per capita output. Deathrates fell steeply, while birthrates seem if anything to have risen. The rate of natural increase rose to 2.1 percent in the 1950s, 2.4 percent in the 1960s, and 3.2 percent in the 1970s. There was a substantial inflow of French private capital after 1945, as well as increased allocation of French government funds for development. Export agriculture grew even more rapidly than before, while factories producing light consumer goods appeared in considerable numbers. In the decade 1950–60, GDP grew at 6.5 percent per year and GDP per capita at 4.4 percent, much above pre-1940 rates. This increase partly reflects the post-1945 resurgence of the French economy, with which Algeria was so closely linked.

Let us look briefly at the structure of the economy near the close of the colonial era. Amin (1970) and Sa'igh (1978) give somewhat differing estimates of the sector composition of GDP, but it appears that the economy was already heavily oriented toward service production. Sa'igh estimates that as of 1955 trade and private services was 36 percent of GDP and public administration 11 percent. Agriculture produced about 29 percent of GDP, "industries and crafts" 12 percent, and other types of material production 13 percent.

More than one-quarter of the cultivated land was owned by Europeans, in farms averaging 307 acres compared with an average of 32 acres for Moslem farms. This land was also of better quality on average, and the European owners made greater use of modern inputs and cultivation methods. Foreigners thus produced about 60 percent of agricultural output—90 percent of the wine, 60 percent of the citrus crops and other fruits and vegetables, 40 percent of the cereals. The per capita income of Europeans engaged in agriculture was about one-third higher than that in France itself and ten times as high as the average income of Moslem agriculturalists.

Only about 10 percent of the French population, however, was engaged in agriculture, compared with 74 percent of the Moslem population. The French congregated rather in the cities, where they formed one-third of the labor force and dominated the higher-level occupations. The percentage of the French labor force engaged in professional and administrative occupations was three times as high as that in France itself, and it is not surprising that these people wanted Algeria to remain French. As far down the ladder as skilled labor and white-collar work, the French slightly outnumbered the Moslems. Moslems predominated in semiskilled and unskilled labor and in domestic service, but only about half of urban Moslems worked in such jobs. As of 1955, about 20 percent were white-collar workers, while 25 percent were small businessmen engaged in trade, crafts, small industries, and other fields.

The French-Moslem income gap was much smaller in the cities than in the countryside. Urban wages were not much below the French level, and the comprehensive French minimum-wage system applied to Algeria as well. As of 1960, rates for skilled labor were only about double the unskilled level. Amin estimates average Moslem earnings in manufacturing, transportation, and construction at about 40 percent of non-Moslem earnings. Thus the depressed economic status of the Moslem population was due mainly, though not entirely, to its heavy concentration in agriculture. While economic growth may have brought little benefit to the average Moslem farmer, many urban Moslems did work their way up to higher levels of skill and earnings. Algerians employed in France at French wage levels must also have benefited substantially.

It is often said that revolutions break out not when conditions are deteriorating but when they are improving. At any event, a guerrilla struggle against French control broke out in 1954 and continued with increasing ferocity until 1962. The large number of Algerians in France and the large number of French in Algeria (many of them third-generation residents who considered themselves as "Algerian" as anyone else) made the struggle unusually bitter. It was ended by President de Gaulle's decision, highly controversial within France, to terminate hostilities and to grant independence as of July 1, 1962.

Intensive Growth, 1962–80

The war for independence brought much physical destruction; and after the war about 90 percent of French residents left Algeria, removing most of the country's human capital. Abandoned French farms and factories were often taken over by former employees, causing much confusion and interruption of production. In the first two years after independence national output dropped sharply. But interestingly enough, while income *per capita* dropped from 1960 to 1963, income *per Algerian* seems to have risen as Algerians moved into higher-paid jobs vacated by the French. From 1964 onward growth was resumed, and the GDP growth rate in the 1970s was a bit higher than it was in the 1950s. Recent growth, strongly propelled by oil and OPEC, has been somewhat unbalanced and needs to be examined sector by sector.

It is perhaps not surprising that the weakest performance has been in agriculture. The former French-owned estates are now collective farms, owned by the state, and managed by a director and a workers' committee. Workers receive a cash wage and are allowed to cultivate small private plots. The collectives occupy about 30 percent of the cultivated land and employ 20 percent of the agricultural labor force but produce about 60 percent of agricultural output, ratios close to those which prevailed in the French period. In private farming there is still substantial inequality of ownership. There has been some redistribution through ceilings on landholdings and distribution of state land; but land reform has not been as thoroughgoing as, for example, in Egypt. The private-farm sector has not been favored by government policy and has had little access to improved inputs and technical assistance. The favored collective farms, on the other hand, have not performed well because of the managerial and incentive problems involved in this type of agriculture.

Total agricultural output, then, has been stationary or slightly falling, and agriculture's share of GDP had fallen by 1980 to 7 percent. There have been increases in production of animals and livestock products, fodder crops, fruits and vegetables, and a number of industrial crops. But cereal output has fallen in absolute terms and even more in per capita terms. This has had predictable results. The internal terms of trade have shifted sharply in favor of agriculture, reaching 161 in 1979, on a base of 1969 equaling 100. Although this may be encouraging to farmers, it poses obvious difficulties for the urban sector. A second consequence has been rising food imports, which amounted to 12 percent of total imports in 1979. Imports have made possible an improvement of diets—average daily calories per capita rose from 2,040 in 1960–62 to 2,369 in 1977–79—in the face of declining domestic food production. The ease with which food imports can be financed from oil exports has encouraged inattention to the agricultural sector, which could pose long-term difficulties.

Industry, a favored sector, has shown rapid output growth and considerable diversification of production. From the consumer-goods industries of the French period, Algeria has expanded into petrochemicals, iron smelting, automotive, building materials, engineering, electrical, and machinery products. By 1979 some 400,000 workers, or about 15 percent of the nonagricultural labor force, were employed in manufacturing, and manufacturing plus mining and energy produced 16 percent of GDP. The public-private ownership mix is about fifty-fifty, but there is a large difference in scale of enterprise. As of 1970 there were 30 public companies, essentially holding companies operating a number of enterprises. These enterprises tend to be the larger plants, many of them formerly French-owned and nationalized after independence. Industry has typically received about 30 percent of government investment funds in successive four-year plans. There were also in 1970 some 1,816 enterprises in the private sector, much smaller in average size but employing about as many workers as the public sector.

Oil was discovered in 1958 and was developed initially by private companies. These were nationalized gradually after independence, and government undertook all new development, with the result that by the early 1970s the industry was almost completely in public hands. Export revenue and government revenue from oil have soared dramatically, first through an increase of export volume from eight million tons in 1960 to 50 million tons in 1974 and then through the very large price increases of 1974 and 1979. Production volume was leveled off deliberately after 1974 because of a desire to stretch out known reserves over a longer period in the future. As of 1979 the oil sector accounted for 31 percent of GDP, and this should be borne in mind when looking at other sector shares. For example, the manufacturing-mining-energy share of *nonoil GDP* was 23 percent, and agriculture's share was almost 10 percent. The oil sector has typically received one-quarter to one-third of public-sector investment, and its share has grown over time.

Exports are about one-third of GDP, and oil and natural gas provide more than 90 percent of the total. Exports of manufactures and agricultural goods are small, and wine output in particular has fallen sharply. Like some other oil countries, Algeria has managed to spend money even faster than it has earned it. Imports typically exceed exports, the deficit being covered mainly by commercial borrowing. By 1979 the debt-service ratio had risen to about 25 percent of exports. Imports are predominantly capital goods and intermediates, with food forming 12 percent of the 1979 total and other consumer goods 10 percent. Like Venezuela, Algeria is "sowing the oil" through a high rate of investment in development projects, racing against the date when oil revenues must inevitably decline.

The public sector is relatively small in consumption terms but much larger in investment terms. In 1980 public consumption was only 14 percent of GDP; but fixed investment was 41 percent, and most of this flowed through the public sector. Government revenue, predominantly oil revenue, amounts to 35–38 percent of GDP and government saving to 22–25 percent of GDP. But government spends so heavily on direct investment and loans to public enterprises that the overall budget balance is typically negative. The deficit is covered partly by drawing on private savings through bond issues, the postal savings system, and other channels. But in the late 1970s there were also substantial borrowings from the central bank, which brought increases of more than 20 percent per year in money supply and an acceleration of inflation.

The growth rate of GDP per capita since the mid-1960s has been in the range of 2–3 percent per year, a good though not spectacular performance. Because of the marked shift toward investment, the growth rate of personal consumption has been lower; but the population has clearly benefited, and income growth has been more widely diffused than during the colonial period. The economy is still beset by problems. Sa'igh, a friendly critic, notes overdependence on oil, a sluggish agricultural sector, inefficient management in many public-sector enterprises, heavy unemployment (15.8 percent of the nonagricultural labor force in 1979, despite the surplus-labor outlet to France), and "the growing strength of bureaucrats and technocrats." On the horizon, too, is the eventual depletion of oil reserves and the question of how well the economy will be positioned for greater self-sufficiency when that time arises.

MOROCCO

Morocco, which resembles Algeria in some respects, differs from it significantly in others: a long-standing monarchy, which persisted throughout the French period and continues today; a shorter period of French domination because of late colonization; a French population that peaked at about 5 percent of the total, as opposed to Algeria's 10 percent; a friendlier attitude toward private enterprise since independence, despite the presence of a large public sector; a lack of Algeria's oil wealth, but a good supply of farm and pasture land as well as phosphates and other mineral resources.

Before colonization, the population was part Arab, part Berber and included also many Jews of Spanish origin who had fled from persecution in that country. The Jews engaged in banking, which was forbidden to Moslems by their religion, as well as in trade and the jewelry crafts. Settled farming, mainly of wheat and barley, prevailed in the western lowlands. In the High Atlas were tribes practicing both agriculture and animal raising, often migrating between farm and pasture lands with the season. East of the Atlas were only nomadic tribes.

A well-developed handicraft system, employing some 10 percent of the population, was controlled by "corporations" resembling European guilds. Ports were few and poor, and so trade was mainly internal, centering on Fès and to a lesser extent on Meknes and Marrakech. The royal court rotated regularly among these three cities, bringing purchasing power in its train. There was some foreign trade, initially mainly with Britain, but after 1900 mainly with France. The chief imports were cloth, sugar, tea, glassware, and hardware. In return Morocco exported cereals, wool, and hides to Europe, and djellabas, shoes, and silks to North Africa and Senegal.

Rough estimates show population growing even in the eighteenth century and then rising from 2.5 million in 1800 to 3 million in 1850 to 5 million in 1900. Morocco was clearly experiencing extensive growth, aided by plentiful land supplies, a stable polity, and close proximity to Europe.

Turning Point: *circa* 1920

Because of its proximity Morocco was a natural object of rivalry among the European powers. The Act of Algeciras in 1906 provided that all powers should receive equal treatment in trade with Morocco. French political predominance was conceded in a treaty of 1912 as part of a deal that gave Germany a freer hand in Central Africa, allotted a stretch of Atlantic coastline to Spain, and placed Tangier under international control. Most of the country was effectively occupied by 1922, though fighting continued in the mountains until 1934. In movies of the 1920s resolute members of the Foreign Legion regularly confronted Riff tribesmen riding down from the High Atlas. Unlike Algeria, Morocco was never an integral part of France but rather a protectorate, with the sultan exercising at least nominal authority.

Intensive Growth, 1920–56

As in Algeria, the French implanted a second economy on top of the indigenous one. The colonial government took over by decree considerable amounts of ''superfluous tribal land'' and resold it to French settlers, who also bought land from individual Moroccans. European settlers thus came to dominate the best agricultural areas in the northwest. Moroccans tended to be squeezed out toward marginal lands to the south and east having lighter and more variable rainfall. By 1953 European holdings amounted to about one million hectares, in farms averaging 170 hectares in size. While this was only about 10 percent of all crop land, it produced 25 percent of gross agricultural output. The European farms concentrated on high-value crops—such as citrus products, wine, fruits, and vegetables—oriented toward local European consumption with some overspill into exports to France. The Moroccan-owned farms, averaging only 17 hectares in size, concentrated on such food crops as hard wheat, soft wheat, barley, and corn.

The area planted to cereals grew from about two million hectares in 1919 to three million in 1929 to 4.4 million in 1952. There is little evidence of improvement in yields over time, though yields on European farms were usually about 25 percent higher than those for the same crop on Moroccan farms. Output of the high-value European crops rose faster than cereal output, and so did output of livestock products. Between 1931 and 1951 the number of cattle increased substantially, while sheep doubled and goats tripled in number. Amin (1970) estimates that between 1920 and 1955 total agricultural output grew at 2.6 percent per year, somewhat above the 2 percent rate of population growth.

There was some development of irrigation, but by 1956 only 56,000 hectares, about one-seventh of the potentially irrigable area, had been brought under irrigation. Credit facilities and technical assistance were oriented toward European farms, and these farms seem to have had little demonstration effect on Moroccan farming. Only after World War II did the French begin to take a serious interest in Moroccan agriculture, and this effort was soon swamped by the independence movement. Continued population growth produced a sizable rural proletariat, of whom some worked on European farms, some sought work in France, and some migrated to ''bidonvilles'' (tin-can towns) on the edge of the cities.

The industrial sector throughout the French period was dominated by hand-icrafts. To the traditional crafts, which employed around 100,000 people in 1920, were added a variety of "modern" crafts and small-scale industries. Factory industry as of 1940 was limited largely to food processing—flour milling, sugar refining, brewing, vegetable canning, sardine canning. Even in textiles, the usual early leader, there was little activity. After World War II there was a short-lived inflow of French capital into enterprises producing light consumer goods for the local market. But as independence loomed on the horizon, capital flight set in by 1954–55.

A substantial mining industry developed, with phosphates in the lead but with a sizable output also of coal, oil, lead, zinc, iron, and manganese. Phosphate production, operated as a state monopoly, rose from two million tons in 1930 to 18 million tons in 1952. In Algeria and Tunisia phosphate mining was a private industry, but the three areas cooperated in a cartel to regulate output and prices. Florida and the Soviet Union are the only other significant sources of phosphate.

During the colonial period, extensive development of the infrastructure was undertaken. By 1956 there were 50,000 kilometers of highways, of which 15,000 were hard-surfaced. There were 1,756 kilometers of railways, eight ports, seven airports, good telephone and postal facilities. This cheapening of transport for passengers and goods brought a multiplication of markets and some reduction of the social and economic gap between city and country.

Foreign trade played its usual role of a leading sector. Between 1920 and 1955 exports increased 11 times, rising from 8 percent to 31 percent of the country's material product. Agricultural exports predominated, but phosphates were about one-third of export receipts and were also a major source of government revenue. There was typically a substantial trade deficit, which was closed in a variety of ways: French (and later American) military expenditures, remittances from Moroccans employed in France, French government grants (increasingly generous after 1945), private capital inflow, and foreign borrowing.

Taxation was lighter in Morocco than in Algeria or Tunisia, and the public sector remained relatively small. Revenue came mainly from customs, land taxes, and other indirect taxes plus the phosphate monopoly. The ratio of government expenditure to GDP rose from about 8 percent in 1920 to 12 percent in 1955. With the appearance of foreign aid after 1945, an "extraordinary" or development budget, heavily French-financed, was added to the regular budget. Over the period 1947–56 about one-third of this budget was allocated to agriculture and irrigation, one-third to infrastructure, and the balance to education, health, housing, and other services.

By the end of the French period Morocco had been transformed into a semimodern economy. The investment rate in 1955 was about double the 1920 level, and investment was going more heavily into industry, mining, and the infrastructure than had been true earlier. Agricultural output had shrunk to 32 percent of GDP, trade and private services were 31 percent, "industries and crafts'' were 14 percent. The number of handicraft workers was still substantially larger than the number of factory workers. Sa'igh (1978) estimates that the ''modern sector'' was producing 68 percent of GDP, though it employed only 29 percent of the labor force. The racial division of labor resembled that in Algeria. The French formed only 5 percent of the population, but two-thirds of them were employed in manufacturing, public administration, the professions, and commerce. Among Moroccans, on the other hand, 70 percent were employed in agriculture, 10 percent in handicrafts, and the remainder in petty trade, laboring, and minor clerical activities.

Regarding output growth, Samir Amin's venturesome estimates may be worth citing, since they are all we have. Over the period 1920–55, Amin estimates that agriculture grew at 2.6 percent per year, ''industries and crafts'' at 6.0 percent, services at 3.7 percent, and total output at 3.7 percent. A population growing at 2.0 percent would mean a 1.7 percent growth of output per capita. It seems likely that per capita income did rise significantly over the period. But it is also clear that the benefits were unequally distributed and that Moroccan farmers, in particular, may have made little progress.

Intensive Growth, 1956–80

The 1956 transfer of power to an independent Moroccan government under the king was relatively peaceful; and the new government, fearful of frightening away capital and skills, moved more slowly than that in Algeria to transfer assets and jobs from Europeans to Moroccans. Still, the European population dropped from 575,000 in 1955 to 260,000 in 1960, while the Jewish population dropped from 210,000 to 160,000 as about 50,000 emigrated to Israel. Much French land, especially land held by absentee owners, passed to Moroccans through private sale, though the government did not force such sales. By 1974 the amount of French-owned land had fallen to 250,000 hectares, or about one-quarter of the 1956 level. There was also gradual Moroccanization of the civil service, the professions, and business management, retarded mainly by the initial shortage of educated people. Even today, after a generation of independence, there is still a marked shortage of administrators and technicians, which will be corrected only gradually by educational progress.

Even peaceable decolonization produces some disruption in the economy, and it is not surprising that output increased little in the first five years of independence. But after 1961, with a new king and a more active development policy, the growth rate began to rise. It averaged 4.4 percent per year during the 1960s and 5.6 percent during the 1970s. Meanwhile population growth had accelerated to 2.5 percent in the 1960s and 3.0 percent in the 1970s. Thus over the period 1960–80, per capita output grew at 2.5 percent per year.

The agricultural sector has been sluggish. Neither the cultivated acreage nor the livestock population has increased appreciably. About 150,000 hectares of land have been added to the 65,000 under irrigation in 1960, but only about half of the irrigation potential has been realized. There has been no significant land redistribution and, despite much talk of rural development, agricultural policy in practice remains hesitant. Food output appears to have fallen behind domestic demand, and in the late 1970s food imports were about 10 percent of total imports. Agriculture's share of GDP has fallen to 16 percent.

The mining sector has continued to expand, though only at 3.4 percent per year. The handicraft sector has been stagnant, though it is still important in employment terms. Modern industry grew slowly until the late 1960s, more rapidly during the 1970s, but the "crafts and industries" share of GDP has risen only slightly to 16.5 percent. The government professes to look kindly on private investment and has established an investment code and a development bank. But entrepreneurs, both Moroccan and foreign, have been hesitant to invest in an atmosphere of etatism and comprehensive government control. The public sector is quite large, having domain over phosphates and other mining enterprises, banking and insurance, a tobacco monopoly, transport and electric power, and a number of industrial enterprises. Public enterprises as a whole contribute a net profit to the treasury, though most of this comes from the phosphate company.

Exports have been a bright spot, growing at around 6 percent per year and also showing gradual diversification. Phosphates are still the largest single item but are almost equalled by agricultural products, which include output from expanding citrus-fruit and sugar-beet industries. Tourism has emerged as important, averaging around 20 percent of exports in the late 1970s. Manufactured exports have also grown rapidly from a small base, rising from 3.4 percent of total exports in 1967 to 11.9 percent in 1977. Imports continue to exceed exports by a substantial margin. Consumer-goods imports other than food are now quite small. More than 80 percent of imports are capital goods, fuels, intermediate products, and military supplies (important since 1975 because of continuing tension in the Sahara). The trade deficit is closed partly by substantial remittances from Moroccan workers employed in France, partly by a continuing foreign-aid inflow— originally mainly from France but now also from the United States, West Germany, the World Bank, and the Arab development banks. There has also been some borrowing from commercial banks, and by the late 1970s the debt-service ratio was nearing 20 percent.

The public sector has expanded in current expenditure as well as investment terms. The GDCF/GDP ratio in 1980 was 21 percent; and about 60 percent of investment comes from government and public enterprises. The public-consumption share of GDP rose from 12.2 percent in 1967 to 22.0 percent in 1980. There has been heavy expenditure on education, health, and housing to service the growing population. Primary school enrollments have risen dramatically, though secondary enrollments are still low. Defense expenditures shot up after 1975 and take about one-quarter of the budget. There are also substantial consumption subsidies, reflecting a strong welfare element in government policy. Chronic budget deficits are closed mainly by foreign borrowing, though there is some domestic borrowing from the public and the central bank.

The economy is not without problems. Agricultural performance has been weak. The number of unemployed has risen by one-third since 1960, though it has declined as a percentage of the labor force to about 8 percent in 1977. On the other hand, the country's credit rating has been strong because of good export performance. There is political stability under the monarchy. Public administration is reasonably competent, despite continuing personnel shortages in middle management. The resource base is good, and Morocco's geographic location and its close ties to the European Economic Community (EEC) are advantageous. Except for some agricultural and textile products, Moroccan goods have free access to the EEC and there is also free movement of labor. The economy should continue to grow at a moderate rate, though not at a superior rate, over the foreseeable future.

9

Nigeria, Ghana, Ivory Coast

Sub-Saharan Africa differs in many ways from Asia or South America. Most Asian states have a history going back for hundreds of years, usually predating the era of European colonization. The Latin American countries, too, have a long history as colonial provinces of Spain or Portugal and later as independent nations. They *emerged* from colonial rule a half-century before Africa *entered* on colonial rule. In Africa there were no nations in the modern sense before the colonial era, but rather hundreds of tribal chiefdoms, some having substantial and others tiny domains. Other distinctive African characteristics were: thin population and abundant land; primitive and land-intensive agricultural techniques; poor transport facilities in the interior and heavy reliance on head porterage; contacts with the international economy limited largely to the slave trade.

A further distinction can be drawn between West Africa and East and Central Africa. West Africa is low-lying, hot and humid, with rain forest along the coast shading into savanna grasslands farther north. East and Central Africa are mainly high-plateau country having moderate temperatures even at the equator. From an economic standpoint, West Africa in 1800 was considerably more "advanced" than other regions. It had a denser population, a better-developed trade network, and earlier and closer contacts with Europe via Atlantic shipping routes.

It will save space and reduce repetition to outline first the general features of West African development in the precolonial and colonial eras. These features were broadly similar for Nigeria, Ghana, and Ivory Coast. After completing this outline I shall turn to individual countries, providing additional detail for the earlier period and continuing the story through the era of independence.

SOME COMMON FEATURES OF WEST AFRICAN ECONOMIC GROWTH

The Era of Extensive Growth

In chapter 2, I noted the inaccuracy of stereotyped pictures of precolonial African economies as static, tradition-bound, unresponsive to change. In the basic industry, agriculture, there is much evidence of successful adoption and diffusion of new crops imported from Asia and South America. There existed a range of handicraft industries resembling those of preindustrial societies in other parts of the world and a well-established system of local markets and long-distance trade routes.

Exports of slaves from West Africa to the Americas began very early, and one might wonder why this trade did not generate export-led growth. Although the trade involved several million people over the centuries, it was never very large in dollar terms and the proceeds were not widely distributed. The suppliers of slaves, mainly tribal chiefs who sold captives from other tribes or even their own subjects, were consumers rather than investors. Hopkins (1973) concludes that the trade neither promoted development nor seriously disrupted economic activity.

Trading in slaves was prohibited by Britain in 1807, by the United States in 1808, by Holland in 1814, and by France in 1815. Although Portuguese traders continued active for some time, the trade died a lingering death over the first half of the nineteenth century. But as slaving declined there was a remarkable growth in primary-product exports from 1815 onward. These included ivory, gum, gold, and timber from Sierra Leone; palm oil from the Niger Delta; and groundnuts from Senegal. As the British became more hygienic and soap-conscious, their imports of palm oil rose from 107 tons in 1807 to 31,457 tons in 1853. Trade was stimulated by rising manufacturing productivity in Britain and France, which cheapened manufactures and improved the terms of trade for primary products. Britain's net barter terms of trade fell almost 50 percent between 1800 and 1855. Cheap manufactures spread out from the coastal ports of West Africa through local trade networks to ordinary farmers and petty traders, stimulating production of cash crops in return. This activity, however, involved a narrow strip of land ranging from 50 to 100 miles inland from the coast. Beyond that transport costs made trade unprofitable, and the northern savanna areas remained largely untouched before 1900.

The terms-of-trade movement was reversed around 1860, partly because of recurrent depressions in the "developed" economies from 1873 to 1896. Prices of primary products fell about 50 percent between 1860 and 1890, while prices of manufactures fell less. This decline in the terms of trade of primary products was largely offset, however, by a continued rise in export volume. In addition, ocean shipping costs were being reduced steadily as steam replaced sail.

Even before the colonial era, then, West Africa seems to have been involved in a process of extensive growth that is readily explained in terms of staple theory. Population estimates are very rough, but they suggest a slow upcreep of population in the nineteenth century. Total exports and exports per capita were clearly rising. That there is no evidence of deterioration in food supply must mean that more land and labor were being used in agricultural production. Moving large amounts of heavy commodities raised employment in transport, and trading activity also increased. About three-quarters of the import flow consisted of four items—

textiles, liquor, salt, and iron—but there were also sizable imports of hardware, tobacco, and firearms. Britain, as industrial leader, was able to dominate this trade. It was estimated that in 1868 about 60 percent of West African trade was with Britain and an additional 20 percent with France.

A new development from about 1850 onward was the appearance of European wholesalers in coastal ports. Initially, the Europeans had been seamen first and traders only incidentally; but as trade became more profitable, shipping concerns began to establish permanent merchant houses. Other European merchants, with no previous connection with West Africa, discovered the opportunities opened up by cheaper steam transport. There were also African wholesalers, some of whom had converted from wholesaling slaves to wholesaling palm oil, while others were newcomers. And there was a large network of intermediary traders involved in assembling export products and distributing imports to the interior.

The depression of 1873–96 intensified competition among European merchants of different nationalities and between them and African merchants. There were disputes over spheres of influence. Some European companies tried to move inland—for example, up the Niger River—in order to buy more cheaply closer to the source. Some African merchants tried to bypass the Europeans and sell directly to Europe. This rivalry was partly responsible for increasing pressure on European governments to "do something," in which the merchants were often joined by the missionaries. It was not very clear what that "something" was supposed to be, but it seems to have included: pacifying the interior, where tribal warfare caused loss of trade as well as loss of life; abolishing the internal tolls levied by the numerous African chiefs; improving transport through port, river, and railway development; moving inland to reduce the number of middlemen and reduce trading costs; establishing political boundaries to reduce competition by traders of other European nationalities.

The standard doctrines of imperialism are not very helpful in explaining European penetration. Africa was always rather marginal from a European standpoint. It was not an important outlet for European capital *à la* Hobson and Lenin. Because of its small population and low per capita income, it was not a major market for manufactures. Rather, it was more important as a source of raw materials. On this front, the British would probably have preferred continuation of free trade, which was working well for them. But this would have required French and German agreement, which was not forthcoming. France moved in a protectionist direction after 1870 and established a preferential tariff system that included its African possessions. In 1879 a French military column started eastward from Senegal, which eventually reached Lake Chad 2,000 miles away, meanwhile sending fingers southward to the Ivory Coast and other areas. In the mid-1880s Germany moved actively to solidify its control over Togo and the Cameroons. The British then moved belatedly to protect their holdings in Ghana and Nigeria. By 1900, the partition of Africa was over.

Colonialism and Intensive Growth, 1890–1950

The years 1890–1915 stand as a watershed in West African economic history. The "national" boundaries that exist today were drawn for the first time. Tribal warfare was brought under control and order was established in the interior. Port facilities, river transport, and railroad building expanded rapidly. Export volume grew at an accelerated rate and, because the terms of trade of primary products were once more rising from 1896 to 1914, capacity to import rose even faster. There was a considerable capital inflow through both government and private channels, railroad building typically being financed by bond issues in the home country. By 1914 West Africa, and indeed most of the rest of Africa, had been welded firmly into the international economy.

The strongest impression one gets from an examination of West African economic growth after 1890 is one of *continuity*—continuity within the period and continuity with the precolonial era. Export expansion came from agricultural products, which had been known in the nineteenth century and which were produced in ever-increasing volume by peasant smallholders. Economies were open and trade-oriented, currency systems were linked to the metropolis, government policies were laissez-faire and not concerned directly with stimulating production. The colonies were expected to be self-supporting and, since a large part of government revenue came from export and import taxes, this expectation strengthened the protrade bias of public policy. There was a marked absence of structural change. Apart from some food processing and raw-materials processing, manufacturing was still virtually absent in 1945. As Hopkins (1973, p. 235) points out, "Colonial rule did not create modernity out of backwardness by suddenly disrupting a traditional state of low-level equilibrium. On the contrary, the nature and pace of economic development in the early colonial period can be understood only when it is realized that the main function of the new rulers was to give impetus to a process which was already underway."

The barter terms of trade changed course several times over the period, tending on the whole to deteriorate against primary products. The more sluggish heartbeat of the world economy from 1914 to 1945 brought a retardation of the export growth rate. In current dollars, West Africa's exports *quadrupled* between 1897 and 1913, *doubled* between 1913 and 1929, and rose by *50 percent* between 1929 and 1945.

Infrastructure continued to expand. Colonial governments were still pushing railways in the 1920s, not fully appreciating the dawn of the motor era; but after 1945 road building was to dominate the scene. The area embraced by the trading system was pushed farther and farther north from the coast. There was increasing specialization of agricultural production, as many farmers chose to concentrate on commercial crops and to buy much of their food. Within the European merchant class there were numerous mergers and failures of smaller firms, which by the

1920s had produced a tight oligopoly with two dominant British firms and one major French firm. The larger firms could afford to establish more branches in the interior, to hire better expatriate staff, to finance the activities of an increasing number of indigenous traders, to finance large inventory holdings, to withstand trade fluctuations, and to take advantage of vertical integration with manufacturing and shipping concerns. They also tended to receive preferred treatment from administrators, who liked the convenience of dealing with few people rather than many.

This oligopolistic position no doubt enabled the large merchants to maintain wider spreads between buying and selling prices than would have existed under pure competition. But they were subject to some competition from smaller firms, which managed to survive, and from Lebanese merchants, who entered in growing numbers after 1900. Nor did African wholesalers pass from the scene. Their *share* of the wholesale trade declined between 1880 and 1930; but trade increased so much that their volume of sales probably rose, and there were some notable success stories. Below the wholesale level, African traders flourished and multiplied. Although there were frequent complaints of "unnecessary middlemen," this trade network seems to have been quite efficient.

The failure of manufacturing to develop is not hard to explain. Nigeria was the only country with a substantial population, and domestic markets were small before the 1950s. Trading profits were more attractive than riskier forms of industrial investment, and the merchant houses were rather opposed to domestic industries, which would reduce their import flow. Labor scarcity was also a continuing problem. Agricultural incomes were high enough to hold up the opportunity cost of labor to urban activities. European employers tended to explain their labor-recruitment difficulties in terms of "the target worker" and "the backward-bending supply curve of labor." Research studies suggest that the main explanation was simply that employers' wage offers were too low.

Since export expansion was central to economic growth, we should ask where the exports came from. Why, to begin with, was there little development of large, European-owned farms such as occurred in parts of East and Central Africa? Climatic factors may be partly responsible. The hot, humid, malaria-prone areas of West Africa were less attractive to Europeans than were the highlands of Kenya or Rhodesia. The merchant houses were not favorable to plantations, which might have tended to monopolize supplies, preferring rather to buy from many small producers. The plantations that were established in the early years usually failed after a short time. Their problems included ignorance of tropical agriculture, shortage of capital, labor scarcity and high wage rates, and the wide fluctuation of product prices on the world market. Meanwhile, peasant producers had shown that they were capable of sustaining vigorous export growth. So, partly by drift rather than decision, colonial policy crystallized in favor of smallholder production.

There were some large African-owned farms, usually belonging to tribal chiefs or other notables. But most of agriculture was in the hands of small cultivators who did not "own" land in the Western sense but were entitled to cultivate a certain area as members of a village. The ready response of these small cultivators to cash-crop opportunities is central to the development story. But the story should not be oversimplified. It is sometimes portrayed as a process in which food producers, who needed to work only a few hours per day to produce the conventional diet, were induced by cash rewards to offer more hours of labor and cultivate more acres of land. Thus cash-crop production was simply "added on" to the established pattern of production. This is an important part of the story, but not the whole of it. Many of the coffee and cocoa innovators in Ghana and the Ivory Coast were in fact migrants who moved to areas with suitable unoccupied land. These enterprises were thoroughly capitalistic from the start, and it was food production that had to be "added on" rather than vice versa. In other cases the innovators were nonfarmers. The Hausa traders of northern Nigeria, perceiving good market opportunities, persuaded and financed nearby farmers to go into groundnut production.

In addition to absorbing more labor time, cash-crop production also involved changes in the division of labor between the sexes. Hoeing and other food-production activities were traditionally "women's work," though the heavier labor of tree felling and ground clearing was done by men. But much of the activity involved in export production—for example, planting and tending cocoa or coffee trees—was defined as "men's work." Even with men working more than before, labor supply was a continuing problem. Labor scarcity was eased somewhat by the freeing of slaves, which was still going on in 1900 and was not completed until around 1930. The main reliance, however, was on seasonal migrant labor from rain-scarce areas farther north. Senegal groundnut farms employed 60,000–70,000 temporary immigrants each year, and by the 1950s Ghana cocoa farms employed 150,000–200,000 migrant workers, a large number relative to the country's population. Thus income derived originally from exports was eventually distributed rather widely through the savanna and southern Sahara regions.

In general, there was little diversion of land from food production. In northern Nigeria, however, some land was diverted from food crops to groundnuts, and this happened also in Senegal, which eventually became a substantial food importer. Technical change was not prominent, but again examples can be found. Expansion of Nigerian groundnut production involved changes such as shorter fallows, increased manuring, and increased interplanting of groundnuts with other crops.

During the 1930s and 1940s there was a marked movement away from free trade and laissez-faire. France's African possessions were locked more tightly into the French trading system, and trade with France rose from 40 percent of their total trade in 1900 to 75 percent in 1935–60. Britain's introduction of imperial preferences in 1932 had a similar effect. The agricultural distress of the 1930 led governments to intervene in the market with stockpiling and price-support operations. Market intervention increased further during World War II, when it typically took the form of a government marketing board for each major crop, which profited considerably from the gap between the export price and the price paid to farmers. While this was rationalized as a way of insulating farmers against world-market fluctuations and stabilizing their incomes, it also amounted to a substantial tax on agriculture.

Gradual recovery from war in the late 1940s was followed by a strong export boom in the 1950s. Exports rose at rates that had not been seen since 1914, reflecting the remarkable upsurge of output in the "developed" countries. While colonial governments encouraged and profited from the rise of exports, the rising supply was generated mainly by the decentralized efforts of small producers, as it had been in earlier decades. At the same time there were new developments after 1945. These included:

1. a heightened interest in colonial development by the metropolitan powers, particularly France and Britain, and the first substantial infusion of development funds;
2. the first appearance of light manufacturing industries, aided by expansion of the domestic market through rising export income;
3. continuation of the marketing boards for key crops and allocation of part of their surpluses for development purposes;
4. a marked expansion of the public sector, in regard to both current expenditure and capital formation; and
5. the appearance of five-year development plans financed from varying combinations of metropolitan aid, marketing-board surpluses and other local revenue, and borrowing from the IBRD and other sources. Plan expenditures emphasized infrastructure but gave some attention also to education, health, and urban housing. Directly productive activities, presumably the domain of private enterprise, received lowest priority. Agriculture typically received only a few percent of development expenditure.

I shall not attempt to explain why movements for national independence gathered force not when African populations were particularly oppressed but when they were getting visibly better off. Whatever the reasons, the colonial powers pulled out rather abruptly, and in the era 1955–65 one African state after another embarked on self-government, usually with a very inadequate supply of African administrators and technicians.* No part of Africa had anything approaching the Indian Civil Service or the large stock of educated manpower that enabled the new government of India to get off to a running start.

---

*A personal note may be of interest here. In 1952 I was asked by the Carnegie Foundation to organize a group of Yale social scientists for a three-month summer tour of sub-Saharan Africa. The colonial administrators who were our hosts in each country assured us repeatedly that the Africans, often described in unflattering terms, were quite incapable at that stage of governing themselves. Independence, if it ever came, was necessarily in the distant future. We accepted most of this at face value and were as surprised as anyone else to discover within a decade that most Africans were in fact governing themselves. This story has no moral.

We turn now to three countries that together accounted for three-quarters of West Africa's output in 1960. Their postindependence paths have been different—strong economic performance in Ivory Coast; moderate, somewhat precarious success in Nigeria; poor economic performance in Ghana. Reasons for these differences, which have more to do with politics and administration than with resources, will appear as we proceed.

NIGERIA

Like other parts of West Africa, the areas that eventually became part of Nigeria had a long-established traditional society. There were many local rulers, who assigned land for cultivation, controlled trade, and collected taxes. (Later on, the British authorities typically chose to govern indirectly through these African rulers rather than to displace them.) Agriculture, using shifting cultivation and simple implements, was mainly for subsistence, though there was some exchange of surpluses in local markets. Handicraft industries produced the usual array of consumer goods. The larger towns had guilds of skilled craftsmen who trained apprentices and regulated admission to the trade. There was a network of village markets in which farmers could exchange produce for handicrafts. Longer-distance trade moved mainly along the rivers or by head porterage, and transport costs restricted trade to high-value objects.

After about 1830 exports of palm oil and kernels, primarily to Britain, gradually replaced the dying slave trade. Although the initial base was small, the growth rate of exports and imports was high. Imports of cotton cloth through Lagos, for example, rose from 2.4 million yards in 1831 to 17 million yards in 1850, while salt imports more than doubled. Palm oil was the export staple throughout the nineteenth century. Cocoa appeared in the 1890s, and after 1900 we shall see a diversification into other export products.

Turning Point: circa 1890

British penetration first occurred through shipowners and chartered merchant companies such as the Royal Niger Company, with political authority developing later. The initial contacts were confined to coastal areas because of transport difficulties, endemic malaria, and tribal warfare in the interior. Discovery of quinine as an antimalarial improved the situation. The first expedition to use quinine penetrated the interior in 1854. Lagos was ceded to Britain in 1861. In 1886 an "Oil Rivers Protectorate" (later Southern Nigeria) was established over the Niger Delta. The northern territories centering on Kano were taken over from the Royal Niger Company in 1900 and became the Protectorate of Northern Nigeria. The northern and southern protectorates were merged in 1914.

Modern Nigeria, like most other African states, is thus a colonial creation. Although it was occupied by stages, the southern region, which provided most of the exports, was under British control by 1890. Intensive growth, then, can reasonably be dated from the 1890s.

Intensive Growth, 1890–1945

The period 1890–1945 saw modest growth in population and per capita income, with marked continuity in the main trends of economic development. Although population data are poor, Ekundare (1973) estimates that population increased from 16.8 million in 1900 to 27.4 million in 1945, a growth rate of 1.1 percent per year. Since land was abundant, it is reasonable to suppose that food output grew in line with population. While export growth occupies the spotlight, food output was always much larger in absolute size.

Export growth was certainly rapid. From 1900 to 1929 Helleiner (1966) shows export volume rising at 5.5 percent a year and export value at 7 percent a year. He speculates that exports may have been 2 percent of GDP in 1900 and that by 1929 its share may have risen to 5–7 percent of GDP. Export volume, after the post-1929 slump, rose sharply again in the late 1930s and remained high throughout World War II. The main problem of these years was persistent deterioration in Nigeria's terms of trade, which were lower in 1942–45 than at the bottom of the Great Depression.

Rapid export growth was made possible partly by continuing diversification of exports. Cotton and groundnuts expanded in the north, cocoa and rubber in the south. Mines on the Jos Plateau provided substantial tin exports. By 1929 the palm-products share of exports, initially near 100 percent, had fallen to 47 percent, and this decline was to continue in later years. Imports kept pace with exports, rising from £2 million in 1900 to £16 million in 1945. These imports, mainly of consumer goods, also became more diversified over time, with the share of cotton piece goods falling from 31 percent in 1900 to 19 percent in 1938. The initial regime of free trade was followed by growing import restrictions after inauguration of the ''imperial preference'' system in 1932. One reason for the shift was that Japan was beginning to compete seriously with Britain in textile exports.

The public sector, while small, also showed a high growth rate, with government revenue rising from £2.7 million in 1900 to £13.2 million in 1945, about half of which came from customs revenues. Direct taxes on land, cattle, and people were collected by the local rulers under British supervision and a certain percentage, usually one-quarter, of the collections were paid to government. An income tax on non-Africans was imposed in 1931, with later increases in rates, so that by 1945 personal and business income taxes formed 20 percent of total revenue.

The most important government activity was infrastructure development, financed partly by borrowing in London. There was considerable dredging and demolition of logs and other obstacles on the Niger and other inland waterways. Railroad building began in 1901, the main Lagos–Kano line was completed in 1911, and by 1930 there was a network of 2,100 miles. Helleiner comments that the railroads were "built far ahead of development events," but they did induce development along corridors adjacent to the railroad. A road-construction program was started in 1905 and accelerated as motor vehicles entered the country in increasing numbers. By 1940 there were 3,800 miles of government roads and about 25,000 miles of lower-quality roads maintained by the local authorities. Truck traffic, mainly in the hands of small African owners, was substantial enough so that in 1932 the operators formed a Nigerian Motor Transport Union. The port of Lagos was improved, and ship tonnage entering the port tripled between 1914 and 1937–38.

While directly productive activities were largely left to private enterprise, the government did develop and operate coal mines at Enugu, mainly to supply the railways. By 1930 employment of Africans in all types of government work averaged about 50,000. Export promotion led government to take an interest in the technology of export crops. Numerous agricultural research and experiment stations were established, which attacked cocoa disease and other plant diseases and distributed improved plant varieties. Government encouraged cooperative credit organizations; established systems for inspecting and certifying the quality of export crops, which was essential to their acceptability in world markets; and aided the introduction of small palm-oil pressing machines by advancing purchase money to the farmers. Cotton growing was promoted by a private organization, the British Cotton Growing Association, founded in 1902 to increase the empire's supplies and reduce dependence on the United States. The association established an experimental farm, built ginneries along railway lines in the north, and distributed improved seed through these ginneries.

Apart from agriculture, the main private activities were trading and handicrafts. Factory industry was virtually absent, amounting in 1945 to a few soap factories, a cigarette plant, a few sawmills, and a few cotton ginneries.

So who had benefited from development up to this point? A substantial proportion of the farming population participated in the export boom, either directly by growing export crops or indirectly by supplying food to specialized cash-crop producers. Farmers' higher incomes were used partly to buy larger amounts and a greater variety of imported consumer goods. The 50,000 government employees also had higher incomes than they would have earned in agriculture. African traders, truckers, and other small businessmen participated in the growth of commercial activity. For much of the population, however, life must have changed very little. Although we lack reliable estimates of GDP, it seems unlikely that the growth rate of GDP per capita could have exceeded 1 percent per year (Helleiner's estimate for 1900–29 is 0.6 percent).

Intensive Growth, 1945–80

The years 1945–60 saw a quickened tempo of political and economic change, which in retrospect appears as a preparation for independence though few can have expected independence to come as rapidly as it did. The governmental system had been revamped in 1934 into a federation, with three regional legislative councils added to the federal one. While the councils were still European-dominated and had only limited powers, there was now a minority of elected African members. Many internal functions were delegated to the regions, financed partly by federal "revenue sharing."

On the economic side, the "development movement" gathered headway. Under the influence of reform-minded Labour governments, Britain for the first time made substantial development grants to the African colonies. A system of government marketing boards for major export crops, established during World War II and continued in the postwar period, yielded substantial surpluses available for government expenditure. In addition, the colonial government was able to borrow in London. Funds began to be allocated through multiyear development plans, a process entertainingly described in Stolper's (1966) *Planning without Facts*.

A peaceable transition to independence in 1960 brought no immediate change in the growth pattern. But the new nation soon encountered political difficulties arising from rivalry between the Moslem Hausa and Fulani in the northern region, the Ibo in the eastern region, and the Yoruba and other groups in the western region. Parliamentary deadlocks and turnover of governments led to two military coups in 1966, and the nation remained under military government until civilian rule was restored in 1979. In 1967 an effort by the Ibo to secede and form an independent state of Biafra led to civil war, which ended only in early 1970. After 1970 there was a rapid economic recovery, aided by growing oil exports. Nigeria is a member of OPEC, and the large oil-price increases of 1974 and 1979 swelled export totals and government revenue, while also distorting the economy in ways to be described.

The economic story, then, is best divided into two periods: 1945–66, during which export-led growth proceeded along traditional lines with little structural change; and the 1970s, which saw the appearance of an oil-dominated economy, with many of the problems that seem to characterize such an economy.

Although the general pattern of growth from 1945 to 1966 resembled that in earlier decades, its tempo was considerably higher. Population growth accelerated after 1945 and, while the data are poor, seems to have been somewhat above 2 percent per year. GDP seems to have risen at something above 4 percent. But total resource use rose faster than this, as a typical trade surplus turned in the mid-1950s into a growing deficit, financed by drawing down accumulated reserves and by foreign-capital inflow. Helleiner estimates that from 1950–51 to 1960–61 total resource use rose at 5.1 percent per year. There was a marked shift in resource use, however, toward investment and public consumption, which rose at more than 12 percent per year compared with a 3.6 percent growth rate for private consumption. Even so, per capita consumption was certainly rising faster in the 1950s than before 1945.

The growth process continued to be fueled by exports, which rose considerably faster than GDP. The export/GDP ratio rose from 10.3 percent in 1950 to

14.3 percent in 1960. Between 1946 and 1963 export volume rose about two-and-one-half times. The net barter terms of trade also rose sharply until the peak of the primary-products boom in 1954 and, although it then dropped by 20 percent, it remained well above the level of the late 1940s. Thus the economy's capacity to import increased about fourfold between 1947 and 1963.

The major exports as of 1964 were cocoa (19.1 percent), palm kernels and palm oil (15.1 percent), and groundnuts and groundnut oil (20.0 percent). But petroleum, first exported in 1958, was already 15.2 percent of exports by 1964. In addition, there were substantial exports of tin, timber, cotton, and rubber. The export list was thus more diversified than in earlier times; but the main nonoil exports were still products of rural origin produced by small farmers.

Producers of export crops did not benefit as much as the economy in general because of the spread between buying and selling prices. The marketing boards earned large surpluses up to 1954 and even after the price drop of that year continued to earn smaller surpluses. By now the boards had clearly come to be viewed as revenue-producing devices. The severity of what amounted to export taxation is suggested by the fact that in 1964 the real price to producers of palm oil and palm kernels was below the levels paid during the Great Depression. Cocoa, groundnuts, and cotton producers fared somewhat better, but not nearly as well as they would have done at world price levels.

While exports rose rapidly, imports rose even faster. Import volume increased about sixfold between 1947 and 1963. Beginning in 1955, imports pulled ahead of exports and produced a growing trade deficit. For some time the deficit could be covered from the large foreign-exchange reserves yielded by marketing-board surpluses, which at their peak in 1955 amounted to about two years' worth of imports. By the mid-1960s, however, reserves had been drawn down to low levels. It was then necessary to turn toward heavier foreign borrowing and to import restriction through higher tariffs and other policies. There was a moderate shift in the composition of imports. By 1964 machinery and transport equipment were 26 percent of the total, and raw materials and intermediates were another 20 percent. But consumer goods were still more than half of the total, suggesting the limited extent of import substitution at this point.

More broadly, one can say that there was little structural change up to the mid-1960s. Although the agriculture-forestry-fisheries share of GDP had fallen a few points, it was still almost two-thirds. Modern manufacturing, which was smaller than handicraft production until around 1960, amounted to only 3.5 percent of GDP; and the shares of infrastructure and public services were also modest. The economy remained heavily rural and agricultural.

Government was more activist than before, particularly after 1960 brought an independent Nigerian government committed to the ideology of development. The bulk of government revenue continued to come from the foreign sector—import duties, export taxes, marketing-board surpluses. The foreign-trade proportion of government revenue fluctuated in the range of 60–70 percent, with no downward trend, and was even higher than the 56.7 percent of 1930–31 and the 53.9 percent of 1938–39. The declining contribution of marketing-board surpluses after 1954 was offset by a rising contribution of import duties, which by the early 1960s provided almost half of government revenue. British development grants, while running in the range of £2–3 million a year during the 1950s, never amounted to more than 5 percent of the revenue collected from domestic sources, and by 1960 they amounted to only 2 percent.

Since trade was doing well, government revenues were buoyant and formed a rising percentage of GDP. But government expenditure rose even faster. From 5.4 percent of GDP in 1950–51, it rose to 15.1 percent in 1960–61, well above the 12.2 percent collected in revenue. By the 1960s budget deficits had become habitual and were covered by a varying combination of foreign borrowing, domestic bond issues, credit creation, and, after its creation in 1959, loans from the Central Bank of Nigeria.

Development objectives were increasingly prominent in expenditure allocation. Helleiner compiled public-sector tables that include expenditures by the three regional governments as well as the federal government. These show that by the early 1960s about one-quarter of government expenditure was going into transport and communications and another 10 percent into agricultural and industrial development. The 18 percent for education and 7 percent for health could also be considered developmental in a broad sense. The share of general administration, defense, and police had by this time fallen below 30 percent.

Government capital formation amounted to more than 60 percent of total capital formation, and the capital formation/GDP ratio had roughly doubled from 7 percent in 1950 to 13 percent in 1964. Government funds went heavily into road building, the road network growing from 25,000 miles in 1946 to 40,000 in 1960, of which about 5,500 miles was hard-surfaced. In addition there was some extension of the railway line, considerable river and port development, electrification, and the modest beginnings of manufacturing industry.

The new independent government moved to encourage industrial investment in several ways. Tax incentives and import-duty exemptions were provided for "pioneer" industries. The government gave preference to domestic producers in its own purchases. Import duties were raised, with an eye to protection as well as revenue. A Federal Loan Board and three Regional Development Corporations were established to provide capital, often in the form of equity participation in foreign-owned enterprises. "Industrial estates" were laid out in the larger cities. In response to these efforts, plus the atmosphere of optimism and political stability in the early 1960s, a sprinkling of factories appeared for the first time—for canning, brewing, textiles, cement, cigarettes, tanning, iron work, tin smelting, plywood, foundry works, and railway engineering. New industries were encouraged mainly to promote import substitution in light consumer goods, which was made possible by growth of the domestic market and evidenced by a gradual decline in the share of consumer goods in total imports.

Kilby (1967) estimates that about 70 percent of the capital in the "organized'' industrial sector as of 1964 was foreign private (primarily British), 20 percent was Nigerian public, and 10 percent was Nigerian private. Most of the British-financed factories were set up by merchant houses accustomed to whole-saling British-produced goods in Nigeria. After 1945 these houses encountered growing competition from Indians, Levantines, and other new wholesalers, posing a serious threat to profits. The solution, as it seemed, was to set up a factory in Nigeria and request a tariff high enough to shut out competition, thus securing a monopolistic or oligopolistic position. Kilby judges that this consideration was more important than the tax holidays and other inducements offered by government.

As of 1965, however, large factories by no means dominated the scene. The ''industrial sector'' at this time included: (1) rural cottage industries, with an estimated 900,000 households engaged in food processing, palm-oil extraction, and production of textiles, clothing mats, and metal products—employment in which, plus the travel and trade required to market household output, helped to fill in periods of slack labor demand in the agricultural cycle; (2) urban small-scale industry, in shops employing less than ten people, with an estimated employment of 100,000; and (3) firms employing ten or more people, with an estimated employment of 76,000, a tiny number for a country of 40 million people.

Official policy was to encourage small-scale, Nigerian-owned enterprises. But this effort had disappointing results, and available loan funds were often undersubscribed. The main reason, Kilby (1967, p. 336) judges, was inadequate absorptive capacity: ''the problem of inadequate absorptive capacity can be restated as the problem of deficient entrepreneurial capabilities.'' This took such forms as poor equipment maintenance, poor supervision of workers, unwillingness to delegate authority, profits eroded by embezzling and pilfering by members of the clerical staff. In addition to deficiencies of education and technical skills, there seem to be cultural factors at work. Visible wealth, however attained, commands high status in the society; but diligent managerial performance does not.

As often happens in early industrialization, there was a large and growing wage gap between the ''organized'' and ''unorganized'' sectors. Helleiner estimates that wage rates for unskilled and semiskilled labor doubled in the eastern region and tripled in the northern and western regions between 1948 and 1964. Wages for skilled labor rose less, apparently because the main impact of the minimum-wage system was on the lowest wages. Kilby also notes that real wage rates in the organized sector have increased at more than twice the rate of GDP. Government not merely sets minimum wages but also acts as wage leader, paying its own employees at rates well above the market-clearing level, which are then imitated by private employers. Unions achieve wage gains not through direct collective bargaining but by urging government to raise its own pay scales and then pressuring private employers to fall in line.

There must also have been a considerable increase in the rural-urban income gap, though I have not seen data on this point. There is indirect evidence in the heavy migration to cities, particularly of young people with primary-school education, and the growth of both open and concealed unemployment in the cities.

The 1967–69 civil war brought a drop in production, including oil production, which was located mainly in the war-torn eastern region. When peace was restored in early 1970, however, production recovered and by 1972 was back on its previous trend line. The story of the 1970s is one of rapid, unbalanced growth propelled by oil exports. Population growth has not yet begun to slacken, the 1970–80 rate of increase being 2.5 percent per year. GDP rose at 6.5 percent per year and GDP per capita at 4.0 percent. Living standards and employment opportunities rose at a rate that attracted some two million migrant workers from neighboring Ghana.

Oil was discovered in 1958 and by 1965 was already the largest single export, accounting for about 25 percent of export receipts. The industry recovered rapidly after 1970, and export volume continued to rise through 1973. Volume then levelled off, but the huge price increases of 1974 and 1979 brought a great increase in foreign-exchange availability and federal government revenues. At the same time, the oil boom created problems. The high value of the currency, resulting from balance of payments surpluses, attracted imports and discouraged nonoil exports. Traditional agricultural exports decreased and by 1980 exports of palm products had ceased, all the output being used at home. Imports of both foodstuffs and consumer goods flooded in, and by 1980 Nigeria was *less* self-sufficient in both areas than it had been in 1970. The ease with which imports could be financed encouraged neglect of agriculture, whose output rose at only 2.1 percent per year during the 1970s. Government also embarked on very large investment projects, such as the new capital city of Abuja in the center of the country, at a rate that created supply bottlenecks and forced up construction costs.

The influx of oil income went heavily into investment and expansion of public services. Between 1973–74 and 1978–79, gross investment grew at 25.6 percent per year and public consumption at 12.3 percent, compared with an 8.2 percent growth rate of private consumption. As government discovered new ways of using money, the current budget surplus shrank from 2,229 million naira in 1973–74 to 995 million in 1978–79. Since government investment in 1978–79 was 6,502 million naira, there was a large public-sector deficit. Private saving, on the other hand, had risen by 1978–79 to 8,228 million naira, compared with private investment of 4,194 million. But after borrowing as much as it could from the private sector, government still had to resort to the central bank. Data on the allocation of public investment from 1975 to 1980 show about one-quarter going to transport, another quarter to manufacturing, power, and other infrastructure, only 3 percent to agriculture. There is a large unexplained residual, presumably including such things as the new capital city.

Competence in public administration is variable, tending to decline as one moves from top-level toward grass-roots operations. There is considerable capacity for macro planning but less ability to convert plans into operational projects and still less to complete these projects efficiently. *Ex post facto* evaluation of projects is virtually absent. Bribery is pervasive in public service, even such low-level activities as mail delivery usually requiring a "tip" to the postman.

Agriculture, relatively neglected by government, has changed little from earlier times. Sixty percent of the holdings are less than 2.5 acres in size and 30 percent are less than one acre. Technology is primitive, relying basically on the hoe. Bullock plowing is not used even in the north, where there is no tsetse-fly problem and bullocks are available. Few modern inputs are used, and crop yields are low and stagnant. An examination of yield tables for cereal crops over the period 1963–77 shows no upward trend. The estimated 1.5 percent per year increase in food output during the 1970s thus resulted almost entirely from expansion of cultivated acreage. Even with large and growing imports, food supplies are inadequate and prices are high.

While still primitive in many respects, Nigerian agriculture also shows considerable specialization and commercialization. In the western region, for example, a farm survey reported 54 percent of farmers growing only annual (primarily food) crops, 23 percent growing only tree (export) crops, and 13 percent growing both. Overall, about 40 percent of farm output was being marketed either for export or for domestic consumption.

Another long-standing characteristic is the intermingling of agricultural and nonagricultural activities in rural households. A labor-force survey found that, in rural Nigeria as a whole, about 66 percent of households are engaged only in farming, 8.5 percent only in business, and 23 percent in both. There is considerable regional variation, with the proportion of households engaged solely in farming highest in the north, whereas in the western state 40 percent of households combine farming with business. Even those who report agriculture as their main activity usually have one or more side activities that absorb considerable time, especially in the slack season.

Agricultural Change in Tropical Africa by Anthony, Johnston, and others (1979) reports results of many studies of farming in Nigeria and other African countries. For example, a sample of families in the cocoa-growing region of Nigeria reported that their net cash income from trade, home industries, and service activities was on average about 60 percent of their net cash income from cocoa farming, or almost 40 percent of their total income. Again, a study of three villages near Zaria, in northern Nigeria, found that men in farming families worked about 255 days per year. But only about half of these days were spent in farming. Of the remaining days, about one-third were spent in trading, one-quarter in "manufacturing" (as blacksmiths, tailors, carpenters, spinners, potters, leather workers, cigarette makers, mat weavers, sugar makers), and 40 percent in service activities (as builders, thatchers, firewood cutters, butchers, bakers, hunters, washermen, Koran teachers).

These rural activities—a blend of farming, handicrafts, and trade—are still the heart of the economy. While the urban population has a high growth rate, it is only a small percentage of the total population. And within the urban labor force, the two million people employed in the "modern" or formal sector in 1980 were greatly outnumbered by the 5.2 million in the informal sector.

Manufacturing has been the favored sector in development policy. Government-owned manufacturing enterprises have increased considerably, partly through buying out of foreign-owned enterprises under an "indigenization" program. Private investment in manufacturing has not been as vigorous as might have been expected given the rapid expansion of markets. Trade, urban real estate, and other activities continue to yield higher and quicker profits. A large share of private saving, as already noted, has been drawn off to cover government deficits. With substantial inflation, with wages tending to outrun inflation, and with virtually no increase in labor productivity, Nigeria remains a high-cost producer. An index of net labor costs relative to manufacturers' selling prices rose from 95 in 1965 to 127 in 1976. Behind this lies the lag in agricultural output, which has pushed up food prices and money wages, producing a typical Ricardian squeeze on manufacturing profits.

The index of manufacturing output more than doubled during the 1970s, but domestic demand grew so much faster that self-sufficiency decreased. The ratio of manufactured imports to value added in domestic manufacturing was 2.10 in 1973 and had risen to 3.47 in 1978. In the important cotton-textile field, import substitution is now substantially complete. But in most other consumer goods there was reverse substitution in the 1970s—that is, the share of imports in domestic supply *rose* substantially. For example, the percentage of domestic consumption still being imported in 1977 was 89.2 for sugar, 84.0 for cement, 29.9 for paint, 28.7 for soap and detergents, 22.7 percent for footwear, 40.7 percent for beer, 27.1 for soft drinks. These products are not difficult to make and are usually in the forefront of import substitution. But in Nigeria, at least for the time being, import substitution has gone into reverse.

The mushrooming of urban activities has considerably widened the urban-rural income gap. The ratio of average urban income to average rural income per capita was estimated in 1960–61 at 2.6. By 1977–78 it had widened to 4.6. This has naturally stimulated rural-urban migration. Virtually all primary-school graduates leave agriculture, which has caused the schools to be labeled "kidnapping centers." This drain of talent from agriculture helps to reinforce agricultural stagnation.

The outlook for the economy, then, is unclear. Even with the decline of oil prices in the early 1980s, Nigeria is by no means poor. But whether political stability will continue, whether the capacity of public administration can be raised, whether the economic distortions of the 1970s can be remedied, whether Nigeria can "sow the oil" effectively before the oil runs out—these are still unanswered questions.

GHANA

Intensive Growth, 1895–1945

The Gold Coast, comprising what is now southern Ghana, was declared a British colony in 1874. There followed the same gradual northward penetration as occurred in Nigeria. The Ashanti kingdom was subdued in 1896, and by 1900 the whole of present-day Ghana was under British control. As in Nigeria, intensive growth can be dated from the 1890s.

We need say little about the pre-1945 period, because the process of export expansion and associated infrastructure development has been adequately described in previous sections. Exports expanded rapidly from a small base. Their average annual growth rate from 1882 to 1913 was 9.2 percent. The area's colonial name suggests that the country had substantial gold deposits, and gold still formed 25 percent of exports in 1913. But the main specialty was always cocoa, whose share of exports was 50 percent in 1913 and was to rise still higher in later years. The process of smallholder expansion into cocoa production has been recorded in studies by Polly Hill and others. Cocoa was very profitable from the outset, the basic techniques were simple, and small farmers needed little urging to plant more trees on the plentiful available land. The government's contribution consisted mainly in improving transport facilities and establishing experiment stations, which worked on disease control and distribution of improved seeds.

Growth and Decline, 1945–80

As in other parts of West Africa, in Ghana the end of World War II brought accelerated economic growth, a substantial infusion of development funds, and a gradual loosening of colonial controls. Internal self-government was granted by a new constitution in 1951, and full self-government followed in 1957. The first prime minister (and first president after the declaration of a republic in 1960) was Kwame Nkrumah, a charismatic politician who aspired to a pan-African leadership role. Within Ghana, he showed a penchant for showcase projects, such as impressive public buildings in Accra and a national airline. By force of personality and with the usual battery of foreign economic advisers and multiyear development plans, he created at least an impression of economic development, including a modest growth of (mainly foreign-owned) manufacturing enterprises. Even in the 1950s, however, the GDP growth rate was only about 4 percent, and after 1960 the economy began to deteriorate.

Nkrumah was overthrown in 1966 by a military coup, and the political situation has remained unstable since that time. Civilian government was restored in 1969 under President Busia, but he was ousted by a military coup in 1972. Since then there have been further coups and countercoups as rival military factions have struggled for power. Instability has prevented continuity in economic policy. Instead, there has been a concentration on short-term expedients to surmount recurring crises and hold onto office.

There is no general monograph on the economy of Ghana since 1945. There is a volume by J. Clark Leith (1974) in the National Bureau of Economic Research series on trade regimes and economic development, but it focuses on trade policy and extends only through 1969. Thus we must make what we can from the statistical record plus scattered articles and World Bank mission reports.

Population has grown at a reported annual rate of 2.4 percent in the 1960s and 3.0 percent in the 1970s. But national output has failed to keep pace with population. Indeed, the growth rate of GDP has fallen decade by decade, from 4.1 percent in the 1950s to 2.1 percent in the 1960s to −0.1 percent in the 1970s. Thus GDP per capita in the 1970s *fell* at about 3 percent per year. This record of economic deterioration is confirmed by other data. The index of food output per capita fell by 18 percent between 1970 and 1980. Average calorie availability per capita fell from 2,160 in 1960–62 to 1,996 in 1977–79, a decline of 8 percent.

There is further confirmation in the virtual absence of structural change. Thus agriculture's percentage share of GDP fell between 1950 and 1980 by only 3 percentage points, while the share of manufactures was virtually constant. The investment/GDP ratio, after rising during the 1950s, declined steadily after 1960 and by 1980 was well *below* the 1950 level. The public-consumption share rose somewhat over the period, but remained below 10 percent.

Leith (1974, p. 87) attributes poor economic performance partly to a strong import-substitution and antiexport bias in the trade regime, which has pulled resources out of exports and into import-competing sectors. "In nominal terms, output in the expanding sectors rose; but higher and higher cost resources were called upon to increase the output, so that the relative real expansion of output did not keep pace with the nominal. As a result, the real productivity of the resources drawn into the favored sectors deteriorated." Falling productivity of capital is indicated by the fact that the estimated output/capital ratio for the economy as a whole fell continuously from 1.80 in 1955 to 0.69 in 1969.

Aspects of economic mismanagement suggested by more recent observers include:

1. Failure to reduce export dependence on cocoa. A sharp drop in the world cocoa price, which is not infrequent, immediately precipitates an economic crisis. At the same time cocoa output has stagnated because of adverse public policies.
2. Pegging the value of the cedi at an artificially high level. In addition to the normal economic effects of overvaluation, this provides a strong incentive to smuggling. Cocoa slips through the porous land border to neighboring countries, and the government loses tax revenue.
3. Comprehensive regulation of prices, which among other things discourages agricultural production by taxing farmers too heavily. Retail-price ceilings are intended to protect the consumer but fail to do so because they are so widely evaded. Black-marketing appears to be universal.
4. Poor fiscal performance. By the late 1970s government revenue was only about two-thirds of government expenditure, with a consequent high inflation rate, pressure on money wages, and discouragement of private saving. The large deficits result partly from heavy overstaffing of government agencies, plus large wage increases that attempt, but recently have failed, to outrun living costs. In addition to the usual pressure for expansion of education, health, and

other public services, there are substantial consumer subsidies and other transfer payments to individuals. Political leaders have attempted to maintain popular support by operating a welfare state, but without the productive capacity needed to support it.

5. Stagnant foreign-exchange earnings, plus the fact that the country is unable to attract either private or official capital, severely restricts Ghana's capacity to import. Thus farmers cannot secure the modern inputs needed to raise productivity, manufacturing industries operate below capacity for lack of materials, and the transport system is undermaintained. The process of deterioration thus becomes circular: lack of imports and poor transport leads to a still lower level of exports, which further tightens the foreign-exchange constraint. With heavy currency overvaluation and all imports licensed, these licenses have high cash value, and there appears to be much corruption in their administration.

Ghana's situation was eased for a time by its ability to sell labor to prosperous Nigeria. Some two million Ghanaians migrated to Nigeria in the 1970s, usually illegally, and their remittances to families at home became an important source of foreign exchange. But after the 1981–82 drop in oil prices and revenues, Nigeria in early 1983 ordered all illegal entrants to leave the country within two weeks. The Ghanaians were shipped out, intensifying the problem of underemployment and declining incomes in their home country.

IVORY COAST

Ivory Coast's geography resembles that of Ghana and Nigeria. Rain forest in the south shades off into savanna grasslands in the north. Export crops are grown mainly in the south, while the north grows food crops by traditional methods and also serves as a source of labor supply. Population density is only about half that of Ghana, and labor scarcity is the main constraint on production. The economy has always depended heavily on foreign labor supplies. Europeans are prominent in the higher occupational strata, migrant Africans in lower occupations, such as hired agricultural laborers.

Ivory Coast resembles its West African neighbors in the timing of colonization. French control was established in the south in 1893 and was extended gradually to the north over the next twenty years, bringing more than fifty distinct ethnic groups under common political control. As in other Francophone African countries, colonial policy emphasized assimilation of the local population into French culture, the creation of "black Frenchmen." Racial distinctions and tensions were never as severe as in the British colonies. A native elite was trained to occupy many of the intermediate positions in government and the economy, incidentally being imbued with French values and outlook. This may help to account for the lack of violent nationalist outbursts, the peaceable transition to independence, and the continuing good French-Ivoirian relations.

Intensive Growth, 1895–1945

Ivory Coast was a significant exporter even in precolonial days, sending palm oil to Europe and kola nuts to its northern neighbors. Miracle (in Robson and Lury, 1969) judges that the income generated by these exports equalled that from the slave trade. Rapid expansion of primary exports, however, dates from the early 1890s, which can be taken as the turning point to intensive growth. The tonnage exports of palm kernels increased about six times between 1892 and 1913, and timber exports also rose more than sixfold. To these traditional exports were soon added coffee and cocoa, introduced by the French and exported in rapidly growing volume from 1900 onward. With temporary dips due to war and depression, export volume grew at a high rate throughout the colonial period. From what must have been only a few percent of GDP in 1890, exports had risen to 28.6 percent of GDP by 1960. Agricultural export crops were by that time roughly equal to domestic food production, each contributing about one-quarter of GDP.

Logging is a large-scale operation carried on mainly by foreign companies. But palm oil, coffee, cocoa, and other agricultural exports are peasant crops, income from which is widely distributed among the rural population. As in other parts of West Africa, output was expanded mainly by cultivating additional land, which was freely available throughout the period. Labor scarcity, the main constraint, was met to some extent by migrant labor from northern Ivory Coast, but in large measure by migration from Upper Volta, Niger, and other less-prosperous countries to the north and west.

Little need be said about other sectors of the economy. The trade network expanded with the growth of foreign and internal trade. Export and import trade was largely French-controlled; but internal trade was carried on mainly by Africans, supplemented by Lebanese and Syrian traders, who entered the country in considerable numbers after 1900. Manufacturing remained a handicraft activity, with virtually no development of factory industry before 1940. As late as 1960, handicraft output was estimated as equal in value to factory output, and handicraft workers outnumbered factory workers by a wide margin. The colonial government concentrated on infrastructure development—ports and waterways, railroad construction beginning in 1904, and a road network, which became increasingly important with time.

Intensive Growth, 1945–80

We have already noted that 1945 marked something of a watershed in colonial policy. In the Ivory Coast a large investment program was undertaken with French technical and financial assistance. The Vridi Canal, opened in 1950, gave Abidjan an excellent deep-water port. The Abidjan–Niger railway, started in 1904, finally reached Ouagadougou in 1954. The road network was further expanded, particularly in the forested area centering on Abidjan. Export growth continued at a high rate. Between 1950 and 1960 the volume of coffee exports tripled and timber exports increased sixfold, though cocoa showed only a small increase. Rising consumer incomes stimulated a modest growth of consumer-goods manufacturing. As of 1960, however, factory industry was limited mainly to textiles and foodstuffs plus first-stage processing of primary products, and factory output was still only equal in value to handicraft output. Lack of an indigenous skilled labor force, lack of experienced management, and a relatively high wage level associated with agricultural prosperity tended to make domestic manufacturing noncompetitive with imports. Also, government continued to follow a liberal trade policy reflecting Ivory Coast's comparative advantage in primary exports.

Political independence was achieved in 1960. The country's first (and thus far only) president was Felix Houphouet-Boigny. He had been politically active during the colonial period and had in fact represented Ivory Coast in the French senate, under the French policy of affiliating the colonies with the metropole. Later he organized and led the Ivory Coast's only political party, which is broadly based and has wide public support. His policy has been one of conciliation and dialogue with the French government, French residents of Ivory Coast, and foreign business concerns. In a poll of foreign business executives, political stability was listed as the most important consideration in their decision to locate in Ivory Coast, while tax incentives were listed in fifth place.

The main lines of economic policy show no marked break with the colonial period. While there are moderately high protective tariffs, the economy is still relatively open and outward-looking. President Houphouet-Boigny, himself owner of a substantial farm, has been proagriculture and proexport. The country has remained in the franc zone, with the currency tied to the French franc at a stable 1:50 rate. There are virtually no restrictions on financial transfers. Foreign investment is welcomed and encouraged by a battery of tax and tariff incentives. About two-thirds of manufacturing industry is foreign-owned. There is still a strong French presence in the country. French advisers are prominent in the economic ministries and the central bank. While Ivorization is proceeding at a moderate pace, French residents form a substantial proportion of top managers, technicians, and even skilled craftsmen and foremen.

This structure could easily be criticized as a continuation of colonialism under the guise of independence. But the country has turned in a strong economic performance, probably the best in tropical Africa. This will appear evident from a brief sector-by-sector review.

Government devotes substantial resources to agriculture through research and extension, credit facilities, and rural infrastructure development. It appears, however, that agriculture rather more than pays for this. There is a net resource transfer out of agriculture, mainly through the operation of the price-stabilization system, which yields a substantial surplus to government. Den Tuinder (1978) estimates that, using 1.0 to indicate a situation in which the product is neither taxed nor subsidized, values less than one for products that are taxed, and values greater than one for products that are subsidized, "coffee and cocoa have values between 0.5 and 0.6, palm oil and copra between 0.8 and 0.9, cotton, maize, and rice about 1.0, and the median for industry is 1.45." During the 1970s coffee and cocoa farmers seem to have averaged about 50 percent of the export price of these crops.

The prices offered to farmers have nevertheless been sufficient to induce a continuing expansion of acreage and output. Between 1960 and 1974 cocoa plantings rose from 600,000 to 920,000 hectares, while coffee increased from 700,000 to 1,235,000 hectares. In addition to expansion of these staples, there was considerable diversification into other crops—mainly oil palm, cotton, and pineapple. Cotton growing was made feasible in the north by development of selected seed varieties and crucial insecticides in the early 1960s and by introduction of ox-drawn cultivation. Cotton, usually grown in rotation with food crops, has become a major element in integrating the backward north with the rest of the country and reducing the regional income gap.

Overall, agricultural output grew at 4.6 percent per year during the 1970s, while food production grew at 5.1 percent. But with migration plus natural increase producing a 4.3 percent rate of population growth in the 1970s, and with a continuing rise in per capita incomes, food output has not kept up with domestic demand. Food imports form about 20 percent of total Ivory Coast imports. Given the strong balance-of-payments position, these imports are apparently not considered worrisome. They have contributed to a considerable rise in nutritional levels, from an average of 2,290 calories per capita per day in 1960–62 to 2,528 calories in 1977–79.

Industrialization has been stimulated by high and well-distributed cash incomes arising from peasant exports, by the atmosphere of political stability, by investment incentives offered by government, and by a rising level of effective protection. The average rate of effective protection in the mid-1970s was 42 percent for manufacturing as a whole, but exceeded 100 percent for some products, including flour milling, footwear, rubber products, and cement. From a small initial base, manufacturing output grew at about 11 percent per year from 1960 to 1976, its share of GDP rising from 4 percent to 15 percent. While real manufacturing output quintupled over the period, manufacturing employment quadrupled, yielding an estimated employment elasticity of 0.8. This high figure may reflect the fact that much of manufacturing is still relatively small-scale and labor-intensive, oriented toward agricultural processing and light consumer goods.

The modern manufacturing sector is not without problems. It is heavily concentrated in Abidjan. Some industries have relatively high costs on a world scale, with no clear tendency for the "infants" to grow up. Protection is high enough to reduce pressure to cut costs; and when the initial ten-year concessions provided by the investment code run out, they tend to be extended for an additional period. Some industries have excess capacity for the local market, and some can probably never achieve comparative advantage. In 1975 some 68 percent of industry was foreign-owned; and of the remainder, about three-quarters was owned by government. Private Ivoirian investment, though favored in principle, has been slow to develop, most people preferring the quicker returns available in real estate, trade, and other activities.

Exports have continued to grow faster than GDP, the export/GDP ratio reaching an all-time high of 35 percent in 1976. In addition to a high growth rate of the "big three"—coffee, cocoa, and logs—there has been successful diversification in several directions: through local processing of cocoa, coffee, and timber before export; through development of new natural-resource-based exports, including palm products, cotton, and fruit; and through development of manufactured exports. About one-quarter of Ivory Coast exports of manufactures go to other African countries, which are at a still lower level of industrial development.

Imports are typically below exports but have grown at roughly the same rate. Their composition has not changed much over the years. Food imports are about 20 percent of the total, other consumer goods about 25 percent (down from 34 percent in 1960), capital goods about 30 percent, raw materials and semifinished goods about 20 percent. France is still the largest trading partner, but its share of both exports and imports has fallen substantially since 1960, while the share of other EEC countries has been rising. Free access to the EEC market under the Lomé Convention of 1975 is a definite advantage, particularly since this trade concession is nonreciprocal, the Ivory Coast and other countries covered by the convention being allowed to levy duties on EEC products.

The favorable merchandise balance is more than offset by financial transfers out of the country. The largest single drain is workers' remittances, which amounted to about 14 percent of export earnings in 1975. (Profit remittances, on the other hand, were only 8 percent of exports.) About 60 percent of these remittances were by Europeans, about 40 percent by non-Ivoirian Africans. The overall payments deficit is closed mainly by public-sector foreign borrowing. Given the country's strong export performance and good credit rating, moderate borrowing has presented no problem.

Turning to the public sector, we note first a relatively high current revenue/GDP ratio, averaging 25.4 percent in the years 1970–75. More than half of revenue comes from taxes on foreign trade and most of the remainder from value-added taxes (VAT) and other indirect taxes. Taxes on income and wealth contribute only about 20 percent. Current expenditures, which typically amount to only about 80 percent of current revenue, are rather welfare-oriented. Education and public health receive about 40 percent of the total, while agriculture and public works get only 11 percent and national defense, 9 percent.

The country's investment rate has been high and rising, increasing from 15 percent in the 1950s to 28 percent in 1980, about 60 percent of which is public-sector investment, representing mainly investment by a variety of public enterprises. These include agencies involved in research, technical assistance to farmers, regional development, and the like, which for various reasons have been detached from the general budget; publicly owned financial institutions; and public utilities, manufacturing concerns, and other institutions engaged directly in production.

Contrary to experience in many countries, Ivoirian public enterprises earn a substantial profit, sufficient to finance about two-thirds of their investment requirements. The remainder comes from foreign borrowing. General government investment is financed mainly by the current budget surplus plus profits of the crop-stabilization funds, which are treated as a separate item. It has not been necessary to resort heavily to borrowing from the central bank. Ivory Coast has not suffered from the inflationary pressure endemic in some other countries, and this has no doubt contributed to its good economic performance.

The overall investment level is only loosely controlled. The four-year development plans set firm limits only for investment by general government (which is about 40 percent of public-sector investment, or one-quarter of total investment). While there are plan targets also for investment by public enterprises, these are not effectively enforced. Targets for private investment are still looser, in the French tradition of "indicative planning." Private-sector investment is almost entirely self-financed, with little reliance on foreign funds. Even after the drains of profit remittances and workers' remittances, private-sector saving is roughly equal to investment.

Much has been made of Ivoirian commitment to private enterprise, particularly in comparison with some other African states. But Ivory Coast is clearly a mixed economy, with government playing a role not unlike that in France itself.

The upsurge of growth since independence shows up clearly in the tables to be presented in chapter 15. The average annual increase in real GDP rose from 3.6 percent in the 1950s to 8.0 percent in the 1960s and 6.7 percent in the 1970s. The rate of population growth has also been unusually high, with heavy immigration attracted by prosperity in Ivory Coast being added to natural increase. Even so, the growth of per capita income has been above average for third-world countries and well above average for Africa. The GDP estimates on this point are confirmed by such physical indicators as calorie intake, school enrollments, health-care facilities, (falling) mortality rates, and rising life expectancy at birth.

10

Kenya, Uganda, Tanzania, Zimbabwe, Zambia

The British came into East Africa in the late nineteenth century from a foothold in Zanzibar, where the sultan had long ruled under British "protection" and which in due course was formally annexed as a colony. The Central African colonies of Southern Rhodesia (Zimbabwe) and Northern Rhodesia (Zambia) were penetrated from South Africa, initially by a private company organized by Cecil Rhodes.

The motivation for colonization was partly strategic. The Cape, Zanzibar, and the East African coast were stepping-stones to India, always the key British colony. Uganda contained the headwaters of the White Nile and served as a buffer against the Germans, who were coming into Tanganyika (Tanzania) to the south. The Rhodesias drove a wedge between Angola and Mozambique, thwarting Portugal's hope of a solid belt of territory across Central Africa. But there were commercial motives as well, mainly a desire for secure imports of cotton, coffee, sisal, and foodstuffs from within the empire. The procurement of materials was considered more important than gaining the small African market for British manufactures.

KENYA

The east coast of Africa had long had trade relations with India and the Arab countries through the entrepôt of Zanzibar. Ivory and slaves were exported from Africa while British, Indian, and other manufactures were imported. There were also Arab plantations along the East African coast, operated with slave labor, which became unviable when British occupation brought the abolition of slavery.

Intensive Growth: 1895–1960

The British moved into the mainland from Zanzibar after 1884, partly to counter the German movement into Dar es Salaam. As in some other parts of Africa, the area was initially occupied by a private company, which eventually went bankrupt, leading to a takeover by government in 1895. A 600-mile railroad from

Mombasa to Lake Victoria was started in 1897 and completed in 1901. Many of the Indian laborers employed on this project stayed on to become traders and artisans, initiating the three-tier racial structure that continued throughout the colonial period. The railroad had the usual cost-reducing and trade-stimulating effect. The ratio of prices in Uganda to prices in Mombasa, previously 3:1 or even higher, was drastically reduced.

The population record is obscure. (The first census was taken only in 1948.) There may have been little population growth in the nineteenth century, and some observers surmise that population actually declined in the early decades of British rule. During the 1920s and 1930s, however, population began to grow, perhaps at a rate of 1.0–1.5 percent per year. But land continued to be abundant.

After briefly considering peopling Kenya with Indians, the authorities decided instead to encourage British settlement. So substantial tracts of land were designated for transfer to white settlers on 99-year lease. Settlers in the "white highlands" eventually came to occupy about 20 percent of the "good" agricultural land, that is, land with a minimum annual rainfall of 30 inches. There were successive waves of white settlement from 1901 to 1914, during the 1920s, and (most substantially) after 1945 under a settlement scheme for ex-servicemen. All other land, designated as "native reserves," was set apart for African use.

European farms were large, as can be inferred from the fact that in 1930 1,700 farms occupied more than five million acres. Wolff (1974) estimates that only about one-eighth of this land was cultivated, the rest being in pasture or unused. Most of the product was marketed, and much of it was exported. After experimenting with various crops, some of which proved unsatisfactory, the landowners concentrated on corn, sisal, coffee, and wheat. The first three of these provided about three-quarters of exports in 1930.

The colonial administration aided European agriculture by building roads and marketing facilities and by providing technical assistance. During the severe depression of the early 1930s government intervened with support prices. Government helped also with labor supply, which was always the largest production problem. The Africans, who could do well enough in their tribal areas, were not much inclined to wage labor. Partly on this account, government imposed hut and poll taxes that required some cash earnings. The amount collected in this way rose from £105,000 in 1910 to £591,000 in 1930. District officers also "encouraged" wage employment and did a certain amount of direct recruitment, though the methods used were not as forcible as those in some Belgian and Portuguese territories. By 1930, an average of 125,000 African workers were employed on European farms in a typical month. In addition, African families often squatted on unused European land and were allowed to remain on condition of supplying a specified amount of labor.

Although European farming was thus well established by the 1930s, its real boom period was 1945–60. The number of white farmers doubled, the number of cattle tripled, and fertilizer use increased 25 times. Some £46 million was invested in agriculture and supporting infrastructure. The output of grain and sisal doubled, coffee output rose three times, sugar four times, milk three times, and meat seven times. The shift away from cereals toward mixed farming is suggested by the fact that by 1960 livestock and dairy products formed 25 percent of marketings, cereals only 15 percent. The main export crops—coffee, tea, and sisal—were 45 percent of the total.

Meanwhile, in the "native reserves," food growing by traditional methods remained largely unchanged. The Africans were not encouraged to grow export crops in competition with whites and were steered rather toward food production. Encouragement of food crops in the reserves resulted in some marketed surplus, and African farmers benefited to some extent from increasing food demand in urban centers. Only after 1945 did government begin to pay serious attention to African agriculture, partly because of the more progressive spirit of the times, but partly also because of the Mau Mau uprising in the early 1950s and other signs of political unrest. A program of shifting from tribal to individual land tenure, involving consolidation of scattered strip holdings, was carried out in the Kikuyu area in the late 1950s, partly to reward those who had remained loyal to government during the uprising. The program probably benefited mainly the larger and wealthier African farmers, who were able to consolidate their holdings into substantial farms. A program of buying out European land and subdividing it among African smallholders was initiated in 1960. Both lines of policy were to continue after independence.

The Masai and several other tribes were pastoralists rather than farmers, valuing cattle as a symbol of wealth and a medium of exchange. In precolonial days, these more warlike tribes had dominated the settled agriculturalists. But under the British their relative position deteriorated, until by 1960 they were clearly subordinate. In addition to preventing tribal warfare, the colonial authorities established fixed boundaries, which interfered with free migratory grazing. To prevent African cattle from spreading disease to European-owned cattle, they established quarantine laws, which often interfered with profitable marketing. And as land scarcity appeared and "overstocking" became an increasingly serious problem, the authorities sometimes intervened to reduce overstocking by simply taking away cattle. Pressure on the land had begun to appear by 1940 and with the population upsurge after 1945 was to grow steadily.

Manufacturing in the precolonial period consisted of traditional crafts. Smiths smelted iron and produced knives, spears, and swords. This was a skilled occupation that involved an apprenticeship system. Extraction of salt from lake water was a substantial industry. Clothing was produced mainly from animal skins and wattle bark. Other crafts included pottery, basket work, house building, boat building, fish traps and nets, and silver working. Some of these crafts probably suffered at least a relative decline in the face of import competition, but little documentation is available.

Factory industry appeared only slowly. As of 1939 it consisted of a few plants producing beer, cigarettes, soap, cement, and a few other necessities. Beyond this the British were not much interested in building up competition for their home industries. After 1945 the attitude toward industrialization was more favorable. Industrial estates were laid out in Nairobi and other urban areas, and financial aid was available from the Industrial Development Corporation. Domestic demand was growing rapidly because of farm prosperity. Industrial growth was aided also by the common market with Uganda and Tanganyika. In principle, there was supposed to be an equitable distribution of new industries among the three territories; but Kenya had the largest internal market and for this reason, together with its superior transportation and financial services, it was usually chosen as the best location. In the 1950s, about 20 percent of Kenya's manufacturing output was exported to the other two East African colonies.

At this stage, however, industry was still heavily oriented toward agricultural processing. The food-beverage-tobacco group accounted for about half of manufacturing output. The remainder consisted of railroad and motor-vehicle repair, cement, shoes and clothing, and other consumer goods. By 1960 there were 3,380 private companies, with a total capital of £120 million. A few of these were sizable branches of multinational corporations, but most were quite small, owned either by Europeans or Asians residing in Kenya. Both in government and business the three-tier occupational division of labor was well established. The British were owners, administrators, and professional people as well as farmers. The Indians were junior officials, clerks, foremen, artisans, and traders. Africans not in agriculture were mainly employed as semiskilled and unskilled laborers.

In government the colony was expected to be self-sufficient. The small public revenues came from head taxes, excise taxes, and taxes on foreign trade; they were spent on administration and policing, building and maintenance of roads and urban infrastructure, and limited education and health facilities. Substantial government outlays with a development orientation appeared only after 1945.

An elaborate network of local markets and longer-distance trade existed in precolonial days that included intertribal transactions, such as exchange of Kikuyu food for Masai animal products. With improvement of transport and growth of domestic demand after 1900, the trade network grew in scope and volume. As Europeans came into the country, Indian traders usually followed close behind and took over most of the larger and more profitable trading opportunities. But African markets did not disappear; and small African traders often functioned as intermediaries between the farmer and the Indian trader.

Foreign trade rose rapidly in percentage terms from a small initial base. Kenya's exports rose from less than half a million pounds in 1914 to more than four million pounds in 1940 and seventeen million pounds in 1950. These exports were almost entirely agricultural and came mainly from the European farms. The imports, mainly of consumer goods, also went primarily to European and Asian residents of Kenya. But rising incomes from farm marketings and wage labor enabled Africans also to increase their consumption of a few items, which gradually became "necessities"—bicycles, watches, radios, tin roofing for houses, colorful cotton cloth. There was a consistent trade deficit, which was closed by tourist receipts, money brought in by white settlers, and other private investment. The years 1945–60 appear in retrospect as a period of transition to independence, though it was not evident at the time. There was an increasing flow of development funds from London. The road network was improved and expanded. European farming boomed, but there was at the same time increasing attention to African agriculture and the beginnings of land transfer to small African farmers. Manufacturing growth was encouraged, and plants producing consumer goods appeared in considerable numbers. African representation in the colony's legislative council was increased substantially. The transition to independence in 1963 was peaceable and did not break the continuity of economic development.

Intensive Growth, 1960–80

Kenya's economic record since independence is one of the most successful in Africa. GDP grew at 6.0 percent per year during the 1960s and at 6.5 percent in the 1970s. Despite unusually rapid population growth of more than 3 percent per year, per capita income rose at 2.7 percent per year from 1960 to 1980. Consumption rose less rapidly because of a shift toward investment, but it still rose substantially. Moreover, a larger share of the increased income accrued to Africans, as against Europeans and Asians, than had been true in earlier times.

Political stability and competent administration contributed importantly to economic performance. Kenya's founding father, Jomo Kenyatta, served as prime minister for fifteen years after independence, providing strength and continuity of leadership. The civil service developed in colonial days was Africanized gradually, but a substantial number of Europeans and even Americans continued to serve as senior administrators and policy advisers. Economic policies were generally moderate and pragmatic.

In agriculture, the tenure changes initiated in the 1950s were continued after independence. Registration of individual titles of ownership was accelerated and by 1980 was substantially complete in the "good" agricultural regions, which because of rainfall and soil deficiencies in most of the country comprise only about one-sixth of the total agricultural-pastoral area. In the "white highlands," which at their peak included 3.1 million hectares, some 1.25 million hectares had been transferred to African ownership by the late 1970s. While European landowners were not forced out, many withdrew voluntarily; and about half of the land transfers were by private sale rather than under official settlement schemes. Many of these sales were in large tracts to new African owners. There is now a substantial group of well-to-do commercial African farmers, some of whom are absentee owners living in cities. The government, interested in maintaining agricultural exports, which come predominantly from the larger farms, has not interfered with this tendency.

Most farms, however, are very small. About 85 percent of the rural population are smallholders, cultivating some 3.5 million hectares in farms averaging about two hectares in size. About one million hectares is occupied by medium-sized farms, averaging 25 hectares each, and 1.1 million hectares is in large farms or plantations averaging about 500 hectares.

The smallholders should not be thought of as subsistence farmers. On the contrary, they are quite commercialized, marketing on average close to half their output. Farm surveys in the late 1970s showed the following distribution of output: food crops for own use, 38 percent; livestock and milk for own use, 17 percent; food-crop sales, 20 percent; livestock and milk sales, 16 percent; export-crop sales, 9 percent. The percentage of agricultural exports coming from smallholders, who now produce about half of the coffee and sugarcane and about one-third of the tea, has been growing steadily. The percentage of output marketed varies in the usual way by size of farm. Some 10 percent of the largest holdings provide about two-thirds of the domestic supply of corn, meat, milk, and other foodstuffs. The marketed percentage varies also by region, being lower in the remote eastern regions than in districts closer to Nairobi.

Farm surveys show the usual relation between farm size and land productivity. Output per hectare is highest on the smallest farms and diminishes steadily with increasing size. The acreage in large farms (300 hectares and above) is in fact substantially underutilized. Only about 19 percent of large-farm area was under crops in 1976, while 66 percent was in uncultivated meadow and pasture, 5 percent in temporary meadow and fallow, and 10 percent in forest. Rapid growth of population and food demand will no doubt produce increasing pressure for subdivision of land and intensification of cultivation.

Much the largest marketed crop as of 1975 was coffee (26 percent), followed by tea (10 percent), corn (11 percent), cattle (12 percent), dairy produce (7 percent), wheat (5 percent), and sugarcane (5 percent). The total value of marketed produce rose from £60 million in 1964 to £162 million in 1975, large and small farms contributing about equally to this latter total. During the 1970s, however, food output lagged increasingly behind domestic demand. Agricultural output grew at only 3.2 percent per year and food output at only 2.3 percent, well below the 3.4 percent rate of population growth. It is significant that data on calorie availability per capita show a slight decline between 1960–62 and 1977–79 and that the index of per capita food output dropped by 15 percent during the 1970s. Thus, in this heavily agricultural economy, the population-food balance is still the central economic issue.

Manufacturing, typically, has grown faster than GDP—at 8.1 percent per year from 1963 to 1972 and at 10.8 percent from 1972 to 1979. By 1980 its share of GDP had risen to 13 percent. Government has supported manufacturing development in several ways. There are the usual tax credits, including rapid write-off of new plant investment. Financial aid has been made available through the Development Finance Company and the Industrial Development Bank, and government has an equity participation in many of the larger enterprises. There is moderate tariff protection. Perhaps most significant, there is free repatriation of profits for "approved enterprises." This has encouraged multinational investment, and about 60 percent of gross manufacturing output comes from foreign-owned firms. Unlike the situation in many third-world countries, in Kenya only 15 percent of manufacturing output comes from wholly-owned government enterprises, which include the railway workshops, meat-packing plants operated by the Kenya Meat Commission, and the government Printing Office. But government also has varying amounts of equity participation in about half the private companies with more than 200 employees.

About two-thirds of manufacturing output consists of consumer goods. The food-beverage-tobacco group alone accounted for 40 percent in 1980. Textiles and clothing, with 10 percent, are underdeveloped relative to other third-world countries of comparable size and income level. Import substitution in consumer goods is now largely completed. In 1975, imports of consumer goods as a proportion of domestic supply had already fallen to 16 percent and must be still lower today. About 28 percent of intermediate goods and 56 percent of capital goods were still imported in 1975.

The main impetus to manufacturing growth has been rising domestic demand, based on agricultural prosperity. But through most of the period Kenya also had a substantial export trade to Tanzania and Uganda under the East African Community (EAC) customs union. Advent of the Idi Amin regime in Uganda in 1971, however, disrupted the Ugandan economy and reduced its foreign trade. In 1977 Tanzania, desiring a larger share of both manufacturing and tourism, closed its border with Kenya. Soon afterward armed conflict developed between Tanzania and Uganda, and the EAC effectively ceased to exist. The proportion of Kenya's manufactured output that was exported fell from 22 percent in 1972 to 12 percent in 1979.

The "formal" manufacturing sector is dominated by establishments of considerable size. While only 12 percent of the establishments have more than 100 employees, they provide 70 percent of employment and 75 percent of value added. The smaller size categories remain rather hollow, despite official statements of encouragement to small business. Part of the explanation may be that in colonial days small business was mainly in the hands of Asians, who are now in disfavor, while the number of potential African entrepreneurs is still limited. The "informal" or aritisan sector, however, seems to be holding its own in absolute size and provides a good share of consumer necessities, especially in more remote areas. Nor is this sector merely "traditional." On the contrary, much artisan activity now consists of producing goods previously unknown in Kenya from materials equally unknown. An example is metalworking using scrap from discarded cars.

Data on the public sector give an impression of good fiscal management. Tax revenue as a percentage of GDP has been raised substantially, reaching 23.8 percent in 1980. The tax structure has also been modernized, with income taxes now providing about 40 percent of revenue, a general sales tax 25 percent, and customs duties only 20 percent. Current output of public goods was 20 percent of GDP in 1980, a large increase over the 7.4 percent of 1950. Rapid population growth means a large number of primary-school enrollees, and so education takes about 20 percent of the current budget. Agriculture, roads, health services, and defense each receive about 10 percent. The effect of health and education expenditure shows up in physical-development indicators. Primary-school enrollments as a percentage of the relevant age group have risen from 32 percent in 1950 to 97 percent in 1979. The adult literacy rate has risen from 20 to 45 percent. The child mortality rate has been more than cut in half, and life expectancy at birth has risen from 41 to 55 years.

Government capital expenditures are substantial, running recently at 8–10 percent of GDP, or close to half of all investment. There is normally a modest surplus in the current budget, sufficient to finance 25 percent or so of capital expenditure. About two-thirds of the remaining funds are raised through domestic borrowing, about one-third through foreign borrowing. The debt-service ratio has remained relatively low.

There are more than 200 parastatal organizations, with functions ranging from advice and regulation through marketing and financing to direct involvement in production. The profitability of these bodies varies substantially. Electricity, water, finance, insurance, real estate, and business services do best. Mining and quarrying, wholesale and retail trade, and restaurants and hotels servicing the tourist trade typically lose money. Overall, there is a net budgetary outflow to the parastatals, which rose from £9 million in 1971–72 to £48 million in 1977–78. Profitability, of course, is not the only test of performance. For example, in the operation of the marketing boards for farm products the most serious issue is whether the prices offered to farmers provide adequate production incentive and lead to an economic allocation of land among alternative products.

Kenya is quite export-dependent, the export/GDP ratio running typically at around 40 percent. As of 1979, 63 percent of exports went to the industrialized countries, 21 percent to sub-Saharan African countries, and 15 percent to other third-world countries. The composition of exports has been somewhat distorted by establishment of a large oil refinery at Mombasa that, in addition to serving the Kenyan market, exports refined products to neighboring countries. Thus fuels constituted 18 percent of exports in 1978; but the crude oil is imported, and value added in Kenya is quite small. Manufactures were 13 percent of exports in 1978 and primary products (with coffee and tea predominant), 69 percent.

There is typically a substantial negative balance on merchandise trade, plus a growing negative item from repatriation of profits. This gap is offset by a positive item for tourism and a sizable inflow of long-term capital. In a typical year, exports provide some 65 percent of foreign-exchange requirements, invisibles (mainly tourism) 15 percent, and capital inflow 20 percent. The long-term capital inflow is typically about 60 percent private, 40 percent public, reflecting the generally private-enterprise tone of policy.

Several developments during the 1970s could be construed as unfavorable. Export volume, which had been rising at 7.2 percent per year from 1960 to 1969, declined at −0.5 percent from 1970 to 1979. At the same time exports became more concentrated in a few products, increasing the vulnerability of the economy. The share of the three principal commodities in total exports rose from 34.2 percent in 1961 to 52.5 percent in 1976–78, contrary to the desirable diversification that many other countries have achieved. Significantly, too, there has been increased concentration of imports in capital goods, fuels, and intermediates— that is, in essential inputs for industry and infrastructure. Consumer goods, including food, were only 11.6 percent of imports in 1979. Thus a foreign-exchange shortage does not impinge seriously on consumption but can have a disruptive effect on industrial output and investment.

Some might criticize the pattern of development since independence as "neocolonial," pointing to such features as continued participation of Europeans in the top civil service, the favorable attitude toward foreign private investment, and continued export-dependence and involvement in the international economy. But in Kenya, as in Ivory Coast, one could reply that the policies followed seem to have worked.

Whether they will work equally well in future is by no means certain. We may note in particular:

1. The possible onset of political instability. Tribal bickering, held in check by the prestige of Jomo Kenyatta, has been renewed under his successor, Prime Minister Daniel arap Moi, who recently banned rival political parties and announced establishment of a one-party state. An attempted Air Force coup, quickly suppressed, may not be the last of its kind.
2. The staggering rate of population growth, one of the highest in the world, is already bursting the walls of the primary schools and the limits of the government budget, as well as producing rising unemployment and political unrest.
3. The serious lag of food production behind food demand has already been noted. Unless productivity can be raised substantially, it may be necessary to divert land from export crops to food crops or to import larger amounts of food, either of which would tighten the foreign-exchange constraint.

UGANDA

For lack of documentation, this will be a brief report. Writers on East Africa tend to focus on Kenya, tossing in a chapter on Uganda almost as an afterthought. While the broad outlines of development are clear, many details are not adequately reported.

Uganda differs from Kenya in several ways. It is a remote, landlocked country, with road and rail access to the sea only through Kenya. On the other hand it has superior agricultural resources. The amount of well-watered farmland per head of population is about twice as large as that in Kenya. Agriculture has remained largely African agriculture. The colonial authorities decided early not to push European settlement, and the "white settler" aspect of Kenya's development is absent here. Finally, Uganda was always a "protectorate" rather than a colony, with the British ruling indirectly through tribal chiefs. Much the most important of these was the kabaka (king) of Buganda, which occupies most of central Uganda surrounding the royal capital of Kampala. Strong persistence of tribal loyalties and organization is not unrelated to the later hardships of the Idi Amin regime, which had a marked tribal aspect.

Intensive Growth: 1900-60

In order to cement a political alliance with the kabaka, the British by a treaty in 1900 allocated about half the Baganda land in freehold to the kabaka and several hundred lesser chieftains. These people became capitalist farmers, using their subjects as tenants. Cotton seeds were brought in soon after 1900 at the initiative of the British Cotton Grower's Association, which had been formed to stimulate cotton production within the empire. Seeds were distributed through the Uganda Company to the chiefs, who were directed by government to order their peasants to plant it. The chiefs obediently beat the drums, assembled their subjects, and told them to plant cotton. Very soon, however, the economic gains from planting cotton were so clear that the crop spread rapidly on a voluntary basis.

Land availability was no problem, and peasant families simply added cotton growing to their production of traditional food crops. Output expansion came almost entirely from increased acreage. There is no evidence of any appreciable increase in yields before 1940. Marketing was done by Asian traders and British export houses. Still, returned value to the peasant producers was substantial. By 1927 the British felt sufficiently well established to pass a tenant-protection law, after which peasants in effect owned cultivation rights to their land in return for a moderate cash payment. This naturally strengthened production incentives.

The British did not encourage cash-crop production in the outlying areas of Uganda. If members of those tribes wanted cash, they could earn it by wage labor, as many of them did. Their function in the economy was to provide a reservoir of migrant labor for both farm and urban employment.

In the early decades of colonial rule there was some prospect of white settlement, which was actually recommended by a royal commission. By 1920 there were 220 large estates, covering about 126,000 acres. But these early settlers were hard hit by the 1920-21 slump. Government did not bail them out, as was done in Kenya, and so white acreage shrank substantially. One reason government did not intervene to protect and promote white settlement was that by this time the African peasant had proved to be a dependable producer of exports. During the 1920-21 slump, indeed, the peasant cotton growers doubled their output to offset the price decline and maintain their cash income.

Exports grew rapidly in volume and value. Total exports from Uganda rose from £212,000 in 1910 to £3,956,000 in 1940. In most years Uganda's exports were larger than Kenya's and, unlike Kenya, Uganda consistently had a positive trade balance. Cotton was the dominant export, varying from 75 to 90 percent of the total. Coffee had been introduced in 1922 and became dominant later on, but in 1940 it still formed only 10 percent of exports.

Regarding other sectors of the economy, what has already been said about Kenya would apply here. Government maintained order, built roads, and provided urban amenities in the only sizable cities, the British capital of Entebbe and the Baganda capital of Kampala. Artisan productions of household necessities continued as before. Asian traders bought farm produce and distributed imported consumer goods.

As they did in other colonies, the British authorities after 1945 followed a more active development policy. Grants were provided from the British budget. New lending institutions were established for agriculture and industry. The authorities encouraged both expansion of established export crops—cotton and coffee—and diversification into new crops, such as tobacco. A program was initiated for registration of land titles and consolidation of fragmented holdings, but it did not arouse strong peasant interest and was only moderately successful. Modern tractor services were provided through government-owned tractors rented out to farmers; but this proved to be a high-cost program, since the tractors could be used only for a short time each year.

Exports continued to grow at a good rate, and exports from Uganda continued to exceed those from Kenya. Exports rose from £4 million in 1940 to £29 million in 1950, part of this increase, to be sure, due to a rise in prices rather than in volume. (The export figure was to rise further to some £66 million by 1968.) Robusta coffee had by this time replaced cotton as the largest export crop, but it was grown in essentially the same way—by small peasant producers alongside food-crop production.

The largest nonagricultural development involved damming the White Nile at its exit from Lake Victoria and building a large power station at Jinja in 1954. It was hoped that ample low-cost power would stimulate manufacturing development. The Uganda Development Corporation stood ready to provide capital for new ventures, drawing partly on profits accumulated by the agricultural marketing boards. Foreign investors, however, did not show strong interest, preferring the larger market and preexisting industrial base of Kenya. Thus most of the new plants established at Jinja were government-owned.

Early estimates of GDP show it rising at 3.4 percent per year from 1950 to 1960, modestly above estimated population growth of 2.8 percent.

Growth and Decline, 1960–80

In 1962 power passed peaceably to a parliamentary government under Prime Minister Milton Obote. At this time Uganda was one of the strongest and most promising economies of sub-Saharan Africa; and during the first decade of independence, economic growth speeded up considerably. Between 1960 and 1970 GDP grew at 5.6 percent per year, and GDP per capita rose at 2.7 percent. The domestic savings rate rose to 13 percent, which, together with some foreign borrowing, was sufficient for an ambitious public-investment program. Export volume—now primarily coffee, but also cotton and tobacco—continued to grow and the country maintained its traditional export surplus. Government revenue rose faster than current expenditure, and the current surplus was sufficient to finance a good share of development expenditure.

All this changed dramatically in 1971 when a military coup installed Idi Amin as dictator of Uganda. The usual conditions of orderly government—security from arbitrary arrest, security of property from looting or confiscation, merit as a criterion in civil-service appointments, responsible accounting for public funds—disappeared overnight in an atmosphere of violence and intimidation.

The Asian population, which had provided much of the business, professional, and clerical labor force, was expelled forcibly from Uganda in 1972. Many of the best African administrators, entrepreneurs, teachers, and traders also left the country. Those who remained went into hiding or were harassed, imprisoned, or killed. While there was much physical destruction, the loss of human capital was even more devastating.

Abandoned or confiscated businesses were taken over haphazardly by a bloated parastatal sector, with little concern for management problems. The administrative system, both in parastatals and in general government, was geared increasingly to fear and favoritism. Appointments were wholly political and utterly insecure, subject to instant termination, sometimes with extreme prejudice. Fiscal responsibility was virtually nonexistent.

This dismal era is instructive as a case study in reverse development, or "undevelopment." All the indicators that one expects to see moving in certain directions in the course of economic growth now reversed course and moved in the opposite direction. The monetized sector of the economy shrank while the subsistence sector expanded. One reason was the population's flight to the countryside in search of personal safety and food supplies. A less-obvious reason was the shrinkage of government revenue, from 14 percent of GDP in 1971–72 to 9 percent by 1975–76. With expenditure for the police and the military continuing unrestrained, there was a current budget deficit amounting typically to 40 percent of expenditure. Since external assistance was largely cut off, the shortfall was financed by borrowing from internal banks, leading to a high rate of inflation. With little adjustment of official wage levels, incentive to work in the money economy decreased rapidly. Many people turned to full-time or part-time subsistence production or to black-market activity. The comment of a 1982 survey mission that "absenteeism among civil servants was widespread" is no doubt an understatement. Comprehensive control of prices led simply to comprehensive evasion. Most goods and services moved through nominally illegal channels in a "parallel market," at prices much above official levels.

Official data for this period are unavailable, since the government statistical apparatus virtually disappeared. So quantitative statements made here are simply the best judgment of the 1982 mission of outside experts. They estimate that from 1970 to 1978 monetized output fell at −2.0 percent per year. Subsistence production, on the other hand, grew at 3.4 percent per year, rising from 31 to 37 percent of GDP. Overall, GDP fell slightly, which means that per capita GDP fell substantially. The national savings rate fell from 13 percent in 1964–70 to 7.7 percent in 1971–78. The drop in government revenues has already been noted. There was a sharp decline in "official" exports, since the low fixed producer prices made such exports unprofitable, though smuggling continued across Uganda's porous borders with neighboring countries. Lack of foreign exchange to buy imported inputs, plus the drying up of domestically produced inputs, crippled manufacturing operations. As late as 1981, two years after the fall of Amin, about 40 percent of the industrial establishments were not operating at all, while the remainder were operating much below capacity.

Uganda invaded Tanzania in late 1978, and Tanzania responded in early 1979 with a counteroffensive. Tanzanian troops entered Kampala in April 1979, and the Amin regime fled, leaving the economy in shambles. Everything that could be looted had been looted—cars, trucks, tools and machinery, household furniture. School supplies and office records were lost or destroyed. The most severe drop in GNP, indeed, occurred in 1979 and 1980. Not until mid-1981 did a new elected government, once more under Milton Obote, announce a package of policy reforms aimed at restoring economic stability and production levels. It remains uncertain how long it may take for Uganda to emerge from the wreckage of the 1970s.

TANZANIA

Compared with Kenya and Uganda, colonial Tanganyika appears in some respects as an intermediate country. It had more white settlers than Uganda, but not as many as Kenya. Its agricultural resources are only moderately good and its agricultural exports were considerably smaller than those of well-endowed Uganda. In regard to industry, it was less centrally located and had a smaller domestic market than Kenya, and before 1960 it was essentially an industrial dependency of Kenya. Its political history is also different—it was a German colony until 1918, then a British-mandated territory under the League of Nations until 1945, then a trust territory under the United Nations Trusteeship Council, and finally in 1961 the first independent nation in East Africa. Political pressures operating through the United Nations had some influence on British administration of the territory and also accelerated the date of independence.

At the 1885 conference of the European powers devoted to carving up Africa, Britain conceded German's prior rights in Tanganyika in return for acceptance of Britain's rights in Kenya. Uganda was left in limbo, but in 1890 British occupation of that area was traded off against German possession of the North Sea island of Helgoland.

Much of what has been said earlier about ninteenth-century Africa applies to Tanganyika. Because much of the interior is poorly watered, and because of the poor transport system and widespread prevalence of tsetse fly, Tanganyika was lightly populated. But there was the usual tribal organization, a settled subsistence agriculture, the usual array of artisan industries, and markets for internal and external trade. There were long-established trade relations with southwestern Asia and India, handled mainly by Arab traders using the Sultanate of Zanzibar as an entrepôt. The largest trade item in the nineteenth century was ivory, which was exchanged for textiles, guns, and other items.

The first forerunner of colonialism was a private German trading company that began operations in 1885. But the company soon ran into financial difficulties, as well as armed conflict with local tribes, and in 1891 handed over authority to government. The Africans were not readily subdued, and sporadic fighting continued through the Maji Maji rebellion of 1905–07. But meanwhile, infrastructure development and agricultural expansion had got under way.

Intensive Growth: 1900–60

Although the period of German occupation was relatively short, much of the country's infrastructure was laid down during German rule. Among the projects undertaken was a rail line across the center of the country from Dar es Salaam to Lake Tanganyika and a line northwest from the port of Tanga to Moshi and Arusha in the Kilimanjaro area. Others were the development of ports in Tanga and Dar es Salaam, a road network, which was to become steadily more important in the motor age, and 14 administrative and trading centers in the interior, with modern buildings, electricity, water supply, and sewers.

Reasoning much like the British, the Germans regarded Tanganyika as essentially a source of raw-material supplies. Agriculture was developed along three main lines:

1. *Plantations.* Sisal seeds had been smuggled in from Brazil in 1892. The crop was well adapted to local conditions, and sisal plantations spread rapidly in areas northwest of Tanga and west of Dar es Salaam. By 1910 there were already 54 plantations (later to grow to 150), exporting some 20,000 tons of sisal per year. Most of these enterprises were owned by German companies and operated by salaried managers with African wage labor. The economies of scale in sisal production arise from the need for substantial investment in machinery for decortication of the stalks to extract the fiber.

2. *Settlers* were allowed to come in and take up land, but they were not particularly encouraged, and their number never approached Kenya's proportions. The amount of land alienated to whites seems not to have exceeded 1 percent of total agricultural acreage, compared with Kenya's 20 percent. But European-owned farms were a significant source of export products—mainly coffee, but also rubber (until the collapse of rubber prices in 1913) and cotton. Tanganyikan rubber production was not competitive with the lower-cost output of South and Southeast Asia, and after the price collapse the industry dwindled away.

3. *Peasant* producers entered energetically into export production where soil and climate were favorable. The Chagga tribe, living on the slopes of Kilimanjaro, soon became important coffee producers. The western area around Lake Victoria and bordering on Uganda also had good soil and rainfall. Peasant producers there were soon turning out a large supply of cotton, coffee, and other export crops as the interior was opened up by transport lines and a network of Indian traders. German administrators liked the Ugandan model of "the peasant as economic man," and later British administrators followed the same line. By the time of independence, and even more after independence, peasant production was to overshadow estate and settler production.

World War I brought a British invasion from Kenya, with both attackers and defenders consisting largely of white-led African troops. At the end of the war the territory was assigned to British administration under a League of Nations mandate. The war produced a ten-year economic hiatus, the 1914 output level not being regained until 1924. There were also some property transfers. The sisal estates were confiscated and sold at auction, with the former owners forbidden to bid. Later, however, some German owners returned and bought back into the industry.

The British otherwise made little change in economic structure or policy. Export expansion continued along established lines. Between 1913 and 1938 the value of exports more than doubled from £1,778,000 to £3,708,000. There was some change in the composition of exports. By 1938 gold had appeared, whereas rubber had vanished. In 1938 sisal was 38 percent of exports, gold 16 percent, and cotton and coffee each 10 percent.

Most African countries are heavily rural, but Tanganyika was unusually so. As late as 1948 only 2.6 percent of the population lived in areas classified as urban. The only real city, Dar es Salaam, had a population of only 70,000. Apart from agricultural processing, there was hardly any manufacturing development before 1940. The British did not encourage industry, partly because it might lead to an influx of "detribalized" Africans into the towns, which was considered politically dangerous. Much better for Africans to remain on the farm under tribal organization. The customs union with Kenya, established in 1927, also hampered local industry. Manufacturing enterprises usually preferred to locate in Kenya for transport and market reasons, and Tanganyika ended up importing most of its manufactures from Kenya and shipping primary products in return. Tanganyika was in this sense a "colony" of Kenya.

There was creeping import substitution during World War II. Although in 1945 a majority of plants were still processing agricultural products for export or home use, there were also several dozen plants producing such things as salt, cigarettes, beer, soda water, furniture, and jewelry. Interestingly, although cotton was a major crop, not even cotton spinning had appeared in Tanganyika before independence.

Wage labor was virtually absent before the German occupation. But by 1951 there were 443,600 wage earners, or about 10 percent of the economically active population. Of these 52.5 percent were in agriculture, 20.2 percent in government, 4.6 percent in household service, and 22.7 percent in other private activities. Only about 5 percent were in manufacturing and electric power. Of the agricultural workers, about 70 percent were employed on the sisal estates, which frequently ran to 1,000 acres or more, each employing upwards of 500 workers.

Most of the employment opportunities were located in the Dar es Salaam-Tanga-Moshi triangle in the northeast, favored by rainfall, soil fertility, and good infrastructure. Peasant export production also tended to cluster there for the same reasons. Further, peasants in this region had an opportunity to grow and sell cash food crops to feed the estate laborers. The result was that, despite relatively dense population in the northeast, the opportunity cost of labor was higher than estate owners were willing to pay, and few farmers were willing to become estate workers. Thus about 70 percent of the agricultural wage laborers were long-distance migrants from areas in the south and west, where farmers were prevented by distance and poor transport from becoming competitive in commodity production.

During the colonial period employers complained constantly about the scarcity of wage labor. The main reason for the supposed scarcity seems to have been a low-wage policy, rationalized by the concepts of the "target worker" and the backward-bending supply curve of labor. There is much evidence that Africans were in fact responsive to higher incomes, which would permit purchase of cloth, cooking pots, guns and gunpowder, knives, hoes, and other imported consumer goods. But in an oligopsonistic labor market, employers and government used their power to administer wages below the market-equilibrating level. Naturally enough, this produced a scarcity despite the existence of a forward-sloping labor-supply curve.

African families could earn extra income in three ways: by selling export crops, by selling food crops in the local market, and by selling labor for wages. While Europeans and Asians gained most from development, many Africans gained as well. Median per capita income rose, this taking the form of larger consumption of "modern" consumer goods plus some improvement in health facilities and a modest amount of primary education. It is also clear, however, that there was growing income inequality within the African population. Peasant farmers in the northeast gained more than those in the west, and both gained more than those who were forced to depend on wage labor.

As elsewhere in Africa, for Tanganyika the period 1945–60 was one of accelerated growth—in population, exports, total and capita output. Between 1950 and 1960 population grew at 2.2 percent per year, GDP at 6.0 percent, and GDP per capita at 3.8 percent. In addition to rapid expansion of traditional exports, cashew nuts and diamonds appeared as important new export products. Export volume increased as follows:

	Sisal	Coffee	Cotton (thousand tons)	Ground Nuts	Cashew Nuts	Diamonds (thousand carats)	Total Value (million shillings)
1948	117	11.3	9.9	3.1	5.6	148	324
1960	205	26.2	32.2	14.6	55.3	555	958

Note that peasant crops grew substantially faster than output from the sisal estates.

There was greater emphasis after 1945 on import substitution and development planning, and larger development grants were made available by the British government. Even so, the industrial sector remained very small. Of the 20,000 manufacturing workers in 1958, about 40 percent were in sawmilling and furniture, 30 percent in the food-beverage-tobacco group, and 13 percent in motor-vehicle repair and engineering. Clothing and footwear employed only 448 people, and textiles were still absent.

The most serious deficiency of the colonial period was in education. Less than half of African children ever saw a primary school (the enrollment rate in 1957 in grades 1–4 was 40.7 percent), and few of those remained long enough to acquire functional literacy. As of 1957 there were more Asians than Africans in high school, despite the tiny Asian population. There were only 290 Africans in grades 11 and 12. Only 15 Tanganyikan students graduated in 1957 from Makerere College in Uganda, the only institution of higher education in East Africa. It is not surprising, then, that a 1962 census table of "employment in selected professions" lists 438 Europeans, 103 Asians, and only 30 Africans (of whom 16 were doctors and 9 veterinarians).

Despite this lack of educated leadership, there were stirrings of African organization during the 1950s. The Chagga coffee cooperative continued to flourish, and new cotton cooperatives had by 1959 taken over control of all marketings from the Lake Victoria area. A trade-union movement, spearheaded by the Dar es Salaam dockworkers, achieved substantial strength. A rural-based political party, the Tanganyika African National Union (TANU), quickly achieved status as African spokesman on political matters. Julius Nyerere and other TANU leaders took their case for political independence to the British public and the United Nations Trusteeship Council. In the end, the British relinquished control with remarkable speed. The first steps toward phasing Africans into government were taken only in 1958, and by 1961 the country was fully independent. In 1963 the Africans in Zanzibar, who were a large majority of the population, revolted against Arab rule and deposed the sultan, after which they sought union with the mainland. When this was granted, the country's name was changed to Tanzania.

Intensive Growth, 1960–80

To an unusual degree the hopes of the new nation were embodied in Julius Nyerere, who became president in 1962 and has held that office ever since. A brilliant man, who had been a student leader at Makerere and later won a scholarship to Edinburgh University, Nyerere returned to Tanganyika as a teacher and political organizer. In addition to his stature within Tanzania as statesman and philosopher, he has gained international prominence as spokesman for a distinctive approach to development often labeled "African socialism." Nyerere's socialism, in the British Labour Party tradition, emphasizes equalization of incomes, public ownership of key industries, and a leading role for government in the economy. Further, as is natural in a very rural economy, Nyerere attaches great importance to rural development, and his most distinctive contribution has been the "villagization" program described below.

Despite Nyerere's moderate and humane approach, his regime does not correspond to Western liberal ideals. Tanzania is a one-party state and, though rival candidates can compete in elections, they are all TANU members. Serious dissent is not permitted, and dissidents have been imprisoned in substantial numbers. Appointed officials dominate elected representatives at all levels of government. After several large strikes in the early 1960s, the right to strike was eliminated and trade-union functions severely curtailed. The villagization program, affecting some two-thirds of the rural population, involved a considerable amount of coercion. To any criticism on these scores, President Nyerere would no doubt reply that strong controls are necessary at this stage of African development and that Western-style institutions would not be appropriate.

The new regime did not bring any immediate change in the development pattern, which continued along familiar lines through 1967. Many of the white settlers departed on independence, part of their land being taken over by African farmers and part reverting to bush. Sisal output stagnated because of a dramatic drop in the world price between 1964 and 1967. But coffee and cotton exports grew at 13 percent per year, and most other peasant crops grew at around 10 percent. The new government for a time encouraged this growth and tried to provide better service to the peasant producers, even though President Nyerere did not like the growing inequality of peasant incomes incidental to export growth.

By 1967, however, the governing group had turned against what it considered an unsatisfactory growth pattern: a widening rural-urban income gap; growing inequality within the peasant population; relative neglect of food crops in favor of export crops; and continued reliance on primary exports rather than movement toward economic independence. President Nyerere, in the Arusha Declaration, announced a shift to a different policy course that would emphasize broad-based rural development, cooperative rather than individualist agriculture, intensified industrialization under public ownership and control, and movement toward national self-reliance.

In agriculture, government turned its back on the prosperous peasants, who had hitherto provided a large share of export production. It turned its back also on the strategy of gradual improvement in agricultural techniques and opted for what has been called the "transformation approach"—a rapid shift to modernized agriculture, using larger amounts of machinery and other modern inputs. The centerpiece of the new approach was the villagization program. The 1967 statement contemplated voluntary movement of families into "ujamaa villages," in which land would be held and cultivated in common. But this scheme did not prove attractive to peasants, and the program moved slowly. So in 1973 the biennial conference of TANU decreed that the whole rural population should live in villages by the end of 1976. President Nyerere announced that "to live in villages is now an order."

Through this crash program some 13 million rural people were moved into villages by the end of 1975. Exceptions were made for urban areas, for villages that already had 700 or more families, and for some highland areas, such as the Kilimanjaro region. Few of the new villages, however, actually practice communal cultivation. The great majority are "Stage 1 villages," in which the block of land surrounding the village is divided into individual family holdings. Collective ownership and cultivation is still held out as an ideal for the future, but whether there will be much movement in this direction is uncertain.

Apart from ideology, the main motive for villagization seems to have been bureaucratic convenience. A local administrator can more readily exercise authority over a village than over many dispersed farmsteads. There are scale economies in centralized provision of health facilities, primary education, and other public services. (Those who were reluctant to move to a village were informed that they would not be eligible for any public services in future.) It was also stated that villagization would make for larger agricultural output, but no clear reasons were given for this belief. There are in fact some production disadvantages. Continuous intensive cultivation of the same plot, rather than the old pattern of shifting cultivation, will exhaust soil fertility sooner unless offset by increased fertilizer supplies. There is little indication that these will be forthcoming in adequate volume. Further, location of plots at some distance from the home consumes travel time and makes it more difficult to protect tools and crops against theft.

The recent performance of agriculture has been disappointing. Between 1969–71 and 1979–81, food output grew at only 2.0 percent per year, well below the 3.4 percent rate of population growth, and diets have been maintained only by large cereal imports. Total agricultural production, including export as well as food crops, grew even more slowly, at 1.6 percent per year. Output of some export crops declined substantially. Coulson (1982) estimates that between 1966–67 and 1977–78, sisal production (which was nationalized after the Arusha Declaration) grew at −7.5 percent per year, while the rate for cotton was −4.1 percent, for coffee 1.0 percent, and for cashew nuts 0.5 percent.

Although the villagization program probably contributed to this poor showing, other factors were also at work. Despite the announced emphasis on rural development, government support for agriculture remained limited. Budget allocations were small relative to those for industry and infrastructure. Agricultural research was skimpy and extension services inefficient. The parastatal organizations charged with marketing farm output and supplying agricultural inputs were not very well managed. Prices offered to farmers were held down by the marketing-board system, while the policy of import-substituting industrialization raised the prices they had to pay. Coulson estimates that the rural-urban terms of trade declined about 25 percent between 1969–70 and 1978–79. Other observers comment on the frequent reshuffling of government institutions, which failed to provide a stable environment for peasant producers.

Industry, on the other hand, was favored by high tariffs, generous capital allocations, and other measures. Along with government, manufacturing is the only sector showing substantial growth during the 1970s. Even so, it produced only 9 percent of GDP in 1980. Manufacturing is heavily concentrated in Dar es Salaam and limited largely to consumer goods (now including textiles) and some intermediates. The progress of import substitution is suggested by a drop in the consumer-goods share of imports from 36 percent in 1967 to 19 percent in 1977. Domestic productions of capital goods, however, has scarcely begun.

There is substantial government participation in manufacturing. Immediately after the Arusha Declaration the government nationalized eight grain-milling firms, seven of which were Asian-owned, and bought a 51 percent interest in seven subsidiaries of multinational corporations that produced shoes, beer, tobacco, cement, and other products. Several new public manufacturing enterprises have been started since that time. Clark (1978) estimated the public-sector share of manufacturing in 1972 at 33 percent, and it is probably higher today. The public-sector enterprises tend to be large, while private enterprises are on average smaller and less capital-intensive.

Evidence on the efficiency of public manufacturing enterprises is mixed. Clark reports their average profit rate in the early 1970s as 13 percent. On the other hand, they were able to finance only about one-quarter of their new investment. More than half of their new capital came from foreign borrowings and the remainder from government allocations. A World Bank study reports man-hour output in government manufacturing as only 70 percent as high as in private enterprises with comparable capital/labor ratios. This suggests that there may be serious overstaffing in government enterprises, apart from any management difficulties.

Manufacturing is a high-wage sector. The real hourly wage in manufacturing tripled between 1955 and 1970, and in 1970 it was more than double that for wage labor in agriculture. In addition to government pressure, exerted through minimum-wage legislation and government pay scales, Sabot (1979) suggests that employers have raised wages voluntarily to stabilize the labor force and to justify investment in training. These wage costs, of course, are passed on in prices by quasi-monopolistic manufacturing concerns operating behind tariff protection.

Export performance, as suggested earlier, has been poor. Export volume stagnated between 1965 and 1975, and exports fell from 22 percent to 14 percent of GDP. The usual surplus on merchandise trade turned into a deficit after 1967, and the deficits became very large from 1973 onward, partly reflecting the "oil crunch." Imports, including substantial food imports after 1974, have been sustained only by a large volume of foreign grants and loans. The Scandinavian countries, West Germany, and other countries that find President Nyerere's philosophy attractive have thus far been willing to supply substantial funds on concessional terms. The "national self-reliance" that is still proclaimed as a policy goal seems as far distant as ever.

Perhaps the most important post-1967 development is the politicization of the economy, the pervasive and growing importance of government in all areas. Through sharp increases in income taxes, a new general sales tax, higher import duties, and other measures, tax revenue was raised from 11 percent of GDP in 1967–68 to 18.5 percent in 1979–80, a substantial achievement for a very poor country. This was more than offset, however, by an explosive increase in current expenditure. A current budget surplus of 1.6 percent of GDP was converted into a budget deficit of 1.8 percent. The increase in current expenditure arose partly from a (commendable) increase in the real level of educational, health, and other public services; but also from a marked increase in defense expenditure, sharp wage and salary increases for the civil service, and overstaffing of government agencies under the pressure of rising urban unemployment.

In addition to the activities of general government, public corporations are prominent in many sectors of the economy. Immediately after Arusha, government nationalized all banks, insurance companies, and import-export houses, in addition to the manufacturing enterprises noted earlier. As early as 1972 Clark estimated the public-sector percentage of value added as follows: agriculture, 2.3; mining, 71.4; manufacturing, 33.4; public utilities, 65.5; construction, 3.9; commerce, 15.0; transport, 11.8; financial services, 47.2. In view of the commitment to socialism as a long-term goal, these percentages are probably higher today.

Because of these activities, government's share of capital formation is substantial. Public investment has been oriented heavily toward manufacturing (54 percent) and transport (29 percent). More than half of this investment is foreign-financed. The largest single project, the railroad from Dar es Salaam to the Zambian border, involved an interest-free loan from China, use of imported Chinese equipment, and employment of many Chinese on the construction work.

Given the small stock of human capital the country inherited at independence, it is not captious to suggest that the expansion of government activities has outrun the administrative capacity of government, leading to poor performance of many tasks and much frustration of private initiative. Coulson (1982, pp. 194–95), who is not unsympathetic with President Nyerere's professed objectives, comments: "The overall picture is one of government taking increasing control of the economy, putting great emphasis on provision of social services and on increasing the rate of investment through use of foreign capital transfers and high rates of domestic taxation, but being frustrated by failures in agricultural production and by low productivity in manufacturing."

Education and health levels have been raised considerably, and this clearly is a gain in welfare. The investment rate has been raised from about 15 percent in 1965 to 22 percent in 1980. It is somewhat puzzling that the investment rate has been rising while the GDP growth rate has been falling. A partial explanation may be that investment has been oriented toward high-ICOR activities: transport, communications, mining, and large-scale manufacturing. But there are also indications that total factor productivity has been falling in manufacturing and indeed throughout the nonagricultural economy.

One of the less encouraging features of the present situation is that population growth continues unchecked, at an estimated rate of 3.4 percent per year from 1970 to 1980. The course of total and per capita GDP in the 1970s is not known with any precision. Coulson (1982, pp. 188–89) notes that the official figures seem to rest on an implausibly high growth rate for subsistence production in agriculture. The official figures show gross *material* product (omitting service activities) growing at 3.9 percent per year from 1971 to 1977. But this assumes that subsistence production was growing at 6.5 percent per year, which is scarcely credible. The growth rate of *monetized* GNP for this period was only 2.0 percent. If the growth of subsistence production is adjusted downward to a plausible level, any increase in per capita output during the decade disappears. This conjecture of stagnant per capita output is supported by comments of Sabot, Coulson, and other observers, as well as the fact that food availability per capita was slightly *lower* in 1977–79 than in 1960–62.

It is possible, of course, that performance may improve in future. But it remains to be demonstrated that the new institutional structure, however attractive in equity terms, is compatible with sustained economic growth. Even in equity terms, there is some doubt whether income differentials have been reduced significantly since 1967.

ZIMBABWE

Zimbabwe has had an unusual political history: it was a property of the British South Africa Company until 1923; then the colony of Southern Rhodesia, effectively under white-settler control, from 1923 to 1954; then united with Northern Rhodesia and Nyasaland in the self-governing Federation of Rhodesia and

Nyasaland from 1954 to 1963; then, after the Unilateral Declaration of Independence (UDI), the independent and still white-governed nation of Rhodesia from 1964 to 1979. Finally, after a seven-year civil war, a negotiated peace was concluded in late 1979 and a new African-controlled government was installed in early 1980, at which time the country was renamed Zimbabwe and its capital, Salisbury, became Harare.

The economic chronology is somewhat different. Until 1939 the country was an agricultural and mining economy with a strong export orientation. The years 1945–74 were marked by large inflows of capital and white settlers, the rise of a manufacturing sector, which eventually reached 25 percent of GDP, and a high growth rate, which persisted through changes of political regime. The economic sanctions imposed by most other countries after UDI, in accordance with a United Nations resolution, had little effect and the economy flourished as never before. Intensification of the civil war, however, brought a substantial drop in GDP between 1974 and 1979. The end of the war brought some recovery of production, along with institutional changes whose eventual effect cannot be assessed at this time.

Intensive Growth, 1900–45

The British South Africa Company was chartered by Cecil Rhodes and others in 1889. Rhodes was a businessman, but even more an empire builder. He dreamed of a British-controlled Central Africa that would link up with other British-controlled areas from Kenya to Egypt, the whole joined together by a 6,000-mile Cape-to-Cairo railroad. The railroad never materialized, but political control of Central Africa did become a reality.

Rhodes's "pioneer column" from South Africa reached Salisbury in September 1890. To cover its military and administrative expenses, the company was entitled to appropriate and sell off farmland. The initial distribution was partly to soldiers, partly to land speculators and adventurers, who later resold it to settlers from Britain and elsewhere. European settlement eventually extended to more than half of the better farmland on the high plateau. As European land titles were confirmed, Africans previously living on the land were obliged to become tenants or laborers or else to move to the "tribal reserves" assigned to Africans. What developed was a Kenya-like situation, with additional overtones of South Africa—passes for "natives," restrictions on their residence in "European" areas, legislation that effectively barred them from skilled labor, and so on.

The company was never a financial success and never paid a dividend. Military and other expenses more than ate up the land revenue. When control was transferred to the Colonial Office in 1923, the company had assets of only £8 million against borrowings of more than £14 million, leading the British government to award it a severance grant of £3.75 million.

The economy, as it developed from 1890 to 1940, was export-oriented and strongly dualistic, with a white-dominated money economy expanding and increasingly overshadowing the indigenous subsistence economy. The Europeans controlled mining, initially of gold, later of chrome, asbestos, and other minerals. As of 1940, gold was about 52 percent of all exports and other minerals, about 30 percent. The Europeans also had more than half of the good agricultural land, laid out in farms averaging several thousand acres in size. They produced mainly maize, tobacco, and cattle. Cattle predominated until about 1925, but after that field crops pulled ahead. By 1940 crop output was almost double the output of meat and dairy products, and by 1950 it was five times as large. Tobacco was essentially an export crop, but there were also large and growing exports of maize.

In the African areas agricultural production continued along traditional lines involving shifting cultivation, simple tools, and a division of labor in which women did most of the farm work. The heavier ground-clearing work done by men needed to be done only at intervals, which enabled men to be absent for extended periods as wage laborers.

Africans entered the money economy as wage laborers and as producers of marketed agricultural products, which were added to subsistence production. African money income was negligible in 1900. But by 1914 Africans were already paying £248,000 in taxes and buying £460,000 of imported goods. Their participation as farmers is suggested by the fact that the number of African-owned cattle rose from 55,000 in 1902 to more than 400,000 in 1914. In addition, the number of African-owned plows rose from zero to about 5,000. The plow permitted extensive cultivation on larger tracts of land. Between 1900 and 1920 land cultivated by Africans more than doubled, far exceeding any reasonable estimate of population growth.

The Europeans did not entirely welcome the Africans as agricultural competitors. Africans' right to plant the profitable tobacco crop was restricted; and when the white settlers succeeded in winning a government support price for maize during the Great Depression, African farmers were paid less than the full support price, the balance going into a government fund for "African improvement."

African participation in wage labor showed a marked inverse relation with agricultural opportunities. Barber (1961) notes that "in areas in which agricultural production for market can be carried on successfully, the absence of male labor for wage employment is relatively lower than in the provinces in which agricultural production is a less profitable alternative." Wage labor also grew over the course of time. The number of male African wage earners roughly doubled between 1926 and 1946, from 173,598 to 356,868. Some 44 percent of these were employed in European agriculture, 24 percent in mining, and the remainder in other occupations. The percentage of adult male Africans in Southern Rhodesia who worked as wage laborers rose from 29 percent in 1929 to 44 percent by 1942. Even so, local labor supplies were insufficient to meet the demand of European employers. The deficit was met by attracting migratory labor from Nyasaland, Northern Rhodesia, and Mozambique, where employment opportunities were more limited. As of 1946, about 60 percent of male Africans employed in Southern Rhodesia came from these other areas.

Aggregative data on economic performance are scarce before the 1920s. But from that time on all the indicators suggest a high growth rate of total and per capita output. Gold exports (in thousand ounces) rose from 582 in 1925 to 826 in 1940. Over the same period chrome-ore exports (in thousand tons) rose from 136 to 273, and asbestos exports from 34 to 56. Crop output from European farms tripled between 1925 and 1940, while output of meat and dairy products rose about 80 percent. Barber (1961, p. 101) cites an early estimate by S. H. Frankel and H. Herzfeld of net national income in the monetized economy in 1929 prices that shows it rising from £11,161,000 in 1924 to £28,594,000 in 1943, an average annual growth rate of 4.7 percent.

The economy was open and export-oriented. Foreign capital was brought in by settlers and through government borrowing for railroads and other infrastructure development. The ratio of exports to GDP in the money economy was typically between 45 and 55 percent. Almost all manufactures were imported, including substantial imports of processed food to meet the tastes of the European population. Barber considers at some length the criticisms that have been brought against this type of export-led growth, concluding that "Central African experience does not bear out this pessimistic diagnosis."

Intensive Growth, 1945–80

World War II brought difficulties in trade with Europe, some decline in exports, and an intensification of local manufacturing activity to replace foreign supplies. There was a noticeable shift toward greater self-reliance, which was to continue in the postwar period.

The end of the war initiated a thirty-year period of accelerated growth, which continued through the various changes of political regime. Southern Rhodesia maintained and strengthened its position as the economic hub of Central Africa. The federation with Northern Rhodesia and Nyasaland in 1954 was advantageous in broadening the market for Southern Rhodesia's manufactures and also in enabling it to tap the tax revenue from Northern Rhodesia's copperbelt for development purposes. But there was continuing political tension between white-dominated Southern Rhodesia and the other two territories, in which African influence was much stronger, and this led in time to breakup of the federation when the other two areas opted for independence.

As in Kenya, there was an accelerated inflow of white settlers into Southern Rhodesia after 1945, resulting partly from soldier-settlement schemes. The white population rose from 84,000 in 1946 to 220,000 in 1960. Net white immigration, indeed, remained positive through 1975, though the white population at its peak was only 3.8 percent of total population. The growth rate of African population also accelerated. Although data are imperfect, they suggest that population growth was close to 4 percent per year in the 1950s and 1960s.

All sectors of the economy show high growth rates from 1945 onward. Between 1945 and 1957 alone the value of meat and dairy marketings from European farms increased fourfold, while crop marketings rose almost fivefold. While part of this represents higher prices, the volume increase was also substantial. African output of marketed crops appears to have increased even faster. African maize marketings rose from 21 percent of European marketings in 1934–35 to 58 percent by 1955–56.

Growth continued to be export-led. Chrome-ore tonnage increased about three times between 1945 and 1959, while asbestos tonnage more than doubled. While the volume of gold exports changed little, higher gold prices contributed to a rising value total. The export value of these three minerals rose from £7,096,000 in 1945 to £17,517 in 1959. Added to this was a large increase in agricultural exports, principally tobacco and maize. Total exports from Southern Rhodesia ran consistently at about 40 percent of estimated GDP.

The most distinctive feature of this period, however, was the rise of manufacturing industry. Very small in 1939, manufacturing was stimulated initially by the reduction of foreign supplies during World War II. After the war tariff protection was provided for the first time, an Industrial Development Commission was established, several public enterprises were initiated, and a series of rolling four-year government investment programs was started in 1949. Key industries expanded or initiated by government included iron and steel, cotton spinning and weaving, industrial alcohol, sugar refining, and molasses by-products to improve cattle feed. Most industries, however, were privately initiated and financed. These included wire drawing, fencing materials, cables, cutlery and surgical instruments, steel and earthenware piping, asbestos, cement, plywood and paper, chemicals, rubber products, boots and shoes, soap, starch, and edible fat products. Southern Rhodesia became a sizable exporter of manufactures to Northern Rhodesia, Nyasaland, and Mozambique and in time was able to compete in some parts of the South African market. Even in the 1950s, about 20 percent of manufacturing output was exported.

This economic expansion was supported by an unusually high rate of investment. Estimates for the whole federation area from 1950 to 1959 show investment usually in the range of 30–40 percent of GNP. About half of this investment was financed from foreign sources, with foreign investment especially prominent in manufacturing. The remainder came from domestic saving, which included undistributed corporate profits, substantial surpluses in the current government budget, and personal savings running at about 10 percent of consumers' disposable income. Use of foreign capital, of course, involved some outflow of interest and dividends to foreign lenders, which typically amounted to 15–20 percent of export proceeds.

Government was a major investor. During the federation period, the federal government's current expenditure was in the range of 10–13 percent of GNP, the percentage tending to rise over time. But government capital expenditure, including investment by public corporations, was typically larger than current expenditure. The government share of total capital formation was usually in the range of one-third to one-half. Given a rapidly expanding economy and a rather modern tax structure relying heavily on corporate and personal income taxes, tax revenue was buoyant and yielded substantial surpluses over current expenditure. In addition, there were large foreign borrowings, amounting to £101 million between 1954 and 1959 alone. The largest project of this period was the Kariba Dam and hydroelectric project on the Zambezi. Rhodesian Railways also received a good share of the investment budget, which included a new line through Mozambique to Maputo to relieve congestion at the port of Beira.

Economic expansion involved a continuing rise in African wage employment. The number of African wage earners rose from 376,868 in 1946 to 609,953 in 1956. In addition, possibly because of more rapid population growth, the proportion of these workers who were residents of Southern Rhodesia began to rise, reaching about 50 percent by 1956. Most of this employment was in farm labor and other low-skilled jobs. A legislative provision that employers must pay Africans the "European wage" in skilled jobs had the effect of barring Africans almost completely from those jobs. Even so, Africans' total wage income for the federation as a whole was estimated in 1959 at £101.1 million. Part of this, to be sure, was in the form of housing and food rations, which employers were required to supply, and part leaked away through remittances to home areas outside the federation. But the remaining cash income, combined with the growing income from farm marketings, made the Africans significant consumers of modern manufactures.

Unlike most parts of Africa, the federation was not administered as a colony. It was a self-governing entity, with its own parliament, operating under only nominal British control. Self-government, however, meant essentially white government, with virtually no African participation at the national level. In the early 1960s the demands for African self-rule, which were rising in other regions, reached the federation as well. The British government, in line with its policy elsewhere, entered into negotiation with federation leaders, looking toward a phasing in of African political participation and an eventual transfer of power. The white population of Southern Rhodesia, however, under the leadership of Premier Ian Smith, put up a stubborn resistance to these proposals. The upshot was that Northern Rhodesia (renamed Zambia) and Nyasaland (renamed Malawi) did pass into control by African-elected leaders. But Ian Smith broke off negotiations with the British and issued a defiant Unilateral Declaration of Independence.

Rhodesia thus became an independent, still white-governed, country, supported by South Africa, but in disfavor in Britain, the United States, and most other countries. A trade boycott was imposed under United Nations auspices, but this proved surprisingly ineffective. Goods destined for Rhodesia were shipped through South Africa or through Mozambique, which until 1975 was still under Portuguese control, and Rhodesian exports moved out through the same channels. Export growth was slowed, to be sure, the volume index rising only 23 percent between 1964 and 1974, indicating that the export/GNP ratio was falling. But exports and imports did grow, and the GNP growth rate was somewhat higher than before UDI.

The excellent Barber study ends in the late 1950s, and nothing comparable has been published since. The story for the UDI period has to be pieced together from a 1980 study prepared under United Nations auspices, and from IBRD mission reports. Population is estimated to have grown at 3.5 percent per year from 1965 to 1979. Real GDP is estimated to have grown at 7.0 percent from 1965 to 1974, though the United Nations estimate is even higher. Equally impressive is the even distribution of growth across the economy. Real agricultural output rose 7.3 percent per year from 1964 to 1974, compared with a 10.2 percent rate for manufacturing. The manufacturing share of GDP rose to 25 percent, and its share of "formal" employment to about 15 percent (150,000 manufacturing workers). While light industry still predominates, metals and metal products by 1974 formed 28 percent of manufacturing output and chemicals, 12 percent.

The foreign-payments account continued in approximate balance, a surplus on merchandise trade being roughly offset by a deficit on services. Capital movements after UDI were small. On the export side, minerals still predominated in 1970 at 48 percent, followed by agricultural products with 35 percent, and manufactures with 12 percent. Imports show the usual shift toward capital goods and intermediates. By 1974 capital goods were 26 percent of imports, fuels and other intermediates 55 percent, and consumer goods only 19 percent.

Rapid economic growth, however, did little to allay political discontent. Guerrilla warfare developed in the early 1970s, one faction under Joshua Nkomo operating from bases in Zambia, the other under Robert Mugabe from bases in Mozambique. For the white settlers, security of life and property diminished, and there was a net outflow of white population from 1975 onward. As guerrilla strength grew, the economy came under increasing strain. The government budget, swollen by military expenditures, showed growing deficits, which finally reached 40 percent of current expenditure. The inflation rate, previously moderate, averaged 11.5 percent from 1975 to 1979. Real GNP is estimated to have declined at 2.7 percent per year from 1974 to 1979. Output on the increasingly insecure European farms dropped especially sharply, and agriculture's share of GDP fell from 18 percent in 1974 to 12 percent in 1979.

At the end of 1979 a conference convened by the British foreign secretary negotiated an end of the war and a new constitution for the country, providing for an elected parliament in which the black population by force of numbers has a large majority. Although the first elected premier, Robert Mugabe, made reassuring statements to the white population, the net outflow of whites that had begun in 1975 continued. A major problem facing the new government is whether it can contain factional strife between Mugabe and Nkomo supporters, which has a strong tribal basis. On the economic front, it remains to be seen how far the new regime, which is socialist in orientation, will push nationalization of industry and how rapidly it will move to transfer land from large European-owned farms to African smallholders.

ZAMBIA

After reaching Salisbury in 1890, Rhodes's British South Africa Company in 1891 sent agents north of the Zambezi to negotiate agreements with tribal chiefs in what later became Northern Rhodesia. The chiefs granted concessions over large stretches of territory, permitting mineral exploration and alienation of farmland to white settlers. On the basis of these agreements, the company claimed the whole area for Britain. The British government welcomed this costless acquisition of territory, since the company bore all military and administrative expenses. There was some local opposition, and in 1898 a pitched battle was fought against 10,000 Ngoni warriors. After this the area was "pacified" and was administered by a very small staff, consisting in 1917 of 27 British sergeants and 750 African police.

During the thirty years of company administration, which ended in 1924, Northern Rhodesia remained very much a frontier area. A line of rail from Salisbury reached the border in 1905, was extended to Broken Hill in 1906, and reached the border of Katanga Province of the Belgian Congo in 1909. Small lead and zinc mining operations were developed at Broken Hill, and white farm settlers began to trickle in. But in 1925 there were still only 504 European farmers, living along the line of rail and growing mainly corn. The indigenous economy had as yet been little affected.

Intensive Growth: 1925–60

The turning point to intensive growth can be dated from discovery of major copper deposits in 1925. Two large companies, one owned by British and South African interests, the other with 51 percent ownership by the American Metal Climax Company, undertook exploration and mine development. By the early 1930s Northern Rhodesia ranked second as copper producer after the United States. Exports in 1934 were 138,000 tons, which was 13.4 percent of copper output outside the Soviet Union.

The economy has always been unusually dependent on copper. World demand for copper continued to grow at about 4 percent per year, with Northern Rhodesia slightly improving its market share (1960 exports were 579,000 tons, or 15.7 percent of non-Soviet output). Export revenues, of course, fluctuated with the price level. A cartel of copper-producing countries has at times restricted output to stabilize prices, but this effort has not been very successful because the cartel controls only about 60 percent of world output. Copper has consistently furnished 80–90 percent of exports from Northern Rhodesia and has been the major source of government revenue.

Profit rates have been high and returned value to the domestic economy relatively low. In the late 1940s Phyllis Deane (1953) estimated returned value at about 35 percent of the value of output, but this was still a substantial amount. Deane estimated copper company expenditures within Northern Rhodesia in 1949 at £12,500,000. The largest items were income tax and customs payments to government, £3,600,000; wages, salaries, and bonuses of European mine workers, £4,100,000; wages and rations of African mine workers, £2,000,000; and freight payments to Rhodesian Railways, £1,800,000. Later estimates by Baldwin (1966) for 1956–57 show the copper industry accounting for 61 percent of purchases of railway services, 63 percent of electric power purchases, 66 percent of government tax revenue, 38 percent of European wages, 24 percent of African wages in the monetized sector, 29 percent of construction activity, 56 percent of purchases of ferrous and other metal products, 24 percent of chemicals, and 24 percent of wood products.

The earliest market for maize exports from Northern Rhodesia was the Katanga mining area of the Belgian Congo. But the rapid growth of employment in the copperbelt and the custom of paying African workers a maize ration as part of their wage provided a growing domestic market, which stimulated agricultural development. The number of European farms rose to more than a thousand. Government discriminated in favor of European agriculture and against African agriculture in land allocations, pricing policies, and input supplies. By the mid-1930s the available land had been divided into:

1. Some 8 million acres alienated to Europeans. This tended to be the better land, located along the line of rail and having superior transport facilities.
2. Some 71 million acres in "native reserves" for African use. While some of this was good land and some was along the line of rail, much of it was remote from transportation. Much of it, too, was infested by tsetse fly, which prevented animal raising.
3. Unallocated land, forest, and game reserves totaling about 105 million acres.

In the more remote areas African agriculture continued to be traditional slash-and-burn, with the whole output consumed locally. But in areas closer to transport, African farmers practiced more-intensive cultivation and made their way into the money economy by marketing part of their output. African maize marketings rose faster than those of European farms, and by 1935 African farms were providing about one-third of the total supply. Crop yields were low, however, averaging only about half of those on European farms.

The depression of the early 1930s, which cut mine employment and maize demand, created a problem of oversupply. Government's response was to institute a system of marketing boards and controlled pricing, which was to continue in later decades. Its main features were: (1) a guaranteed price to European farmers, which was frequently above the world price; (2) a lower price to African farmers, with the difference between this and the European price going into a fund for agricultural improvement; (3) a subsidized retail price, designed to ensure cheap food and low labor costs for the mine employers.

The initial effect of this system was to discourage expansion of production, as prices paid to farmers lagged behind the rate of inflation. Maize deliveries to the marketing board show no uptrend from 1935 through 1948, and substantial imports were needed to meet local demand. Between 1949 and 1952, however, producer prices were raised by about one-third. Output then rose substantially and by 1954 the country was once more in an export position.

An almost unique attempt to develop modern social accounts for a backward area was undertaken around 1950 by Phyllis Deane of Cambridge University. Covering Northern Rhodesia and Nyasaland, Deane's study provides estimates of several dimensions of these economies as of the late 1940s. Mining was estimated at 47 percent of Northern Rhodesia's GNP in 1948, while agriculture and forestry provided 20 percent; trade, 11 percent; manufacturing (including handicrafts), 4 percent; and government services, 3 percent.

Within agriculture, African agriculture was judged to produce about six times as much as the European farms. In industry, village handicrafts were estimated to produce more than twice as much as European factories. Village industries included pots, beds, chairs, baskets, mats, beer, shoe repair, bicycle repair, smithing, tailoring, leather goods, wood and ivory curios. There was a modest development of factory industry, centered at Ndola in the copperbelt and dominated by the food-beverage-tobacco group. Factory products included milled grain, sawn timber, furniture, plywood, veneer, bricks, ferroconcrete pipe, soap, mineral waters, baked goods, chocolate, clothing, blankets, and iron.

By this time Africans had been drawn thoroughly into the money economy via farm marketings and wage labor. Close to half the adult males were working as wage laborers either within Northern Rhodesia or as migrants to Southern Rhodesia. Deane estimated that the African population, numbering at this time about 1.5 million, had a total income in 1945 of £10,270,000, categorized as follows: subsistence agriculture, £4,050,000; traded crops and livestock, £940,000; fish and fish trade, £275,000; village industries, £666,000; other independent work, £375,000; earnings of employees within Northern Rhodesia, £3,369,000; and earnings of migrant workers, £595,000. Subsistence agriculture thus provided only about 40 percent of African income; and as for cash income, wage earning was about four times as important as farm marketings.

The Deane study also reaveals the disequalizing impact of development, the pulling apart of the African income structure, and the opening of a wide gap between mine workers at the top and pure subsistence farmers at the bottom. Within wage employment there was a three-tier structure: African mine workers in 1945 earned £41.2 per year, including food rations and housing; workers in manufacturing, transport, and government averaged about £19; workers in European agriculture averaged £10.3. Lower still were the earnings of self-employed rural Africans. Deane estimates their average annual income at £4.8 per head, of which £3 was accounted for by subsistence agriculture, and concludes that "the average cash value of total incomes per head was three to four times as much in the urban areas as in the rural areas."

Even among villagers there were substantial differences among districts, related partly to opportunity for cash sales. Thus estimated cash income per head in Southern Province, on the line of rail, was two-and-one-half times as high as in remote Barotseland to the west.

While the African mine worker was highly privileged within the African population, his earnings were still much below those of European workers. The European skilled mine workers early formed a strong union, one of whose objectives was to prevent upgrading of Africans to skilled jobs, an effort that was largely successful throughout the colonial period. The standard of living of Europeans was at least as high in Northern Rhodesia as in England; and maintaining this standard required that money incomes be above British levels, since most consumer goods were imported.

From 1945 to independence in 1964, the economy grew rapidly along familiar lines. Population growth speeded up to an estimated 2.4 percent per year from 1950 to 1960. GDP rose at 5.6 percent per year during the decade, yielding per capita income growth of 3.2 percent. These aggregative estimates are confirmed by physical indicators for major products. Output of blister and electrolytic copper (in thousand long tons) rose from 194 in 1945 to 375 in 1958. Maize marketings from European farms (in thousands of 200-pound bags) rose from 274 in 1945–46 to 1,190 in 1956–57, while African marketings rose from 230 to 710 over the same period.

The central position of copper in the economy warrants a word on the economic characteristics of this industry. It has a moderately high capital coefficient (about 2:1) and a very low labor coefficient. In 1959 employment per thousand dollars of output was 0.146 in copper, 0.404 in textiles, 0.681 in construction, and 1.30 in maize and tobacco growing. European mine workers, almost all in the skilled category, formed 15.3 percent of the labor force in 1961.

Africans were initially reluctant to face the dangers of underground work, but from 1930 onward there was always a large surplus of applicants for jobs. Despite this labor surplus, the companies raised the real wage of African employees about two-and-one-half times between 1935 and 1960. The European real wage rose about 50 percent over this period so that the wage gap, while still very large, was somewhat reduced. Baldwin attributes the large increase in African wages to pressure by the African Mineworkers' Union, formed in 1949, as well as to an Industrial Conciliation Act under which commissioners sent out from Britain tended to make large wage awards. By the late 1950s the African wage was high enough to encourage active capital-labor substitution. Thus while copper output at the Roan Antelope mine rose 23 percent between 1951 and 1960, African employment dropped by 33 percent. The high-wage policy of the mines, which tended to spread to manufacturing and other sectors, probably reduced the growth of wage employment in those sectors.

Structural change in the economy from 1945 to 1960 was moderate. Copper continued dominant, producing an estimated 44 percent of GDP in 1961. The share of agriculture had declined a little since 1945. Manufacturing had expanded a little but, apart from products needed by the mines, it still consisted largely of small-scale, consumer-oriented industries based on local raw materials. The public sector also expanded modestly, especially as regards infrastructure investment. A ten-year development plan was launched in 1947, consisting essentially of departmental requests rather loosely stitched together. After federation with Southern Rhodesia and Nyasaland in 1954 a more ambitious federal plan was drafted, in which the largest items were the Kariba Gorge project (60 percent of the total) and rehabilitation and extension of the railroads (25 percent). Funding came from the British Colonial Development and Welfare Fund and from the World Bank, in addition to local resources.

Meanwhile, the political situation had been evolving. An African Mineworkers' Union had been formed in 1949 to bargain both for wages and for upgrading of Africans to better jobs. This led to a broader interest in politics. The first African members were appointed to the legislative council, a policy under way in other British African colonies. The federation proposal was implemented over the opposition of the Africans, who viewed it as an extension of Southern Rhodesia's white-dominated policies to all of Central Africa. African political activity increased during the federation period, and Africans achieved some electoral successes and moved toward demands for national independence. When the British government eventually decided to accede to these demands, the federation was dissolved in 1963 and Northern Rhodesia became the independent state of Zambia in 1964.

Southern Rhodesia, as noted earlier, went its own way by issuing its Unilateral Declaration of Independence. Zambia thereupon closed its border with Rhodesia, which among other things required rerouting of rail traffic. The short-term solution was to ship westward through Angola. A longer-term solution was construction of the Tanzania-Zambia railroad in the early 1970s, which gave access to the port of Dar es Salaam. (Still more recently, the reconstitution of Rhodesia as Zimbabwe has led to normalization of relations and reopening of the route to the south.)

Intensive Growth, 1960–80

Kenneth Kaunda, the first and thus far only leader of independent Zambia, inherited a copper-dominated economy that is exposed to external shocks and offers only limited employment opportunities; an agriculture divided between European farming, African commercial farming, and subsistence agriculture; and, most serious, a great shortage of human capital. African education had been badly neglected under colonial rule. At independence the country had less than 100 university graduates and only about 1,500 high school graduates to man the administrative posts in government and industry previously occupied by Europeans.

The government's economic policy led it into an initial period of quarreling with the copper companies, with the government insisting on higher taxes and the companies responding by withholding investment. By 1969 the effective tax rate had risen to 73 percent of profits. At this point the industry was nationalized, with a government holding company taking over 51 percent stock ownership in the companies. The former owners were given a management contract to continue operating the mines. These contracts were terminated in 1975 for a lump sum payment of $78.6 million, and the industry is now fully Zambianized.

The government also moved to establish Zambian control over other sectors of the economy. In 1968 retail trade and liquor licenses outside the major towns were reserved for Africans. Bus, trucking, and taxi licenses could go only to companies with 75 percent Zambian ownership. Sand, gravel, and clay extraction could be done only by Zambians. Twenty-six of the larger firms—in building supplies, brewing, road transport, logging, and newspaper publishing—were asked to "invite" the government to join their enterprises with 51 percent ownership, the cost of the acquisition to be paid out of future profits. These enterprises were placed under a governemnt conglomerate, the Industrial Development Company (INDECO), though the expatriate managements were retained. In 1969 came the nationalization of copper, the mines being placed under another conglomerate (MINDECO). State corporations and statutory boards were given import monopolies in building supplies, textiles, and a number of other consumer goods. In 1970 the government took over 51 percent ownership of all banks, which were put under still another holding company (FINDECO). Seven more major companies were put under INDECO. Government thus became the dominant force in the economy, owning copper, finance, and about 60 percent of manufacturing and exercising pervasive control over private economic activities. A comprehensive control system for wholesale and retail prices was put in place in 1969. Agriculture, too, is tightly controlled with regards to prices, marketing, and input supplies.

The crucial copper industry has been beset by problems. The ore grade of the mines has been declining, hampering production and raising unit costs. The closing off of Rhodesia and the rerouting of rail shipments raised transport costs about 30 percent. When Rhodesia tried to exact a sharply increased price for coal, new supplies had to be developed elsewhere. Zambianization of personnel has made slow headway because of the shortage of qualified Africans. But the announced goal of Zambianization and the consequent insecurity felt by European personnel has led to increased turnover, serious difficulty in recruiting new expatriate workers, and a consequent shortage of key people, especially skilled maintenance workers. Personnel problems have contributed to equipment breakdowns and delays in production.

It is not surprising, then, that the industry's performance has been disappointing. Copper output rose at 7.7 percent per year from 1950 to 1959, but only 2.5 percent from 1960 to 1969 and 0.5 percent from 1970 to 1978. The fact that employment rose from 48,500 in 1970 to 59,300 in 1977, with virtually no increase in output, suggests substantial overstaffing. Since copper still forms 90 percent of exports, exports are now static, and the foreign-exchange constraint is increasingly serious. Copper's contribution to government revenue, formerly above 50 percent, fell to less than 10 percent by 1976; its contribution to real GDP fell from 38 percent in 1965 to 21–23 percent in 1974–76.

Although there has been lip service to rural development, government has in fact concentrated on mining and manufacturing and agriculture has been relatively neglected. A government marketing board has a monopoly of maize sales (which are 60–70 percent of all marketings) and also of several minor crops. It also controls supplies of fertilizers and other modern inputs. Dodge (1977) reports that the board's operations are quite high in cost and inefficient—input supplies sometimes arrive late, the board is not ready to handle crops at the time of harvest, and so on. Producer prices are typically well below world market levels and are not differentiated regionally to take account of large differences in transport costs. Rural terms of trade have deteriorated, more so for field crops than for livestock or fruits and vegetables. Fertilizer prices are subsidized, but agricultural credit is often difficult to obtain. Budget allocations to agriculture have not been generous. In the first (1966–70) development plan, "agriculture and lands" received only 15 percent of the funds, compared with 38 percent for infrastructure and 21 percent for industry and mining. In the second (1972–76) plan, the Ministry of Rural Development received only 11.3 percent of the funds. There has been a substantial exodus of expatriate farmers, who previously supplied a large share of food marketings. Agricultural research and extension services are poorly funded and short of skilled staff.

All this has contributed to low and unbalanced output growth and rising food imports. Between 1969–71 and 1979–81, agricultural output grew at only 2.2 percent per year and food output at 2.3 percent, well below the 3.0 rate of population growth. Moreover, the output increases have been mainly in livestock, dairy products, and fruits and vegetables. Because of the price discrimination against field crops, farmers have tended to shift away from them. Dodge estimates that crop sales grew at only 1.1 percent from 1964 to 1973. The result was a rapid rise of food imports, from one million metric tons in 1975 to 49.9 million tons (about nine kilos per capita) in 1979. Virtually all the country's supply of wheat, barley, and rice is imported, and more than half the supply of vegetable oils, dairy products, cotton, beef, and potatoes. By the late 1970s food imports were about 10

percent of all imports and about 40 percent of the value of domestic food marketings. Despite this supplementing of domestic supplies, FAO data indicate that
calorie availability per capita declined 12 percent between 1960–62 and 1977–79.

The manufacturing sector has grown from about 6 percent of GDP in 1960 to
17 percent in 1980. It is still oriented toward light industry and engaged mainly in
processing local materials for local use. The fastest-growing components have
been printing, textiles and clothing, chemicals, plastics, and petroleum products.
About 60 percent of manufacturing is government-owned. Government enterprises appear to be plagued by the usual problems of inadequate management,
overstaffing, political pressure on wage and price setting, and poor financial
returns. There is an elaborate incentive system for "approved" private enterprises; but government clearly prefers public or mixed enterprises, and the inflow
of foreign private capital has been small. There is very high effective protection of
domestic industries, through both tariffs and controlled allocation of foreign
exchange.

Urban labor appears to be substantially overpriced. Wage rates have been
forced up by union pressure to narrow the African-European wage gap in copper
mining (which is still large) and the wage gap between copper and other sectors.
Between 1969 and 1977, mining wages rose at 7.4 percent per year, while non-
mining wages rose at 9.9 percent. Wages rose much faster than productivity,
forcing up unit labor costs, especially in mining. Between 1965 and 1977 the wage
index in mining rose to 252.3 while the productivity index fell to 54.6, so that the
index of unit labor cost rose to 462.1. High wages have stimulated heavy rural-
urban migration while at the same time restricting urban employment opportunities. Between 1969 and 1978, total paid employment rose by only 43,000,
while the available labor force grew by 458,000. Rising unemployment remains
an explosive political problem.

As part of the expansion of the public sector, government consumption as a
percentage of GDP rose from 12 percent in 1965 to 28 percent in 1980. Government revenue, on the other hand, has been falling because of the virtual disap-
pearance of copper revenue, and by the late 1970s government expenditure was
running about 50 percent above revenue. Government borrowing from banks
increased rapidly from 1974 onward, contributing to a 15 percent inflation rate
from 1974 to 1978.

Difficulties in the copper industry have also put a severe squeeze on the
balance of payments. While export volume fell only slightly between 1970 and
1980, copper prices fell about 18 percent. Despite efforts to reduce imports, which
have cut into necessary inputs for the domestic economy, Zambia's foreign reserves were quickly exhausted and its foreign indebtedness tripled over the
decade.

To sum up: during the 1970s population grew at 3.1 percent per year. Real
GDP, however, grew at only 0.7 percent, which means that GDP per capita
declined at 2.4 percent per year. Agriculture did somewhat better than the rest of

the economy, growing at 2.3 percent. But mining, manufacturing, and private services grew very little.

On the brighter side, we should note that the expansion of current government expenditure brought substantial improvements in education and health services. The primary-school enrollment rate, which was only 34 percent in 1950, had risen to 98 percent by 1978. High-school enrollments had risen from less than 1 percent to 16 percent. The infant mortality rate was cut by one-third between 1960 and 1979, while life expectancy rose from 40 to 47 years, which is still well below the median of 55 for all countries in our sample. But continuing progress on these fronts may prove difficult in the face of an eroding production base.

PART III
RECENT DEVELOPERS, 1950–80

During the "first golden age" of 1870–1914, 23 of the countries in our sample, or rather more than half the total, reached the turning point to intensive growth. This period was followed by an era, punctuated by two major wars and the Great Depression, of much slower growth in world output and trade. Thus countries that had been growing quite rapidly before 1914 now grew more slowly, contributing to the "life began in 1945" illusion that pervaded the development literature of the 1950s. Further, for countries that had not reached the turning point before 1914, the 1914–45 economic environment was not conducive to doing so. Only three additional countries "took off" during this period, and these cases depended heavily on special circumstances—oil discoveries in Venezuela, copper discoveries in Zambia, and belated French colonization in Morocco.

After a period of postwar recovery in the late 1940s the world economy entered a "second golden age" from 1950 to 1973. In addition to an unprecedented growth of world output and trade, favorable circumstances included the emergence of most colonies as independent states, development of new international organizations such as the IMF and IBRD, and expansion of bilateral aid programs by most of the developed countries. Thus in the "early developers" of the pre-1914 era the tempo of growth quickened appreciably, and the number of additional countries reaching the turning point rose substantially. The task of this section is to consider, with respect to each of these countries, why their turning point was so long delayed, what changes around 1950 precipitated the beginning of intensive growth, and the main outlines of this growth up to 1980.

Because of their great size and extensive literature, China and India will receive a chapter each. I shall then consider more briefly the cases of Egypt, Turkey, Iraq, Iran, Pakistan, and Indonesia. Finally, I shall comment even more briefly on the seven countries in our sample that still show no sign of reaching the turning point. Answers to the question "why" are elusive and would no doubt differ from case to case; but my comments may suggest a few clues.

11

China

"China is different." How often we hear this said. Yet in some respects China resembles a number of other Asian countries. It is a land-scarce economy with a high man/land ratio, very labor intensive techniques in agriculture, and a continuing threat of declining output per capita because of diminishing returns. In this respect it resembles other fully settled, densely populated areas such as Java, India, and Egypt. The population is still overwhelmingly rural. Over the long span of centuries most production has been household production, including a substantial handicraft component. Yet the economy has long been commercialized and monetized, with a substantial amount of local trade and a smaller volume of interprovincial and foreign trade. None of these things is in any way unusual.

There are, however, two characteristics that might be considered special to China. The first is sheer size, for China's hinterland extends thousands of miles from the coast. This means a wide variety of climatic zones, soils, topography, and agricultural products. The "rice south" differs in important ways from the "wheat north"; and Manchuria, Inner Mongolia, Sinkiang, and Tibet are again different.* A further consequence is the importance of regional economies and regional governments. The central government has always had difficulty in maintaining a firm grasp on the outlying provinces, which tend to slip out of control as a new dynasty loses its initial momentum.

Size and distance impose heavy transport costs. Until recently most goods moved by water, especially over the vast Yangtze network. But in much of northern and western China, where river transport is unavailable, goods had to move over crude roads in carts pulled by people or animals. The high ton-mile cost limited most trade to the immediate locality, and a low ratio of foreign trade to national output followed as a consequence. Scholars who have analyzed why Japan developed rapidly in the late nineteenth century while China did not suggest

*For spelling of Chinese proper nouns I use the Wade-Giles system of romanization, which prevailed until recently. The new pinyin system is similar phonetically but differs in spelling.

that transport was an important factor. Almost all points in Japan have ready access to low-cost ocean transport.

A second special feature of China is its long history as a unified country and its tradition of centralized rule through an educated elite. Successive waves of invaders—most recently the Mongols and the Manchus—established new dynasties but in the end were absorbed into the dominant Han population. Nor has China ever been successfully subordinated by a foreign power. This is partly a matter of historical accident. By the time the Western powers got around to China in the late nineteenth century, competiton among them was so intense that none would allow another to establish a dominant position. This rivalry was symbolized in the treaty ports by the existence of distinct foreign enclaves or "concessions"—British, French, Japanese, American, and others. While these foreign powers had an important impact on economic life in the treaty ports, this influence did not penetrate very far into the agricultural hinterland.

EXTENSIVE GROWTH, 1368–1949

In a history going back for several millennia, the year 1368 is significant in that it marked the beginning of the Ming dynasty. From that time on there was a recognized central government, a reasonable level of peace throughout the country, and a sustained rise in population, which was broken only by the Manchu invasions in the seventeenth century and the Taiping Rebellion in the midnineteenth century. Although this rebellion was localized in a few provinces on the east coast, it is estimated to have reduced the population of those provinces by more than 20 million.

Population and Food

Population estimates for earlier centuries are rough. After a careful review of the data, Perkins (1969) estimates the population in 1368 at between 65 and 80 million. His estimate for 1913 is 430 ± 25 million. This would mean a cumulative increase of 0.4 percent per year between 1368 and 1913. The rate of population growth fluctuated with the incidence of war, disease, and famine, in addition to the two major checks already mentioned. But the trend was clearly upward.

Evidence on food production is also fragmentary. Perkins argues, or at times seems simply to assume, that per capita grain consumption, short-term fluctuations apart, did not change appreciably over the centuries. For the period after 1870, for which records are somewhat more complete, Feuerwerker's study (1969) supports the Perkins hypothesis. "While it is certain that rural living standards between 1870 and 1911 did not improve, there is no conclusive evidence that population growth and declining average farm size were accompanied by a drastic secular fall in the peasant standard of living." This standard of living was low, in that more than 90 percent of food intake consisted of cereals. But per capita availability of cereals was above that in some other Asian countries. In 1957–59, per capita grain supply in China was estimated at 285 kilos per year, compared with 289 in Japan, 191 in India, and 230 in Pakistan.

If we accept the hypothesis that food output grew roughly in line with population, then food output must have increased eight to nine times between 1368 and 1949. About half of this increase seems to have come from expansion of cultivated acreage, which increased about fourfold over the period. As of 1368, population was heavily concentrated in the lower Yangtze Valley and along the eastern seaboard. From there it spread out gradually onto the North China Plain (which had been devastated by the Manchus), west to Szechwan, and into the southern and southwestern provinces. This process of territorial expansion was still going on in 1900, with extension of cultivation in Manchuria and Sinkiang. The soil resources and crop yields in these areas, however, were inferior to those in the areas settled earlier, indicating that the specter of diminishing returns was clearly visible. By 1950 the frontier was virtually closed, while at the same time the rate of population growth was accelerating.

The second source of increased output was an approximate doubling of yields per acre over the period. The puzzling thing is that this occurred with little change in the organization of agriculture. By 1400 the land tenure system, production methods, and marketing arrangements had fallen into a shape that was to change little over the next five centuries.

The main reasons for the increase in yields seem to have been:

1. Some spread of improved seed varieties, introduced either from abroad or from other regions of China.
2. Introduction of new crops from America after 1600, of which corn and potatoes were particularly important. Corn can be grown in areas not hospitable to other crops. Potatoes yield many more calories per acre than grain crops.
3. Gradual extension of double-cropping—two rice crops or a rice crop followed by wheat or barley. Double-cropping required water-control projects, which were going on throughout the period, and by 1900 covered almost all the feasible acreage. It also imposes heavy labor requirements at the "switchover point," at which harvesting and replanting must be completed quickly. Perkins argues that population growth in a sense *produced* more double-cropping by removing the labor constraint, providing labor both for seasonal peaks of cultivation and for building dikes and irrigation canals.
4. Some increase of inputs per acre, especially labor and fertilizer inputs.

Structure of the Traditional Economy

The organization of the economy remained largely unchanged up to the late nineteenth century, and in most respects right up to 1949.

In agriculture, most farmers were owner-operators working very small holdings—two to three acres in the rice south, three to four acres in the wheat north. A farm often consisted of five or six separate strips, so smallness of holdings was aggravated by waste of land between strips. Lack of a system of primogeniture contributed to fragmentation of holdings.

Although large estates did not develop, there were by 1900 perhaps two million local elite families with median holdings of 20–25 acres, most of which was rented to tenants. There were also a substantial number of absentee land-lords—officials, army officers, merchants—who invested in land for prestige and security. Growth of landlordism was restrained, however, by the fact that land was not a very profitable investment. Feuerwerker estimates that the rate of return was typically only half what could be earned in trade, moneylending, and other urban activities.

The prevalence of tenancy varied by region. It was only 20 percent or so in northern China, where crop yields did not make land a very profitable investment. It was higher in the well-watered south, southwest, and Yangtze Valley, reaching some 50 percent in Szechwan. A further reason for greater tenancy in some areas than in others was that, because the tenant paid in grain (the commonest pattern), which the landlord could eat only within limits, landlordism was more profitable where there was some way of marketing the surplus. Thus areas close to river or ocean transport were more favorable to tenancy systems.

While landlordism scarcely promoted agricultural productivity, it does not seem to have reduced it materially, one reason being substantial continuity of tenure. Where a three-year rotation was practiced, tenancy contracts were also typically for three years. In regions where water control was important and the long-term payoff to tenant investment was high, tenure periods tended to be longer. At the extreme, there were systems of lifetime and even inheritable tenure. A second important reason for continued productivity in tenant agriculture was extensive use of fixed rents: rents fixed in kind covered about half of all rented acreage, rents fixed in money about 25 percent, and sharecropping only the remaining 25 percent. A fixed-rent system enables the tenant to gain for at least a few years from productivity improvements and hence provides stronger incentive for such improvements.

The living standard of the average peasant was certainly low and stationary. But this was not owing to exploitation by landlords or to oppressive taxation; the main explanation was simply low output from traditional technology.

There were large regional differences in farm output per capita, which are still a prominent feature of the economy. Writing of the republican period 1912–49, Rawski (1978) estimates that grain output per capita in the richest region was *six* times as high as that in the poorest region. Within each region there were substantial variations by size of holding. "Rich peasants" produced more than twice as much grain per capita as did "poor peasants."

By admittedly crude calculations, agriculture during this era provided about two-thirds of national output. The next largest sector was handicraft production.

Handicrafts were carried on overwhelmingly in individual farm households, in combination with farm work. At the seasonal peak of farm activity most people were fully employed on the land, but handicraft activity increased in the slack season. There is also evidence that the proportion of family income derived from handicrafts varied inversely with size of farm. Production of goods and services in the household served as a kind of sponge, soaking up labor time left over from agriculture. In addition to individual household production, there was cooperative activity by a number of households in such activities as salt and pottery production and rice and wheat milling. There were also small organized workshops, especially in urban areas.

Cotton spinning and weaving was much the largest handicraft activity and was especially well developed in cotton-growing areas of the lower Yangtze Valley. These areas exported both raw cotton and yarn to other parts of China, which made possible widespread dissemination of weaving throughout the country. Cotton cloth was also exported from the Yangtze area, after having been shipped long distances by traditional transport. Maintenance of minimum living standards for the dense rural population in this region was heavily dependent on the market for raw cotton, yarn, and cloth.

Other important handicraft activities were preparation of foods, such as milled rice, wheat flour, soybean sauce, and other edible oils; lumber and wood products; clothing and knit goods; tobacco, wine, and liquor; paper and printing; stove, clay, and glass products. All consumer requirements, indeed, had to be produced in this way in the absence of factory industry or substantial imports.

In terms of employment, trade and transportation were only slightly less important than handicrafts. Transport was simple, costly, and labor-intensive, employing 4–5 percent of the labor force. River transport involved everything from one-man sampans to sailing vessels of considerable size. Overland transport was by carts pulled by animals or humans, and hand-drawn vehicles were also standard in the towns and cities.

Trade, which absorbed another 5–6 percent of the labor force, was carried on in a hierarchy of markets, ranging from local to international. Probably three-quarters of all trade took place in some 70,000 basic local markets, where farmers and handicraft workers exchanged their surplus produce. The system was thoroughly commercialized and monetized, but each market was restricted in geographic scope. It appears that in most markets there were enough buyers and sellers to ensure effective competition, though this may not have been true in the more remote areas.

Long-distance trade, which moved mainly along waterways, was feasible only for objects of sufficient value to bear the transport costs. Perkins estimates that about 20 percent of farm output was marketed and that this percentage changed little over the centuries. But only 5–7 percent of farm output went into interprovincial trade and perhaps 1–2 percent into foreign trade, which was heavily weighted toward silk, tea, and other luxury goods.

Government did little to stimulate economic development. The public sector was small. Rough estimates for the 1890s suggest that all levels of government were raising revenues equal to about 7.5 percent of national product. But of this the central government got only about 40 percent, or only 3 percent of GNP. The main revenue sources were land taxes, customs duties, an internal transit tax on movements of merchandise, and the salt tax.

This 7.5 percent is not out of line with tax ratios in Europe and the United States in the midnineteenth century, and those economies did develop. One difference is that in China hardly any of the revenue went for productive purposes. Virtually all of it was spent on administration, the military, and (after about 1900) interest and repayment of foreign debt. The estimate for the 1890s shows less than 2 percent of expenditure allocated to public works and scarcely anything to railway construction, which was booming in other parts of the world.

The Beginnings of Change, 1890–1949

Did China experience a significant rise in per capita income during the first half of the twentieth century? While economic historians of China are not in full agreement on this point, my own judgment suggests a negative answer. There was some increase in the tempo of political change, some acceleration in the rate of population growth, some development of textiles and other light industries, some increase in the foreign-trade ratio. But these changes affected a limited number of people along the eastern seaboard and did not penetrate far into the heartland. There is little evidence of a significant improvement in living standards; and estimates of national income for the 1930s (Liu and Yeh, 1965) reveal an economic structure little different from that in earlier centuries.

It appears, then, that the period of intensive growth should be dated from the 1949 revolution. The changes during the years 1890–1949 might be regarded as preconditions for growth in the sense of being helpful to the later acceleration of growth, but not in the sense that they would by themselves have led to such an acceleration.

On the political side, China's defeat by Japan in 1895 marked a further step in foreign penetration of the economy; and for the next fifty years foreign companies and governments were prominent in the small "modern" sector. In 1912 the emperor was deposed and a republic established. This ushered in a period of civil strife, warlordism, and banditry, which was scarcely conducive to economic development. Establishment of the Nanking government under Chiang Kaishek in 1926 brought only a brief period of stability. The Japanese occupied Manchuria in 1931, fought pitched battles in Shanghai in 1932, and in 1937 began a full-scale war that lasted until 1945. There followed several years of civil war before the communist victory in 1949. By that time the living standard of the average Chinese was probably lower than it had been in 1900.

It is not clear just when the rate of population growth began to rise. Feuerwerker (1968) estimates a growth rate of 0.78 percent per year from 1912 to 1953, almost double the average rate of previous centuries. The increase probably came about mainly through a modest decline in mortality rates. New medical technology and hospital services, provided partly by Western missionaries, may have had some effect. Improvements in rail and road transport may have helped to alleviate localized famines. At any rate, population growth did accelerate.

At the same time the frontier was gradually closing. New land was available mainly in Manchuria and Inner Mongolia, and cultivated acreage grew much more slowly than population. Since 80 percent of the population was engaged in agriculture, there was intensified pressure on the land. One result was a decrease in average size of farm, particularly in northern China. There was also an intensified effort to squeeze out more output from each acre through a shift toward crops yielding more nutrition per acre, some expansion of high-value export crops, further development of irrigation systems and double-cropping, and an increase in labor and organic-fertilizer inputs per acre. Commercial fertilizer was still almost unknown in 1949.

The foreign presence was felt in several ways. China was limited by treaty to low import duties, so that even if import substitution had been desired it would not have been feasible. Only in 1925 did the Nanking government recapture some control over rates of duty and begin to levy protective tariffs. The new and shaky republican government engaged in substantial foreign borrowing. In return, British and other foreign officials were given control over collection of customs, and the revenue was used to guarantee interest and debt repayments. Foreign concessions in the major ports established the right of foreigners to residence, property ownership, investment, and business activity. Many of the new industrial enterprises that began to appear from the 1890s onward were foreign-owned; and foreign banks, trading companies, and shipping lines were prominent in the coastal cities.

These foreign activities, however, did not penetrate into the interior of the country, which was protected by high transport costs. The foreign sector was always small. In 1933 export plus imports were estimated at less than 7 percent of GNP. This is dwarfed by the amount of goods exchanged on local markets. Nor does the contention that foreigners "drained" China of its wealth stand up to close examination. Rawski points out that China typically had an import surplus and that there was also a consistent *inflow* of gold and silver to the country. This comfortable balance-of-payments situation was due partly to remittances by overseas Chinese, who were prospering in Hong Kong, Java, Malaya, and other parts of Asia.

The story of handicrafts having been "crushed" by imports and domestic factory production has been much overdrawn. One branch, cotton spinning, was indeed seriously affected. Imported yarn began to enter the country in about 1860, first from India and later from Japan. The first domestic spinning mill was established in 1890, and after 1895 foreign investors came in increasingly. As of 1936,

Chinese owners had 52 percent of spindle capacity and Japanese companies 44 percent, the British and everyone else having been squeezed out. Factory production increasingly displaced both imports and handicraft production. By 1933, 84 percent of all yarn was factory-produced.

But the availability of cheap machine-made yarn actually helped handloom weaving, which continued to expand absolutely while declining somewhat in market share. In the 1930s about 70 percent of all cotton cloth was still hand-produced. Factors contributing to the survival of handloom weaving included:

1. The fact that it was a sideline to agriculture. It paid to employ surplus labor time in this way even if the marginal productivity of labor was less than a subsistence wage.
2. Substantial technical progress, including successive introduction of an improved wooden loom, the iron loom, and the Jacquard loom. With an iron loom and machine-made yarn, the productivity advantage of factory weaving was only about 4:1. In spinning, on the other hand, the productivity advantage of the factory was estimated at 44:1, which made hand production unviable. The comparative advantage of household workers thus shifted from spinning to weaving.
3. Considerable development of the putting-out system, which provided yarn supplies, marketing channels, and quality control. This system seems to have been operating in the China of 1930 in much the same way that it was in the England of 1750.

Two other handicrafts suffered somewhat. Iron and steel products were largely wiped out by factory equivalents. Tea declined somewhat in competition with tea from India and Ceylon, where the colonial authorities maintained better quality control. But many activities, such as oil pressing, rice milling, flour grinding, silk weaving, and mining by native methods were little affected by domestic or imported manufactures. Feuerwerker (1968) concludes that total demand for handicrafts did not decrease in the twentieth century. Thus there is no indication that handicraft industry as a whole was seriously undermined. In 1933, handicrafts still accounted for 68 percent of industrial output and, because of market growth, the labor time devoted to handicrafts had increased over the years.

Factory industry expanded from the 1890s onward, but not very rapidly. The main barrier to manufacturing growth was weakness of demand from the low-income rural population. Other obstacles were absence of a modern banking system and inability of the government to provide law and order. Chinese firms, which predominated in most industries, were typically family businesses rather than corporations, and they were dependent on willingness of family members to provide finance. Manufacturing had to compete for money with other attractive opportunities—trade, moneylending, speculation in commodities, foreign exchange, government bonds, and investment in land. Competent managers were also in very short supply.

Industry was heavily concentrated in the treaty ports, preeminently Shang-hai, and in Manchuria, where Japanese influence was growing. Output was mainly consumer goods, with textiles as usual in the lead. In 1933 producers' goods accounted for only 25 percent of value added. The average size of factory was small, and smaller for Chinese than for foreign-owned firms. A 1933 sample survey found the average number of employees per firm to be 202, which is clearly an averaging of a few quite large establishments with a multitude of smaller ones. Total factory employment was only about a million, out of a labor force of some 205 million in 1933.

Poor transportation and high transport costs continued as a major problem. Liu and Yeh's national income estimates for 1933 show "traditional" transporta-tion still contributing three times as much as "modern" transportation to value added. Railway building began late, and in 1939 this huge country still had only 13,000 miles of track, of which 40 percent was in Manchuria. Maintenance was poor, and railroad operations were frequently disrupted by bandits, warlords, and the "regular" army, who simply appropriated stretches of railway and pocketed the fares. A good deal of surfaced road had been built, especially from 1928 to 1937, but this amounted to only 25,000 miles in 1937. The main reliance was still on water transport, as it always had been.

The Nationalist government was unable to channel much of national income through the public sector. On average, for the years 1931–36, central government expenditure was only 3.5 percent of GNP, and part of this was financed by foreign borrowing rather than tax revenue. Some 25 percent of expenditure went for civil administration, 41 percent for military purposes, and 25 percent for debt service, leaving little for productive investment.

The first national accounts estimates available are the Liu-Yeh estimates for 1933. These show agriculture as contributing 65 percent of net value added; traditional nonagricultural activities (handicrafts, transport, trade), 19.6 percent; "modern" nonagricultural activities, 12.6 percent; and government administra-tion, 2.8 percent. The distribution by end uses was personal consumption, 92 percent; government consumption, 3 percent; and gross domestic investment, 5 percent. Except for a rise in the contribution of factory industry from zero to 5 percent, there is no evidence that these proportions had changed appreciably since 1870. Nor is there evidence of a secular uptrend in average per capita income. Perkins estimates that per capita income in 1933 was 10 percent above what it had been in 1913, but by 1952 it was back to the 1913 level.

For these reasons I date intensive growth from 1949, but a number of devel-opments before this time were helpful in subsequent growth. Features of the 1949 economy that were not present in 1900 include: (1) several urbanized industrial regions, notably Shanghai, which continued after the revolution to be a leading center of industrial growth; (2) a considerable pool of skilled industrial labor and experienced management, not only in textiles but also in engineering repair work, machinery, weapons, chemicals, and the nascent Manchurian iron and steel industry; (3) an enlarged system of modern transport and communications, including the road and railway mileage already noted; (4) a network of modern higher education and research institutions; and (5) an embryonic system of agricultural research and extension work.

As in other countries, intensive growth did not take off from zero but from a modest platform of previous accomplishments.

INTENSIVE GROWTH, 1949–80

Introduction

In 1949 the economy was still devastated by the war with Japan and the subsequent civil war. The years 1949–52 were years of gradual recuperation during which the new regime did not press institutional changes. From 1952 onward the tempo of institutional change and economic growth quickened appreciably. So discussions of postwar growth usually take 1952 as the base year.

The statistical documentation is by no means precise. The Chinese government itself has difficulty in assembling data from such a large area. While release of government statistics to the outside world has increased substantially since the mid-1970s, it is still selective. In this section I rely heavily on estimates of experienced China specialists, such as the late Alexander Eckstein, Dwight Perkins, and Thomas Rawski. These are adequate, I believe, to reveal the broad contours of economic events since 1952.

A word should be added on the political context. In many third-world countries political power has gravitated into, or remained in, the hands of middle-class and upper-class people. China, by contrast, experienced a revolution fought in the interest of the poor. Although the Communist Party tried to appeal to everyone except the hated landlord, its hard core of support came from the poorest strata of the population. After the revolution, a person's class origin remained an important criterion for admission to education and for movement up the career ladder. People of ''poor peasant'' origin tended to dominate the political structure. If middle or rich peasants had been dominant, as they were briefly in the early 1950s, it might have been impossible to carry through the pooling of land into cooperatives in the mid-1950s and the organization of communes in the late 1950s.

Under the surface of the monolithic ruling party there has been a continuing political struggle, which is by no means ended. Two polar views can be distinguished, though there are of course intermediate shadings. One view attaches main importance to economic objectives and economic performance, to efficient management of the economy. It is willing to use material incentives for contributions to higher output and to tolerate the consequent differentiation of incomes and occupational status. Chou Enlai, and more recently Deng Xiaoping, are representative of this view. Against this view stands the Maoist position that political and social objectives should be preeminent. The Maoist group is strongly egalitarian in outlook. It is suspicious of material incentives and believes in the development of a "new socialist man" who will work for the good of the community. It dislikes status distinctions and emphasizes participatory democracy in the workshop rather than administrative control from above. (Thus during the Cultural Revolution era all organizations were run by a "revolutionary committee," though in fact there was usually a "principal responsible person" with managerial functions.) It exalts political purity and downgrades technical expertise.

The relative influence of these two views has varied over time. When the Maoist view has been strongly predominant, production has been adversely affected. Thus the Great Leap Forward campaign of 1958–59 involved projects and expectations that proved quite unrealistic. Agricultural and industrial output dropped substantially and took several years to recover. Again, the onset of the Cultural Revolution in 1966, which encouraged challenges to managerial authority, brought a two-year drop in industrial output, which ended only when the excesses of political activists had been curbed. Thus there have been sizable short-term fluctuations in the growth rate, associated partly with political turbulence.

The radical wing was heavily reliant on Mao's personal authority. After his death their power collapsed, and "the gang of four" was under arrest within three weeks. The Chinese polity seems now to be evolving toward the pragmatist pole, and the radical wing may be in permanent eclipse. But continuation of this shift depends partly on whether the pragmatists can deliver the goods in terms of production.

Economic Organization

In describing the administrative structure of the economy, we must remember that it has recently been subject to much discussion and some change. Especially in agriculture there have been innovations that may turn out to be quite significant.

Agricultural Organization. After the 1949–52 recovery period, the regime moved in stages toward full collectivization of agriculture. Initially, peasants were nudged and persuaded to pool their land and animals into cooperative units. Production was planned and carried out in common; but in the first instance each family's share of the proceeds was related to the amount of land it had contributed. Within a few years, however, this arrangement was superseded by a system of "advanced cooperatives" in which the initial land contribution was ignored and income payments were based on labor services only. This sequence of events involved a redistribution of assets and income away from "middle" and "rich" peasants in favor of the poor peasants and their allies in the political power structure.

Finally, the central feature of the Great Leap Forward campaign of 1958 was the establishment of "people's communes," much larger in size than the previous cooperatives and having industrial and local government functions as well as agricultural functions. Although some of the initial expectations—"steel furnaces in every backyard''—proved unrealistic and were soon abandoned, the commune system survived and became the main framework for the rural sector, in which 80 percent of the population lives and works.

A commune involves three levels of authority—the *commune* itself, the *production brigade,* and the *production team*—among which there is a rather clear division of labor. The commune is a large unit, including on average some 15,000 people and several thousand hectares of land. Under the province and the county, it is the basic unit for provision of social services. It typically operates a hospital with a medical staff, runs a high school serving the commune population, and performs other local government services. Industrial establishments, which are an important feature of the rural sector and especially important in producing inputs for agriculture, are typically managed at the commune level. The commune is not much involved in crop production, though it does take a hand in larger-scale projects such as fish farming, forestry, horticulture, and animal husbandry.

The *production brigade,* typically including 1,500 people or so, is a center of rural economic and political life. It operates primary schools and medical dispensaries staffed by paramedical personnel (''barefoot doctors''), who are qualified to dispense standard medications, screen patients, and pass those who need treatment to the commune hospital. It houses the local Communist Party unit and the local militia unit. It participates in production planning and distribution of quotas to the production teams. It organizes credit, input supplies, and marketing services. It mobilizes labor for roads, canals, and other public works. It usually has industrial sideline activities, such as food processing and workshops for repairing farm equipment.

The *production team* averages perhaps 200 people and corresponds to a traditional village. It is the basic unit for organizing agricultural production and distributing the resulting income. Its members work cooperatively in carrying through the seasonal cycle of farm operations in the area under its control. When the output has been marketed and taxes and necessary costs deducted, the net income is distributed to team members according to how many ''work points'' each has accumulated. A work point is a labor day, adjusted by a coefficient reflecting the skill, strength, experience, and diligence of the individual. These judgments of individual merit are obviously rather touchy, involving a good deal of group discussion and no doubt a certain amount of politics. (''Class background'' still crops up as a factor in assigning points.)

The primacy of the production team assures a rather close link between effort and reward; and planning officials use price incentives as well as output targets to guide production in desired directions. The general level of farm prices has been raised several times since 1960 to stimulate output as well as to reduce the urban-rural income gap; and relative crop prices are also adjusted from time to time as an aid in redirecting production.

In addition to its contribution to group production activities, each commune family works a private plot large enough for production of vegetables, fruit, chickens, even pigs. This output is sold in the nearest town market at a free market price; and while these private plots amount to only 5 percent of the arable land, they provide about 20 percent of the income of the average farm household.

An important innovation of the Deng Xiaoping regime in 1979 was to allow the production team to "contract out" output from a given plot of collective land to individual households. The household agrees to deliver part of its crop to the state but can keep anything they grow above this quota. This "responsibility system" comes close to a restoration of tenant farming with the state as landlord. It has been adopted most enthusiastically in the lush rice-growing areas of Canton province, but it is spreading also in other parts of the country. It appears to have stimulated larger output of basic crops as well as diversification into sidelines, such as raising ducks for the Hong Kong market. The possibility of higher incomes through greater effort has become respectable.

It appears also that communes are being deemphasized in that some of their governmental functions are being transferred to the traditional townships.

Industrial Organization. Socialization of industry was considerably easier to carry out than socialization of agriculture. Most of the industrial enterprises existing in 1949 were owned either by foreign companies or by rich Chinese who fled the mainland at the time of the revolution. These were simply nationalized; and new enterprises started after 1949 were socialized from the start. Many small-scale industrial, repair, trading, and service enterprises were permitted to remain in private hands through the early 1950s, but these were gradually swept into the net, with the result that by the late 1950s the nonagricultural sector was virtually 100 percent socialist.

Since Mao's death and consolidation of the Deng regime, however, small-scale private economic activities have been allowed to reappear. It is now legal to start your own business provided you employ only family members (a definition that in China is rather extensible!) so that you are not "exploiting" the wage labor of others. The result has been a multiplication of private restaurants, sidewalk stalls, repair services for bicycles, shoes, furniture, and other service establishments. These enterprises have helped to ease urban unemployment and at the same time to provide the population with a wide range of consumer services that in the Soviet Union are provided only clumsily or not at all by state enterprises.

The administrative structure of industry and the central planning procedures are quite Sovietesque, so little need be said about them, and in any case our space limits preclude any detailed discussion. Physical-output targets are assigned to each enterprise in considerable detail, along with limits on its use of materials, labor, and credit. The planning organization drafts "material balances" for supplies and allocations of several hundred key materials, though a considerably smaller number than in the Soviet Union. Use of these techniques has produced problems familiar to any student of Soviet planning. Emphasis on quantity of output has sometimes led to deterioration of quality. Inability of an enterprise to obtain inputs that have been allocated to it can cause slowdowns or interruption of production. To guard against such bottlenecks enterprises tend to integrate vertically, to produce as much as possible of the materials and equipment they need, which may be quite inefficient from a broader standpoint. They also tend, as in the Soviet Union, to carry large inventories as a security device, larger than would be necessary if supplies were more assured. Supply of efficient managers for the rapidly growing industrial sector has been a continuing problem. The present managers often have no production experience or technical qualifications for their jobs. Many are simply Party officials or army officers who have been rewarded with managerial positions. Although this situation is widely recognized within China, there is no simple solution. Even if politically influential incumbents could be dislodged, an adequate number of replacements is not yet in sight.

The efficiency-minded people who have dominated the government since 1976 have been much concerned with improving the management of industry. Systematic management training is being undertaken for the first time. In 1981 several leading Chinese universities established departments of management and sent emissaries to tour United States business schools in search of curriculum ideas. Shorter courses for midcareer executives have been established, staffed by foreign professors, and some Harvard-type ''business cases'' from China have been collected.

There has been widespread discussion of ways to give enterprise managers greater autonomy and stronger incentives. Possible measures include giving enterprises greater freedom to vary their product mix and to initiate new products outside their official plan; permitting enterprise expansion through bank credits rather than central allocation of investment funds; allowing the enterprise to retain a larger share of profits resulting from above-plan performance; greater use of managerial bonuses, which thus far have been used very little as compared with Soviet practice. In some regions, notably Szechwan, there has been considerable experimentation with such techniques. Overall, however, there has thus far been much more talk than action. Any substantial freeing up of the planning system would have to overcome strong political and bureaucratic resistance, the kind of resistance that has largely impeded ''economic reform'' in the Soviet Union.

Economic Performance: An Overview

While different writers give somewhat different estimates of output growth, these estimates converge on a figure of 6 percent per year over the period 1952–79. This is somewhat above the growth rate of the OECD countries over the same period and is well above the average for all third-world countries.

The 6 percent figure, of course, conceals considerable variation by sector and by time period. Growth was unusually rapid, at more than 7 percent per year, from 1952 to 1957. From 1957 to 1965 the growth rate fell by about one-third because of the turbulence during and following the Great Leap campaign. Since 1965 the growth rate has been noticeably more stable, apart from year-to-year variation in harvest size. Industry has grown most rapidly, at 9–10 percent per year. But agricultural output has also grown at more than 3 percent per year (Perkins cites 3.4 percent for the years 1952–74), well above the rate of population growth. China entered the era of population explosion rather abruptly. Before 1940 the growth rate, restrained by disease, hunger, and war, was below 1 percent per year. Under the new regime, with establishment of civil peace, improved health services, and a guaranteed minimum of food under the rationing system, population growth accelerated quite rapidly. It seems to have peaked in the mid-1960s, at well over 2 percent, and then to have declined somewhat as China's population-control policies took hold. Over the period 1952–79 the growth rate was probably close to 2 percent per year. The growth rate of *per capita* output over the period would thus have been about 4 percent per year.

Living standards rose less rapidly, since much of the increased output was directed to investment and military purposes. But some improvement is evident, not only from aggregative statistics but from a variety of physical indicators.* Per capita availability of grain rose only slightly and of cooking oil not at all. But most other foodstuffs show an increase, though from a low base. Thus per capita availability of sugar and tea tripled and of meat products doubled (from 5.9 kilos per person per year in 1952 to 12.3 kilos in 1980). Fish and fruit supplies per capita rose about 50 percent. Supplies of cotton cloth have grown at about 2 percent per year, and there has also been an improvement in styling and variety. Production of the favorite light consumer goods—bicycles, sewing machines, radios, wrist-watches—has grown very rapidly, at rates between 15 and 25 percent per year. The amount of modern urban housing has increased substantially, and there has been a great expansion of free educational and health services.

Population, Food, and Agriculture

The new regime in 1949 faced an unusually difficult situation. Population growth was accelerating in this already densely populated country. At the same time China was land-scarce in two senses. There was virtually no room for further expansion of acreage. Further, as a result of past progress, crop yields per acre were already above the average for third-world countries, leaving less room for future improvement. China had done about all it could with traditional technology and had to look increasingly toward technical change.

There were two aspects of the agricultural problem: a *food problem,* a need to raise output at a faster rate than population was growing to permit some improvement of diet, and an *employment problem.* The rural labor force as of 1949 was seriously underemployed. And over the years 1952–78 population growth was to

---

*Most of the data that follow are from IBRD Report No. 3391–CHA, June 1, 1981, vol. 1. They are presumably drawn from official statistics made available to the IBRD mission, but they are reasonably consistent with reports by Eckstein and others.

add another 90 million to the agricultural labor force. What use could be found for this additional manpower under conditions of stationary acreage?

I have already noted that food output did grow at some 3.4 percent a year. Food-grain output grew at 2.6 percent, somewhat faster than population. Other food products—meat, fish, dairy products, sugar, fruits, and vegetables—grew typically at 3–4 percent per year, though Chinese consumption of animal products remains very low. The increase in sown area from 1952–1970 is estimated at only 0.2 percent per year. Thus increased output came almost entirely from higher output per acre.

How was this accomplished? Several factors seem to have contributed:

1. An increase of traditional inputs per hectare. Population growth and livestock growth produced increasing supplies of night soil. Collecting and spreading this fertilizer required additional amounts of labor—indeed, this is one of the most labor-consuming farm activities. The plentiful labor supply was also used to intensify cultivation in various ways: closer planting; greater use of transplanting, for wheat, corn, cotton, and other crops as well as for rice; more weeding, spraying, and pruning; more intercropping in the same plot. Chinese agriculture is more like gardening than like farming, and the amount of tender loving care can be increased almost indefinitely. The agricultural labor force was growing at about 2 percent per year; and since there is evidence that man-days worked per year were also increasing, labor inputs per hectare must have risen at more than 2 percent.

2. Continued progress in water control, making possible an expansion of double-cropping and even triple-cropping. Over the years 1957–78 some 1.8 million tube wells were installed. The amount of electricity used to run irrigation and drainage equipment rose from a negligible level to 65 million horsepower. Some 13 billion cubic meters of earthworks were constructed. Irrigated area rose from less than 30 percent to more than 40 percent of arable land. The multiple-cropping index rose from 1.31 in 1952 to 1.50 in 1978.

3. Improvement of seed varieties, mainly by selective breeding within China, but also by borrowing from IRRI and other foreign research centers.

4. A rapid increase after 1960 in the application of modern inputs to agriculture. Chemical fertilizer output, negligible before 1960, had reached 48 million tons by 1978. As of 1977 China was applying 64 kilos of chemical fertilizer per arable hectare, intermediate between Japan's 428 kilos and India's 25 kilos. (By 1980, the Chinese figure had already risen to 128 kilos.) It is not surprising that China occupies the same intermediate position in crop yields. The average Chinese rice yield (tons per hectare) in 1977–79 was 3.95. The average for other less-developed countries was 2.10 tons, while the average for the advanced industrial countries was 5.54 tons.

Rawski estimates that the supply of industrial inputs to Chinese agriculture—such as fertilizers, tube wells, cement, electric power, and a growing volume of farm machinery—grew at 20–25 percent per year between 1957 and 1978. By 1980 there were some 750,000 large and medium tractors on Chinese farms and an even larger number of power-driven hand tillers. Extensive mechanization under surplus labor conditions may appear strange. But power-driven threshing machines, plows, and cultivators help to speed up operations at the switchover point between crops and can make triple-cropping possible when otherwise it would not be. Machinery also lightens the burden of farm labor, which is a considerable benefit. Tractors are even used to transport produce and people to the nearest market, which saves walking and heavy carrying in a situation where automobiles are unavailable.

Turning to employment, we should note first the Chinese policy of restricting migration to the cities. People cannot simply wander into the city and settle in a shantytown as happens in many other developing countries. Hiring of labor by urban employers is controlled through a central employment bureau in each city. An enterprise needing aditional labor sends a requisition to the employment bureau. The bureau must satisfy itself that the employer actually needs the labor and must then seek recruits within the urban area. In principle, an applicant from the countryside cannot get a job unless those already in the city are fully employed. And without a job, the person is not eligible for housing accommodation or food rations.

The result is that surplus labor is largely dammed up in the countryside. Some net migration has occurred, and the urban population is estimated to have grown from something like 13 percent of total population in 1953 to 19 percent in 1975. Between 1957 and 1975, the Chinese labor force grew by some 148 million. Of these, about 58 million are estimated to have entered industry and other non-agricultural employment, mainly though not entirely in urban areas. This left some 90 million to be employed in agriculture. To approach full employment in the rural sector, then, it would have been necessary to find enough jobs to (1) absorb the initial underemployment existing in 1949; (2) provide for 90 million new entrants to the labor force; (3) offset some displacement of labor through farm mechanization; and (4) offset a reduction in time devoted to handicraft activity.

The most careful estimates of rural labor supply and labor use are those of Thomas Rawski (1979). Rawski first chooses a standard of full employment for a farm worker. Setting this standard at 275 days of work per year, he estimates that the degree of full employment in 1957 was only 0.58, meaning that more than 40 percent of the available labor time was unutilized. By 1975, he estimates that the degree of full employment had risen to 0.75 percent (on very conservative assumptions) or to 0.99 percent (on considerably more liberal assumptions).* Thus China, if it has not yet reached full employment, has come considerably closer to

---

*The conservative assumption is that 200 man-days per year are necessary to cultivate a hectare of land, and 100 man-days a year are required to manure that hectare. The liberal assumption sets these requirements at 300 and 130 man-days, respectively. The actual figure is probably between these limits, but the available farm survey data do not permit a precise estimate.

it. Again, the question is how this was accomplished. Factors that seem to have been important include:

1. The changes in agricultural techniques noted earlier—more labor used to spread more fertilizer, more careful cultivation, more labor needed to harvest and market the larger crop yields, expansion of double- and triple-cropping. These changes accounted for perhaps half of the increased employment.
2. A faster growth rate of more labor-intensive products—cotton, sugarcane, tobacco, tea, silk, vegetables, hogs, poultry, dairy products. Output of all these have grown faster than that of the basic grain crops. These labor-intensive products, while only one-third as large as grain output in 1957, were almost half as large by 1974.
3. A large amount of rural public-works activity. There are annual campaigns to carry out water conservancy, land improvement, reforestation, and other projects during the winter months. In recent years these efforts have involved some 30 percent of the rural labor force, or about 100 million people. Farmers seem on the average to allocate about 20 percent of their available workdays to these activities. A favorable side effect of collective agriculture is that it facilitates this mass mobilization of labor.
4. This suggests the further point that labor activity within a commune is by no means synonymous with agricultural activity. A good deal of rural small-scale industry is managed at the commune level. The rapid expansion of education, health facilities, and other social services in the communes has also absorbed substantial amounts of labor. This diversion of rural labor time from agriculture clearly eases the employment problem.

A cautionary note: application of larger labor inputs to a fixed land area seems to have encountered diminishing returns. Rawski estimates that labor's average gross productivity (yuan per man-day) was 1.46 in 1957. By 1975 it had fallen to between 1.24 and 0.94, depending on which of the employment assumptions mentioned earlier is chosen. A similar estimate of total factor productivity shows that, taking 1957 as 100, productivity had fallen by 1975 to between 64 and 74.

With the number of man-days lavished on a fixed land base rising at an estimated 4.6 percent per year from 1957 to 1975, it is perhaps surprising that productivity did not fall even more. In many regions the marginal productivity of labor must be substantially below these estimates of average productivity. In view of the limited alternatives, however, intensified use of labor even at very low productivity rates seems a reasonable course. The evidence also underlines the economic rationale for the population-control policies the government is presently pursuing.

Industrial Development

China's postwar industrial development started from a modest base that had been established in earlier decades. Factory textile production dates from the 1890s, and by the 1930s Shanghai had some 100,000 textile workers. The development of this industry before and after 1949 followed a sequence familiar from other countries—a sequence the Japanese call the "wild-geese flying" pattern, in which the curves of yarn imports, cloth imports, and textile-machinery imports turn down one after the other. The cotton-yarn cycle was completed by 1928, when China became a net yarn exporter. In cotton cloth, imports were falling as a percentage of domestic supply from 1920 onward and were falling absolutely after 1930. By 1955 China was a large net exporter of cloth. The final phase was a sharp acceleration of textile-machinery production after 1949, with China attaining a net export position by 1960.

China also had a light engineering industry dating from prewar days. In 1933 Shanghai had 972 such establishments with an employment of 20,000. Most of these had started out as repair shops for railroad equipment, shipyards, and textile machinery. Entrance to these fields was easy and scale economies were almost absent. Workshops were small, family-owned, dependent on internal finance for expansion. The more successful moved on from repairing textile machinery to making textile machinery, and before 1949 a few had already expanded into machine-tool production. After 1949, with the infusion of state funds, some of these small enterprises rapidly became very large enterprises. The nucleus of skilled workers and managers built up earlier was an important resource facilitating this expansion; and Shanghai has continued to be a major source of innovation in the engineering field.

In Manchuria, Japan had developed a substantial complex of iron and steel works, coal mining, chemicals, arsenals, shipyards, and railway repair shops. When Japan pulled out in 1945, these industries and the associated rail, road, and power infrastructure fell into Chinese hands.

The years 1949–57 saw a rapid buildup of industry. The Soviet Union provided equipment for some 200 major projects and also provided engineering, managerial, and planning training and advice. Much of the increase in chemical and engineering output, however, came from expansion and fuller utilization of preexisting enterprises. Partly on this account 1957 chemical output was 87 percent *above* the official plan targets, while machinery output was 78 percent above target. But the typical Soviet emphasis on quantity over quality, and the absorption of millions of untrained workers into the labor force, also produced considerable inefficiency.

The Great Leap years 1958–60 brought substantial disorganization of production. Normal planning, and even accurate recording of output, virtually disappeared. But the "efficiency people," led by Chou Enlai, gradually regained control. From early 1961 on political study was de-emphasized, careful management was restored, and the "quantity first" policy was reversed by a decree that goods not up to standard quality could not be counted in factory output. Monetary controls were tightened and financial criteria of performance were emphasized.

There has been substantial continuity of policy since that time. True, the first years of the Cultural Revolution brought renewed heckling of management and disruption of production. Between 1966 and 1968 industrial output dropped 14 percent. But although the Red Guards destroyed university operations for a decade, they were less successful in industry. Chou Enlai and others fought back and continued to assert the importance of systematic management. By 1969 production was once more 14 percent above 1966. As against those who criticized "placing profit in command," a 1970 official statement concluded that profits are an important measure of efficiency, which cannot safely be ignored. The initially successful Maoist attack on material incentives was undermined by the early 1970s and openly reversed in 1977, when the Deng leadership revived interest in bonuses and piece rates.

Despite these fluctuations industrial output, and particularly output of producer goods, continued to grow rapidly. Producer-goods output in 1975 was more than ten times as high as that in 1957. In addition to producing more of the same, there was a significant movement into *new* industries, notably petroleum and chemical fertilizers. Petroleum output grew 15 times between 1962 and 1977. China was able to dispense with oil imports after the mid-1960s, while at the same time raising the share of oil in total energy consumption from 5 percent to 25 percent. Chemical-fertilizer production increased tenfold between 1962 and 1977, about two-thirds of the added production coming from relatively small plants dispersed throughout the countryside.

The Chinese growth pattern since 1949 resembles the Soviet growth pattern after 1930—a strong autarkic tendency, a high rate of investment, a strong bias toward capital goods—dictated in both cases partly by military requirements. Producer-goods output since 1952 has grown at more than 15 percent per year, much above the rate for consumer goods. In consequence, producer goods' share of total industrial output rose from about 30 percent in 1949 to almost 80 percent in 1975. This is much higher than would be normal for a country of China's per capita income. As Bela Balassa remarked about the East European socialist countries, China is prematurely heavy-industry oriented. Total industrial output now forms more than 50 percent of China's gross material product, with agriculture contributing perhaps 35 percent and "material services" constituting the remainder.*

A high rate of growth in output of producer goods means by definition a high rate of investment. Investment as a proportion of national output rose from 11 percent in 1952 to a peak of 30 percent in 1958. After a collapse in the early 1960s,

---

*These ratios are influenced by which year's prices are used as a basis, and so rather different figures appear in different sources. The industry share is usually estimated in the range of 50–60 percent, the agriculture share in the range of 25–35 percent. It is clear that industry passed agriculture some time ago and has been widening its lead. There is a further implication: since three-quarters of the labor force is still engaged in agriculture, output per worker must be *much* lower in agriculture than in industry.

it recovered and has fluctuated between 25 and 30 percent since that time, the figure depending somewhat on which year's prices are used in the calculation. Until recently the development pattern was quite autarkic. Exports plus imports were typically below 10 percent of GDP, as compared with Kuznets's "large country" norm of 21 percent. More recently, however, the Deng regime has taken a more favorable view of foreign trade and invesment. Contracts have been let to foreign firms for construction of fertilizer plants, hotel building, oil drilling, and other purposes. Investment by mixed (foreign and Chinese) enterprises has been encouraged. Two export-processing zones have been established in Canton province, and others are in the planning stage. Since 1977 foreign trade has grown at 20–40 percent per year, and the trade/GDP ratio is now well above 10 percent.

Regarding composition of trade, most of the imports are requisites for development: metals and metal manufactures, 28 percent; machinery and transport equipment, 16 percent; chemicals, 10 percent; crude materials (largely textile fibers), 18 percent. But food and beverage imports are about one-fifth of the total. China normally imports wheat while exporting rice to other Asian countries, the net food balance varying with harvest conditions in a particular year. On the export side, manufactured goods form about half the total, food and beverages about 25 percent, and crude materials 20 percent.

Until recently China was reluctant to borrow and insisted on a pay-as-you-go policy. The merchandise balance of payments typically showed a small surplus. Beginning in 1974, however, foreign medium-term borrowings increased considerably, mainly for the import of entire plants, including fertilizer plants from Japan, and also for airplanes from the United States to replace aging Soviet equipment. China, unlike the Soviet Union, has also joined the IMF and the IBRD and is eligible for World Bank loans.

China's industrial growth resembles that of other third-world countries in that output has grown much faster than employment. Between 1952 and 1975, the gross output of industry increased more than ten times. But employment only tripled, rising from 12.7 million to 39.6 million workers. Industry absorbed only about 15 percent of total labor-force growth over the period.

Capital inputs to industry have risen at something like four times the rate of labor inputs, with a consequent sharp rise in the capital/labor ratio. Chinese industry is still considerably more labor intensive than American or European or Japanese industry. There is much more use of labor in supporting operations outside the central machinery processes. The small-scale rural industries are also considerably more labor intensive than city industries. The general *trend,* however, is toward growing substitution of capital for labor. A natural correlate of this trend is a high rate of increase in output per worker. Average gross output per worker rose from 2,703 yuan per year in 1952 to 9,558 yuan in 1975. With a relatively stable money wage level, this must have meant a large increase in the industrial profits remitted to government, which have helped to finance the high investment rate as well as current government operations.

Growing capital intensity is associated partly with the changing structure of industry. The fastest-growing sectors have been petroleum, machinery, chemicals, ferrous metallurgy, and electric power. All of these except machinery have capital/labor ratios above the all-industry average. In addition, however, several factors operate to restrict the employment of labor within particular establishments:

1. The planning system encourages managers to economize on *all* resources, including labor.
2. There are bureaucratic obstacles. To get more labor a manager must persuade the central employment bureau that the extra workers are really needed.
3. The restrictive attitude of government toward rural-urban migration has already been noted. In addition to putting more pressure on housing and other urban facilities, transferring a worker from agriculture to industry means a substantial increase in income and hence in demand for consumer goods, which militates against investment.
4. Plant workers naturally respond favorably to innovations that make work easier, including mechanization of strenuous activities. This is one thing a manager can do for his workers, though he is barred from changing the official wage scales.

A word should be added on the role of small and medium-sized plants operated by China's 2,000-odd counties. Rawski reports that most counties are now active in one or more branches of consumer-goods production. In addition virtually all counties have farm-machinery repair shops, 80 percent have small cement plants, 55 percent operate coal mines, 50 percent manufacture chemical fertilizer, and over half engage in a whole range of producer-goods enterprises. These enterprises have lower capital/labor ratios and lower output per worker than the larger urban establishments. They produce a high percentage of certain outputs, particularly those entering into agricultural production. As of 1972 they produced 50 percent of the building materials, 60 percent of the chemical fertilizer, 67 percent of the farm machinery, 28 percent of the coal, and 18 percent of iron and steel products. Their percentage of all industrial output, however, was only 6.3 percent.

The rural communes also operate a variety of industrial establishments. In addition to producing some goods produced also by the county industries, they do most of the agricultural processing—cotton ginning, flour milling, rice hulling. Many operate small hydroelectric power plants to meet their own requirements. They also turn out handicraft products for market or for their own consumption. These activities are quite labor intensive: average output per worker in "collective industry" is only about one-quarter as high as that in "state industry." Much of the labor supply comes from part-time work by people who are fully employed in agriculture at the peak season. Commune industries thus help to fill in valleys in the seasonal cycle—Rawski estimates that such employment is perhaps equivalent to 15 million full-time workers, which is still only 5 percent of the agricultural labor force—and they produce perhaps 10–15 percent of total industrial output.

The rapid expansion of industry has necessarily been accompanied by rapid development of economic infrastructure. Electric power generated rose from 7,261 million kilowatt-hours in 1952 to 133,800 million kilowatt-hours in 1974. Transportation has consistently received 15–20 percent of the investment budget, with more than half of this going to railroads. The rail network has grown from 22,000 kilometers in 1949 to 50,000 kilometers in 1980 and is still expanding. Motorable roads have increased from 80,000 kilometers in 1949 to about 900,000 kilometers.

But China is still very railway-oriented, and water transport also retains its traditional importance. In 1979 the railroads still carried 53 percent of freight traffic and the waterways 44 percent, while only 3 percent moved by road transport.

The Distribution of Income

Income equalization ranks high among official policy objectives, and it is usually said that China has done better in this respect than most other low-income countries. To what extent is this view supported by hard evidence?

Two things seem clear. First, China has succeeded in establishing a poverty floor through rationing of certain necessities—grain, cooking oil, cotton cloth—and through free or heavily subsidized provision of health facilities, education, urban housing, and urban transport. This minimum standard of living is low, but extreme poverty has been eliminated. One does not see in Chinese cities the ragged clothing, emaciated bodies, running sores, people sleeping on sidewalks or in parks, and other evidence of human misery common in many other parts of Asia.

Second, with regard to incomes above the minimum, there was a marked shift toward greater equality in the 1950s. In the countryside, rich landowners disappeared and income differences based on land ownership were eliminated. In the cities, property income and private business income disappeared, and the new salary scales for managers and officials provided lower salary premiums than had existed previously. The lower end of the income distribution was raised through minimum wages and a rather generous pension system.

But substantial income differences remain, and it is not certain that there has been much further movement toward equality since the 1950s. Let us look briefly at the rural distribution, the urban distribution, and the size of the rural-urban gap.

In agriculture, the overriding fact is wide geographic differences in output per agricultural worker. The richest provinces, in the northeast and the Yangtze Delta, have outputs per worker more than twice as high as those in some provinces in the south and southwest. And there are further differences among counties within provinces. Perkins states that the six richest agricultural counties in the country have a per capita income six times as high as that of the six poorest counties. These productivity differences show up in the average income distributed to commune members and hence in private consumption. Disparities in provision of health, education, and other public services are mitigated, however, by fiscal transfers through the national budget. The richer provinces are required to remit a high proportion of their tax collections to Peking, while the poorer provinces receive substantial subsidies.

Regional differences in industrial output per worker are even wider than those in agriculture. In Tientsin and Peking, output per industrial worker is five times as high as that for the country as a whole, and in Shanghai it is more than ten times the national average. Disparities arise from differences in industry mix, scale of plant, level of technology, and experience of the labor force. There is a marked correlation between regional differentials in industry and agriculture. Provinces with relatively high agricultural output per worker tend also to have relatively high industrial productivity, but the regional variations in industry are more extreme.

But in industry, unlike agriculture, there is no necessary connection between productivity levels and personal income levels. There are standard wage and salary schedules for industry, and indeed for all state enterprises, which are applied rather uniformly throughout the country. Productivity differences, then, show up mainly as differences in profits rather than in income distributed to workers. The skilled-unskilled wage differential is about 3:1, which is not unusual for countries at an early stage of industrialization, though considerably wider than what prevails in the advanced industrial countries. The highest salaries, for top managers and officials, are about four times the earnings of skilled workers, but very few receive these salaries.

The distribution of income among urban households seems to be substantially more even than among rural households. Household sample surveys show a Gini coefficient of about 0.16 in urban areas, compared with 0.31 in rural areas.* An important factor in the urban distribution is the number of wage-earners per household. Because of greater availability of jobs, plus reduction of sex discrimination and the opening of careers to women, the labor-force participation rate in cities has risen from about 42 percent in the 1950s to 55 percent at present. A family with two or three wage-earners will obviously have more income than a single-earner family and can live rather comfortably by Chinese standards.

The wage-salary structure has remained rather stable over the years. Wage adjustments are infrequent because the price level has been held stable and there has been no need for the frequent cost-of-living adjustments that occur in most other countries. When wages are raised, there is a mild tendency to raise the lower

---

*These estimates, which appear in the IBRD mission report cited earlier, should be viewed with caution.

labor grades more than the higher grades on a percentage basis, with a consequent compression of skill differentials. But this tendency is not strong enough to have a marked effect on the urban income distribution.

The rural-urban income gap varies considerably by region. It is widest in the agriculturally poor regions, because of the substantial uniformity of urban wage scales. For the nation as a whole, the IBRD study reports that urban per capita income is currently 2.2 times as high as rural per capita income. This gap arises mainly from higher earnings per worker, but also partly from the higher labor-force participation rate, which is about 55 percent in urban areas compared with 42 percent in rural areas. If this estimate for China is roughly correct, it seems in line with corresponding estimates for other low-income countries. On a *household* rather than a per capita basis, the urban/rural ratio is estimated as follows: China, 1.7; Bangladesh, 1.5; India, 1.8; Sri Lanka, 1.7; Indonesia, 2.1; Malaysia, 2.1; Philippines, 2.3.

Regarding trends over time, it appears that the rural-urban gap has been somewhat narrowed. Procurement prices for farm crops have been roughly doubled since the 1950s (which has meant ever-larger budget subsidies to hold retail prices stable and avoid upsetting the money wage level). Meanwhile the prices paid by rural households for industrial goods have risen only about 10 percent. This improvement in agriculture's terms of trade has added more to real farm income than the increase in physical quantities marketed. On the other side, the provision of public services in the cities is clearly more ample than in the countryside, and here the gap may have widened over time. The gap in labor-force participation rates has also widened, pushing up relative per capita income in the cities. Overall, the rural-urban gap has probably narrowed, but this is not completely certain.

To sum up: China has succeeded in cutting off the two tails of the income distribution. Extremes of wealth and poverty have been eliminated. Substantial differences in income remain. But these seem if anything to be narrowing rather than widening, contrary to Kuznets's hypothesis that income distribution tends to become more unequal in the early stages of accelerated economic growth.

12

India

India, like China, is rather more than a country. The common term *subcontinent* is suggestive. Again like China, India is very large, densely populated, predominantly rural with (until recently) poor communications from the interior to the seacoast, and with marked regional differences in income levels and rates of growth. In a thorough economic history, which cannot be undertaken here, these regional differences would stand out as predominant.

But India differs from China in important respects. The population is less homogeneous, in terms of religion, language, and ethnic origin. Hereditary castes and the linkage of caste with occupation impose unusually strong barriers to economic mobility. Further, India had a long period of British colonial rule. The conventional wisdom, enshrined in Indian nationalist writings, contrasts economic stagnation under the British with rapid growth since independence. Continuing poverty of the Indian population is attributed to colonial economic policies, which focused on advancing Britain's economic interests and, apart from this, took little interest in modernizing the economy for the benefit of Indians. Only with independence was it possible for the country to adopt policies leading to sustained economic growth.

We shall find that this picture needs revision with regard to both the earlier and the recent period. The Indian economy from 1800 to 1947 was by no means stagnant. Significant internal changes took place as India was welded into the international economy. There was even, during certain periods, a creeping rise of per capita income. While domestic economic development was not the prime concern of the colonial rulers, they did some things that laid the foundations for later development. And accelerated economic growth after 1947, while owing something to the greater freedom of maneuver permitted by independent government, also owed much to the world economic boom of 1945–73 and the increased availability of foreign loans and grants.

Having said this, we must recognize that 1947 was a watershed date and that it is reasonable to take it as marking the turning point to intensive growth.

EXTENSIVE GROWTH, 1800–1947

India came under the domination of the British East India Company in the eighteenth century. The company controlled foreign trade, and its auxiliary activities penetrated gradually into the interior. It was supported by British troops to the extent necessary to protect its property and trade routes. A significant revision of the company's charter in 1833 ended its economic monopoly and opened the way to private British enterprise. After the Indian Mutiny of 1857, administrative responsibility was transferred from the company to the Crown. India became formally a British possession, with political authority exercised by a British viceroy. The discussion here relates mainly to the period after 1857, though I shall also note significant earlier developments.

Population Growth

Population growth was intermittent, interrupted frequently by famines and epidemics. Deepak Lal (1984) lists 61 famines, usually regional in scope, between 1800 and 1950, with an estimated mortality of 38.7 million. The influenza epidemic after World War I is estimated to have caused 9–18 million deaths.

The long-term trend, however, was upward. Durand (1974) estimates the population at 190 million in 1800, 235 million in 1850, and 285 million in 1900. Lal estimates the average annual rate of increase at 0.46 percent per year from 1840 to 1881 and at 0.44 percent from 1881 to 1921. These figures indicate a crude birthrate in the high forties, near the biological maximum, combined with a high and secularly stable mortality rate. No acceleration of population growth is evident before 1920.

Agriculture and Food Output

Agriculture has always been the dominant sector of the economy; it occupies the bulk of the population and until recently generated more than half of national output. An estimate for 1901 shows 69.4 percent of the labor force employed either as cultivators (50.3 percent) or agricultural laborers (19.1 percent). By 1951 this proportion had *risen* slightly, to 73.3 percent.

How did the slowly growing population manage to feed itself? The main explanation, during the period we are considering, was expansion of cultivated acreage. The land was heavily settled, but not yet fully settled. Nineteenth-century data are fragmentary, but for years after 1900 we can speak with more confidence. Alan Heston (in Kumar and Desai, 1983) estimates that from 1891 to 1941 crop acreage increased at 0.40 percent per year. Output of commercial crops grew faster than that of food grains, but food-grain acreage grew at 0.31 percent per year. Sown area grew somewhat faster than cultivated area because of gradual extension of irrigation and double-cropping. There was also a modest increase in yields. Heston estimates that agricultural output grew at about 0.60 percent per year. Even with some bias toward commercial crops, then, food-grain output grew at roughly the same rate as population, which permitted a low, essentially stationary, level of diets, with marked year-to-year fluctuations.

Agricultural methods changed little. There was continued heavy reliance on manure, and supplies of chemical fertilizer were very small. The colonial administrators attempted to supply better seeds for rice, wheat, sugarcane, cotton, and jute, mainly in Punjab and Sind provinces. In 1938–39 acreage in improved seed as a proportion of total acreage was 32.9 percent in Greater Punjab and 15.8 percent in Bombay-Sind, but only 6.2 percent in Greater Bengal, 5.0 percent in United Provinces, and 11.1 percent for the country as a whole.

The main source of higher yields, however, was more-intensive cultivation, application of more labor inputs per acre. As in China, population growth provided both the need and the inputs required for larger output. Lal estimates that, from 1901 to 1941, total area sown rose by 4.5 percent, the agricultural labor force by 12.6 percent, and net agricultural output at constant prices by 31.6 percent. There was thus a significant rise in the labor/land ratio and a substantial rise in both the output/land and output/labor ratios.

British colonial policy was initially very laissez-faire. But after about 1870, with the harsh experience of repeated famines, the government began to promote irrigation schemes. These were financed in London but were expected to be self-supporting through water charges. Government also encouraged private irrigation through wells and smaller irrigation projects. The amount of irrigated land rose from 13.2 million hectares in 1900 to 18.9 million hectares in 1930, by which time it was approaching 20 percent of total crop acreage. These schemes were developed mainly to supplement rainfall in drier areas such as the Punjab, rather than in wetter monsoon areas or the Gangetic floodplain. Thus the percentage of land irrigated varied from 55.5 percent in Greater Punjab to 15.0 percent in Greater Bengal and 4.8 percent in the Central Provinces. Lal argues that this policy directed irrigation investment toward areas in which its marginal yield was highest.

After independence, Punjab continued to be in the forefront of agricultural progress. Its success was not a new development but one which took shape during the colonial period.

Industrial Growth

Throughout the colonial period, "industry" was dominated by small-scale production by artisans and "cottage industries." Textile mills were built from the 1850s onward, and a variety of other factory industries emerged after 1900. But even in 1920, factories employed less than 1 percent of the labor force. Of the 10 percent classified as engaged in manufacturing at that time, the great majority were handicraftsmen. The factory share of manufacturing output, however, was considerably higher than its share of employment because of markedly higher capital/labor and output/labor ratios.

India's handicraft tradition goes back for centuries. In addition to supplying the domestic market, India had long-standing trade connections with East Africa, the Persian Gulf region, and the Far East. Indeed, India was more important as a textile exporter before 1800 than it has been at any later time. Descriptions of the organization of cotton-cloth production read much like descriptions of the putting-out system in England or Western Europe. An Indian merchant typically supplied yarn to the weaver and bought the cloth output, paying what amounted to a piece rate. Sometimes a number of weavers were brought under one roof in a "factory," but since economies of scale were small the incentive to do this was not strong. Factories for dyeing and finishing, however, were often of substantial size. Cloth for export was typically resold to a British foreign trade house, which usually confined itself to the export trade. Some of the British houses, however, also engaged in putting-out operations.

The impact of imported factory goods on handicraft production after 1800 was adverse but uneven. It was felt first and most severely in the coastal cities rather than in the interior, which had poor communications with the coast before the 1860s. It was felt more severely in cotton spinning than in weaving, because it is in spinning that the technological superiority of the factory is largest. The Indian handloom weavers, indeed, survived rather better than their English counterparts. They survivied partly by concentrating on coarser cloth and on the rural market, partly by taking advantage of cheap machine-made yarn. Eventually they lost ground to Indian textile mills, which after 1850 cut increasingly into both imports and handicraft production. As late as 1900, however, handloom production was still twice as large as factory production. Even in the years 1900–40, handicraft production does not seem to have fallen in absolute terms, though its market share diminished because of the faster growth of factory output.

In other areas of marked technological inferiority, such as iron smelting and metalworking, handicrafts also declined in the face of factory competition. But handicraft producers held onto many fields through product adaptation, improvements in tools and techniques, availability of new types or sources of raw materials, markets sheltered by transport cost, or consumer attachment to traditional products. Gadgil (1971) notes that in fields where production and demand were both widespread—textiles, metalworking, woodworking, leather products—a kind of stratification developed. Handicraftsmen continued to produce luxury goods for the urban market. The mass urban market was served largely by factory-produced goods. But handicraft products continued to supply a large share of the rural market. Blacksmiths, carpenters, leather workers, and potters were generally local, as were resource-based industries such as forest products, paper, and glass. With urbanization and industrialization new types of artisan production developed—for the making of cigarettes, soap, trunks, safes, cupboards, furniture, electroplating, locks, cutlery, auto parts. Further, factory output at an earlier stage of production often helped handicraft workers to survive at a later stage. Machine yarn helped the handloom weavers. Synthetic dyes aided cloth dyeing. Factory production of sheet metal helped the brass and coppersmiths. The blacksmiths took advantage of rolled iron, and sewing machines increased the productivity of tailors.

Factory industry, in addition to facing import competition without tariff barriers, was hampered by internal circumstances. Except for railway building from the 1850s onward, infrastructure was poorly developed, and new industries often had to provide their own. In attracting capital, industry had to compete with the large and quick profits available in trade. The banking system was little developed, and the British banks concentrated on foreign trade rather than domestic finance. In addition to Brahmin distaste for commerce, the humanistic bias of Indian universities, which had been patterned on British lines, was not conducive to producing entrepreneurs, engineers, and managers. Educated Indians aspired rather to the civil service, which carried high prestige in India as in Britain. Labor was plentiful but entirely untrained. Since it appeared cheap, management used it wastefully, with little concern for training, discipline, and productivity. There is abundant evidence that the ''labor problems'' of early industrialization are mainly management problems; and this was as true in India as anywhere else.

The two centers of industrial growth were the Bengal Presidency and the relatively new port city of Bombay. After the East India Company's monopoly was ended in 1833, private British enterprise began to come into Bengal, mainly in the form of the ''managing agency system,'' under which each agency managed a variety of enterprises on behalf of absentee British owners. By the late 1830s British enterprise already extended to sugar manufacture, rice and flour mills, indigo and tea plantations, shipyards, and mining, as well as foreign trade, banking, and insurance. British capital was to dominate Bengal for a long time. The first jute factory, for example, was started by a Scot in 1854.

But in Bombay, which became the main textile center, Indian entrepreneurship was dominant. The first cotton mill was started in 1854 by a Parsi family previously engaged in foreign and internal trade. The great majority of the early mills were founded by Parsi merchants engaged in the yarn and cloth trade at home and in the East African and Chinese markets abroad. By 1890, 69 additional mills had opened, and there was a slower but steady expansion thereafter. Thus India, which had lost to Lancashire on the handicraft side, began to get its own back through factory output. After 1875, India was once more a textile exporter; and the domestically produced proportion of cotton-cloth consumption rose from 8 percent in 1896 to 76 percent in 1945 (part of this, of course, still being handicraft production).

Cotton textiles were a natural area for Indian enterprise for several reasons: a local source of raw materials, a large domestic market already pioneered by imports, standardized machinery that could be purchased abroad and whose operation required little skill, and an ample labor supply. Indian mills rapidly became competitive in the coarser grades of cloth, and after 1900 moved into higher counts as well. Profit rates were high. A 1905 survey showed them averaging more than 50 percent of paid-up capital, which provided both incentive and finance for continued expansion.

Another Parsi, Jamsetji Tata, founded a company that established India's first steel mill in 1911 and that became what is still the largest industrial dynasty in the private sector. The example of this firm initiated a gradual but definite shift toward heavier types of industry. The years 1914–45 saw diversification of manufacturing into foundries; metallurgical plants; ordnance factories; the production of cement, paper, bicycles and motorcycles, textile machinery; and other fields. A shift of colonial policy in the 1920s permitted imposition of import duties for the first time. Although this was done for revenue purposes, it had an incidental protective effect.

In 1946, however, 43 percent of factory employees were still in cotton textiles and 23 percent in jute textiles, compared with 5 percent in steel and 7.5 percent in engineering. Total factory employment of 1.5 million was still only 1 percent of the labor force, though another million employed in coal mining and railroading could be considered part of the "modern" sector. The manufacturing share of total employment *fell* slightly between 1901 and 1951, as agriculture continued to absorb rather more than its share of the growing labor force.

I should add a word on wage behavior, since it plays a considerable role in development theory. The evidence suggests two-way flexibility of both money and real wages, in both the urban and rural sectors, in response to changing demand and supply conditions. Thus wages shot up temporarily after the plague of 1898 and again after the influenza epidemic of 1921. Real wages also fluctuated because of price fluctuations, with money wages generally lagging behind the movement of prices. Lal finds no clear trend in real agricultural wages before 1910. After that there appears to have been a mild uptrend, but one having violent fluctuations—including a collapse of wages from 1933 to 1942, followed by a recovery to 1947. In industry, Morris (1965) finds no trend in the real hiring wage for unskilled labor from 1870 to 1920. After that, there was a distinct upward movement in the real unskilled wage. This phenomenon of rising real wages in the face of ample labor supplies is common in developing countries; it is usually attributed to institutional elements in wage determination—minimum-wage legislation, trade-union pressure, and overpricing of labor in the public sector.

Infrastructure and Foreign Trade

Railway building began in the 1850s, and by 1869 some 6,000 miles of track had been laid. The rail network continued to expand gradually in later decades, reaching 43,000 miles by 1932. The initial policy was to encourage private railway construction by guaranteeing a minimum profit rate of 5 percent. Somewhat later government began to assume ownership of lines, while continuing to contract out management to private companies. The railways were fully taken over by government in the 1920s. The location of lines, as well as the freight rate structure, was oriented toward moving raw materials to the ports; and not until the 1920s was the rate structure revised to give more-equitable treatment to internal trade. Even so, reduction of transport costs had an important internal impact. It stimulated commercialization and specialization in agriculture. Instead of producing all their requirements, farmers could now sell some things and buy others. The result was not so much a displacement of food acreage by nonfood acreage as a general reorganization of production. Better transportation also materially reduced the risk of localized famines. Although the railroad injured some handicrafts by facilitating the movement of imported factory goods into the interior, it benefited Indian-made factory goods as these grew in importance.

Government investment in irrigation has already been noted. There was also extensive road building, as motor transport became more important. By 1939 there were 64,000 miles of hard-surfaced roads. There was substantial investment in port facilities. Electric power receives little attention in the literature, the implication being that many of the new industries maintained their own generating facilities.

Overall, infrastructure investment was moderate rather than impressive. As late as the 1930s, public investment was only 1–2 percent of GNP. (For comparison, this rose rapidly after independence, reading 6.6 percent of GNP in 1960–61.) The British taxed relatively lightly, and colonial finances were always precarious, being subject in particular to ''monsoon shocks.'' About 40 percent of expenditure went for military purposes, and most of the rest for general administration and current services. Investment was estimated at 27 percent of government expenditure in 1927, and 15–18 percent in the 1930s.

India, like other very large countries, has always had a relatively low trade ratio. Maddison (1972) estimates exports at 10.7 percent of GNP 1913, though this seems on the high side. There was some drain on Indian resources through a typical export surplus. Maddison estimates this surplus at 1.5 percent of GNP, a not inconsiderable amount.

The main export products as of 1911–13 were jute, 21 percent; cotton, 21 percent; food grains, 15 percent; hides and skins, 11 percent; oilseeds, cake and oil, 10 percent; tea, 7 percent; and opium, 4 percent. This list is more diversified than that of most developing countries. But the growth rate of exports was low. During the years 1870–1914 many tropical countries were raising exports at 3–4 percent a year. India's agricultural exports, on the other hand, were growing at only 1.4 percent a year. Neither the size nor the growth rate of exports was sufficient to provide a strong stimulus to the economy.

Why did primary exports grow so slowly? Lal's diagnosis is that India lacked not wetlands as such, but rather *unoccupied* wet lands, that is, land not already devoted to rice cultivation. Continuation of rice growing was not due to any irrational preference among subsistence farmers, but rather to the fact that it paid better than the new commercial crops, based on relative prices. The problem was not faulty public policy, but rather soil and climate constraints, within which farmers probably responded appropriately to the opportunities open to them. India's comparative advantage has probably never lain in any massive expansion of tropical exports.

But what about labor-intensive manufactured exports? We have already noted that India began to export factory textiles around 1875, and by 1913 manufactures were about 20 percent of total exports. But here, too, India failed to mount a sustained drive against foreign competition. In yarn exports to China it lost out to Japanese competition, and by the 1920s Japanese cloth was coming into India at an ominous rate, largely replacing the earlier Lancashire menace. This new challenge was countered by imposition of tariffs in the 1920s and by trade agreements between Japan and Britain to restrict textile imports in the 1930s. But these measures were scarcely an adequate answer to the underlying lack of competitiveness. Writings on the industry by Morris and others suggest that part of the problem lay in loose management, including poor management of the labor force. Although Indian wages were relatively low, output per worker was still lower. This problem, and the tendency to respond to it by protectionist, inward-looking policies, has continued into the postindependence period.

National-Income Estimates

It is now time to pull this sectoral discussion together by looking at estimates of national income and income per capita. These estimates are very rough for the nineteenth century, partly because of inadequate agricultural statistics, but somewhat better from 1900 onward. Further, the data have been reviewed carefully by Mukherjee (1969), Heston (in Kumar and Desai, 1983), Lal (1984), and others.

There seems to have been no significant trend in per capita income before about 1860. For the period 1860–1920, the data suggest a slight and intermittent uptrend. Estimates of the increase in per capita income over this period fall in the range of 0.4–0.6 percent per year. This increase seems to have ceased after 1920, partly because of a speeding up of population growth. Per capita income in 1950 was if anything a bit lower than that in 1920.

One cannot argue, then, that there was any marked improvement in welfare during the colonial period. But neither can one make a case for immiserization of the population. The impression of a very modest improvement in living standards is supported by several physical indicators reported by Lal. For example, the male literacy rate rose from 9.8 percent in 1901 to 25.6 percent in 1951, though the female literacy rate fell from 10.7 to 7.9. The infant mortality rate fell from 295 per thousand in 1901 to 199 in 1951. Male life expectancy rose from 23.7 to 32.5 years, and female life expectancy from 25.6 to 31.7 years.

I judge that these improvements are too small to justify dating the turning point to intensive growth before 1947. This view is supported by the fact that before 1947 the economy did not experience the structural changes in composition of output that normally accompany intensive growth. There is a striking similarity in the industrial distribution of the labor force in 1875, 1900, and 1950. Data for 1901 and 1951, estimated originally by J. Krishnamurty and reported in Lal, are as follows:

| | *Distribution of Labor Force (percent)* | |
	1901	*1951*
Cultivators	50.3	52.2
Agricultural laborers	19.1	21.1
Livestock, forestry, fisheries	3.8	2.4
Mining	0.1	0.4
Manufacturing	10.1	8.7
Construction	1.0	1.3
Trade and commerce	5.1	5.2
Transport and communications	1.1	1.5
Other services	9.3	7.2

Modest changes there certainly were. The urban population grew from 10.8 percent to 17.6 percent of the total. Industrial output grew somewhat faster than agricultural output; and within the industrial sector, factory output grew faster than handicraft output. But factory industry was still on the fringes of the economy rather than central to its operation. Thus any argument for a pre-1947 "takeoff" would be hard to sustain.

It should be added that the figure of average per capita income conceals wide variation around the average. The Heston study includes an appendix on estimates of regional per capita income. The range is typically greater than 2:1, with Bombay at the top and Bengal, Bihar, and Orissa at the bottom. The variation by type of occupation is even wider. Heston's estimates of value added per worker, in rupees per year at 1946/47 prices, are as follows:

	1900	*1947*
Agriculture	273	297
Manufacturing	1,196	1,900
Small-scale industry	289	488
Professional	330	559
Transport and commerce	568	874

Note that small-scale industry, reasonably in line with agriculture in 1900, had pulled considerably ahead by 1947, and factory industry had pulled ahead even more markedly.

The Impact of Colonialism

Did British rule, in addition to preventing national independence, seriously retard the growth of the economy? Here one must choose carefully among arguments that seem clearly warranted and others that are less well grounded. Much has been made, for example, of the decline of Indian handicrafts in the face of imported factory goods. We have noted that this impact was limited to certain types of handicraft, notably cotton spinning and weaving. The decline of home production of textiles was a universal feature of the nineteenth century, in independent countries as well as in colonies. The fate of Indian home spinners and weavers would not have been very different if they had faced competition not from Lancashire mills but from Indian mills, as they did increasingly after 1850. Any effort to protect home spinning and weaving could scarcely have been more than a delaying action, with questionable economic justification.

In regard to agriculture, it has been argued that British policies led to concentration of land ownership, increased exploitation of the peasants by landlords, moneylenders, and government, the growth of a landless class, and immiserization of the rural population. But after surveying the evidence, Lal comes to the following conclusions.

1. The British introduced a new class of "tax farmer"—the zamindars—between landowner and tenant. But it can be shown that, if this new group is less risk-averse than the owners and if there is some cost sharing with tenants, the effect of zamindari on output will be favorable and the tenants' income may quite possibly increase.
2. The tax burden declined substantially. Under Moghul rule, the land tax was about 15 percent of national income. By the end of the colonial period, land taxes were only 1 percent, and total taxes only 6 percent, of national income. This is one reason for land prices rising substantially.
3. Data on land ownership show a continuous gradation from large to small holdings, rather than the sharp dualism characteristic of Latin American countries. Sample surveys typically find 10 percent of owners holding about 50 percent of the land. But there is no evidence of increasing concentration over time—the Gini coefficients remain rather stable.
4. Neither is there evidence that landless laborers increased as a percentage of the rural population. The proportion remained rather stable, in the range of 15–20 percent.
5. It is sometimes argued that growing commercialization of agriculture led to a shift away from food grains toward cotton and other cash crops, a reduction of domestic food supplies, and increased exposure to famine. But there is little evidence that the absolute amount of land planted to food grains decreased; and railroad construction certainly reduced the famine risk.

The British clearly did not encourage development of Indian manufacturing. The policy to "Buy British," applied most rigorously on the railroads, interfered with normal backward linkages that might otherwise have led to earlier development of Indian capacity in iron and steel, transport equipment, and machinery. (Not until the Depression of the 1930s were the Tata interests able to win an agreement that the railroads would use Indian steel.) It has been argued also that an independent government could have used protective tariffs to accelerate the pace of import substitution. But tariff arguments, as is well known, are always two-edged. Lal believes that free trade was not adverse to Indian development and that "by contrast the creeping protection offered to Indian industry in the twentieth century . . . began that process of inward-looking industrial development which was to reach both its height as well as its limits within a decade of India achieving its independence."

Morris Morris (in Kumar and Desai, 1983) concludes that slow development of manufacturing was the result of complex Indian conditions and of weaknesses on both the demand and supply sides, rather than of specific British policies: "No single act of policy or single change of behavior could have made for much more rapid progress than did occur."

A stronger criticism might be that British rule tended to bar Indians from occupational advancement. This was notably true in the higher levels of the civil service and the army, where British staffing prevailed. It was somewhat less true in the private sector. British enterprise no doubt precluded Indian enterprise in some areas. But Indian merchants and manufacturers were always prominent, and the relative importance of Indian enterprise increased as the twentieth century wore on.

British domination of the administrative and military establishments involved some resource drain on the economy. Most of these services could have been performed equally well by Indians, paid in local currency at local salary scales.

Against any adverse effects of British rule must be set a number of positive accomplishments. The British established political unity over the subcontinent, and even the struggle against their rule contributed to a growing sense of nationhood. They established the law and order that is a precondition for economic growth and developed an effective administrative service that could be carried over largely intact to the postindependence era. They introduced joint-stock companies, modern banking, and other economic institutions. They linked the economy with the world market. They built substantial amounts of infrastructure. Not least important was the development of human infrastructure through an educational program that includes the largest university system in the third world.

I noted in chapter 3 that colonialism raises several distinct issues. We might ask: would the Indian economy have advanced faster if the British had never appeared on the scene? This counterfactual question is unanswerable. No one can say whether some Indian ruler would have established political and administrative control over the subcontinent, whether this hypothetical ruler would have been interested in economic growth, and whether he would have fashioned effective economic policies.

Suppose instead we ask: did British rule, on balance, retard or accelerate the development of the economy? Did it postpone the beginning of intensive growth?

This requires a weighing of pros and cons, some of which have been suggested above, and careful scholars might well come out with differing judgments. Although intercountry comparisons are suspect, it may be relevant to note that China, which was never a colony, did not do notably better than India before 1950.

Finally, we may ask: could the colonial rulers have done more to develop the economy and to initiate intensive growth? The answer to this is clearly yes. The London authorities understandably treated India as a source of raw materials, a market for British manufactures, an arena for British enterprise, and a strategic anchor post of the empire. Had they instead concentrated on developing the Indian economy for the benefit of its residents, both policies and results would have been different.

INTENSIVE GROWTH, 1947–80

The question of whether colonial policies served as a precondition of growth can be interpreted in different senses. It could mean: was the Indian economy in 1947 in a better position to embark on intensive growth than it had been fifty or a hundred years earlier? The answer to this question is yes. Several features that were to prove helpful in later decades had their roots in the previous century: an educated elite, readily capable of assuming the responsibilities of government; an effective administrative service, increasingly Indian-staffed; a tradition of peaceable settlement of political and economic differences; a large and growing entrepreneurial class; the beginnings of a factory labor force; established linkages with foreign markets; a road and rail network that facilitated internal commerce; introduction of banks, corporations, and other modern economic institutions; and substantial commercialization of the rural sector.

But these circumstances, while favorable, were in no way compelling. They would not have led inevitably to the beginning of intensive growth. The decisive event was national independence, conceded voluntarily by Britain in 1947 after decades of internal pressure. Even with the separation of Pakistan, India retained most of the area of the subcontinent and a more than proportionate share of its industry, entrepreneurship, infrastructure, and administrative staff. The new Indian government had a charismatic leader, Jawaharlal Nehru, an ideology that attached high priority to economic growth, an abundance of economic advice from both Indian and foreign economists, and a fund of international goodwill that included willingness to provide capital on concessional terms.

The new India also stood at the threshold of a great boom in world output and world trade, which was to last for a generation. As it turned out, India did not take advantage of this favorable environment as fully as did some other economies. But it did achieve a moderate, sustained rise in per capita income.

Population Growth

Population growth began to accelerate several decades before independence. In the 1920s the growth rate rose above 1 percent, and it continued to creep upward thereafter. By the 1950s it had risen above 2 percent, and then leveled off at about 2.2 percent in the 1960s and 1970s. While the crude birthrate fell from 44 per thousand in 1960 to 36 in 1980, the crude deathrate also fell from 22 to 14, leaving the rate of natural increase essentially unchanged.

There is substantial interstate variation in both mortality rates and birthrates. In 1976–78, the crude birthrate was 40.3 per thousand in Uttar Pradesh but only 26.4 in Kerala. Factors responsible for the lower rate in Kerala include: an unusually high literacy rate, with little difference between men and women; an unusually high educational level for women; perhaps partly on this account, an average age at marriage of 21, compared with 16 in some other states; and a high proportion of wage workers as against farm-family workers.

India has an active family-planning program, which seems to be making modest progress. It is estimated that some 24 percent of married couples were practicing family planning in 1980, though with wise interstate variation. In Kerala, which is near the top, it is estimated that about 40 percent of the decline in the crude birthrate can be attributed to family planning, the remaining 60 percent to "natural causes." But this distinction is somewhat artificial, since such "natural causes" as literacy and education must have made women more receptive to family planning.

Total and Per Capita Output

It will be useful to look at overall economic results before examining sector performance. The GNP growth rate varies considerably from year to year, mainly because of weather-induced fluctuations in agricultural output. On average, however, it has run in the range of 3.6–3.8 percent per year since 1950. With population growing at a bit over 2 percent, this has meant an increase of around 1.5 percent per year in per capita income. Lal's estimates of annual increases in per capita income are as follows: 1951–55, 1.7 percent; 1956–60, 2.0 percent; 1961–65, 0.0 percent (there were two bad monsoons at the end of this period); 1966–69, 1.8 percent; 1970–74, 1.1 percent; 1974–80, 1.5 percent. The impression is one of moderate but persistent growth. The index of real per capita output rises from 100.0 in 1950 to 145.4 in 1980, with only a few declines associated with crop failures.

This picture of moderate but sustained improvement is confirmed by physical indicators of health and education. For boys, the percentage of the relevant age group in primary school rose from 59 in 1950–51 to 98 in 1976–77; in middle school, from 21 to 49 percent; and in secondary school from 9 to 29 percent. The percentages for girls show an even sharper increase, though they are still only about half as high as for boys. University enrollment has increased tenfold, from 300,000 in 1950–51 to 3,200,000 in 1976–77. The literacy rate has risen from 25 percent to 46 percent for males, and from 8 percent to 25 percent for females.

Regarding health, the crude deathrate fell from 27 per thousand in 1950 to 14 in 1980. Infant mortality has dropped from 199 per thousand in 1951 to 125 at present; and life expectancy at birth has risen from 32 years to 51 years.

There have been substantial changes in the composition of output, again confirming the reality of intensive growth. Agriculture's share of net domestic product, which was still 57.0 percent in 1950–51, had fallen to 40.0 percent by 1980–81. The manufacturing share has risen from 10.0 to 15.4 percent, while services have risen from 26 to 36 percent. The service-sector total includes public administration and defense, 11 percent; transport, communications, and trade, 19 percent; and banking, insurance, and real estate, 6 percent.

The distribution of the labor force, as usual, differs considerably from the distribution of output. As of 1978, 49.1 percent of the labor force were farm operators and 22.3 percent farm laborers, for a total of 71.4 percent in agriculture. An additional 19 percent worked in the "unorganized sector" of the economy— 12.4 percent as self-employed, 6.7 percent as wage or salary earners. Less than 10 percent are wage and salary earners in the "organized sector," in which public employees (5.7 percent) decidedly outnumber private employees (3.8 percent). These figures suggest both the limited development of "modern" employment and the dominant weight of the public sector.

The changes in end uses of output are also familiar. The gross investment/GDP ratio has risen from 13 percent in the 1950s to 23 percent in 1980. More than half of this is public-sector investment, which peaked at 63.6 percent of all investment in the third (1961–65) plan period, but fell back to 57.6 percent in the fifth plan period. Government production of current services has increased from 7 to 10 percent of GDP. Thus the share of private consumption, which was close to 90 percent in 1950–51, has fallen to around 70 percent today.

There are substantial regional differences in per capita income, which have probably become somewhat wider since 1950. In 1975–76 Punjab, which had pulled ahead of Maharashtra as the richest state, had a per capita income of 551 rupees, compared with 201 rupees in Manipur and 214 in Bihar.

Agriculture and Food Supply

Although manufacturing has been the glamour sector since 1950, agriculture continues as the basic underpinning of the economy and employs over 70 percent of the labor force. The race between population and food supply is still a central fact of life. Food supply has been gaining slightly in this race, particularly since the late 1960s, but the future remains uncertain.

The growth rate of agricultural output has been uneven because of monsoon fluctuations, but overall has averaged about 3 percent per year. The growth rate was higher in the 1970s than in previous decades, and the sources of growth changed materially, with increases of sown acreage less important and yield increases considerably more important. From 1949–50 to 1964–65, sown area increased at 1.6 percent per year, partly through cultivation of more unirrigated land and partly through extension of irrigation. Yields per acre rose at 1.5 percent per year, giving an output growth rate of 3.1 percent. Between 1967–68 and 1977–78, on the other hand, sown acreage rose at only 0.7 percent a year while yields rose at 2.7 percent per year, for an output growth rate of 3.4 percent. Food-grain output has grown at about the same rate as non-food-grain output. Among food grains, however, wheat has become more important relative to rice as a result of a breakthrough in wheat technology from the late 1960s onward.

The fact that food output has at least kept pace with demand is confirmed by other indicators. Over the years 1951–79 the terms of trade between manufactures and foodstuffs have fluctuated considerably, but there is no clear trend in either direction. Data on availability of cereals and pulses (in grams per capita per day) since 1950 show considerable year-to-year fluctuations but no upward trend. This is not inconsistent, however, with a modest improvement of diets through increased per capita consumption of nonstaples, such as fruits, vegetables, poultry, fish, and dairy products.

The government of India has often been criticized for underinvesting in agriculture. The percentage of planned investment allocated to rural development has usually been less than 20 percent, well below the allocations to industry and infrastructure. Apart from irrigation, however, the opportunities for capital investment in agriculture are limited. Technical progress, based on agricultural research and extension, requires mainly people, expertise, and organization rather than substantial amounts of physical capital. Moreover, much of the investment in roads, marketing facilities, fertilizer factories and other areas has been of direct benefit to agriculture.

The emphasis of public policy has changed considerably over the years. In the early 1950s a program of land reform raised the proportion of owner-cultivators from about 40 percent to 75 percent, while the remaining tenants were better protected with regard to tenure and rent levels. The resulting agricultural structure, while based on family farming, is by no means egalitarian. About one-third of the rural population have less than an acre of land or no land at all. Another third are small farmers with holdings of one to five acres. Most of the remaining third, with holdings of more than five acres, cannot be considered rich, though they are comfortably above the poverty line. The really large landowners still have disproportionate economic and political influence; but they do not dominate the scene as in some Latin American countries.

Other developments of the 1950s included substantial investment in irrigation. Expansion of the irrigated area is estimated to have accounted for 30 percent of the increase in agricultural output between 1950 and 1960. (Expansion of irrigation has continued in subsequent decades. The irrigated area rose from 22.6 million hectares in 1950–51 to 51.0 million hectares in 1978–79, about half the estimated potential of 112 million hectares.) A system of agricultural credit cooperatives was established to reduce dependence on rural moneylenders. Borrowings through this system rose from about 6 percent of all farm borrowings in 1950 to 40 percent in 1970–71. The system has probably been most useful to the larger farmers, who tend to dominate the local coop boards and naturally give themselves priority in credit allocations.

By the early 1960s the tendency was to view the farmer as a rational decision maker who would respond well to adequate incentives. The previous policy of holding down food prices for the benefit of consumers gave way to a policy of offering better price incentives to farmers, and growing emphasis was put on increasing the supplies of modern inputs, notably fertilizer inputs. A high point of this period was a "package program," the Intensive Agricultural Development Program, which involved selecting well-watered areas with superior output potential and proceeding to saturate them with inputs and technical advice. The production results were somewhat disappointing, apparently because of overemphasis on fertilizer and inadequate attention to management, water control, and improved seed varieties. The program was nevertheless an important milestone, yielding useful information and insights as well as some increase in output.

Up to the mid-1960s, then, higher yields per acre were achieved mainly by larger inputs per acre, notably larger labor inputs. The population upsurge provided both the means and the incentive for larger labor inputs. After 1950 there was also increasing availability of fertilizer, pesticides, and other nonlabor inputs. Lal interprets this development in terms of the Boserup hypothesis that farmers adjust to declining land/man ratios by more-intensive cultivation methods, which raise output per acre about enough to offset the decline in acres per man. Yield per hectare moves upward to the left along the Ishikawa curve discussed in chapter 2, with output per farm worker roughly constant.

Since the mid-1960s, however, new agricultural technologies have paved the way for accelerated growth of output. This "green revolution" is more properly described as a "wheat revolution," its impact on rice cultivation being still quite limited. Dwarf wheat varieties were distributed widely to experiment stations in 1963–64 and to farmers in the following year. By the crop year 1968–69, the new seeds were widely and amply available. Between 1964–65 and 1970–71, wheat production increased by 90 percent, or 11 percent per year. Although wheat was only 14 percent of food-grain production at the beginning of the period, it accounted for 60 percent of the *increase* in food-grain production over the period. The average wheat yield per acre rose about 43 percent over the period and accounted for 62 percent of the output growth. The growing profitability of wheat induced some diversion of acreage from other crops; it also induced farmer investment in irrigation. The percentage of wheat land irrigated rose from 33 percent in 1960–61 to 48 percent in 1967–68. Diffusion of the new varieties was aided by geographic localization and by a superior wheat research system. (Expenditure for wheat research, as a percentage of commodity value, was two-and-a-half times as high as that for rice research.) While Punjab, Uttar Pradesh, and Haryana have been the core area of the wheat revolution, there has been a rather dramatic spread of wheat eastward from this core.

Who benefits from the output increase? Consumers presumably benefit through lower food prices than would exist otherwise. On the producer side, land and capital are the scarce factors of production and some two-thirds of the output increase is typically imputed to these factors. It follows that the incidence of benefits is (largely) proportional to the distribution of land and capital ownership, which is quite unequal. But the new technology is labor-using and, while labor receives a small *percentage* of the increase in farm income, it benefits substantially in absolute terms. Studies typically show cash and imputed payments to labor rising by 35–50 percent. Demand for labor in the core wheat areas has risen substantially, wage rates for farm labor in these states have risen relative to other states, and in-migration of labor has been substantial. These developments will not solve the landless-laborer problem in the foreseeable future, but they are helpful.

Data on landless laborers, farm sizes, and so on for the post-1950 period present the same picture of massive stability that was noted earlier for the pre-1950 period. The percentage of landless workers has not changed appreciably, nor has there been any appreciable drift toward greater concentration of land ownership. Since rural income distribution is highly correlated with land ownership, one would not expect it to have changed much either. Unpublished data provided by T. N. Srinivasan suggest a slight *decrease* in the Gini coefficient for rural household incomes, from 0.34 in 1957–58 to 0.28 in 1973–74. This shift apparently does not result from any improvement in the bottom stratum of the population. The percentage falling below the poverty line remains rather stable at about 40 percent. But it appears that the top 15 percent of the distribution have suffered a decline in relative living standards, while the middle-income groups have gained. It is interesting also that the rural Gini coefficient is consistently quite close to the urban Gini coefficient, contrary to experience in many developing countries.

The labor-absorbing capacity of manufacturing and other "modern" sectors of the Indian economy has been low. So the great bulk of labor-force growth has continued to accumulate in agriculture and to a lesser extent in the "unorganized sector"—petty trade, handicrafts, and service activities. This raises a question whether wages and labor supply have behaved as Lewis's "surplus-labor" model predicts. Lal, after a careful review of the evidence, concludes that:

1. There is no evidence of wage constancy. On the contrary, the data show a marked uptrend in both the rural and industrial real wage. The industrial workers' share of income produced in industry has *not* fallen, as it would in the Lewis model, but has remained stable at 53–54 percent.
2. The behavior of relative wage rates is well explained by a demand-supply framework. Both demand and supply curves for rural labor seem to be quite inelastic, with the result that small shifts produce substantial wage changes. Interstate variations in farm wages are readily explained on this basis. The variables that influence interindustry wage differences in the urban sector include output per worker, capital-intensity, average size of firm, and profitability—all presumably affecting demand. If supply curves were horizontal, demand shifts would affect only employment and not the wage rate; but in fact wages are responsive. The implication is that labor supply curves are upward-sloping.

3. The Indian Sample Survey for 1970–71 included questions on how many rural people would accept industrial employment and what wage they would expect. Hypothetical supply curves constructed from these data show a definite upward slope. Farm-management surveys also show substantial use of permanent hired labor, even on small farms. Thus surplus family labor, which could exist only in families making no use of hired labor, must be relatively small. Lal uses the Little-Mirrlees method to estimate the shadow wage rate of industrial labor and finds it to be typically 50–75 percent of the market wage.

4. Recent estimates of urban unemployment show it running at around 9 percent. But these estimates, based on registrants at the public employment service, must be interpreted with caution. Their service makes 85–90 percent of its placements in the public sector, which workers prefer because it offers a wage premium of 20–25 percent over comparable jobs in the private sector. So the employment service register is essentially a queue of people awaiting public-sector jobs, some of whom are already employed in the private sector but wish to improve themselves. Its size is influenced by people's estimate of the probability of getting such jobs, which in turn is related to the growth rate of public employment.

In sum, the agricultural sector has performed better than might have been predicted twenty years ago; but substantial problems remain. Progress has benefited mainly the large and medium-sized farmer, and some economists urge policies aimed more directly at small farmers and landless laborers. The technical revolution has as yet had relatively little impact on rice growing. To do more on this front would require, among other things, improved flood control on the Gangetic plain involving a substantial commitment of public resources. Supplies of some modern inputs, notably fertilizer, remain limited. Scarcity of foreign exchange restricts the possibility of either importing fertilizer or importing components for India's fertilizer plants. Despite these difficulties the future is not unhopeful, especially if there is some deceleration of population growth.

The Industrial Sector

Industrialization enjoys high priority among Indian economic objectives. Before looking at accomplishments in this area, it will be useful to say something about the ideological and institutional background.

The political framework is democratic and federal. Although observers tend to focus on what happens in New Delhi, state political leaders are also important. Pressure-group influence on political leaders can conflict with economic efficiency. For example:

1. Decisions about location of both public and private enterprises (which are controlled through the system of industrial licensing) are influenced by pork-

barreling among the states. The notion that every state is entitled to a fertilizer plant can lead to the operation of plants below optimum scale.

2. Union pressure exerted through government on managers of public enterprises has led to substantial overstaffing, overpayment, and resistance to efficient work rules.

3. Large landowners, who have particular influence on state governments, have used their position for economic advantage.

4. Large private industries have also used government regulation, notably the licensing system for imported inputs, to strengthen their market position and freeze out potential competitors.

5. Managers of public enterprises and other economic officials are open to political attack, and even the most competent and honest may be attacked illegitimately. This leads naturally to bureaucratic timidity, lack of initiative, a refusal to do anything that cannot be justified as clearly within established rules.

These tendencies, of course, are not specifically Indian. They are found in the United States and other economies operating under democratic governments. But they stand out prominently in India because government controls pervade the economy and make it unusually profitable to manipulate the political levers.

In the early years of independence thinking about economic development, and more particularly about industrial development, was shaped by an ideology which can be characterized as:

1. *Inward-looking*. There was a strong desire to reinforce political independence by achieving economic independence. This was interpreted as involving a reduction of the international economic linkages that had been so prominent in colonial times. The export pessimism of Prebisch and Myrdal, part of the conventional wisdom of the 1950s, was widely accepted. The moral appeared to be autarkic development and comprehensive import substitution, achieved through across-the-board industrialization.

2. *Socialist,* in the British Labour Party tradition of favoring public ownership of basic industries. At the time of independence, indeed, one wing of opinion advocated immediate and comprehensive nationalization. Prime Minister Nehru compromised this issue by declining to nationalize existing industries while promising that the bulk of future industrial expansion would be within the public sector. This was to be accomplished by reserving a list of industries, including virtually all of heavy industry, for the public sector and by mobilizing large amounts of money for planned public investment. Thus the private sector would gradually be encircled and its relative importance reduced.

3. *Antimarket*. Planning was to replace the market as the main instrument for economic coordination. Many Indian leaders were impressed by the Soviet example of rapid industrialization through successive five-year plans. So India not only opted for planning but tended to interpret this as Soviet-style planning, involving

reliance on physical targets with prices playing only a secondary role and involving also a strong priority for capital goods over consumer goods.

Given the existence of private agriculture and a substantial private industrial sector, however, the Indian five-year plans could scarcely approximate the Soviet plans. They are considerably more macroeconomic and also more monetary, with sources and uses of investment funds occupying a central position. In large measure, they are investment plans for the public sector. The figures for private-sector output and investment are projections rather than the firm targets; and not infrequently private-sector performance has exceeded the plan figures.

A final important feature of the institutional environment was the existence of the Indian civil service, a well-staffed organization patterned on British lines. This was one of the more important legacies of the colonial period. It was perhaps partly the existence of a ready-made administrative organization that encouraged government to embark on pervasive and detailed regulation of the economy. But the service turned out to be in some ways ill-adapted to the regulatory task, in addition to being overloaded by the sheer mass of detail. Its performance has been criticized, for example by Bhagwati and Desai (1970), on such grounds as:

1. The generalist tradition carried over from Britain, the belief that an intelligent administrator can turn his hand to anything, is not well suited to the specialized tasks of industrial management. Assigning someone to manage a steel mill because he has the proper civil-service rank though he lacks any experience of the industry may not produce good management. In a system ruled by generalists, people with specialized technical competence tend to be downgraded, underutilized, and underrewarded.
2. A wide gap between plans and performance. Civil servants proved much better at developing impressive and plausible projects than at following through and ensuring their execution. The comment by Bhagwati and Desai that "taking the word for the deed is a feature of the Indian temperament" is perhaps unfair. The practice of announcing a project and then neglecting to do anything about it is common in many developing countries, as in Latin America, where it is known as "projectismo."
3. A strong preference for physical planning and for the detailed controls of the private sector that follow from it. As Bhagwati and Desai (1970, p. 134) remark: "The bureaucrats, especially at the top levels, have traditionally taken to this doctrine with some enthusiasm, for it has conferred on them great power and re-emphasized their inherited notions of omnipotence. For much the same reason, many politicians in power (and in search of patronage) have also embraced these policies of detailed regulation."

Turning from institutions to accomplishments, we note first that the savings rate of the economy rose substantially after independence. Net savings/net domestic product rose from 6.0 percent in 1950–51 to 16.9 percent in 1980–81, a high rate for such a low-income country. Interestingly enough, most of this rise represents an increase in household saving, which has consistently provided 60–70 percent of all saving. This suggests a high marginal savings rate out of increases in per capita incomes, facilitated by a good network of savings institutions as well as by possibilities of reinvesting savings in farms and small businesses. The private corporate sector has on average contributed only about 10 percent of savings. Government saving has also turned out to be smaller than initially planned. Public corporations have quite low earnings and contribute little to the budget. Government has done a good job of increasing tax revenue, which rose from about 5 percent of GNP in 1950–51 to 10 percent in 1978–79. But current expenditure has risen even faster than revenue, with the result that the contribution to saving has not been commensurate with the tax effort. Public-sector saving as a proportion of national saving peaked at 29.3 percent in 1964–65 but then began to decline and was less than 20 percent throughout the 1970s.

Government's share of gross investment, on the other hand, has typically been 50–60 percent. To pay for this investment government has required substantial borrowing from domestic sources and to a lesser extent from foreign sources. Foreign aid was important in the 1950s and 1960s, peaking in 1964–65 at about 3.5 percent of GNP (of which about 1 percent was food shipments under the United States' P.L. 480). It then fell rather sharply to 1 percent of GNP in 1970–71 and has remained low during the 1970s.

Public-sector investment has gone heavily into manufacturing and infrastructure, with smaller allocations to other sectors. Within manufacturing, there has been a marked preference for heavy industry. Steel and engineering have received about 60 percent of manufacturing investment; chemicals and petroleum, about 10 percent each; mining and minerals, 7.5 percent; leaving only about 10 percent for all other purposes. There has, of course, been substantial private investment in light industry. Even so, output of capital goods has risen about twice as fast as output of consumer goods.

During the first three plan periods, when the heavy push for industry was at its height, the index of industrial production rose quite rapidly: at 5.7 percent per year from 1951 to 1955, 7.2 percent from 1956 to 1960, and 9.0 percent from 1961 to 1965. But growth then decelerated to 3.7 percent from 1966 to 1970, 3.7 percent from 1970 to 1975, and 5.7 percent from 1975 to 1979. Fortunately, the performance of agriculture improved as manufacturing slowed, sustaining the overall growth rate of the economy.

The new industries in the "organized sector" are quite capital-intensive. There has been a massive increase in the capital stock and a sharp increase in the capital/labor ratio. Between 1950–51 and 1970–71 alone, fixed capital per worker in constant prices more than tripled. Slow growth of employment has been a natural consequence. Employment has risen less than half as rapidly as industrial output.

There is marked dualism between industries in the "registered" sector and small-scale or unorganized manufacturing. In 1970–71, capital per worker in the organized sector was *eight* times as high as in the unorganized sector. Earnings per worker, however, were only twice as high in the organized sector, suggesting substantially higher productivity of capital in small-scale industry.

The economic performance of the public-sector industries has been disappointing. The private rate of return is typically low, though in some cases this results from deliberate underpricing of public-sector products, the efficiency of which would have to be evaluated on a case-by-case basis. The social rate of return also appears to be low and declining. Assuming a shadow wage of 60 percent of the market wage, Lal estimates that the average social rate of return to Indian manufacturing in 1968 was 5.4 percent. If the shadow wage is assumed equal to the market wage, the social rate of return drops to -6.1 percent. These results he attributes to the heavy-industry, public-sector, import-substitution bias of investment policy.

Bhagwati and Desai are also critical of public-sector performance. Major projects have been undertaken without systematic analysis of costs and of alternative designs and technologies. Where cost-benefit studies were made, government often went ahead with the project despite a low estimated rate of return. So long as the proposed output contributed to some physical plan target, all else was forgiven. Long delays in plant completion and serious inflation of costs have been common. Management has suffered from a variety of ills already noted: use of unqualified generalists as top administrators; shortages of technical personnel, due partly to salary scales not being competitive with those in private industry; political heckling of administrators, leading to cautious management and lack of innovation; political decision-making on plant location; union pressure through political channels for overstaffing and overpayment.

In rebuttal, government officials could point out that much has been accomplished. There has been an impressive growth of manufacturing capacity. Import substitution is virtually complete in consumer goods and has gone a long way in capital goods. What the critics are saying is that more could have been accomplished with the resources available. The criticism is similar to that often made of investment policy in Eastern Europe and the Soviet Union: great effort, low returns. In particular, India has not capitalized on its labor resources to penetrate the vast world market for manufactures, as some other developing countries have done.

The Foreign Sector: Trade and Aid

India has followed a policy of fixed exchange rates, with only rare devaluation. A substantial devaluation in 1966, urged on the government by foreign-aid donors, was followed by fixed parities at a lower level. Exchange-rate policy becomes involved in both domestic and international politics. Suggestions from abroad for devaluation or a floating rate tend to be attacked as an unwarranted intrusion in

Indian affairs. Within India, the political left assails such proposals as "rightist tendencies" involving capitulation to international capitalism and a loss of Indian independence. Policymakers have to navigate within these political constraints.

A fixed (and usually overvalued) rate for the rupee produces foreign-exchange "scarcity" and a need for exchange rationing. Indian industry is subject to a dual set of controls:

1. The industrial licensing system, which is applied in a very detailed manner. A government license is required not merely to establish a new plant but to increase capacity or to make a change in product lines. Thus normal responses to changing market conditions are delayed or even prevented.
2. The foreign-exchange allocation system covers all imported inputs for current operation as well as plant construction. Foreign exchange is available only for "essential" products for which there is no indigenous source of supply, a system which makes established Indian producers virtually immune to foreign competition. Although allocations are supposed to be guided by priorities, these have proved almost impossible to establish—everything becomes "essential." In practice, allocations seem to be guided by the concept of "fairness." If ten firms use an imported raw material, each firm tends to receive a share based on plant capacity, which among other things encourages overexpansion of capacity. In principle, the system gives equal treatment to large and small firms; but in practice large firms with established government connections and the know-how to cope with bureaucratic procedures seem to enjoy an advantage.

The operation of the system has been generally criticized by economists, most recently in a study by Bhagwati and Srinivasan (1975), who point out that:

1. The system imposes substantial administrative costs on both government and industry and involves uncertainty and delay in procurement of supplies. It is also inflexible. Import licenses are very specific and nontransferable, though there is some informal evasion of this provision.
2. The system is thoroughly anticompetitive. Existing producers are completely sheltered from import competition. It is difficult for new firms to enter an industry. The "fair shares" principle for imported materials prevents more-efficient firms from expanding at the expense of the less-efficient.
3. The system discriminates against exports. In addition to the antiexport bias of an overvalued exchange rate, export products must often be produced with high-cost or inferior domestic inputs. The impossibility of getting more imported inputs by bidding in the market makes the supply of exports quite inelastic.
4. Government loses the revenue that might have been obtained through a tariff system. Instead, the scarcity value of the import licenses is converted into industrial profits.

The political climate is not favorable to foreign private investment, which has had little part in Indian industrial development. In addition to direct restrictions imposed by government, the climate of a highly regulated economy is uncongenial to foreign firms and reduces their willingness to invest. Thus capital flows to India have mainly taken the form of government-to-government transfers, used largely to finance public-sector investment. Loans by Western countries and the World Bank are coordinated by an "India Consortium" managed by the Bank. In addition, India has received a good deal of Soviet aid.

While India is the world's largest aid recipient in absolute terms, per capita aid is low because of the great size of the country. Some of the smaller developing countries have received much more in per capita terms. At the height of aid activity in the mid-1960s, India's foreign borrowings (exclusive of P.L. 480 food aid) were about 2.5 percent of GNP. This apparently small figure, however, amounted to 46 percent of India's imports, 23 percent of gross investment, and close to half of public-sector investment. From this high point aid declined to about 1 percent of GNP in 1970–71 and has remained at this lower level during the 1970s. India's balance-of-payments position has been eased considerably by large remittances from Indian workers employed in the Middle East.

A marked feature of the Indian economy since independence has been poor export performance. Between 1948 and 1970, world exports increased more than five times while India's exports rose by only 50 percent. India's percentage of world exports dropped from 2.6 percent to 0.72 percent. Performance with regard to manufactured exports was especially weak. Between 1960 and 1978, manufactured exports from developing countries grew at 11.6 percent per year. India's manufactured exports, however, grew at only 6.8 percent.

A particularly striking case is that of textiles. In 1953, India accounted for 38 percent of all textile exports from developing countries. By 1970 India's share had fallen to 7 percent. The absolute level of textile exports was about what it had been in 1953, while several other countries had made sensational progress. By 1970 South Korea's textile exports were 50 percent above India's, and Taiwan's exports were more than double. Even Japan, an "old exporter" that might have been presumed to be losing comparative advantage, increased its textile exports fivefold to more than ten times the Indian level. In addition to the antiexport policy biases already noted, India invested little in textiles, failed to modernize antiquated plants and equipment, and did not move quickly into synthetic fabrics as other countries were doing.

India has gradually developed a system of export incentives parallel to the import-restriction system described earlier. The system is quite complicated, and some of the incentives appear counterproductive; for example, the farther a plant is from a port, the larger is its transport subsidy. The incentives are also applied rather indiscriminately to all types of exports, with the usual result of negative value added in some cases.

Concluding Comment

Space has limited this chapter to a fragmentary discussion of a large and complex economy, but I have tried to highlight both accomplishments and shortcomings. The tone of professional discussion, as suggested at several points, has been rather critical. In a concluding chapter on the lessons of Indian experience, Bhagwati and Desai (1970, p. 499) comment as follows:

> Indian planning for industrialization suffered from excessive attention to targets down to product level, and a wasteful physical approach to setting and implementation thereof, along with a generally inefficient framework of policies designed to regulate the growth of industrialization. . . . India did not plan too much; in certain important ways it just planned inadequately. Physical, cost-benefit ignoring and choice-negligent planning, combined with detailed regulation of such inefficiently-determined targets, really proved to be a negation of national planning.

But such criticisms cut in two directions. The more mistakes have been made in the past, the more room for improvement in the future. Indian policymakers will perhaps learn from experience, and may begin to pull away from detailed regulation in the interest of concentrating on a limited number of central decisions while leaving a larger area of decision making to people outside government.

13

Egypt, Turkey, Iraq, Iran

Having considered the two largest of the recent developers, India and China, we now look more briefly at other countries that entered the phase of intensive growth after 1945. The four countries examined in this chapter are all located in the Middle East, and all except Iran were part of the former Ottoman Empire, which collapsed after World War I.

EGYPT

Egypt was ruled for several centuries as a suzerainty of the Ottoman government in Istanbul. The desire for autonomy was always strong, however, and Egypt finally achieved effective autonomy around 1875. But the Egyptians escaped from the Turks only to fall into the hands of the British. The Suez Canal, opened in 1869, was a vital link on the route to India and other British possessions in the Far East. In addition, successive khedives had borrowed heavily from French and British lenders, to the point where interest on their debts amounted to about half of government revenue. The British intervened openly in 1882, nominally to ensure interest and debt repayments. In the great power politics of the day, the French accepted British control of Egypt in exchange for a freer hand in North Africa and parts of West Africa. After 1882, then, the British resident in Cairo, who controlled government revenues and foreign economic transactions, was the effective ruler of the country. This quasi-colonial situation continued through 1945.

Extensive Growth, 1800–1952

The population of Egypt has been growing for a long time. Mead (1967) comments that during the nineteenth century the population more than tripled; and the rate tended to rise because of modest reductions in mortality. Rough estimates put total population at 2.5–3.0 million in 1821, 5.25 million in 1871, and 12.75 million in 1907. From 1897 to 1937, population grew at about 1.2 percent a year.

Food production was kept roughly in line with population growth by irrigation development, which first extended the cultivated area and later permitted increased double- and triple-cropping. There were two main bursts of irrigation activity. The first occurred under Muhammad Ali, a progressive ruler who held power from 1805 to 1848. The cultivated area rose from 2,032 thousand feddans (one feddan approximately equals one acre) in 1821 to 4,160 thousand feddans in 1852. After a thirty-year interregnum, progress was resumed around 1880 under British auspices with the building of the first (low) Aswan Dam and of the "Nile barrage" at the mouth of the delta. Better control of the annual Nile flood permitted for the first time a substantial development of multiple-cropping. Thus while the *cultivated area* increased by only half a million feddans between 1877 and 1902, the *cropped area* increased by almost three million feddans, from 4,762 thousand in 1877 to 7,429 thousand in 1902.

Each wave of irrigation enabled agricultural output for the time being to pull ahead of population growth. But population then proceeded to catch up, requiring a new wave of investment in irrigation. The rural economy ran into difficulties after about 1910, however, when a major new wave failed to develop. Crop yields, which had been rising from 1870 to 1900, began to fall, apparently because of inadequate drainage. It was not realized for a long time that a drainage system to remove excess salinity is a necessary complement of irrigation. There was some further improvement of irrigation, including heightening of the Aswan Dam, and the cropped area rose by another million feddans to 8,522 thousand in 1939. With increased application of fertilizer in the 1930s, plus the beginnings of drainage work, crop yields recovered. Even so, over the period 1910–45 crop production grew at only about 1 percent per year, well short of population growth, which by the late 1930s had reached 1.8 percent per year and was still accelerating. Hansen and Marzouk (1965) estimate that per capita income *fell* by 20 percent between 1910 and 1945.

During the second half of the nineteenth century long-staple cotton, introduced from abroad, emerged as the country's main export product. Cotton exports, in million kantars (one kantar approximately equals 100 pounds), rose from 0.50 in 1853–57 to 2.52 in 1873–77 and to 6.72 in 1908–12. To anticipate a possible question: why do we not take this increase in exports as marking a turning point to intensive growth? This is of course a matter of judgment. I reached a negative conclusion for several reasons: the export growth rate from 1873 to 1912 was only about 2.8 percent per year; it was confined to a single crop, which formed a small percentage of GNP; it appears that most of the export proceeds were skimmed off in government revenue and trading profits without reaching the peasant; and there is no evidence of substantial improvement in living standards for the mass of the population. Issawi (1966) comments that "the large increase in [cotton] production and exports during the period was absorbed partly by the population increase and partly by a sharp rise in the level of living of the upper and middle classes and a small rise in that of the mass of the population; little of it was reinvested." The main imports for mass consumption were cotton textiles, tobacco, and coffee, though consumption of wheat also increased somewhat. But whatever improvement may have been achieved during this period must have been more than lost by the marked decline from 1910 to 1945.

Government policy was timid and nondevelopmental. A large share of the revenue flowing into the treasury from export taxes and other sources went abroad in interest and debt repayment. The surpluses accumulated during the export boom of World War I were used largely to liquidate old debts and were not available for development. (The outflow of private dividends and interest, however, was at most times more than offset by new private investment and did not constitute a net drain on the economy.) Education was seriously neglected, typically receiving only about 1 percent of the budget. In 1907, 92 percent of the population aged 10 and over were illiterate.

British and French investors did finance a good deal of infrastructure. By 1858 Cairo was linked to Alexandria and Suez by rail. By 1913 there were some 2,953 kilometers of standard-gauge railways and 1,376 kilometers of light railways. The Nile and some of its canals were navigable yearround. The port of Alexandria was further improved and new ports were built at Suez and Port Said. Opening of the Suez Canal in 1869 brought a greatly increased flow of traffic through Egypt.

Slow development of manufacturing is not difficult to explain. Wealthy Egyptians invested in land but showed little interest in industry, trade, or finance. Foreigners also found that they could make quick profits in speculation, trade, and banking, whereas industry promised only slow and uncertain returns. The British did not favor local manufacturing development. They imposed an 8 percent limit on tariff duties, so this device for industrial promotion was not available.

Growth of manufacturing in the 1930s can be traced partly to the Great Depression, which reduced exports and hence import possibilities. It was aided also by greater freedom in tariff matters. When the British-imposed restrictions expired in 1930, duties were promptly raised to 25 percent. Although this was done mainly to increase revenue, there was an incidental protective effect. A substantial cotton-textile industry developed during the 1930s. In addition, plants were established to produce cement, chemicals, petroleum products, paper, processed foods, and a variety of other consumer goods. Egyptian capitalists and entrepreneurs displayed an interest in industry for the first time. These changes were too small, however, to alter the general structure of the economy. Agriculture's share of the labor force held steady at around 70 percent and its share of GNP at about 50 percent.

By the late 1930s, too, government was becoming more development-minded, in line with British colonial policy in other parts of the world. Health and education, which had traditionally received about 3 percent of the budget, were allocated 20 percent in the 1938–39 budget. Irrigation's share had also risen. Mead estimates that about 35 percent of that year's budget could be regarded as "developmental expenditure."

Was the Egyptian economy in 1950 in a better position to embark on intensive growth than it had been in 1900? The answer is mixed. On the positive side were substantial development of infrastructure; the beginnings of manufacturing and an industrial labor force; and modest improvements in education and health. On the negative side were accelerating population growth; an ominous lag in food production; heavy dependence on a single export product; domination of the modern sector by foreign owners and managers; and shortage of Egyptian managerial and technical expertise, which was not encouraged during the British era.

Certainly nothing in the economic setting in 1950 would have led one to expect a speedy transition to intensive growth. The transition was set off rather by dramatic and unexpected political events.

Intensive Growth, 1952–80

I date the turning point from the 1952 revolution. This revolution, which exiled the king and installed Gamal Abdel Nasser as president in 1956, was both populist and nationalist. It brought about the emancipation of the country from foreign economic tutelage and the emergence of an independent government committed to development for the benefit of Egyptians. This commitment was embodied in two major institutional changes: a reorganization of agriculture, going considerably beyond "land reform" in the usual sense; and nationalization of the Suez Canal, large-scale industry, and banking.

A 1952 land-reform law, enacted soon after the revolution, set a ceiling of 200 feddans on individual holdings, which was later lowered to 100 feddans (1961) and 50 feddans (1969). The owners were compensated by interest-bearing bonds, but in 1964 interest payments were discontinued and the bonds became worthless. About a million feddans of land obtained in this way and by expropriation of Crown and foreign-owned land was redistributed to 342,000 families in plots averaging 2.4 feddans. The recipients were forbidden to sell or sublet this land or to subdivide it through inheritance. They were expected to repay the cost of the land over 30 years at 3 percent interest, but this requirement was later liberalized to one-quarter the original cost with zero interest. The 1952 law also gave tenants greater protection in regard to tenure (a minimum of three years) and rent (a maximum of 50 percent of the crop, with equal sharing of production costs).

The reform produced a considerable equalization of land ownership. The Gini coefficient fell from 0.61 in 1952 to 0.38 in 1965. The number of smallholders (those owning less than five feddans) rose from 2.6 million to 3.0 million, their average size of holding increased by 50 percent, and their share of total farm acreage rose from about 33 percent to 60 percent. At the top of the structure, 5,000 large holdings of 100 feddans or more, which had occupied 25 percent of the available acreage, disappeared through subdivision. Some 150,000 medium-sized holdings, accounting for 40 percent of the acreage, continued undisturbed.

This redistribution of land assets led to a substantial equalization of rural income. Abdel-Fadil (1975) estimates that the percentage of agricultural income received by landless farm laborers rose from 5.3 percent in 1950 to 9.7 percent in 1961. The share received by smallholders with less than five feddans rose from 15.0 percent to 28.0 percent. Middle peasants with 5–50 feddans also improved their position. The share received by large landowners with 50 feddans or more fell from 39.0 percent to 17.0 percent, while rental payments to owners dropped from 15.7 to 13.0 percent.

Recipients of redistributed land were required to join cooperative associations, and in 1957 this requirement was extended to all agriculturalists. These agricultural cooperatives gradually became exclusive agencies for input supplies, provision of credit, and marketing of outputs. Although cooperative in form, they are actually the lowest level of the government's agricultural bureaucracy. The coop manager is selected and assigned to an area by higher officials. He supervises production operations in considerable detail. Farmers are required to coordinate their crop patterns by planting the same crop in adjacent plots (which facilitates various joint operations while maintaining individual ownership), to practice triennial rotation (rather than biennial rotation, which depletes soil fertility), and to cooperate in such activities as fumigation of crops and pest control. The farmer benefits by lower production costs and greater availability of credit. Loans through the system, mainly crop-year loans to finance input purchases and wage labor costs, rose from £E18 million in 1954 to £E81 million in 1970. On the other hand, the system involves a certain amount of bureaucratic inefficiency. Moreover, a government that controls prices of both inputs and outputs is obviously in a position to tax farmers at will. How reasonably this power has been exercised will be considered later.

The nationalization of major industries came about through a series of *ad hoc* measures and was more nationalist than socialist in inspiration. The first major step was nationalization of the highly profitable and foreign-owned Suez Canal in 1956. The abortive military intervention by British, French, and Israeli forces, which was repudiated by the United States and came to nothing, confirmed the Egyptian government in its antipathy to foreign ownership in general. So the foreign-owned industries and banks that constituted most of the modern sector were soon taken over; and in the early 1960s government took the last step of nationalizing Egyptian-owned "big business" as well. The idea that government knows best, and that planned economic development will proceed faster under government auspices, is naturally congenial to politicians and bureaucrats. It was also, as was noted in the case of India, part of the conventional wisdom in development economics at this time.

Turning from institutions to events, we note first an acceleration of population growth, which had already set in before the revolution. The crude deathrate fell from 27.8 per thousand in 1934 to 12.0 in 1980, while the crude birthrate fell only from 44 to 37. Over the years 1950–80, population grew at 2.5 percent per year, and a significant decrease in this rate is not yet in sight.

The largest single step toward helping food output once more overtake population was construction, with substantial Soviet aid, of the Aswan High Dam. This project increased the country's electric power capacity by about three times. Potential capacity at the dam is 10,000 million kilowatt-hours, or double the 5,000 million capacity of existing thermal stations. Considering that actual power usage in 1970 was only 7,000 million kilowatt-hours, there is enough excess capacity to last for some time.

On the agricultural side, the high dam permitted a better distribution of the Nile water both *within* the year and *between* years, since there is considerable year-to-year variation in the size of the Nile flood. Lake Nasser, behind the dam, is large enough to achieve "century storage." The dam itself had to be complemented by expanding the canal system for water distribution and the drainage system to dispose of waste water; and there were some unfavorable side effects. Silt from the upper Nile no longer reaches land on the lower Nile, collecting instead in Lake Nasser. The loss of this natural fertilizer will have to be offset by increased applications of chemical fertilizer. The salinity of water reaching the land may also increase because of evaporation in Lake Nasser.

But there were three substantial benefits: (1) about 800,000 feddans of land were reclaimed between 1960 and 1970, increasing the cultivated area by almost 15 percent; (2) the sown area increased even more, through the introduction of multiple-cropping, to an additional 500,000 feddans; (3) perhaps equally important are changes in crop allocation resulting from larger and more regular water supplies. Better water supplies will permit some profitable (privately and socially) switching from cotton to sugarcane in Upper Egypt, from wheat to rice in parts of the delta, and from flood maize to summer maize, which has a 20 percent higher yield.

In addition to acreage increases there have been substantial yield increases for most crops. Mabro (1974) reports that between 1952 and 1971 the yield per feddan rose 50 percent for cotton, 65 percent for wheat, 74 percent for maize, 47 percent for millet, 27 percent for barley, and 50 percent for rice. A major source of higher yields was a sharp increase in farmers' use of modern inputs, which were partly imported, partly supplied by the growing industrial sector. Between 1960 and 1971 alone the use of pesticides doubled, use of fertilizer quadrupled, and use of improved seed increased six times. The growing rural population, which rose from 12.6 million in 1947 to 19.3 million in 1970, also permitted larger labor inputs per feddan, some of which was required by the new technology. Despite substantial out-migration, the rural labor force has continued to grow at close to 2 percent per year, compared with 3–4 percent for urban population.

The agricultural sector operates under comprehensive government regulation. The acreage of cotton, wheat, rice, and sugarcane is controlled through the cooperative joint planting system and through allocations of irrigation water. The acreage of most other crops reflects farmers' choices. The government also controls prices for most crops either through direct purchase (as in cotton and sugarcane) or through support prices (as in wheat or maize). With both price and output controlled, one might expect that the economy would often be off the demand curve; but this problem is mitigated by export and import possibilities plus maintenance of internal buffer stocks.

Government has considerably altered the domestic price structure relative to international prices. Hansen and Nashashibi (1975) estimate that the export crops—cotton, rice, onions—have received "negative protection"—that is, they have been taxed at rates varying by crop and by year from 20 to 50 percent. On the other hand the big food crops, wheat and corn, have usually had positive protection of 30–40 percent. Prices of minor crops, such as fruits and vegetables, are not controlled, which has led to some diversion of acreage in their direction. Overall, however, Hansen and Nashashibi conclude that the misallocation effect of government controls amounts only to about 8 percent of total acreage. They find also that, for owner-cultivators operating without hired labor, the net return per feddan is rather uniform across crops, which would presumably also be a "competitive" result.

After the encouraging results of the 1960s, agricultural performance deteriorated once more in the 1970s. The growth rate of food production, which was 3.1 percent per year in the 1950s and 3.8 percent in the 1960s, dropped to 1.5 percent in the 1970s. Lack of drainage and inadequate water management have apparently led to growing salinity and a drop in the water table. Government investment in agriculture was lower in the 1970s than the 1960s. An IBRD report comments on institutional deficiencies in applied research, extension, and marketing.

For whatever reasons, food output is once more lagging markedly behind demand, which is propelled by population growth and rising per capita incomes. Comparing 1960 with 1981, self-sufficiency ratios (domestic supply as a percentage of domestic consumption) have declined as follows: wheat, from 69.8 to 24.8; maize, 94.0 to 71.1; sugar, 114.2 to 53.2; beans, 100.4 to 69.8; vegetable oils, 95.4 to 31.6. The exportable surplus of cotton, rice, and other field crops has also fallen sharply. The rise after 1974 in foreign-exchange receipts from oil exports and other sources may have produced some complacency toward the rapid growth of food imports. But the situation remains precarious because the Nile is now quite fully exploited and the sources of foreign exchange that finance food imports at present may not continue at the same level in future.

Manufacturing was already growing quite rapidly in the prenationalization period. Between 1947 and 1960, output per employed worker doubled, and capital per worker also doubled, with little change in the capital/output ratio. Money and real wages rose but lagged behind productivity, so that the wage-salary share of value added fell from about 40 percent to 32 percent. Profit rates, already high, rose still further, and this provided a persuasive rationale for nationalization. Public ownership would not only prevent exploitation of labor but would raise the national savings rate by appropriating profits previously distributed, largely to foreigners, as private dividends.

Industrial growth since 1960 has followed predictable lines: industrial output rising faster than agricultural output; the industrial share of GNP rising gradually; a rise in output of capital goods and intermediates relative to consumer goods (though textiles remains much the largest industry); employment in large-scale industry rising a good deal less rapidly than output and making only a limited contribution to labor absorption. The manufacturing share of GDP has risen from about 10 percent in 1950 to 28 percent in 1980, by which time it exceeded agriculture's 23 percent.

The structure of industry is markedly dualistic, with "big business" dominated by public corporations while many thousands of smaller businesses remain in private hands. All imports and exports are subject to licensing and pass through public companies at controlled prices. Prices of public-sector products are also fixed, apparently on a "fair margin" basis. Wage rates, on the other hand, are largely market-determined, though government has been trying to develop a more-systematic wage scale for nationalized industries. Public-sector investment decisions are quite centralized. Profits are remitted to government, and investment allocations must be obtained from government. Current production decisions, on the other hand, are relatively decentralized and determined mainly by current market demand. Public enterprises seem to function somewhat as profit-maximizing enterprises, within the framework set by import licensing, price fixing, and other controls. This is true especially in consumer-goods industries, where demand is mainly private. Where a plant sells to the public sector, on the other hand, a government decision to buy becomes automatically an order to produce. As in Soviet-type economies, the system apparently tends to produce shortages of most domestically produced goods.

Most observers judge the management of public enterprises to be quite inefficient, partly because of the top-heavy Egyptian bureaucracy. Despite a large expansion of university capacity since 1952, government has maintained its commitment that every university graduate is entitled to a government job. The result is heavy overstaffing in all public operations. Hansen and Marzouk point out that in the very large textile industry the public-sector enterprises, which have about three-quarters of total employment, are notably inefficient relative to privately owned plants. The ratio of administrative and service employees to actual operatives is 60 percent in the public sector, 20 percent in the private sector. The average wage rate in the public sector is more than twice as high as that in the private sector. And inventories are huge, amounting to 67 percent of fixed assets in the public sector, compared with 15 percent in the private sector.

There have also been major mistakes in selection of new industries for promotion. Hansen and Nashashibi found that the new pulp and paper plants are very uncompetitive, frequently showing negative value added. The integrated steel mill at Helwân is also highly uneconomic, as is a small auto-assembly plant. On the other hand there are success stories: sugar refining is quite competitive; cement is highly competitive and has in fact become an important export industry, which should have been expanded more rapidly; fertilizers, which have taken advantage of the ample electricity supply, are a successful "infant industry" with export potential; and a tire plant has also done well. Thus, the criticism is not of government promotion *per se*, but of indiscriminate promotion that ignores cost-benefit analysis and fails to capitalize on comparative advantage.

I should add that, since the "opening to the West" and the expulsion of Soviet advisers in 1974, there has been at least a potential resurgence of the private sector. In addition to some liberalization of trade and exchange controls, a new investment law provided incentives for both foreign and domestic private investment. How far private companies have taken advantage of this shift in policy, and how much this has altered the public-private mix in manufacturing, is not yet apparent from the literature.

The government budget plays a large and central role in economic affairs. In 1962–63, government current and capital expenditure already amounted to one-third of GDP, and of 1979 it was more than half of GDP. The components of this total are:

1. Output of current services, which had risen to about 20 percent of GDP in 1980.
2. Consumer subsidies, especially food subsidies, which have been widely used to restrain living costs during the inflationary 1970s. Partly because of this item, there is a sizable deficit in the current budget. Against this one can set a certain amount of public-sector saving. The profits of state enterprises make some contribution, though this has been declining, from 7.8 percent of GDP in 1974 to 4.6 percent in 1979 (of which 60 percent was Suez Canal earnings). Government borrows also from the current surplus of the social-security system.
3. Public investment is a large item, typically amounting to more than public consumption. In 1980, total investment was 31 percent of GDP, and about three-quarters of this was public-sector investment. Investment allocations are embodied in an annual plan, five-year planning having been abandoned after an abortive effort in the early 1960s. The sector allocations of public investment are not unusual. In the 1970s manufacturing was getting about 35 percent of the total, infrastructure (including the Suez Canal) about 25 percent, agriculture a bit under 20 percent.

Public-sector saving, after providing for the current budget deficit, typically covers only about one-quarter of the investment budget. So, in addition to heavy foreign borrowing, there is also substantial domestic bank borrowing, with consequent inflationary pressure.

As for the foreign sector, Egypt normally has a deficit in merchandise trade. Until the oil boom, the export/GDP ratio was falling, declining from about 19 percent in the early 1950s to 12 percent by 1969. But with the discovery of oil and the rapid increase in oil prices, exports shot up again to 34 percent of GDP in 1980.

Imports, however, have shot up even faster, amounting in 1980 to 47 percent of GDP. The sources of finance for this large trade gap will be noted in a moment. The export bill has been steadily diversified over time. Cotton has lost its predominant position and agricultural exports in general have fallen as a percentage of total exports. Meanwhile exports of manufactures have risen sharply, and by 1980 they exceeded exports of agricultural products. For the time being, at least, Egypt has assumed the position of leading manufacturer in the Moslem world and has been able to cash in on the oil wealth of its neighbors. The most recent and spectacular newcomer is oil, which in 1980 was larger than all other exports combined.

On the import side, food has typically constituted 20–25 percent of the total, the balance consisting almost entirely of capital goods, raw materials, and intermediates. Except for some consumer durables, Egypt is virtually self-sufficient in consumer goods.

The directions of trade have varied with political conditions. Trade with the Soviet bloc rose substantially after the Czechslovak arms deal of 1955 and the Soviet commitment to aid in constructing the Aswan Dam. The Soviet bloc's percentage of Egyptian exports rose from 11 percent in 1950 to 42 percent in 1960 and 61 percent in 1970; but these countries, being weak exporters, never provided more than 40 percent of Egypt's imports. With the decline of Soviet influence and the turn toward the West in the 1970s, trade with the Soviet bloc dropped sharply and Western Europe and the Middle East became Egypt's major trade partners.

In the late 1970s several favorable developments eased Egypt's balance-of-payments position, leading to higher import and investment levels and a marked rise in the GNP growth rate. The reopening of the Suez Canal, recovery of the Sinai oil fields and additional oil discoveries, large remittances from Egyptian workers employed in the Middle East, and substantial amounts of foreign aid from the United States and other sources, have all contributed. By 1980, the sources of foreign exchange available to Egypt looked very different from the distribution a decade earlier. The percentage distribution in 1980–81 was as follows: agricultural exports, 5.2; manufactured exports, 5.3; nonfactor services (including tourism), 9.0; petroleum exports, 21.2; Suez Canal receipts, 6.2; workers' remittances, 21.1; other factor income, 3.4; direct foreign investment, 6.6; official and private loans and transfers, 22.0. Three items—oil exports, worker remittances, and foreign aid—now dwarf the traditional export sources.

Egypt's growth record is above average for the countries in our sample. Real GDP rose at 3.3 percent per year in the 1950s, 4.3 percent in the 1960s, and 7.4 percent in the 1970s. After the explosion in oil prices, the growth rate from 1975 through 1980 averaged above 9 percent. Allowing for population growth, real per capita income grew from 1960 to 1980 at 3.4 percent per year, with the rate accelerating toward the end of the period.

Egyptian economic growth presents something of a puzzle. The country has all kinds of apparent disadvantages: a very small usable agricultural area; severe population pressure; a top-heavy bureaucracy; rather inefficient state industries; complicated economic controls, some of which appear counterproductive. On the other hand, it has a strategic geographic position, which causes it to be courted by powerful neighbors; a stable government with strong popular support; proximity to newly rich nations that provide a growing market for both labor and goods; control of the vital and profitable Suez waterway; and bits of good fortune, such as oil discoveries. Thus far, the balance has tilted toward growth.

TURKEY

Assignment of Turkey to the post-1945 period is a matter of judgment. The decisive political event—the Turkish Revolution—occurred in the early 1920s, and several important development measures were enacted in the late 1920s and the 1930s. The first significant rise in per capita income seems to have occurred from 1935 to 1939; but this growth was cut short by World War II, and per capita income in the late 1940s was still at about the prewar level. A sustained rise in per capita income, then, can reasonably be dated from around 1950.

Extensive Growth to 1950

Turkey was the core of the Ottoman Empire, which at its peak comprised most of the Balkans, North Africa, and the Middle East. By 1914 North Africa and most of Europe had been lost. After World War I the Asian empire was fragmented into a half-dozen states, leaving Turkey, under a new revolutionary government, as the shrunken survivor.

Issawi (1966) attributes the economic backwardness of the empire partly to the Ottoman rulers' view that economic affairs were an inferior kind of activity that should be left to the subject races; partly to intense rivalry among the European powers, which led each European government to oppose and frustrate any projects in Turkey started by nationals of another country; partly to the "capitulations" imposed by these powers, which limited Turkey's economic freedom, including its authority over foreign traders and its power to levy tariffs.

As of 1914 Turkey's economy was still primitive in the extreme. Population was growing. Data for the earlier period are unreliable, but by 1923–38 population was already growing at about 2 percent per year. Additional land was being brought under cultivation. About three-quarters of farmland was in small peasant holdings. Land was nominally state-owned, but the peasant's position was secure so long as he payed the customary taxes, which were the government's main concern. There was also a good deal of landlordism. Courtiers secured large grants from the Crown; rich merchants and other townspeople invested in land; peasants got into debt and sold their holdings. Cultivation methods were very traditional. Wooden plows drawn by oxen produced only a shallow furrow. There was no use of fertilizer, animal dung being too valuable as fuel, and no use of machinery.

Farm products were exchanged in small amounts at local village markets. Some export trade had developed, however, in tobacco, cotton, grain, raisins, and figs, mainly from Anatolia.

Railroad building had commenced. The line connecting Istanbul with Europe, over which the Orient Express rolled for many years, was completed in 1888. By 1913 there were some 6,000 kilometers of railways in present-day Turkey. But these lines were built by a number of European companies, for differing economic and strategic reasons, and did not constitute an efficient national network. Factory industry was almost absent. The industrial sector in 1913 consisted mainly of 7,765 textile workers and 4,281 workers in food processing.

The Ottoman Empire's defeat as an ally of the Central Powers in World War I decisively undermined the authority of its rulers. Large parts of the empire were carved out as French (Syria) or British (Iraq, Palestine) mandates. Within Turkey, a 1919–22 revolutionary war led by Mustafa Kemal (later Kemal Atatürk) drove out both the Ottoman rulers and the Greek and Armenian minorities, which had previously supplied most of the country's businessmen. The revolution also involved separation of church and state; the unveiling of women; seizure of the sultan's land and much of the church land, which thus became available for redistribution to smallholders; a new capital at Ankara, replacing the sultan's capital of Istanbul; and gradual nationalization of foreign-owned mines, railways, and other enterprises. In 1923 the victorious Atatürk signed the Treaty of Lausanne with Britain, France, Italy, Greece, and other powers providing for interchange of Turkish and Greek populations, an end to the capitulations and foreign concessions, repayment of the Ottoman debt, and restrictions (until 1929) on Turkey's right to levy tariffs.

The new government was nationalist and xenophobic. It aimed not just to eliminate foreign ownership and influence but to alter Turkey's role of exchanging primary products for manufactures and to make Turkey a self-sufficient industrial nation. This autarkic outlook was soon reinforced by the collapse of exports during the Great Depression.

The initial effort was to stimulate private industrial enterprise. A 1927 Law for the Encouragement of Private Industry provided a typical battery of incentives for "approved" enterprises—free grants of land, exemption from customs duties on materials, exemption from profits taxes, and numerous other concessions. Before this program had gotten off the ground, however, the Depression intervened and so actual accomplishments were limited. This strengthened the hand of those who argued that "private enterprise had failed" and cited the Soviet example as showing that *rapid* industrialization could be achieved only through state action. It is relevant to note that the ruling oligarchy consisted of military men and high officials who had no business experience and were not friendly toward business. The long Turkish tradition of centralized rule from above was also important.

The 1930s was a period of protectionism, expansion of government-owned industrial enterprises, and pervasive government control of the economy; a pattern was set that to some extent has continued ever since. When the tariff restrictions on Turkey expired at the end of 1929, a general tariff of 40 percent was imposed, with higher rates on specified commodities. This was soon followed by foreign-exchange rationing, import licensing, and government control of all foreign transactions. These measures gave strong protection to local production and reversed the traditional negative balance of payments; but they did not contribute to rational allocation of resources.

Government now took the lead in industrial development through state-owned enterprises and state investment banks, which had managerial as well as financing functions. New private enterprise was barred *de facto* from many branches of activity. A five-year plan (more correctly, a project list without much coordination) in 1934 was aimed at developing industries using local raw materials, especially textiles and other consumer-goods industries. A second five-year plan, announced in 1938, emphasized mining, machinery, ports, electricity, and other infrastructure projects. Supervision and financing of the new enterprises was turned over to government banks—the Sümer Bank, which was dominant in manufacturing; the Eti Bank, which concentrated on mining; and the Is Bank, or "bank of business." Credit seems to have been extended rather easily. If an enterprise lost money, the supervising bank simply provided cash as needed. This arrangement removed any pressure on enterprise managers to be concerned with costs and also led to excessive money creation with inflationary consequences.

The state industrial enterprises (hereafter SEEs) apparently suffered from overstaffing and other typical inefficiencies. A large iron and steel project built by the Krupp firm was an economic disaster. Industrial output nevertheless grew quite rapidly from 1933 to 1939, especially in coal mining, cotton textiles, sugar refining, and cement. Employment rose at almost the same rate as output, indicating little improvement in productivity. Output per industrial worker in 1939 was estimated at 40 percent of the British and 20 percent of the United States level.

Although agriculture did not figure in the five-year plans, it was not entirely neglected. There was a modest land-redistribution program, an agricultural bank to provide low-interest loans, a price-support program for wheat and some other crops, and some effort in irrigation and seed improvement. Net agricultural output in constant prices rose about 20 percent between 1929 and 1939, roughly matching the 2 percent rate of population growth. This was accomplished almost entirely through extension of cultivated acreage, with little change in yields.

National-income estimates for this period are weak. It appears, however, that there was little change in per capita income from 1923 to 1929; a drop during the Depression followed by a return to about the 1929 level by 1935; a rather sharp upturn of some 15 percent from 1935 to 1939; then a World War II drop followed by recovery, which restored per capita income in 1950 to about the 1939 level. This checkered history, including only one four-year period of marked improvement, warrants a conclusion that intensive growth should be dated from around 1950. It is also true, however, that by 1950 some foundations had been laid both in infrastructure and manufacturing. In addition, economic institutions and traditions had been established that were to continue in later decades: a strong government role in the economy, a generally autarkic tendency, predominance of SEEs in the industrial sector, and a central role for government banks in the financial system.

Intensive Growth, 1950–80

Although Turkish economic policies since 1950 show continuity with those of earlier decades, there have also been considerable changes. Agriculture has received relatively more attention, particularly under the liberal regime of the 1950s. Infrastructure investment has increased relative to manufacturing investment. Despite the continued prominence of SEEs, private enterprise has not withered away, and its share of industrial investment and output has increased.

Population growth accelerated moderately after 1945, from around 2 percent per year in the 1920s and 1930s to 2.9 percent in the 1950s and 2.6 percent in the 1960s and 1970s. The main reason, as usual, was a falling mortality rate and a failure of birthrates to respond immediately. By the late 1970s, however, the rate of natural increase had begun to decline. The crude deathrate fell from 14.6 per thousand in 1963 to 10.0 in 1978, which leaves little room for further decline, while the crude birthrate fell from 39.6 per thousand in 1963 to 32.2 in 1978. Thus the rate of natural increase will probably drop below 2 percent in the 1980s. The fact that the population is now almost half urban, plus rising levels of education and income, have contributed to declining birthrates.

Among the steps taken to encourage agriculture in the late 1940s and 1950s we may note:

1. A new land-redistribution law in 1945, including among other things a ceiling of 500 hectares on individual holdings, which after 1950 began to be seriously enforced. By 1956 some 1.3 million hectares had been distributed, constituting about 5 percent of cultivated area in the country.
2. The tax on agricultural income was abolished in 1945, though this benefited large landowners more than farmers near subsistence level.
3. Favorable price policies, under which government maintains prices of major crops above world levels while subsidizing both exports and sales to domestic consumers. Prices of fertilizer and some other farm inputs are also subsidized.
4. Farm mechanization and fertilizer use accelerated quite sharply from 1950 onward.

Over the years 1950–80, agricultural output grew at an average rate of 3.2 percent per year, running slightly ahead of population growth. Calorie consumption per capita has risen substantially and is now above prescribed nutritional requirements. The area sown to basic cereal crops has not increased materially, though the acreage of fruits, vegetables, and other minor crops rose about 50 percent between 1962 and 1977. The main source of increased output has been a substantial increase in crop yields. Between 1962 and 1977 yields per hectare rose about 35 percent for rice, 50 percent for barley, 75 percent for wheat, and 80 percent for corn. Most of the major industrial crops also show substantial increases over the same period: 50 percent for tobacco, 70 percent for sugar beets, and almost 100 percent for cotton. These increases reflect a substantial infusion of improved inputs and production technology. In addition to larger crop production, there has been an increase of about one-third in sheep and 80 percent in poultry, contributing to diversification and improvement of diets.

Turkey is now approaching the limits of acreage expansion. Remaining land is rather poorly watered, permitting only low and variable crop yields. Much of it is suitable only for pasturage. Nor are Turkey's rivers well suited to irrigation. Irrigation potential is estimated at only 2 percent of the land area. Even more than in the past, therefore, Turkey will have to rely on yield increases, reduction of fallow (still considered excessive by some observers), shifts in the crop mix, and expansion of animal production.

In manufacturing, Turkey has continued to push import substitution within a highly protectionist framework. The growth rate of manufacturing output has been close to 10 percent per year, much above agriculture's 3.2 percent. In the 1970s manufacturing was receiving about 25 percent of public-sector investment and about 35 percent of the (somewhat smaller) private-sector investment. Private manufacturing industry, which by 1980 accounted for about 70 percent of value added in manufacturing, has grown faster than state industry. Private-sector enterprises are on average much smaller than the SEEs and more oriented toward consumer-goods production, whereas the public sector is dominant in heavy manufacturing. Most of the SEE output is accounted for by eight large holding companies in charge of sugar, textiles, pulp and paper, petrochemicals, nitrogen fertilizer, cement, iron and steel, machinery, and chemicals.

Although the range of industries has expanded and the composition of output has changed gradually, capital goods are still a minor part of the total. In 1978, consumer goods were still 42 percent of manufacturing output, with food processing and textiles forming four-fifths of this total; intermediate goods were 41 percent of output, two-thirds of this total consisting of petroleum products, chemicals, cement, and wood products; and investment goods were only 17 percent. Import needs for metals, machinery, and transport equipment remain high.

The growth rate of manufacturing employment has been well below the growth rate of output, running at 3–4 percent per year. Trade policy has apparently contributed to this result. Capital goods are admitted at low rates of duty and are sometimes subsidized in addition. This policy has encouraged use of capital-intensive techniques. Labor use has been discouraged by a high rate of increase in wages, plus substantial social security and other benefits. Labor costs have risen considerably faster than capital costs over time, encouraging substitution of capital for labor.

Turkey's export performance is not impressive. Even in 1950–52 exports were only 7.6 percent of GDP, much below the Chenery norm of 16 percent for a country of this size and income level. Moreover, the export ratio has declined over time, falling to 3.9 percent of GDP in 1978–80. Partly because of relative inefficiency in manufacturing, Turkey has not moved strongly into manufactured exports. Only about 5 percent of manufacturing output is exported, well below the level of comparable countries. Two-thirds of Turkey's exports still consist of agricultural products (wheat, tobacco, cotton, fruits, and vegetables).

Imports typically exceed exports, requiring chronic resort to infusions of foreign capital. This is mainly "official" capital, since there has been little private long-term investment. Turkey's strategic location as part of NATO gives it considerable leverage in obtaining direct United States loans and loans from international agencies sponsored by the United States. There is no apparent tendency for this need for foreign capital to diminish over time, and debt obligations have now reached a high level.

This payments imbalance has been accentuated by a chronic overvaluation of the Turkish pound, with only rare and inadequate devaluations. Overvaluation is accompanied by detailed quantitative control of imports. The effects of this system resemble those noted earlier in the case of India. Anne Krueger (1974) criticizes the system on several grounds:

1. It produces a general bias against exports and in favor of import substitutes.
2. Indiscriminate, across-the-board protection has distorted resource allocation and led to wide differences in social rates of return to the factors of production.
3. Foreign competition has been stifled, since a product is put on the "prohibited list" whenever a domestic source of supply is available. Internal competition has also been reduced, since efficient producers cannot expand at the expense of the inefficient. The result is high-cost, low-quality output, which reduces exports competitiveness. The cry that "we can't export" then becomes a further justification for import restriction, and the circle is closed.
4. Producers suffer excess costs from red tape, delay, uncertainty, and excess inventory holdings.

To the argument that the manufacturing growth rate remained high, Krueger responds that it could have been higher. She estimates that a balanced strategy with no antiexport bias could have raised the manufacturing growth rate by about one-third. It would also have helped the balance of payments by producing more exports and requiring fewer imports than the policies actually followed.

The economy is subject to persistent inflation. Prices doubled between 1950 and 1958 and doubled again between 1958 and 1970. The inflation rate in the 1970s was even higher, frequently exceeding 50 percent per year. The prime source of inflation is a large public-sector deficit, amounting typically to 3–4 percent of GNP, which is financed by monetary expansion. In addition to a chronic deficit in the current budget, the SEEs overall show a deficit even larger in absolute size. The same is true of the agricultural procurement agency, Toprak, which operates the price-support system. Prices to farmers are set high on income and incentive grounds, and the produce is sold at subsidized prices to urban consumers or for export, often at a large loss. Farmers also receive subsidized credit and subsidized fertilizer supplies.

There is a minimum-wage system and, though the minimum is not very effectively enforced, increases in it generate union pressure to raise wages above the minimum to preserve skill differentials. Real wage rates have risen substantially since 1960 despite an apparent surplus of workers. Wage rates in the public sector are well above those in the private sector, and the gap appears to be increasing. Between 1960 and 1977 the average real wage in the public sector doubled while in the private sector it rose only about 50 percent. Turkey also has an extensive social-security system and an array of other legislated fringe benefits. The cost of hiring a worker is about double the basic wage, which naturally tends to restrict employment.

The employment problem has been alleviated in two ways. Some 800,000 workers have been exported to Europe as 'guest workers," whose remittances are an important source of foreign exchange. Further, the labor-force participation rate has declined substantially, which is unusual for third-world countries, though the Philippines shows a similar phenomenon. This may be partly a "discouraged worker" effect arising from slack demand for labor. Despite these developments, it was estimated in 1979 that out of a labor force of 16 million there were 800,000 surplus agricultural workers and 1.5 million urban unemployed. The urban unemployment rate has tripled since 1960.

An important step was the decision to join the European Economic Community. Turkey was admitted as an associate member in 1970 and, after a provisional period, was scheduled to achieve full membership in 1982. When this decision is fully implemented, there will be heavy pressure on some Turkish industries to become more competitive or go out of operation. On the other hand there will be increased export opportunities for both agricultural and manufactured goods.

In view of its numerous difficulties and inefficiencies, the growth rate of the economy has been surprisingly high. Real GDP grew at 6.3 percent per year in the 1950s, 6.0 percent in the 1960s, and 5.9 percent in the 1970s. Real per capita income has thus risen at about 3.5 percent per year. There have been the usual shifts in sector shares. Agriculture, which in 1950 still contributed about half of GDP, had fallen to 23 percent by 1980. Meanwhile the manufacturing share had risen to 21 percent and that of industry in the broader sense to 30 percent. There has been a considerable rise in the services share, from 35 percent in 1950 to 47 percent in 1980. Overstaffing in government agencies, plus absorption of surplus labor into low-productivity urban activities, may partly account for this result.

In terms of end uses, public consumption has remained rather stable at 13–14 percent of GDP. The investment ratio has risen substantially from 14 percent of GDP in the 1950s to 27 percent in 1980. The public-sector share of total capital formation has risen from around 40 percent to 55 percent in recent years; and the machinery and equipment share has fallen gradually to around 30 percent. Most capital formation represents construction activity: dwellings, about 22 percent of capital formation; government buildings, 14 percent; other construction, 26 percent.

Looking back over the thirty-year record leaves two impressions. First, as in the case of Egypt, it seems that the country has grown faster than it ''should'' have grown. There has been considerable political turbulence, with military rule prevailing most of the time since 1960. Many things have been done wrong. The bureaucracy is top-heavy, the SEEs are relatively inefficient, fiscal and monetary management is loose, inflation rates are high, trade and exchange policies have in some ways been counterproductive. But these things have apparently been overborne by a strategic location that induces substantial external support, by increasingly close ties with the vigorous economies of Western Europe, and perhaps by elusive sources of strength in the private sector, including a strong farmer response to technical opportunities.

Second, despite the statistical record, the country is still struggling to get over the hump to economic maturity. The large and chronic government-budget gap, the savings-investment gap, and the foreign-exchange gap do not suggest an economy that has achieved self-sufficiency and internal growth capacity.

IRAQ

Iraq, a seat of ancient civilizations, has seen several cycles of prosperity and decline. It is very dependent on irrigation. Only the northeast has adequate natural rainfall, while the west is largely desert. Crop potential is thus limited mainly to the irrigable area between the Tigris and Euphrates rivers. Over the centuries population and output have tended to grow when the irrigation works were kept in good repair and to decline when they were neglected.

Two other features of modern Iraq have an important bearing on its economic development. First, its political problems, internal and external, are unusually severe. It is deeply involved in the politics of oil and the politics of the Arab world. It has had recurrent disputes with its western neighbor, Syria, and in 1980 became involved in a protracted and costly war with its eastern neighbor, Iran. Internally, the country has seen the military overthrow of the monarchy in 1958, the Baathist coup of 1964, a brief return to civilian rule, and a second Baathist coup in 1968. The ruling Baath ''party'' is more nearly a palace clique, heavily military, without a broad base of popular support. There has been intermittent civil war with the Kurdish minority in the north, whose territory overlaps into Iran; the Kurds aspire to independent nationhood, a situation that provides fertile soil for meddling by foreign powers.

Second, economic growth since 1950 has been entirely oil-propelled. A great bonanza of oil revenue descended on the government and, although this revenue has not been very efficiently used, some economic growth was inevitable. But this has been lopsided, industry-oriented growth, with agriculture so neglected that Iraq is now heavily dependent on food imports. Little has been done to insulate the economy against short-term fluctuations in oil revenue or to prepare for the eventual tapering off of this revenue. Thus continued intensive growth in Iraq remains more precarious than in most other countries in our sample.

Extensive Growth, 1850–1950

Until World War I Iraq was part of the Ottoman Empire, and little more need be said to explain its slow growth up to that point. After World War I, as part of the division of the Middle East into British and French spheres of influence, Iraq became a British-mandated territory and remained so from 1918 to 1932. In 1932 authority was transferred to an independent monarchy, with continuing foreign tutelage and intervention, particularly during World War II. The monarchy continued into the 1950s and was ended by the coup of 1958.

Iraq's population in 1867 has been estimated at 1.25 million. Of these, some half-million were nomads, another half-million were classified as "rural" (that is, settled agriculturalists or pastoralists), and the remainder were townspeople. Population was growing at an appreciable rate, with some acceleration after 1900. The annual percentage rate of increase is estimated at 1.3 percent from 1867 to 1890, 1.8 percent from 1890 to 1905, and 1.7 percent from 1905 to 1919. The population was also becoming more settled, with the percentage of nomads declining gradually and the percentage classified as "rural" rising from 41 percent in 1867 to 68 percent in 1930. After 1930, the main trend was an increase in the urban percentage through cityward migration—the "push" of an overcrowded countryside, the "pull" of incipient industrialization.

The Ottoman rulers pushed registration of individual titles of land in Iraq, as they did in Turkey and other parts of the empire. But if the intent was to create a system of smallholders, it had only limited success. Tribal sheikhs registered large tracts of land in their own names, and a good deal of tribal land was acquired by influential townsmen. Land, previously not regarded as an asset, became increasingly attractive with the emergence of cash-cropping, and there was competition between sheikhs and townsmen to lay claim to it. The actual small cultivators seem to have remained at the bottom of the heap, as share-cropping tenants. A comment in Issawi (1966) that "the economic position of the cultivator during this period and particularly in the irrigation zone was unenviable" is probably an understatement.

There is no firm information about agricultural output. One can surmise that it grew reasonably in line with population, since land was still relatively abundant. It is known that Iraq passed from being a wheat importer in 1800 to being a wheat exporter in 1900. It appears also that during the years 1850–1914 there was a gradual growth of other agricultural exports, including dates, barley, wool, hides and skins, live animals. Iraq's main trading partners at this stage were Britain and

India. But total exports remained small, amounting in 1912–13 to only about £3 million.

Some irrigation work was undertaken by the Ottoman rulers from 1890 onward. Under the British, and later under the monarchy, there was continued attention to irrigation. The irrigated area rose from one million hectares in 1918 to 5.6 million hectares in 1953. This must have helped to keep food supply in line with population and to permit a modest export surplus.

Throughout this period manufacturing remained largely a handicraft activity. A few factories, led as usual by textiles, appeared in the 1920s and 1930s to produce light consumer goods. But the census of 1947 shows 57 percent of the occupied population engaged in primary industries, 35 percent in service industries, and only 7.4 percent (some 95,923 workers) in the industrial sector. And of these, a substantial majority were handicraft workers—tailors, carpenters, leather workers, woodworkers, metalworkers, and so on.

By this time oil had already made its appearance. The first concessions were granted in 1925, the first oil was struck in 1927, and a small amount of oil revenue began to flow into the treasury. But the real revenue flood dates from 1951, when the deal with the companies was revised to Iraq's advantage.

National-income estimates for this period are unavailable. Statements in Issawi suggest a slow growth of output to 1900 and a somewhat faster growth from 1900 to 1914, stimulated partly by British-German rivalry. Germany perceived Iraq as a cotton producer for the German economy, much as Egypt supplied British mills. The Berlin-Baghdad railway project was launched, and construction was well under way by 1914. A study by Penrose and Penrose (1978) describes the years 1932–52 as a period of slow development—a war-induced boom in agriculture, continued growth of rail and road infrastructure, a gradual increase of public revenue (though customs revenue was still four times as large as oil revenue).

Nowhere does one find a statement that living standards for the mass of the population changed appreciably before 1950. At most, there may have been improvement for a small number of merchants, landowners, bureaucrats, and professional people. This lack of widespread growth before 1950 warrants a judgment that intensive growth should be dated from around that date.

Intensive Growth, 1950–80

We begin with oil, which in recent decades has constituted one-third to one-half of Iraq's GDP and which provides the great bulk of both foreign exchange and government revenue. The Iraqi story is part of the larger story of how the oil-producing nations gradually asserted sovereignty over their oil resources and reduced the foreign oil companies to the status of junior partners in the industry.

The first oil concessions in 1925 were granted to the Turkish Petroleum Corporation, later renamed the Iraq Petroleum Corporation. This was owned jointly by several United States and British companies, the leaders being Standard Oil of New Jersey, Royal Dutch Shell, and Anglo-Iranian. The corporation agreed to build a pipeline to the Mediterranean and to pay a fixed annual amount in lieu of taxes. It retained full control over pricing, production, and profits, and the production level was varied in accordance with the interest of the international oil cartel.

After World War II, with Iraq now an independent monarchy and with economic development very much in the air, there was growing pressure to revise this (from Iraq's standpoint) very unfavorable deal. In 1951 the corporation agreed to a fifty-fifty sharing of profits with government, an arrangement that had already been pioneered in Venezuela and in Saudi Arabia, where Aramco had accepted a fifty-fifty sharing. The role of oil revenue in financing development expenditures dates from this point. Under the profit-sharing arrangement, government's oil revenues rose from £32 million in 1952 to £186 million in 1970, mainly because of a quadrupling of oil output.

The agreement, however, did not end controversy between the corporation and the government, whose first taste of wealth whetted its appetite for more. Especially after the overthrow of the monarchy and establishment of the Kassem regime in 1958, there was continuing pressure on the corporation to accept equity participation by government, to increase the government's profit share, and to relinquish concession areas that it had failed to exploit (amounting to about 99 percent of the original concession). When the corporation proved unyielding on this last point, the government in 1961 simply took over the unexploited concessions. The corporation retaliated by freezing oil output for three years, then raising it more slowly than in other Middle Eastern countries through the 1960s.

Continuing controversy with the government in an atmosphere of growing OPEC militancy, nationalizations by radical Arab governments in Algeria and Libya, and emergence of the vaguely socialist Baathist regime in Iraq led the corporation in early 1972 to concede a 20 percent equity participation by the Iraqi government. In retaliation, however, it once more cut Iraq's oil output and continued to demand compensation for the seized concessions. So in mid-1972 the government simply nationalized the corporation and transferred all its operations to a new Iraqi National Oil Company. The new company moved quickly to sign drilling agreements with a French firm and the Soviet Union, to negotiate bilateral export agreements with Japan, Brazil, and several other developing countries (thus bypassing the major companies' control of marketing channels), to build a new pipeline through Turkey to reduce dependence on Syria, and to establish its own tanker fleet.

The flow of oil profits to government was greatly increased by the two rounds of oil price increases in 1974 and 1979, which raised the price of crude oil from $2 per barrel to about $35 per barrel. For the time being, at least, Iraq was able to develop with "unlimited supplies of capital."

Iraq first tried a device used also in Iran. In 1950 it created a semiautonomous Development Board, which was to receive the bulk of oil revenue and channel it to development purposes. This much of a divorce from politics proved impractical, however, and in 1953 a Ministry of Development was created to handle allocation of funds. The ministry's poorly paid and inefficient civil-service staff was never able to spend as much money as was available. More serious, completed projects were handed over to other government ministries, such as the Irrigation Department, which were also too poorly staffed to administer them effectively. Poor management in government is a major and continuing problem.

The development programs of the 1950s involved mainly construction, flood control, transport, communications, and other infrastructure. But factory industry, very small in 1950, was also encouraged through tax concessions to private investors and creation of an Industrial Bank. The existing textile industry was further expanded. New industries included oil refining, bricks and cement, food processing and beverages, furniture, metal products, and shoes. Between 1952 and 1964 manufacturing output grew at better than 15 percent a year, though from a very small base, and by 1964 amounted to 10 percent of GDP. The response of Iraqi entrepreneurs, however, was below initial expectations. Land and trading were the traditional ways of making money and were still favored. Businessmen were also fearful (rightly, as events proved) that government would move into manufacturing. So they tended to hold back; and this strengthened the hand of those who argued that government *must* intervene to ensure rapid growth.

The Baathist regime installed by the 1964 coup was socialist in outlook and was also influenced by Nasser's example of nationalization in Egypt. So it promptly nationalized all large-scale industries, grouping them into 30 state companies, still involved mainly in consumer-goods production. The immediate effect was to reduce the growth rate of industrial output, which was lower from 1964 to 1969 than from 1952 to 1964. Growth speeded up again after 1970, however, as oil revenue flowed in increasing volume. There was a strong push into heavier industries: petrochemicals, fertilizers, pulp and paper, vehicles and assembly of vehicles, electrical appliances, electronics, iron and steel, glass, artificial fibers, tires, engineering, chemicals, and construction materials. Most of these were turnkey projects, built by contractors from Eastern Europe, Western Europe, and the United States. Manufacturing continued to increase its share of GDP, and indeed became the largest component of nonoil GDP.

As of the mid-1970s, the public sector had about 70 percent of industrial employment, in some 1,330 relatively large establishments. Private enterprises are more numerous but also smaller in average size. The difficulties of state industrial management are severe. There are several levels of bureaucracy above the enterprise level. There is a high turnover of personnel, extending all the way up to cabinet ministers. Many enterprise directors are army officers with little industrial experience. Workers cannot be laid off and overstaffing is endemic. So, as we have noted in a number of other countries, heavy commitment of resources has yielded disproportionately small returns.

In agriculture, the Kassem regime in 1958 introduced a conventional land reform patterned on the earlier reform in Egypt. A ceiling was imposed on land-holdings and excess land was to be sold to smallholders, who were to pay for it over a 20-year period. The program, however, was much less successful than the Egyptian program. There were endless disputes over land titles, which are less clear than in Egypt, over which tracts were to be retained by landowners, and over proper compensation to owners. Government had a very limited staff to deal with these disputes. So land redistribution has been very slow, and most of the seized land has continued to be administered by the Ministry of Agrarian Reform. The ministry has not been able to replace the farm management and input-supplying functions previously performed by landlords, though some landlords have con-tinued these functions on an informal basis. Further, the farmers' cooperatives which were expected to take over the landlords' functions, and which have worked effectively in Egypt, failed to materialize. By 1963 only 25 had been established out of a planned 2,000. So illiterate farmers have been thrown very much on their own.

The ceilings on farm size were lowered further by a new land-reform law of 1970, which led to sequestration of 1.1 million hectares on top of the previous 1.5 million. Adding some 0.75 million hectares of state land, about 60 percent of the cultivated area has come under state control. Distribution has been slow, however, and in the early 1970s about one-third of the total land area was still being administered by the Ministry of Agrarian Reform, which has apparently been even more unhelpful to tenants than the previous landlords.

While government has spent heavily on irrigation and drainage, little has been done as regards agricultural research and extension, supplying modern in-puts, and motivating the individual farmer. Government's response to any prob-lem is apparently to create a new agency; and heavy-handed bureaucracy, bad enough in industry, has even worse effects in agriculture. Land under cultivation dropped about 15 percent between 1958 and 1961 as a result of the first land reform and has continued to decline over time. Some crops show a modest uptrend in yield. Total agricultural output was stationary in the 1950s and grew at 4.5 percent per year in the 1960s but at only 2.2 percent in the 1970s. Meanwhile food demand has risen substantially through population growth and rising per capita incomes. The result has been growing imports of grain and other foodstuffs, which can be financed readily enough from oil revenue but which should not have been neces-sary in such a potentially rich country.

Population growth shows the acceleration we have observed in other coun-tries, the growth rate rising from 3.1 percent per year in the 1950s to 3.6 percent in the 1970s. But GDP rose at 6 percent per year in the 1960s and 12 percent in the 1970s. The IBRD estimates that from 1960 to 1980 per capita income rose at an average annual rate of 5.3 percent. Physical indicators also confirm a substantial improvement of living standards.

The investment share of GDP is high and rising, estimated at 33 percent in 1980. About half of total investment is public and half private. Public consumption has increased only moderately, to about 12 percent of GDP. Defense takes 35–50 percent of the "ordinary" budget, but education ranks next with 15–25 percent. There are in addition several "supplementary" budgets for economic purposes. All of these budgets are financed largely from oil revenue, and there has been little effort to increase nonoil revenues. On the trade front, too, there has been little effort to develop nonoil exports, since oil exports normally yield a comfortable balance-of-payments surplus. Traditional exports—dates, raw wool, tobacco, hides and skins—show a low growth rate.

Looking below the surface, then, one sees that the growth record is less impressive than the statistics suggest. Poor agricultural performance, poor export performance, and poor tax performance can scarcely be offset indefinitely by the golden flood of oil. In addition, there is a critical need to improve the quality of public administration in this very government-dominated economy.

IRAN

Iran's growth story begins a bit earlier than that of Turkey or Iraq. Oil exports had already appeared in significant volume by 1913. A modernizing ruler, Shah Pahlevi, took power in 1921. There was a noticeable rise in per capita income from 1925 to 1939. Thus I could not disagree strongly with anyone who wished to date Iran's turning point from the mid-1920s. But there was a further sharp acceleration of growth after 1945 under the Shah's son, who was installed as Shah Reza Pahlevi after his father had been deposed by the Allied occupation forces. A 1945 dating, then, is at least equally reasonable.

Extensive Growth to 1950

Iran is somewhat remote from the mainstreams of commerce, cut off from the Persian Gulf by a mountain chain. As of 1900 it could scarcely be considered a country, but was rather a decentralized tribal society, with one-third of the population living as nomads. The dryness of the country, much of which is desert, is conducive to a nomadic pastoral life. There are no good rivers for navigation or irrigation, and most of the land is unusable for agriculture. The country's long history is one of repeated subjugation by foreign invaders (Greeks, Arabs, Mongols, Turks), dynastic cycles, successive periods of prosperity and decay.

The eighteenth century was a period of decline, but the nineteenth century saw gradual recovery. However, Iran remained a laggard in development compared with more accessible parts of the Middle East, such as Egypt, Lebanon, and Turkey. Issawi (1971) comments that "its military forces were far weaker, its administration less efficient, its fiscal system much more archaic, and its educational institutions much less developed." Another stultifying factor was British-Russian rivalry. Any development project in Iran proposed by one power was effectively nullified by the other. Not until 1907 did a treaty divide the country into southern (British) and northern (Russian) spheres of influence. So Iran was generally neglected by European capital and enterprise. In 1914 Egypt had 250,000 European residents, Iran only a few hundred. Minority groups such as Jews and Armenians, who were spearheads of enterprise elsewhere, were small and isolated in Iran.

Population seems to have grown from five or six million in 1800 to about ten million in 1900, a growth rate of about 0.5 percent per year (compared with Egypt's 1 percent). Plagues recurred throughout the century and famine was also endemic, since internal transport was completely undeveloped. Bharier (1971) estimates that by the period 1875–1900 the population growth rate had risen to 0.75 percent. There was also a gradual settling of the population, with nomads falling from perhaps half the population at the beginning of the century to one-third at its end.

In agriculture, traditional land-tenure systems continued unchanged. Most land belonged to the Shah, court nobles, tribal leaders, or other large landowners, who extended their holdings as growth of cash crops made agriculture increasingly profitable. The actual cultivators were mainly tenants, paying rents in kind or, as the century wore on and monetization spread, increasingly in cash. The impact of government was, on the whole, negative. In addition to extortionate taxation and inability to maintain law and order, Issawi (1971) notes that "neglect of irrigation, the complete indifference to improvement of agricultural techniques and the high cost of transport, the system of land tenure, by depriving farmers of incentive to improve methods or expand output, was a strong drag on economic development." Agricultural output figures are unavailable. But the fact that Iran, previously a net exporter of cereals, had by 1900 become a net importer (food constituting about 30 percent of total imports) suggests that domestic food output was lagging behind population growth.

Foreign trade was growing intermittently through the century, increasing perhaps 12-fold in real terms between 1800 and 1914. (In Turkey, however, the increase was 15–20-fold, in Egypt 50–60-fold, and world trade also increased about 50-fold). There were marked changes in the composition of trade. Textiles rapidly became the leading import and had the usual adverse effect on local handicraft production. There was also a sharp rise in imports of "colonial goods," especially tea and sugar. The growth of food imports has already been noted. On the export side there was a marked rise in such cash crops as opium (for China and Europe), rice (for Russia), and cotton. Dried fruits and livestock continued important. Carpet production also grew steadily, and by 1900 carpets were a major export item. There were changes also in the direction of trade. In 1800, Iran's main trading partners were Afghanistan, the central Asian principalities, Turkey, and India. After 1800 British trade rose rapidly and by 1860 probably accounted for half of the total. But Russia then came increasingly onto the scene, and by 1914 its share of Iran's trade had risen to 65 percent while Britain's share had fallen to 20 percent. As in many other countries, there were foreign-imposed "capitulations" limiting Iran's tariff rates to 5 percent.

Industry at this stage was almost entirely handicraft industry. In 1914 only 1,700 people were employed in "factories," of whom 400 were in cotton ginneries and 300 in sugar plants. Handicraft employment at this time is estimated at 100,000, with carpet makers and textile weavers the largest groups. The "decline" of handicrafts in the face of import competition is more properly described as a shift in the composition of handicraft output. While foreign trade did injure certain import-competing crafts, it stimulated other crafts directed partly to the export market: leather processing, opium processing, silk goods and other textiles for export, and above all carpet making.

Public revenue, meaning the income of the royal court, is estimated by Bharier at about 2 percent of GNP. The main tax was the land tax, whose assessments were archaic, inequitable, and income-inelastic. About 40 percent of expenditure went for military purposes, 20 percent for court expenses, and 15 percent for payments to nobles and Islamic mullahs. Virtually nothing was spent for economic and social purposes.

The 1914 economy, in short, was about as primitive as could be imagined. Ninety percent of the population were farmers or pastoralists. Ninety-five percent were illiterate. There were no railroads and no electric power. Internal transport relied on mule tracks, there being only 800 miles of improved roads. Different parts of the country were quite isolated from each other. Capital formation is estimated by Bharier at 8 percent of GNP. Half of this was housing and only a tiny part was imported machinery and equipment.

With the installation of the Pahlevi regime in 1921 the economy began to emerge from this rudimentary state. Population growth accelerated in two distinct spurts, the first in the mid-1920s, the second in the 1940s. In the mid-1920s trucks began to be imported and extensive road building was undertaken, with the result that food supplies could be moved around the country and localized famines prevented. Perhaps mainly on this account, the estimated growth rate of population rose from 0.80 percent from 1900 to 1926 to 1.50 percent from 1927 to 1940. In the 1940s the deathrate was further reduced by malaria control and other health improvements, introduced initially by the Allied military forces and later by the World Health Organization and other agencies. The falling mortality rate, together with a continued high birthrate, raised the population growth rate to 2.2 percent from 1941 to 1956 and 2.9 percent from 1956 to 1970.

Government continued to pay little attention to agriculture, its modernizing bent being directed toward industry and infrastructure. The tenure system continued essentially unchanged, with about 70 percent of the fertile land controlled by a small number of large landowners, members of the ruling class. Agricultural output seems nevertheless to have kept pace with population, and the country remained essentially self-sufficient throughout the period. This was accomplished largely through extension of acreage, with little change in crop yields or crop mix. The cultivated area rose from about four million hectares in the mid-1920s to five million in 1940. Additional large increases after 1945 indicate that Iran was not as yet a land-scarce country. About half of the output consists of a few staples: wheat, barley, rice, tobacco, cotton. Production figures assembled by Bharier indicate that, over the twenty-year period 1925–29 to 1945–49, there were production increases of 68 percent in wheat, 50 percent in barley, 60 percent in rice, and 100 percent in both tobacco and cotton. There were also substantial increases in the animal population.

Oil development was carried on by the British-owned Anglo-Iranian Oil Company operating under concession from the Shah. Oil was struck in 1908, the pipeline to the coast completed in 1911, and the Abadan refinery opened in 1913. Production (in thousand tons per year) rose from 43 in 1912 to 1,385 in 1920 to 5,929 in 1930 to 10,195 in 1938 (though a more sensational expansion was to come after 1945). The initial modest payments to government were increased by renegotiation of the concession in 1932, and government oil revenue rose from £0.5 million in 1920 to £10 million in 1940. Apart from this tax contribution, however, the oil economy was a self-sufficient enclave, importing everything it needed. The oil fields and the port of Abadan became British oases. The multiplier effect on the Iranian economy was negligible because of a high propensity to import by both the company and its employees.

Oil already dominated the foreign trade scene. The value of oil exports increased more than seven times between 1920 and 1939, by which time it formed more than three-quarters of all exports. But nonoil exports also tripled over this period. Carpets were the largest item, followed by a variety of primary products: raw cotton, fresh and dried fruit, wool, rice, animal skins, fish, opium. Rising exports permitted large increases in imports. Between 1928 and 1939 alone the volume index of imports increased almost three times. Especially significant is the fact that imports of capital goods, which were only 12 percent of the total in 1928, had risen to 33 percent by 1938. Due mainly to rising oil exports, the balance of visible trade was consistently favorable from 1922 onward. Britain and the Soviet Union continued as the main trading partners.

An important development was reorganization of the royal finances by an American adviser, Dr. A. C. Millspaugh, who served as Director-General of Finance from 1922 through 1927. He raised revenues rapidly, partly through new taxes and partly through better collection of existing taxes, and also carried through a reorientation of government expenditure. Between 1928 and 1938 the "ordinary" budget increased by almost six times. The military share was cut from 40 to 25 percent, and the pensions to nobles and priests were cut almost to zero. In the new order, industry and infrastructure got about one-third of the budget. Agriculture, public health, and education, which previously had gotten virtually nothing, now received about 10 percent of the total.

In addition to the ordinary budget there was a "special budget," which was almost half as large and which was financed from oil revenues plus special sugar, tea, and road taxes. About one-third of this budget was spent on military equipment, but almost all the remainder went to road, rail, and factory construction. This reorientation of public finances continued through the 1940s. By 1949, the public-sector share of GNP had risen to 15 percent, and increasing amounts were being allocated to development purposes.

Only eight modern manufacturing plants were established before 1925. But after 1925 the pace of expansion accelerated. By 1947 there were 136 factories employing some 40,000 workers, of whom 28,000 were in textiles. This was still overshadowed, of course, by the much larger amount of handicraft employment. Private industry was encouraged by sharply higher tariff rates, free imports of machinery, and a variety of tax exemptions. But government also established a number of state factories, which in 1947 accounted for about half of industrial employment. Sugar, cement, and tobacco were state monopolies, and government also had a share of the dominant textile industry as well as of flour milling, rice milling, and tea processing. Most of the state enterprises lost money consistently and were a considerable drain on the budget.

More important for the future was the substantial investment in infrastructure. The Trans-Iranian Railway was built by foreign contractors between 1927 and 1938. By 1938 some 13,370 miles of road had been built, of which about one-quarter was rated as first class. Substantial amounts were spent also on communications, electric power, and human capital. Between 1924 and 1947 the number of primary schools increased five times, the number of high schools tripled, and the low literacy level began gradually to rise.

There are no reliable figures on national income or its composition during this period. Although Bharier's estimate that GNP doubled between 1925 and 1938 seems overoptimistic in view of the slow growth of the large agricultural sector, there probably was a significant rise in per capita income during this period. There was also a considerable rise in the investment share of national income. Bharier estimates that the GDCF/GNP ratio rose from 8–9 percent in the first quarter of the century to 15–20 percent by 1939. This was associated with the rise noted earlier in capital-goods imports as a proportion of total imports. Income per capita fell during World War II, then recovered, and by 1949 was perhaps back to the 1939 level.

Developments since 1950 show marked continuity with the 1920–50 period. By 1950 the main features of Iran's political economy were well established: prominence of oil as a source of foreign exchange and government revenue; large government expenditures for economic development, using the device of assigning much of oil revenue to a separate development budget; rapid industrial expansion, with the public sector continuing to play a prominent role; a lagging agricultural sector; a centralized, court-dominated administrative structure; and continuation of Iran's position as a buffer state, with the United States replacing Britain as the main counterweight to Soviet influence.

Intensive Growth, 1950–80

The recent period falls into three subperiods:

1. *1950–72*. This was a period of rapid, oil-propelled growth along "normal" lines. The data have now been worked over rather thoroughly, and most of my discussion will relate to this period.

2. *1973–78*. The oil-price explosion of 1973–74 set off an avalanche of revenue, which in retrospect was clearly beyond the absorptive capacity of the economy and society.

3. *1979 to the present*. No reliable data are available for this period. Oil production was disrupted by the Iranian revolution and the war with Iraq, oil exports at times falling close to zero. National output fell, and output per capita probably fell, but we cannot say by how much.

From 1920 to 1950 oil production grew at a high rate, but government oil revenue rose less rapidly than output because of meager royalty arrangements. Oil never provided more than 15 percent of government revenue, which continued to come mainly from customs duties, excises, and fiscal monopolies. As in other countries, there were continuing disputes with the foreign oil company and pressure for a larger government share of profits. When the Anglo-Iranian Oil Company proved resistant to these demands, the government in 1950 proceeded to nationalize the company. This led to a prolonged stoppage of production and eventually, in 1954, to a new agreement that sharply raised the government's share of sales proceeds. After this time oil dominated both exports and government revenue.

Foreign-exchange receipts from the petroleum sector increased tenfold between 1955 and 1970. Even though other exports increased fivefold, oil by 1970 formed three-quarters of Iran's exports. The buoyancy of exports permitted a relatively open trade regime. A unified exchange rate was adopted in 1956, and restrictions on exchange transactions were gradually phased out. So imports rose along with exports. The composition of imports shifted in the usual way. By 1970 Iran was virtually self-sufficient in consumer nondurables, and only 12 percent of imports fell in this category. Some 46 percent of imports were capital goods and consumer durables, while 42 percent were intermediate goods. West Germany (22 percent) and the United States (18 percent) by this time ranked as the main sources of imports, though Britain (13 percent) and Japan (8 percent) also had appreciable shares.

Rising oil exports should have produced a comfortable balance-of-payments position, and this was true most of the time. But the demands of industrialization and modernization were import-intensive, the Shah spent heavily on military equipment, and consumer demand for imports was essentially unrestricted. So in the late 1950s and again in the late 1960s there was a deterioration in the balance of payments, which required resort to foreign funds. These were easily obtained, however, because of Iran's apparently strong repayment capacity and because of its strategic location as a buffer state whose army was regarded by American strategists as a check on Soviet expansion. (In one year alone, 1965–66, the United States provided $712 million in military grants, $445 million in economic grants, and $392 million in economic loans.) Thus there was little restraint on the Shah's propensity to spend even beyond his ample oil revenues.

Oil became the main pillar of government finance and especially of public-sector investment. A central institution here was the Plan Organization (Planorg), staffed by young Iranian technocrats reinforced by foreign economic advisers. Its function was to receive the bulk of oil revenue, normally 75–80 percent, and to allocate this revenue among development projects, using a multiyear planning framework. These extensive powers naturally led to bureaucratic infighting with the regular ministries, which wanted to divert more oil money to the current budget and also to control the planning and execution of investment projects. Planorg was quite successful in maintaining both its share of oil revenue and its allocating and budget-making functions, though preparation and execution of investment projects was in time transferred back to the ministries.

While government's current revenue was rising rapidly, from both oil and nonoil sources, current expenditures rose even faster. One reason was a swollen military establishment, which in 1969–70 took 45 percent of the current budget. Administration took about 10 percent, education 16 percent, health 5 percent, other economic purposes 16 percent. A deficit in the current budget was thus normal. In 1970, for example, there were revenues of only 115 billion rials against current expenditures of 126 billion. This deficit was financed mainly by borrowing private-sector savings, but also by some extension of bank credit.

Most of the public-sector deficit, however, resulted from Planorg operations. In 1970, for example, Planorg spent 120 billion rials, or about as much as the current budget. But against this Planorg had only 70 billion rials of revenue, of which 95 percent was oil revenue. Of the deficit, about 20 billion was financed by net foreign borrowing, the remaining 30 billion by domestic bank credits, with resulting inflationary pressure.

The sector allocations of Planorg expenditure shifted over time. During the 1950s agriculture received about 25 percent, with smaller allocations to industry and other sectors. By the late 1960s, however, industry's share had risen to 20 percent, reflecting the first substantial push into heavy industry. Infrastructure received 40 percent and agriculture only 14 percent.

Manufacturing output rose gradually from 1947 to 1955, then much more rapidly, growing at about 15 percent a year from 1956 to 1970. The industrial labor force, only about 40,000 in 1947, had risen to 1,402,000 by 1968. Development still largely benefited light industry, with textiles employing 48 percent of the total, and food processing, tobacco, and footwear an additional 29 percent. An appreciable shift toward heavy industry, however, occurred in the late 1960s. The fourth plan, for 1968–72, provided for a steel-mill complex, a heavy-metals plant, an aluminum smelter, a machine-tool plant, a tractor factory, and three petro-chemical complexes. There was a substantial amount of foreign investment, about half of which came from the United States. By 1970, 90 foreign companies were operating in tires, auto parts, chemicals, pharmaceuticals, and other fields. Efficiency in these foreign-owned plants was reportedly a good deal higher than in Iranian enterprises.

The public-sector share of industry has varied over the years. In 1946, 50 percent of factory workers were employed in state factories, almost all of which managed to lose money. Perhaps partly on this account state enterprise was deemphasized, and virtually all the plants established after 1960 were private. Government began to come back into the picture in the late 1960s, however, partly because of the sheer volume of investment funds flowing through government channels. The new heavy industries initiated in the late 1960s and early 1970s were mainly state industries, with the result that after 1970 government's share of output was rising once more.

While government has a considerable share of "big business," little business is private and almost entirely oriented toward consumer goods. And little business continues important, producing a strongly dualistic manufacturing sector. As late as 1972, establishments with less than ten workers still employed more than twice as many people as establishments above that size level—633,000 compared with 303,000. Moreover, employment in these small businesses had grown as rapidly as employment in larger businesses over the preceding ten years. Industries with a high percentage of value added coming from small establishments include textiles and carpets (40 percent), clothing (71 percent), wood and wood products (63 percent), leather products (63 percent), metal products (51 percent), electrical machinery (34 percent), nonelectrical machinery (77 percent), and food processing (36 percent). On the other hand the small-business percentage is below 10 percent in beverages, tobacco, rubber and plastic products, basic metals, and motor vehicles.

Value added per worker rises steeply with size of enterprise. The wage level also rises, but less steeply, indicating that unit labor cost decreases with size. Because of lower output per worker the enterprises with less than ten workers, while they have two-thirds of manufacturing employment, produce only about one-third of manufacturing output.

In agriculture, land reform was undertaken seriously for the first time. The Shah led the way during the 1950s by redistributing about 500 villages from the royal estates. A wave of land reform after 1960 redistributed about 30 percent of the cultivated area to smallholders, and a second wave after 1965 redistributed another 10 percent. Considerable attention was paid to irrigation. The traditional system of underground channels was supplemented increasingly by deep-well pumps. Cultivated area continued to expand from about 5 million hectares in 1940 to 7 million in 1970, of which 3 million was irrigated. The country's land potential is still by no means fully exploited. Out of an estimated 22 million hectares of potentially productive land in 1970, some 7 million were cultivated, 5 million were in fallow, 7 million were used as pasture, and 3 million remained unutilized.

Agricultural output figures are unreliable; but output seems to have grown during the 1950s and 1960s at about 3 percent per year, barely keeping ahead of population. Increased output was obtained mainly by expansion of acreage, with little productivity improvement. Agricultural performance, indeed, resembled what normally occurs during extensive rather than intensive growth. Fertilizer use was rising rapidly in percentage terms during the 1960s but was still small in absolute terms; and there was little use of other modern inputs. Rural living standards remained abysmally low, and the rural-urban gap was clearly increasing. The ratio of output per worker in agriculture to the economy-wide average dropped sharply. Because of agriculture's inability to keep up with rising food demand, imports of food increased substantially during the 1970s.

National-income estimates suggest a GDP growth rate of 5.9 percent per year in the 1950s and 11.3 percent in the 1960s. High growth continued through most of the 1970s but, because of the 1979–80 collapse, the growth rate from 1970 to 1980 was only 2.5 percent. Even in the boom days, however, growth was highly skewed—3 percent in agriculture, 15 percent in industry, even higher in the oil sector. The proceeds of growth were also quite unequally distributed, with most of the increased income going to business owners, private and public administrators, urban professionals and technicians, and skilled workers in modern large-scale industry. Unskilled workers and farmers did not do very well.

In addition, a sizable share of the increased output did not go into private consumption. Public consumption, which includes the large military establishment, rose from less than 10 percent of GNP in 1950 to more than 20 percent in 1970. The capital-formation rate had risen above 20 percent by 1970 and shot up to over 30 percent after the oil-price revolution. Public investment normally formed 55–60 percent of total capital formation.

Little need be said about the period of 1973–78, which in most ways was "more of the same." The sharp increase in revenue after the 1973–74 oil-price increase (in which the Shah, always a "price hawk" in OPEC circles, was a prime mover) led to a sharp rise in the investment rate, massive government expenditure on armaments and heavy-industry projects (with a correspondingly large increase in the "take" of members of the royal family), imports at a rate beyond port and transport capacity, and a general overstraining of the economy. Among OPEC countries, Iran was notable in its rush to spend income even before it came in.

In a study (1977) published, ironically, on the eve of the Iranian revolution, I included Iran among fifteen countries with unusually successful records of economic development. Had we not all been taught that economic development would bring political stability, growing prominence of a modernizing middle class, and an almost automatic continuation of "self-sustained growth?" In Iran, events proved otherwise. Quite suddenly and unexpectedly, the Shah and his entourage were swept away, and power passed to a group of religious fundamentalists whose outlook was antiforeign, antimodern, and antieconomic.

Iran's impressive physical infrastructure and manufacturing facilities are still there. But how far they will be reactivated, and how effectively they will be managed, by a regime whose central interests are religious and political remains unclear at this point.

14

Pakistan, Indonesia, and Seven Nonstarters

Until 1947 what is now Pakistan was part of undivided India. The discussion in chapter 12 of the reasons India did not reach a turning point before 1947 applies to Pakistan as well, so in this chapter I will consider only the period of intensive growth, which set in after independence and partition.

At partition, the new state of Pakistan consisted of two distinct regions, West Pakistan and East Pakistan, separated by 1,200 miles of Indian territory and having direct communication only by sea. In 1970 East Pakistan split away, with Indian encouragement and assistance, and was renamed Bangladesh. The economy of East Pakistan—Bangladesh—will be discussed later in the chapter. This section focuses on what was West Pakistan from 1947 to 1970 and simply Pakistan after that date. Where figures refer to the old, undivided country, this fact will be noted.

Intensive Growth, 1947–80

Pakistan's political history has been moderately turbulent. A short period of multiparty government was ended by a coup in 1958 and installation of a military regime. Except for a brief return to civilian rule under Prime Minister Bhutto, who was later overthrown and executed, military rule has continued and seems likely to continue indefinitely. Externally, there has been continuing tension with India, which has led to substantial military expenditure on both sides. A dispute over possession of Kashmir at the time of independence was never resolved, and a military truce line has hardened into a *de facto* boundary. War with India broke out in 1965 and again in 1970 apropos of the Bangladesh secession. More recently, the Soviet invasion of Afghanistan has produced tension on the northwestern border and a large influx of Afghan refugees.

The former Indian provinces constituting present-day Pakistan were heavily agricultural. With the 1947 partition, India inherited almost all of the manufacturing industry and the great bulk of the experienced civil servants, business administrators, and professional people. Pakistan was left with soldiers and farmers. But the fact of limited prior manufacturing development made import substitution for a time natural and easy. There was also a substantial migration of Moslem traders and artisans from India to Karachi as part of the great interchange of Hindu and Moslem population following partition. These people were to form the nucleus of a new Pakistani industrial class.

In addition, West Pakistan benefited from a quasi-colonial relationship with East Pakistan. Karachi, and later the new planned capital of Islamabad, became the seat of government and the center of military and bureaucratic power. Manufacturing development centered on Karachi and other cities of West Pakistan, while East Pakistan remained heavily agricultural and continued to supply the bulk of the country's primary exports. Government policies, which tended to transfer income from agriculture to industry, thus also transferred income from East to West. I shall estimate the size of this transfer when I discuss the absence of intensive growth in Bangladesh.

There was a typical acceleration of population growth after 1945, as continuing declines in mortality were not matched by any appreciable change in birthrates, which continue to reflect uncontrolled fertility. The annual growth rate of population in (present-day) Pakistan is estimated at 2.3 percent from 1950 to 1960, 2.8 percent from 1960 to 1970, and 3.1 percent from 1970 to 1980.

The policies of the new government were at first unfavorable to agriculture. Both farm and retail prices of key foodstuffs were controlled at a low level, with a view to maintaining cheap food and low money wages for the nascent industrial sector. There was also a cumbersome system of food distribution through government channels. An overvalued exchange rate, supported by strict import licensing, discriminated against agricultural exports while yielding windfall profits to the manufacturing sector. Agriculture's internal terms of trade were only about 40 percent of what they would have been at world prices during the 1950s. It is not surprising that production was discouraged. Agricultural output rose during the 1950s at only 1.4 percent per year, and by 1960 Pakistan was a substantial food importer.

These adverse policies were relaxed increasingly after 1960. Farm prices were raised somewhat, and an export tax on agricultural products was removed. There was movement toward returning distribution of foodstuffs to private channels. Government began to subsidize farm credit along with fertilizer and other input supplies. Agriculture's terms of trade improved considerably, though remaining below world levels. As one would expect, there was a favorable production response. During the 1960s, agricultural output grew at 3.8 percent per year. The growth rate fell somewhat in the early 1970s, then recovered later in the decade. Between the crop years 1969–70 and 1980–81, the growth rate averaged 3.1 percent, but improved toward the end of the period.

This modest increase in output has come mainly from a growth of cropped acreage, associated with irrigation development. In addition to canal irrigation from the Indus River dams, there has been a substantial development of tube-well irrigation, and rural small-scale industries have sprung up to provide tube-well components. During the 1970s wheat acreage increased 11 percent, cotton 17 percent, rice 18 percent, and sugarcane 33 percent. Modern technology has as yet had only a limited impact. Wheat yields did rise about 40 percent during the 1970s, reflecting increased use of fertilizer and new seed varieties; but they are still low relative to other wheat-growing countries, and most other crops show little yield improvement.

The sluggish performance of agriculture is confirmed by FAO data, which show virtually no change in per capita food output or per capita calorie availability since 1950. It is significant also that the real wage of agricultural laborers shows little change. This may be partly because there has been considerable mechanization of production by the larger farmers, facilitated by trade policies that make machinery imports artificially cheap. Mechanization has reduced demand for farm labor while at the same time, because of industry's limited absorptive capacity, the rural labor force has continued to grow inexorably.

Information about industrial growth is limited to "organized," relatively large-scale, establishments. Little is known about the substantial amount of artisan and small-workshop activity. The convention in the national accounts is to show output of this sector growing at the same rate as population. But in view of the apparent multiplication of rural workshops producing tube wells, farm implements, and other agricultural inputs, this may well be an underestimate.

The growth rate of recorded industrial output has been high but declining over time, as one might expect in a series starting from an almost zero base. It was above 25 percent per year from 1950 to 1955, fell to 15 percent by 1965, and after a drop to almost zero during the oil crisis of 1973–75 recovered to about 8 percent in the late 1970s. Industrial growth was accelerated by government policies that made manufacturing highly profitable. The price of wage goods was kept low; the industrial sector got access to the foreign exchange earned by the agricultural sector at less than its opportunity cost to the economy; and the protection afforded by high tariffs and import licensing permitted high domestic prices for manufactures. While part of the gap between domestic and world prices was absorbed by the relative inefficiency of Pakistani industries, much of it was reflected in high profits.

Pakistan came into existence with abnormally low industrial output for a country of its population and income. Industry's share of GNP was far below the Chenery norm. So much of early industrial growth could be regarded as readjustment to a "normal" economic structure. Stephen Lewis's (1969) analysis of individual industry growth rates concludes that the most important single determinant was the extent to which an industry depended on domestic rather than imported raw materials, access to which was restricted by an import-licensing system.

Thus jute and cotton were increasingly converted domestically and a growing proportion of the materials was exported as cloth rather than in raw form.

Size of the domestic market was also an important determinant. At the outset the main market was for consumer goods, so import substitution proceeded rapidly and by 1965 Pakistan was already 90 percent self-sufficient in this area. Only in the 1960s, with the rapid rise in investment as a percentage of GNP, was there a sizable market for investment and related goods. Thus one observes the usual shift from lighter to heavy industries. By the 1970s there was substantial movement into metals, machinery, chemicals, and fertilizers. Government policies were generally autarkic and protectionist, emphasizing import substitution and reflecting the export pessimism of the 1950s. But protective policies were haphazard, and different industries received widely differing rates of effective protection. Lewis concludes, however, that this did not have a major effect on differential industry growth rates, which were determined mainly by market size and raw-material supplies.

After the foreign-exchange crisis of 1952–53, due to the collapse of raw-materials prices at the end of the Korean War, a strict import-licensing system was imposed, which had an important effect on industrial development. In addition to differential effects on industry growth rates, the general shortage of imported materials led to very low rates of plant utilization in the 1950s. The situation improved in the 1960s with some liberalization of import controls and greater availability of foreign exchange as a result of increasing foreign aid. But in 1968–69 the median rate of plant utilization was still only 60 percent.

Beginning in 1955, Pakistan embarked on a series of five-year plans. These were largely collections of public investment projects, but they were incorporated in a macroeconomic framework including saving-investment and balance-of-payments estimates. Size of the public investment program was a central issue. On one hand, a large program was regarded as helpful in securing foreign aid. But a large plan also implied a greater tax effort and larger public-sector savings. Nurul Islam (1981, p. 9), who was close to the planning operation, comments that "the debate for and against a big public investment program became a debate between the Ministry of Finance and the Planning Commission, the former urging caution and conservatism and the latter advocating bold, new departures and larger programs. The State Bank of Pakistan threw its weight on the side of conservatism, since failure to raise taxes implied deficit financing and militated against the pursuit of monetary discipline." The plans included output targets for particular manufacturing industries, which were largely in the private sector; but there is little indication of any serious effort to enforce these targets.

Government policy has emphasized private industrial development; but this is not inconsistent with a good deal of government initiative. A common pattern was for government, through the Pakistan Industrial Development Corporation, to contract with a foreign company for a turnkey project. When the plant was finished and in operation, efforts were made to sell it off to a private concern, thus replenishing PIDCO's capital for further ventures.

The initial industrial entrepreneurs were mainly Moslem immigrants from India. Studies in the 1960s showed that about 80 percent of large-scale industrialists and 70 percent of smaller industrialists were immigrants. Most of these people had previously been merchants, but some had backgrounds in small-scale industry and some had been agriculturalists. Immigrants from India also formed 70 percent of the professionals, technicians, and managers and 65 percent of the skilled workers.

About three-quarters of the initial capital was family money transferred from other areas, most of which had been accumulated in trade. Government, commercial banks, and scattered stockholders provided the remainder. Reinvested profits have been the main source of increases in capital, providing an estimated 70 percent of the total. The industrial sector has thus developed along the lines of W. Arthur Lewis's (1954) model. By 1965 the corporate sector was providing about one-third of national savings.

Because of heavy reliance on imported technology, the new industries are quite capital-intensive. The capital/labor ratio is typically much above that in Japan and often near United States levels. In the textile industry, for example, Islam (1981, p. 181) notes that capital per worker is $2,760 in the United States, $2,418 in Pakistan, $475 in Japan. Smaller firms are better adapted to Pakistan's factor endowment than larger firms in the same industry. They have markedly lower capital/labor ratios, higher capital productivity, and not necessarily lower labor productivity. The trade system and the credit system discriminate against small businesses. For example, unincorporated enterprises do not qualify for "tax holiday" benefits. Yet they continue to flourish, particularly in rural areas, partly because of family willingness to accept incomes below the large-industry wage scale.

Because of capital intensity, accompanied by heavy immigration of skilled and even unskilled workers from India, the industrial sector has made only a small contribution to labor absorption in Pakistan. Events have not conformed to growth models that depict a substantial labor transfer from agriculture to industry. During the 1950s and 1960s industry absorbed only an estimated 5 percent of labor-force growth. Perhaps because of the abundance of labor, real wages in industry have risen little and the labor share of value added has been falling.

Turning to the foreign sector, we see that exports have been somewhat sluggish. During the 1950s and 1960s the export/GNP ratio remained almost unchanged at around 7 percent. Performance during the 1970s was better, with the export ratio rising from 7.8 percent in 1969/70 to 12.0 percent in 1979/80, largely through growth of manufactured exports. But imports have risen even faster than exports, with the import ratio typically several points above the export ratio. The situation has been saved only by substantial capital inflows, mainly of "official" capital channeled through government. Foreign private investment is viewed with suspicion and its volume has been small.

In the early 1950s foreign aid was less than 1 percent of Pakistan's GNP. But by 1960 it had risen to 3 percent, by 1965 to more than 5 percent, and it has fluctuated around 5 percent ever since. For a long time the United States and other Western aid donors were predominant, Pakistan's position as a presumed buffer against Soviet expansion making it a preferred customer for both economic and military transfers. Since the oil-price revolution of 1973–74 Pakistan, as a fellow-Moslem country, has received increasing amounts of aid from the Arab oil states. During the 1970s, too, immigrant remittances from Pakistanis employed in the oil states became an important factor. By 1980 some 500,000 Pakistanis were employed in the Middle East and immigrant remittances were three-quarters the size of merchandise exports. But this windfall has apparently led to further relaxation of import restrictions, leaving the balance-of-payments gap and the "need" for foreign aid still around 5 percent of GNP.

There have been substantial changes in the composition of exports and imports. The consumer-goods share of imports has fallen steadily, amounting to only 16 percent in 1979–80. By that time imports of capital goods had risen to 36 percent and of industrial raw materials to 49 percent of total imports. On the export side, raw cotton, which was 40 percent of all exports in 1950–55, had fallen to 14 percent by 1979–80. Rice has appeared as an important export crop, its value being now somewhat larger than cotton. Most important, however, exports of finished manufactures are now as important as primary exports, each being about 42 percent of the total in 1979–80. The remaining 16 percent is exports of semimanufactured goods, notably yarn and leather. There has also been considerable diversification in the directions of trade. About 30 percent of trade is now with Western Europe, 15 percent with the Middle East, 15 percent with the United States, and 10 percent with Japan.

Several things have contributed to expansion of manufactured exports. Some of the early import-substituting industries gradually improved their efficiency, as evidenced by cost declines ranging from 5 to 60 percent and by declining relative prices. By the early 1960s, some of these industries had already begun to export. Stephen Lewis (1970) reports that the largest declines in relative prices between 1955 and 1965 were in edible oils, cigarettes, cotton textiles, soap, matches, pharmaceuticals, and metal products. Low and stable wage rates were helpful, as was the growth of markets in the newly rich oil states during the 1970s. Exports were helped also by two currency devaluations, introduction of an export bonus scheme in 1958, and liberalization of import controls as the foreign-exchange situation improved. Many export products now receive high rates of effective subsidy, which vary considerably by product and no doubt involve some resource misallocation.

With regard to the public sector, the tax effort has been impressive. Tax revenues rose from 7.6 percent of GNP in 1952 to 16.2 percent in 1980. The tax system is regressive, with customs duties providing about 30 percent of revenue, sales and excise taxes another 30 percent, and direct taxes only 15 percent. About 40 percent of current expenditure is for military purposes. The growth rate of current expenditure has been held below that of current revenue, permitting some margin of saving in the current budget. But this margin is more than eaten up by public-sector investment. In 1980–81, "development expenditure" amounted to 9 percent of GNP. With a current budget surplus of 4.8 percent of GNP, there was an overall public-sector deficit of 4.2 percent of GNP, covered by net external finance of 3.0 percent and domestic bank borrowing of 1.2 percent of GNP. Thus whether we look at the balance-of-payments gap, the aggregate investment-savings gap (typically 3–6 percent of GNP), or the public-sector resource gap, we come back to the key role of large inflows of foreign aid.

The allocation of development expenditure seems reasonably balanced among sectors. In 1980–81, infrastructure received about 34 percent of the total, agriculture and water 23 percent, industry 15 percent, fuels 6 percent, social sectors and housing 16 percent. Islam (1981, p. 12) notes that intersectoral allocations depend somewhat on the initiative and efficiency of the ministries involved. "The competent and powerful civil servants habitually gravitated toward economic ministries rather than ministries in charge of social sectors. . . . Because competence in project preparation and implementation was a vital factor in determining allocations, the social sectors suffered. . . . Health and education always suffered when a cut in the development program was needed."

A word, finally, about overall growth of GDP and GDP per capita. The growth rate in the 1950s was low. GDP rose at only 2.4 percent per year, and GDP per capita rose hardly at all. The main reason was the unusually poor performance of agriculture during this decade. With better agricultural performance in the 1960s, however, and with a heavier weight for the rapidly growing industrial sector, GDP rose at 6.7 percent per year and per capita income at 3.9 percent. Growth slowed somewhat in the 1970s, averaging growth rates of 4.7 percent in terms of output and 1.6 percent in output per capita.

The investment share of GDP has risen substantially, from about 12 percent in the 1950s to 18 percent in 1980. Public investment typically exceeds private investment, though this varies from year to year, depending somewhat on the aid inflow, which mainly supports public-sector projects. The savings/GDP ratio has also risen substantially but remains several points below the investment rate, foreign aid again serving a gap-filling function.

Overall, Pakistan gives the impression of a "middling" country in several important dimensions: a medium growth rate, a medium investment level, a medium inflation rate, a middling agricultural performance, public industrial corporations that do better than in some other countries but still not very well. The most distinctive characteristic is perhaps the continuing heavy dependence on foreign aid. The point at which the aid/GDP ratio begins to fall, already reached in many other countries, has not yet been reached in Pakistan. Nor has there yet been a real breakthrough in the agricultural sector.

INDONESIA

Each of our country cases is "special" in one way or another. But Indonesia is special in several senses.

First, it is at least two countries rather than one: (1) Java, the populous heart of the country, long the main focus of Dutch colonial activity and dominated by irrigated rice cultivation; and (2) the "outer islands," of which there are hundreds stretching over several thousand miles of sea, Sumatra being most important. These islands are much more thinly populated than Java, rice is not important, and the traditional method of cultivation is slash-and-burn. Dutch control was not firmly consolidated even in Sumatra until around 1900 and in some other islands even later. When referring to the nineteenth century, then, I shall be talking mainly about Java; the outer islands increase in relative importance from 1900 on.

Second, we know Indonesia's past better than its present. There have been several good studies of the colonial period, and we can give a convincing account of events up to 1940. There is no equally thorough study of the post-1945 period, and the statistical framework that would be needed for such a study is quite defective.

Third, the location of Indonesia in my chronology of turning points is debatable. There was a substantial expansion of coffee and sugar exports from Java from 1850 to 1900 and even faster export expansion after 1900 because of rising exports of tea, palm oil, rubber, petroleum, and other products from the outer islands. On these grounds one might argue that Indonesia had reached the turning point even before 1914. The main reasons for my contrary conclusion are that only a small proportion of the export proceeds accrued to the local population and that there is no evidence of appreciable improvement in living standards before 1950.

By my reckoning, then, intensive growth in Indonesia is recent and still precarious. In the postwar cases considered up to this point, intensive growth began in the years 1945–50 and so has been going on for about three decades. In Indonesia, on the other hand, intensive growth began only around 1965 and the impressive GDP figures since that time are heavily weighted with oil exports. The longer-range future is still uncertain.

Extensive Growth to 1965

The East Indies were never a promising market for manufactures, and Holland was in any case inferior to Britain in manufacturing expertise. The main object of Dutch colonial policy, then, was to extract a marketable surplus of primary products by building a capitalist export economy on top of the traditional economy of home agriculture, cottage industry, and petty trade. The object, as Geertz (1963) says, was "to pry agricultural products out of the archipelago, and particularly out of Java . . . without changing fundamentally the structure of the indigenous economy . . . to bring Indonesia's crops into the modern world, but not her people." The concept of a "dual economy" was first elaborated by the Dutch economist Boeke on the basis of the Indonesian experience.

The Dutch pursued this objective initially through the so-called culture system. Under a law of 1830, native cultivators in Java were required to set aside one-fifth of their land for the growing of prescribed crops, such as coffee, sugar, tea, pepper, and tobacco. This produce was purchased by the government at a low fixed price or was taken in payment of taxes. The produce was then shipped to Holland by a government corporation, in which the king was the chief stockholder, and sold at a large profit.

With the advent of a "liberal economic policy" around 1870, this older system was phased out in favor of development through private corporations. An Agrarian Law of 1870 decreed that all land not already in private ownership—a large acreage, about half of which was in the outer islands—was state property and could be leased out for periods up to 75 years. Much of this land was leased to Dutch corporations, mainly for coffee plantations, which require permanent planting and operate with wage labor. Another law of 1871 provided for leasing of land from actual cultivators for a maximum of 21.5 years. This land was mainly in Java and was leased for sugar and other crops that could be integrated with native agriculture. In the dominant sugar industry, the system operated as follows: a sugar corporation entered into a 21.5-year lease with a village, no doubt involving some coercion by government administrators and village leaders. Under the lease, one-third of the village land was planted to cane for the 15-month production cycle. This land was then returned to the village and another one-third planted to cane; and so on. The company built a sugar mill and hired large amounts of labor for planting, harvesting, and mill operations. In 1930, sugar companies employed some 800,000 Javanese men, women, and children at one point or another during the year. While this brought additional cash income to the village, the diversion of land from food crops intensified the problem of raising food output in line with population growth.

Coffee was the major export until about 1880 but, partly because of a coffee-plant disease which struck in the 1870s, sugar then pulled ahead as the leading export. In addition to expansion of sugar acreage, there was a doubling of sugar yield per acre between 1870 and 1900 as a result of experimentation with improved varieties and techniques. Java, indeed, was the earliest source of innovation in sugar, from which improved varieties spread to Taiwan, Philippines, and other sugar producers.

Sugar expansion continued after 1900, with additional yield increases and with output rising from 744,000 tons in 1900 to 2,915,000 tons in 1929. The most important developments after 1900, however, were growing diversification of exports, growth of the export share of the outer islands, and increasing peasant participation in export production. In the outer islands, notably Sumatra, two parallel systems developed: plantations on large tracts of land assigned by government and from which any native farmers were firmly removed; and alongside this, peasant producers who added production of export crops to their previous production of food crops. The earliest plantation crop in Sumatra was tobacco, which was important from the 1860s onward and by 1900 equalled coffee in export value. Rubber was introduced in the 1900s and became a major export after 1910. By 1929, Indonesia's exports of rubber were approaching the level of Malaya's. The main problem of plantation production in the outer islands was labor scarcity, which was met initially by importing indentured labor from China and Java. Later, as the settled population increased, there was considerable recruitment of "free" labor.

In addition to agricultural exports, there was a substantial development of tin mining and coal mining in Sumatra and adjacent islands after 1900. Petroleum was important from the 1920s onward. By 1930, the outer islands had about 56 percent of total exports, compared with 13 percent in 1870. Further, an increasing proportion of these exports were coming from small peasant producers. While corporations usually did the initial plantings, peasants quickly found that rubber, coffee, and a number of other crops were suited to small-scale production. Geertz estimates that the peasant share of total Indonesian exports rose from 10 percent in 1894 to 50 percent in 1937. Smallholders produced about 60 percent of exports from the outer islands, though only about 20 percent of those from Java.

The situation that had developed by the 1930s, then, involved a two-way division of labor. Geographically, Java specialized in labor-intensive products, notably sugar, while the land-abundant outer islands specialized in land-intensive products. Further, there was a division of products between plantations and smallholders, described by Allen and Donnithorne (1957) as follows: "the estates were responsible for all the latex and palm-oil products, nearly all the sugar, cinchona and cocoa, the greater part of the tea and tobacco, and rather more than half the dry rubber. The native producers supplied all the exports of maize, rice, areca nuts, peanuts and peanut oil, and cassava, and most of the exports of coco-nut products, coffee, pepper, kapok, tapioca, essential oils, nutmegs and mace." Geertz estimates that about 60 percent of 1938 rubber exports came from some 800,000 smallholder producers.

Figures on total exports are available only in current values. This is not too bad for data from before 1914, when price levels were reasonably stable, but is less useful for figures from after that time. Furnivall (1939) shows exports (in million florins) rising from 98 in 1856 to 185 in 1885 to 258 in 1900. This is a growth rate of 2.15 percent per year, rather below the average for tropical countries in this period but slightly above the rate of population growth. Allen and Donnithorne show a further sharp increase to 671 million florins in 1913, then the usual sequence of war boom, postwar price collapse, and recovery to a 1925 peak of 1,801 million. With adjustments for price level changes, export volume in 1925 must have been somewhat above the 1913 level. Export values fell sharply after the collapse of prices in 1929, and export volume must have grown little if any in the 1930s. Export expansion, in short, was much slower after 1914 than before that time, reflecting the lower rate of world economic growth.

Meanwhile, what about indigenous agriculture and food production? Here the story is quite different for the two subeconomies. The outer islands, by which I mean mainly Sumatra, were very thinly populated as of 1850. Sumatra entered on a period of rapid expansion in the late nineteenth century, which accelerated further after 1900. Between 1905 and 1930 the population of the outer islands rose from 7.6 million to 19.0 million, reflecting considerable in-migration as well as a high rate of natural increase. Yet land continued abundant. Even after withdrawal of more than a half-million hectares for plantations, the peasants were able not only to feed themselves but to develop a large export trade. As of 1930, about 45 percent of the land acreage was devoted to peasant export crops. This compares with only 9 percent of the land area of Java, where population pressure forced heavy concentration on food crops.

If Sumatra were a separate country, we could outline an export-led growth process in which smallholders were deeply involved, similar to that in neighboring Burma, Malaya, and Thailand. And we could date the turning point in the late nineteenth century, as we did for these other countries.

But this picture would not be correct for Java, which had 90 percent of the total population in 1900 and still about 70 percent in 1930. Here a rapidly growing population was confined within a limited land area, and export crops competed directly with food production. Java's population, estimated at 4.8 million in 1815, had by 1905 risen to 30.4 million, a compound growth rate of some 2.0 percent per year. Midnineteenth-century Java was still far from fully settled, and population could spread out into additional land of good quality. The population growth rate accelerated further after 1900, as the colonial government became more welfaristic and introduced a variety of health improvements.

Assuming for the moment that food output kept pace with population, we must ask where this increased output came from. The sources are familiar, though their relative importance cannot be measured precisely:

1. Continued expansion of acreage, as terraced rice cultivation spread from east Java to central and west Java and as drier land was put to use for other crops. This expansion continued for a surprisingly long time. A 1937 commission concluded that there were still about three-quarters of a million acres of cultivable land not in use.
2. Continued expansion of irrigation systems and multiple-cropping. The sugar companies pushed irrigation because of sugarcane's heavy water requirements; but peasant cultivation, which continued alongside cane in the same areas, also benefited. The irrigated acreage in Java roughly doubled between 1885 and 1930, by which time about three-quarters of all rice land was irrigated.

3. A steady increase in labor inputs per hectare, a process we have observed in China and elsewhere. Geertz has termed this process in Indonesia "agricultural involution," and he gives a fascinating list of the things that can be done just a little better: terrace building and repair, planting, water regulation, weeding, "razor blade" harvesting, and so on.

4. A gradual penetration of dry-farming annual food crops into village agriculture. The new crops included soybeans, unirrigated rice, maize, cassava, sweet potatoes, and peanuts (all introduced by Europeans). These crops were grown partly on nonirrigable land, but also as a second crop in the irrigated rice cycle. The acreage planted to these crops grew faster than rice acreage and by 1938 formed about 55 percent of the harvested area. Thus rice monoculture was replaced by a crop pattern that was considerably more diversified than that in the rice areas of Thailand, Burma, or the Philippines.

Were these developments sufficient to raise food output as rapidly as population was growing? We don't really know. The fact that Indonesia was a consistent rice importer after 1900, with rice forming about 10 percent of total imports, suggests that the race was a close one. Scattered through the literature are statements that living standards for the mass of the population had changed little. Jan Broek (1942) for example, comments that "various studies have shown that the average native standard of living in 1929 was at least as high as some 50 years ago," despite a doubling of population. A number of "welfare surveys" carried out in the years 1900–30, although somewhat noncomparable and hard to interpret, also suggest near-stationary living conditions. Aggregate consumption statistics indicate a small drop in per capita consumption of rice offset by some increase in per capita consumption of other foods. Export-crop production as a percentage of total agricultural production in Java declined somewhat as food needs became more severe.

How can we reconcile this apparent stagnation of living standards with the export-growth figures given earlier? Several comments are relevant:

1. Exports per head of population, or as a percentage of hypothetical GDP, were never as large as in some of the smaller Southeast Asian economies.

2. An unusually high percentage of export proceeds was drained off in various ways: as cash payments to the Netherlands government; in taxes levied to cover expenses of the local colonial administration; as profits of the Dutch plantation companies, plus their supporting banks and export-import houses; as profits of Chinese merchants, who formed most of the commercial middle class; and as payment for imported luxury goods consumed by the European population. Imports were typically only about two-thirds as large as exports, suggesting a substantial foreign drain.

3. The main impact on the local population of incorporation into the world economy was some increase in consumption of imported factory goods, notably cotton cloth. Wage payments to laborers engaged in growing, processing, and

transporting the export crops also enlarged the cash market for foodstuffs and led to a modest increase in commercialization of agriculture.

4. There were marked *regional* differences, as noted earlier. Peasant producers in Sumatra who drew cash income directly from export crops benefited considerably more than rice-growing villagers in Java. Essentially, I am making the judgment that rising per capita incomes in the outer islands were *not* sufficient to outweigh near-stationary incomes in the Javanese heartland.

The literature focuses on agriculture and says little about the rest of the economy. But perhaps not much can be said. The cutting off of supplies during World War I stimulated local industrial production of such goods as cement, canned goods, soap, oil, paper, beer, biscuits, and other processed foods. Industrial growth continued at a slower pace in the 1920s and 1930s. As of 1939 industry was still small, limited largely to Java, and outweighed by a larger volume of handicraft production. In 1939 the number of industrial workers in establishments using mechanical power was estimated at 300,000, of whom three-quarters were employed in food and beverages, textiles, metal products, and repair work. Workers in establishments not using mechanical power were estimated at 600,000; and there were in addition many thousands of individual artisans plus a large amount of household production.

The import pattern was also preindustrial, consisting mainly of rice (10 percent), cotton goods (25 percent), and other consumer goods (40–50 percent). Machinery, tools, and iron and steel formed only 12 percent of 1929 imports, suggesting a low level of investment.

The colonial government built some infrastructure, notably irrigation works and transport facilities. Railroad building began in 1875 and by 1903 a trunk system covered Java. By 1930 there were 2,917 kilometers of railroad in Java and 1,334 in Sumatra. In addition, there were some 1,400 kilometers of private lines built to connect the plantations with the government rail system.

Human development was neglected, reflecting a three-tier occupational stratification of the population. Estate managers, public administrators, bankers, professionals, and technicians were European, most of them Dutch. The Dutch penetrated somewhat lower in the occupational structure, however, than did their British colonial counterparts. They appeared as wholesale and even retail traders, skilled workers, and clerks. The Chinese formed a middle stratum of clerical workers, merchants, moneylenders, and other small businessmen, though many Chinese were employed also as mine and plantation workers. By 1930 there were about 1.25 million Chinese in the country, compared with 0.25 million Europeans, out of the total population of 60 million. The local population was engaged overwhelmingly in agriculture and in low-skilled wage labor, occupations that could be regarded as requiring little or no education.

Whatever the rationale, education in the vernacular was provided for only a small minority of Indonesian children, who typically dropped out after the first few grades. Very few were admitted to the Dutch-language secondary schools, which the Europeans attended and which were the channel to higher education. In 1930–31, only 862 of 4,986 secondary-school students were Indonesian. The same was true of the three higher-educational institutions: a Technical College (founded in 1919), a Law College (1921), and a Medical College (1926). In 1930–31 there were 178 Indonesians in these colleges, out of an enrollment of 374. Thus with the departure of most Europeans at the time of independence, Indonesia was left with virtually no educated class capable of taking over administrative tasks in business and government. Despite great catch-up efforts since 1950, this is still a serious handicap to the economy.

Intensive Growth, 1965–80

The years since 1939 can be divided into (1) a long period of zero or negative growth, which begins with the outbreak of World War II and ends with the overthrow of President Sukarno in 1965; and (2) a period of substantial increase in per capita income since 1965, which is heavily dependent on oil exports and whose permanence remains to be demonstrated.

For Indonesia, the war really began with the Japanese invasion of 1942 and the three-year occupation that followed. The effort of Dutch forces to reoccupy the islands as the Japanese departed encountered strong nationalist resistance, and guerrilla warfare continued until independence was conceded in 1950. There was widespread destruction of physical facilities during these years, which increased investment needs later on. The years 1950–58 were a "democratic" period during which political struggles led to increasing instability and eventual collapse of the parliamentary system. On the economic side, this was a period of reconstruction, marked by severe foreign-exchange shortage and strict quantitative control of imports. In 1958 manufacturing plants were operating on average at only 40 percent of capacity, due mainly to material scarcities.

The years 1958–65 were dominated by President Sukarno, who was averse to foreign capital and to market processes and who favored a "guided economy." But the guidance was not very firm. Sukarno was hemmed in by the army on the right and a strong Communist Party on the left and could not move far in any direction. Lack of experienced administrators was a continuing problem. The economic results were dismal. Per capita output fell at a rate estimated by Thomas Weisskopf (in Dernberger, 1980) at 0.5 percent per year. Inflation was also very high.

The impression of no economic progress before 1966 is confirmed by physical-welfare indicators. The only significant improvement was in school enrollment, especially primary-school enrollment. Food intake per capita declined slightly. It is significant also that there was little change in the sectoral composition of output.

In 1966 President Sukarno was overthrown in a bloody coup, which involved the killing of many thousands of communists and imprisonment of thousands more and which brought the army to power under General Suharto. Generals were placed in charge of most ministries and government corporations. The regime is authoritarian but "liberal" in the sense of favoring reliance on the market mechanism and on private enterprise. It relies rather heavily on a group of young, western-trained economists who occupy key positions in the planning organization, the finance ministry, and the central bank and who framed a successful program of monetary stabilization and trade liberalization. By 1968 output had regained the level of the 1950s, and it has grown quite rapidly since that time.

Population growth had already reached the 2 percent level by 1950 and continued to increase slightly to 2.3 percent per year during the 1970s. Up to 1966, food output was falling behind population growth. Weisskopf estimates that food output rose only 1.7 percent per year from 1953 to 1966 and that *per capita* output fell by 0.6 percent per year.

The Suharto regime brought a turnaround in agriculture as in other sectors. From 1968 to 1972 food output grew at 4.2 percent per year, and it continued to grow faster than population through the 1970s. The average annual increase in food output between 1969–71 and 1979–81 was 3.6 percent. For the first time there was substantial progress in rice output, which rose 53 percent between 1968 and 1979. This came about through a 10 percent increase in harvested acreage plus an increase of more than 40 percent in yields per hectare, reflecting introduction of improved rice strains and greater use of fertilizers and other modern inputs. A government "rice intensification program," which covered only two million hectares in 1969, had been expanded to five million hectares by 1979. Despite this good performance, rice imports have also risen, financed by the flood of oil revenue. In 1978–79, they amounted to about two million tons a year, or 10 percent of total rice supply of 20 million tons. Thus rice availability per capita (kilograms per year), which was 107 in 1960 but had fallen as low as 90 by 1967, had risen to an all-time high of 130 by 1979.

With regard to noncereals, fish output rose more than 50 percent between 1968 and 1979. Animal products also grew rapidly, though from a small base. Milk production more than doubled, egg production tripled, and meat production rose about 60 percent.

Industrial development is at an early, light-industry stage. Manufacturing production grew at more than 10 percent a year during the 1970s and by 1979 amounted to 12.9 percent of GNP. Textiles have played their usual role of leading industry. Between 1969–70 and 1979–80 textile yarn production increased fivefold and production of fabrics almost fourfold. Other important consumer goods include vegetable oils, cigarettes, salt, matches, soap, car and bicycle tires, bicycles and motorcycles, radios and TV sets, and sewing machines. The most important nonconsumer outputs are fertilizer and cement. Cement production rose 14 times between 1967 and 1979, with imports falling from 1974 on and vanishing by 1980. Per capita consumption of cement rose from 4.7 kilograms in 1967 to 29.3 kilograms in 1979, indicating a high level of investment activity.

Oil production rose only from about 500 million barrels a year in the early 1970s to 600 million barrels a year at the end of the decade. But the price increase from $2 a barrel to more than $30 a barrel has brought a very large revenue increase. Exports of liquid natural gas grew about fivefold during the decade; and several other minerals—copper ore, nickel ore, and coal—showed output increases in the range of 50–100 percent. Bauxite output was relatively stable at a high level.

The flood of oil revenue has transformed public finances, providing a large surplus in the current budget and reducing the need for inflationary finance, which had been a chronic problem in earlier years. The inflation rate peaked in 1974 at 33 percent, then began to decline as oil revenue came in and had fallen below 7 percent by 1978. Budget figures for 1980–81 suggest the present fiscal situation. Current revenue (billions of rupiahs) was 9,055.3, against current expenditure of 5,529.2. But development expenditure of 5,027.7 considerably exceeded the current budget surplus of 3,526.1. The gap of 1,501.6 was financed almost entirely by foreign aid of a "project" type, which amounted to 1,436.4.

There has been a modest increase in public consumption as a percentage of GDP, from about 9 percent in 1960–64 to 13 percent in 1980. More than half of the current budget, however, consists of transfer payments rather than provision of services. An oil-price subsidy to consumers took about 15 percent of the 1980 budget, and food subsidies about 3 percent. Debt-service payments took another 14 percent. Transfers to regional governments took 18 percent. The fiscal situation is unusual in that both oil revenues and other revenues (customs, excises, income tax) flow initially to the central government in Jakarta. The outer islands have always complained of insufficient funds to meet local expenditure needs. Geographic transfers in the federal budget are a response to this problem.

The allocations in the 1980–81 development budget reflect the general thrust of government policy. Industry and mining received only 6.7 percent, in accordance with the emphasis on private enterprise in these sectors. Transport and power received 22.5 percent. But agriculture and irrigation received 14.7 percent, and education, health, and housing 18.1 percent, indicating more than usual concern for these sectors. In addition, the 5.9 percent allocated to subsidize migration from Java to the more sparsely populated outer islands, and the 9.6 percent for regional development, reflect Indonesia's unusual geographic pattern.

The export/GDP ratio has risen steadily under the new regime, reaching 31.7 percent in 1980. Due partly to policies that are no longer so severely biased against exports, nonoil exports have been doing very well. Between 1968 and 1979, rubber output increased by 25 percent, copra by 40 percent, coffee by 50 percent, while cane sugar more than doubled, palm oil more than tripled, and timber output grew fivefold. Indonesia has been reclaiming its pre-1940 position as a rich and diversified source of primary exports. Smallholders dominate the exports of rubber, coconuts and copra, and coffee, and also have about one-third of sugarcane acreage. Private plantations are still of some consequence, producing about 12 percent of the rubber, 10 percent of sugarcane, and 25 percent of palm oil. But the former Dutch-owned estates were nationalized at independence, so estate production is now mainly government production. As of 1980 government estates were producing about 20 percent of the rubber, 60 percent of sugarcane, and 75 percent of palm oil. Oil exports increased more than tenfold in value between 1973 and 1980, by which time they were slightly more than half of all exports.

While imports have also increased rapidly under the relatively liberal trade regime, there has been a growing current surplus in the balance of payments. The composition of imports has changed substantially. Consumer goods, traditionally well over half of all imports, have now fallen to about 15 percent. The capital-goods share of imports has risen to about 45 percent, the remaining 40 percent consisting of raw materials and intermediates.

Japan is now the leading trade partner, taking about 45 percent of Indonesia's exports and providing 30 percent of its imports. The United States, the EEC, and the ASEAN group (Association of Southeast Asian Nations) are roughly equal, each having 10–15 percent of Indonesian trade.

While Indonesia has a comfortable current account surplus, it continues to borrow on a substantial scale. Lenders have been quite accommodating, on the principle that "to them that have shall be given." Japan has been the largest lender, followed by the United States and West Germany. The World Bank group has also supplied substantial long-term capital. There has been a modest flow of private direct investment, but this is typically less than 10 percent of the total capital flow. As of 1980, Indonesia's $20 billion debt seemed well within its carrying capacity, with annual debt service amounting to only 12 percent of export receipts.

National-income estimates from 1966 onward show GDP rising at 6–7 percent a year. The average rate during the 1970s was 7.6 percent, yielding a growth rate of about 5 percent in per capita income. This has been accompanied by the normal shifts in composition of output. By 1980 agriculture was providing only about one-third of GNP. "Industry"—mining, manufacturing, infrastructure, construction—provided another one-third; and the remaining one-third consisted of trade and services. The investment share of GDP has risen from less than 10 percent in 1960 to 22 percent in 1980.

Although this performance leads us to include Indonesia in the list of countries that have reached the turning point, a word of caution is in order. Fifteen years is a short span of economic history. Indonesia has all kinds of problems: imperfect control of the sea frontier and widespread smuggling of goods and currency; a limited staff of qualified administrators below the top level; rather widespread corruption; a continuing problem of squeezing more food out of limited land resources; heavy reliance on oil exports, which are likely to grow less rapidly in the future than in the recent past. It may be another twenty years before we can say that continued growth is reasonably assured.

Our sample includes seven sizable economies that still show no sign of reaching the intensive-growth phase: Afghanistan, Nepal, Bangladesh, Ethiopia, Sudan, Mozambique, and Zaire. There are similar cases among the world's smaller countries. The United Nations' euphemism that all poor countries are "developing countries" is a polite evasion of reality, which we are under no obligation to observe.

It is not correct to say that these economies are not growing. They are experiencing extensive growth, their rising populations being roughly offset by rising output; and extensive growth is usually associated with modest changes in economic institutions and processes. But *per capita* output is not rising at an appreciable rate and shows no sign of beginning to do so.

To ask *why* a particular country has not reached the turning point may not be a sensible question. Nonevents are hard to explain. To the extent that one can answer this question, the answer appears to differ from country to country.

My discussion of these economies will be much briefer than those of the "success cases" considered earlier. This reflects partly scarcity of information. I noted in chapter 1 the positive correlation between a country's economic performance, the quality of its economic statistics, and the amount of writing about it. The countries that are doing worst have been little investigated and the quality of statistics available about them is also unusually poor.

Afghanistan

Afghanistan's geographic remoteness and poor internal communications are almost sufficient to explain its limited development. It is a landlocked country far from the main channels of commerce. Most of the country is mountainous and the remainder largely desert. Only about 12 percent of the land can be cultivated because of limited rainfall. There are no railways. There are a few main roads, centering on the capital of Kabul. But most of the country is accessible only by mule tracks and footpaths.

In addition, the country has had a turbulent political history. Control of Afghanistan was long disputed between the British, pushing up from India, and the Russians, pushing down from the north. Driving through the Khyber Pass one still sees monuments to the British regiments that participated in successive Anglo-Afghan wars, which culminated in a 1919 treaty that defined the border with India (today, with Pakistan). Afghanistan remained essentially a tribal society rather than a "country" until well into the twentieth century. From the 1920s on, however, the shah managed gradually to centralize authority and to undertake very limited modernization. After 1945 the traditional Anglo-Russian rivalry was replaced by U.S.–Soviet rivalry, and such development as occurred was largely incidental to this rivalry. The United States built the Kabul airport, a main road south from Kabul to Pakistan, and a large irrigation project (which, however, was seriously mismanaged when it was turned over to local control). The Soviet Union built a main road north from Kabul to the Soviet border and aided the construction of several government-owned industrial enterprises.

The shah was overthrown in 1973 and his cousin, Muhammad Daoud, took over as president; but Daoud was soon overthrown by another coup. The new ruler, soon in domestic difficulties, in 1979 appealed to the Soviet Union for aid. But to his surprise, when Soviet troops arrived they started off by killing him and installing their own preferred ruler in office. It remains to be seen whether the Soviet-backed regime can pacify the country and fit the economy into the conventional Soviet mold.

There are virtually no reliable economic data. Not even the population is known with any accuracy. An IBRD mission in 1977 made a heroic effort to estimate GDP and its components from fragmentary sources.* It estimated government revenue in 1975–76 at 6 percent of GDP and gross investment at 10 percent of GDP, of which 6 percent was public and 4 percent private. Exports and imports were roughly balanced at 15 percent of GDP. The main exports were dried fruits and nuts, fresh fruit, karakul, cotton, carpets and rugs, and natural gas. Cotton textiles and petroleum were the main imports.

The economy is basically rural, even nomadic, and livestock forms an important part of agricultural output. Most of the rural people are illiterate, conservative Moslems of the Sunni sect (which prevails also in Iran) who are largely untouched by the incipient modernization going on in Kabul. Manufacturing is still dominated by handicrafts. Industry is limited to a few state-owned enterprises that produce mainly natural gas, textiles, and cement. These enterprises appear to be poorly managed and tend to drain the state budget rather than contribute to it. Public administration has traditionally been understaffed, inefficient, and corrupt. The country's educational facilities are very limited, and Afghans who do manage to get an education tend to migrate to jobs in other countries.

Whether the Soviet Union will be able to implant economic development in this unfavorable environment, or whether Afghanistan will remain an undeveloped military outpost, is still unclear.

Nepal

When Nepal, long a "hermit kingdom" virtually closed to foreigners, emerged from its self-imposed isolation in the early 1950s, it was almost without infrastructure, physical or human. Transportation was almost entirely on foot. There was no

---

*Country Report no. 1777a–AF, Mar. 17, 1978.

electric power. Less than 10 percent of school-age children were in school. Health facilities were almost nonexistent. The royal government in Kathmandu exercised nominal control over dozens of tribal groups and performed minimal functions of collecting taxes and maintaining law and order. The "country" was no more than a loosely linked series of largely autonomous village economies.

Geographically, Nepal is three rather distinct countries. Going from south to north, they are (1) the *terai*—a flat, grain-growing extension of the North India Plain; (2) the *foothills*—river valleys divided by low mountains, where altitudes increase as one goes northward from about 4,000 to 8,000 feet and where grain is grown on hillside terraces but is insufficient to feed the population, which depends heavily on imports from the terai; and (3) the *Himalaya*—a high mountain chain along the Tibetan border, with villages located as high as 13,000 feet. The Himalaya is also a food-deficit area, but in all other ways these villages are 95 percent self-sufficient. They come as close to the traditional "subsistence economy" as one could find in today's world.

Population growth accelerated from 1.2 percent in the 1950s to 2.5 percent in the 1970s and this rate may increase further as health facilities improve. Family planning is official policy, but the small medical staff can do little to implement this policy. Population per hectare of cultivable land is even denser in Nepal than in India or Bangladesh. The resulting severe ecological pressure has led to over-cutting of timber for buildings and firewood, leading in turn to soil erosion on the denuded hillsides, and increasing use of animal dung for fuel rather than fertilizer, with adverse effects on crop yields.

Agricultural performance has been poor. During the 1970s per capita output of the basic foodstuffs, cereals and potatoes, fell at about 1 percent per year. This is confirmed by FAO statistics showing declining per capita availability of both calories and protein despite increasing food imports to Nepal. Output of cash crops has grown at a moderate rate, mainly through increases in acreage; but these crops still occupy less than 10 percent of the cultivated area. In addition to an overall food problem, there is a problem of regional distribution. The terai, with about 40 percent of the population, produces 60 percent of the food and normally exports grain to India and Bangladesh as well as to the higher regions of Nepal. The growing food deficits in the foothills and Himalaya region could conceivably be met by larger transfers from the terai, achieved by some combination of greater output and reduction of foreign exports. But transport into the foothills and mountains is still limited to donkey back and human porterage. The only motor roads are the "Chinese road" from Kathmandu to Lhasa and a short spur westward from Kathmandu to Pokhara. Available transport is not up to the task of moving food northward in sufficient volume.

Industry still means mainly handicrafts. The factory share of GDP has risen slightly over the years, to a level of about 9 percent. But about 70 percent of industrial output is agriculture-based. Rice mills and oilseeds mills alone account for about half of industrial value added. Thus slow growth of agricultural output means slow growth in these branches of industry. Other industries of some consequence include sugar refining, jute goods, leather goods, and cement. On the whole, industry shows little promise as a leading sector, partly because of Nepal's proximity to the well-developed Indian industries. Nepal's ability to restrict imports from India is limited, since it depends entirely on India for access to the sea.

Export performance has not been good. Exports declined substantially from 1975 to 1980, due mainly to a sharp drop in rice exports. The deterioration of the current balance has been checked somewhat by rising receipts from tourism; and foreign transfers have been generally sufficient to close the remaining deficit. Nepal's strategic location between China and India makes it a favorite candidate for foreign aid. China built the Kathmandu–Lhasa road, provided Kathmandu with a modern electrified bus system, and built a hydroelectric power development north of Kathmandu. When China offered to help also in building roads in the terai, India intervened with an offer, which was accepted. The Swiss operate an agricultural experiment station, including cheese-making and sawmill facilities, in the high foothills at Jiri. The Japanese have built a beautiful, impractical tourist hotel on a 13,000-foot ridge looking toward Everest. The British provide medical centers and dispensaries, while the Hilary Foundation of New Zealand builds primary schools, hospitals, and bridges for the Sherpa population of the Himalaya. The Germans, the Russians, the Americans—everyone is into the act. The Nepalese economy seems unlikely to grow, but it will probably not be *allowed* to deteriorate.

Nepal has a core of young economic technocrats, aided by the usual foreign advisers, with Americans especially prominent in the agricultural area. Fiscal performance is one of the brighter spots in the economy. Government revenue as a percentage of GDP has been rising, though it was still only 8 percent in 1980. Equally significant, current expenditure has been held within bounds, leaving a substantial surplus for transfer to the development budget. Even so, the development program is sufficiently ambitious to require foreign finance. Out of total expenditures under the most recent five-year plan, 44 percent was financed from foreign sources, 34 percent from current budget surpluses, and 22 percent from domestic borrowing. The sector allocations of the development budget appear reasonable, with agriculture receiving an unusually large share. But capacity for project implementation is well below capacity for project design, and plan targets are typically underfulfilled.

National-income estimates have a large probable error. Taken at face value, they show GDP rising at 2.5 percent a year from 1950 to 1980. This was slightly above population growth in the 1950s and 1960s but only equal to population growth in the 1970s. The negative fact of declining food availability has already been noted. Nepal thus appears to be still in the phase of extensive growth, and just treading water successfully will require continued effort in the years ahead.

Bangladesh

I have already noted that this region, which was East Pakistan from 1947 until its breakaway from West Pakistan in 1970, was seriously disadvantaged in its economic relations with West Pakistan. Government policy favored import-substituting industries, located mainly in Karachi and other cities of West Pakistan, at the expense of agricultural output and agricultural exports, on which East Pakistan was heavily dependent. In addition, East Pakistan received considerably less than its share of public development expenditure, government bank lending, and allocations of foreign exchange.

This policy bias shows up in a variety of indicators. The distortion of the agriculture-industry terms of trade has already been documented. While East Pakistan provided 60 percent of the exports, it received only about 30 percent of the imports, including vital imports of industrial raw materials and capital goods. In West Pakistan, imports were about 12 percent of gross regional product during the 1960s, while in East Pakistan they were only 6 percent. East Pakistan received only about 30 percent of the lending by government development agencies. In government's current budget, West Pakistan consistently received 4–5 times as much as East Pakistan. In the development budget, per capita expenditure in 1950–55 was 4.9 times as high in West Pakistan as in East Pakistan, though by 1965–69 it had fallen to 2.2 times as much.

In view of all this, it is not surprising that the investment rate was markedly higher in the West than in the East. In 1960–65, the investment rate averaged 21.5 percent in West Pakistan but only 12.7 percent in East Pakistan. Moreover, while East Pakistan financed 80 percent of its own investment, West Pakistan financed only about 60 percent, since allocations of foreign aid were slanted in its direction.

National-income estimates show per capita income in East Pakistan falling slightly during the 1950s and rising slightly during the 1960s but remaining essentially stationary over the 1947–70 period. Meanwhile, West Pakistan was pulling ahead as described earlier. At the time of partition from India in 1947, per capita income in West Pakistan was already 17 percent higher than in East Pakistan. The gap widened over the years, and by 1970 West Pakistan's income advantage had increased to 33 percent. This is no doubt helped to strengthen the secession movement, which achieved success in 1970.

Since the "second independence" of 1970, Bangladesh has been on its own. One might expect things to have gone better, and economic performance has been somewhat better, though with unusually large infusions of foreign aid. Continuing political turmoil, with several coups since 1970 and much turnover of economic officials, has not been helpful in framing long-term programs.

The dominant form of agricultural organization is small peasant proprietorships, with the median size group 2.5–5.0 acres and with 80 percent of the acreage in farms of 10 acres or less. Only about 15 percent of the land acreage is under tenancy. This structure favors operation of economic incentives in production. Almost all cultivable land is cultivated, and about half of it is double- or triple-cropped. The cropping intensity index is 1.53. Government has promoted irrigation, and irrigated acreage rose by about 50 percent between 1970 and 1980. Even by 1980, however, only 16 percent of cultivable land was irrigated, about half by "modern" methods, including tube wells, and half by "traditional" flooding from the great rivers that traverse the country and occasionally bring devastating floods. Fertilizer use increased about eightfold during the 1970s but in 1980 was still less than a million tons.

As in India and Pakistan, technical progress has been most rapid in wheat, where yields per acre more than doubled during the 1970s. Farmers responded quickly to the increased profitability of this crop, so that wheat acreage tripled and output increased eightfold. Rice yields, on the other hand, have increased only about 10 percent. Food output in constant dollars is estimated to have risen by 40 percent between 1972 and 1980, with livestock growing most rapidly, crop output at a lower rate, and fishery output being essentially stagnant. Meanwhile, however, population is growing at almost 3 percent a year. So Bangladesh remains a food-deficit country. In a good crop year, the country almost succeeds in feeding itself. In a bad year large food imports are necessary and have sometimes exceeded 25 percent of the total import bill.

There is a small industrial sector, with textiles making up about half of the total; food, beverages, and tobacco, about 25 percent; chemicals (including fertilizer), 10 percent; and iron and steel, 10 percent. Industry is dominated by public corporations, and public investment is several times as large as private investment. The financial performance of the public corporations is not impressive, the textile corporations in particular usually showing sizable losses.

Raw jute and jute goods still form two-thirds of exports, but jute acreage and output have been falling moderately. Tea, leather, and fish are minor exports. On the import side, the fastest-growing item is imports of capital goods, which more than doubled during the 1970s. Food imports are also important in most years. The current account deficit is huge, with imports typically two to three times as large as exports. This deficit is possible only because of a large foreign-aid inflow, which is becoming more important over time. In 1973–74, net external assistance was 4.2 percent of GDP. By 1979–80 this figure had risen to 8.8 percent, though we should note that this was an unusually poor crop year.

Government has done a good job of raising current revenue, which in 1978 amounted to 16.6 percent of GDP. It has also managed to hold current expenditure below current revenue, yielding a modest surplus for transfer to the development budget. But the development budget is very large—50 percent larger than the current budget—and is financed almost entirely by foreign aid. The allocation of development expenditures during the most recent plan period were about 33 percent to infrastructure, 30 percent to agriculture, 14 percent to industry, and the balance to other purposes. Considering the meager infrastructure that Bangladesh inherited from the past and the vital importance of raising food output, this distribution seems to reflect a reasonable judgment of priorities.

The national-income accounts suggest modest growth during the 1970s. GNP rose at 3.9 percent per year, population at 2.6 percent, income per capita at 1.3 percent. It would be premature, however, to conclude that Bangladesh has passed the turning point. Any withdrawal or reduction of the foreign-aid crutch could have a shattering effect. The prospects for political stability and sustained economic leadership are cloudy. A generation from now it may be possible to make a firmer judgment.

Sudan

The Sudan, like Egypt, was long under British tutelage; it emerged as an independent nation only in 1956. There followed a period of political instability, marked by a prolonged civil war between the black Nilotic peoples in the south and the dominant Arab majority. This period ended with suppression of an attempted coup in 1971. Only since then has there been a relatively secure government able to concentrate on economic objectives.

Sudan achieved independence with a primitive infrastructure, which continues to be a serious constraint. Hard-surfaced roads are still limited mainly to the vicinity of Khartoum. Railroad capacity is quite inadequate. Even Nile river transport and Red Sea port facilities are quite underdeveloped. Electric-power output is the smallest of all the Arab countries, despite a large hydroelectric potential. Human capital is also undeveloped. There is a high illiteracy rate, a small educational establishment, and severe shortages of every kind of skilled and technical manpower. In 1950 only 14 percent of the relevant age group was in primary school. The adult literacy rate was about 10 percent and even today is only 20 percent.

While only 5 percent of the population is foreign, Europeans still dominate import and export trade, banking, and insurance. Other expatriate groups— Greeks, Armenians, Lebanese, Syrians—are legally excluded from land ownership and so have concentrated on trade, manufacturing, and moneylending. Sudanese, of course, dominate the civil service, and Sudanese entrepreneurs are gradually becoming more important. Migrants from Central and West Africa provide part of the common labor. Sudan is a labor-scarce economy, partly because of the ease with which Sudanese can take to subsistence farming or animal breeding. Labor is especially scarce at the peak of the cotton harvest.

To say that labor is scarce implies that land is abundant, and the cultivated area is still well below potential. Much of the unused land requires irrigation, but this is not an insuperable problem. It is estimated that the Aswan Dam alone will enable more than a million hectares to be brought under cultivation. There is already substantial use of pump irrigation and much room for further expansion.

Population growth shows the usual acceleration since World War II, from about 1.9 percent per year in the 1950s to 3.0 percent in the 1970s. The foodstuffs for this growing population include a substantial amount of livestock products plus wheat, rice, beans, sorghum, and minor crops. To say that food output has kept rough pace with population is only a surmise, but in the absence of land scarcity it is a reasonable surmise. FAO estimates show a modest improvement in calorie availability between 1960 and 1980. Food does not figure prominently on either the export or import list.

Cotton is the major cash crop. Cotton accounts for 50 percent of the irrigated area, 15 percent of the total area under cultivation, 20 percent of government revenue, and 40–50 percent of foreign-exchange earnings. Most of this output comes from the British-initiated (1924) Gezira project, located in the triangle between the Blue Nile and White Nile and rightly regarded as a success story in agricultural development. Government functions as a benevolent landlord, providing housing and community facilities, water, other production inputs, and supervision. The tenant provides labor and receives better than 40 percent of crop proceeds, while government receives a similar share, the balance going for management expenses. While the Gezira continues to deliver a dependable amount of cotton output, there has been little improvement in productivity. Yield per feddan was almost stationary from 1925 to 1965.

At independence virtually no factory industry existed. A central bank was created in 1959, as were three development banks for agriculture, industry, and "estates." Government also passed an industrial promotion act offering the usual tax advantages. From 1959 on there was a modest amount of private and public investment in industrial projects: three tanneries, a foundry, a textile mill, a dairy-products factory, several sugar mills, and some other processing activities. As of the early 1970s a Public Industrial Development Corporation controlled nine enterprises. These have experienced a variety of difficulties: faulty initial planning with regard to location, capacity, and adaptation to the market; inadequate specification of machinery quality and installation dates; serious underestimation of costs; and insufficient trained personnel at the skilled-labor, supervisory, and administrative levels. Sa'igh (1978) concludes that government entrepreneurship by coming in too early and too heavily discouraged private entrepreneurs and also set them a bad example of poor industrial performance. Even in the early 1970s industrial output was still dominated by handicrafts. While 5 percent of the labor force was classified as in "industry," 4 percent of these were in handicrafts and only 1 percent in the modern sector.

The growth rate of exports was only 2.6 percent in the 1950s and 3.4 percent in the 1960s, though it rose to 7.4 percent in the 1970s. Although cotton still forms about half of exports, there has been some diversification into gum, groundnuts, sesame, cattle and hides. Imports have tended to rise faster than exports, with capital goods and raw materials now dominating the list. The current balance is typically negative and is offset mainly by capital inflow from the United States,

Soviet Union, West Germany, the World Bank, and development banks in the Arab countries. Development aid from Arab sources increased sharply from 1974 onward, permitting a more rapid increase of imports and a larger trade deficit. The Arab connection is helfpul also in providing a growing market for Sudanese raw materials. The Arab development banks seem to be interested in the Sudan's large untapped agricultural potential, which could help to meet the food needs of the oil-rich countries.

Government revenue increased about six times between 1958 and 1974, and most of this was a real increase, since the price level was relatively stable. The current budget is typically balanced, but little more than that. There have been a series of development plans, in which public investment typically exceeds estimated private investment and which are heavily dependent on foreign financing. Domestic savings, both public and private, have run well below estimated levels and have been mainly responsible for underfulfillment of plan targets. In the 1960–70 plan, for example, actual investment was only 70 percent of the projected level. The domestic savings/GNP ratio is only about 7 percent, and the investment/GNP ratio not much above 10 percent.

Little can be said about the behavior of national output. The current-value GNP estimates are not of high quality, and the price deflators available for conversion to real terms are defective. Sa'igh expresses the opinion that the growth rate of per capita income from 1955 to 1972 was close to zero. IBRD tables show the growth rate of GNP per capita from 1960 to 1980 as −0.2 percent. It seems reasonable to conclude that the Sudan remains in the era of extensive growth.

The future outlook is not unhopeful. Substantial resources are available to a relatively sparse population. Oil and gas discoveries on the Red Sea coast may prove substantial. The Sudan may also achieve a division of labor within the Arab economies of the Middle East that will enable it to share in the expansion of those economies.

Mozambique

Although seacoast trading posts were established very early in both Angola and Mozambique, the Portuguese had little interest in developing the interior. The main economic activity for several centuries was the slave trade, the slaves being destined mainly for Brazil. Portugal gave up this trade later than did other countries, and then only under severe pressure from Britain.

During the nineteenth century a few Portuguese soldiers and adventurers penetrated the interior, where they set up what amounted to private baronies, especially along the Zambezi River. A continuing military presence and organized administration of the interior began only toward the end of the century and was not completed until about 1915. Even after that, white settlement was minimal before World War II. The 1940 Portuguese population of 27,500 was tiny relative to the

African population of five million. In effect, Mozambique missed the 1900–40 expansion in which many other African colonies participated.

Mozambique before 1940 was essentially a labor reservoir. Labor migration to the Transvaal mines began in the 1880s. The colonial authorities signed an agreement allowing South African agents to come into the territory and recruit up to a maximum number of workers each year but requiring that workers be repatriated at the end of their term of service. In return, the South African authorities agreed that a certain percentage of their freight traffic would be shipped through Mozambique to the port of Lourenço Marques. Much of the freight traffic from Southern Rhodesia also passed through Mozambique, and many thousands of Mozambique workers went to Southern Rhodesia for employment, though not as a matter of formal agreement.

Domestically, the end of slavery was succeeded by a system of obligatory labor. Laws passed in the late nineteenth century specified that each African must pay an annual head tax. Unless he could find cash for this tax from some other source, he was liable to be drafted for public or private employment at a low wage rate. The population was controlled through a pass system, in which every male African was obliged to carry a pass and to show it if he wished to move to another area. This resembled the South African system and seems to have continued right up to the time of independence in 1975.

Development efforts began only in the 1950s. They included some development of electric power, roads, and communications; a number of irrigation schemes; and an effort to settle both Portuguese and African farmers in planned new settlements. White-farmer settlement, which had begun much earlier in other parts of Africa, finally reached Mozambique. The Portuguese population rose from 27,500 in 1940 to some 60,000 in 1960. By the advent of independence, there were 4,738 farms classified as "commercial" and held under Portuguese civil law rather than tribal custom. These varied in size from small farms to large plantations, and the actual cultivation was done by African labor. By the 1950s the labor laws had been liberalized to provide that only public authorities could impose obligatory labor on tax delinquents. Private employers had to recruit through labor contractors, but this recruitment was not entirely voluntary. Pressure was put on Africans by local administrators and compliant chiefs to sign up for work, often at a considerable distance from home. There were also truly voluntary labor contracts, usually for work within the home area.

The Portuguese at this time embraced the traditional French approach to African populations. The Africans were to be acculturated, to become Portuguese in speech and thought. Those who met the educational and other requirements could become Portuguese citizens. But much of this was shadow play. Education of Africans was so backward that there were less than a thousand high school students in Mozambique in the mid-1950s. Those who qualified to become "assimilados" numbered only a few thousand out of the five million population.

These belated development activities were soon overwhelmed by the independence movement. By the early 1960s most African colonies were independent, and Mozambican Africans were not willing to be left behind. When the Portuguese authorities proved unresponsive, guerrilla warfare broke out, leading to eventual evacuation by the Portuguese and installation of a new African government in 1975.

The new regime inherited what was still a primitive economy. Agriculture, the dominant sector, was strongly dualistic. The rural village population planted corn, cassava, rice, sorghum, peanuts, beans, and cotton using traditional slash-and-burn methods, usually involving interplanting of crops. A United States Department of Agriculture study (1976) reports that "in good crop years, caloric intake is sufficient," implying that it is insufficient in poor years. There is no indication of an uptrend in food output per capita. The only important cash crop was cotton, which provided cash income for some 283,000 small producers in 1973. The average planting was less than one hectare, usually interplanted with food crops. Only about one-third of the cotton crop came from these smallholdings, the balance coming from the commercial farm sector. The gathering of cashew nuts, an important export, from millions of wild trees in lowland coastal areas is also an African occupation.

On the other hand were the farms classified as "commercial." These included some 4,000 farms owned by individuals plus 561 corporate farms, averaging 2,164 hectares in size. The area occupied by these farms was slightly larger than that devoted to African agriculture, though only about 30 percent of the commercial acreage was actually in use. These farms produced most of the country's tea and sisal output, a large part of the sugar and copra, about two-thirds of the cotton, and a number of food crops, notably corn, rice, and peanuts.

Factory industry was little developed. The national accounts show the manufacturing share of GDP as 9 percent in 1979, an increase from 8 percent in 1950. But industrial activity was largely processing of agricultural raw materials, plus manufacture of a few consumer goods.

The country continued to get foreign exchange from two sources in addition to exports: (1) cash remittances by an estimated half-million workers employed in South Africa; and (2) payment for railroad services on the lines running from South Africa to Lourenço Marques and from Rhodesia to Lourenço Marques and Beira.

Several other features of the new nation were not conducive to high economic performance. Portuguese administrators and commercial farmers left the country in large numbers. The number of trained African administrators was unusually small. Through 1979 Mozambique continued to be used as a base by the Mugabe forces fighting in Rhodesia, leading to frequent reprisal raids from the Rhodesian side. The new regime, Marxist in orientation, was particularly unsuccessful in agriculture. The effort to impose a system of collective cultivation proved quite disorganizing to production.

It is not surprising, then, that the economic indicators turned sharply negative. While the population growth rate accelerated moderately, the rate of GDP growth fell from 4.6 percent to −2.9 percent. Per capita income in 1980 was virtually the same as in 1960. Agricultural output dropped between 1970 and 1980 at −1.1 percent per year. Per capita food availability in 1978–80 was 11 percent below the 1964–66 level. Exports dropped from 1970 to 1979 at a remarkable −16.6 percent per year. It is not very comforting that imports also dropped at −14.4 percent.

As of the early 1980s, then, the economy remained mired in poverty and nondevelopment, with government unable to offer more than rhetorical solutions.

Zaire

Here again little documentation is available in English. Statistical information is fragmentary and unreliable. Although one might argue for a turning point during the Belgian period, the case would be weak. Economic performance since independence in 1960 has been dismal.

Leopold II sent troops into the Congo in 1884, not as king of the Belgians but to make money for his personal Fondation de la Couronne. Directly through his emissaries, and indirectly through companies to which he granted concessions, he compelled the Africans to deliver specified amounts of wild rubber, ivory, and palm oil at arbitrarily determined prices. Physical violence was often involved. Eventually a public outcry in Britain and elsewhere brought pressure on Leopold to turn the colony over to Belgium in 1908.

Roger Anstey (1966) suggests that Belgium never especially wanted the colony, never took much interest in it, and did not develop any coherent policy toward it. Even in the 1950s there was no sign in the Belgian Congo of the systematic preparation for independence that was under way in the British colonies. When African political unrest developed in the late 1950s, the government was entirely unprepared. In effect, Belgium dumped the colony precipitately and departed, leaving a vacuum of trained African leadership.

Exploitation of resources was left entirely to private enterprise. Mining activity was centered in Katanga Province (now Shaba Province), adjacent to Zambia. While there was some exploration as early as 1906, large-scale production got under way only in the 1920s as rail links were laid through Rhodesia and Angola. The industry was dominated by three Belgian companies, notably the Union Minière du Haut-Katanga, a subsidiary of the powerful Société Générale in Belgium. Production was less specialized than in Zambia (then Northern Rhodesia). Copper formed only about half of mineral output. Other important products were industrial diamonds, cobalt, manganese ores, and gold, and there was some production of tin, lead, and zinc. The industry had a strong enclave character, and returned value was relatively small.

The main agricultural export was palm oil. A subsidiary of Lever Brothers had large plantation holdings, and there were other sizable plantations in the north and east of the country. About 15,000 Belgian settlers were given smaller land grants, especially in the eastern Kivu Province, whose high altitude provides a healthful climate. African farmers were engaged mainly in traditional food-crop production. But cotton was an important cash crop, much of the output going for local use; and there was some peasant production of palm oil, rubber, and coffee for export. Belatedly, in the 1950s, government began to pay some attention to peasant agriculture. About 100,000 African farmers were resettled on new holdings with individual tenure and were given better access to credit, marketing facilities, and technical assistance. But this touched only a small percentage of the population in this very large country.

Infrastructure development was hampered by terrain and climate. Zaire is a country of large and turbulent rivers, dense jungle over much of the area, and torrential downpours in the rainy season that wash away roads and bridges. Some 2,000 miles of rail were built during the Belgian era, to link Katanga with Northern Rhodesia and Angola as well as with river ports within the country. Road building was actively pursued from the 1920s on. But the country still does not have, and perhaps never can have, the integrated transport grid that exists in most other countries.

Although a few industries were established in the 1920s, manufacturing was mainly a post-1945 development. Between 1947 and 1958, manufacturing output increased about three-and-a-half times. By 1958, agricultural processing was estimated at 4.9 percent of GDP and other manufacturing at 8.1 percent. The main outputs were foodstuffs, beverages, tobacco, textiles, clothing, footwear, and other light consumer goods; but, there was also some production of chemicals and building materials. Manufacturing employment in 1958 was 205,358, or about 18 percent of all wage employment in the country. Plants were heavily concentrated in Léopoldville (Kinshasa), the only major urban center, and in the Katanga mining areas.

Africans participated in the modern economy mainly as wage laborers. The mines were staffed largely with African workers, who were housed in company towns. The companies maintained a superior wage scale and living conditions in order to reduce recruiting costs and retain a settled labor force. This policy was generally successful, and many workers did settle permanently in town with their families. Other Africans settled in the "native cities" attached to Léopoldville, Stanleyville, and other urban areas. About half of these workers held unskilled jobs as servants, porters, and manufacturing and construction laborers. About 40 percent, however, held semiskilled or skilled jobs. The Belgians were more permissive than the British in permitting Africans to penetrate the upper grades of manual labor, though only 5 percent or so of the more educated rose to clerical and minor administrative positions. These urban Africans, in addition to earning cash wages, had relatively good access to primary schooling, medical facilities, and modern housing.

There was also considerable peasant production of cash crops for market. An official report issued in 1960 showed African farmers producing most of the cotton, about half the palm oil, one-third of the rubber, one-fifth of the coffee. European farm area in 1958 is reported as 840,000 hectares, compared with African area of 5,980,000 hectares. The great bulk of the African acreage was in food crops, cassava alone accounting for about one-quarter. Cash-crop acreage was only about one million, and even here cotton, the largest crop, was typically interplanted with food crops.

In important respects, however, Africans were walled off from the modern sector. Retailing, transport, and small business generally was dominated by Europeans and Indians, unlike in West Africa, where the traders were predominantly African. Very little high school education was available, which precluded going on to university. Africans could go to Belgium only to study medicine, and the first local university was founded only in 1955. At the time of independence, this vast country had 17 university graduates.

Worst off were the majority of rural Africans who continued to rely on subsistence agriculture, often in areas remote from transport or communications. Anstey suggests that their situation may even have deteriorated during the colonial period. They received a little missionary-supplied education, very little medical care, and were dominated by local chiefs acting as agents for the Belgian administrators. A special hardship was that villagers were subject to compulsory labor under a corvée system and were often forced into the arms of company labor recruiters. Desire to escape from this system was a strong incentive for moving to town. Anstey estimates that by 1958 about one-quarter of the African population lived "outside the sway of custom."

Whether the economy reached a turning point during the colonial period is debatable. On the positive side, one could point to high export growth during the 1920s and again in the 1950s. Export volume doubled between 1950 and 1958, with exports about equally divided between minerals and agricultural products. One could point also to the benefits that accrued to a minority of Africans working as wage laborers or producing cash crops.

A negative case could be based on the stagnant situation of the large majority of Africans who remained in the bush. Most serious was the lack of investment in human capital, the failure to develop a group of educated Africans who could provide leadership for an independent nation. This was a general shortcoming of the colonial powers in Africa, but here it reached heights paralleled only in Angola and Mozambique.

One's judgment is bound to be influenced also by the dismal economic performance since independence, which stems partly from failures of the colonial period. If the economy did take off briefly in the years 1945–60, it soon landed again. I prefer to say that it did not take off at all.

The Belgian decision to hand over the country in 1960 was very abrupt and immediately raised the question, "Hand over to whom?" The mass of the population had no sense of nationhood. The "parties" that had emerged in the late 1950s were little more than tribal confederations. Virtually the only African professionals were professional soldiers, and it is not surprising that they soon assumed control. The years 1960–65 were marked by civil war, the murder of the first prime minister, Patrice Lumumba, an effort at secession by Katanga Province (stimulated by the mining companies in the hope of avoiding nationalization), and the suspicious "accidental" death of Dag Hammarskjöld, who had been sent out by the United Nations to resolve the Katanga problem. In 1965 General Sese Seko Mobutu took power in a coup d'etat. His main qualification for office was his command of the troops in the Kinshasa area, a trump card in time of crisis. Although Mobutu has managed to retain power since 1965, the political situation has scarcely been tranquil. Katanga (now Shaba) Province has twice been invaded by secessionist forces based in neighboring Angola, and these uprisings have been put down only by emergency airlifts of foreign troops.

The nature of the Mobutu government goes far to explain stagnation, or even decline, in the economy since independence. There have reportedly been large accumulations of funds for personal use by members of the inner circle. But corruption is perhaps less serious than outright incompetence. The early cabinet ministers had virtually no education except military training. Although Lovanium University in Kinshasa has since 1960 been producing a stream of better-qualified people, these are inadequately utilized, partly because the less educated are fearful of hiring their educational betters. Government intervention in the economy is both pervasive and ineffectual. Trade and exchange controls have produced a large increase in smuggling activity across Zaire's long and porous frontiers. The agricultural marketing apparatus, which apparently controls sale of consumer goods to farmers as well as purchase of their cash crops, is reported to be bribe-ridden and inefficient.

The inflation of the public sector, with "public consumption" rising to 20.9 percent of GDP by 1977, does represent some increase in provision of public services, in that both education and health levels show modest improvement. But it also represents heavy overstaffing. During the 1970s the bureaucracy was growing at about 10 percent per year, virtually the only area of expanding employment. Public-sector growth also includes much misappropriation of public funds. Budget deficits have been large, with revenues typically only about two-thirds of current expenditure. It is not surprising, then, that the average inflation rate was 29.9 percent per year from 1960 to 1970 and 31.4 percent from 1970 to 1979.

In the crucial mining sector, the Union Minière du Haut-Katanga was nationalized in 1967, with compensation set initially as a percentage of sales but later commuted to $100 million. A new national company—Général de Carrières et des Mines de Zaïre (GECAMINES)—now produces 90 percent of the copper and cobalt and most of the zinc and tin. Its Belgian parent company, Société Général de Minérals, still provides technical assistance and marketing facilities but is expected to help GECAMINES toward self-sufficiency in marketing and refining.

The number of European personnel is being steadily reduced. Zaire has also entered into joint ventures with foreign firms, notably a copper-mining concern which is 85 percent Japanese-owned and whose whole output is exported to Japan.

Mineral output, then, has been reasonably well maintained. Zaire's share of world copper output has fallen only slightly since 1960. Because agricultural exports have fallen off substantially, Zaire has become more mineral-dependent than before, minerals now forming three-quarters of total exports. Government has focused its limited capacity on maintaining mining as a source of foreign-exchange earnings and government revenue. Revenue from export taxes on minerals helps to support current public services. Investment funds, raised partly through foreign borrowings, go heavily into power and transport infrastructure to support mining operations, as well as into mining itself. Government investment in other directions appears to be minimal. In the 1970–75 period, agriculture, health, and education combined received less than 10 percent of investment allocations. Rural transport has been decaying since 1960. One recent study estimates that only about 15 percent of roads are being maintained.

Statistical data on the economy are remarkably bad. But such as they are, they paint a discouraging picture. Although the population is not really known, the growth rate in the 1970s is estimated at 2.7 percent. GDP growth is estimated at 3.4 percent per year from 1960 to 1970 and 0.1 percent from 1970 to 1980. During the 1970s, then, GDP per capita fell rather sharply.

These aggregative estimates are confirmed by sectoral data. Agricultural output grew during the 1970s at only 1.2 percent, well below the rate of population growth. Government control over prices and marketing has worked against the farmer. Farm prices of marketed produce have fallen, and the margin between farm price and retail price has widened. Farmers who find themselves squeezed in this way have tended to revert to subsistence agriculture. Zaire was a net exporter of corn before independence, but by 1968 imports of corn had risen to 125,000 tons and by 1975 to 306,000 tons. By this time food imports were taking about 20 percent of the available foreign exchange.

Large plantations were nationalized in 1973, and the former owners were left in place temporarily as managers. In 1975, however, the system was "radicalized," meaning that European managers were replaced by Zairians as rapidly as possible. Perhaps partly on this account, output and exports have been declining. Agricultural products, which formed 49 percent of all exports in 1962, had fallen to 18 percent by 1978, leaving Zaire more mineral-dependent than ever before.

With agriculture performing poorly and minerals performing only moderately, export volume fell at −1.8 percent per year from 1960 to 1970 and at −1.1 percent from 1970 to 1979. The net barter terms of trade, which had almost doubled during the 1960s, were more than cut in half in the 1970s, falling to about 75 percent of the 1960 level. Even with substantial foreign borrowing, imports fell sharply in the 1970s. Since 35 percent of 1978 imports were food and fuels and another 38 percent were machinery and transport equipment, there was a severe squeeze on imported inputs for manufacturing industries. The industry share of GDP fell during the 1970s and was lower in 1979 than in 1960, again suggesting "development in reverse."

The large deficit in the current balance has been closed by frequent infusions of foreign aid, mainly bilateral aid from the United States and other Western countries interested in maintaining access to Zaire's mineral resources. In 1979 such aid amounted to 5.7 percent of GDP and about three-quarters of gross domestic investment, which had fallen to only 9 percent of GDP by this time. Foreign debt rose from $311 million in 1970 to $4,080 million in 1979 and will almost certainly continue to climb.

In sum: Zaire is a shrinking economy, with rising unemployment and underemployment, which is hampered by a corrupt and inefficient government and propped up for the time being by foreign aid reflecting a blend of economic and political motives. Uncertainty about the future is unusually high.

PART IV
RETROSPECT

15

Comparative Growth Performance, 1950–80

In earlier chapters our actors were brought on stage: countries whose intensive growth began as early as 1850 in some cases, as recently as 1950 in others, plus some countries that have not yet reached the turning point. I want now to look at these countries together over the period 1950–80, because for this period we have a richer store of quantitative data. Statistics have been collected for many countries on a somewhat comparable basis by the United Nations and its specialized agencies, the IBRD, the IMF, and other international organizations. Despite some defects in measurement, these data provide a firmer empirical base than exists for any earlier period.

On the basis of this material I will comment on, and suggest answers to, some of the "big questions" about recent growth performance. For example: (1) Is recent performance related to the *time* at which a country entered on intensive growth? Do early starters have an advantage? (2) Is population a drag? Is the rate of increase in per capita income inversely related to the rate of population growth? (3) Are there other quantitative variables that may help to "explain," in a statistical sense, the intercountry variation in 1950–80 growth rates? Candidates here include country size, initial income level in 1950, export performance since 1950, agricultural performance since 1950, the investment/GDP ratio and its rate of increase over time. In addition to such economic variables, I shall explore the possible significance of political variables.

AGGREGATE MEASURES OF GROWTH

Data Problems

Information about national output and its composition comes from national accounts prepared by statistical agencies in each country. In the late 1940s the Statistics Division of the United Nations began to send an annual questionnaire to each member government, requesting national account estimates in a standard format and supposedly using standard definitions and procedures. The returns are

387

published each year in the *United Nations Yearbook of National Accounts Statistics*. The United Nations staff is forbidden by protocol from revising the estimates of its sovereign members, so these are published essentially as submitted. The IBRD and IMF are less subject to political constraints and devote considerable staff time to revising and reestimating the country data. Wherever possible, then, I shall use IBRD or IMF sources, which reflect careful professional screening.

Revision at higher levels, however, can never fully repair inadequacies in the original estimates. Discussion with professionals in the field suggests that the estimates for countries in our sample differ widely in quality—that is, in the probable error in the estimates of major GNP components and hence, except in the unlikely event of offsetting errors, in GNP itself. For only about half the countries in our sample can the national accounts data be regarded as solid. The accounts of a few, including India, Sri Lanka, and pre-1978 Iran, approach in accuracy those of the OECD countries. Another dozen countries, including most of those with a strong growth record since 1950, show a wider but still moderate margin of error. But below this group are ten countries whose accounts are dubious, with wide error margins, and another ten for which the official data are essentially worthless. As might be expected, there is a marked correlation between poor statistics and poor economic performance. Of the ten countries with poorest data, six are on our list of countries that have not yet reached the turning point.

Especially serious is the problem of deflating money values to measure changes in real GNP. Price indexes in most of these countries do not approach the accuracy of those in the OECD countries. This imprecision is especially serious in countries with a high inflation rate. Argentina, for example, has recently had very high inflation, which has reduced the accuracy of its real product estimates. One finds countries that deflate money GDP by the consumer price index in the capital city or whose price indexes are based on a "market basket" as ancient as 1940.

So there is considerable inaccuracy in the data used here, its degree varying from country to country. There is absolutely nothing I can do about this, but it clearly complicates the problem of trying to explain differences in reported national growth rates. Part of what I will be "explaining" is differing degrees of statistical error rather than differences in economic performance.

In addition, Simon Kuznets has noted that there are several sources of upward bias in GNP estimates for third-world countries.[*] If we follow Kuznets, the rates reported in table 2 should be adjusted downward by at least one percentage point to make them at all comparable with rates for the developed countries. There is less distortion, however, in comparisons *within* the third-world group.

The Reported Growth of Output per Capita

Discussions of national output used to focus on gross national product. More recently, the World Bank and others have tended to focus on gross domestic

---

[*]Simon Kuznets, "Problems in Comparing Recent Growth Rates for Developed and Less Developed Countries," *Economic Development and Cultural Change*, 20 (January 1972):185–209.

product. GDP, which measures what is produced within a country's borders, is the better measure of growth in productive capacity. GNP, which measures how much of what is produced *belongs* to residents of the country, is more closely related to changes in welfare. The distinction is not very important for the "developed" countries; but it sometimes is important in third-world countries, where an appreciable percentage of what is produced may go to foreign suppliers of capital or labor.

Further, one can look at total output or at output per capita. The latter figure will typically run 2–3 percent below the former, since 1950–80 population growth rates for the countries in our sample were typically in this range. To conserve space, I omit any tabulation of total output growth rates and go directly to output per capita.

Two somewhat different measures are presented in table 2. The first column shows average annual growth rates of GNP per capita from 1960 to 1980. I rely most on these figures because they are World Bank estimates, which have undergone the scrutiny and revision noted earlier; because data for the 1960s and 1970s are better on average than those for the 1950s, when statistical staffs had less experience and expertise; and because these are the figures recent writers on comparative growth experience have usually tried to explain.

The remaining columns show growth rates of real GDP by decade plus, in the final column, a simple average of the three decade rates. The decade rates are of interest, since they enable us to sort out countries whose performance improved steadily over the period as against those whose performance deteriorated. The figures in the last column, of course, are not "true" growth rates. A little thought will show that, if we start from a country's real per capita output in 1950 and 1980 and calculate the geometric rate of increase over this period, we will *not* arrive at the same figure as the three-decade average. But the latter figure will usually not be very different from the former, and it provides a rough indicator of performance.

In all the tables in this chapter countries are ranked in order of 1960–80 growth in GNP per capita. A ranking based on the figures in the last column would have been somewhat different, but not greatly different. The reader will note that the tables contain only 37 of the 41 countries in our sample. Omission of Bangladesh is explained by the fact that it came into existence only in 1970. In Cuba the revolution brought substantial change in statistical concepts and measurements, so that pre-1958 and post-1958 data are not readily comparable. China was not included in United Nations and World Bank tables until the mid-1970s, and even now it would be difficult to fill in a "China line" for all the later tables in this chapter. Japan is omitted because by this period it had already passed out of the "less-developed" category.

The first impression one gets from table 15.1 is the wide variation in country growth rates, from countries at the top, which are in the "Japan range," down to those at the bottom having negative growth rates. For convenience in later analysis, I have divided the countries into four tiers: a top group of ten countries and

TABLE 2   Selected Measures of Output Growth (percent per year)

Country	Real GNP Per Capita 1960–80	Real GDP Per Capita			Average of Decade Rates
		1950–60	1960–70	1970–80	
South Korea	7.0	2.0[1]	6.4	7.5	5.3
Taiwan	7.1[3]	4.0	6.4		
Iraq	5.3[2]	3.2[1]	2.4	5.5	3.7
Brazil	5.1	3.6	2.3	5.4	3.8
Thailand	4.7	3.3	5.1	4.2	4.2
Malaysia	4.3	1.1	3.0	5.7	3.3
Nigeria	4.1	2.1	1.5	4.3	2.6
Indonesia	4.0	1.7	0.8	5.1	2.8
Turkey	3.6	2.9	3.4	3.2	3.2
Egypt	3.4	2.9	1.9	3.8	2.9
Iran	n.a.	3.3	6.7	−0.1	3.3
Algeria	3.2	6.0	−1.0	4.9	3.3
Colombia	3.0	1.5	1.9	3.3	2.3
Pakistan	2.8	0.4	3.3	1.9	1.9
Philippines	2.8	3.3	1.9	3.2	2.8
Kenya	2.7	1.1	4.6	0.7	2.1
Mexico	2.6	2.8	3.9	1.9	2.9
Venezuela	2.6	3.5	2.3	1.6	2.5
Ivory Coast	2.5	1.5	2.6	2.9	2.3
Morocco	2.5	−0.8	1.2	2.8	1.1
Sri Lanka	2.4	1.0	2.5	3.1	2.2
Argentina	2.2	1.2	2.8	1.0	1.7
Tanzania	1.9	1.4	5.0	2.0	2.8
Chile	1.6	1.2	2.2	0.8	1.4
India	1.4	1.9	1.2	1.3	1.5
Ethiopia	1.4	2.1	1.9	−0.6	1.1
Burma	1.2	4.4	0.2	1.6	2.1
Peru	1.1	2.9	1.9	0.4	1.7
Zimbabwe	0.7	2.9	−0.6	−2.0	0.1
Zambia	0.2	3.3[2]	5.3	−2.6	2.0
Zaire	0.2	2.1	0.5	−2.6	0.0
Nepal	0.2	1.0	0.2	0.2	0.5
Mozambique	−0.1	1.8	1.4	−0.3	1.3
Sudan	−0.2	2.0[2]	0.2	1.2	1.1
Uganda	−0.7	0.4	1.5	−3.4	−0.5
Ghana	−1.0	2.4	0.0	−2.1	0.1
Afghanistan	n.a.	0.4	0.2	0.2	0.3

(continued)

[1]1953–60   [2]1955–60   [3]1960–77

SOURCES: Column 1: IBRD, *World Development Report*, 1982. Columns 2–5: UNCTAD, *Handbook of International Trade and Development Statistics*, 1960–81; Taiwan [Republic of China], *National Income Accounts, 1981.*

TABLE 2 *(continued)*

	Real GNP Per Capita 1960–80	Real GDP Per Capita			Average of Decade Rates
Country		*1950–60*	*1960–70*	*1970–80*	
Medians					
Tier 1	4.5	2.9	2.7	5.3	3.5
Tier 2	2.8	2.8	2.6	1.9	2.7
Tier 3	1.6	1.4	1.9	1.3	1.7
Tier 4	0.0	2.0	0.2	−2.0	0.3

three lower groups of nine countries each. Although the decline in per capita GNP growth rates from top to bottom is continuous and the dividing lines are in this sense arbitrary, I feel it will be useful to divide the sample into *high-growth economies* (median growth rate, 4.5 percent per year), *moderate-growth economies* (median growth rate, 2.8 percent), *low-growth economies* (median growth rate, 1.6 percent), and *no-growth economies* (median growth rate, 0.0 percent). In all tables of this chapter, countries shall be listed in this same order and median values* computed for each tier so as to enable us to form a quick impression of substantial differences in behavior.

Note that three of the top ten countries and three of the next nine are "oil economies," which benefited from the oil price explosion of the 1970s. Without oil these countries would have ranked considerably lower. The ranking of Mexico and Ivory Coast, on the other hand, appears lower than it "should" be. These are very successful economies that have a high rate of GNP growth. But population growth has also been unusually high, due in Mexico to natural increase and in Ivory Coast to substantial in-migration from neighboring African countries, which has pulled down their ranking in per capita terms.

The middle three columns of table 2 show what was happening to each country decade by decade. In about half the cases, the decade growth rates fluctuate with no marked trend. A half-dozen countries show steady acceleration, with a growth rate for the 1970s much above that for the 1950s. This group includes South Korea, Taiwan, Malaysia, Colombia, Morocco, and Sri Lanka. But there are more cases of deceleration, with the growth rate falling decade by decade. This is true of all nine countries in the lowest group, which indeed is why they ended up in this group. It is true also of Burma, Ethiopia, Peru, and Venezuela.

The medians at the bottom of the decade columns indicate that the dispersion of country growth rates widened over time, and particularly during the 1970s. In the 1950s the median growth rate for countries in tier 1, 2.9 percent, was not

---

*Occasionally a figure is available for a country in, say, 1980 but not in earlier periods. In such cases the country is excluded from the median calculation in both periods.

strikingly above that for countries in tier 4, 2.0 percent. By the 1960s, however, the gap had widened to 2.7 percent *versus* 0.2 percent; and in the 1970s tier 1 countries grew at a remarkable 5.3 percent, while those in tier 4 had negative growth of −2.0 percent per year.

This observation underlines a point made earlier. The most significant development since 1945 is *not* a widening of the average gap between third-world and OECD countries. Some widening seems to have occurred, but more significant is the sharp pulling apart of growth rates *within* the third world itself. As of the 1980s we find a top group of countries that will certainly continue to grow and (probably) to overtake the OECD countries. At the bottom is a group of stagnating or declining economies that are falling farther and farther behind the world average.

Selected Physical Indicators

Suppose that GNP estimates were unavailable. We might then try to judge changes in per capita income by looking at physical indicators of consumption. This is useful in any event as a cross-check on GNP estimates, which as already indicated have a substantial probable error. From the many measures available, I have selected for inclusion in table 3 an indicator of nutrition (calories per capita per day), of education (primary-school enrollment as a percentage of the primary-age population), and of health (life expectancy at birth).

We cannot assume, of course, that measurement of these variables is precise. Calorie availability estimates rest on a prior estimate of food production, with adjustment for exports and imports, and are reduced to a per capita basis by dividing by the estimated population. The meaning of "primary-school enrollment" is unclear. Who is counted: those who show up on the first day? Those who show up at some point in the year? Those who are there at the end? Some fuzziness is evident when we find, as we do find in table 3, that more than 100 percent of the available children are "enrolled." Life expectancy at birth is derived indirectly from mortality rates, with changes in infant mortality having greatest influence on the result.

Look first at food availability. In anything pertaining to agriculture, three-year averages are usually used to even out the effect of harvest fluctuations. And because data for the 1950s are not very complete or reliable, we are limited to the short period from the mid-1960s to 1980. As of the base period 1964–66, 25 of our 37 countries fell within the narrow range of 2,000–2,250 calories per day, though there were extreme values such as Argentina's 3,241 and Indonesia's 1,750. The striking fact, however, is that there was little relation between a country's growth-rate ranking and its nutrition level. The median for tier 4 is only 100 calories below that for tier 1. We must of course bear in mind that calorie *requirements* vary among countries, for climatic and other reasons. Even if all populations were adequately nourished, we would find considerable variation in caloric intake per capita.

TABLE 3 Changes in Welfare: Some Physical Indicators

Country	Food Availability (per capita calories per day)			Primary-School Enrollment (percent of age group)			Life Expectancy at Birth (years)		
	1964–66	1978–80	Change	1950	1980	Change	1960	1980	Change
South Korea	2,100[2]	2,946	+846	53	109	+ 56	54	65	+11
Taiwan	2,008[1]	2,824	+816	48	99	+ 51	63	72	+ 9
Iraq	2,050	2,643	+593	16	116	+100	46	56	+10
Brazil	2,460[1]	2,517	+ 57	28	93[5]	+ 65	57	63	+ 6
Thailand	2,220	2,301	+ 81	52	96	+ 44	51	63	+12
Malaysia	2,430	2,650	+220	45	92	+ 47	57	64	+ 7
Nigeria	2,160	2,335	+175	16	98[5]	+ 82	39	49	+10
Indonesia	1,750	2,295	+545	29	112	+ 83	41	53	+12
Turkey	2,760	2,965	+205	50	101	+ 51	51	62	+11
Egypt	2,605	2,949[1]	+344	26	76	+ 50	46	57	+11
Iran	2,030	2,912	+882	16	101[3]	+ 85	46	59	+13
Algeria	1,890	2,406	+516	15	95	+ 80	47	56	+ 9
Colombia	2,190	2,255	+ 35	28	128	+100	53	63	+10
Pakistan	1,838	2,300[1]	+462	16	57[5]	+ 41	44	50	+ 6
Philippines	1,900	2,315[1]	+415	74	110	+ 26	51	64	+13
Kenya	2,240	2,055	−185	26	108[5]	+ 82	47	55	+ 8
Mexico	2,568[1]	2,803	+243	39	120	+ 81	58	65	+ 7
Venezuela	2,221[1]	2,649	+428	40	104[5]	+ 64	58	67	+ 9
Ivory Coast	2,430	2,623	+193	4	76[5]	+ 72	37	47	+10
Morocco	2,130	2,651	+321	11	76	+ 65	47	56	+ 9
Sri Lanka	2,186[1]	2,249	+ 63	54	100	+ 46	62	66	+ 4
Argentina	3,241[1]	3,386	+145	66	112[5]	+ 46	65	70	+ 5
Tanzania	2,140	2,025	−115	10	104	+ 94	42	52	+10
Chile	2,520	2,732	+212	66	117	+ 51	57	67	+10
India	2,051[1]	1,998	− 53	21	76[4]	+ 55	43	52	+ 9
Ethiopia	2,150	1,729	−421	3	43	+ 46	36	40	+ 4
Burma	2,010	2,286	+276	9	84[3]	+ 75	43	54	+11
Peru	2,256[1]	2,166	− 90	43	112[5]	+ 69	48	58	+10
Zimbabwe	2,550	1,911	−639	44	88	+ 44	45	55	+10
Zambia	2,250	1,982	−258	35	95[5]	+ 60	40	49	+ 9
Zaire	2,040	2,133	+ 93	33	90[4]	+ 57	40	47	+ 7
Nepal	2,030	1,914	−116	3	91	+ 88	37	44	+ 7
Mozambique	2,130	1,891	−239	12	93	+ 81	37	47	+10
Sudan	2,090	2,371	+281	6	51	+ 45	39	46	+ 7
Uganda	2,029	2,016	− 13	18	50[5]	+ 32	44	54	+10
Ghana	2,160[1]	1,862	−298	19	69[5]	+ 50	40	49	+ 9
Afghanistan	2,060	1,833	−227	3	30[5]	+ 27	34	37	+ 3

[1]1961–65   [2]1962   [3]1977   [4]1978   [5]1979

(continued)

SOURCES: Food availability, FAO, *Production Yearbook,* 1960–82. Primary-school enrollment: UNESCO, *Statistical Yearbook,* 1963, 1982. Life expectancy: UN, *Demographic Yearbook,* 1960–82; IBRD, *World Tables,* 1980; and IBRD, *World Development Report,* 1982.

TABLE 3   (*continued*)

Country	Food Availability (per capita calories per day)			Primary-School Enrollment (percent of age group)			Life Expectancy at Birth (years)		
	1964–66	1978–80	Change	1950	1980	Change	1960	1980	Change
Medians									
Tier 1	2,190	2,647	+459	37	99	+ 62	51	63	+12
Tier 2	2,190	2,406	+226	26	80	+ 54	47	59	+12
Tier 3	2,168	2,249	+ 83	21	100	+ 79	47	56	+ 9
Tier 4	2,090	1,914	−176	18	88	+ 70	40	47	+ 7

Over the ensuing fifteen years, most countries show a marked improvement in food availability, and this is strongly correlated with the reported growth rate. In tier 1 countries, median food availability rose by 459 calories; but in tier 4 countries it *fell* by 176 calories. Every country in tier 1 and all but one in tier 2 show an increase in food availability; but seven of the nine countries in tier 4 show a decline. This suggests that the GNP estimates on which our country ranking is based did distinguish rather successfully between fast-growing, slow-growing, and deteriorating economies.

The findings for education and health are somewhat different. As of 1950, the tier 1 countries already had a primary-school enrollment ratio about double that of the tier 4 countries. But it is striking that, over the next thirty years, almost every country brought its enrollment ratio close to the 100 percent* mark. Since the tier 4 countries were lower to begin with, they actually improved *more* than the tier 1 countries over these thirty years. The reality is no doubt less rosy than the statistics suggest. The bare numbers tell us nothing about quality of instruction, length of attendance during the school year, numbers of repeaters, or how many reach a grade 4 or grade 8 level of competence. Still, the impression remains that, even in countries with low or zero growth rates, governments have been under pressure to mount crash programs of primary education and have been able to find funds for these programs.

In regard to life expectancy, too, it is striking that every country in the table shows substantial improvement, ranging for most countries from 7 to 12 years. Here, however, there is some relation between a country's reported growth rate and the degree of health improvement. The median increase in life expectancy is 12 years for tier 1 and tier 2 countries, but only 9 years for tier 3 and 7 years for tier 4 countries.

*A figure *above* 100 percent may indicate a substantial number of repeaters—students above normal primary-school age but still in the primary grades. Or it may simply reflect misreporting.

Table 3 does not reveal many anomalies—that is, cases in which the story told by GNP measures conflicts sharply with that told by physical indicators. Brazil, with a high growth rate, shows little improvement in calorie availability and substandard performance on life expectancy. In Kenya, with a superior growth rate, calorie availability has actually declined. Farther down the table, Burma and Sudan have done *better* on physical indicators than their low growth rate suggests. In general, however, the physical data do not overturn the rankings based on GNP estimates.

Table 3 does suggest that, in drawing conclusions about changes in per capita consumption or welfare, it is important to distinguish among different elements in consumption. It is apparently quite possible for educational opportunities, health facilities, and perhaps other items of public consumption to improve even in an economy whose overall growth rate is low or negative. This serves as some offset to the decline in food availability and perhaps in other items of private consumption.

CHANGES IN THE COMPOSITION OF OUTPUT

From the work of Kuznets and others it is well established that growth of national output is accompanied by systematic changes in the composition of output. Since the data are readily available, it seems worthwhile to present them.

Output by Sector of Origin

The standard sectoral division of output distinguishes (1) agriculture, forestry, and fisheries; (2) industry, including mining, manufacturing, public utilities, and construction; and (3) services, including government, trade, finance, professional and personal services. In addition to showing these major divisions in table 4, I have separated out the manufacturing component of industry.

The agricultural data are well behaved. Agriculture is expected to shrink in relative importance, and it does shrink. Moreover, the rate of shrinkage is directly related to the rate of economic growth. Over the years 1950–80, the median agriculture/GDP ratio for tier 1 countries was cut in half, while for tier 4 countries it fell considerably less. As of 1980, then, agriculture averaged only 21 percent of GDP in the tier 1 countries but was still 41 percent in tier 4 countries. There are a few high-growth countries, including Malaysia and Ivory Coast, in which agriculture has shrunk less than would be expected. This reflects the strong agricultural base of these countries and the importance their governments attach to agricultural development. There are several low-growth countries—Burma, Uganda, Zambia—in which the share of agriculture has *risen,* contrary to expecta-

TABLE 4 Output by Sector of Origin (percent of GDP)

Country	Agriculture 1950	Agriculture 1980	Agriculture Percent Change	Industry 1950	Industry 1980	Industry Percent Change	Manufacturing 1950	Manufacturing 1980	Manufacturing Percent Change	Services 1950	Services 1980	Services Percent Change
South Korea	47[2]	16	− 66	15	41	+179	10	28	+183	38	43	+ 12
Taiwan	19	9	−111	24	46	+ 92	17	43	+153	57	39	− 32
Iraq	22	7	− 68	50	73	+ 45	6	6	0	28	19	− 31
Brazil	27	10	− 63	24	37	+ 57	21	23	+ 10	52	53	+ 2
Thailand	58	25	− 57	16	29	+ 81	10	20	+100	26	46	+ 76
Malaysia	37[4]	24	− 35	18	37	+106	9	23	+156	45	39	− 13
Nigeria	67	20	− 70	6	42	+556	3	6	+100	27	38	+ 41
Indonesia	51[3]	26	− 49	17	42	+154	12	9	− 25	32	32	0
Turkey	49	23	− 53	16	30	+ 88	11	21	+ 91	35	47	+ 35
Egypt	35[2]	23[5]	− 35	15	35	+137	11	28	+146	50	42	− 16
Iran	29[4]	9[6]	− 69	33	52	+ 37	11	12	+ 9	38	35	− 8
Algeria	33	6	− 82	24	57	+139	13	14	+ 8	44	37	− 15
Colombia	39	28	− 27	22	30	+ 39	16	22	+ 35	40	42	+ 5
Pakistan	56	31	− 47	8	25	+198	7	16	+129	33	44	+ 35
Philippines	39	23	− 42	20	37	+ 82	12	26	+111	40	40	0
Kenya	38[2]	34[5]	− 11	21	21	0	10	13	+ 35	41	45	+ 9
Mexico	20	10	− 51	31	38	+ 21	22	24	+ 8	48	52	+ 8
Venezuela	8	6	− 25	47	47	0	10	16	+ 60	45	47	+ 4
Ivory Coast	43[4]	34[5]	− 21	14	22	+ 57	7	11	+ 57	43	44	+ 2
Morocco	30[1]	18	− 40	25	32	+ 30	10	17	+ 72	46	50	+ 9
Sri Lanka	56	28	− 50	10	30	+216	4	18	+414	35	42	+ 20
Argentina	14[2]	12	− 14	38	41	+ 8	29	33	+ 14	48	39	− 19
Tanzania	63	54[5]	− 14	16	13	− 18	6	9	+ 50	22	33	+ 54
Chile	14	7	− 50	37	37	0	24	21	− 12	50	56	+ 13
India	50	37	− 26	16	26	+ 63	11	18	+ 61	34	37	+ 9

Ethiopia	65[4]	51	− 22	12	16	+ 33	11	11	0	23	33	+ 44
Burma	38	46	+ 20	7	13	+ 97	5	10	+100	50	41	− 18
Peru	35	8	− 77	24	45	+ 88	15	27	+ 82	41	47	+ 15
Zimbabwe	18[4]	12[5]	− 33	35	39	+ 11	17	25	+ 47	47	49	+ 4
Zambia	9[2]	15	+ 61	71	39	− 45	3	17	+400	19	46	+138
Zaire	34	32[5]	− 6	28	23	− 19	5	4	− 23	38	45	+ 19
Nepal	69[7]	57	− 17	10	13	+ 30	8	4	− 50	21	30	+ 43
Mozambique												
Sudan	61	38	− 38	11	14	+ 32	4	6	+ 50	29	48	+ 68
Uganda	67[2]	76	+ 14	12	6	− 50	8	6	− 25	21	18	− 14
Ghana												
Afghanistan	58[4]	48[6]	− 17	10	12	+ 20	9	9	0	30	32	+ 7
Medians												
Tier 1	42	21	− 50	16.5	39	+237	10.5	22	+210	36.5	40.5	+ 11
Tier 2	38	23	− 40	22	37	+168	11	16	+145	41	44	+ 7
Tier 3	38	28	− 26	16	30	+187	11	18	+164	41	42	+ 2
Tier 4	58	41	− 29	12	19	+ 58	8	6	− 25	29	42	+ 45

[1] 1952
[2] 1955
[3] 1958
[4] 1960
[5] estimated
[6] 1977
[7] 1966

Note: References in the agriculture column apply to other sectors as well. Industry includes mining, manufacturing, construction, and electricity. Services includes transport, trade, public administration, and other services.

SOURCES: IBRD, *World Tables, 1971*; IBRD, *World Development Report, 1982*.

tions. This typically reflects disorganization of the money economy and a reversion to subsistence agriculture.

The figures for industry are somewhat distorted by inclusion of mineral and oil production, which accounts for the very high 1980 figures for industry in the oil-exporting countries. If we allow for this distortion, the industry figures behave as expected. The industry sector grows in relative importance, and its rate of expansion is directly related to the rate of economic growth. Consequently, by 1980 industry contributed almost twice as much to GDP for tier 1 countries as did agriculture. In tier 4 countries the reverse was true. Again, there are cases in which the industry percentage *fell* between 1950 and 1980. These cases reflect special circumstances, such as the decline of the copper industry in Zambia and general economic disorganization in Uganda and Zaire.

Looking more narrowly at manufacturing, we note first that several Latin American countries were already quite industrialized in 1950. In Argentina, Brazil, Chile, and Mexico, manufacturing already contributed more than 20 percent of GDP. For other parts of the third world, however, this was not true. The typical manufacturing/GDP ratio was only about 10 percent, and for most tier 4 countries it was even lower.

The next thirty years saw a marked relative expansion of manufacturing. By 1980 a dozen countries had manufacturing/GDP ratios above 20 percent, including not only the spectacular cases of Taiwan and South Korea but also Thailand, Malaysia, Egypt, Turkey, Colombia, Peru, and the Philippines. The rate of manufacturing expansion is clearly related to the rate of economic growth. By 1980 the median manufacturing/GDP ratio had reached 22 percent for tier 1 countries, but it was still only 6 percent for tier 4 countries.

This association does not mean that more rapid industrialization was the *cause* of more rapid GNP growth. As I argued in chapter 4, manufacturing growth is more properly regarded as an accompaniment or even a consequence of overall growth. The dominant influence was expansion of consumer incomes and domestic demand fueled by export expansion, which in the 1950s and 1960s was mainly expansion of primary exports. In addition, factory industry gradually won a larger share of the market by displacing both imported manufactures and domestic handicraft production. The widespread prevalence of government policies favoring industrialization was no doubt helpful. But the influence of policy is often overemphasized relative to the autonomous response to market growth.

The "services" sector is very heterogeneous, and to say much about it would require subdividing it into major types of service—such as trade, government output, personal services—and looking separately at each.

Consumption, Investment, Government

We turn now to the division among private consumption, public consumption, and investment (see table 5). This is a distribution not of domestic output but of domestic availabilities. If imports exceed exports, as is usually the case, availabilities will exceed output and the three figures will add to more than 100 percent. The discrepancy is shown in the resource balance (exports minus imports) column at the right of the table.

An additional point is of some importance. The percentage distribution in table 5 reflects nominal (money) values of output. But to discover how well this method reflects the distribution of real resources we must adjust for biases in the pricing system. This is especially necessary for cross-country comparisons, because the price biases are correlated with a country's income level. The prices of investment goods in less-developed countries are high relative to prices of the same goods in industrialized countries, and the discrepancy is greatest for the poorest countries. With regard to government output, on the other hand, the bias is in the other direction. The cost of producing public goods is mainly labor cost; and so a poor country with low wage rates is devoting more resources to public output than the money distribution suggests.

This question has been investigated by the International Comparison Project, sponsored by the Statistical Office of the United Nations. A recent publication* gives the following results for the ratios of *real* to *nominal* income shares for 119 countries:

Country Group	Consumption Ratios		Investment Ratios		Government Ratios	
	1950	1975	1950	1975	1950	1975
Low Income	0.942	0.940	0.905	0.814	2.057	1.434
Middle Income	0.949	0.968	0.955	0.925	1.769	1.351
Industrialized	0.951	1.007	1.060	1.113	1.161	0.862

These figures mean that the nominal ratios shown in table 5 *overstate* the real resources devoted to investment and *understate* the resources devoted to government output, the discrepancy being greatest for the lowest-income countries. Over the twenty-five years covered by the study the discrepancy decreased for the government share but increased substantially for the investment share. Thus for any comparison with ratios for the industrialized countries, which is bound to be in the back of our minds, the nominal investment ratio for low-income countries must be *reduced* substantially, whereas the nominal government share must be *raised* even more substantially.

In the industrialized countries analyzed by Kuznets, the private-consumption share of GDP has tended to fall over the long run, while the other two shares have risen. What does table 5 tell us about trends in third-world countries? Looking first at the gross-investment share of GDP, we see that in the 1950s it tended to run

*Robert Summers, Irving B. Kravis, and Alan Heston, "International Comparison of Real Product and Its Composition: 1950–77," *Review of Income and Wealth,* Ser. 26, no. 1 (March 1980):19–66.

TABLE 5 Output by End Uses (percent of GDP)

Country	Gross Domestic Investment			Public Consumption			Private Consumption			Resource Balance	
	1951–60	1980	Percent Change	1951–60	1980	Percent Change	1951–60	1980	Percent Change	1951–60	1980
South Korea	13[2]	31	+ 148	11	13	+ 18	85	64	− 25	− 9	− 8
Taiwan	16	31	+ 94	19	16	− 16	71			− 6	+ 26
Iraq	18[2]	33	+ 79	15	*		50	41*		+ 16	
Brazil	17	22[5]	+ 29	13	14	+ 8	71	67	− 6	− 1	− 2
Thailand	14	27	+ 93	10	12	+ 15	77	66	− 15	− 2	− 5
Malaysia	12[3]	29	+ 136	14	17	+ 25	61	51	− 16	+ 13	+ 3
Nigeria	10	24	+ 147	5	10	+ 104	86	62	− 28	− 1	+ 4
Indonesia	7	22	+ 201	9	13	+ 41	83	57	− 31	+ 1	+ 8
Turkey	14	27	+ 90	14	13	− 7	73	69	− 6	− 2	− 9
Egypt	13	31	+ 135	17	19	+ 11	68	65	− 5	+ 2	− 5
Iran	4										
Algeria	24	41	+ 70	25	14	− 44	65	44	− 32	+ 14	+ 1
Colombia	18	25	+ 41	6	8	+ 29	75	67	− 11	+ 1	0
Pakistan	12[4]	18	+ 50	11	11	0	84	83	− 1	− 7	− 13
Philippines	13	30	+ 140	7	8	+ 8	81	67	− 17	− 1	− 5
Kenya	20[4]	22[5]	+ 10	11	20	+ 82	72	65	− 10	− 3	− 7
Mexico	17	28	− 61	5	12	+ 131	79	62	− 21	− 1	− 2
Venezuela	26	25	− 5	13	13	+ 2	53	55	+ 5	+ 9	+ 7
Ivory Coast	15[4]	28	+ 87	10	18	+ 80	73	59	− 19	− 5	− 5
Morocco	14[1]	21	+ 53	11	22	+ 104	79	67	− 16	− 4	− 10
Sri Lanka	14	36	+ 157	11	8	− 30	72	78	+ 8	+ 2	− 22
Argentina											
Tanzania	14[4]	22	+ 57	9	14	+ 56	72	78	+ 8	+ 5	− 14
Chile	16	18	+ 15	10	12	+ 17	74	72	− 3	0	− 2
India	13	23	+ 84	7	10	+ 52	83	70	− 15	− 2	− 3

Ethiopia	12	10	− 17	8	15	+ 88	81	80	− 1	− 1	− 5
Burma	19	24	− 26	11	*		70	82*		0	− 6
Peru	24	16	− 33	8	13	+ 55	70	68	− 3	− 3	+ 3
Zimbabwe	30	18	− 41	10	21	+106	69	63	− 9	−10	− 2
Zambia	26	23	− 11	9	28	+229	48	54	+13	18	− 5
Zaire	25	11	− 57	13	12	− 9	58	75	+29	+ 3	+ 2
Nepal	9[4]	14	+ 56	*	*		96	93		− 5	− 7
Mozambique	8[2]	10	+ 24	11	15	+ 43	82	85	+ 4	− 1	−10
Sudan	10	12	+ 24	8	12	− 56	82	85	+ 4	+ 1	− 9
Uganda	11[4]	3	− 73	9	11	+ 22	75	87		+ 5	− 1
Ghana	15	5	− 66	8	9	+ 18	75	86	+14	+ 2	0
Afghanistan	17	14	− 16	6	6	0	86	83	− 3	− 9	− 3
Medians											
Tier 1	13.5	28	+108	13	13	− 0	75	64.5	−14	− 1	− 2
Tier 2	17	28	+ 65	10	12.5	+ 25	74	64	−14	− 1	− 3.5
Tier 3	14	21	+ 50	9	13	+ 44	74	72	− 3	− 0.5	− 5.5
Tier 4	15	12	− 20	9	12	+ 33	75	84	+12	+ 1	− 2.5

*public consumption included in private consumption

[1] 1952–60
[2] 1953–60
[3] 1955–60
[4] 1960
[5] estimated

Note: References in the gross domestic investment columns apply to other columns as well.

SOURCES: IBRD, *World Tables, 1971*; IBRD, *World Development Report, 1982.*

between 13 and 17 percent. Some of the oil-mineral economies were above 20 percent, while a few economic laggards were at 10 percent or less. The interesting thing, however, is that there seems to be no significant relation between a country's investment ratio in the 1950s and its subsequent output growth. The median ratios for the four tiers in the table are not very different.

By 1980 the investment rates for the top three tiers in our sample had increased substantially. The median rate for tier 1 countries more than doubled, the tier 2 median rose 65 percent, and the tier 3 median rose 50 percent. For the unsuccessful economies in tier 4, on the other hand, the median investment rate *fell* from 15 to 12 percent of GDP. The investment rates achieved by the more successful countries are impressive. Even with the downward adjustment suggested earlier, the medians for tier 1 and tier 2 countries would remain above 20 percent, which is in line with medians for the OECD countries.

There does seem, then, to be an association between a country's *growth rate* and the *rate of increase* in its investment ratio. But this observation does not reveal the direction of causation. One could reason that the tier 1 and tier 2 countries, having achieved success in production for a complex of reasons, then had a larger surplus available for investment. Certainly this was true for the oil economies. Their revenues increased sharply, not because of investment, but through the exercise of market power. These revenues, flowing mainly through government channels, made possible a sharp increase in capital expenditure. Conversely, the tier 4 countries, with static or declining per capita incomes, could spare little for investment and did invest little. But low investment was not the *reason* for economic stagnation or decline, which usually had political roots.

The public consumption/GDP ratios in table 5 appear low; but remember the price distortion problem noted earlier. For proper comparison with the industrialized countries, a 13 percent ratio in the table should be adjusted to something like 20 percent. This is still below the developed-country median, but not so far below.

In the case of investment we saw that ratios that were initially rather uniform had by 1980 become unequal. For public-consumption ratios, the behavior is just the reverse, moving from marked disparity in the 1950s to substantial uniformity by 1980. As of the 1950s the median public-consumption ratio for tier 1 countries was 50 percent higher than those for tier 3 and tier 4 countries. But by 1980, the medians for the four tiers are almost identical.

One implication of these results is that the more successful countries exercised restraint in expanding their public sectors. In few cases did the public-consumption ratio rise by more than two or three points, and in several cases it declined. With total output rising rapidly, of course, public services could also be expanded quite rapidly *without* much increase in tax/GDP or current expenditure/GDP ratios. We can speculate that restraint in raising these ratios may have had something to do with these countries' economic success.

The tier 4 countries were in a different situation. They were under the same pressure as other countries to expand primary education, improve health facilities, and provide urban amenities. Popular demand for these public goods is strong and bears little relation to economic resources. Recall the substantial improvement in education and health facilities shown in table 3 by countries at all income levels. In countries with slow or zero growth in GDP, providing these services required raising the government *share* of GDP, often quite substantially.

It is worth noting that the public-consumption figures show only current output of public goods. They do *not* indicate the size of total government revenue or expenditure. These figures have also been rising. IBRD data show that for the middle-income economies central-government revenue as a percentage of GDP rose from an average of 15 percent in 1960 to 26 percent in 1980.* This compares with an average of about 35 percent for the industrial market economies. One reason for the lower budget percentage in LDCs is the much smaller importance of transfer payments. In the industrial market economies, transfer payments constitute about 55 percent of total budget outlays. The corresponding percentage in the middle-income economies is about 15 percent and in low-income countries only a bit over 10 percent. The proportion of the budget going to investment, on the other hand, is substantially higher in these economies than in industrialized countries, averaging 20 percent in middle-income countries and 25 percent in low-income countries, compared with less than 10 percent in the industrial market economies. The LDCs are still building up their capital stock, rather than using their fiscal systems for large-scale redistribution of income.

Little need be said about private consumption. Arithmetically, a rise in the investment and government ratios must mean a decline in the consumption ratio. This decline has been fastest in the high-growth countries. In the 1950s, the median private consumption/GDP ratio in tier 1 and tier 2 countries was about 75 percent. By 1980 this had fallen to 65 percent, not far from typical ratios in the industrialized countries. A corollary is that private consumption per capita has risen a good deal less rapidly than GDP per capita in these countries.

ADDITIONAL DIMENSIONS OF GROWTH: POPULATION, AGRICULTURE, EXPORTS

Demographic Behavior

I have noted at several points that the deathrate tends to change exogenously, in response mainly to advances in medical science. There was a gradual decline in most countries in the late nineteenth and early twentieth centuries, a marked drop after 1920, and another marked drop after 1945. Table 6 indicates that this process was still going on in the years 1960–80. Over this period the crude deathrate dropped five to ten points in most countries. For tier 1 and tier 2 countries, the

World Development Report, 1983 (Washington: IBRD, 1983), pp. 47–48.

TABLE 6   Demographic Behavior (births or deaths per thousand)

Country	Crude Birth Rate			Crude Death Rate			Rate of Natural Increase		
	1960	1980	Change	1960	1980	Change	1960	1980	Change
South Korea	43	24	−19	13	7	− 6	30	17	−13
Taiwan	40	21	−19	7	5	− 2	33	16	−17
Iraq	49	45	− 4	20	12	− 8	29	33	+ 4
Brazil	43	30	−13	13	9	− 4	30	21	− 9
Thailand	44	30	−14	15	8	− 7	29	22	− 7
Malaysia	45	31	−14	16	7	− 9	29	24	− 5
Nigeria	52	50	− 2	25	17	− 8	27	33	+ 6
Indonesia	46	35	−11	16	10	− 6	27	22	− 5
Turkey	43	32	−11	16	10	− 6	27	22	− 5
Egypt	44	37	− 7	19	12	− 7	25	25	0
Iran	46	41	− 5	17	11	− 6	29	30	+ 1
Algeria	50	46	− 4	23	13	−10	27	33	+ 6
Colombia	46	30	−16	14	8	− 6	32	22	−10
Pakistan	51	44	− 7	24	16	−12	27	28	+ 1
Philippines	46	34	−12	15	7	− 8	31	27	− 4
Kenya	52	51	− 1	24	13	−11	28	38	+10
Mexico	45	37	− 8	12	7	− 5	33	30	− 3
Venezuela	46	35	−11	11	6	− 5	35	29	− 6
Ivory Coast	50	47	− 3	26	18	− 8	24	29	+ 5
Morocco	52	44	− 8	23	13	−10	29	31	+ 2
Sri Lanka	36	28	− 8	9	7	− 2	27	21	− 6
Argentina	24	21	− 3	9	8	− 1	15	13	− 2
Tanzania	47	46	− 1	22	15	− 7	25	31	+ 6
Chile	37	22	−15	12	7	− 5	25	15	−10
India	44	36	− 8	22	14	− 8	22	22	0
Ethiopia	51	49	− 2	28	24	− 4	23	25	+ 2
Burma	43	37	− 6	21	14	− 7	22	23	+ 1
Peru	47	36	−11	20	11	− 9	27	25	− 2
Zimbabwe	55	54	− 1	17	13	− 4	38	41	+ 3
Zambia	51	49	− 2	24	17	− 7	27	32	+ 5
Zaire	48	46	− 2	24	18	− 6	24	28	+ 4
Nepal	44	42	− 2	27	20	− 7	17	22	+ 5
Mozambique	46	45	− 1	26	18	− 8	20	27	+ 7
Sudan	47	47	0	25	19	− 6	22	28	+ 6
Uganda	45	45	0	20	14	− 6	25	31	+ 6
Ghana	49	48	− 1	24	17	− 7	25	31	+ 6
Afghanistan	50	47	− 3	31	26	− 5	19	21	+ 2
Medians									
Tier 1	44	31.5	−12.5	16	9	− 7	29	22	− 7
Tier 2	46	41	− 5	17	11	− 6	29	30	+ 1
Tier 3	44	36	− 8	22	13	− 9	22	23	+ 1
Tier 4	48	47	− 1	24	18	− 6	24	29	+ 5

SOURCE: IBRD, *World Development Report*, 1982.

process is substantially completed, their median deathrates now being close to developed-country levels.

It is interesting to note that, although the absolute level of deathrates remains somewhat higher in tier 3 and especially in tier 4 countries, the *decrease* in deathrates from 1960 to 1980 was almost identical for all four tiers. Even the low-growth countries have been able to match the rates of progress in the high-growth countries, partly by drawing on low-cost technical assistance provided by the World Health Organization and other international bodies.

Thus the strong upward pressure on population growth rates, which has been provided by declining mortality since 1900, is now nearing its end. From now on the outcome will hinge mainly on birthrate behavior. Table 6 shows that in 1960 most countries still had birthrates in the 40–50 per thousand range, representing essentially uncontrolled fertility. The only exceptions were relatively high-income Argentina and Chile plus Sri Lanka. Since 1960, the trend has clearly been downward. Only two countries fail to show a drop in the crude birthrate between 1960 and 1980, Uganda and Sudan showing no change. A dozen countries show declines of more than ten points, reaching 19 points in South Korea and Taiwan, a remarkable change for such a short period. The rate of decline in birthrates seems clearly related to the rate of economic growth. Between 1960 and 1980 the median for tier 1 countries dropped 12.5 points, while the median for tier 4 countries fell only one point.

The decline of birthrates in the industrialized countries accompanying their increasing affluence is a familiar story. This process seems now to be setting in throughout most of the third world. The reasons for declining birthrates no doubt differ somewhat from country to country, and many case studies are currently under way. A number of countries have adopted vigorous family-planning programs—China is the most dramatic example—and these have clearly had some effect. But more important in most cases are the factors that were operative earlier in the OECD countries: rising incomes and consumption aspirations, increases in education, improvement in the status of women, urbanization changing the cost-benefit balance from additional children, and so on. At any event, the downtrend in most countries seems well established and likely to continue. The black side of the picture is that the countries with poorest growth performance also show least progress in fertility control. The median birthrate in tier 4 countries in 1980 was still 47 per thousand, with the result that children are appearing in largest numbers in the countries least able to support them.

Changes in the rate of natural increase, shown in the final columns of table 6, reflect the outcome of the race between declining fertility and declining mortality. For tier 1 countries, fertility decline pulled ahead in the race between 1960 and 1980, and the median rate of natural increase dropped from 29 to 22 per thousand. The rate will certainly continue to decline in future. In tier 2 and tier 3 countries, the race was a tie and the median rates of natural increase in 1960 and 1980 were almost identical. But here, too, one can safely predict a decline in the near future.

The most pessimistic prognosis is for tier 4 countries. Here mortality decline won the race by a decisive margin, and the rate of natural increase *rose* by five points. With deathrates still relatively high, there is considerable room for further decline. Thus the population growth rate seems more likely to rise than to fall over the next decade or two.

Agricultural Output and Food Output

We would expect success in raising agricultural output to be an important determinant of overall growth. For a long time after the turning point agriculture remains the largest sector, so its growth rate has heavy weight in the GDP growth rate. But the relationship is more than arithmetical. Except for a limited number of oil-mineral economies, agriculture is the main source of exports; and the export growth rate, as we shall see, is an important determinant of the GDP growth rate. Domestic food supply is also a critical factor. Failure to raise food production as rapidly as food demand tends to produce a relative rise in food prices, which puts upward pressure on money wages, which tends to reduce industrial profits. A lagging agricultural sector also means that farmers cannot provide a vigorously expanding market for domestic manufactures.

In an open economy, of course, the food constraint is relaxed in two ways. First, part of the country's land is usually devoted to export crops—indeed, basic food crops such as rice may also be important exports. The growth rate of domestic food availabilities can thus be raised by diverting land from nonfood export crops to food crops, or by consuming more of the food output at home and exporting less, or both. A notable example is Burma, which at one time had a large export surplus of rice; this surplus has been shrinking since 1945 as more and more of the rice output is eaten at home. Second, there is the possibility of importing food, which some countries in our sample have used on a substantial scale.

I shall concentrate here on the data on food production in table 7. But note that for well over half the countries in our sample the average growth rate of food output is *above* that of total agricultural output. This suggests that diversion of land from nonfood to food crops has been occurring on a substantial scale. The extent to which food output is being eaten at home rather than exported does not show up in the table, but there is evidence that this has also been happening in quite a few countries.

Examination of table 7 reveals a clear relation between agricultural performance and overall economic performance. The median growth rate of both agricultural output and food output declines steadily as we go from tier 1 to tier 4. There is an especially sharp break between tiers 1 and 2, with median growth rates above 3 percent, and tiers 3 and 4, with median growth rates below 2 percent. The tier 1 and tier 2 countries have also improved their performance over time. Their medians for the 1970s are perceptibly above those for the 1950s. The main reason for the increase is probably the introduction of new agricultural technology—improved seed varieties, more fertilizer, better water control—in many countries from the mid-1960s onward, which has substantially raised yields per acre. But

TABLE 7 Growth Rates of Agricultural and Food Production (percent per year)

Country	Agricultural Production				Food Production			
	1952–54/ 1959–61	1959–61/ 1969–71	1969–71/ 1979–81	1952–54/ 1979–81	1952–54/ 1959–61	1959–61/ 1969–71	1969–71/ 1979–81	1952–54/ 1979–81
South Korea	5.4	3.2	4.2	4.4	4.2	4.0	4.3	4.0
Taiwan								
Iraq	0.3	4.5	2.2	2.4	0.1	4.4	2.3	2.4
Brazil	4.7	2.6	4.3	3.7	4.0	4.3	4.4	4.3
Thailand	4.5	5.1	5.1	4.8	3.2	5.3	5.4	4.6
Malaysia	3.0[1]	5.6	4.8	4.4	4.1[1]	5.3	6.1	5.1
Nigeria			2.1				2.3	
Indonesia	1.6	2.2	3.4	2.4	1.9	2.3	3.6	2.5
Turkey	3.2	3.1	3.6	3.2	3.2	3.0	3.7	3.2
Egypt	2.8	3.4	1.2	2.4	3.1	3.8	1.5	2.7
Iran	3.9	2.8	3.5	3.2	3.1	2.6	4.0	3.1
Algeria	−1.2	−0.2	1.3	0.1	−1.4	−0.2	1.3	−0.1
Colombia	2.5	3.0	4.1	3.1	1.9	3.5	4.3	3.2
Pakistan	2.2	3.8	3.1	3.0	2.3	3.6	3.3	3.0
Philippines	3.1	3.4	4.7	3.6	3.1	3.2	4.5	3.5
Kenya			3.2				2.3	
Mexico	5.0	4.5	3.5	4.1	5.1	5.2	3.7	4.5
Venezuela	4.5	5.3	3.8	4.4	4.8	5.7	4.0	4.7
Ivory Coast			4.6				5.1	
Morocco	−0.9	4.0	1.0	1.7	0.0	3.9	1.0	1.7
Sri Lanka	2.4	3.0	3.5	3.0	2.5	3.9	5.7	4.0
Argentina	0.6	1.6	2.7	1.6	0.6	2.1	2.9	1.9
Tanzania			1.6				2.0	
Chile	2.1	−2.0	1.3	1.5	2.1	1.8	1.4	1.7

(continued)

TABLE 7 (Continued)

Country	Agricultural Production				Food Production			
	1952–54/ 1959–61	1959–61/ 1969–71	1969–71/ 1979–81	1952–54/ 1979–81	1952–54/ 1959–61	1959–61/ 1969–71	1969–71/ 1979–81	1952–54/ 1979–81
India	2.6	2.2	2.4	2.4	2.7	2.1	2.4	2.3
Ethiopia	2.4	2.5	0.6	1.7	1.9	2.0	0.5	1.4
Burma	2.3	2.5	2.8	2.4	2.5	2.3	2.7	2.5
Peru	2.6	2.2	0.8	1.7	2.3	3.2	0.7	1.9
Zimbabwe			3.2				2.7	
Zambia			2.2				2.3	
Zaire			1.2				1.3	
Nepal			0.7				0.8	
Mozambique			-1.1				-0.7	
Sudan	4.5	4.6	1.4	3.4	4.1	4.7	3.0	3.8
Uganda			-0.4				1.5	
Ghana			-0.7				-0.3	
Afghanistan	2.7	0.5	2.0	1.6	2.6	0.2	2.2	1.5
Medians								
Tier 1	3.1	3.3	3.9	3.45	3.2	4.15	4.0	3.6
Tier 2	3.1	3.4	3.65	3.2	3.1	3.5	4.0	3.2
Tier 3	2.3	2.35	2.0	1.7	2.2	2.2	1.9	1.9
Tier 4	*	*	1.2	*	*	*	1.5	*

*too few observations
1West Malaysia only

SOURCES: FAO, Production Yearbook, 1955–82.

more-favorable government policies toward agriculture have also contributed. At any event, quite a few of these countries are approaching, or have already reached, a favorable conjuncture of decelerating population growth and accelerating food output. Especially hopeful in this respect are South Korea, Taiwan, Brazil, Thailand, and Malaysia.

Performance has varied widely, both among countries in each decade and from decade to decade in a particular country. A dozen or so countries show steady improvement decade by decade. This group includes Brazil, Colombia, Malaysia, Thailand, Indonesia, Sri Lanka, and Philippines. Another group shows rather steady performance, with no perceptible uptrend. This includes South Korea, Taiwan, India, Turkey, Mexico, and Venezuela. A third group shows deteriorating agricultural performance over the years. These are mainly tier 4 countries, but Chile and Peru are also included.

The low rate of agricultural growth in tier 3 and tier 4 countries is worth underlining for the following reason: the low GDP growth rate of the poorest countries is often attributed to the large weight of their agricultural sector, which tends to grow more slowly than the industrial sector. But the lower growth rate of agriculture itself provides an *additional* reason for their poor performance.

One feature of table 7 may appear puzzling. Many countries were not raising food output fast enough to meet rising consumer demand. How then was demand satisfied? For countries in a strong export position, the main answer was rising imports of food. This is true of all the oil economies in the table and also of prominent mineral exporters, such as Chile and Zambia (copper) and Morocco (phosphates). Here the ready availability of foreign exchange to finance food imports led governments to relax their agricultural effort, a policy that may prove hazardous over the longer run. Another group of countries were able to maintain consumption levels by moderate and intermittent food imports, as in India, or by reducing food exports, as in Burma. Finally, in a regrettable number of countries, the answer was a shrinkage in per capita food consumption. Looking back at table 3 we note that, of the fifteen lowest-ranking countries, ten show a decline in food availability. Seven of these countries are in Africa, where consumption levels generally have been declining despite substantial gifts of food from the developed countries.

Export Performance

A recurrent theme in this book has been the role of foreign demand in stimulating domestic growth, a role that has continued in the post-1945 period. Table 8 shows two indicators of export growth: the growth rate of merchandise exports decade by decade and the ratio of exports to GDP at the beginning and end of the period under study. The two measures are related, since a growth rate of exports exceeding that of GDP will necessarily raise the export/GDP ratio.

The marked relation between export growth and overall growth is apparent

TABLE 8   Export Performance, 1950–80

Country	Growth of Merchandise Exports (percent per year)				Exports/GDP (percent)		Change (percent of GDP)
	1950–60	1960–70	1970–80	1950–80	1950–52	1978–80	
South Korea	1.4	39.6	37.2	29.7	1.2	28.1	+26.9
Taiwan	9.3	21.7	15.7[12]		9.2	53.6	+44.4
Iraq	14.0	5.5	40.2	14.9	24.9	58.0[9]	+33.1
Brazil	−2.0	7.2	21.7	8.9	9.0	9.1	+ 0.1
Thailand	1.5	5.1	24.6	10.1	18.2	18.8	+ 0.6
Malaysia	0.6	4.3	24.5	8.2	52.0[3]	51.7	− 0.3
Nigeria	4.1	8.1	33.1	15.3	26.5	21.1	− 5.4
Indonesia	−1.1	1.7	35.3	9.8	18.4[8]	31.7	+13.7
Turkey	0.0	6.0	16.2	7.7	7.6	3.9	− 3.7
Egypt	0.1	4.5	12.9	5.6	19.2	10.0	− 9.2
Iran	36.4	12.6	22.9	21.2	6.0	26.8	+20.8
Algeria	3.0	3.8	30.6	11.4	24.7	31.0[10]	+ 6.3
Colombia	0.4	4.0	19.8	6.2	12.0	13.1	+ 1.1
Pakistan	−4.2	10.3	13.2	6.9	8.9	9.9	+ 1.0
Philippines	4.5	7.5	17.7	9.1	9.6	14.0	+ 4.4
Kenya	8.0	6.8	16.9	11.0	18.5	18.6	+ 0.1
Mexico	3.4	5.9	25.7	8.6	9.8	6.1	− 3.7
Venezuela	8.1	1.2	19.9	7.6	34.1	26.0	− 8.1
Ivory Coast	4.5	11.7	22.2	11.9	28.3[5]	30.1[11]	+ 1.8
Morocco	5.0	3.7	15.9	7.2	19.6	15.7	− 3.9
Sri Lanka	0.9	−1.4	13.0	2.5	33.9	27.7	− 6.2
Argentina	2.3	5.0	20.4	7.9	5.8	10.8	− 5.0
Tanzania	3.5	5.0	7.6	5.7	26.0[2]	10.9	−15.1
Chile	3.7	10.2	16.0	7.9	15.3	17.8	+ 2.5
India	0.0	3.7	15.9	6.0	6.7[7]	4.9	− 1.8
Ethiopia	6.6	5.1	13.6	7.6	7.6[6]	9.9	+ 2.3
Burma	1.0	−8.8	14.1	−0.2	20.6	6.2	−14.4
Peru	6.2	8.4	13.9	9.0	18.0	25.6	+ 7.6
Zimbabwe	5.3	5.6	12.9	9.0	n.a.	25.6	n.a.
Zambia	6.6	13.4	4.7	7.3	74.6	36.4	−38.2
Zaire	4.5	6.1	7.9	4.9	38.8	20.8	−18.0
Nepal						6.0[11]	n.a.
Mozambique	6.2	7.0	−4.0	5.2			n.a.
Sudan	2.6	3.4	7.4	5.5	17.5[4]	7.0	−10.5
Uganda	3.1	7.1	4.2	5.2	27.9[1]	4.2	−23.7
Ghana	3.1	2.2	10.9	5.4	32.2	10.4[10]	−21.8
Afghanistan	2.6	4.3	20.6	8.2	4.1	11.7[10]	+ 7.6

(*continued*)

[1]1950   [2]1954   [3]1955   [4]1956–58   [5]1960–62   [6]1961   [7]1966–68   [8]1967   [9]1975
[10]1977   [11]1978   [12]1970–77

SOURCES: Columns 1–4: UNCTAD, *Handbook of International Trade and Development Statistics*, various issues. Columns 5–6: *UN Yearbook of International Trade Statistics*, 1980; IMF, *International Financial Statistics*, various issues; IBRD, *World Tables*, 1980; Taiwan [Republic of China], *National Income of the Republic of China, 1982.*

TABLE 8   (*continued*)

Country	Growth of Merchandise Exports (percent per year)				Exports/GDP (percent)		Change (percent of GDP)
	1950–60	*1960–70*	*1970–80*	*1950–80*	*1950–52*	*1978–80*	
Medians							
Tier 1	1.0	6.0	24.5	10.0	18.3	24.6	
Tier 2	4.5	6.8	19.9	9.1	12.0	18.6	
Tier 3	3.5	5.0	14.1	7.2	18.0	10.9	
Tier 4	3.8	5.8	7.9	5.2	30.0	11.1	

from table 8. Over the period 1950–80, the median growth rate of exports was 10.0 percent per year in tier 1 countries and 9.1 percent in tier 2 countries, compared with only 5.2 percent in tier 4 countries. Even if we omit the oil economies as well as the spectacular cases of South Korea and Taiwan, most tier 1 and tier 2 countries managed to increase exports at rates of 7–11 percent per year. The median export/GDP ratio for both groups rose substantially, while for the two lower tiers it deteriorated.

The reasons for high export growth rates differ from country to country, but two factors deserve special emphasis. The first is a tendency during the 1960s and 1970s for one country after another to turn away from highly restrictive trade policies toward outward-looking policies more favorable to exports. These reform "packages" typically included such elements as: adoption of a unified and realistic exchange rate and in some cases a floating or "crawling peg" system; reduction of tariff rates and import quotas; liberalization or abandonment of foreign-exchange allocation systems; and new export incentives such as tax rebates, cheap credit, and free import of raw materials and capital goods. The result was to raise the profitability of exports relative to import-substituting activities, and exports typically responded strongly. Countries that moved in this direction include Taiwan, South Korea, Brazil, Colombia, Pakistan, Turkey, Egypt, and Sri Lanka. A number of other countries, such as Malaysia and Thailand, had always been export-oriented and simply continued their liberal trade policies.

The second important fact is that countries that adopted policies favorable to exports were generally successful not only in raising exports of primary products, but also in penetrating the world market for manufactures. The spectacular examples are South Korea and Taiwan, where manufactures now form 90 percent of total exports. But quite a few other countries have succeeded in raising exports of manufactures from a few percent to 20 percent or more of total exports as of 1980. Examples include Mexico (25.5 percent), Brazil (32.6 percent), Pakistan (48.2 percent), Egypt (19.7 percent), Thailand (22.6 percent), Turkey (26.2 percent), Philippines (21.6 percent), Colombia (19.6 percent), and Sri Lanka (18.6 percent). Manufactured exports are continuing to rise more rapidly than traditional exports, and these percentages will be considerably higher by 1990.

Although we have data also on merchandise imports, little would be gained by presenting them here. In general, the import/GDP ratio tracks the export/GDP ratio, rising where exports are buoyant, falling where exports are doing poorly. Most countries have a deficit on merchandise trade in most years; and except for the oil economies these deficits, as a percentage of GDP, were typically larger in 1978–80 than they had been in 1950–52. Deficits are closed in a variety of ways. Some countries now benefit greatly from remittances from their nationals employed abroad (Turkey, Egypt, Sudan, Pakistan, Sri Lanka, Mexico). Kenya, Mexico, and a few others have substantial revenues from tourism. But the trade gap is closed mainly by transfers of short-term and longer-term capital. Some idea of the size of these transfers can be obtained from the final two columns of table 5. These "resource balance" columns show the export surplus (+) or deficit (−) as a percentage of the country's GDP.

WHY DO GROWTH RATES DIFFER?

Although our tables suggest factors that may have had an important effect on country growth rates, one would like to have some measure of their relative importance. The standard procedure is to regress the growth rate against possible explanatory variables. I selected twelve variables that might plausibly be related to economic growth and ran a large number of regressions to test their significance. As one might expect, some of these variables turned out not to be statistically significant. The ordinary least-squares regression, which performed best for the countries examined, was as follows:

$$\text{GNP growth rate} = -0.5 + 0.8 \text{ agricultural production growth rate}$$
$$(2.4)$$
$$+ 0.09 \text{ export growth rate}$$
$$(2.8)$$
$$- 0.005 \text{ population density in 1960}$$
$$(-0.8)$$
$$+ 0.01 \text{ GDI/GDP growth rate.}$$
$$(1.7)$$

All growth rates are annual average growth rates from 1960 to 1980. The GNP figures used are the World Bank estimates shown in table 2. It turned out not to matter much whether the growth rate of GNP or of GNP per capita was used as the dependent variable. The coefficients and t-statistics were very similar in the two cases. GDI/GDP is the share of gross domestic investment in gross domestic product. R^2 is equal to 0.70, and it is significant at 1.2 percent.

In general, the variables that emerged as significant were those which stand out in the tables presented earlier. Together, success in promoting (merchandise) exports, encouraging agriculture, and increasing the share of investment in national income accounts for about 70 percent of growth in GNP over the twenty-year period.

Some degree of multicollinearity between the variables has lowered their individual significance. This mattered particularly, as might be expected, for the investment and agriculture variables; the importance of both rose significantly as one or the other was dropped. Nonetheless, except for population density, all explanatory variables were, even in this equation, significant at the 10 percent level. Tested separately, they were all significant at the 1 percent level.

So, as noted earlier, international competitiveness matters for growth, as do both the level (result not shown) and growth rate of investment, though the direction of causality between these latter and GNP growth is not clear. The existence of a healthy agricultural sector is probably both a reflection of and a catalyst to growth.

The variable used for population density was hectares of arable land per head of population in 1960. I surmised that a country with less arable land per capita might on this account have a lower growth rate. This hypothesis is weakly supported here. It appears that, when a zero restriction is imposed on the density variable, the negative effect of increasing population density is found in company with, and offsets to some extent, the positive effects of high investment and exports.

Several apparently plausible hypotheses were not confirmed by the analysis. Population growth is often assumed to operate as a drag on progress, in the sense that a higher population growth rate is negatively related to growth of output per capita. I ran a variety of regressions—for GNP, for GNP per capita, for the entire period, for several decades—using the population growth rate as independent variable. None of these yielded significant results. This is in line with Kuznets's (1966) earlier findings for a sample of "developed" countries over the period 1860–1960, in which he found no significant relation between growth rates of population and per capita income.

Again, one might think that it is easier for a small country to develop than for a large country. This theory was tested using 1960 population as a crude indicator of size. The coefficient was insignificant. Or one might expect a low-income country to grow faster than a high-income country, on the basis of a "catching-up" hypothesis. But income per capita in 1960 did not prove to be significantly related to the 1960–80 growth rate.

Missing Variables: The Political Element

Even though we know that growth of agricultural output, growth and diversification of exports, and a high investment rate seem to be important, the sources of sustained growth remain mysterious. It is clear from table 5 that countries with apparently similar investment rates can have very different growth rates. Compare

Brazil and Tanzania, or Thailand and India. Some countries extract more output from capital than do others. An effort to explain why quickly leads us beyond the boundaries of economic analysis.

Some of the most important variables excluded from economic models can be labeled as political. Government matters. When we ask in precisely what ways it matters, the answer seems to include at least the following: strength of nationhood; degree of continuity in political leadership; degree of interest in economic growth by the governing group; administrative competence of government; and general stance of economic policy. Without professing to be at all complete, I shall turn now to exploring these variables.

1. *Nationhood.* The term *nation* carries connotations derived from Western experience, which are often inappropriate in the third-world setting. In Europe and North America, a nation was a well-defined geographic area whose residents usually shared a common language and a sense of cultural identity. This sense of nationhood had been consolidated gradually over the centuries, usually before the outset of intensive growth.

Third-world countries range all the way from those which are nations in the full sense to those which are scarcely nations at all. The Latin American countries have substantial linguistic and cultural unity, though in some countries the admixture of European and Indian groups has produced social and political stratification. They also have a tradition of self-government over a century and a half. Some Asian countries—Japan, China, Korea, Thailand—also have a strong sense of national identity. But India, more nearly a continent than a country, has great ethnic and religious diversity; and so do Indonesia, Malaysia, the Philippines, and some other Asian countries. Diversity is even more evident in sub-Saharan Africa. Here the precolonial political boundaries were tribal, and the new boundaries drawn by the colonial powers were quite artificial. Tribal allegiances persisted during the colonial period, which in any event was rather short, and have been affirmed strongly in the era of independence. African governments today often represent a large and dominant tribe, and other tribes remain outside the power structure.

Thus for the ordinary person in Africa, in many parts of Asia, and even in certain Indian regions of Latin America, the notion that the government is "his" government, or that he should make sacrifices for the future of "his" country, probably has little acceptance. This alienation is reinforced by the fact that most third-world countries are governed by a military group, a civilian oligarchy, or even a personal monarch. A continuous tradition of selecting government leaders through open and broadly based elections is unusual. The inability of many governments to rely on a developed sense of citizenship, and their consequent inability to mobilize initiative or impose economic sacrifices for the sake of national goals, is characteristic of what Myrdal has labeled "the soft state."

2. *Continuity of Political Leadership.* The need for continuity is almost self-

evident. Frequent and abrupt transfers of power make it difficult to develop a coherent economic strategy. They may also involve loss of life, destruction of property, and disruption of production.

Continuity can be and is achieved in a variety of ways: through peaceable transfer of power as a result of elections, as in India, Sri Lanka, Malaysia, and (recently) Colombia and Venezuela; through continuous rule by a single dominant party, as in Mexico, Ivory Coast, Tanzania, Kenya, Algeria, and Taiwan, plus China and other communist-led countries; through personal dictatorship, usually by a military leader, as in South Korea, Indonesia, Pakistan, Iraq, Zaire, and (recently) Argentina, Brazil, and Chile; or through a personal monarchy, as in Nepal, pre-1978 Iran, and Morocco.

Dislike of military government is (rightly) built into American ways of thought. But I have not seen clear evidence that military rule *per se* is either favorable or adverse to economic growth. It should be noted that in some third-world countries the army is virtually the only effective administrative organization; that it provides one of the few channels by which an able young man from a poor family can rise to a position of leadership; and that, since it uses modern technology embodied in modern weapons, it serves to develop both technical skills and attitudes favorable to modernization throughout the economy.* One can easily construct a box score of countries which have progressed substantially under military rule, as in Brazil, Pakistan, Indonesia, and South Korea, as against countries in which military rule has debauched the economy, as in Argentina, Uganda, Ghana, and Zaire. But such anecdotal evidence is scarcely conclusive.

A number of countries, particularly in Africa, have had a turbulent political history, including anticolonial wars, civil wars, coups and countercoups. Examples are Ghana, Nigeria, Uganda, and Mozambique, where political instability in itself is sufficient to explain mediocre or poor economic performance. But neither does stability necessarily provide any *guarantee* of growth. The governments of Burma under the generals, Nepal under the king, Ethiopia in the Haile Selassie era, and Zaire under Mobutu have been quite stable, but growth has been minimal. Continuity of leadership seems to be a necessary but not a sufficient condition for good performance.

3. _Orientation of Leadership_. The interests and orientation of the governing group can also be decisive for economic growth. Historically, most governments have concentrated on staying in power, putting down dissenters, and perhaps making war on neighboring nations. Attaching high priority to economic progress might be regarded as unusual, even eccentric. Yet it does happen. It makes a difference whether government is dominated by a landowning class interested

*See Lucian W. Pye, ''Armies in the Process of Political Modernization,'' in *The Role of the Military in Underdeveloped Countries*, ed. John J. Johnson (Princeton: Princeton University Press, 1962).

mainly in drawing customary rents from the land or whether merchants and nascent industrialists also have substantial influence. The growing power of the mercantile-industrial bourgeoisie was very important in northwestern Europe, North America, and Japan in the nineteenth century; and it is important today in most Latin American and some Asian countries.

Nationalist motivation—economic growth as a basis for national independence and military power—has been important on occasion, notably in Japan and China. In South Korea and Taiwan, fear of "the enemy" has reinforced leadership pleas for economic effort. In communist-led countries, of course, economic growth is a secular religion, and effort in this direction can be taken for granted.

4. *Administrative Competence.* A key requirement for success is a competent administrative staff, not only at top government levels but at lower levels as well, so that policies and projects developed at the top are carried out effectively. All the requisites for economic progress—effective collection of taxes, execution of public works and other infrastructure projects, dissemination of modern technology and inputs to farmers, expansion of education and health facilities— require competence and continuity in staffing. The capacity of third-world governments in this respect ranges all the way from near-European levels to virtually zero. The difficulties of most African countries arise partly from the fact that colonial administrative staffs were dominated by Europeans with little African participation. Thus when the Europeans departed they left almost a vacuum, which will take a long time to fill. In India, on the other hand, economic performance has been aided by the strong professional tradition of the Indian civil service, which over the years came to consist increasingly of Indian rather than British personnel. If one could develop a quantitative indicator of administrative capacity, it would probably show a high correlation with economic performance.

A much-discussed question, which cannot be considered adequately here, is the widespread acceptance of bribes by public officials. This sometimes arises from low civil-service salaries, which over time tend to be eroded by inflation and which must be supplemented in some way to provide even a minimal standard of living. Another source is the tendency of third-world governments to regulate private economic activity in detail. When almost any transaction requires a license, or a permit, or a ration, or an allocation of inputs or foreign exchange, there is a natural tendency to speed the transaction by a payment to the official in charge. The payment may be to get him to do something that is already his duty (tipping the postman to get delivery of your letter), to speed up a legitimate transaction, to get preferential treatment where claimants exceed supplies, or to get an extralegal exception to the rules. Such payments have sometimes been defended as necessary grease on the wheels of a slow-moving bureaucracy. But they also introduce an element of uncertainty. How much must I pay? Will it work? And they can even cause a slowdown of action, as when a bureaucrat declines to do anything until the right payment is forthcoming. Myrdal, after looking at the matter closely in the Asian setting, reached a clearly negative verdict.

A particular weakness in most third-world countries is a shortage of middle management. There may be good economic technocrats at the top of the government structure but, as one goes down the hierarchy, capacity diminishes rapidly. The result can be what Latin Americans call "projectismo"—the development of ambitious plans at the top that are executed only partially or not at all. Thus along with considering what government *should* do, given an ample supply of angelic administrators, one must always bear in mind what government is *able* to do in the real world.

5. *Policy Stance.* By *policy stance* I mean mainly the extent to which government encourages and relies on private economic initiative or, on the contrary, the extent to which it tries to substitute government decisions for private decisions. There is evidence that such policy orientation can have substantial effect on the growth rate. Where government concentrates on maintaining an appropriate structure of incentives and relies on private economic agents to respond, the production response is usually strong. On the other hand, an effort to control private economic activity in detail usually has a stultifying effect. This point is so important that I shall devote most of the next chapter to exploring it and so will say nothing more here.

These five variables might be regarded as measurable, in principle, with values ranging from 1 to 0 for a particular country. It was tempting to try to assign numerical grades to each country on each variable and to see whether the consolidated scores were closely related to growth rates. But to do this at all accurately would have meant much additional research and consultations with country specialists, which time did not permit.*

On an impressionistic basis, however, the importance of political variables stands out strongly. Omitting the oil economies, the top five performers in table 2 are South Korea, Taiwan, Brazil, Thailand, and Malaysia. It would be fair to characterize all these countries as displaying the following traits: a strong sense of national identity (though with some Chinese-Malay dissension in Malaysia); continuity of political leadership (though with a civilian-military shift in Brazil in 1964 and occasional disturbances in Thailand moderated by the influence of the king); a growth orientation of leadership, partly because of the influence of a business middle class in these countries; good institutions of higher education and competent administrative staffs (though perhaps least strong in Thailand); a favorable view of private economic activity and generally astute economic policies.

Look on the other hand at the nine countries with lowest growth rates (tier 4 in table 2). In varying degrees these countries are characterized by: weak national identity; serious political instability (except in Nepal, where the stability is that of an old-fashioned oriental kingdom); leadership that is either uninterested in eco-

*For an interesting effort at quantification of political and social variables, using A–D ratings, see Irma Adelman and Cynthia Taft Morris, *Society, Politics, and Economic Development: A Quantitative Approach* (Baltimore: Johns Hopkins University Press, 1967).

nomic growth or unable to pursue it effectively; poor performance in higher education and administrative staffing; and a tendency to overregulation, which discourages private activity (least evident in Nepal, most evident in Ghana, Zambia, and Uganda under Amin).

Overall, then, consideration of political variables brings us closer to an explanation of growth performance than we could get by looking at economic variables alone.

A Concluding Word

We all know that statistical association does not reveal causation. Examination of table 5, for example, suggests that countries with apparently similar investment rates can have very different growth rates. Compare Brazil and Tanzania, or Thailand and India. Some countries clearly extract more output from capital than do others. But to explain why would lead us beyond the bounds of regression analysis.

The variables analysts have been unable to quantify seem largely political— continuity of governments, growth orientation (or its absence) in the political leadership, administrative competence of government, effectiveness of policies in agriculture, foreign trade, and other key sectors. The importance of these things is almost self-evident from table 2. Of the twenty countries with highest 1960–80 growth rates, most (not all) would get good scores on political stability, administrative staffing, and effectiveness of economic policies. But the opposite is true of the nine countries in tier 4. Almost all these countries have been wracked by civil wars, by coups and countercoups, or by serious misgovernment and major policy errors. The only country in the group that has enjoyed political stability is Nepal, but this is the stability of an oriental kingdom that cheerfully accepts foreign aid from all comers but otherwise shows minimal interest in economic development.

For good or ill, government seems central to economic growth. For this reason I will devote the final chapter to government activity.

16

The Functions of Government

In the long tradition of political economy, economists have always taken account of government actions. But the tone of the discussion has changed over the years. In the eighteenth and early nineteenth centuries, government was the enemy. The problem was to liberate private production and exchange from the stranglehold of government controls. This emancipation of the market was in large measure accomplished, and most economists thought that it contributed to acceleration of growth in the now "developed" countries. Even Marx looked to capitalism to transform heavily agricultural economies into modern industrial states. Socialism would arrive only after capitalism had developed a powerful engine of production.

Even after free-market economies were in place, government was of course always in the background. It was expected to protect life and property and to establish a legal framework for economic activity. It usually went ahead pragmatically to encourage development of railroads and other infrastructure. It provided national defense, plus a growing amount of education and other public services, financing these activities by a tax system. These minimal functions of government continue in today's developing countries, and we shall largely take them for granted.

In the late nineteenth century government began to reemerge as a more prominent economic actor. The spread of socialist ideas, the gradual extension of the suffrage, a growing popular belief that economic performance was somehow the responsibility of government, all contributed to this trend. The expansion of government functions took several forms: use of taxation and public expenditure to redistribute income; some expansion of public ownership of industry; an increase in the number of wages and prices subjected to public control; a retreat from the high point of free trade around 1870 and a partial return to mercantilist policies; acceptance of government responsibility for the general level of output and employment after the debacle of the Great Depression.

This trend toward creeping interventionism of the state in economic affairs was considerably accelerated by the two world wars. War is the great socializer. Nations discovered that the private economy could be subjected to detailed public control. They discovered also that the tax system could yield revenues much in excess of previous expectations and, as military demands abated, these revenues left room for increased government spending in other directions. In most countries (except for the United States, Canada, and Japan) socialist parties began to alternate in office with conservative parties; and although government functions were sometimes cut back a bit by conservative regimes, the expansionist trend continued.

These changes in the older industrial countries set the stage for economic policy in third-world countries after 1945. In most countries it was accepted with little debate that government is the main instrument for promoting economic development. The old enemy, government, had become the friend and promoter of economic progress. The reasons for this drastic shift from the view held (and practiced) in the older industrial countries during their takeoff periods would form an interesting chapter in the history of economic thought; but I cannot write that chapter here. Rather, I shall examine how well the expanded functions of government are being performed and how fully the record warrants the new faith in government's competence and beneficence.

THE FRAMEWORK OF ECONOMIC INSTITUTIONS

It would be hard to say anything new or interesting about the conventional functions of government—as tax gatherer, infrastructure builder, and supplier of public services—beyond what has been said in earlier chapters. I shall simply take these functions for granted. But I must comment briefly on an important function that is often overlooked: development of an effective framework of economic institutions. I have in mind here a "mixed economy," in which most productive equipment is privately owned and most economic transactions take place in private markets. What economic institutions are needed in such an economy, and how can government midwife their development?

The concept of a competitive, price-guided, market economy is an attractive utopia, one that has been perfected by economists over more than two centuries. Many people fall in love with it and, in so doing, fall into several kinds of error. The results of the market machinery depend partly on initial conditions, notably the distribution of asset ownership, and what constitutes a proper distribution of wealth cannot be decided on economic grounds alone. There is a tendency to understate the imperfection of markets, the importance of public goods and external economies, and other things that may require government action. Finally, there is a tendency to think that the highly developed market institutions that we see in the more-developed countries sprang spontaneously from the brow of Zeus—or of Adam Smith. But in fact they evolved over a long period; and in third-world countries, at the outset of economic growth, they are usually quite underdeveloped. The most basic task of government—assuming that the goal is a (mainly) private economy—is to foster laws, procedures, and organizations that encourage private initiative and enable producers to reap its rewards.

Since agriculture is usually the largest sector, the institutions governing land ownership and use are especially important. Many third-world economies have always had a system of family farming, which permits effective operation of income incentives. This is true in some (not all) Latin American countries, in most of Africa (where land use is allocated to families even when ownership remains tribal), and in most of Southeast Asia. Some other countries in which land ownership was initially quite unequal have undergone land reforms, as in Taiwan, South Korea, Egypt, and Mexico. Though these reforms differ in detail, they typically involve some combination of (1) subdivision of large, often absentee-managed landholdings into smaller, family-sized units; (2) provision for tenants to become farm owners through long-term government financing; and (3) arrangements for giving the remaining tenants greater security of tenure, a larger share of output, better access to credit, and greater economic independence. Such a restructuring, which enables the cultivator to make price-guided production decisions and to reap the rewards of innovation, seems to be a necessary, though not a sufficient, condition for raising productivity in agriculture. In some countries, particularly in Latin America, the distribution of ownership is still quite unequal; and this is a source of lagging output growth as well as political instability.

In the area of industry and trade there is need for a legal and judicial system to protect property, to ensure enforceability of contracts, and to permit modern forms of business organization. There are still countries in which debts are not legally collectable and where in consequence a person can go into business only with family members over whom he has some moral hold. Thus large private enterprises are almost precluded. Development of the corporate form was vital to growth of large-scale industry in the presently developed countries; and spread of this form can be expected to play a similar role in third-world economies.

A further need is creation of a modern financial structure. A developing country does not need instant Wall Street. But it does need a central bank; a system of commercial banks, lending preferably at flexible, market-determined rates; facilities for long-term investment finance, usually including one or more government development banks; a system of savings institutions providing security and an attractive real rate of interest; and a public market for government securities, which can gradually be extended to cover high-grade private securities.

Another important institution is the government's own budget-making machinery. In the economies we are considering here, government usually produces 10–15 percent of national output, and it often accounts for one-third to one-half of gross capital formation. We tend to assume that resources flowing through government channels will be allocated rationally; but this cannot be taken for granted. It is quite possible for the allocation to be whimsical and unstable, following lines of personal influence rather than any economic rationale. The critical factor here is the top political leadership. Bad leadership cannot be remedied by redrawing organization charts. But given reasonable competence and continuity in leadership, one can design budget procedures that will aid rational decision-making.

Rationalization of government's role in the economy is the main function of the multiyear "development plans" used by many third-world countries in recent decades. While these plans are professed to be global, containing macroeconomic targets for the entire economy, their control power over the private sector is usually quite limited. The "hard" part of a development plan relates to the public sector and is essentially a multiyear budget, covering capital expenditures and often current expenditures as well, which serves as a guide for preparation of annual budgets. Making development plans directs attention to long-run priorities rather than simply to immediate pressures. It requires each department of government to document its budget requests more fully and to relate this year's budget to the preceding and following years. This can scarcely fail to improve resource allocation.

The institutional requirements for economic development by the capitalist route were outlined long ago by John Stuart Mill (1848) in a passage that is still highly relevant:

> The desideratum for such a [less-developed] country, economically considered, is an increase of industry and of the effective desire of accumulation. The means are, first, a better government; more complete security of property; moderate taxes, and freedom from arbitrary exaction under the name of taxes; a more permanent and more advantageous tenure of land, securing to the cultivator as far as possible the undivided benefits of the industry, skill, and economy he may exert. Secondly, improvement of the public intelligence. . . . Third, the introduction of foreign arts, which raise the returns derivable from additional capital . . . and the importation of foreign capital, which renders the increase of production no longer exclusively dependent on the thrift or providence of the inhabitants themselves . . . and by instilling new ideas and breaking the chains of habit . . . tends to create in them new wants, increased ambition, and greater thought for the future. These considerations apply more or less to all the Asiatic populations, and to the less civilized and industrious parts of Europe, as Russia, Turkey, Spain, and Ireland.

Most of what we talk about today—orderly government, land reform, a tax system that does not encroach unduly on incentives, technology transfer, foreign aid, capital accumulation, rising consumer expectations—is encompassed in Mill's meaty paragraph.

In this as in so many other respects, Japan is the model of a successfully developing economy. Between 1868 and 1900 the Japanese government created almost from scratch a new institutional structure that provided a favorable setting for private economic initiative. Major reforms included abolition of the rigid system of five social classes, membership in which was determined by birth and each of which was limited to prescribed economic activities, and substitution of a more fluid class structure open to men of talent from diverse social origins; abolition of barriers to internal movement of goods and people and dissolution of the restrictive craft guilds; displacement of the feudal lords who, in lieu of their former revenues from agriculture, received allotments of government bonds whose value was later eroded by inflation; replacement of farmers' payments in kind to the feudal lords by a land tax payable in cash to government and simultaneous abolition of the Tokugawa prohibition against the purchase and sale of land; creation of a modern banking system under the National Bank Act of 1872, accompanied by retirement of the many varieties of Tokugawa paper money and their replacement by a single currency; and development of an efficient budgetary system, which for the first time permitted forecasting and control of revenues and expenditures.

POLICIES TOWARD AGRICULTURE

I have already noted the importance of a tenure system that encourages owner-occupied farms of moderate size and, to the extent that tenant farming continues, provides security of tenure and reasonable rent payments. Why does government need to do any more than this? There is abundant evidence that small farmers are shrewd managers, quite responsive to price signals and to demonstrated possibilities for raising their incomes. So why not just leave them alone to operate as they will?

The problem is that, although agricultural production can be organized efficiently on a small scale, it requires a variety of supporting services that must be organized on a larger scale, and indeed must often be organized by government. The most important of these are:

1. Large-scale programs for water supply, drainage, and other land improvements. These usually require concerted action over an area embracing many farms, as well as large capital investment.
2. Infrastructure investments serving agricultural areas, such as farm-to-market roads, warehouses, and other marketing facilities.
3. Farm credit, especially important where improved technology requires larger purchases of fertilizer and other modern inputs, which farmers with small or zero cash reserves have difficulty in financing. Government can promote the formation of credit cooperatives, which have been quite successful in some countries. Government can also encourage extension of commercial bank lending to rural areas—for example, by *not* imposing interest-rate ceilings that make lending unprofitable, discourage saving, and misallocate capital; or it can set up a system of government-operated farm credit banks.
4. Special mention should be made of agricultural research and extension, which has loomed as increasingly important since 1945. New agricultural technology is a public good in the sense that, once developed, it becomes available to all comers. No one farmer can hope to appropriate it or keep it secret. Further, the social return is usually much larger than any private return to the developer. It

is thus necessary for government to assume main responsibility for agricultural research and development. I should note also that improved technology cannot simply be borrowed from the developed countries or from international research centers. Technology always needs to be adapted to specific soil, rainfall, and sunshine conditions within countries, regions, and districts. Effective borrowing and adaptation thus depends on a strong local network of research centers and experiment stations. Evenson and others have done cross-sectional analyses of countries and of individual states within India. These studies suggest a strong relation between agricultural research activity and rates of increase in agricultural productivity. Rates of return to research activity are typically very high, suggesting that research is usually underfinanced.

This catalog is helpful in detecting ways in which a government may go wrong. It may easily go wrong through neglect, through failing to do the things we have specified as important in stimulating farm output. This may happen because large oil or mineral exports make it easy for the time being to finance food imports, with the result that raising domestic food output does not seem very important. Thus it is not surprising that notable cases of agricultural neglect include oil-exporting Venezuela, Algeria, Iraq, and Nigeria and mineral-exporting Chile, Peru, and Zambia. Neglect may also reflect ideological bias, a view that industry is the hope of the future and that agriculture is naturally a backward and inferior sector. The fact that government is often dominated by city people responsive mainly to pressure from urban interests may be a contributing factor. There may even be an element of laziness—it is easier to build a steel mill than to raise agricultural productivity.

A second way in which government may go wrong involves control of farm prices and farm marketings. This is not common practice in Latin America, but it is practiced by most African and some Asian countries.

In these countries basic food crops, as well as major export crops, are typically bought by a government marketing board at a fixed price. The marketing board is also usually responsible for distributing fertilizer, seeds, and other inputs to the farmers, and it sometimes even distributes consumer goods. The system is supposed to "protect" the peasant against the rapacious middleman, who is portrayed as a monopsonistic buyer enforcing an unduly low price at the farm gate. A second argument is that the fixed price protects farmers against the large world-price fluctuations for primary products. The quantities procured by the marketing board are either exported or resold to domestic consumers, often at a subsidized price.

While such a system may protect farmers against exploitation by private traders, the extent of which is usually exaggerated, it facilitates an even more serious exploitation by government. It would be possible in principle to stabilize prices without affecting their average level over the years. But in practice there is an irresistible temptation to use the system as a method of *taxation,* by systematically paying farmers less than world-price levels and less than they would receive in a free domestic market. The size of this tax varies among countries, but it is usually substantial. It is not unusual to find farmers receiving only half to three-quarters of the world price for their produce.

Further, arbitrary setting of *relative* prices for various farm products can lead to substantial misallocation of resources. Farmers are quite responsive to shifts in relative prices, reallocating their land among products so as to maximize private profit. But this allocation may be socially inefficient, that is, it may produce an output bundle inferior in total value to that which would have resulted from farmer response to market-determined prices. In addition to misallocation among major crops, one often finds an abnormal increase in output of "minor" farm products exempted from price control and government procurement. The free prices for these products often rise to very profitable levels, leading farmers to devote more land and labor to them. The effect is not unlike that in China or the Soviet Union, where farmers lavish time on their private plots, whose produce can be sold at uncontrolled prices.

The cumbersome marketing-board system often leads to higher marketing costs and other inefficiencies. Inability to move the crop promptly at harvest time can lead to crop spoilage. Failure to supply inputs at the time they are needed in the production cycle can also reduce production. The much-maligned private middleman would probably do a better job in most cases. Research studies—for example, studies of rice marketing in Thailand and elsewhere—suggest that private markets are usually (not always) competitive, that traders do not have strong monopsony power, and that their profit margins are small.

Agricultural policies are often reinforced by other policies that reduce farm incomes relative to urban incomes. Many countries have maintained an over-valued exchange rate, which reduces the return in domestic currency of all exports, including agricultural exports. At the same time, tariffs and other trade restrictions raise the price to farmers of manufactured goods and agricultural inputs. The combined effect is often a downtrend in the rural-urban terms of trade, which can scarcely encourage farm production.

This depressing effect has been felt most severely in Africa. For all the sub-Saharan African countries, the median annual rate of increase in agricultural output from 1970 to 1979 was only 1.8 percent, well below the rate of population growth. In addition to countries in the Sahel, which were affected by drought, several other countries show an actual drop in agricultural output during the decade. The list includes Mozambique, Ghana, Zimbabwe, Angola, and Nigeria. A World Bank study* attributes this poor showing partly to inadequate income incentives to farmers. In Tanzania, for example, official prices paid to producers have not kept pace with world prices or domestic production costs. The terms of trade for cash-crop farmers fell by almost one-third during the 1970s. The story is

---

*Accelerated Development in Sub-Saharan Africa (Washington: The World Bank, 1981).

similar in Ghana. Between 1965 and 1979 cocoa output fell by almost 60 percent, and Ghana's share of the world market dropped from one-third to one-sixth. One reason must be that the price paid by the Cocoa Marketing Board rose only sixfold, whereas the price index for consumer goods was rising 22 times. As a result farmers have been neglecting their cocoa trees, trying to shift into other crops, and smuggling cocoa to neighboring countries offering much higher prices.

But we should not paint the picture blacker than it is. Horror stories about agricultural policy can be matched by perhaps an equal number of favorable cases. Ivory Coast has always been proagriculture and proexport. The president, himself owner of a large farm, requires each of his cabinet members to own 12.5 acres of farmland, and each member of parliament must own 7.5 acres. Mexico, in addition to its major land reform, invested heavily in rural infrastructure from 1930 onward and has also been unusually active in agricultural research and development. In Taiwan, the active agricultural policy initiated by the Japanese has continued into the independence period. In addition to the land reform of the early 1950s, government has pursued a comprehensive development policy involving improvement of rural health and education, development of agricultural research and extension, expansion of irrigation facilities, development of farmers' self-help organizations and government lending institutions, and provision of growing amounts of modern inputs. Malaysia, in addition to a massive program of rubber-tree replanting, has moved energetically to raise domestic food production. Large amounts have been spent on land clearing and settlement, feeder-road construction, irrigation, and rural electrification.

The motivation for these programs is no doubt partly political. The Chinese dominate business activity while the Malays are mainly farmers and also control the government. A pro-Malay policy thus tends to be a proagriculture policy. Other countries that have been favorable to and successful in agriculture are South Korea and Thailand. One could say, of course, that these six countries have had relatively high growth rates and so could afford to devote resources to agriculture. But attention to, and success in, agriculture may also be one reason for the high growth rates.

China should also be included in the list of proagriculture countries. Mao, who began as a peasant leader, always counted on the rural population as his main political base. The tilt of policy toward agriculture has if anything increased since his death, with sizable increases in official prices for major crops and increased latitude for peasants to grow and sell additional produce at market prices.

In addition to these clear success cases, we should note several countries whose policies have been moderately favorable toward agriculture, or at least not markedly unfavorable. This group includes India, Sri Lanka, Pakistan, Egypt, Philippines, and Kenya. There are also several cases of "latter-day conversion," that is, countries that neglected agriculture before the mid-1970s but have now shifted to stimulative policies. In Brazil, for example, agricultural policy was until recently neglectful or actually exploitative. Export taxes, an overvalued exchange rate, and price ceilings on domestic food products had an adverse affect on farm income. The military regime that took power in 1964 shifted policy in a favorable direction. Agriculture benefited from abolition of export taxes, adoption of a floating exchange rate, and lifting of food-price ceilings. There was also a marked increase in rural credit facilities. The real value of loans increased six times between 1960 and 1975. These policies must be partly responsible for the 5 percent growth rate of agricultural output since 1960.

In Burma, there was a marked policy shift around 1975. A "package program" was introduced for rice that included dissemination of high-yield varieties, increased supplies of fertilizer at a subsidized price, and a doubling of the government purchase price. Controls over private sales to the free market were also relaxed. The program produced a rise of 40 percent in rice output within a few years, and this success led to its being extended to groundnuts, maize, wheat, sesame, cotton, beans, and pulses, most of which have also shown substantial increases in yields and output.

In Indonesia, the Suharto regime after 1966 introduced a "rice intensification program," which by 1979 covered about five million hectares. Between 1968 and 1979 rice yields per hectare rose by 40 percent, and rice output by 53 percent. Food output as a whole grew during the 1970s at 3.6 percent per year, compared with a rate of only 1.7 percent from 1953 to 1966.

These examples suggest that agriculture, far from being an inherently laggard sector, is quite responsive to well-conceived government programs.

TRADE AND EXCHANGE POLICIES

Because of their small economic size, most third-world countries are heavily dependent on foreign trade. This dependence is not forced on them by the more-developed countries. It is inherent in the fact of small output and small purchasing power.

Writers on international economics usually distinguish between "outward-looking" and "inward-looking" trade and exchange policies. The main features of an outward-looking policy are: a realistic and flexible exchange rate; a free market for foreign exchange, rather than government-determined allocations; and efforts to promote exports, including in time exports of manufactured products. The term *outward-looking* connotes a favorable view of trade possibilities and reliance on a growing flow of exports to earn the foreign exchange needed for domestic development.

Inward-looking policies are the opposite of those just described: a fixed exchange rate, which usually becomes increasingly overvalued as a result of domestic inflation; a consequent "scarcity" of foreign exchange, which is then allocated among claimants by a government agency; high and often indiscriminate protection of manufacturing industries, by quantitative restrictions on imports as well as tariff rates, with a view to speeding up import substitution in manufactures;

and a pessimistic view of exports, which are neglected or even penalized through export taxes and the exchange-rate system. This policy package tends to produce sluggish growth of exports, which is then used to justify continuation of the restrictive policies.

The difference between the two is not a simple black-and-white contrast. Both policy sets are matters of *degree*. Inward-looking policies may be highly restrictive or only moderately so. Further, there are protariff as well as antitariff arguments. All the developed countries except Britain were quite protectionist while building up their own industries, and so doctrinaire preaching of free trade to currently developing countries has a hollow ring. The size of the economy makes considerable difference. Strong emphasis on import substitution makes more sense for India or Brazil than for Ivory Coast or Peru.

The fact remains that expert opinion is generally critical of highly inward-looking or import-substituting policies. The adverse effects, of course, vary with the severity of the restrictions imposed and with the stage of industrialization. They apply most strongly after "easy import substitution" in nondurable consumer goods is largely completed and the issue is how rapidly to move into consumer durables, chemicals, metals, machinery, and transport equipment. The adverse effects are usually stressed as follows.

1. The overvalued exchange rate, a hallmark of inward-looking policy, taxes exporters and discourages exports. Because there is excess demand for foreign exchange at the official rate, exchange rationing becomes necessary, and those who receive allocations of exchange get a windfall profit. The antiexport bias usually means also an antiagriculture bias, even when the country has comparative advantage in one or more agricultural goods. This discourages agricultural production. Thus apart from any limitations of foreign demand, export expansion may be slowed from the supply side. Export pessimism, which was urged as a reason for import substitution, can readily become self-fulfilling.
2. A common defect is that protection and other incentives are provided not to a limited number of the most promising "infants" but to any and all branches of manufacturing. Studies of Argentina in the Perón era, for example, show little relation between indicators of comparative advantage for a particular industry and the degree of government support it received. Similar results have been reported by Krueger for Turkey, by Lewis and others for Pakistan, and by Bhagwati and Srinivasan for India. At the extreme, one finds cases of "negative value added"—that is, cases in which the value of inputs exceeds that of outputs when both are valued at world prices. It appears also that the cost of the resources used to save a dollar of foreign exchange by import substitution is often well above the cost of using the same resources to earn a dollar of foreign exchange in export production.
3. Foreign competition is stifled. In some countries a product is put on the "prohibited" list as soon as a domestic source of supply has been created. The

domestic monopolies or oligopolies thus created have no incentive to efficiency, and comparative international studies often show that their unit costs are far out of line with those of foreign sources of supply.

4. The way in which foreign-exchange allocation systems are operated tends to produce additional inefficiency. Very common is the "fair shares" principle, in which foreign exchange to buy imported inputs is allocated among firms in an industry in proportion to their installed capacity. This protects firms already established in an industry against newcomers who might be more efficient. It also encourages overbuilding of capacity to obtain larger quotas, and everybody ends up producing below capacity for lack of inputs. This phenomenon helps to explain the paradox that, in countries where capital is supposedly scarce, industrial capital is often seriously underutilized.

5. Systems of quantitative controls, operated by bureaucracies ranging from moderately efficient to quite inefficient, involve uncertainty, delay, excessive paperwork, bribery, and other economic costs. They also tend to favor large producers with good connections over small and unknown producers, regardless of relative efficiency. Thus government's verbal encouragement to small business is negated in practice by the difficulty of finding one's way through the maze of government controls.

6. The supposed aim of reducing import dependence is not necessarily accomplished by inward-looking policies. Some manufacturing industries, especially of the "finishing touches" type, are heavily dependent on imported inputs. So a crash program of import substitution may in the first instance raise import requirements rather than lower them. Even the objective of raising the growth rate of manufacturing output may not be accomplished. Krueger's study of Turkey concluded that a different, balanced strategy with no antiexport bias would have *raised* the manufacturing growth rate by about one-third. It would also have helped the balance of payments by producing more exports and requiring fewer imports than the policies actually followed.

We should not suppose that third-world governments are blind to these problems or that they cannot learn from experience. Some countries in our sample never embarked on highly restrictive trade policies, preferring a generally outward-looking stance. Ivory Coast, Malaysia, and Thailand are prominent examples. In quite a few others there has been a marked shift in policy over time. The doctrine and practice of import substitution peaked in the 1950s. From 1960 onward, one country after another moved in a liberalizing direction. This evolution of policy is important enough to warrant citing a few examples.

A new policy package was introduced around 1961 in Taiwan and around 1965 in South Korea. The main steps taken were: (1) a substantial currency devaluation and substitution of a unified for a multiple exchange rate; (2) liberalization of import quotas and reduction of tariff rates; and (3) a variety of export incentives, with special attention to exports of manufactures. In Taiwan, for example, these incentives included creation of duty-free processing zones; rebate of customs duties and indirect taxes on imported inputs for export products; reduction of the corporate income tax on export earnings; loans at low interest rates; export insurance; a government institute for market research; and a direct subsidy to some industries, administered through manufacturers' associations.

Taiwan's economic success, of course, has been due to a number of factors, including land reform and progressive agricultural policies. But the shift to outward-looking trade policies has certainly contributed. The response of industrialists to the new policies was strong and rapid. Manufacturing output, exports, and productivity rose at spectacular rates after 1960. Manufactures rapidly came to dominate the export list, replacing primary products, which maintained their volume but fell in percentage terms, a process usually termed "export substitution." The same sequence of events occurred in South Korea after 1965. Hong Kong and Singapore since its separation from Malaysia are also quite open economies. It is striking that, as of 1980, about half of all exports of manufactures from the third world came from this Far Eastern "gang of four."

In the late 1960s Brazil and Colombia moved toward more export-oriented policies. The Colombia policy package included a tax rebate system, refund of import duties on inputs, credit at a low rate of interest (usually slightly negative in real terms), and a movable exchange rate system under which the rate was devalued frequently to reflect differential movement of foreign and domestic prices. In Chile, after replacement of the Allende regime in 1973, there was a wholesale removal of price controls and other government controls over the economy. Tariff and nontariff barriers to imports were reduced dramatically. The exchange rate was massively devalued in 1973, with frequent downward adjustments after that, and exchange controls were eliminated. Under the new regime GDP grew rapidly in the late 1970s, exports rose from 40 percent to 50 percent of GDP, and nontraditional exports did particularly well, with copper falling below half of all exports for the first time.

Pakistan liberalized trade somewhat in the early 1960s, then slid back, then returned to a proexport stance in the mid-1970s. Exports, which had been growing at less than 2 percent a year, grew from 1976 to 1980 at 15.3 percent per year. By 1980 finished manufactures were half of all exports, semimanufactures 30 percent, and primary products only 20 percent. Egypt, after the "opening to the West" in 1974, adopted more liberal policies as regards both foreign trade and private investment. The export/GDP ratio rose from about 14 percent in 1970 to 34 percent in 1980, partly but not entirely due to rising oil revenues. There was a general liberalization of economic policies in Sri Lanka in 1978, when a conservative government was installed after a long period of socialist rule. The new policies included exchange-rate unification and devaluation and a liberalization of import controls. Turkey launched a reform program in January 1980 designed to move toward greater reliance on market forces as against quantitative controls and a more outward-looking policy stance.

Since 1960, in short, the trend has been away from extreme import substitution and toward greater integration into the world economy along lines of comparative advantage. A policy shift in this direction has typically led to a sharp spurt in export growth. Meanwhile countries that have clung to inward-looking policies have experienced slow export growth and a shrinking share of world markets.

PUBLIC OPERATION OF INDUSTRY

In the developed countries railroads, electric power systems, and other public utilities are normally government-owned, though the United States is an exception in this respect. Other sectors are predominantly under private ownership, though there is some government ownership of manufacturing in Britain and France and rather more in Italy. Government enterprises are normally organized as semi-autonomous public corporations whose managers are not subject to day-to-day political intervention by government. They are expected to operate on business principles and to earn enough so that they do not become a burden on the general budget.

In third-world countries, too, government ownership of public utilities is virtually universal. But many governments have gone beyond this into agricultural marketing, banking, mining, and manufacturing. Even in countries with a predominantly capitalist orientation, government is usually the main investment banker. In Brazil, for example, government banks are estimated to provide 70 percent of all investment funds. In a number of countries government has also taken over the commercial banking system. Oil and mineral enterprises are usually government-owned. The historical reason is that before 1940 these enterprises were almost all owned by private foreign companies. Nationalizing them thus seemed the most direct way of asserting the country's control over its natural resources and also of appropriating the large profit streams these enterprises usually yield.

One indicator of the importance of state-owned enterprises in the economy is their investment as a percentage of gross fixed capital formation. In the late 1970s this was 23 percent in Brazil and 23 percent in South Korea, countries with a generally private-enterprise orientation. But it was 33 percent in India, 45 percent in Pakistan, 61 percent in Burma and Zambia, and 68 percent in Algeria.*

The main concern here is with manufacturing, in which practice varies most from country to country and the merit of public ownership is perhaps most debatable. In most countries of our sample the government-owned share of value added in manufacturing is below 20 percent, and often below 10 percent. But it is about 20 percent in India, 25 percent in Ivory Coast, 30 percent in Mexico and Turkey; and it reaches 40 percent in Tanzania, 50 percent in Algeria, 55 percent in Burma, 65 percent in Egypt, and 70 percent in Iraq.

In a dozen or so countries, then, state enterprises and private concerns share

World Development Report, 1983 (Washington: IBRD, 1983), p. 49.

the manufacturing sector. The division is to some extent along product lines, with government tending to dominate in capital goods and intermediates while consumer-goods production is mainly in private hands. The government enterprises are relatively few in number but large in scale. Private enterprises are larger in number but much smaller in average scale. They are also more labor-intensive, and their share of manufacturing employment is well above their share of output. Private businesses are at some disadvantage relative to state enterprises with regard to allocations of credit, foreign exchange, and material inputs. Despite this, the private sector has managed to survive and in some countries shows surprising vigor. The public-private percentages are thus not frozen forever but may be expected to change in response to the evolution of market demand and shifts in public policy.

A number of country studies have tried to appraise the economic performance of state economic enterprises. Several possible criteria are available. Profit performance alone is not conclusive, because marginal-cost pricing may sometimes be socially efficient and may involve financial loss. But when one sees most enterprises losing money most of the time, one is bound to have doubts. In some cases private and state enterprises operate side by side in the same industry, which means that comparative appraisal is possible. It is relevant also to compare unit costs and prices of state enterprises with world price levels, and with unit costs of comparable plants in other countries.

The evidence is somewhat mixed. In South Korea and Ivory Coast, for example, there are some government manufacturing enterprises that seem to operate with reasonable efficiency. These are labor-scarce economies in which there is no incentive for overstaffing; and their governments are stable, pragmatic, and outward-looking. In many other countries, however, observers judge the efficiency of state enterprises to be relatively low. A few examples may be cited.

In India, the private rate of return in public-sector industries is typically low, though this sometimes results from deliberate underpricing, which may have an economic rationale. The social rate of return also appears to be low and declining. Assuming a shadow wage of 60 percent of the market wage, Lal estimates that the average social rate of return to Indian manufacturing in 1968 was 5.4 percent. If the shadow wage is assumed equal to the market wage, the social rate of return drops to −6.1 percent. Bhagwati and Desai are also critical of public-sector performance. Major projects have been launched without a cost-benefit analysis and, where such an analysis was made, government often went ahead with the project despite a low estimated rate of return. So long as the proposed output contributed to some physical target in the five-year plan, all else was forgiven. Long delays in plant completion and serious inflation of costs have been common. Current management has suffered from a variety of ills: use of unqualified generalists from the Indian civil service as top administrators; shortages of technical personnel, due partly to salary scales not competitive with private industry; political heckling of administrators, leading to cautious management and lack of innovation; political decision-making on plant location; and union pressure through political channels for overstaffing and overpayment.

In Egypt, observers judge the management of public enterprises to be quite inefficient, partly because of the top-heavy Egyptian bureaucracy. Despite a large expansion of university capacity since 1952, government has maintained its guarantee of a government job for every university graduate. The result is heavy overstaffing in all government operations. Hansen and Marzouk note that in the large textile industry the government enterprises, which have about three-quarters of total employment, are notably inefficient relative to privately owned plants. The ratio of administrative and service employees to actual operatives is 60 percent in the public sector, 20 percent in the private sector. And government wage scales are more than twice as high.

In Iraq, where government has more than 70 percent of industrial employment, the difficulties of industrial management have been severe. There are several levels of bureaucracy above the producing enterprise. There is high turnover of personnel, extending all the way up to cabinet ministers. Many enterprise directors are army officers with little industrial experience. Workers cannot be laid off, and overstaffing is large. So government's heavy investment of oil revenue in manufacturing has yielded disproportionately small returns.

In Tanzania, the evidence of efficiency of public manufacturing enterprises is conflicting. Clark reports their average profit rate in the early 1970s as 13 percent. On the other hand, they were able to finance only about one-quarter of their new investment. More than half of their new capital came from foreign borrowings, and the remainder from government allocations. A World Bank study reports that man-hour output in government manufacturing is only 70 percent as high as that in comparable private enterprises. This suggests that there may be serious overstaffing in government enterprises.

There is similar evidence from Turkey, Zambia, and other countries. The weight of the evidence suggests that the difficulties of government manufacturing enterprises are built in rather than accidental. They result from a combination of too many levels of bureaucracy above the enterprise, poor selection of and inadequate rewards for industrial managers, and failure to shield the enterprise against day-to-day political intervention. Such intervention is pervasive, including pressure for underpricing, for unduly high wage scales, for hiring of unnecessary workers or prohibition of layoffs, for appointment of managers on the basis of connections rather than qualifications. Most serious is the lack of a budget constraint, since deficits can always be made up from the government budget. Enterprise revenues often fail even to cover operating costs, including depreciation allowances, and constitute a continuing drain on the treasury. An IMF study of 64 public corporations in all parts of the world found that, after providing for depreciation, they had on average a net operating *loss* equal to 8 percent of revenue.

This operating deficit, plus all net investment, had to be covered by outside funds, of which about half came from the general government budget.*

A negative verdict on public enterprise does not suggest any immediate remedy. Disillusionment has certainly set in in some countries, and a good deal of rethinking is going on. Selling off public manufacturing concerns to private investors is often not a viable political option, though it has been done on occasion. What government usually could do is to slow down or stop expansion of the public manufacturing sector and leave future increments in capacity largely to private concerns. Thus a 50 percent government share of manufacturing today could readily shrink to 25 percent over two or three decades. Some countries seem presently to be moving in this direction, and others may do so in future.

Private producers, of course, are not necessarily efficient either. Efficiency depends partly on how far they are exposed to the chastening effect of competition. So the argument for privatization is strongest for large economies and for industries of relatively small optimum scale. Even a private monopolist, however, faces a budget constraint; and increases in efficiency are profitable even if not essential.

OTHER TYPES OF MARKET INTERVENTION

In addition to the policy areas already considered, many third-world governments intervene heavily in the pricing of commodities and factors of production. It would be charitable to attribute this to sophisticated reasoning about market failure and the need for offsetting action by government. But it probably stems mainly from political pressures, which operate also in the richer countries. People want larger incomes and lower prices, and any government that depends at all on public favor is likely to respond. I shall comment briefly on consumer-goods pricing, industrial licensing systems, interest-rate policy, and wage policy.

1. *Pricing.* Subsidized pricing of consumer goods is widespread, especially for basic foodstuffs such as rice, wheat, and bread, for passenger transport and other public-utility services, and recently for petroleum products. This distorts demand patterns. In some countries subsidized bread is the cheapest form of animal food and is so used. The subsidies are a heavy drain on the government budget, making it difficult to finance current services and infrastructure development. And the controls are usually evaded to some extent. In Ghana and in Uganda under Amin, attempts at universal price control led to universal evasion, with actual transactions conducted in unofficial or ''parallel'' markets.

Subsidies are usually justified as a way of protecting the real income of the poorest groups in the population. But the subsidized price is available to everyone, regardless of income level. In recognition of this, the new conservative government of Sri Lanka drastically reduced the long-standing rice subsidy while at the

_____

*Andrew H. Gault and Guiseppe Dutlo, ''Financial Performance of Government-Owned Corporations in Less Developed Countries,'' *IMF Staff Papers,* March 1968, pp. 102–42.

same time introducing a United States–type food-stamp system applying only to those below a certain income level. Some countries, too, have had the political courage to raise rail and bus fares and other public-utility prices to levels bearing some realistic relation to production costs. Courage is indeed required, for even in such tightly controlled countries as Poland any effort to raise prices toward market-clearing levels can lead to street riots.

2. *Licensing*. In many African and Asian countries, any new industrial enterprise must apply for a government license. Some branches of industry may be reserved for the public sector. But even within the private sector it is argued that investment decisions should conform to an overall national plan. The difficulties arising from such a system, especially well documented in the case of India, are similar to those noted earlier for exchange-allocation systems: uncertainty and delay, the temptation to speed things up or bend the rules through bribery, stifling of initiative, barring of new competitors, a bias toward large as against small producers. The idea that governments know better than private individuals how to use capital effectively was roundly denounced by Adam Smith. His critique of European government decisions in the eighteenth century seems at least equally applicable to third-world governments in the late twentieth century.

3. *Interest Rates*. Interest rates, like controlled consumer prices, have been afflicted by a tendency toward underpricing. Interest-rate ceilings are often so low as to result in a negative real rate. This naturally leads to large excess demand and the allocation of loans, instead of being guided by which projects can afford to pay the market rate, is determined by bank officials whose decisions are bound to be somewhat arbitrary. Low interest rates combined with imported capital goods, which are made artificially cheap by low duties, overvalued exchange rates, and other policies, also produce a capital-intensive bias in investment projects. It is notorious that the manufacturing sectors of third-world countries often create little employment and fail to make effective use of the ample labor supply. This is due partly to underpricing of capital and (as we shall see) overpricing of labor. Low interest rates also discourage private saving, making it harder to raise the national savings rate to an adequate level. Countries that have raised interest rates sharply to reflect the real scarcity of capital in the economy, as South Korea did in the mid-1960s, have been rewarded by a marked increase in saving as well as more effective utilization of capital.

4. *Wages*. In many third-world economies one observes a marked rise of real wages in "modern-sector" activities and a growing rural-urban income gap. This occurs even in the face of ample labor supplies and growing open unemployment. Private employers often raise wages voluntarily, partly to attract and stabilize a labor force of good quality and perhaps also because it seems inequitable that the much higher productivity of labor in "modern" than in traditional activities should be reflected entirely in profit, as it is in the Lewis model. But government often forces the pace through minimum-wage laws and through generous wage scales for government employees. Especially in Africa, government employees

often form one-third to one-half of the modern-sector labor force; and government, under political pressure to be a "good employer," tends to serve as wage
leader for the private economy.

Whatever the mechanism, the result is often a wage scale for modern-sector
employees well above any market-clearing level. This encourages substitution of
capital for labor in industry, thus reducing employment opportunities. At the same
time the growing urban-rural income gap stimulates heavy migration, which
overcrowds the cities and intensifies both open and concealed unemployment.

The list of possible price distortions is thus a long one. Factor prices are
distorted by interest-rate and wage policies. Product prices are distorted by exchange-rate policy, trade restrictions, farm price ceilings, consumer subsidies,
and underpricing of power, transport, and other services. The circumstances
responsible for each distortion are different, but their effect is cumulative and can
be seriously adverse to economic efficiency and growth.

Researchers at the World Bank have estimated an "index of price distortion"
for each of 30 countries based on ratings by country specialists.* The countries in
our sample with least price distortion were Thailand, South Korea, Malaysia,
Philippines, Kenya, and Colombia (Taiwan, no longer included in IBRD tables,
would probably also fall in this group). The countries with largest price distortions
were Pakistan, Peru, Argentina, Chile, Tanzania, Nigeria, and Ghana.

It is interesting that the average 1970–80 performance of the low-distortion
group was superior to that of the high-distortion group in important respects:
annual GDP growth rate (6.8 percent *versus* 3.1 percent); domestic sav-
ings/income ratio (21.4 percent *versus* 13.8 percent); additional output per unit
of investment (27.6 percent *versus* 16.8 percent); and annual growth rate of
export volume (6.7 percent *versus* 0.7 percent). Although no simple causal relation can be inferred from these data, the association of market-directed prices and
good economic performance seems significant.

CAPITALISM, SOCIALISM, AND ALL THAT

The pure capitalist economy is an abstraction; we shall never see such a thing in
reality. Even in the nineteenth century, Europe and North America deviated
significantly from the capitalist pattern, and these deviations have increased in the
twentieth century. So we speak now of the "mixed economy," an ambiguous
term in that the mix of private initiative and government intervention varies
considerably from country to country. Broadly, we mean an economy that relies
mainly on private ownership of productive assets and on private economic deci-

---

*The technique was to rate each type of distortion in a particular country as low, medium, or high
and to assign numerical values of 1 for low, 2 for medium, and 3 for high. An overall average was then
computed for the country. The averages range from 1.14 in Malawi and 1.43 in Thailand to 2.71 in
Nigeria and 2.86 in Ghana. *World Development Report, 1983* (Washington, DC: IBRD, 1983), pp.
57–63.

sions coordinated mainly through a network of markets and prices. But along with this goes a substantial output of public goods, government ownership of public utilities and sometimes of other industries, government programs aimed at redistributing income, a tax system that collects a substantial percentage of national income, and a variety of government regulations over the private economy.

Of the 34 countries in our sample that have managed to achieve intensive growth, 22 clearly are mixed economies in this sense. The mix varies, just as it does in more-developed countries. Pakistan, Taiwan, Malaysia, and Thailand are more wholeheartedly committed to private ownership than are Turkey, Iran, or Indonesia. Kenya, Ivory Coast, and Nigeria have a stronger private-enterprise orientation than Ghana or Morocco. Argentina, Colombia, and Venezuela are somewhat more capitalist than Mexico or Brazil.

Seven countries profess a socialist orientation. These are Tanzania, Zambia, Algeria, Egypt, Iraq, India, and Burma. These economies are also mixed in that private production is by no means ruled out. It is usually dominant in agriculture, trade, handicrafts, and small-scale manufacturing. But private industry and profit-making are viewed with suspicion, as needing to be kept under careful control. The socialist tilt shows up in an unusually large public sector that encompasses much of large-scale manufacturing, in a propensity to regulate the private economy in great detail, and sometimes in redistributive income policies.

Three countries have changed direction recently and are thus hard to classify. Peru was rather strongly oriented toward private enterprise in the past, but the military regime that took over in 1968 embarked on widespread nationalization of industry. How much of this will last under restored civilian rule remains to be seen. In Uganda, too, the Idi Amin regime confiscated most private industries, though it failed to operate them effectively. The post-Amin economy is still in shambles, and its future structure remains unclear. Sri Lanka would have been classified as socialist in the Indian pattern up to the late 1970s, but the conservative government that has now won two elections has reversed course on many points. We should perhaps add Zimbabwe to the list of uncertain cases. It was strongly capitalist in the past, with much of its industry foreign-owned. The new African prime minister, Robert Mugabe, professes socialism as a goal; but just how, and how rapidly, he will move in this direction is unclear at this date.

This leaves two countries, Cuba and China, in which government is dominated by a communist party and in which virtually all productive assets are state-owned. In other writings* I have explored the economic performance of this type of regime, and nothing need be added here. Suffice it to say that comprehensive socialization, although it is compatible with intensive growth, provides no firm assurance of such growth. China's moderate growth of per capita income puts it in the middle range of third-world countries, well below the star performers but well

---

The Three Worlds of Economics (New Haven: Yale University Press, 1971); and *Image and Reality in Economic Development* (New Haven: Yale University Press, 1977), chap. 15.

above the other Asian giant, India. On the other hand Cuba's economy was badly mismanaged from 1958 through the early 1970s and, though production has since recovered somewhat, per capita income is probably still below the 1960 level. There is little Western literature on North Korea or Vietnam. One has an impression of high growth in North Korea, low or zero growth in Vietnam, not surprising in view of the chronic warfare in which that country has been engaged since 1940.

Returning to the noncommunist countries, one is struck by the degree of ambiguity and internal contradiction in policies toward private business activity. This is most marked in the professedly socialist countries, but it is by no means absent in others. On one hand there is an implicit reliance on private producers to organize resources and raise national output. But on the other hand their efforts are often checkmated by a querulous or hostile government attitude and a maze of government restrictions. Many years ago an office-mate of mine at Harvard, now a distinguished member of the profession, remarked with the air of one discovering an obscure truth, "You know, capitalists have to be allowed to make money." Many third-world governments are reluctant to acknowledge this necessity.

One can well understand suspicion of foreign multinational corporations. It is possible for a country to gain by permitting multinational investment in its territory, but the terms of each deal need to be carefully specified. One wonders, however, whether this suspicion should be extended to indigenous businessmen, who are not really the monsters of Marxist demonology. They are actually rather timid and peaceable creatures who can be tamed to serve the public interest. Instead of repeating Adam Smith's famous paragraph on this point, let me quote Maynard Keynes (1938) in a letter to President Franklin Roosevelt:

> Businessmen have a different set of delusions from politicians; and need, therefore, different handling. They are, however, much milder than politicians, at the same time allured and terrified by the glare of publicity, easily persuaded to be "patriots," perplexed, bemused, even terrified, yet only too anxious to take a cheerful view, vain perhaps but very unsure of themselves, pathetically responsive to a kind word.
>
> You could do anything you liked with them, if you would treat them (even the big ones), not as wolves and tigers, but as domestic animals by nature, even though they have been badly brought up and not trained as you would wish.
>
> It is a mistake to think that they are more immoral than politicians. If you work them into the surly, obstinate, terrified mood, of which domestic animals, wrongly handled, are so capable, the nation's burdens will not get carried to market; and in the end public opinion will veer their way.

We should recall also that Karl Marx, like Adam Smith, considered capitalism a powerful engine for raising productive capacity. Socialism was to take over only after a modern industrial economy had been created. But disciples are rarely as wise as the master. Latter-day Marxists often turn Marx on his head and advocate socialist organization *before* capitalism has had an opportunity to do its constructive work.

"Capitalist" has now become an epithet. It is perhaps difficult for third-world governments to respond to the question "Do you sincerely want to be rich?" by openly espousing capitalism. But perhaps they might do so quietly. They might recall that the most thoroughly capitalist of the developed countries, Japan, also has the strongest growth record. Also, of the 20 third-world countries ranked highest in recent income growth (see table 2), almost all have a clear private-enterprise orientation. Except for Algeria and Iraq, which have kept afloat on a flood of oil revenue, countries with a socialist orientation rank lower in the table.

LESSONS FROM HISTORY?

Perhaps not *lessons,* but something more in the nature of *suggestions.* An initial suggestion is that we stop using the term *third world.* Whatever purpose it may serve in political debate, it has no economic merit. The third world is simply a group of countries, as diverse as may be, each of which should be viewed independently, just as we view Australia or France.

A second suggestion relates to the sources of long-term growth. In the United Nations Commission on Trade and Development (UNCTAD) and other international bodies it has been fashionable for many of the lower-income countries to blame their problems on the higher-income countries. They are poor because we have exploited them in the past, and they can flourish only if we will finance them in future. This is largely shadow play. The fact that some countries have grown so much faster than others in the same international environment is in itself a convincing refutation. The trade and aid policies of the developed countries doubtless have some impact; and one can make a good case that these countries, by following policies that are *in their own interest,* can also contribute to third-world growth. But when we ask *why* a particular country has grown more or less rapidly, we come back invariably to internal factors: the resource base, the structure of economic institutions, the stability and competence of government, the wisdom of policy measures. In large measure a country grows by internal effort, which outsiders can encourage but not replace.

A third suggestion comes dangerously close to advice to third-world governments, which are likely to be unresponsive to outside advice unless it comes from international bankers. Thirty years ago Arthur Lewis noted a tendency for third-world governments to undertake more than they can accomplish:

> The list of governmental functions . . . is even wider in the less developed than in the more developed economies. . . . On the other hand, the governments of the less developed countries are at the same time less capable of taking on a wide range of functions than are the governments of the more

developed. Their administrations tend to be more corrupt and less efficient, and a smaller part of the national income can be spared for government activity. This is another of the paradoxes of economic growth. Just as poor countries need to save more than rich countries, but cannot afford as much, so also poor countries need more and better government activity than rich ones, but are apt to get less and worse. In fact, one cannot usefully consider in an abstract way what functions a government ought to exercise without taking into account the capabilities of the government in question. It is very easy to overload the governments of less developed economies, and it is quite clear that it is better for them to confine themselves to what they can manage than for them to take on an excessive range.*

Experience since Lewis wrote underscores the wisdom of his comment. Most third-world governments are trying to do too much with too little. The range of their administrative controls over the economy is wider than in the developed countries, while at the same time their civil-service staffs are weaker. The common result, in addition to confusion, delay, and waste, is that the paper controls are not enforced effectively and do not have the intended effect. In the worst cases, such as Uganda, Ghana, and Zaire, the control system dissolves in a welter of smuggling, bribery, and evasion. There is need for a clearer recognition that administrative capacity is a scarce resource, which can be enlarged only gradually and which meanwhile needs to be husbanded and focused on high-priority objectives. The best government decision is often a decision to do nothing.

Governments might well restrain their urge to control everything in the economy and consider the advantages of greater reliance on private initiative. The payoff to private initiative is especially large in agriculture, to which most governments pay less attention than they should. But it is large also in trade, road transport, service industries, and manufacturing. The gradual growth of an industrial and commercial middle class, which was the essence of nineteenth-century development, still has much to contribute in the twentieth century and beyond.

*W. Arthur Lewis, *The Theory of Economic Growth* (Homewood, IL: Richard D. Irwin, 1955), p. 382.

Bibliography

GENERAL ECONOMIC STUDIES

Economic Growth

Balassa, Bela. *The Newly Industrializing Countries in the World Economy*. New York: Pergamon Press, 1981.

Baran, Paul. *The Political Economy of Growth*. New York: Monthly Review Press, 1957.

Birnberg, Thomas B., and Resnick, Stephen A. *Colonial Development: An Econometric Study*. New Haven: Yale University Press, 1975.

Boserup, Ester. *The Conditions of Agricultural Growth*. Chicago: Aldine Publishing Company, 1964.

———. *Population and Technological Change: A Study of Long-Term Trends*. Chicago: University of Chicago Press, 1981.

Chenery, Hollis. "Patterns of Industrial Growth." *American Economic Review* 50 (September 1960):624–54.

———. *Structural Change and Development Policy*. Oxford: Oxford University Press for the World Bank, 1979.

Chenery, Hollis, and Ahluwalia, Montek S. *Redistribution with Growth*. Oxford: Oxford University Press for the World Bank, 1974.

Chenery, Hollis, and Syrquin, Moises. *Patterns of Development, 1950–1970*. Oxford: Oxford University Press for the World Bank, 1975.

Clark, Colin, *The Conditions of Economic Progress*. London: Macmillan, 1951.

Cohen, Benjamin J. *The Question of Imperialism: The Political Economy of Dominance and Dependence*. New York: Basic Books, 1973.

Fei, John C. H., and Ranis, Gustav. *Development of the Labor-Surplus Economy: Theory and Policy*. Homewood, IL: Richard D. Irwin, 1964.

Gerschenkron, Alexander. *Economic Backwardness in Historical Perspective*. Cambridge: Harvard University Press, 1962.

Gould, J. D. *Economic Growth in History*. London: Methuen, 1972.

441

Guha, Ashok S. *An Evolutionary View of Economic Growth.* Oxford: Oxford University Press, 1981.

Hicks, John R. *Essays in World Economics.* Oxford: Clarendon Press, 1959.

Hoffman, Walther. *The Growth of Industrial Economies.* Manchester: University of Manchester Press, 1958.

Hoselitz, Bert F., ed. *The Role of Small Industry in the Process of Economic Growth.* The Hague: Mouton, 1968.

International Bank for Reconstruction and Development. *World Development Report.* Washington DC: IBRD, 1982, 1983.

Ishikawa, Shigeru. *Economic Development in Asian Perspectives.* Tokyo: Kinokuniya Bookstore, 1967.

————. *Essays on Technology, Employment and Institutions in Economic Development: Comparative Asian Experience.* Tokyo: Kinokuniya Bookstore, 1981.

Johnson, Harry G. *On Economics and Society.* Chicago: University of Chicago Press, 1975.

Johnson, John J., ed. *The Role of the Military in Underdeveloped Countries.* Princeton: Princeton University Press, 1962.

Johnston, Bruce, and Kilby, Peter. *Agriculture and Structural Transformation: Economic Strategies in Late-developing Countries.* Oxford: Oxford University Press, 1975.

Keynes, John Maynard. Letter to President Franklin D. Roosevelt, February 1938. Roosevelt Library, Hyde Park, NY. Reported in the *New York Times,* May 24, 1983, p. F6.

Krueger, Anne O., et al. *Trade and Employment in Developing Countries.* Chicago: University of Chicago Press, 1981.

Kumar, Joginder. *Population and Land in World Agriculture.* Population Monograph Series, no. 12. Berkeley: University of California Press for Institute of International Studies, 1973.

Kuznets, Simon. "International Differences in Capital Formation and Financing." In *Capital Formation and Economic Growth,* ed. Moses Abramovitz. New York: National Bureau of Economic Research, 1956.

————. "Quantitative Aspects of the Economic Growth of Nations: Capital Formation Proportions." *Economic Development and Cultural Change* 8 (July 1960a): 1–96.

————. *Six Lectures on Economic Growth.* IL: Free Press of Glencoe, 1960b.

————. *Modern Economic Growth: Rate, Structure, and Spread.* New Haven: Yale University Press, 1966.

————. *Economic Growth of Nations: Total Output and Production Structure.* Cambridge: Harvard University Press, 1971.

————. "Problems in Comparing Recent Growth Rates for Developed and Less Developed Countries." *Economic Development and Cultural Change* 20 (January 1972):185–209.

Kuznets, Simon; Moore, W. E.; and Spengler, J. J.; eds. *Economc Growth: Brazil, India, Japan.* Durham, NC: Duke University Press, 1955.

Lewis, W. Arthur. "Economic Development with Unlimited Supplies of Labour." *Manchester School* 22 (May 1954):139–91.

―――. *The Theory of Economic Growth.* Homewood, IL: Richard D. Irwin, 1955.

―――. "The Slowing Down of the Engine of Growth." *American Economic Review* 70 (September 1980):555–64.

Little, Ian M. D. *Economic Development: Theory, Policy and International Relations.* New York: Basic Books, 1982.

Maddison, Angus. *Phases of Capitalist Development.* Oxford: Oxford University Press, 1982.

Malinvaud, Edmond, ed. *Economic Growth and Resources.* Proceedings of the Fifth World Congress of the International Economic Association. New York: St. Martin's Press, 1979.

Mill, John Stuart. *Principles of Political Economy.* London: Routledge and Keegan Paul, 1965 [1848].

Mitchell, Brian. *International Historical Statistics: Africa and Asia.* New York: New York University Press, 1982.

Myint, Hla. *The Economics of the Developing Countries.* London: Hutchinson, 1964.

Myrdal, Gunnar. *Economic Theory and Underdeveloped Regions.* London: G. Duckworth, 1957.

―――. *Asian Drama: An Inquiry into the Poverty of Nations.* New York: Pantheon, 1968.

Paauw, Douglas S., and Fei, John C. H. *The Transition in Open Dualistic Economies: Theory and Southeast Asian Experiences.* New Haven: Yale University Press, 1973.

Ranis, Gustav, ed. *Government and Economic Development.* New Haven: Yale University Press, 1971.

Ranis, Gustav, et al., eds. *Comparative Development Perspectives.* Boulder, CO: Westview Press, 1983.

Resnick, Stephen. "The Decline of Rural Industry under Export Expansion." *Journal of Economic History* 30, 1 (March 1970):51–73.

Reynolds, Lloyd G. *The Three Worlds of Economics.* New Haven: Yale University Press, 1971.

―――, ed. *Agriculture in Development Theory.* New Haven: Yale University Press, 1975.

―――. *Image and Reality in Economic Development.* New Haven: Yale University Press, 1977.

Rosenstein-Rodan, Paul. "International Aid to Underdeveloped Countries." *Review of Economics and Statistics* 43 (May 1961):107–38.

Rostow, Walt W. "The Take-off into Self-sustained Growth." *Economic Journal* 66 (March 1956):25–48.

―――. *The World Economy: History and Prospect.* Austin: University of Texas Press, 1978.

Schultz, T. W. *Transforming Traditional Agriculture*. New Haven: Yale University Press, 1964.

Smith, Adam. *An Inquiry into the Nature and Causes of the Wealth of Nations*. Homewood, IL: Richard D. Irwin, 1963 [1776].

Stolper, Wolfgang. *Planning without Facts: Lessons in Resource Allocation for Nigeria's Development*. Cambridge: Harvard University Press, 1966.

Summers, Robert; Kravis, Irving B.; and Heston, Alan. "International Comparison of Real Product and Its Composition: 1950–77." *Review of Income and Wealth*, ser. 26, no. 1, March 1980, pp. 19–66.

Wallerstein, Immanuel. *The Capitalist World Economy*. Cambridge and New York: Cambridge University Press, 1979.

Winks, Robin W., ed. *British Imperialism: God, Gold and Glory*. Holt, Rinehart and Winston, 1973.

The International Economy

Ashworth, William. *A Short History of the International Economy, 1850–1950*. London: Longmans Green, 1952.

Bairoch, Paul. *The Economic Development of the Third World since 1900*. Berkeley: University of California Press, 1975.

Bhagwati, Jagdish N. "The Theory of Comparative Advantage in the Context of Underdevelopment and Growth." *Pakistan Development Review,* Autumn 1962.

————. *Anatomy and Consequences of Exchange Control Regimes*. Cambridge, MA: Ballinger, 1978.

Chenery, Hollis. "Comparative Advantage and Development Policy." *American Economic Review* 50, 1 (March 1961):18–51.

Fieldhouse, D. K. *Economics and Empire, 1830–1914*. London: Weidenfeld and Nicholson, 1973.

Kenwood, A. G., and Lougheed, A. L. *The Growth of the International Economy, 1820–1960*. London: Allen and Unwin, 1975.

Kindleberger, Charles P. *Government and International Trade*. Essays in International Finance, no. 129. Princeton, NJ: Department of Economics, Princeton University, 1978.

Kuznets, Simon. "Quantitative Aspects of the Economic Growth of Nations: X. Level and Structure of Foreign Trade: Long-Term Trends." *Economic Development and Cultural Change* 15, 2, Part II (January 1967):1–14.

Latham, A. J. H. *The International Economy and the Underdeveloped World, 1865–1914*. Totowa, NJ: Rowman and Littlefield, 1978.

Lewis, W. Arthur. *Aspects of Tropical Trade, 1883–1965*. Stockholm: Almqvist and Wiksell, 1969.

————, ed. *Tropical Development, 1880–1913: Studies in Economic Progress*. London: Allen and Unwin, 1970.

————. *The Evolution of the International Economic Order.* Princeton: Princeton University Press, 1978a.

————. *Growth and Fluctuations, 1870–1913.* London and Boston: Allen and Unwin, 1978b.

Maizels, Alfred. *Industrial Growth and World Trade.* London: Cambridge University Press, 1963.

————. *Exports and Economic Growth of Developing Countries.* London: Cambridge University Press, 1968.

Myint, Hla. "The 'Classical Theory' of International Trade and the Under-developed Countries." *Economic Journal,* June 1958, pp. 317–37.

Population

Boserup, Ester. *The Conditions of Agricultural Growth: The Economics of Agrarian Change under Population Pressure.* Chicago: Aldine, 1965.

————. *Population and Technological Change: A Study of Long-Term Trends.* Chicago: University of Chicago Press, 1981.

Durand, J. Dana. *Historical Estimates of World Population: An Evaluation.* Philadelphia: Population Studies Center, University of Pennsylvania, 1974.

Easterlin, Richard A., ed. *Population and Economic Change in Developing Countries: A Conference Report.* Universities–National Bureau Committee for Economic Research, no. 30. Chicago: University of Chicago Press, 1980.

Kuznets, Simon. *Population, Capital and Growth.* New York: Norton, 1973.

McEvedy, Colin, and Jones, Richard. *Atlas of World Population History.* New York: Facts on File, 1978.

Population Problems. Proceedings of the American Philosophical Society, vol. III, no. 3. Philadelphia, 1967.

Tilly, Charles, ed. *Historical Studies of Changing Fertility.* Princeton: Princeton University Press, 1978.

European Economic Development

Ashton, T. S., ed. *An Economic History of England.* Vol. 3, *The Eighteenth Century.* New York: Barnes and Noble, 1955.

Bairoch, Paul, and Lévy-Leboyer, Maurice, eds. *Disparities in Economic Development since the Industrial Revolution.* New York: St. Martin's Press, 1981.

Deane, Phyllis, and Cole, W. A. *British Economic Growth, 1688–1959: Trends and Structure.* Cambridge: Cambridge University Press, 1962.

Jones, Eric L. *The European Miracle.* London: Cambridge University Press, 1981.

Kerridge, Eric. *The Agricultural Revolution.* London: Allen and Unwin, 1967.

Milward, Alan S., and Saul, S. B. *The Development of the Economies of Continental Europe, 1850–1914.* Cambridge: Harvard University Press, 1977.

————. *The Economic Development of Continental Europe, 1780–1870*. London: Allen and Unwin, 1979.

Pollard, Sidney. *Peaceful Conquest: The Industrialization of Europe, 1760–1970*. Oxford: Oxford University Press, 1981.

Rich, E. E., and Wilson, C. H., eds. *The Cambridge Economic History of Europe*. Vol. 4, *The Economy of Expanding Europe in the Sixteenth and Seventeenth Centuries*. Cambridge: Cambridge University Press, 1967.

Woodruff, William. *Impact of Western Man: A Study of Europe's Role in the World Economy, 1750–1960*. New York: St. Martin's Press, 1967.

ASIA

General

Allen, G. C., and Donnithorne, Audrey G. *Western Enterprise in Indonesia and Malaya: A Study in Economic Development*. London: Allen and Unwin, 1957.

Dernberger, Robert F., ed. *China's Development Experience in Comparative Perspective*. Cambridge: Harvard University Press, 1980.

Fisher, Charles, *Southeast Asia: A Social, Economic and Political Geography*. New York: E. P. Dutton, 1964.

Shand, R. T., ed. *Agricultural Development in Asia*. Canberra: Australian National University Press, 1969.

Burma

Andrus, J. Russell. *Burmese Economic Life*. 1948. Reprint. Stanford: Stanford University Press, 1956.

Furnivall, J. S. *An Introduction to the Political Economy of Burma*. 3rd ed. Rangoon: People's Literature Committee-House, 1957.

Silverstein, Josef. *Burma: Military Rule and the Politics of Stagnation*. Ithaca: Cornell University Press, 1977.

China

Eckstein, Alexander. *China's Economic Revolution*. London and New York: Cambridge University Press, 1977.

Feuerwerker, Albert. *The Chinese Economy, 1912–1949*. Michigan Papers in Chinese Studies, no. 1. Ann Arbor: University of Michigan, Center for Chinese Studies, 1968.

————. *The Chinese Economy, ca. 1870–1911*. Michigan Papers in Chinese Studies, no. 5. Ann Arbor: University of Michigan, Center for Chinese Studies, 1969.

Liu Ta-Chung and Yeh K'ung Chia. *The Economy of the Chinese Mainland: National Income and Economic Development, 1933–1959.* Princeton: Princeton University Press, 1965.

Perkins, Dwight M. *Agricultural Development in China, 1368–1968.* Chicago: Aldine Press, 1969.

————, ed. *China's Modern Economy in Historical Perspective.* Stanford: Stanford University Press, 1975.

Rawski, Thomas G. *China's Republican Economy: An Introduction.* Discussion Paper no. 1. Toronto: University of Toronto–York University Joint Centre on Modern East Asia, 1978.

Rawski, Thomas G. *Economic Growth and Employment in China.* New York: Oxford University Press for the World Bank, 1979.

————. *China's Transition to Industrialism.* Ann Arbor: University of Michigan Press, 1980.

India

Bhagwati, Jagdish, and Desai, Padma. *India: Planning for Industrialization: Industrialization and Trade Policies since 1951.* London and New York: Oxford University Press for the Development Centre of the Organization for Economic Cooperation and Development, 1970.

Bhagwati, Jagdish, and Srinivasan, T. N. *India (Foreign Trade Regimes and Economic Development).* New York: National Bureau of Economic Research, distributed by Columbia University Press, 1975.

Cassen, Robert H. *India: Population, Economy, Society.* New York: Holmes and Meier, 1978.

Gadgil, D. R. *The Industrial Evolution of India in Recent Times, 1860–1939.* 5th ed. Bombay: Indian Branch, Oxford University Press, 1971.

Ganguli, B. N., ed. *Readings in Indian Economic History.* Proceedings of the All-India Seminar on Indian Economic History. New York: Asia Publishing House, 1964.

Kumar, Dharma, and Desai, Meghnad. *The Cambridge Economic History of India: Volume 2, c. 1757–1970.* London: Cambridge University Press, 1983.

Lal, Deepak. *The Hindu Equilibrium: Cultural Stability and Economic Stagnation, India 1500 B.C.–1980 A.D.* Oxford: Oxford University Press, 1984.

Maddison, Angus. *Class Structure and Economic Growth: India and Pakistan since the Moghuls.* New York: Norton, 1972.

Mellor, John W. *The New Economics of Growth: Strategy for India and the Developing World.* Ithaca: Cornell University Press, 1976.

Morris, Morris D. *The Emergence of an Industrial Labor Force in India: A Study of the Bombay Cotton Mills, 1854–1947.* Berkeley: University of California Press, 1965.

Mukherjee, M. *National Income of India: Trends and Structure.* Calcutta: Statistical Publishing Society, 1969.

Raychaudhuri, Tapan, and Habib, Irfan, eds. *The Cambridge Economic History of India: Volume I, c. 1200–c. 1750.* New York: Cambridge University Press, 1982.

Thorner, Daniel. *The Shaping of Modern India.* New Delhi: Allied Publishers for the Sameeksha Trust, 1980.

Indochina

Robequain, Charles. *The Economic Development of French Indo-China.* London and New York: Oxford University Press, 1944.

Indonesia

Broek, Jan O. *Economic Development of the Netherlands Indies.* New York: International Secretariat, Institute of Pacific Relations, 1942.

Furnivall, J. S. *Netherlands Indies: A Study of Plural Economy.* 1939. Reprint. London and New York: Cambridge University Press, 1967.

Geertz, Clifford. *Agricultural Involution: The Process of Ecological Change in Indonesia.* Berkeley: University of California Press for the Association of Asian Studies, 1963.

Japan

Allen, George C. *Japan's Economic Recovery.* London and New York: Oxford University Press, 1958.

Emi, Koichi. *Government Fiscal Activity and Economic Growth in Japan, 1868–1960.* Tokyo: Kinokuniya Bookstore, 1963.

Klein, Lawrence, and Ohkawa, Kazushi, eds. *Economic Growth: The Japanese Experience since the Meiji Era.* Homewood, IL: Richard D. Irwin, 1968.

Lockwood, W. W. *The Economic Development of Japan: Growth and Structural Change.* Princeton: Princeton University Press, 1954.

Ohkawa, K. *Differential Structure and Agriculture: Essays on Dualistic Growth.* Tokyo: Kinokuniya Bookstore, 1972.

Ohkawa, Kazushi; Johnston, B. F.; and Kaneda, H.; eds. *Agriculture and Economic Growth: Japan's Experience.* Princeton: Princeton University Press, 1969.

Ohkawa, Kazushi, and Rosovsky, Henry. *Japanese Economic Growth: Trend Acceleration in the Twentieth Century.* Stanford: Stanford University Press, 1973.

Ranis, Gustav. "The Financing of Japanese Economic Development." *Economic History Review* 11, 3 (April 1959):440–54.

Rosovsky, Henry. *Capital Formation in Japan, 1868–1940*. New York: Free Press of Glencoe, 1961.

————, ed. *Industrialization in Two Systems: Essays in Honor of Alexander Gerschenkron*. New York: Wiley, 1966.

Shinohara, Miyohei. *Growth and Cycles in the Japanese Economy*. Tokyo: Kinokuniya Bookstore, 1962.

————. *Structural Change in Japan's Economic Development*. Tokyo: Kinokuniya Bookstore, 1970.

Tsuru, S. "The Take-off in Japan, 1868–1900." In *The Economics of Take-off into Sustained Growth: Proceedings of a Conference Held by the International Economic Association,* ed. W. W. Rostow. New York: St. Martin's Press, 1963.

Malaysia

Hoffman, Lutz, and Fe, Tan Siew. *Industrial Growth, Employment and Foreign Investment in Peninsular Malaysia*. Kuala Lumpur and New York: Oxford University Press, 1980.

Lim Chong-Yah. *Economic Development of Modern Malaya*. New York and Kuala Lumpur: Oxford University Press, 1967.

Lim, David, ed. *Readings in Malaysian Economic Development*. Kuala Lumpur and New York: Oxford University Press, 1975.

Snodgrass, Donald R. *Inequality and Economic Development in Malaysia*. A Study Sponsored by the Harvard Institute for International Development. New York: Oxford University Press, 1980.

Pakistan

Falcon, Walter P., and Papanek, Gustav, eds. *Development Policy II—The Pakistan Experience*. Cambridge: Harvard University Press, 1971.

Islam, Nurul. *Foreign Trade and Economic Controls in Development: The Case of United Pakistan*. New Haven: Yale University Press, 1981.

Lewis, Stephen R., Jr. *Economic Policy and Industrial Growth in Pakistan*. Cambridge: M.I.T. Press, 1969.

————. *Pakistan: Industrialization and Trade Policies*. Oxford: Oxford University Press for the Development Centre of the Organization for Economic Cooperation and Development, 1970.

Philippines

Baldwin, Robert E. *The Philippines (Foreign Trade Regimes and Economic Development)*. New York: National Bureau of Economic Research, distributed by Columbia University Press, 1975.

Hooley, R. W. "Long-term Growth of the Philippine Economy, 1902–61." *Philippine Economic Journal,* First Semester, 1968.

Power, John H., and Sicat, Gerardo P. *The Philippines: Industrialization and Trade Policies.* London and New York: Oxford University Press for the Development Centre of the Organization for Economic Cooperation and Development, 1971.

Ranis, Gustav, ed. *Sharing in Development: A Program of Employment, Equity, and Growth for the Philippines.* Geneva: International Labour Organization, 1973.

Valdepenas, Vincente B., Jr., and Bautista, Gemelino M. *The Emergence of the Philippine Economy.* Manila: Papyrus Press, 1977.

South Korea

Frank, Charles R., Jr.; Kim Kwang Suk; and Westphal, Larry. *South Korea (Foreign Trade Regimes and Economic Development).* New York: National Bureau of Economic Research, distributed by Columbia University Press, 1975.

Kim Kwang Suk and Roemer, Michael. *Growth and Structural Transformation.* Cambridge: Council on East Asian Studies, Harvard University; distributed by Harvard University Press, 1979.

Kuznets, Paul W. *Economic Growth and Structure in the Republic of Korea.* New Haven: Yale University Press, 1977.

Sri Lanka

Karunatilake, H. N. S. *Economic Development in Ceylon.* New York: Praeger, 1971.

Snodgrass, Donald R. *Ceylon: An Export Economy in Transition.* Homewood, IL: Richard D. Irwin, 1966.

Taiwan

Fei, J. C. H.; Ranis, Gustav; and Kuo, S. *Growth with Equity: The Taiwan Case.* New York: Oxford University Press for the World Bank, 1979.

Ho, Samuel P. S. *Economic Development of Taiwan, 1860–1970.* New Haven: Yale University Press, 1978.

Thailand

Ingram, James C. *Economic Change in Thailand, 1850–1970.* Stanford: Stanford University Press, 1971.

Marzouk, G. A. *Economic Development and Policies: Case-Study of Thailand 1952–1970.* Rotterdam: Rotterdam University Press, 1972.

LATIN AMERICA

General

Cortes Conde, Roberto. *The First Stages of Modernization in Spanish America.* New York: Harper and Row, 1974.

Furtado, Celso. *Economic Development of Latin America: A Survey from Colonial Times to the Cuban Revolution.* 2d ed. Cambridge: Cambridge University Press, 1976.

Prebisch, R. *Change and Development: Latin America's Great Task.* Report Submitted to the Inter-American Development Bank. New York: Praeger, 1971.

Sanchez-Albornoz, Nicholás. *The Population of Latin America: A History.* Berkeley: University of California Press, 1974.

Stein, Stanley J., and Stein, Barbara H. *The Colonial Heritage of Latin America.* New York: Oxford University Press, 1970.

Argentina

Diaz Alejandro, Carlos F. *Essays on the Economic History of the Argentine Republic.* New Haven: Yale University Press, 1970.

————. "Not Less Than One Hundred Years of Argentine Economic History." In *Comparative Development Perspectives,* ed. Gustav Ranis et al. Boulder, CO: Westview Press, 1983.

Brazil

Baer, Werner. *The Brazilian Economy: Its Growth and Development.* Columbus: Grid, 1979.

Bergsman, Joel. *Brazil: Industrialization and Trade Policies.* London and New York: Oxford University Press for the Development Centre of the Organization for Economic Cooperation and Development, 1970.

Furtado, Celso. *The Economic Growth of Brazil: A Survey from Colonial to Modern Times.* Berkeley: University of California Press, 1963.

Leff, Nathaniel. *Economic Policy-making and Development in Brazil, 1947–1964.* New York: Wiley, 1968.

————. *Underdevelopment and Development in Brazil.* Vol. 1, *Economic Structure and Change, 1822–1947.* London and Boston: Allen and Unwin, 1982.

Merrick, Thomas W., and Graham, Douglas H. *Population and Economic Development in Brazil: 1800 to the Present.* Baltimore: Johns Hopkins University Press, 1979.

Winpenny, J. T. *Brazil—Manufactured Exports and Government Policy: Brazil's Experience since 1939.* London: Latin American Publications Fund, distributed by Grant and Cutler, 1972.

Chile

Behrman, Jere R. *Chile (Foreign Trade Regimes and Economic Development)*. New York: National Bureau of Economic Research, distributed by Columbia University Press, 1976.

Mamalakis, Markos. *The Growth and Structure of the Chilean Economy: From Independence to Allende*. New Haven: Yale University Press, 1976.

Mamalakis, Markos, and Reynolds, Clark. *Essays on the Chilean Economy*. Homewood, IL: Richard D. Irwin, 1965.

Colombia

Berry, R. Albert, and Urrutia, Miguel. *Income Distribution in Colombia*. New Haven: Yale University Press, 1976.

Diaz Alejandro, Carlos F. *Colombia (Foreign Trade Regimes and Economic Development)*. New York: National Bureau of Economic Research, distributed by Columbia University Press, 1976.

International Labour Organisation, *Towards Full Employment: A Programme for Colombia*. Prepared by an interagency team organized by the International Labour Office, Geneva: 1970.

McGreevey, William Paul. *An Economic History of Colombia, 1845–1930*. London and New York: Cambridge University Press, 1971.

Nelson, Richard; Schultz, T. Paul; and Slighton, Richard L. *Structural Change in a Developing Economy*. Princeton: Princeton University Press, 1971.

Cuba

Dominguez, Jorge J. *Cuba: Order and Revolution*. Cambridge: Harvard University Press, 1978.

Mesa-Largo, Carmelo. *The Economy of Socialist Cuba: A Two-Decade Appraisal*. Albuquerque: University of New Mexico Press, 1981.

Wallich, Henry C. *Monetary Problems of an Export Economy: The Cuban Experience, 1914–1947*. Cambridge: Harvard University Press, 1950.

Mexico

Hansen, Roger D. *The Politics of Mexican Development*. Baltimore: Johns Hopkins University Press, 1971.

Reynolds, Clark W. *The Mexican Economy: Twentieth Century Structure and Growth*. New Haven: Yale University Press, 1970.

Singer, Morris. *Growth, Equality and the Mexican Experience*. Austin: the University of Texas Press for the Institute of Latin American Studies, 1969.

Peru

Thorp, Rosemary, and Bertram, Geoffrey. *Peru, 1890–1977: Growth and Policy in an Open Economy*. New York: Columbia University Press, 1978.

Venezuela

Brito Figueroa, Federico. *História Económica y Social de Venezuela: Una Estructura para su Estudio*. Caracas: Dirección de Cultura, Universidad Central de Venezuela, 1966.

Martz, J., and Myers, D., eds. *Venezuela: The Democratic Experience*. New York: Praeger, 1977.

Tugwell, Franklin. *The Politics of Oil in Venezuela*. Stanford: Stanford University Press, 1975.

NORTH AFRICA AND THE MIDDLE EAST

General

Amin, Samir. *The Maghreb in the Modern World: Algeria, Tunisia, Morocco*. Harmondsworth: Penguin, 1970.

Issawi, Charles. *The Economic History of the Middle East, 1800–1914*. Chicago: University of Chicago Press, 1966.

———. *An Economic History of the Middle East and North Africa*. New York: Columbia University Press, 1982.

Sa'igh, Yusif A. *The Economies of the Arab World: Development since 1945*. New York: St. Martin's Press, 1978.

Egypt

Abdel-Fadil, Mahmoud. *Development, Income Distribution and Social Change in Rural Egypt, 1952–1970: A Study in the Political Economy of Agrarian Transition*. Cambridge and New York: Cambridge University Press, 1975.

Hansen, Bent, and Marzouk, G. A. *Development and Economic Policy in the UAR*. Amsterdam: North-Holland, 1965.

Hansen, Bent, and Nashashibi, Karim. *Egypt (Foreign Trade Regimes and Economic Development)*. New York: National Bureau of Economic Research, distributed by Columbia University Press, 1975.

Mabro, Robert. *The Egyptian Economy, 1952–1972*. Oxford: Clarendon Press, 1974.

Mead, Donald C. *Growth and Structural Change in the Egyptian Economy*. Homewood, IL: Richard D. Irwin, 1967.

Iran

Amuzegar, Jahangin, and Fekrat, W. Ali. *Iran: Economic Development under Dualistic Conditions*. Chicago: University of Chicago Press, 1971.

Bharier, Julian. *Economic Development in Iran, 1900–1970*. London and New York: Oxford University Press, 1971.

Issawi, Charles, ed. *The Economic History of Iran, 1800–1914*. Chicago: University of Chicago Press, 1971.

Iraq

Penrose, Edith, and Penrose, E. F. *Iraq: International Relations and National Development*. Boulder, CO: Westview Press, 1978.

Morocco

Steward, Charles F. *The Economy of Morocco, 1912–1962*. Cambridge: Harvard University Press, 1964.

Turkey

Hershlag, Z. Y. *Turkey: An Economy in Transition*. The Hague: Van Keulen, 1958.

Krueger, Anne O. *Turkey (Foreign Trade Regimes and Economic Development)*. New York: National Bureau of Economic Research, distributed by Columbia University Press, 1974.

Thornburg, M. W., et al. *Turkey: An Economic Appraisal*. New York: Twentieth Century Fund, 1949.

SUB-SAHARAN AFRICA

General

Anthony, K. R. M.; Johnston, Bruce F.; Jones, William O.; and Uchenda, Victor C. *Agricultural Change in Tropical Africa*. Ithaca: Cornell University Press, 1979.

Duffy, James. *Portuguese Africa*. Cambridge: Harvard University Press, 1959.

Duignan, Peter, and Gann, L. H., eds. *Colonialism in Africa, 1870–1960*. 2 vols. London and New York: Cambridge University Press, 1969, 1970.

Fieldhouse, Daniel K. "The Economic Exploitation of Africa: Some British and French Comparisons." In *France and Britain in Africa: Imperial Rivalry and Colonial Rule,* ed. Prosser Gifford and W. Roger Louis, pp. 593–662. New Haven: Yale University Press, 1971.

Hopkins, Anthony G. *An Economic History of West Africa*. New York: Columbia University Press, 1973.

International Bank for Reconstruction and Development. *Accelerated Development in Sub-Saharan Africa*. Washington, DC: IBRD, 1981.

Munro, J. Forbes. *Africa and the International Economy, 1800–1960*. Totowa, NJ: Rowman and Littlefield, 1976.

Robson, P., and Lury, D. A., eds. *The Economies of Africa*. London: Allen and Unwin, 1969.

Ghana

Leith, J. Clark. *Ghana (Foreign Trade Regimes and Economic Development)*. New York: National Bureau of Economic Research, distributed by Columbia University Press, 1974.

Ivory Coast

Suret-Canale, Jean. *French Colonialism in Tropical Africa, 1900–1945*. London: C. Hurst, 1971.
den Tuinder, Bastian, ed. *Ivory Coast: The Challenge of Success*. Baltimore: Johns Hopkins University Press for the World Bank, 1978.

Kenya

Hazelwood, Arthur. *The Economy of Kenya*. Oxford and New York: Oxford University Press, 1979.
Van Zwanenberg, R. M. A., and King, Anne. *An Economic History of Kenya and Uganda, 1800–1970*. London and New York: Macmillan, 1975.
Wolff, Richard D. *The Economics of Colonialism: Britain and Kenya, 1870–1930*. New Haven: Yale University Press, 1974.

Mozambique

United States Department of Agriculture. *Mozambiqués Agricultural Economy in Brief*. Foreign Agricultural Economics Report no. 116. Washington, DC: USDA, 1976.

Nigeria

Ekundare, R. Olufemi. *An Economic History of Nigeria, 1860–1960*. New York: Africana, 1973.
Helleiner, Gerald. *Peasant Agriculture, Government, and Economic Growth in Nigeria*. Homewood, IL: Richard D. Irwin, 1966.
Kilby, Peter. *Industrialization in an Open Economy: Nigeria, 1945–1966*. New York: Cambridge University Press, 1967.

Tanzania

Clark, W. Edmund. *Socialist Development and Public Investment in Tanzania, 1964–73*. Toronto and Buffalo: University of Toronto Press, 1978.

Coulson, Andrew. *Tanzania, 1800–1980: A Political Economy*. New York: Oxford University Press, 1982.

Sabot, R. N. *Economic Development and Urban Migration: Tanzania, 1900–1971*. New York: Oxford University Press, 1979.

Stephens, Hugh W. *The Political Transformation of Tanganyika, 1920–1967*. New York: Praeger, 1968.

Zaire

Anstey, Roger. *King Leopold's Legacy: The Congo under Belgian Rule, 1908–1960*. London and New York: Oxford University Press, 1966.

Facts about the Congo Economy. Brussels: Belgian Congo Information and Public Relations Office, 1960.

Grau, Guy, ed. *Zaire: The Political Economy of Underdevelopment*. New York: Praeger, 1979.

Zambia

Baldwin, Robert E. *Economic Development and Export Growth: Northern Rhodesia, 1920–1960*. Berkeley: University of California Press, 1966.

Beveridge, Andrew A., and Oberschall, Anthony R. *African Businessmen and Development in Zambia*. Princeton: Princeton University Press, 1979.

Deane, Phyllis. *Colonial Social Accounting*. Cambridge: Cambridge University Press, 1953.

Dodge, Doris Jansen. *Agricultural Policy and Performance in Zambia: History, Prospects and Proposals for Change*. Berkeley: Institute of International Studies, University of California, 1977.

Obidegwy, C. F., and Nziramasanga, M. *Copper and Zambia*. Lexington: Lexington Books, 1981.

Zimbabwe

Barber, William J. *The Economy of British Central Africa: A Case Study of Economic Development in a Dualistic Society*. Stanford: Stanford University Press, 1961.

Zimbabwe. "Towards a New Order—An Economic and Social Survey." Working Papers. New York: United Nations, Economic and Social Council, 1980.

Index

Abdel-Fadil, Mahmoud, 322
Adelman, Irma, 417n
Afghanistan:
  Extensive growth in, 367–68; agricultural
    sector, 368; industrial sector, 368; hand-
    icraft production, 368; state-owned enter-
    prises, 368; foreign sector, 368
Africa, intensive growth in, 32, 203, 206–08
Agriculture, as precondition for intensive
  growth, 8–9, 15–16, 24, 25; in West Africa,
  203, 206–08
Agriculture, increase in yields, 24–26
Agriculture and food output, comparative rec-
  ord *1950–80,* 406–09; table, 407–08
Ahluwalia, Montek S., 180
Algeria, 191–96, 431
  Turning point in, 191
  Surplus labor in, 191, 196
  Real wages in, 193
  Income distribution in, 192, 193–94, 195
  Intensive era in, 191–96; population growth,
    192
  —agricultural sector, 191–92, 193, 194;
    acreage expansion, 191–92; increase in
    yields, 194; input intensification, 192
  —industrial sector, 192, 194–96; handicraft
    production, 191, 192; factory production,
    192; small-scale *vs.* large-scale, 192, 194;
    sources of capital, 192, 193–94, 195;
    state-owned industries, 194, 195
  —foreign sector, 195–96; export growth
    rates, 195; export composition, 195; im-
    port composition, 194, 195
  —public sector, 192, 195; revenue sources,
    195
Allen, George C., 359

Allende Gossens, Salvador, 111, 112, 430
Amin, Samir, 192, 199
Anglo-Iranian Oil Company, 344, 346
Angola, 425
Anstey, Roger, 378, 380
Anthony, K. R. M., 217
Argentina, 7, 8, 10, 85–91, 405, 428, 436
  Turning point in, 85
  Surplus labor in, 87
  Intensive era in, 85–91; population growth,
    87
  —agricultural sector, 86; acreage expansion,
    86; technical progress, 86–87
  —industrial sector, 88–89; factory produc-
    tion, 88–89; import substitution, 88–89;
    sources of capital, 87–88
  —foreign sector, 86–87; export growth
    rates, 85–86; export composition, 87; im-
    port composition, 87
  —public sector, 90–91
Asia, intensive growth in, 32
Ataturk, Kemal, 329

Baer, Werner, 98
Balassa, Bela, 287
Baldwin, Robert E., 186, 256, 258
Ballesteros, Marto, 109
Bangladesh:
  Extensive growth in, 371; population growth,
    371
  Real wages in, 371
  Agricultural sector, 371–72; input inten-
    sification, 372; technical progress, 372
  Industrial sector, 372; factory production,
    372; import substitution, 371; sources of
    capital, 371

Bangladesh (*continued*)
Foreign sector, 372; export composition, 372; capital transfers, public, 372
Public sector, 372; revenue sources, 372
Barber, William J., 250, 251, 254
Bergsman, Joel, 96
Berry, Charles, 70
Berry, R. Albert, 117
Bertram, Geoffrey, 128, 130
Bhagwati, Jagdish, 312, 314, 315, 317, 428, 432
Bharier, Julian, 342, 343, 344, 345
Birnberg, Thomas B., 122
Boeke, Julius Herman, 358
Boserup, Ester, 25, 28, 308
Brazil, 10, 91–99, 395, 409, 411, 412, 417, 426–27, 430, 431
Extensive growth in, 91–92; population growth, 91
Turning point in, 10, 92
Real wages in, 96
Income distribution in, 93, 98
Intensive era in, 61, 92–98; population growth, 92
—agricultural sector, 92–94, 97–98; acreage expansion, 97–98; technical progress, 93
—industrial sector, 93–94; factory production, 93–94; normal sequence of industries, 93; import substitution, 93, 95–96; sources of capital, 94; sources of entrepreneurship, 94; state-owned industries, 98
—foreign sector, 61, 92–94, 96–97; export growth rates, 92–93; export composition, 94, 96–97; import composition, 61, 94–95; capital transfers, public, 94
—public sector, 98
Broek, Jan, 361
Burma, 135, 142–50, 391, 395, 406, 409, 427
Extensive growth in, 142
Turning point in, 142
Surplus labor in, 142–43
Income distribution in, 142, 145
Intensive era in, 143–50; population growth, 142, 144, 147
—agricultural sector, 142, 143–45; acreage expansion, 144; increase in yields, 147, 149
—industrial sector, 145, 148–49; handicraft production, 145; factory production, 145,

149–50; sources of capital, 143, 148–50; import substitution, 147–48; state-owned industries, 148–49
—foreign sector, 143, 145; export growth rates, 142–43, 145; export composition, 145; import composition, 145; capital transfers, private, 146
—public sector, 143, 145, 148–49; composition, 148; revenue sources, 149–50

Capitalist and socialist growth rates, 436–39
Cárdenas, Lázaro, 102
Carnegie Foundation, 208n
Castro, Fidel, 124, 125
Ceylon. *See* Sri Lanka
Chenery, Hollis, 8, 13, 59, 155, 177, 180, 333, 352
Chile, 108–12, 405, 409, 430, 436
Turning point in, 108
Real wages in, 110
Intensive era in, 108–12; population growth, 109
—agricultural sector, 109
—industrial sector, 109–12; handicraft production, 111; factory production, 110–11; normal sequence of industries, 110; import substitution, 111–12; sources of capital, 110; state-owned industries, 109–10, 112
—foreign sector, 109–10; export growth rates, 109–11
—public sector, 109–10, 111, 112
China, 11, 247, 268–92, 370, 405, 416, 426, 437
Extensive growth in, 17–19, 25–26, 268–77; population growth, 269, 273–74, 282–83
Turning point, 9, 276, 277; events connected with, 276–78
Surplus labor in, 280, 282–83, 284
Real wages in, 282, 291
Income distribution in, 290–92
Intensive era in, 7, 277–92; population growth, 7, 282–83
—agricultural sector, 269–72, 274, 278–80, 282–85, 290–92; acreage expansion, 270, 274; increase in yields, 270, 283, 285; input intensification, 270, 274, 279, 283–85; technical progress, 270, 283
—industrial sector, 280–81, 285–90, 291–

92; handicraft production, 271, 272, 274–75; factory production, 274–76, 282, 287–90; small-scale *vs.* large-scale, 276, 286; normal sequence of industries, 286; import substitution, 274; sources of capital, 288; sources of entrepreneurship, 273, 286; state-owned industries, 280, 290
—foreign sector, 272, 274, 288; export growth rates, 288; export composition, 272, 288; import composition, 288; capital transfers, public, 288; capital transfers, private, 274, 288
—public sector, 273, 276; size, 276; composition, 276, 282; revenue sources, 273, 276
Chou Enlai, 277, 286
Clark, Colin, 13
Clark, W. Edmund, 246
Colombia, 112–19, 391, 409, 411, 430, 436
Extensive growth in, 112–13; population growth in, 112
Turning point in, 112, 113; events connected with, 113–14
Surplus labor in, 113
Income distribution in, 113, 116–17
Intensive era in, 114–19; population growth, 114, 116
—agricultural sector, 113–14, 116–17; input intensification, 116; technical progress, 116
—industrial sector, 114–15, 117–19; handicraft production, 114–15, 118; factory production, 115–19; small-scale *vs.* large-scale, 114, 118; normal sequence of industries, 114; import substitution, 117; sources of capital, 114, 119; sources of entrepreneurship, 114
—foreign sector, 113, 114–15, 117, 118–19; export growth rates, 114, 118; export composition, 115, 118; capital transfers, public, 114, 115
—public sector, 119
Colonialism, effect on economic growth, 10, 32, 34n, 35, 36, 39, 41–43, 74; East Africa, 227; West Africa, 202–09; Southeast Asia, 135; Algeria, 191, 192; Burma, 142–43, 145, 147; Ceylon, 150, 152, 153; Cuba, 119–21; India, 293–95, 301–04; Indonesia, 357–63; Kenya, 228; Morocco, 196–97; Mozambique, 375–77; Nigeria, 212; South

Korea, 174–76; Taiwan, 167, 169, 170; Tanzania, 239–44; Uganda, 235–37; Zaire, 378–80; Zimbabwe, 248–50, 253
Comparative growth record, *1950–80,* 387–418; aggregate measures of growth, 387–403; data problems, 387–88; explanatory variables, 412–13; additional dimensions of growth, 403–13; political element, 414–17; summary, 418
Population growth, 403–06; table, 404
GDP growth, 388–92; table, 390
Output by sector, 395–98; table, 396–97
Output by end use, 399–403; table, 400–01
Agriculture and food output, 406–09; table, 407–08
Physical indicators of consumption, 392–95; table, 393–94
Export growth rates, 409–12; table, 410–11
Explanation of growth differences, 412–18; explanatory variables, 412–14; missing political element, 414–17; summary, 418
Congo. *See* Zaire
Core-periphery theory, 11, 31–32
Coulson, Andrew, 246, 248
Cuba, 119–26
Extensive growth in, 119–20; population growth, 120
Turning point in, 119
Surplus labor in, 123, 125
Real wages in, 123, 126
Income distribution in, 126
Intensive era in, 120–26; population growth, 121
—agricultural sector, 120–22, 123–24; acreage expansion, 122, 124
—industrial sector, 121–22, 124, 125–26; handicraft production, 122; factory production, 121–22, 124, 125–26; normal sequence of industries, 122; sources of capital, 121, 123; state-owned industries, 123–26
—foreign sector, 121, 122–23, 124–25; export growth rates, 121–22, 124–25; export composition, 121–22, 124–25; import composition, 122, 124; capital transfers, public, 122, 124; capital transfers, private, 121, 124
—public sector, 122, 123–24, 125–26; size, 122, 123–24; composition, 122, 124, 126; revenue sources, 122, 124

Deane, Phyllis, 256, 257, 258
Demographic behavior. *See* Comparative
growth record; Population growth
Deng Xiaoping, 277, 280, 287
Den Tuinder, Bastien, 223
Dependency theory, 11, 44
Dernberger, Robert F., 363
Desai, Padma, 300, 303, 432
Díaz, Porfirio, 99–102
Diaz-Alejandro, Carlos, 89, 90, 91, 117, 118,
119
Dodge, Doris Jansen, 261
Dominguez, Jorge J., 123
Dom Pedro I (Brazil), 92
Donnithorne, Audrey G., 359
Durand, J. Dana, 12, 13, 82
Dutlo, Giuseppe, 434

Eckstein, Alexander, 17, 277, 282n
Economic growth eras:
1850–1914, 26–28, 33–35, 49; Latin America, 34, 81–85; Asia, 34, 135; Africa, 35,
202–04; countries reaching turning point
in, 36
1914–45, 33, 35–36; West Africa, 104–09;
countries reaching turning point in, 36
1945–80, 33, 36–38, 49–51; China, 30, 37;
Egypt, 30, 37, 318; India, 29, 37, 304–
17; Indonesia, 37; Pakistan, 30, 37
Economic growth:
Extensive, 7–8, 15–30, 79. *See also* Exten-
sive growth
Intensive, 8, 79. *See also* Intensive growth
Turning point concept, 8–10, 31–48
Turning point dates, 9–10, 31–33, 38–39,
267, 367; table, 10
Events connected with, 6–7, 8, 12–13, 23–
24, 27–30, 38–39, 79
Cross-section analysis, 13
Time-series analysis, 10–14
Comparative record, *1950–80,* 387–414
—Tables: *Selected Measures of Output
Growth,* 390–91; *Changes in Welfare:
Some Physical Indicators,* 393–94; *Output
by Sector of Origin,* 396–97; *Output by
End Uses,* 400–01; *Demographic Behav-
ior,* 404; *Growth Rates of Agricultural
Production and Food Production,* 407–08;
Export Performance, 410–11

Egypt, 318–28, 411, 412, 426, 430, 433
Extensive growth in, 318–21; population
growth, 318–19, 321
Turning point in, 321; events connected
with, 319–22
Surplus labor in, 325
Real wages in, 324, 327
Income distribution in, 321–22
Intensive era in, 321–28; population growth,
322–24
—agricultural sector, 318–19, 321–24;
acreage expansion, 319; increase in yields,
323; input intensification, 322–23; technical progress, 322–23
—industrial sector, 324–26; factory production, 320, 324; small-scale *vs.* large-scale,
325; normal sequence of industries, 320;
sources of capital, 320; state-owned industries, 321, 322
—foreign sector, 325, 326–28; export
growth rates, 327; export composition,
324, 327; import composition, 324; capital
transfers, public, 325–26; capital transfers, private, 324, 325–26
—public sector, 321–22, 325–26; revenue
sources, 322, 324
Ekundare, R. Olufemi, 210
Ethiopia, 391
Europe, intensive growth in, 31–32
European Economic Community (EEC), 201,
225, 334
Evenson, Robert E., 424
Exports:
As growth stimulus, 10, 12, 43–48; Latin
America, 83–84; Argentina, 88; West Af-
rica, 203, 205, 206–07; Colombia, 114;
Cuba, 120, 122–23; Malaysia, 151–52;
Mexico, 100; Nigeria, 212; Philippines,
181; Zimbabwe, 249–51, 252
Returned value concept, 47; Mexico, 100;
Chile, 110; Colombia, 114; Peru, 130;
Thailand, 157–58; Taiwan, 168–69; South
Korea, 179; Philippines, 184; Venezuela,
189; Ivory Coast, 224; Uganda, 236; Zam-
bia, 256
Export growth rates, comparative record,
1950–80, 409–12; table, 410–11
Extensive growth:
Economic organization in, 7, 8–9, 16–23,

26, 28; West Africa, 203–04; China, 19–21, 270–73; Nepal, 21–23
Household production in, 16–17, 268–77; China, 268–77
Population growth in, 7–8, 23–24, 82, 203
Subsistence economy view, 16–17, 238–39, 240, 248, 369–70
Traditional economy view, 15–16, 202–03, 328–29

Fe, Tan Siew, 155
Fei, John, 9, 72, 172, 173
Fei-Ranis model, 9
Feuerwerker, Albert, 17, 269, 271, 274, 275
Food and Agriculture Organization (FAO), 90, 262, 352, 374, 394, 408
Frankel, S. H., 251
Furnivall, J. S., 143, 144, 359
Furtado, Celso, 84, 92, 95

Gadgil, D. R., 296
Gault, Andrew H., 434n
Geertz, Clifford, 357, 359, 361
Ghana, 218–21, 425, 436
Turning point in, 219
Surplus labor in, 221
Intensive era in, 218–21; population growth, 220
—agricultural sector, 219, 220, 221; industrial sector, 219–21; foreign sector, 219–21; public sector, 220–21
Goldsmith, Raymond, 92, 92n
Government economic intervention, 54, 60, 64–68, 419–40; institutional structures favorable to development, 421–23; mixed economies, 436–37; socialist economies, 437; summary, 439–40
Agricultural marketing, 56, 423–27
Land reform, 54–55, 321–22, 421–22, 423, 426
Price controls: food products, 56, 71, 74, 424–25, 434–35; other products, 56, 74, 424–26, 434–35
Wage rates, 71, 74, 419, 435–36
Interest rates, 56, 421, 423, 435
Public ownership of industry, 58, 60, 74, 321–22, 419, 431–34
Trade controls, 56, 60, 419, 426–27, 427–31

Foreign exchange rates, 56, 419, 426–27, 427–31
General evaluation, 60, 67–68, 74, 439–40
Growth record. *See* Comparative growth record
Guha, Ashok, 7

Haddad, Paulo Roberto, 92
Hammarskjold, Dag, 381
Hansen, Bent, 319, 324, 325, 433
Hansen, Roger, 100, 101, 103, 105, 189
Helleiner, Gerald, 210, 211, 212, 214
Herzfeld, H., 251
Heston, Alan, 295, 301, 399n
Hilary Foundation (Nepal), 370
Hill, Polly, 219
Ho, Samuel, 166, 167, 169
Hoffman, Lutz, 155
Hoffman, Walther, 13, 59
Hong Kong, 430
Hooley, R. W., 181, 183
Hopkins, Anthony G., 19, 20, 205

Income distribution, 6, 39–41, 69–73; Brazil, 98; Mexico, 101, 103, 104; Colombia, 115; Cuba, 123, 126; Peru, 133; Malaysia, 156; Taiwan, 173; South Korea, 180; China, 290–92; India, 309; Iraq, 337, 340; Iran, 349
India, 293–317, 409, 426, 428, 431, 432–33
Extensive growth in, 294–304; population growth, 293–94
Turning point in, 293, 300; events connected with, 293–304
Surplus labor in, 309–10
Real wages in, 298
Income distribution in, 309
Intensive era in, 304–17; population growth, 304–05, 310
—agricultural sector, 294–95, 306–10; acreage expansion, 306–07; increase in yields, 306, 308; input intensification, 307–08, 310; technical progress, 307, 308
—industrial sector, 295–98, 310–14; handicraft production, 296–97, 302; factory production, 296–98; small-scale *vs.* large-scale, 313; normal sequence of industries, 313–14; import substitution, 314; sources of capital, 297, 312–13, 315–16; sources of entrepreneurship, 311; state-owned industries, 298, 311

India (*continued*)
—foreign sector, 298–300, 314–16; export growth rates, 299, 316; export composition, 299; import composition, 296, 315; capital transfers, public, 299, 316; capital transfers, private, 299
—public sector, 306, 312, 313–17; revenue sources, 306, 312–13
Indonesia, 357–67, 427
Extensive growth in, 357–63; population growth in, 359, 360
Turning point in, 357, 363, 366; events connected with, 357
Real wages in, 361
Income distribution in, 357, 361–62
Intensive era in, 363–67; population growth, 364
—agricultural sector, 61, 360–61, 364; acreage expansion, 360–61, 364; increase in yields, 364; input intensification, 360
—industrial sector, 359, 364–67; factory production, 364; normal sequence of industries, 364–65; import substitution, 364; sources of capital, 365, 366
—foreign sector, 357–60, 365–66; export growth rates, 357–59, 365; export composition, 358–59, 365; import composition, 362, 364, 366; capital transfers, public, 361, 366
—public sector, 362–63, 365–67; revenue sources, 365
Intensive growth:
Patterns of, 4, 31–32, 49–64, 68–69, 73–75; Mexico, 104, 105; Ceylon, 138; West Africa, 205–09; Nigeria, 212; Pakistan, 354
Population growth in, 7–8, 9, 10, 50, 60–61, 139; table, 404
Agricultural sector, 8–9, 32–56, 203, 206–08; acreage expansion, 8–9, 55; increase in yields, 25, 55–56; input intensification, 25; technical progress, 54
Industrial sector, 56–60; handicraft production, 56–57; factory production, 57; small-scale *vs.* large-scale, 57–58; normal sequence of industries, 59–60; import substitution, 57; sources of capital, 59; sources of entrepreneurship, 58–59; state-owned industries, 58, 60

Foreign sector, 32, 33–35, 60–64, 205–06, 208; export growth rates, 36–38, 43, 60–63; export composition, 33–37, 61–62, 63; capital transfers, public, 63–64; capital transfers, private, 64
Public sector, 64–68, 74, 205–06, 208; size, 64–65; composition, 65–66; revenue sources, 66–68
International Bank for Reconstruction and Development (IBRD), 13, 40, 73, 90, 117, 267, 282n, 291n, 292, 316, 340, 368, 391, 394, 397, 401, 403, 404, 411, 425n, 431n, 433, 436, 436n
International Labor Organization (ILO), 71, 117
International Monetary Fund (IMF), 13, 90, 267
Iran, 341–49, 388
Extensive growth in, 341–45
Turning point in, 341; events connected with, 341–43
Real wages in, 345, 348
Income distribution in, 344, 348, 349
Intensive era in, 346–49; population growth, 343
—agricultural sector, 342–44, 345, 348; acreage expansion, 344, 349; increase in yields, 342, 344, 345–49; input intensification, 348; technical progress, 342, 348
—industrial sector, 343–45, 346–49; handicraft production, 343, 345; factory production, 343, 344, 345; small-scale *vs.* large-scale, 348; normal sequence of industries, 348; sources of capital, 344–45, 347, 348; sources of entrepreneurship, 342; state-owned industries, 345, 346, 348–49
—foreign sector, 343–44; export growth rates, 342, 344; export composition, 342, 344; import composition, 344; capital transfers, public, 345, 346–7
—public sector, 342–43, 344–45, 346–48, 349; size, 346–48; composition, 347; revenue sources, 343, 344, 346–47, 349
Iraq, 335–41, 431
Extensive growth in, 335–37; population growth, 336
Turning point in, 337; events connected with, 337

Surplus labor in, 336
Real wages in, 340
Income distribution in, 337–41
Intensive era in, 337–41; population growth, 340
—agricultural sector, 336, 340; acreage expansion, 337; increase in yields, 340; input intensification, 340; technical progress, 340
—industrial sector, 335, 337–41; handicraft production, 337; factory production, 337; small-scale *vs.* large-scale, 339; normal sequence of industries, 337, 339; sources of capital, 335, 338, 340–41; sources of entrepreneurship, 339; state-owned industries, 339–41
—foreign sector, 335–36, 337, 340–41; export growth rates, 336–37, 341; export composition, 336, 341; import composition, 336, 340; capital transfers, public, 338, 340; capital transfers, private, 338, 340
—public sector, 337, 339, 340–41; revenue sources, 338, 340, 341
Ishikawa, Shigeru, 25, 308
Islam, Nurul, 353
Issawi, Charles, 319, 328, 336, 337, 341, 342
Ivory Coast, 221–26, 395–96, 426, 429, 431, 432
Turning point in, 222
Real wages in, 222, 224
Income distribution in, 222, 224
Intensive era in, 222–26; population growth, 224, 226
—agricultural sector, 221–24; acreage expansion, 224; technical progress, 224
—industrial sector, 222–26; handicraft production, 222; factory production, 223, 224–25; sources of capital, 222, 224–25, 226; state-owned industries, 225
—foreign sector, 62, 222–26; export growth rates, 222–23, 225; export composition, 222, 225; import composition, 62, 224, 225; capital transfers, private, 223
—public sector, 222, 225–26; composition, 225–26; revenue sources, 223–24, 226

Japan, 6, 11, 25, 34–35, 416; and Taiwan, 166, 167–69, 170; and Korea, 174, 175, 176; and China, 273

Johnson, John J., 415n
Johnston, Bruce F., 217
Jones, Eric, 29
Jones, Richard, 82n

Kaunda, Kenneth, 259
Kenya, 227–35, 395, 426, 436
Turning point in, 227
Surplus labor in, 235
Real wages in, 230
Intensive era in, 227–36; population growth, 232, 235; white settlement, 227–28
—agricultural sector, 228–29, 231–32; acreage expansion, 228; increase in yields, 228–29; input intensification, 228–29
—industrial sector, 229, 232–36; handicraft production, 229, 233; factory production, 229–30, 232; large-scale *vs.* small-scale, 233; normal sequence of industries, 230; import substitution, 230; sources of capital, 232–33; state-owned industries, 227–28
—foreign sector, 230, 234–35; export growth rates, 230; export composition, 230, 232; import composition, 233; capital transfers, private, 231
—public sector, 230, 233–34; composition, 234; revenue sources, 230, 234
Keynes, John Maynard, 45, 438
Kilby, Peter, 215
Kim, Kwang Suk, 176
Kindelberger, Charles, 45
King, Timothy, 105
Korea. *See* South Korea
Kravis, Irving B., 45, 399n
Krishnamurty, J., 301
Krueger, Anne, 333, 428, 429
Kumar, Dharma, 300, 303
Kuo, S., 72, 172, 173
Kuznets, Paul, 174, 175, 178
Kuznets, Simon, 6, 7, 8, 12, 13, 14, 40, 50, 68, 69, 70, 156, 288, 292, 388, 388n, 395, 402

Lal, Deepak, 298, 299, 300, 301, 302, 303, 305, 308, 310, 314
Latin America, early growth in, 81–85; intensive growth in, 31–32, 34
Leith, J. Clark, 219, 220
Lewis, Stephen R., Jr., 352, 353, 355

Lewis, W. Arthur, 9, 12, 34, 44, 45, 137, 354, 428, 439, 440, 440n; Lewis surplus labor model, 51, 70, 90, 104, 309, 435
Little, Ian M. D., 4, 4n
Liu, Ta-chung, 276
Lopez Mateos, 103
Lotz, Joergen, 179
Lury, D. A., 222

McEvedy, Colin, 82
McGreevey, William Paul, 112, 114
Maddison, Angus, 299
Maizels, Alfred, 12
Makerere College (Uganda), 243
Malaysia, 135, 150–56, 391, 395–96, 409, 411, 417, 429, 430, 436
    Extensive growth in, 150; population growth, 150
    Turning point in, 150
    Surplus labor in, 156
    Income distribution in, 156
    Intensive era in, 150–56; population growth, 150, 153, 154
    —agricultural sector, 151, 154; acreage expansion, 151–54
    —industrial sector, 150, 154–56; factory production, 150–51, 154–56; import substitution, 155; sources of capital, 152, 155, 156; sources of entrepreneurship, 150–51
    —foreign sector, 151–52, 153, 154; export growth rates, 151, 152, 154; export composition, 151, 152, 154; import composition, 152, 154; capital transfers, private, 152–53, 155
    —public sector, 152, 156; revenue sources, 155, 156
Mamalakis, Markos, 48, 108, 109, 111
Mao Tse-tung, 278, 426
Martz, J., 189
Marx, Karl, 438
Marzouk, G. A., 319, 325, 433
Mead, Donald C., 318
Mesa-Largo, Carmelo, 123
Mexico, 98–106, 409, 412, 431
    Extensive growth in, 98; population growth, 98–99, 102
    Turning point in, 10, 98, 101; events connected with, 98–99

Surplus labor in, 99, 104
Real wages in, 101–02, 106
Income distribution in, 103, 104
Intensive era in, 99, 101–07; population growth, 101–02, 104
    —agricultural sector, 104–05; acreage expansion, 104; increase in yields, 104; input intensification, 104–05; technical progress, 105
    —industrial sector, 100–01, 105–06; factory production, 100; normal sequence of industries, 105; import substitution, 100; sources of capital, 100, 106; sources of entrepreneurship, 106; state-owned industries, 99–101
    —foreign sector, 100–01, 105–06; export growth rates, 100, 106; export composition, 100, 105, 106; import composition, 62, 100; capital transfers, public, 181, 185; capital transfers, private, 99, 100–01
    —public sector, 99, 100–01, 106–07; size, 107; composition, 104–05; revenue sources, 100, 107
Mill, John Stuart, 422
Millspaugh, A. C., 344
Mobutu, General Sese Seko (Zaire), 381
Morocco, 196–201, 391, 409
    Extensive growth in, 196–97; population growth, 196
    Turning point in, 196; events connected with, 196–99
    Surplus labor in, 197, 201
    Intensive era in, 197–201; population growth, 199
    —agricultural sector, 197–99, 200, 201; acreage expansion, 197, 199–200; increase in yields, 197; input intensification, 197
    —industrial sector, 198, 200, 201; factory production, 198, 199, 200; sources of capital, 200; state-owned industries, 200
    —foreign sector, 198–200; export growth rates, 198, 200; export composition, 198; import composition, 200; capital transfers, public, 198, 200; capital transfers, private, 198, 200
    —public sector, 198, 200; revenue sources, 198, 200–01
Morris, Cynthia Taft, 417n

Morris, Morris D., 298, 300, 303
Mozambique, 375–78, 425
  Intensive growth in, 376–78; population
    growth in, 375, 376, 378; economic orga-
    nization in, 377–78; agricultural sector,
    377; factory industry, 377; foreign sector,
    377–78
Mugabe, Robert (Zimbabwe), 254, 437
Mukherjee, M., 300
Myers, D., 189
Myint, Hla, 146, 171
Myrdal, Gunnar, 11, 311, 415, 417

Napoleon Bonaparte, 91
Nashashibi, Karim, 324, 325
Nasser, Gamal Abdel, 321
Nation, as key unit, 10–11
Nationhood, sense of, in West Africa, 205,
  208; in Nigeria, 211–12, 214; in Ivory
  Coast, 223, 226; in Turkey, 329; in Tan-
  zania, 244
Nehru, Jawaharlal, 304
Nepal, 21–23, 368–70
  Extensive growth in, 21–23, 370; population
    growth, 369
  Agricultural sector, 369; acreage expansion,
    369
  Industrial sector, 369–70; handicraft produc-
    tion, 369; factory production, 369–70;
    normal sequence of industries, 370;
    sources of capital, 370
  Foreign sector, 370; capital transfers, public,
    370
  Public sector, 370; revenue sources, 370
Nigeria, 209–18, 425, 436
  Extensive growth in, 19, 209–10
  Turning point in, 209; events connected
    with, 209–10
  Surplus labor in, 215
  Real wages in, 215
  Income distribution in, 211, 215
  Intensive era in, 210–18; population growth,
    210, 212, 216
  —agricultural sector, 217–18; acreage ex-
    pansion, 217–18; increase in yields, 217
  —industrial sector, 214–16; handicraft pro-
    duction, 211, 215; factory production,
    211, 214, 215, 217–18; small-scale *vs.*
    large-scale, 215; normal sequence of in-

dustries, 214; import substitution, 213,
  214, 218; sources of capital, 214, 218;
  sources of entrepreneurship, 215; state-
  owned industries, 210–11
—foreign sector, 210–16; export growth
  rates, 210, 212, 216; export composition,
  210, 213, 216; import composition, 213;
  capital transfers, public, 214; capital transfers, private, 215, 216
—public sector, 210, 213–14, 216; size,
  210; composition, 210–11, 214; revenue
  sources, 210, 213–14, 216
Nkomo, Joshua, 254
North Atlantic Treaty Organization (NATO), 3
Nyerere, Julius, 243, 244–45

Ohkawa, Kazushi, 69
Oil economies (OPEC), growth record, *1950–
  80,* 330, 391, 424
Organization for Economic Cooperation and
  Development (OECD), 5, 13, 281
Organization of Petroleum Exporting Countries
  (OPEC), 36, 189, 194, 330

Pahlevi, Shah Reza, 341, 346–47, 348
Pakistan, 350–57, 411, 412, 426, 430, 431,
  436
  Turning point in, 350; events connected
    with, 350
  Surplus labor in, 351, 354
  Real wages in, 352, 354, 355
  Intensive era in, 350–57; population growth
    in, 351
  —agricultural sector, 351–53, 356–57;
    acreage expansion, 351–52; increase in
    yields, 351, 352; input intensification,
    352; technical progress, 352
  —industrial sector, 352–57; handicraft pro-
    duction, 352; factory production, 353–54;
    small-scale *vs.* large-scale, 352, 354; nor-
    mal sequence of industries, 353; import
    substitution, 351, 352–53, 355; sources of
    capital, 353–54; sources of en-
    trepreneurship, 354
  —foreign sector, 62, 352, 353, 354–55,
    356; export growth rates, 354; export com-
    position, 355; import composition, 354;
    capital transfers, public, 351, 354–55;
    capital transfers, private, 353, 355

Pakistan (*continued*)
—public sector, 353, 355–56; revenue sources, 355, 356
Panama, 115n
Penrose, E. F., 48, 337
Penrose, Edith, 48, 337
Perkins, Dwight, 17, 18, 269, 277, 282, 291
Perón, Juan, and regime in Argentina, 90
Peru, 126–34, 409, 436
Extensive growth in, 127
Turning point in, 127; events connected with, 127–28
Real wages in, 133
Income distribution in, 133
Intensive era in, 128–34; population growth, 131
—agricultural sector, 127, 131–32; acreage expansion, 131; technical progress, 130
—industrial sector, 127, 128, 130–34; factory production, 132–34; normal sequence of industries, 132–33; import substitution, 132–33; sources of capital, 132–34; sources of entrepreneurship, 126, 130, 132; state-owned industries, 131, 133–34
—foreign sector, 126–27, 128–31, 132; export growth rates, 126–27, 128–31; export composition, 127, 128–29; import composition, 132–33; capital transfers, public, 130–31, 134; capital transfers, private, 127, 128, 130–33
Philippines, 180–87, 409, 412, 426, 436
Extensive growth in, 180–81
Turning point in, 181; events connected with, 181
Real wages in, 186
Income distribution in, 182, 186
Intensive era in, 181–87; population growth, 183
—agricultural sector, 181–83, 184–85; acreage expansion, 182, 184; increase in yields, 182, 184; input intensification, 182, 184; technical progress, 184
—industrial sector, 182, 184–86; handicraft production, 181, 182, 186; factory production, 182, 184–86; import substitution, 185, 187; sources of capital, 182, 186; sources of entrepreneurship, 186
—foreign sector, 184, 185, 186; export growth rates, 184, 186; export composition, 181, 187; import composition, 187;

capital transfers, public, 186; capital transfers, private, 182–83, 186
—public sector, 187; revenue sources, 187
Political variables, as explanation for comparative growth differences, 7, 414–18
Population growth, comparative record, *1950–80*, 403–06; table, 404
Power, John, 185
Prebisch, Raoul, 45, 61, 96, 311
Pye, Lucian W., 415n

Ranis, Gustav, 9, 67n, 71, 72
Rawski, Thomas G., 53, 271, 274, 277, 283, 284, 285, 289, 290
Real wages, 9, 59, 70, 72; in Cuba, 123, 125–26; in Peru, 133; in India, 298
Resnick, Stephen A., 122
Reyes, Raphael (Colombia), 113
Reynolds, Clark, 48
Reynolds, Lloyd G., 67n, 437n
Rhodes, Cecil, 227, 249
Rhodesia. *See* Zambia; Zimbabwe
Ricardo, David, 52
Richter, Hazel V., 146
Ridley, H. N., 151
Robson, P., 222
Roosevelt, Franklin D., 438
Rosovsky, Henry, 69
Rostow, Walt, 9, 10

Sabot, R. N., 247, 248
Sa'igh, Yusif I., 192, 196, 199, 374, 375
Sanchez-Albornoz, N., 82n
Schumpeter, Joseph, 27
Shand, R. T., 146
Sherpa economy, 21–23. *See also* Nepal
Siam. *See* Thailand
Sicat, Gerardo P., 185
Silverstein, Josef, 146
Singapore, 430
Slavery, in West Africa, 19, 203; in Brazil, 92, 93; in Cuba, 120; in Peru, 127; in Thailand, 161; in West Africa, 203; in East Africa, 227; in Mozambique, 376
Smith, Adam, 28, 420, 435, 438
Smith, Ian, 253
Snodgrass, Donald, 71, 138, 156
South Korea, 6, 10, 173–80, 391, 405, 409, 411, 417, 429–30, 431, 432, 435, 436
Turning point in, 173, 174

Surplus labor in, 174, 178
Real wages in, 178
Income distribution in, 176, 180
Intensive era in, 174–70; population growth, 176, 180
—agricultural sector, 174–75; acreage expansion, 175; increase in yields, 177; input intensification, 175, 177; technical progress, 175
—industrial sector, 175, 178–79; handicraft production, 175; factory production, 175; small-scale *vs.* large-scale, 175, 178; normal sequence of industries, 175, 178; import substitution, 177; sources of capital, 177, 178, 179; state-owned industries, 178
—foreign sector, 175, 176, 179–80; export growth rates, 175, 176, 179; export composition, 176, 179; capital transfers, private, 176, 180
—public sector, 176, 179, 180; revenue sources, 179
Sri Lanka, 135–42, 388, 391, 405, 409, 411, 412, 426
Extensive growth in, 136
Turning point in, 136
Surplus labor in, 141
Real wages in, 141
Income distribution in, 136
Intensive era in, 136–42; population growth, 139
—agricultural sector, 136–37, 139–40; acreage expansion, 140; increase in yields, 140
—industrial sector, 140–42; handicraft production, 141; factory production, 140–41; import composition, 62; sources of capital, 137, 139, 140, 141; state-owned industries, 140–42
—foreign sector, 62, 136–38, 140, 142; export growth rates, 136, 137, 138; export composition, 136–38, 142; import composition, 137, 138, 139; capital transfers, public, 138, 140–41; capital transfers, private, 141
—public sector, 138, 140–42; size, 138, 141; composition, 140–41; revenue sources, 138, 139, 141
Srinivasan, T. N., 309, 315, 428
Stolper, Wolfgang, 212

Subsistence economy. *See* Extensive growth, subsistence economy view
Sudan, 373–75, 395, 405
Extensive growth in, 373; population growth, 374; agricultural sector, 374; factory production, 374; export growth rates, 374; capital transfers, public, 374–75; public sector, 375
Sukarno, President, 363
Summers, Robert, 399n
Surplus labor, 9, 50–51, 59; in China, 282–84; in India, 309; in Colombia, 118–19; in Cuba, 123, 125

Taiwan, 6, 9, 10, 165–73, 391, 405, 409, 411, 429–30, 436
Extensive growth in, 166–67; population growth, 166
Turning point in, 166–67; events connected with, 167
Surplus labor in, 171, 173
Real wages in, 170, 172, 173
Income distribution in, 170, 173
Intensive era in, 167–73; population growth, 173
—agricultural sector, 167–70, 172; acreage expansion, 168; increase in yields, 168; input intensification, 167–68, 172; technical progress, 168
—industrial sector, 169–70, 171; handicraft production, 169; factory production, 169; small-scale *vs.* large-scale, 169; import substitution, 170; sources of capital, 169, 170; sources of entrepreneurship, 167
—foreign sector, 168, 169–71, 172–73; export growth rates, 168–69, 170, 171; export composition, 169; import composition, 169; capital transfers, public, 168, 171; capital transfers, private, 170
—public sector, 167–68, 171
Takeoff concept, 9–10
Tanganyika. *See* Tanzania
Tanzania, 239–48, 431, 436
Extensive growth in, 240
Turning point in, 240; events connected with, 240–42
Real wages in, 246
Income distribution in, 242–43, 244, 248
Intensive era in, 240–48; population growth, 240, 243, 248; white settlement, 239–41

Tanzania (*continued*)
—agricultural sector, 240–48; acreage expansion, 240
—industrial sector, 243–48; handicraft production, 240; factory production, 242, 243, 246–47; import substitution, 242–43, 246
—foreign sector, 243–45, 247–48; export growth rates, 243; export composition, 242, 243; import composition, 245
—public sector, 243, 245, 247
Tata, Jamsetji, 298
Thailand, 135, 409, 411, 412, 417, 429, 436
Extensive growth in, 156–57
Turning point in, 10, 157
Real wages in, 159–62
Income distribution in, 161–62
Intensive era in, 158–65; population growth, 158, 162
—agricultural sector, 156, 158–60, 161, 165; acreage expansion, 158–59, 162; increase in yields, 159, 162; input intensification, 162, 163; technical progress, 162–63
—industrial sector, 160–61, 163–65; handicraft production, 161; factory production, 161, 164–65; import substitution, 162, 163; sources of capital, 159, 161, 164; sources of entrepreneurship, 159, 160, 164; state-owned industries, 164
—foreign sector, 160, 163–65; export growth rates, 157, 158, 160, 163; export composition, 160; import composition, 160–61; capital transfers, public, 164–65; capital transfers, private, 164, 165
—public sector, 161, 165; size, 161, 165; revenue sources, 161, 164
Thorp, Rosemary, 128, 130
Tugwell, Franklin, 48, 188
Turkey, 328–35, 409, 411, 412, 428, 429, 430
Extensive growth in, 328–31; population growth, 328, 331
Turning point in, 328, 331; events connected with, 328
Surplus labor in, 334
Real wages in, 334
Income distribution in, 331, 334
Intensive era in, 331–35; population growth, 331

—agricultural sector, 328–29, 330; acreage expansion, 330, 332; increase in yields, 330, 331, 332; input intensification, 331–32; technical progress, 331–32, 335
—industrial sector, 329–31, 332–35; factory production, 330, 332; small-scale *vs.* large-scale, 332; normal sequence of industries, 332; import substitution, 332; sources of capital, 329–30; sources of entrepreneurship, 330; state-owned industries, 330
—foreign sector, 329–30, 333, 335; export growth rates, 333; export composition, 333; import composition, 332, 333; capital transfers, public, 333, 335; capital transfers, private, 333, 334–35
—public sector, 332–33, 335; revenue sources, 330
Turning point concept, 8–10

Uganda, 235–39, 398, 405
Extensive growth in, 235–36
Turning point in, 236; events connected with, 235–36
Intensive era in, 236–39; white settlement in, 236
—agricultural sector, 235–37; acreage expansion, 236; input intensification, 237; technical progress, 237
—industrial sector, 237–39; handicraft production, 237; sources of entrepreneurship, 238
—foreign sector, 236–39; export growth rates, 236–37; export composition, 237; import composition, 239; capital transfers, private, 238
—public sector, 238
Union Soviet Socialist Republics, 119; and Cuba, 119, 125; and India, 311–12, 316; and Egypt, 323; and Iraq, 338; and Iran, 344, 345, 347; and Afghanistan, 368
United Nations, 12
United Nations Trade and Agriculture Division (UNCTAD), 391, 411
United States, 115n; and Argentina, 90; and Mexico, 99, 100, 106; and Colombia, 115n; and Cuba, 119–23; and Thailand, 165; and Taiwan, 172; and Philippines, 181, 182–83; and China, 269, 281, 288; and Egypt, 327;

and Turkey, 333; and Iraq, 338, 339; and
Iran, 347; and Nepal, 370
Urrutia, Miguel, 70

Venezuela, 187–90, 391
Turning point in, 187; events connected
with, 187–88
Intensive era in, 188–90; population growth,
190
—agricultural sector, 190
—industrial sector, 189–90; factory production, 190; import substitution, 190
—foreign sector, 188–89, 190
—public sector, 189–90; revenue sources,
189

Wallerstein, Immanuel, 11
Wallich, Henry, 122
Walras, Leon, 27
Weisskopf, Thomas, 363, 364
West Africa, 202–26
Winpenny, J. T., 96
Wolff, Richard D., 228
World Bank. *See* International Bank for Recon-
struction and Development
World Health Organization (WHO), 343, 405

Yeh, K'ung Chia, 276

Zaire, 378–83, 398
Extensive growth in, 378–83; population
growth, 382; agricultural exports, 378;
manufacturing output, 379; subsistence agriculture, 380; export growth rates, 380;
stagnation and decline, 381–83; public
sector, 381; mining sector, 381–83; foreign borrowing, 382–83
Zambia, 255–63, 398, 409, 431
Extensive growth in, 255
Turning point in, 255; events connected
with, 255–56
Surplus labor in, 258, 262
Real wages in, 257, 258, 262

Income distribution in, 257–58
Intensive era in, 255–63; population growth,
257–58, 262
—agricultural sector, 256, 259, 262–63;
acreage expansion, 256; increase in yields,
256, 257; input intensification, 256, 261;
technical progress, 261
—industrial sector, 257–63; handicraft production, 257; factory production, 259,
262; small-scale *vs.* large-scale, 259; normal sequence of industries, 258; sources of
capital, 255–56, 259; sources of entrepreneurship, 255; state-owned industries, 260, 262
—foreign sector, 255–57; export growth
rates, 255–56; export composition, 255–
56; import composition, 261–62; capital
transfers, public, 260; capital transfers,
private, 260
—public sector, 259, 260, 262; revenue
sources, 259, 260–61, 262
Zimbabwe, 248–55
Extensive growth in, 249; white settlement
in, 248–51
Real wages in, 250, 253
Income distribution in, 250, 253
Intensive era in, 249–55; population growth,
251–52, 253
—agricultural sector, 249–51, 252; acreage
expansion, 250; increase in yields, 250,
252; technical progress, 250
—industrial sector, 252–55; factory production, 251, 252, 254; normal sequence of
industries, 252; import substitution, 251;
sources of capital, 251, 252; sources of
entrepreneurship, 249, 251
—foreign sector, 249, 251–52, 254; export
growth rates, 251, 252, 254; export composition, 251, 252, 254; import composition, 251, 254; capital transfers, public,
252–53; capital transfers, private, 251,
252
—public sector, 252–53

Economic Growth Center Book Publications

Werner Baer, *Industrialization and Economic Development in Brazil* (1965). Out of print.

Werner Baer and Isaac Kerstenetzky, eds., *Inflation and Growth in Latin America* (1964). Out of print.

Bela A. Balassa, *Trade Prospects for Developing Countries* (1964). Out of print.

Albert Berry and Miguel Urrutia, *Income Distribution in Colombia* (1976).

Hans P. Binswanger and Mark R. Rosenzweig, eds., *Contractual Arrangements, Employment, and Wages in Rural Labor Markets in Asia* (1983).

Thomas B. Birnberg and Stephen A. Resnick, *Colonial Development: An Econometric Study* (1975).

Benjamin I. Cohen, *Multinational Firms and Asian Exports* (1975).

Carlos F. Díaz Alejandro, *Essays on the Economic History of the Argentine Republic* (1970).

Robert Evenson and Yoav Kislev, *Agricultural Research and Productivity* (1975).

John C. H. Fei and Gustav Ranis, *Development of Labor Surplus Economy: Theory and Policy* (1964). Out of print.

Gerald K. Helleiner, *Peasant Agriculture, Government, and Economic Growth in Nigeria* (1966). Out of print.

Samuel P. S. Ho, *Economic Development of Taiwan, 1860–1970* (1978).

Nurul Islam, *Foreign Trade and Economic Controls in Development: The Case of United Pakistan* (1981).

Lawrence R. Klein and Kazushi Ohkawa, eds., *Economic Growth: The Japanese Experience since the Meiji Era* (1968). Out of print.

Paul W. Kuznets, *Economic Growth and Structure in the Republic of Korea* (1977).

A. Lamfalussy, *The United Kingdom and the Six* (1963). Out of print.

Markos J. Mamalakis, *The Growth and Structure of the Chilean Economy: From Independence to Allende* (1976).

Markos J. Mamalakis and Clark W. Reynolds, *Essays on the Chilean Economy* (1965). Out of print.

Donald C. Mead, *Growth and Structural Change in the Egyptian Economy* (1967). Out of print.

Richard Moorsteen and Raymond P. Powell, *The Soviet Capital Stock* (1966). Out of print.

Kazushi Ohkawa and Miyohei Shinohara, eds. (with Larry Meissner), *Patterns of Japanese Economic Development: A Quantitative Appraisal* (1979).

Douglas S. Paauw and John C. H. Fei, *The Transition in Open Dualistic Economies: Theory and Southeast Asian Experience* (1973).

Howard Pack, *Structural Change and Economic Policy in Israel* (1971).

Frederick L. Pryor, *Public Expenditures in Communist and Capitalist Nations* (1968). Out of print.

Gustav Ranis, ed., *Government and Economic Development* (1971).

Clark W. Reynolds, *The Mexican Economy: Twentieth-Century Structure and Growth* (1970). Out of print.

Lloyd G. Reynolds, *Economic Growth in the Third World, 1850–1980* (1985).

Lloyd G. Reynolds, *Image and Reality in Economic Development* (1977).

Lloyd G. Reynolds, ed., *Agriculture in Development Theory* (1975).

Lloyd G. Reynolds and Peter Gregory, *Wages, Productivity, and Industrialization in Puerto Rico* (1965). Out of print.

Donald R. Snodgrass, *Ceylon: An Export Economy in Transition* (1966). Out of print.